JERKTASTIC PARK

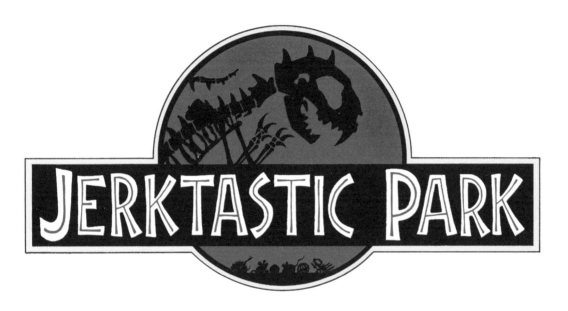

Other *Get Fuzzy* Books

The Dog Is Not a Toy (House Rule #4)

Fuzzy Logic: Get Fuzzy 2

The Get Fuzzy Experience: Are You Bucksperienced

I Would Have Bought You a Cat, But . . .

Blueprint for Disaster

Say Cheesy

Scrum Bums

I'm Ready for My Movie Contract

Take Our Cat, Please!

Ignorance, Thy Name Is Bucky

Dumbheart

Masters of the Nonsenseverse

Survival of the Filthiest

The Birth of Canis

The Fuzzy Bunch

Treasuries

Groovitude: A Get Fuzzy Treasury

Bucky Katt's Big Book of Fun

Loserpalooza

The Potpourrific Great Big Grab Bag of Get Fuzzy

Treasury of the Lost Litter Box

The Stinking

JERKTASTIC PARK

a **GET FUZZY** treasury by darby conley

Andrews McMeel
Publishing®

Kansas City • Sydney • London

Get Fuzzy is distributed internationally by Universal Uclick.

Jerktastic Park copyright © 2014 by Darby Conley. All rights reserved. Printed in China.
No part of this book may be used or reproduced in any manner whatsoever without written
permission except in the case of reprints in the context of reviews.

Andrews McMeel Publishing, LLC
an Andrews McMeel Universal company
1130 Walnut Street
Kansas City, Missouri 64106
www.andrewsmcmeel.com

14 15 16 17 18 SDB 10 9 8 7 6 5 4 3 2 1

ISBN: 978-1-4494-4658-1

Library of Congress Control Number: 2013949468

Get Fuzzy can be viewed on the Internet at
www.gocomics.com/getfuzzy

┌─────────────**ATTENTION: SCHOOLS AND BUSINESSES**─────────────┐

Andrews McMeel books are available at quantity discounts with bulk purchase for educational,
business, or sales promotional use. For information, please e-mail the Special Sales Department:
specialsales@amuniversal.com

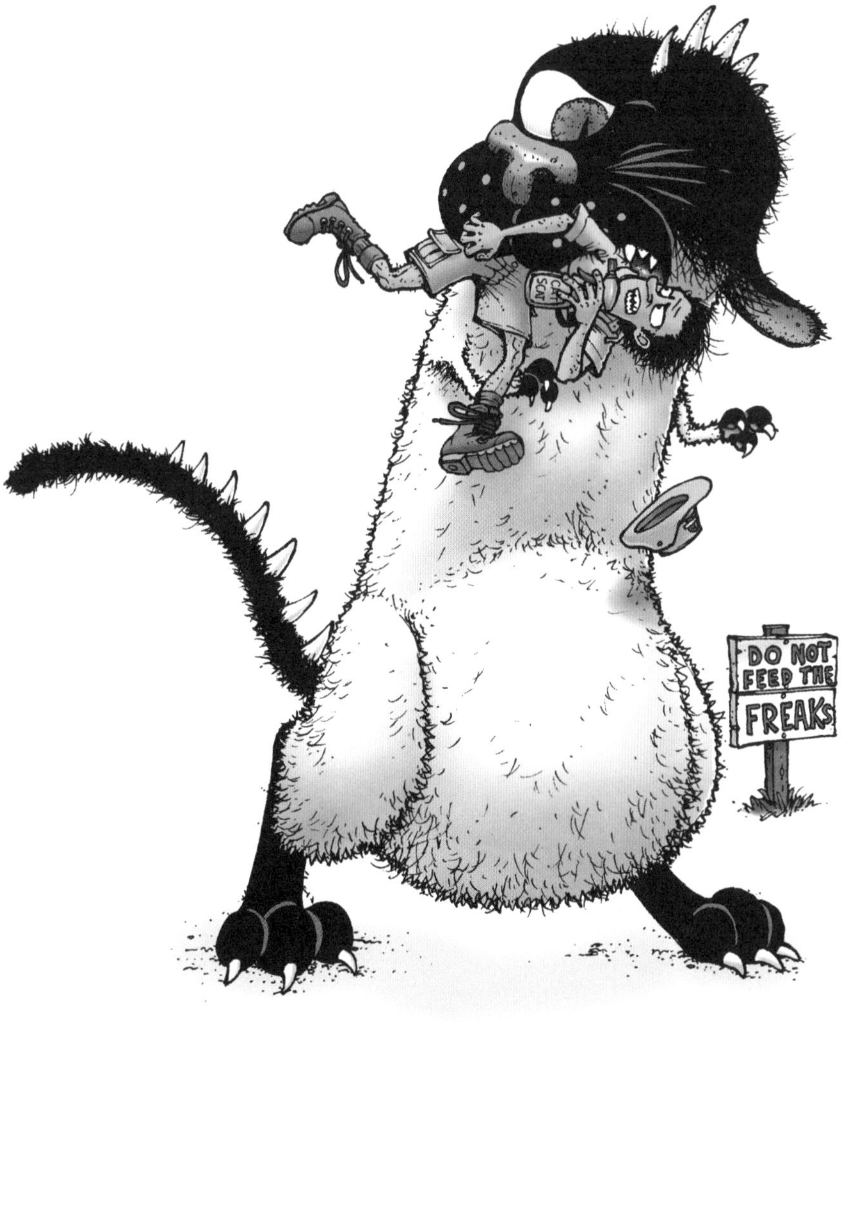
DO NOT FEED THE
FREAKS

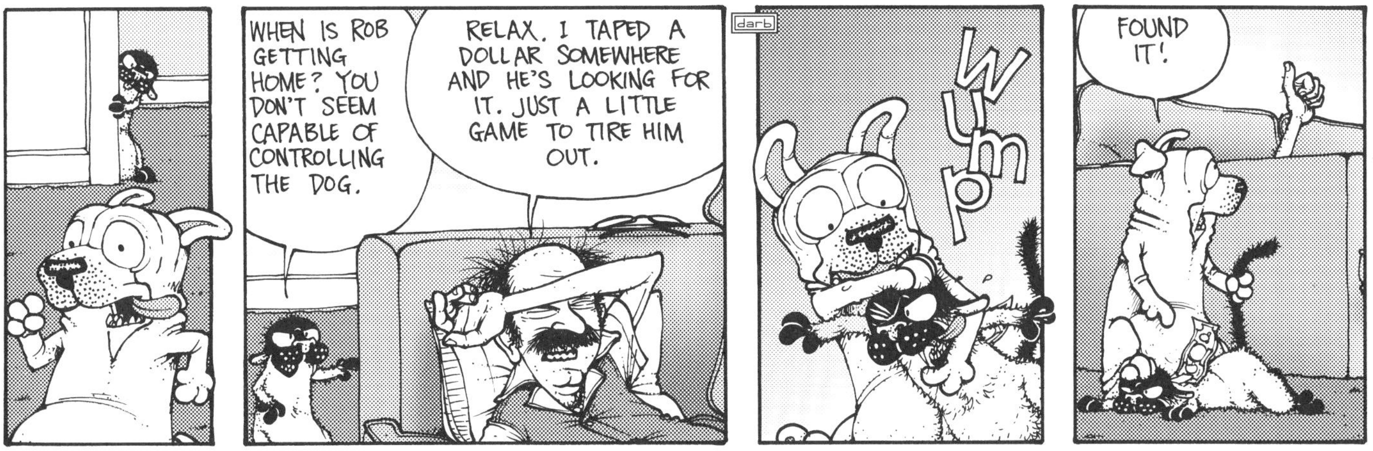
WHEN IS ROB GETTING HOME? YOU DON'T SEEM CAPABLE OF CONTROLLING THE DOG.
RELAX. I TAPED A DOLLAR SOMEWHERE AND HE'S LOOKING FOR IT. JUST A LITTLE GAME TO TIRE HIM OUT.
WUMP
FOUND IT!

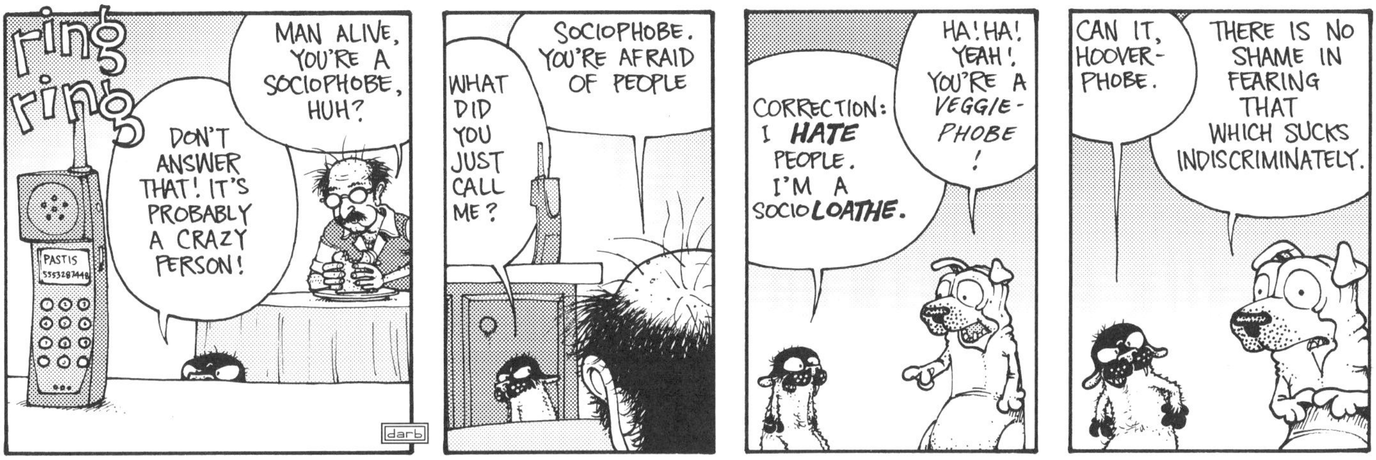
ring ring
DON'T ANSWER THAT! IT'S PROBABLY A CRAZY PERSON!
MAN ALIVE, YOU'RE A SOCIOPHOBE, HUH?
WHAT DID YOU JUST CALL ME?
SOCIOPHOBE. YOU'RE AFRAID OF PEOPLE
CORRECTION: I **HATE** PEOPLE. I'M A SOCIO**LOATHE**.
HA! HA! YEAH! YOU'RE A *VEGGIE-PHOBE*!
CAN IT, HOOVER-PHOBE.
THERE IS NO SHAME IN FEARING THAT WHICH SUCKS INDISCRIMINATELY.

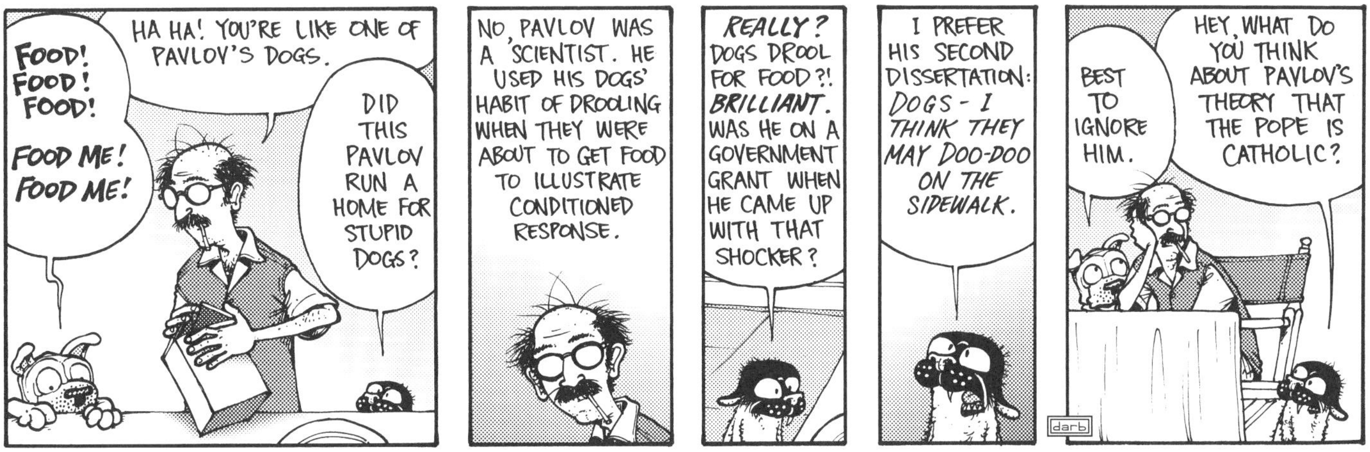
FOOD! FOOD! FOOD!
FOOD ME! FOOD ME!
HA HA! YOU'RE LIKE ONE OF PAVLOV'S DOGS.
DID THIS PAVLOV RUN A HOME FOR STUPID DOGS?
NO, PAVLOV WAS A SCIENTIST. HE USED HIS DOGS' HABIT OF DROOLING WHEN THEY WERE ABOUT TO GET FOOD TO ILLUSTRATE CONDITIONED RESPONSE.
REALLY? DOGS DROOL FOR FOOD?! ***BRILLIANT.*** WAS HE ON A GOVERNMENT GRANT WHEN HE CAME UP WITH THAT SHOCKER?
I PREFER HIS SECOND DISSERTATION: *DOGS - I THINK THEY MAY DOO-DOO ON THE SIDEWALK.*
BEST TO IGNORE HIM.
HEY, WHAT DO YOU THINK ABOUT PAVLOV'S THEORY THAT THE POPE IS CATHOLIC?

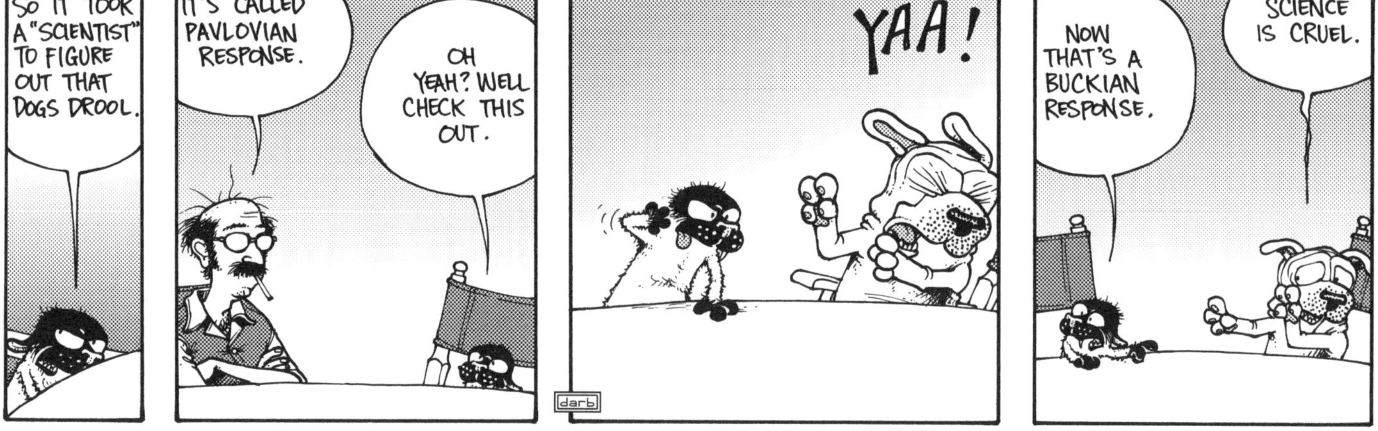
SO IT TOOK A "SCIENTIST" TO FIGURE OUT THAT DOGS DROOL.
IT'S CALLED PAVLOVIAN RESPONSE.
OH YEAH? WELL CHECK THIS OUT.
YAA!
NOW THAT'S A BUCKIAN RESPONSE.
SCIENCE IS CRUEL.
darb

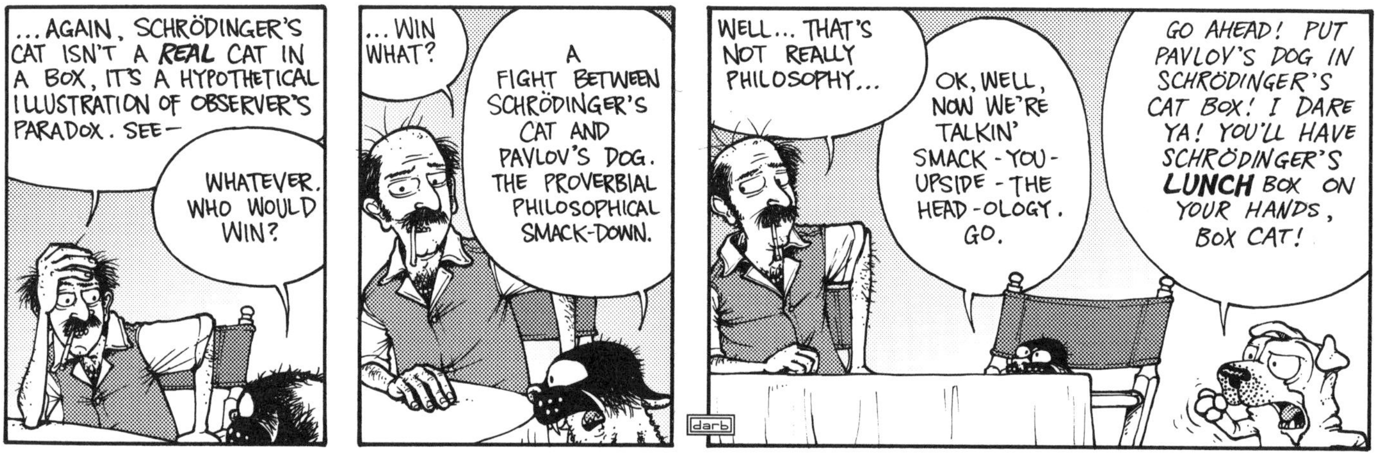
...AGAIN, SCHRÖDINGER'S CAT ISN'T A REAL CAT IN A BOX, IT'S A HYPOTHETICAL ILLUSTRATION OF OBSERVER'S PARADOX. SEE—
WHATEVER. WHO WOULD WIN?
...WIN WHAT?
A FIGHT BETWEEN SCHRÖDINGER'S CAT AND PAVLOV'S DOG. THE PROVERBIAL PHILOSOPHICAL SMACK-DOWN.
WELL... THAT'S NOT REALLY PHILOSOPHY...
OK, WELL, NOW WE'RE TALKIN' SMACK-YOU-UPSIDE-THE HEAD-OLOGY. GO.
GO AHEAD! PUT PAVLOV'S DOG IN SCHRÖDINGER'S CAT BOX! I DARE YA! YOU'LL HAVE SCHRÖDINGER'S LUNCH BOX ON YOUR HANDS, BOX CAT!
darb

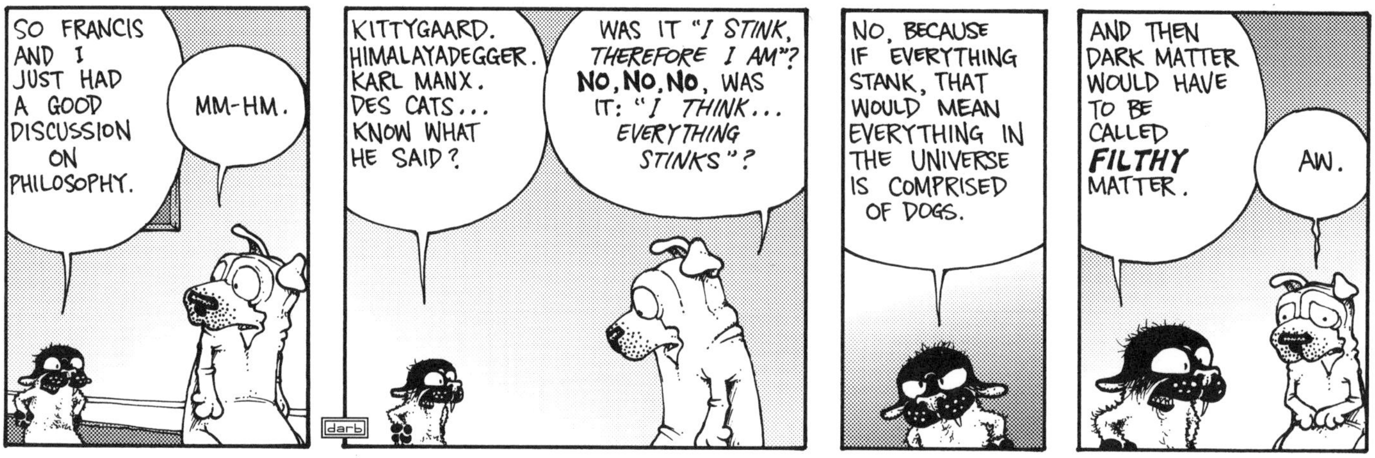
SO FRANCIS AND I JUST HAD A GOOD DISCUSSION ON PHILOSOPHY.
MM-HM.
KITTYGAARD. HIMALAYADEGGER. KARL MANX. DES CATS... KNOW WHAT HE SAID?
WAS IT "I STINK, THEREFORE I AM"? NO, NO, NO, WAS IT: "I THINK... EVERYTHING STINKS"?
NO, BECAUSE IF EVERYTHING STANK, THAT WOULD MEAN EVERYTHING IN THE UNIVERSE IS COMPRISED OF DOGS.
AND THEN DARK MATTER WOULD HAVE TO BE CALLED FILTHY MATTER.
AW.
darb

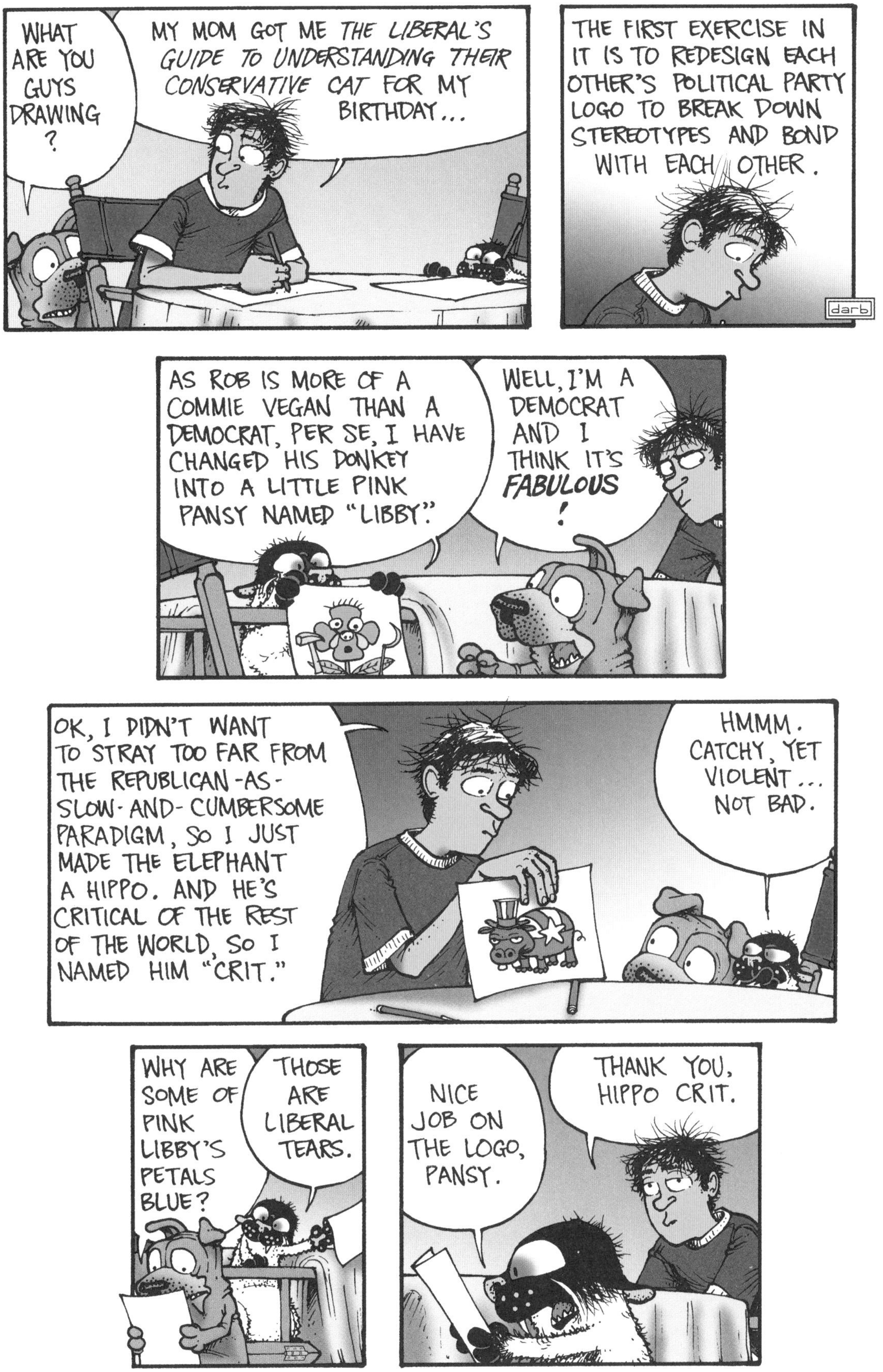
WHAT ARE YOU GUYS DRAWING?
MY MOM GOT ME *THE LIBERAL'S GUIDE TO UNDERSTANDING THEIR CONSERVATIVE CAT* FOR MY BIRTHDAY...
THE FIRST EXERCISE IN IT IS TO REDESIGN EACH OTHER'S POLITICAL PARTY LOGO TO BREAK DOWN STEREOTYPES AND BOND WITH EACH OTHER.
darb
AS ROB IS MORE OF A COMMIE VEGAN THAN A DEMOCRAT, PER SE, I HAVE CHANGED HIS DONKEY INTO A LITTLE PINK PANSY NAMED "LIBBY."
WELL, I'M A DEMOCRAT AND I THINK IT'S **FABULOUS**!
OK, I DIDN'T WANT TO STRAY TOO FAR FROM THE REPUBLICAN-AS-SLOW-AND-CUMBERSOME PARADIGM, SO I JUST MADE THE ELEPHANT A HIPPO. AND HE'S CRITICAL OF THE REST OF THE WORLD, SO I NAMED HIM "CRIT."
HMMM. CATCHY, YET VIOLENT... NOT BAD.
WHY ARE SOME OF PINK LIBBY'S PETALS BLUE?
THOSE ARE LIBERAL TEARS.
NICE JOB ON THE LOGO, PANSY.
THANK YOU, HIPPO CRIT.

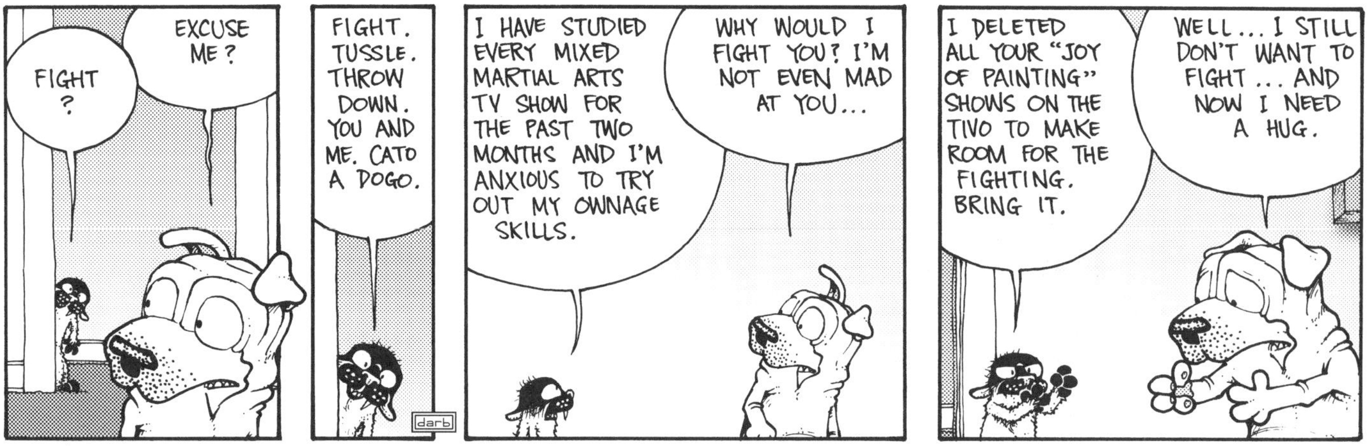
FIGHT ?
EXCUSE ME ?
FIGHT. TUSSLE. THROW DOWN. YOU AND ME. CATO A DOGO.
darb
I HAVE STUDIED EVERY MIXED MARTIAL ARTS TV SHOW FOR THE PAST TWO MONTHS AND I'M ANXIOUS TO TRY OUT MY OWNAGE SKILLS.
WHY WOULD I FIGHT YOU? I'M NOT EVEN MAD AT YOU...
I DELETED ALL YOUR "JOY OF PAINTING" SHOWS ON THE TIVO TO MAKE ROOM FOR THE FIGHTING. BRING IT.
WELL... I STILL DON'T WANT TO FIGHT... AND NOW I NEED A HUG.

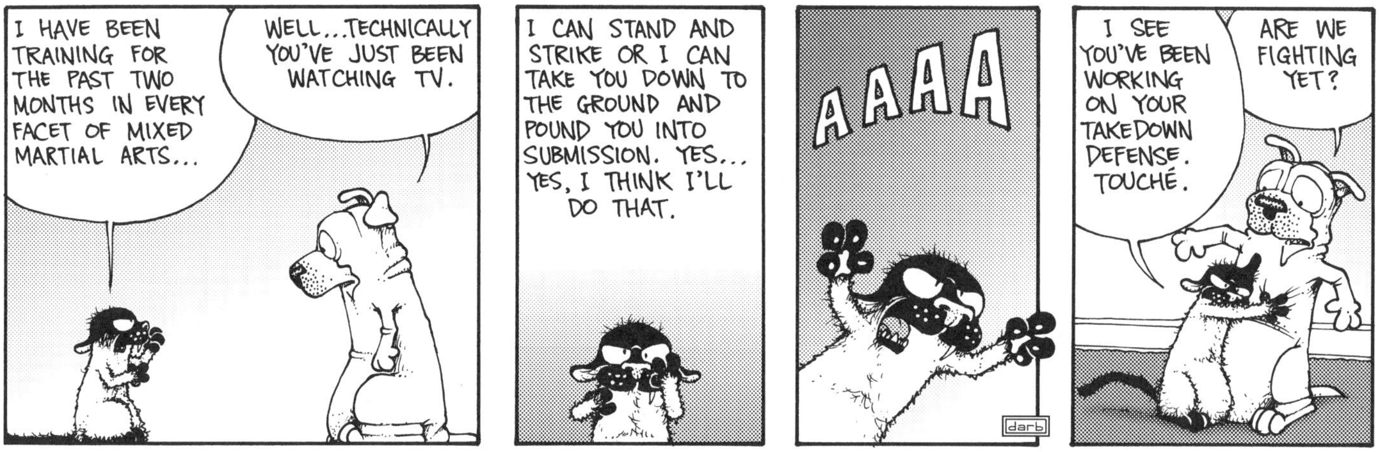
I HAVE BEEN TRAINING FOR THE PAST TWO MONTHS IN EVERY FACET OF MIXED MARTIAL ARTS...
WELL...TECHNICALLY YOU'VE JUST BEEN WATCHING TV.
I CAN STAND AND STRIKE OR I CAN TAKE YOU DOWN TO THE GROUND AND POUND YOU INTO SUBMISSION. YES... YES, I THINK I'LL DO THAT.
AAAA
darb
I SEE YOU'VE BEEN WORKING ON YOUR TAKEDOWN DEFENSE. TOUCHÉ.
ARE WE FIGHTING YET?

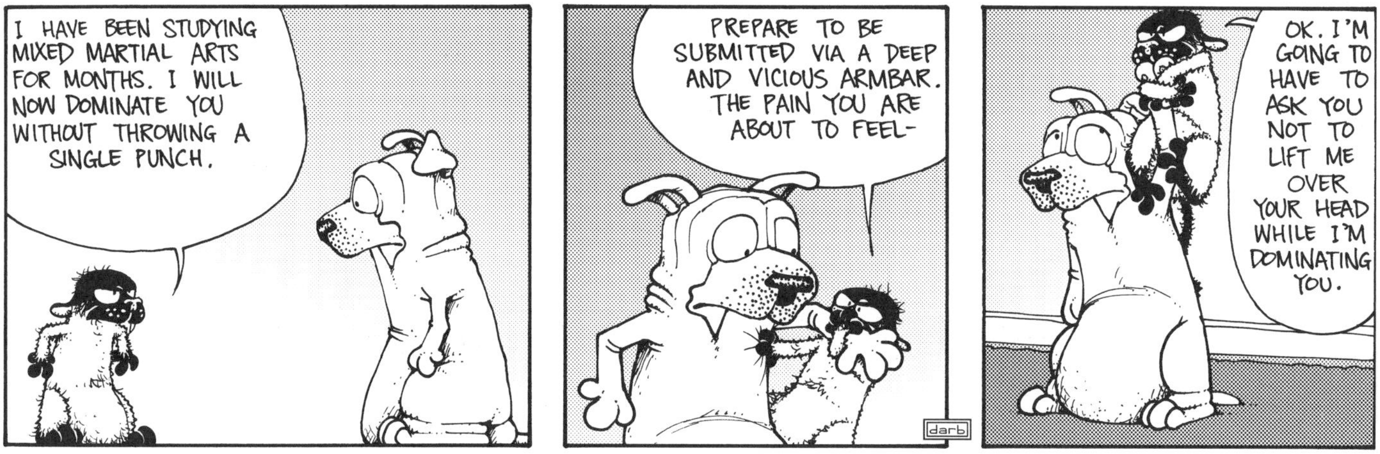
I HAVE BEEN STUDYING MIXED MARTIAL ARTS FOR MONTHS. I WILL NOW DOMINATE YOU WITHOUT THROWING A SINGLE PUNCH.
PREPARE TO BE SUBMITTED VIA A DEEP AND VICIOUS ARMBAR. THE PAIN YOU ARE ABOUT TO FEEL-
darb
OK. I'M GOING TO HAVE TO ASK YOU NOT TO LIFT ME OVER YOUR HEAD WHILE I'M DOMINATING YOU.

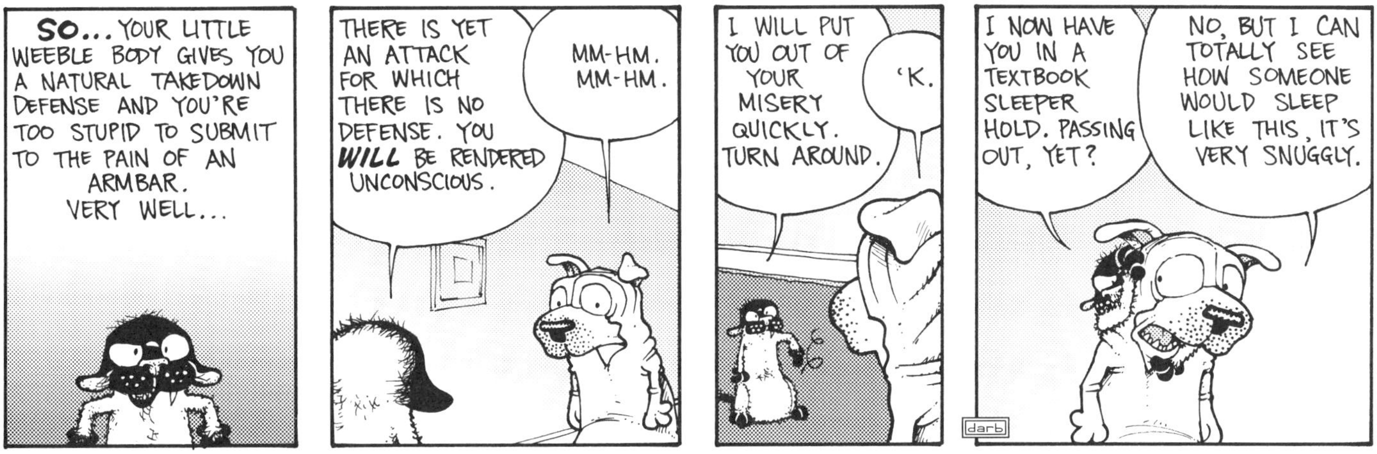
SO... YOUR LITTLE WEEBLE BODY GIVES YOU A NATURAL TAKEDOWN DEFENSE AND YOU'RE TOO STUPID TO SUBMIT TO THE PAIN OF AN ARMBAR. VERY WELL...
THERE IS YET AN ATTACK FOR WHICH THERE IS NO DEFENSE. YOU WILL BE RENDERED UNCONSCIOUS.
MM-HM. MM-HM.
I WILL PUT YOU OUT OF YOUR MISERY QUICKLY. TURN AROUND.
'K.
I NOW HAVE YOU IN A TEXTBOOK SLEEPER HOLD. PASSING OUT, YET?
NO, BUT I CAN TOTALLY SEE HOW SOMEONE WOULD SLEEP LIKE THIS, IT'S VERY SNUGGLY.
darb

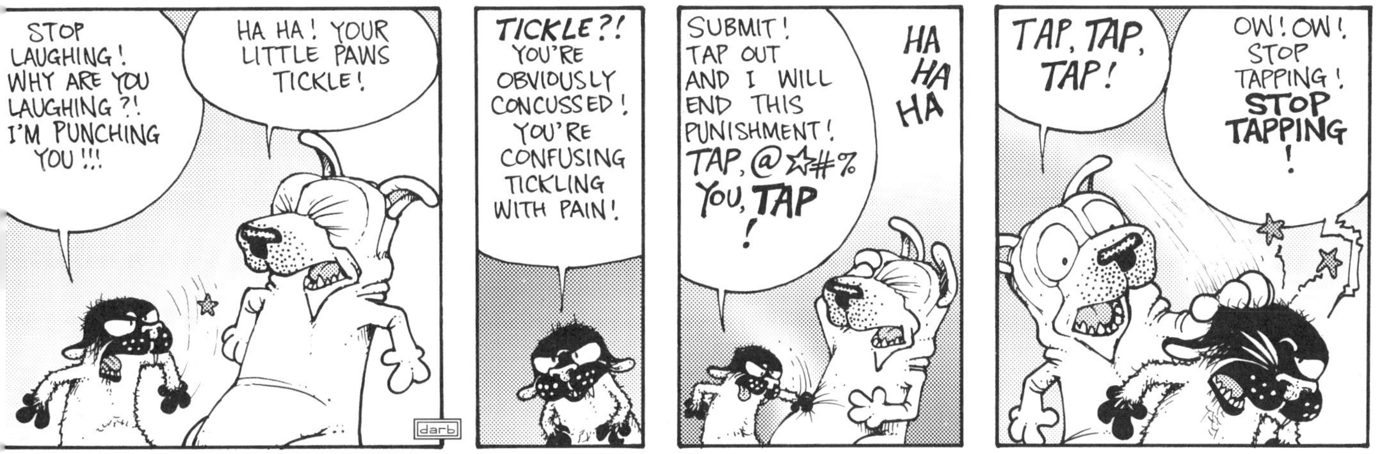
STOP LAUGHING! WHY ARE YOU LAUGHING?! I'M PUNCHING YOU!!!
HA HA! YOUR LITTLE PAWS TICKLE!
darb
TICKLE?! YOU'RE OBVIOUSLY CONCUSSED! YOU'RE CONFUSING TICKLING WITH PAIN!
SUBMIT! TAP OUT AND I WILL END THIS PUNISHMENT! TAP, @☆#% YOU, TAP!
HA HA HA
TAP, TAP, TAP!
OW! OW! STOP TAPPING! STOP TAPPING!

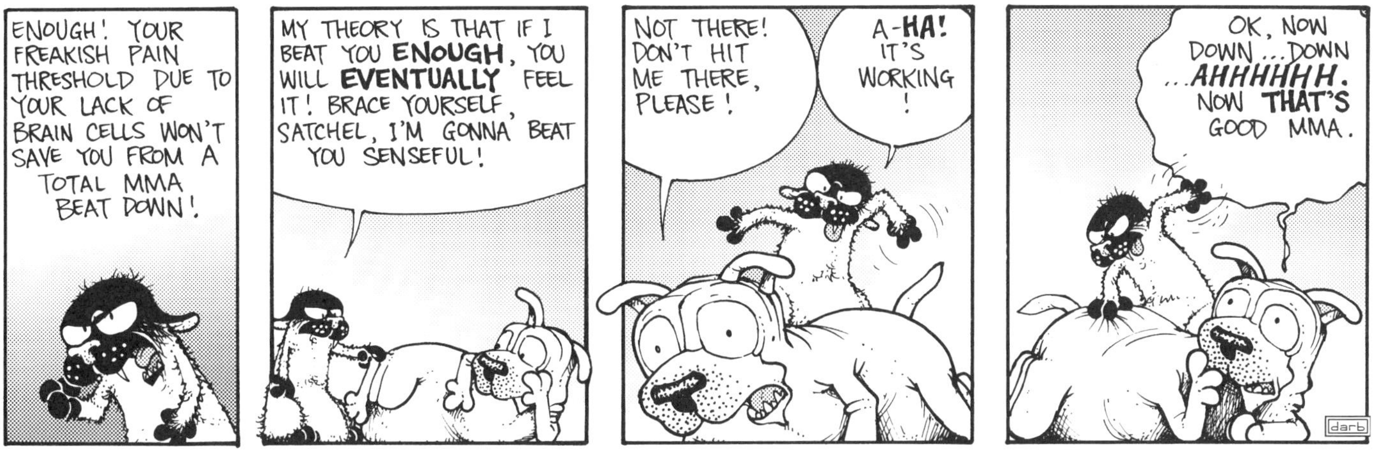
ENOUGH! YOUR FREAKISH PAIN THRESHOLD DUE TO YOUR LACK OF BRAIN CELLS WON'T SAVE YOU FROM A TOTAL MMA BEAT DOWN!
MY THEORY IS THAT IF I BEAT YOU ENOUGH, YOU WILL EVENTUALLY FEEL IT! BRACE YOURSELF, SATCHEL, I'M GONNA BEAT YOU SENSEFUL!
NOT THERE! DON'T HIT ME THERE, PLEASE!
A-HA! IT'S WORKING!
OK, NOW DOWN... DOWN ...AHHHHHH. NOW THAT'S GOOD MMA.
darb

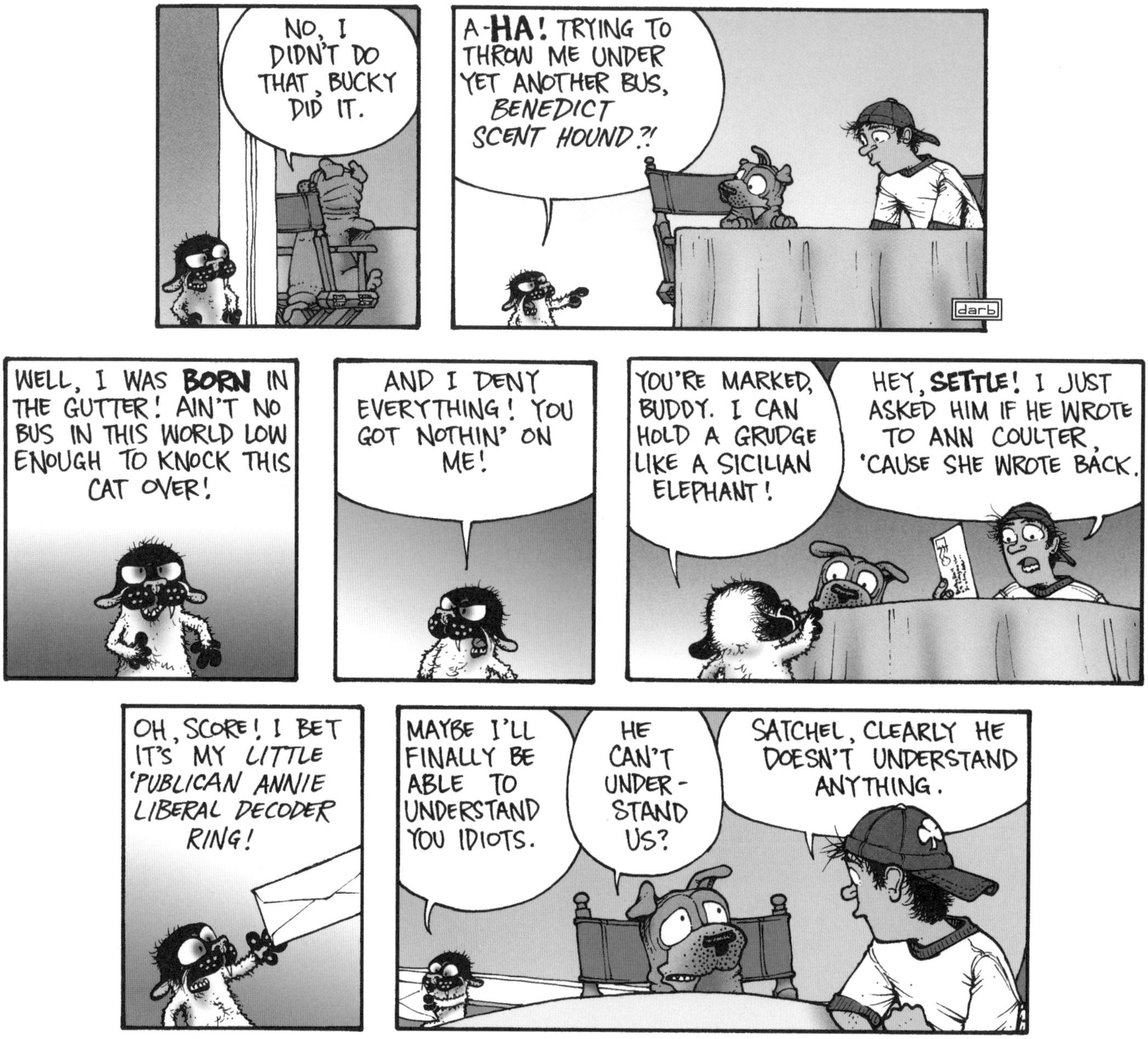
NO, I DIDN'T DO THAT, BUCKY DID IT.
A-HA! TRYING TO THROW ME UNDER YET ANOTHER BUS, BENEDICT SCENT HOUND?!
darb
WELL, I WAS BORN IN THE GUTTER! AIN'T NO BUS IN THIS WORLD LOW ENOUGH TO KNOCK THIS CAT OVER!
AND I DENY EVERYTHING! YOU GOT NOTHIN' ON ME!
YOU'RE MARKED, BUDDY. I CAN HOLD A GRUDGE LIKE A SICILIAN ELEPHANT!
HEY, SETTLE! I JUST ASKED HIM IF HE WROTE TO ANN COULTER, 'CAUSE SHE WROTE BACK.
OH, SCORE! I BET IT'S MY LITTLE 'PUBLICAN ANNIE LIBERAL DECODER RING!
MAYBE I'LL FINALLY BE ABLE TO UNDERSTAND YOU IDIOTS.
HE CAN'T UNDER-STAND US?
SATCHEL, CLEARLY HE DOESN'T UNDERSTAND ANYTHING.

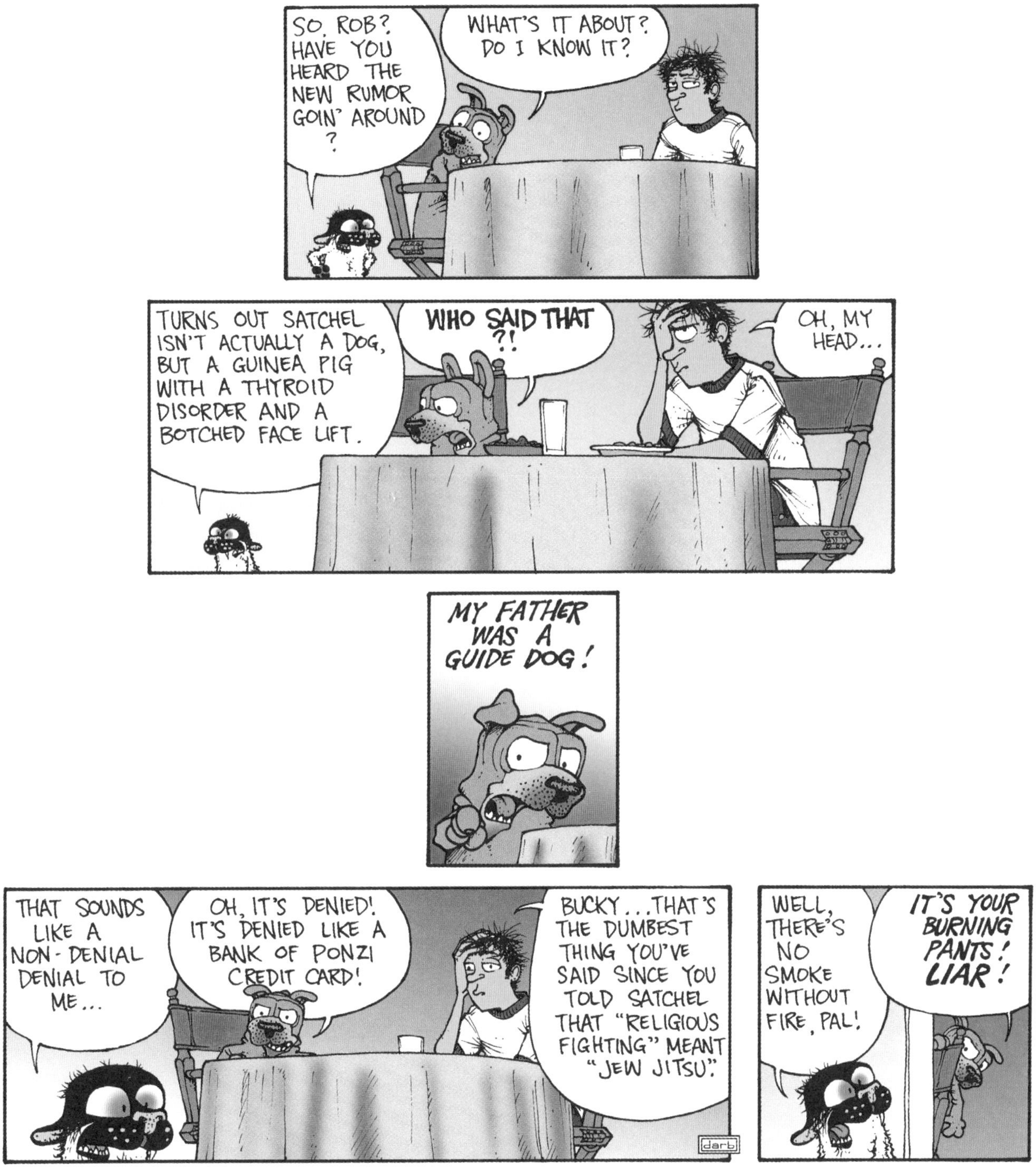
SO, ROB? HAVE YOU HEARD THE NEW RUMOR GOIN' AROUND?
WHAT'S IT ABOUT? DO I KNOW IT?
TURNS OUT SATCHEL ISN'T ACTUALLY A DOG, BUT A GUINEA PIG WITH A THYROID DISORDER AND A BOTCHED FACE LIFT.
WHO SAID THAT?!
OH, MY HEAD...
MY FATHER WAS A GUIDE DOG!
THAT SOUNDS LIKE A NON-DENIAL DENIAL TO ME...
OH, IT'S DENIED! IT'S DENIED LIKE A BANK OF PONZI CREDIT CARD!
BUCKY...THAT'S THE DUMBEST THING YOU'VE SAID SINCE YOU TOLD SATCHEL THAT "RELIGIOUS FIGHTING" MEANT "JEW JITSU".
darb
WELL, THERE'S NO SMOKE WITHOUT FIRE, PAL!
IT'S YOUR BURNING PANTS! LIAR!

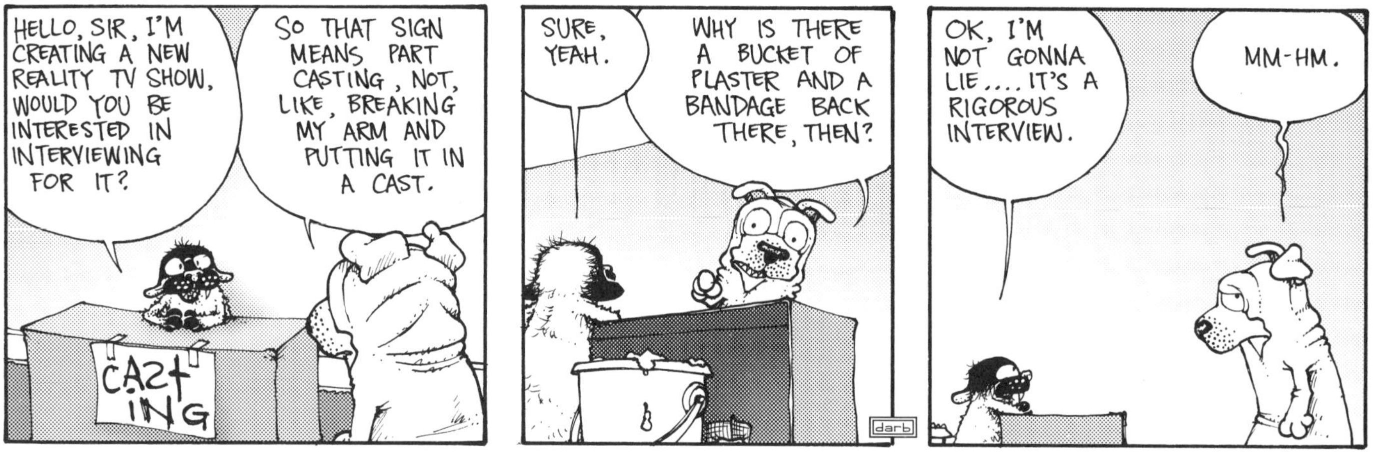
HELLO, SIR, I'M CREATING A NEW REALITY TV SHOW, WOULD YOU BE INTERESTED IN INTERVIEWING FOR IT?
SO THAT SIGN MEANS PART CASTING, NOT, LIKE, BREAKING MY ARM AND PUTTING IT IN A CAST.
CAST ING
SURE, YEAH.
WHY IS THERE A BUCKET OF PLASTER AND A BANDAGE BACK THERE, THEN?
OK, I'M NOT GONNA LIE.... IT'S A RIGOROUS INTERVIEW.
MM-HM.
darb

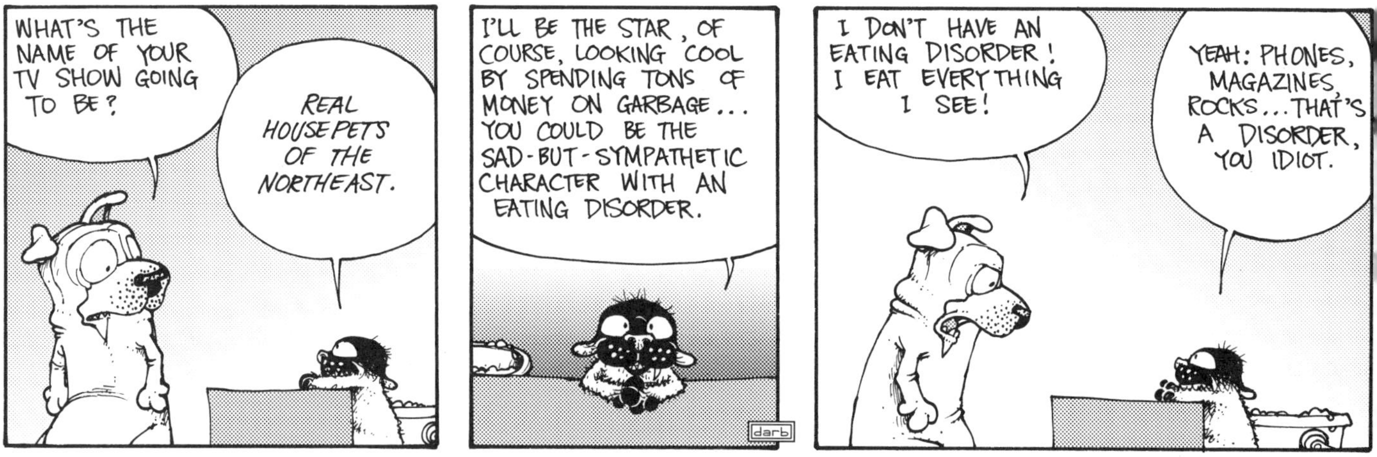
WHAT'S THE NAME OF YOUR TV SHOW GOING TO BE?
REAL HOUSEPETS OF THE NORTHEAST.
I'LL BE THE STAR, OF COURSE, LOOKING COOL BY SPENDING TONS OF MONEY ON GARBAGE... YOU COULD BE THE SAD-BUT-SYMPATHETIC CHARACTER WITH AN EATING DISORDER.
I DON'T HAVE AN EATING DISORDER! I EAT EVERYTHING I SEE!
YEAH: PHONES, MAGAZINES, ROCKS... THAT'S A DISORDER, YOU IDIOT.
darb

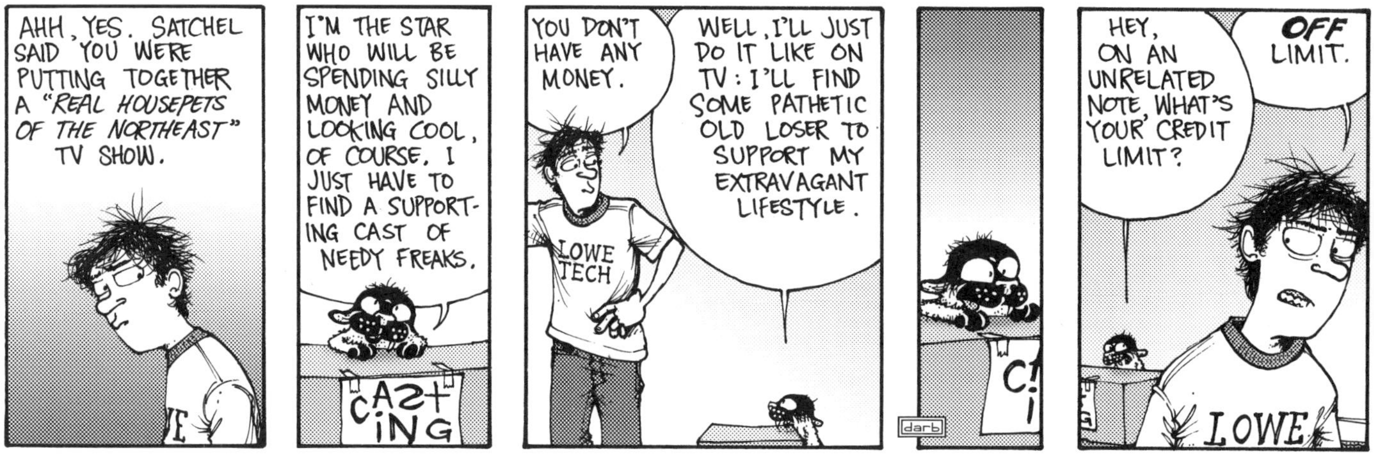
AHH, YES. SATCHEL SAID YOU WERE PUTTING TOGETHER A "*REAL HOUSEPETS OF THE NORTHEAST*" TV SHOW.
I'M THE STAR WHO WILL BE SPENDING SILLY MONEY AND LOOKING COOL, OF COURSE. I JUST HAVE TO FIND A SUPPORTING CAST OF NEEDY FREAKS.
CAST ING
YOU DON'T HAVE ANY MONEY.
WELL, I'LL JUST DO IT LIKE ON TV: I'LL FIND SOME PATHETIC OLD LOSER TO SUPPORT MY EXTRAVAGANT LIFESTYLE.
LOWE TECH
darb
HEY, ON AN UNRELATED NOTE, WHAT'S YOUR CREDIT LIMIT?
OFF LIMIT.
LOWE

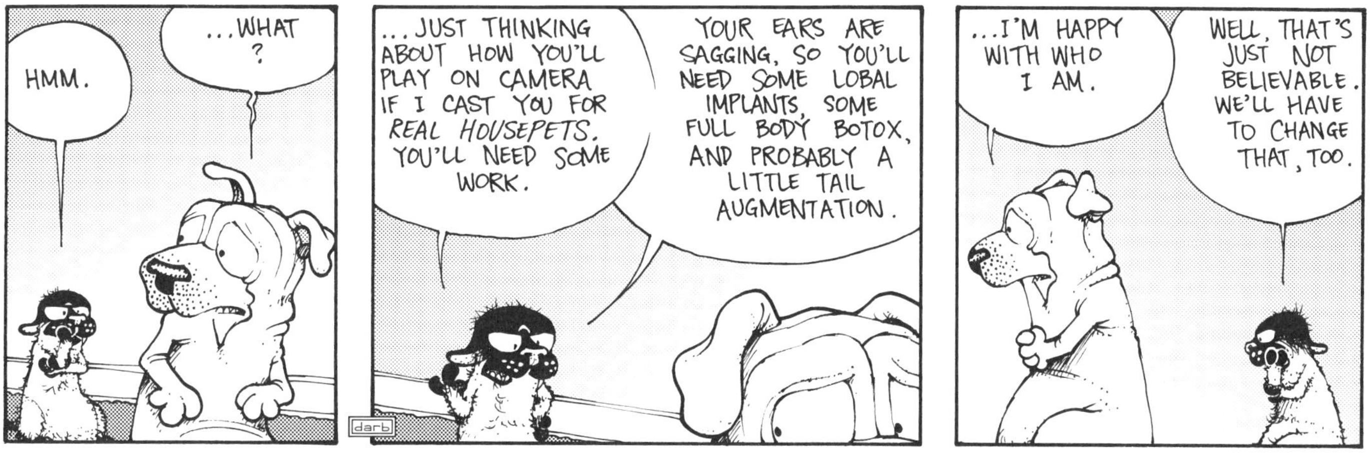
HMM.
...WHAT?
...JUST THINKING ABOUT HOW YOU'LL PLAY ON CAMERA IF I CAST YOU FOR *REAL HOUSEPETS*. YOU'LL NEED SOME WORK.
YOUR EARS ARE SAGGING, SO YOU'LL NEED SOME LOBAL IMPLANTS, SOME FULL BODY BOTOX, AND PROBABLY A LITTLE TAIL AUGMENTATION.
...I'M HAPPY WITH WHO I AM.
WELL, THAT'S JUST NOT BELIEVABLE. WE'LL HAVE TO CHANGE THAT, TOO.
darb

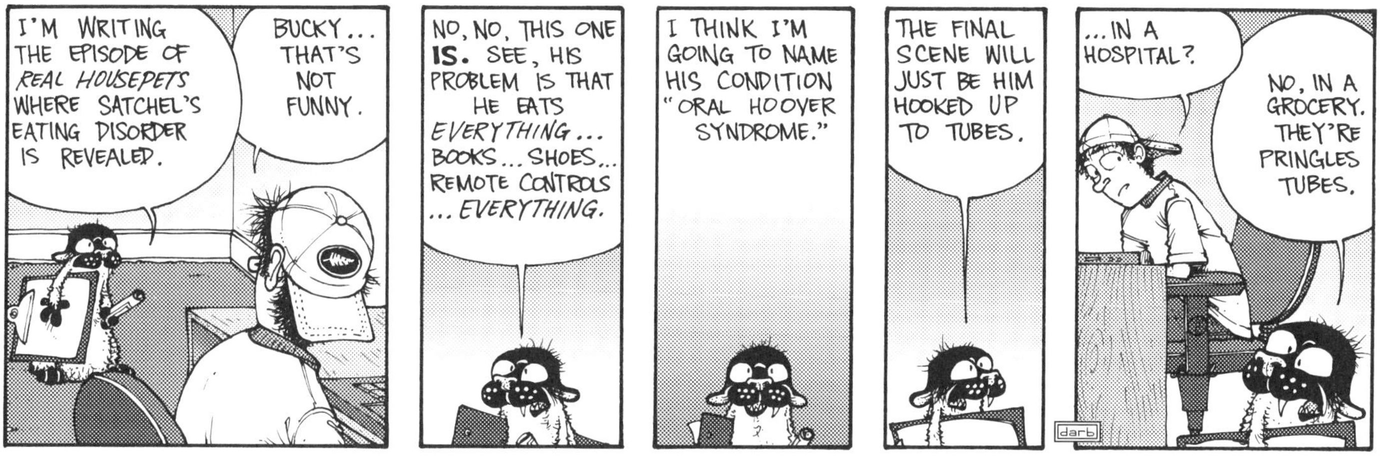
I'M WRITING THE EPISODE OF *REAL HOUSEPETS* WHERE SATCHEL'S EATING DISORDER IS REVEALED.
BUCKY... THAT'S NOT FUNNY.
NO, NO, THIS ONE **IS.** SEE, HIS PROBLEM IS THAT HE EATS *EVERYTHING*... BOOKS... SHOES... REMOTE CONTROLS ...*EVERYTHING.*
I THINK I'M GOING TO NAME HIS CONDITION "ORAL HOOVER SYNDROME."
THE FINAL SCENE WILL JUST BE HIM HOOKED UP TO TUBES.
...IN A HOSPITAL?
NO, IN A GROCERY. THEY'RE PRINGLES TUBES.
darb

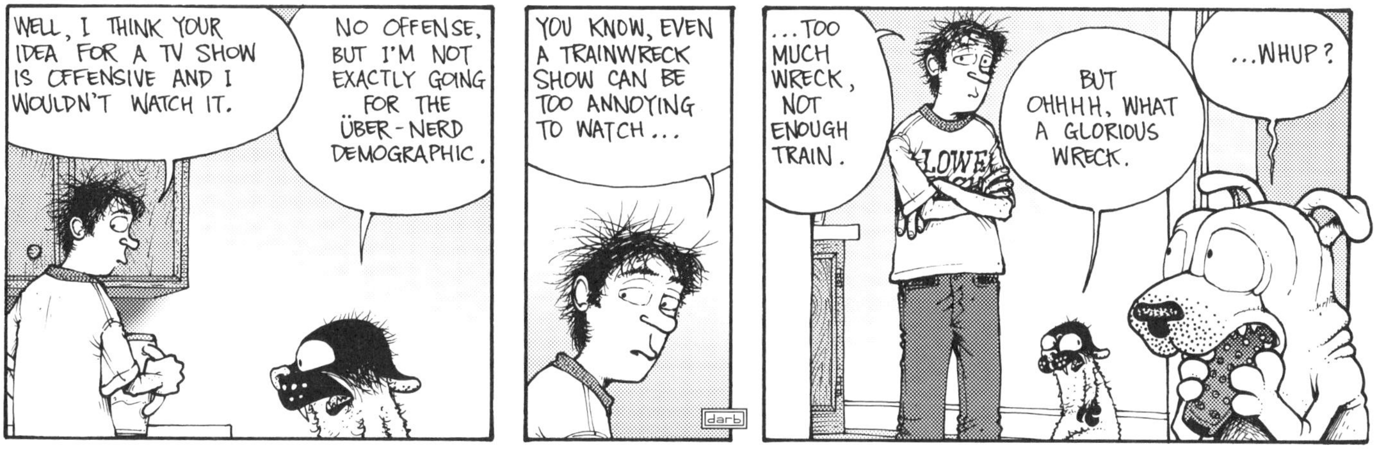
WELL, I THINK YOUR IDEA FOR A TV SHOW IS OFFENSIVE AND I WOULDN'T WATCH IT.
NO OFFENSE, BUT I'M NOT EXACTLY GOING FOR THE ÜBER-NERD DEMOGRAPHIC.
YOU KNOW, EVEN A TRAINWRECK SHOW CAN BE TOO ANNOYING TO WATCH...
...TOO MUCH WRECK, NOT ENOUGH TRAIN.
BUT OHHHH, WHAT A GLORIOUS WRECK.
...WHUP?
darb

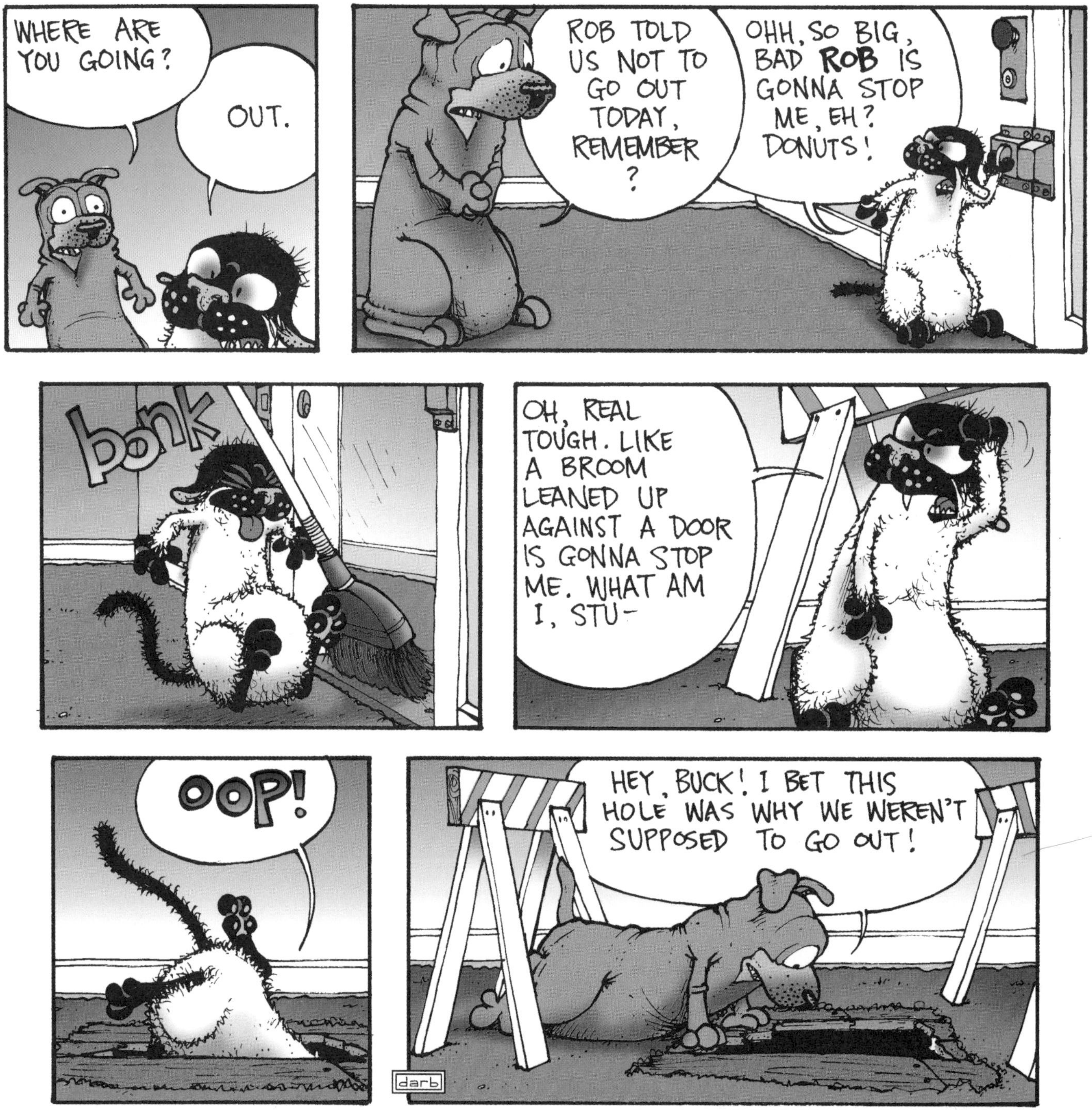
WHERE ARE YOU GOING?
OUT.
ROB TOLD US NOT TO GO OUT TODAY, REMEMBER?
OHH, SO BIG, BAD ROB IS GONNA STOP ME, EH? DONUTS!
bonk
OH, REAL TOUGH. LIKE A BROOM LEANED UP AGAINST A DOOR IS GONNA STOP ME. WHAT AM I, STU-
OOP!
HEY, BUCK! I BET THIS HOLE WAS WHY WE WEREN'T SUPPOSED TO GO OUT!
darb

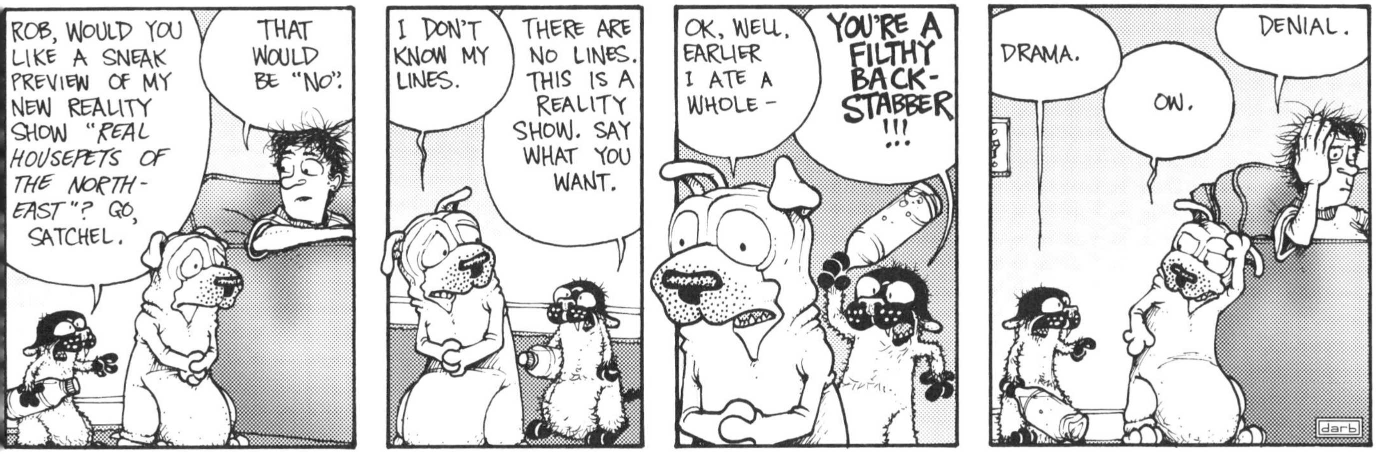
ROB, WOULD YOU LIKE A SNEAK PREVIEW OF MY NEW REALITY SHOW "REAL HOUSEPETS OF THE NORTH-EAST"? GO, SATCHEL.
THAT WOULD BE "NO".
I DON'T KNOW MY LINES.
THERE ARE NO LINES. THIS IS A REALITY SHOW. SAY WHAT YOU WANT.
OK, WELL, EARLIER I ATE A WHOLE-
YOU'RE A FILTHY BACK-STABBER!!!
DRAMA.
OW.
DENIAL.
darb

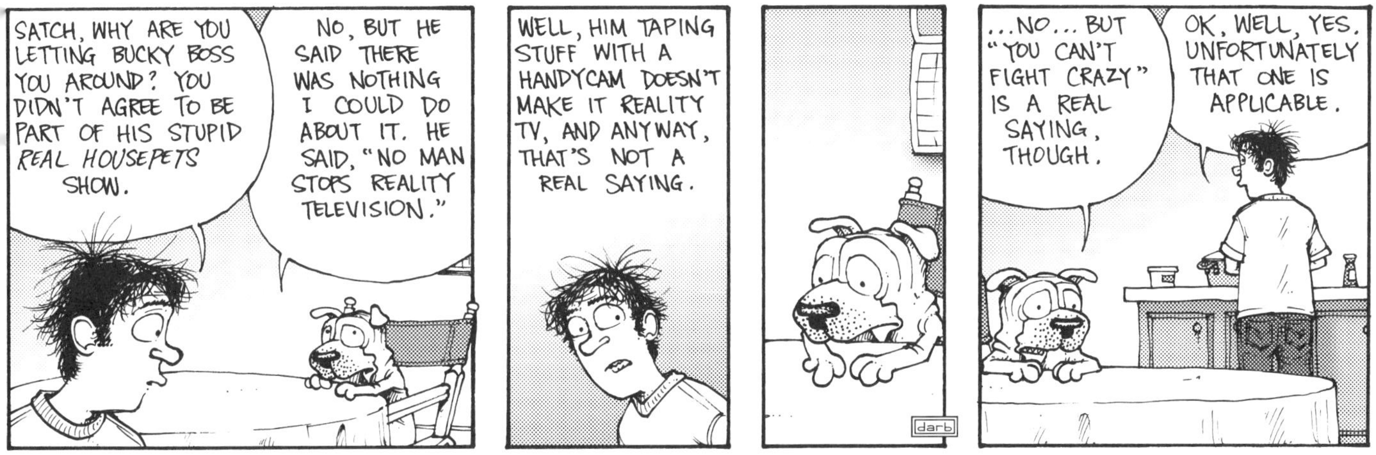
SATCH, WHY ARE YOU LETTING BUCKY BOSS YOU AROUND? YOU DIDN'T AGREE TO BE PART OF HIS STUPID REAL HOUSEPETS SHOW.
NO, BUT HE SAID THERE WAS NOTHING I COULD DO ABOUT IT. HE SAID, "NO MAN STOPS REALITY TELEVISION."
WELL, HIM TAPING STUFF WITH A HANDYCAM DOESN'T MAKE IT REALITY TV, AND ANYWAY, THAT'S NOT A REAL SAYING.
darb
...NO... BUT "YOU CAN'T FIGHT CRAZY" IS A REAL SAYING, THOUGH.
OK, WELL, YES. UNFORTUNATELY THAT ONE IS APPLICABLE.

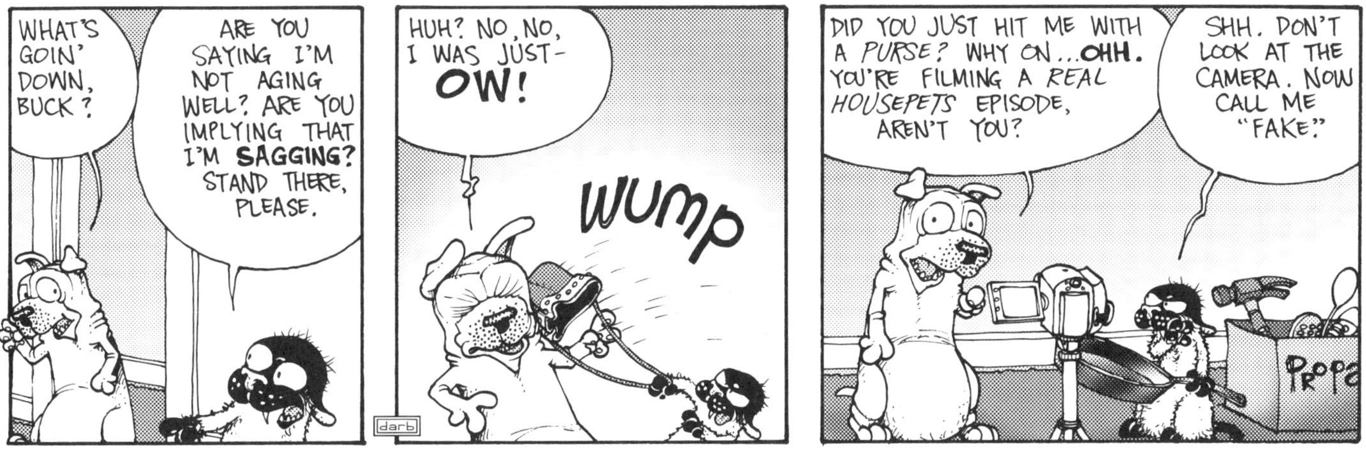
WHAT'S GOIN' DOWN, BUCK?
ARE YOU SAYING I'M NOT AGING WELL? ARE YOU IMPLYING THAT I'M SAGGING? STAND THERE, PLEASE.
HUH? NO, NO, I WAS JUST- OW!
WUMP
darb
DID YOU JUST HIT ME WITH A PURSE? WHY ON... OHH. YOU'RE FILMING A REAL HOUSEPETS EPISODE, AREN'T YOU?
SHH. DON'T LOOK AT THE CAMERA. NOW CALL ME "FAKE."

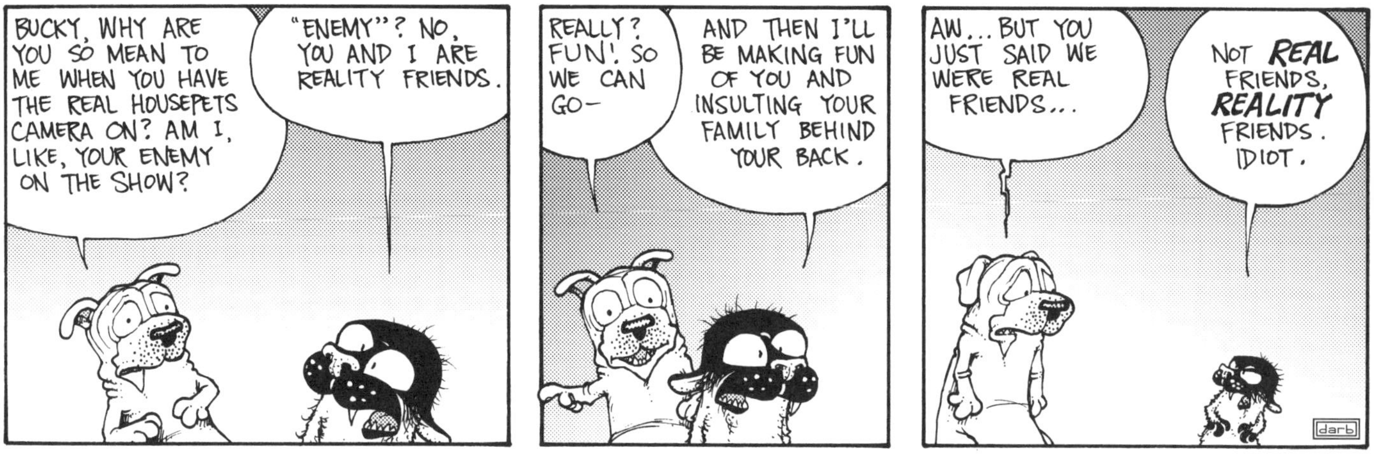
BUCKY, WHY ARE YOU SO MEAN TO ME WHEN YOU HAVE THE REAL HOUSEPETS CAMERA ON? AM I, LIKE, YOUR ENEMY ON THE SHOW?
"ENEMY"? NO, YOU AND I ARE REALITY FRIENDS.
REALLY? FUN! SO WE CAN GO—
AND THEN I'LL BE MAKING FUN OF YOU AND INSULTING YOUR FAMILY BEHIND YOUR BACK.
AW... BUT YOU JUST SAID WE WERE REAL FRIENDS...
NOT **REAL** FRIENDS, ***REALITY*** FRIENDS. IDIOT.
darb

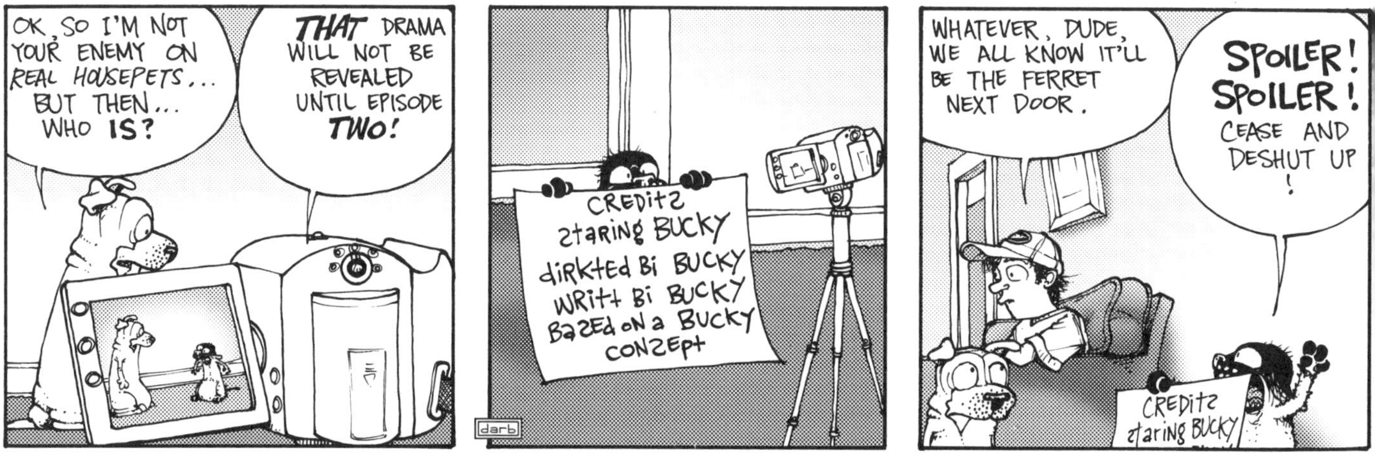
OK, SO I'M NOT YOUR ENEMY ON *REAL HOUSEPETS*... BUT THEN... WHO **IS**?
THAT DRAMA WILL NOT BE REVEALED UNTIL EPISODE ***TWO!***
darb
CREDitz ztaring BUCKY dirKted Bi BUCKY WRitt Bi BUCKY BaZed oN a BUCKY CONZEpt
WHATEVER, DUDE, WE ALL KNOW IT'LL BE THE FERRET NEXT DOOR.
SPOILER! SPOILER! CEASE AND DESHUT UP!
CREDitz ztaring BUCKY

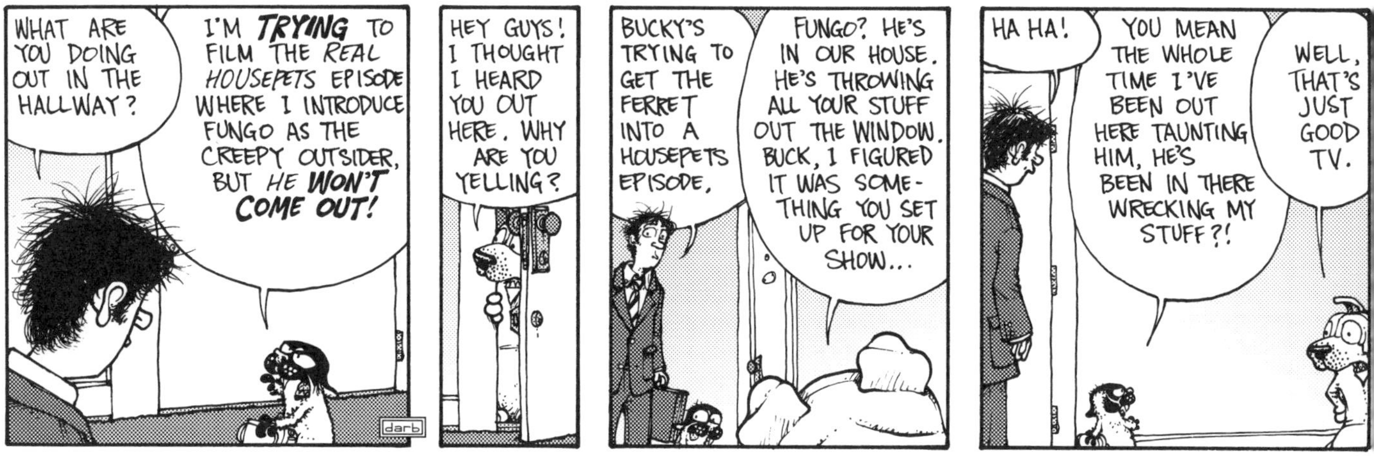
WHAT ARE YOU DOING OUT IN THE HALLWAY?
I'M ***TRYING*** TO FILM THE *REAL HOUSEPETS* EPISODE WHERE I INTRODUCE FUNGO AS THE CREEPY OUTSIDER, BUT *HE* ***WON'T COME OUT!***
darb
HEY GUYS! I THOUGHT I HEARD YOU OUT HERE. WHY ARE YOU YELLING?
BUCKY'S TRYING TO GET THE FERRET INTO A HOUSEPETS EPISODE.
FUNGO? HE'S IN OUR HOUSE. HE'S THROWING ALL YOUR STUFF OUT THE WINDOW. BUCK, I FIGURED IT WAS SOME-THING YOU SET UP FOR YOUR SHOW...
HA HA!
YOU MEAN THE WHOLE TIME I'VE BEEN OUT HERE TAUNTING HIM, HE'S BEEN IN THERE WRECKING MY STUFF?!
WELL, THAT'S JUST GOOD TV.

HMM... I WONDER WHY THE SKY IS BLUE...

SATCHEL, SATCHEL, SATCHEL. THERE ARE SOME QUESTIONS WE CAN NEVER KNOW THE ANSWER TO...

ARE WE ALONE IN THE UNIVERSE? WHY DO BRITISH PEOPLE SING WITH AN AMERICAN ACCENT?

...WOULD A BEAR STILL DUMP IN THE WOODS IF HE HAD ACCESS TO PROPER SANITARY FACILITIES?

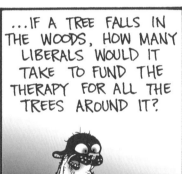

...IF A TREE FALLS IN THE WOODS, HOW MANY LIBERALS WOULD IT TAKE TO FUND THE THERAPY FOR ALL THE TREES AROUND IT?

...IS THE POPE'S HAT ACTUALLY FUNNY, OR IS IT JUST IRONIC?

AND THE BIGGIE: IF A BEAR TRIES TO DUMP IN THE WOODS BUT A TREE FALLS ON HIM WITH NO ONE AROUND, IS THE POPE'S HAT STILL FUNNY?

darb

NO, WHY IS THE SKY BLUE **NOW**? IT WAS SUPPOSED TO RAIN.

OH. I DUNNO. WIND OR SOMETHING, STUPID QUESTION.

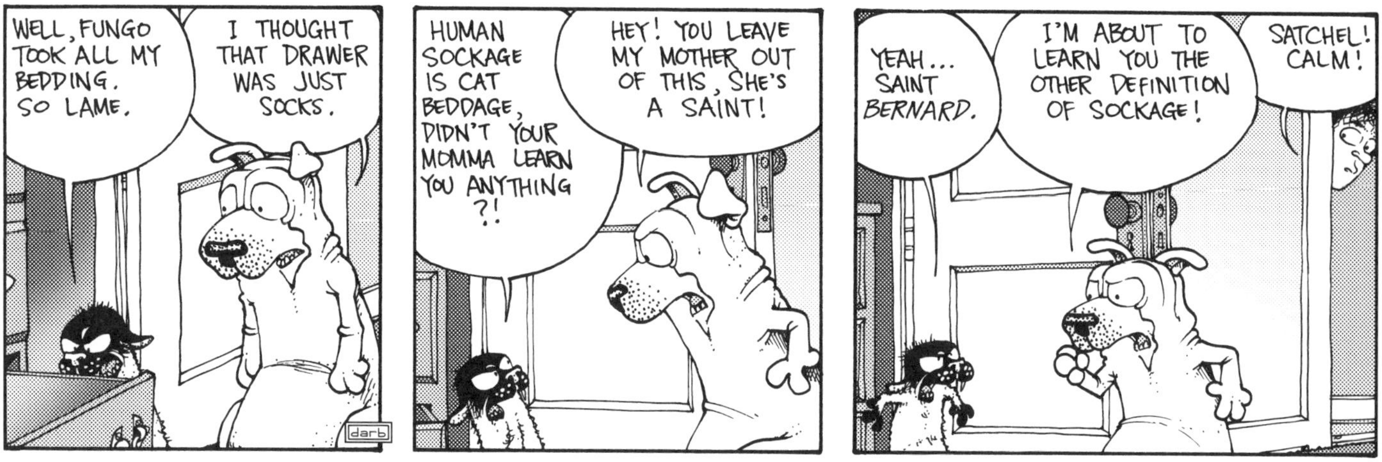
WELL, FUNGO TOOK ALL MY BEDDING. SO LAME.
I THOUGHT THAT DRAWER WAS JUST SOCKS.
HUMAN SOCKAGE IS CAT BEDDAGE, DIDN'T YOUR MOMMA LEARN YOU ANYTHING ?!
HEY! YOU LEAVE MY MOTHER OUT OF THIS, SHE'S A SAINT!
YEAH... SAINT *BERNARD*.
I'M ABOUT TO LEARN YOU THE OTHER DEFINITION OF SOCKAGE!
SATCHEL! CALM!
darb

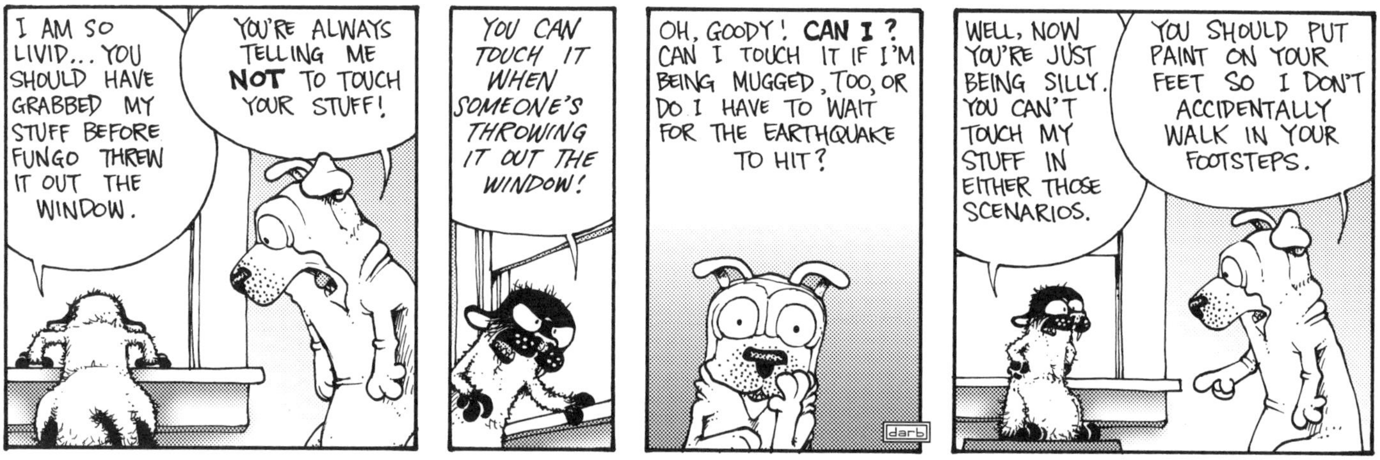
I AM SO LIVID... YOU SHOULD HAVE GRABBED MY STUFF BEFORE FUNGO THREW IT OUT THE WINDOW.
YOU'RE ALWAYS TELLING ME **NOT** TO TOUCH YOUR STUFF!
YOU CAN TOUCH IT WHEN SOMEONE'S THROWING IT OUT THE WINDOW!
OH, GOODY! **CAN I**? CAN I TOUCH IT IF I'M BEING MUGGED, TOO, OR DO I HAVE TO WAIT FOR THE EARTHQUAKE TO HIT?
darb
WELL, NOW YOU'RE JUST BEING SILLY. YOU CAN'T TOUCH MY STUFF IN EITHER THOSE SCENARIOS.
YOU SHOULD PUT PAINT ON YOUR FEET SO I DON'T ACCIDENTALLY WALK IN YOUR FOOTSTEPS.

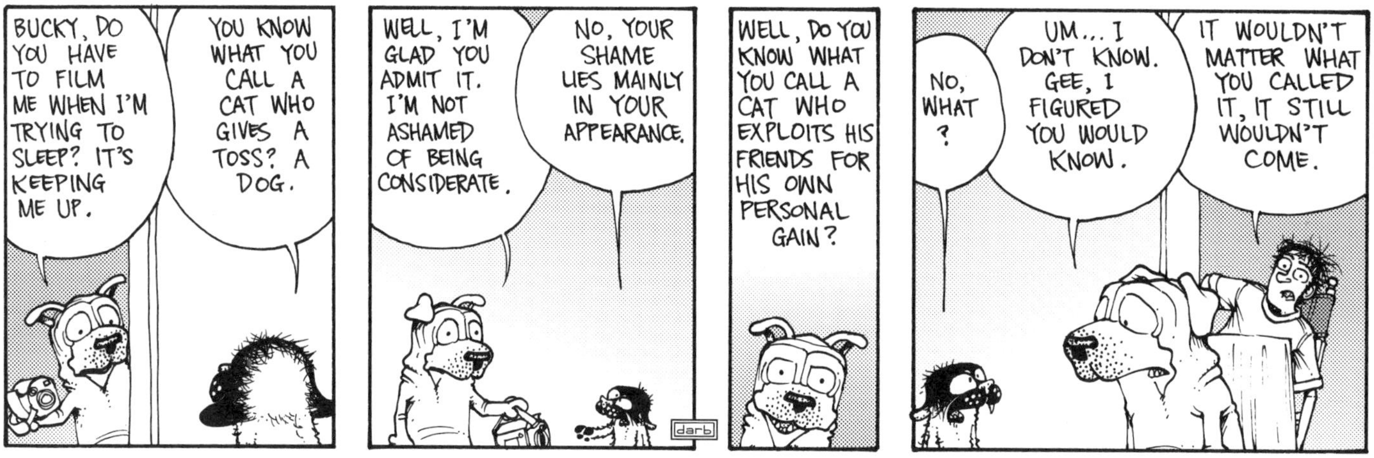
BUCKY, DO YOU HAVE TO FILM ME WHEN I'M TRYING TO SLEEP? IT'S KEEPING ME UP.
YOU KNOW WHAT YOU CALL A CAT WHO GIVES A TOSS? A DOG.
WELL, I'M GLAD YOU ADMIT IT. I'M NOT ASHAMED OF BEING CONSIDERATE.
NO, YOUR SHAME LIES MAINLY IN YOUR APPEARANCE.
darb
WELL, DO YOU KNOW WHAT YOU CALL A CAT WHO EXPLOITS HIS FRIENDS FOR HIS OWN PERSONAL GAIN?
NO, WHAT?
UM... I DON'T KNOW. GEE, I FIGURED YOU WOULD KNOW.
IT WOULDN'T MATTER WHAT YOU CALLED IT, IT STILL WOULDN'T COME.

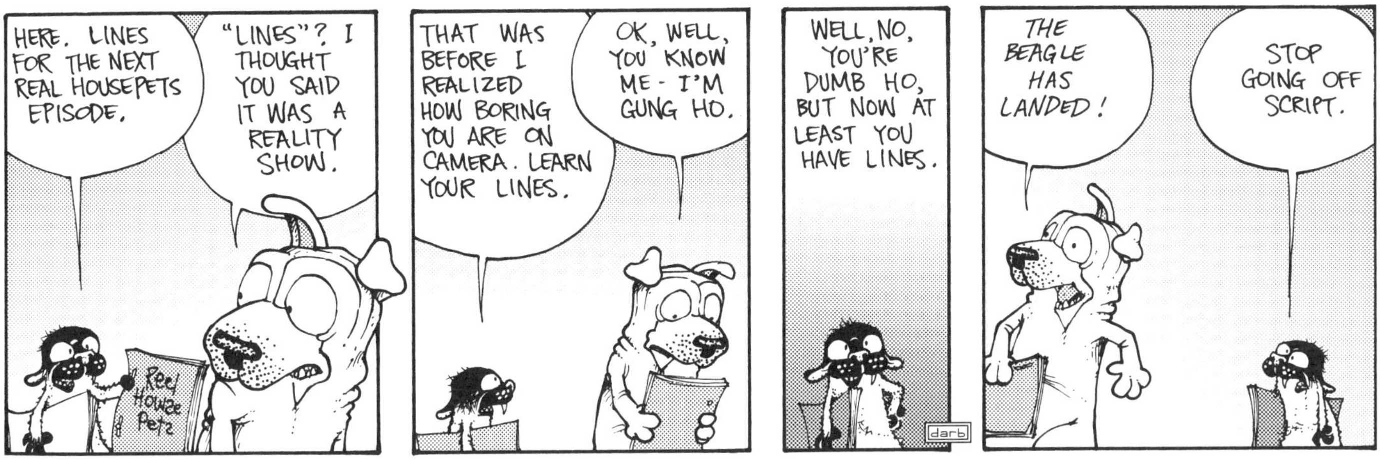
HERE. LINES FOR THE NEXT REAL HOUSEPETS EPISODE.
"LINES"? I THOUGHT YOU SAID IT WAS A REALITY SHOW.
Reel Howze Petz
THAT WAS BEFORE I REALIZED HOW BORING YOU ARE ON CAMERA. LEARN YOUR LINES.
OK, WELL, YOU KNOW ME - I'M GUNG HO.
WELL, NO, YOU'RE DUMB HO, BUT NOW AT LEAST YOU HAVE LINES.
darb
THE BEAGLE HAS LANDED!
STOP GOING OFF SCRIPT.

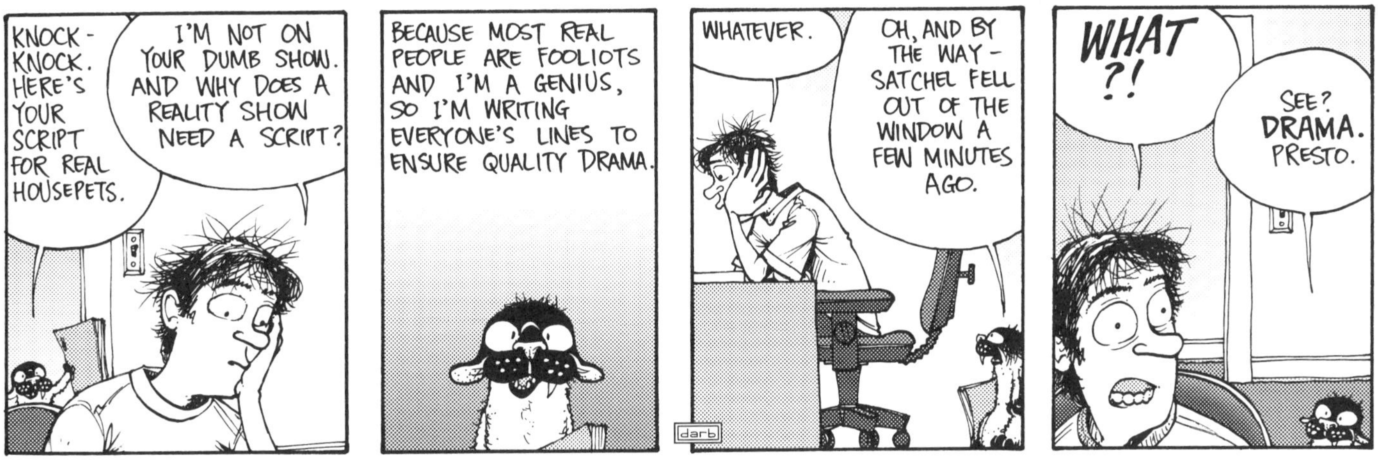
KNOCK-KNOCK. HERE'S YOUR SCRIPT FOR REAL HOUSEPETS.
I'M NOT ON YOUR DUMB SHOW. AND WHY DOES A REALITY SHOW NEED A SCRIPT?
BECAUSE MOST REAL PEOPLE ARE FOOLIOTS AND I'M A GENIUS, SO I'M WRITING EVERYONE'S LINES TO ENSURE QUALITY DRAMA.
darb
WHATEVER.
OH, AND BY THE WAY - SATCHEL FELL OUT OF THE WINDOW A FEW MINUTES AGO.
WHAT ?!
SEE? DRAMA. PRESTO.

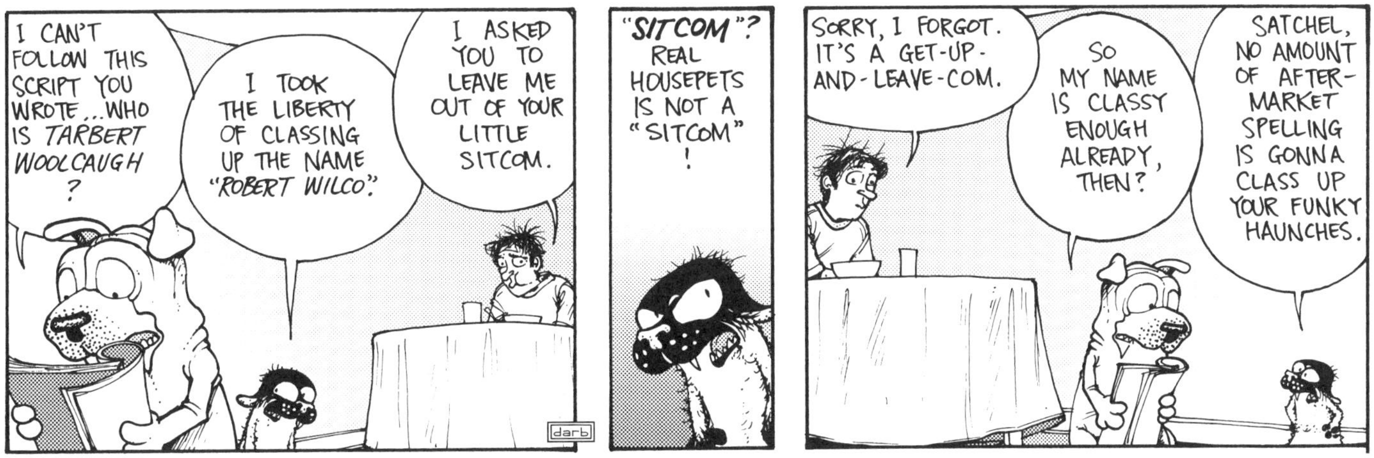
I CAN'T FOLLOW THIS SCRIPT YOU WROTE... WHO IS TARBERT WOOLCAUGH ?
I TOOK THE LIBERTY OF CLASSING UP THE NAME "ROBERT WILCO."
I ASKED YOU TO LEAVE ME OUT OF YOUR LITTLE SITCOM.
darb
"SITCOM"? REAL HOUSEPETS IS NOT A "SITCOM"!
SORRY, I FORGOT. IT'S A GET-UP-AND-LEAVE-COM.
SO MY NAME IS CLASSY ENOUGH ALREADY, THEN?
SATCHEL, NO AMOUNT OF AFTER-MARKET SPELLING IS GONNA CLASS UP YOUR FUNKY HAUNCHES.

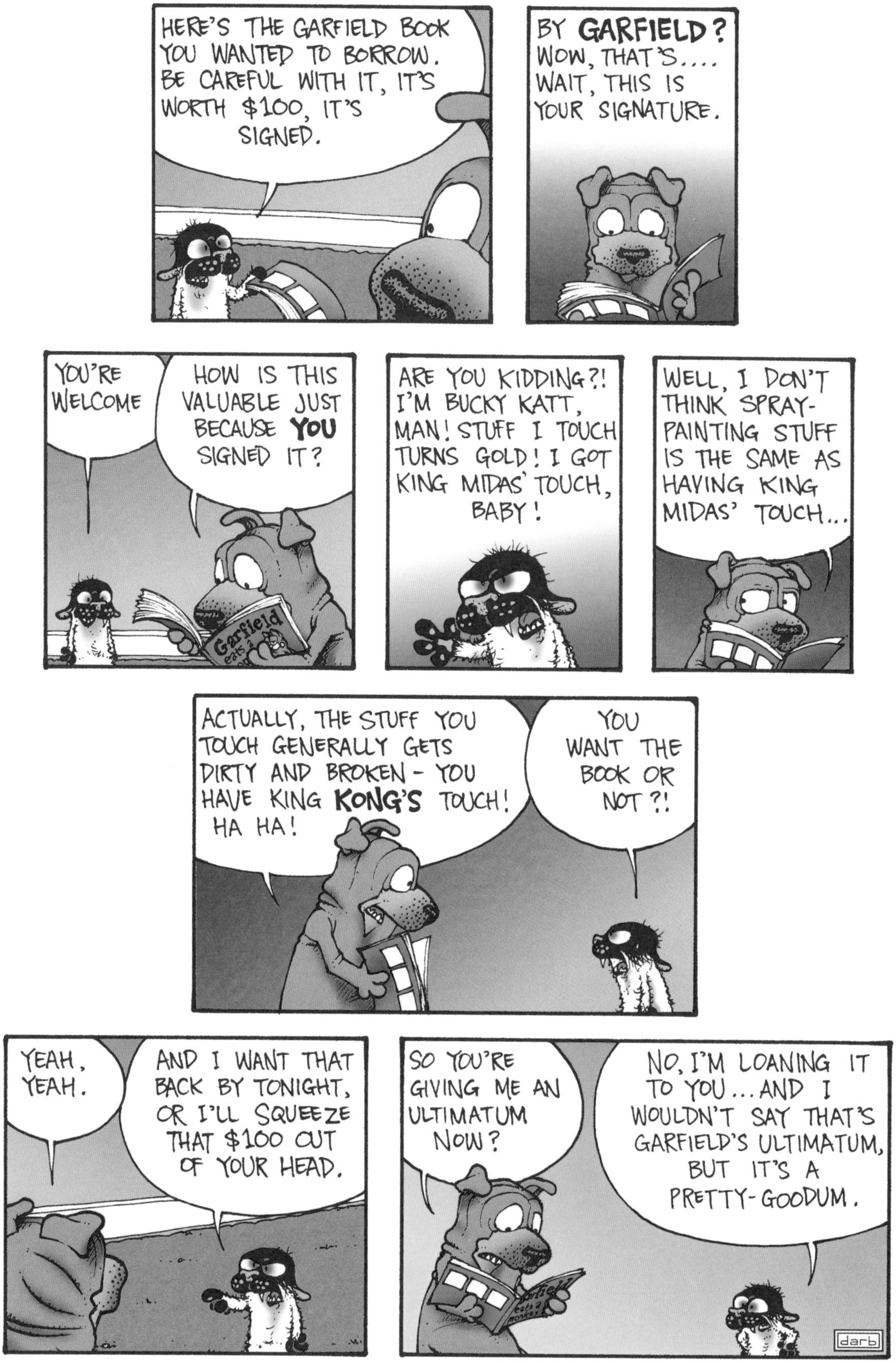
HERE'S THE GARFIELD BOOK YOU WANTED TO BORROW. BE CAREFUL WITH IT, IT'S WORTH $100, IT'S SIGNED.
BY GARFIELD? WOW, THAT'S.... WAIT, THIS IS YOUR SIGNATURE.
YOU'RE WELCOME
HOW IS THIS VALUABLE JUST BECAUSE YOU SIGNED IT?
ARE YOU KIDDING?! I'M BUCKY KATT, MAN! STUFF I TOUCH TURNS GOLD! I GOT KING MIDAS' TOUCH, BABY!
WELL, I DON'T THINK SPRAY-PAINTING STUFF IS THE SAME AS HAVING KING MIDAS' TOUCH...
ACTUALLY, THE STUFF YOU TOUCH GENERALLY GETS DIRTY AND BROKEN - YOU HAVE KING KONG'S TOUCH! HA HA!
YOU WANT THE BOOK OR NOT?!
YEAH, YEAH.
AND I WANT THAT BACK BY TONIGHT, OR I'LL SQUEEZE THAT $100 OUT OF YOUR HEAD.
SO YOU'RE GIVING ME AN ULTIMATUM NOW?
NO, I'M LOANING IT TO YOU... AND I WOULDN'T SAY THAT'S GARFIELD'S ULTIMATUM, BUT IT'S A PRETTY-GOODUM.
darb

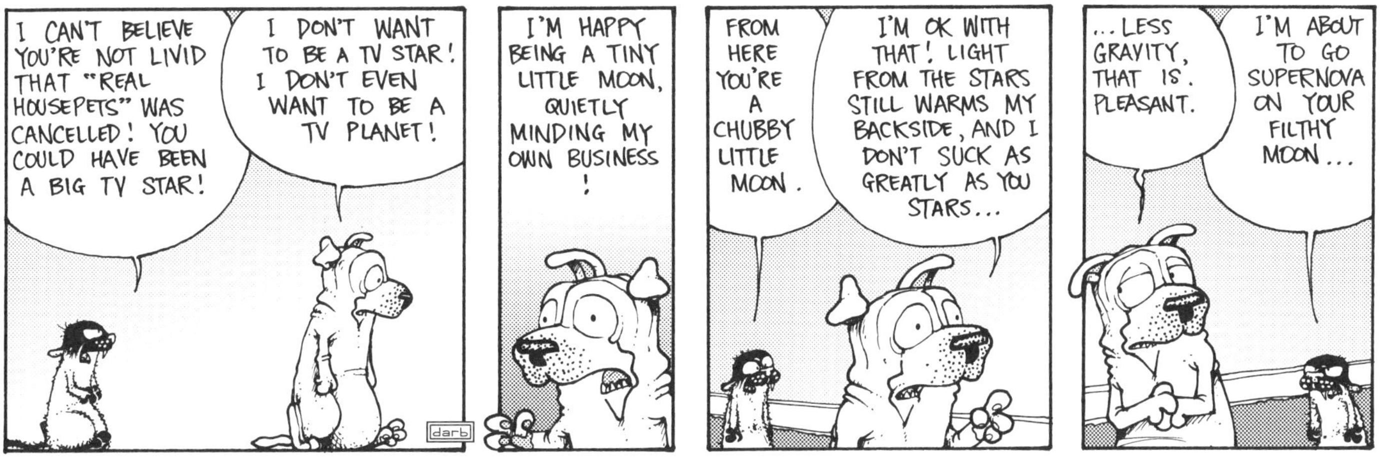
I CAN'T BELIEVE YOU'RE NOT LIVID THAT "REAL HOUSEPETS" WAS CANCELLED! YOU COULD HAVE BEEN A BIG TV STAR!
I DON'T WANT TO BE A TV STAR! I DON'T EVEN WANT TO BE A TV PLANET!
I'M HAPPY BEING A TINY LITTLE MOON, QUIETLY MINDING MY OWN BUSINESS!
FROM HERE YOU'RE A CHUBBY LITTLE MOON.
I'M OK WITH THAT! LIGHT FROM THE STARS STILL WARMS MY BACKSIDE, AND I DON'T SUCK AS GREATLY AS YOU STARS...
...LESS GRAVITY, THAT IS. PLEASANT.
I'M ABOUT TO GO SUPERNOVA ON YOUR FILTHY MOON...
darb

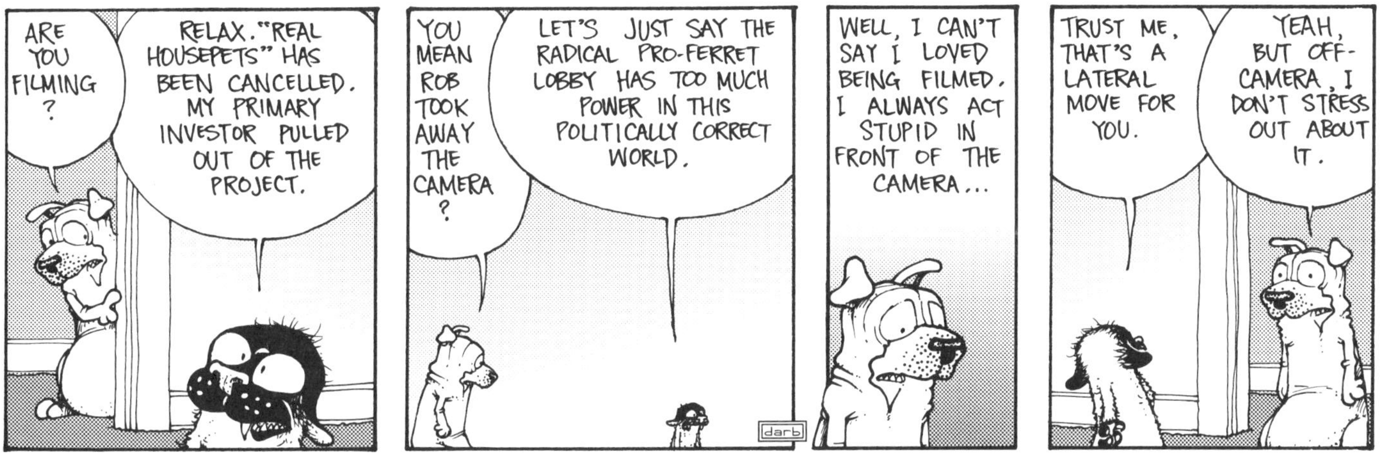
ARE YOU FILMING?
RELAX. "REAL HOUSEPETS" HAS BEEN CANCELLED. MY PRIMARY INVESTOR PULLED OUT OF THE PROJECT.
YOU MEAN ROB TOOK AWAY THE CAMERA?
LET'S JUST SAY THE RADICAL PRO-FERRET LOBBY HAS TOO MUCH POWER IN THIS POLITICALLY CORRECT WORLD.
darb
WELL, I CAN'T SAY I LOVED BEING FILMED. I ALWAYS ACT STUPID IN FRONT OF THE CAMERA...
TRUST ME, THAT'S A LATERAL MOVE FOR YOU.
YEAH, BUT OFF-CAMERA, I DON'T STRESS OUT ABOUT IT.

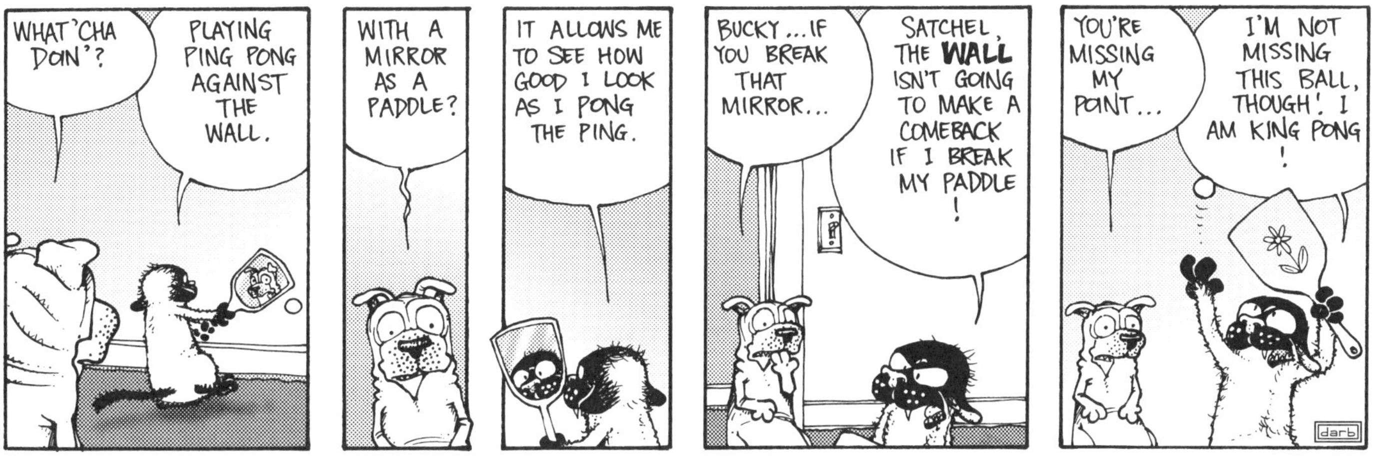
WHAT'CHA DOIN'?
PLAYING PING PONG AGAINST THE WALL.
WITH A MIRROR AS A PADDLE?
IT ALLOWS ME TO SEE HOW GOOD I LOOK AS I PONG THE PING.
BUCKY...IF YOU BREAK THAT MIRROR...
SATCHEL, THE WALL ISN'T GOING TO MAKE A COMEBACK IF I BREAK MY PADDLE!
YOU'RE MISSING MY POINT...
I'M NOT MISSING THIS BALL, THOUGH! I AM KING PONG!
darb

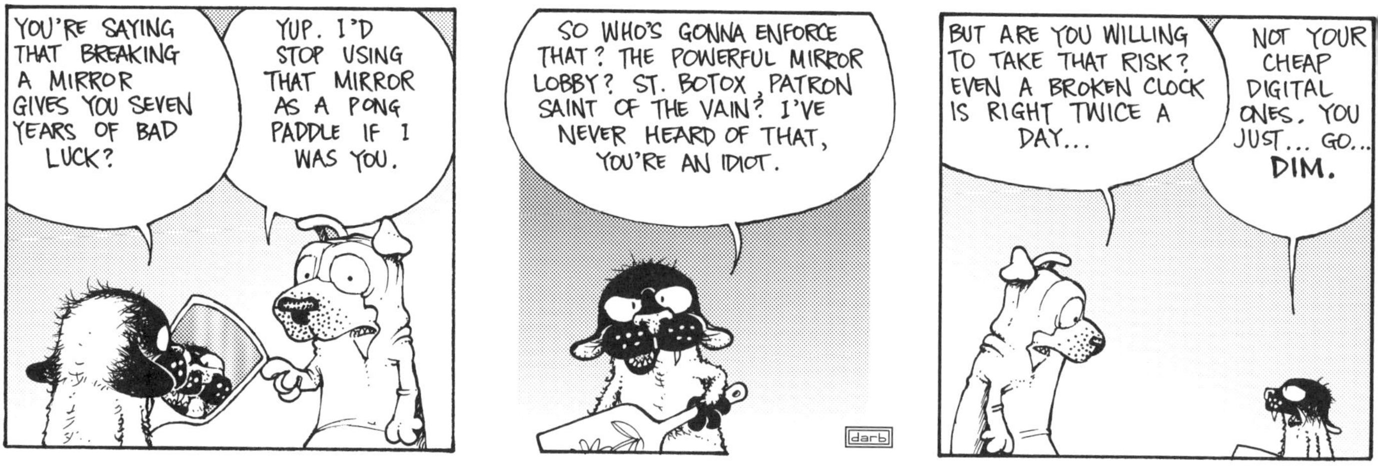
YOU'RE SAYING THAT BREAKING A MIRROR GIVES YOU SEVEN YEARS OF BAD LUCK?
YUP. I'D STOP USING THAT MIRROR AS A PONG PADDLE IF I WAS YOU.
SO WHO'S GONNA ENFORCE THAT? THE POWERFUL MIRROR LOBBY? ST. BOTOX, PATRON SAINT OF THE VAIN? I'VE NEVER HEARD OF THAT, YOU'RE AN IDIOT.
darb
BUT ARE YOU WILLING TO TAKE THAT RISK? EVEN A BROKEN CLOCK IS RIGHT TWICE A DAY...
NOT YOUR CHEAP DIGITAL ONES. YOU JUST... GO... **DIM.**

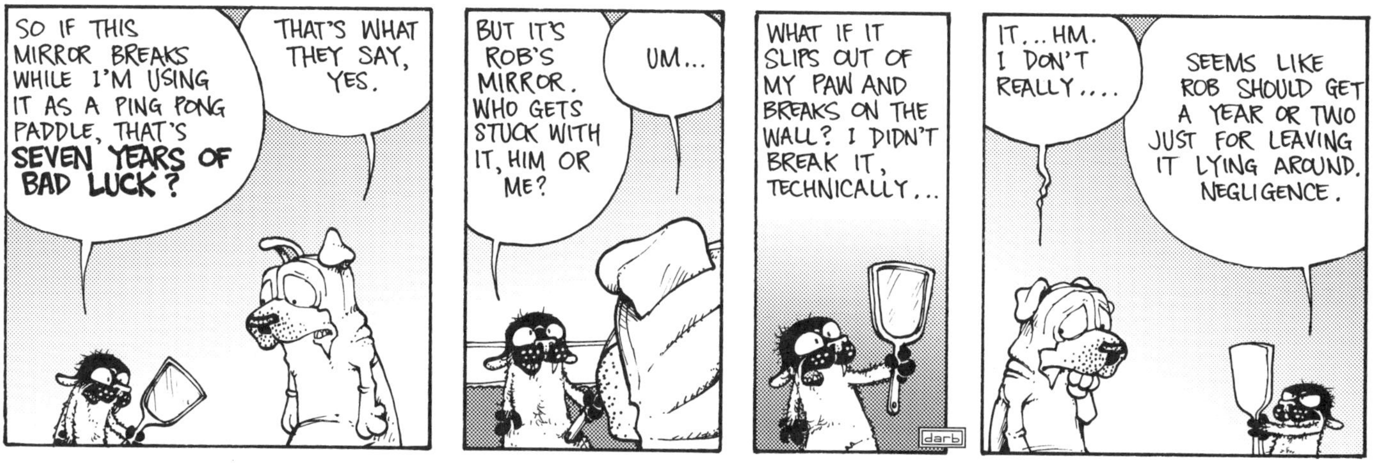
SO IF THIS MIRROR BREAKS WHILE I'M USING IT AS A PING PONG PADDLE, THAT'S **SEVEN YEARS OF BAD LUCK?**
THAT'S WHAT THEY SAY, YES.
BUT IT'S ROB'S MIRROR. WHO GETS STUCK WITH IT, HIM OR ME?
UM...
WHAT IF IT SLIPS OUT OF MY PAW AND BREAKS ON THE WALL? I DIDN'T BREAK IT, TECHNICALLY...
darb
IT... HM. I DON'T REALLY....
SEEMS LIKE ROB SHOULD GET A YEAR OR TWO JUST FOR LEAVING IT LYING AROUND. NEGLIGENCE.

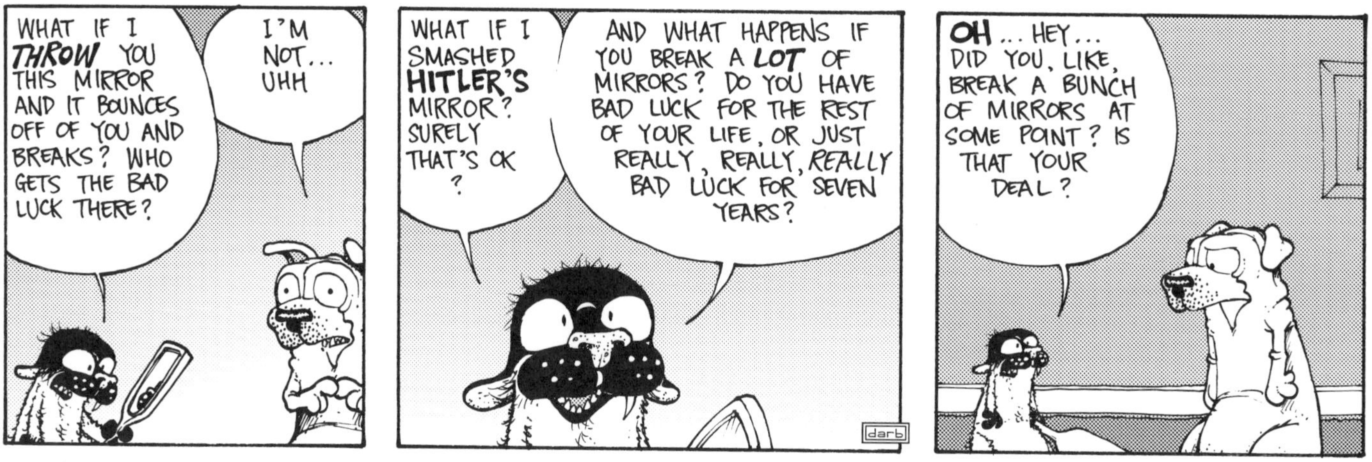
WHAT IF I ***THROW*** YOU THIS MIRROR AND IT BOUNCES OFF OF YOU AND BREAKS? WHO GETS THE BAD LUCK THERE?
I'M NOT... UHH
WHAT IF I SMASHED **HITLER'S** MIRROR? SURELY THAT'S OK?
AND WHAT HAPPENS IF YOU BREAK A ***LOT*** OF MIRRORS? DO YOU HAVE BAD LUCK FOR THE REST OF YOUR LIFE, OR JUST REALLY, REALLY, *REALLY* BAD LUCK FOR SEVEN YEARS?
darb
OH... HEY... DID YOU, LIKE, BREAK A BUNCH OF MIRRORS AT SOME POINT? IS THAT YOUR DEAL?

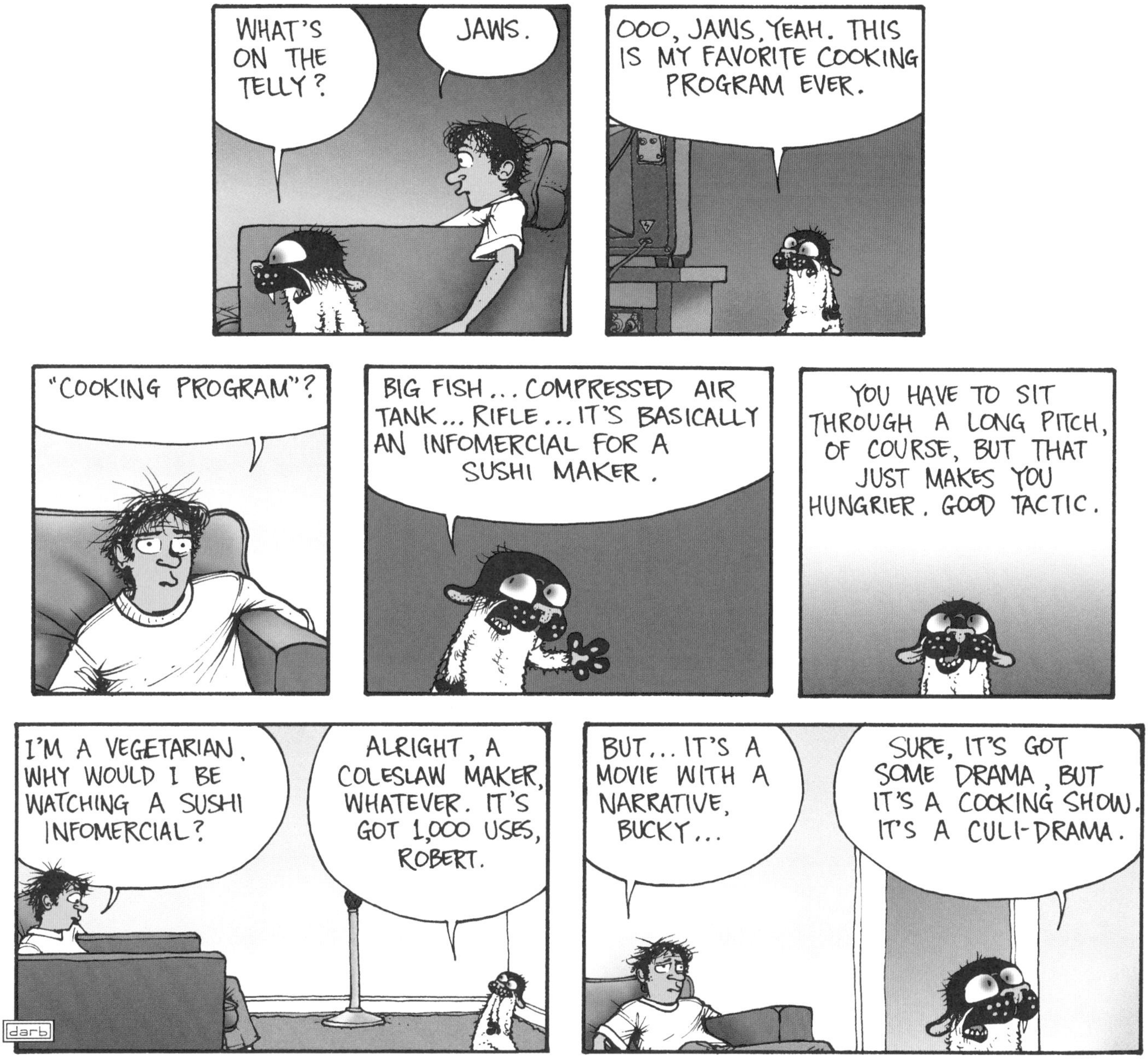
WHAT'S ON THE TELLY?
JAWS.
OOO, JAWS, YEAH. THIS IS MY FAVORITE COOKING PROGRAM EVER.
"COOKING PROGRAM"?
BIG FISH... COMPRESSED AIR TANK... RIFLE... IT'S BASICALLY AN INFOMERCIAL FOR A SUSHI MAKER.
YOU HAVE TO SIT THROUGH A LONG PITCH, OF COURSE, BUT THAT JUST MAKES YOU HUNGRIER. GOOD TACTIC.
I'M A VEGETARIAN. WHY WOULD I BE WATCHING A SUSHI INFOMERCIAL?
ALRIGHT, A COLESLAW MAKER, WHATEVER. IT'S GOT 1,000 USES, ROBERT.
darb
BUT... IT'S A MOVIE WITH A NARRATIVE, BUCKY...
SURE, IT'S GOT SOME DRAMA, BUT IT'S A COOKING SHOW. IT'S A CULI-DRAMA.

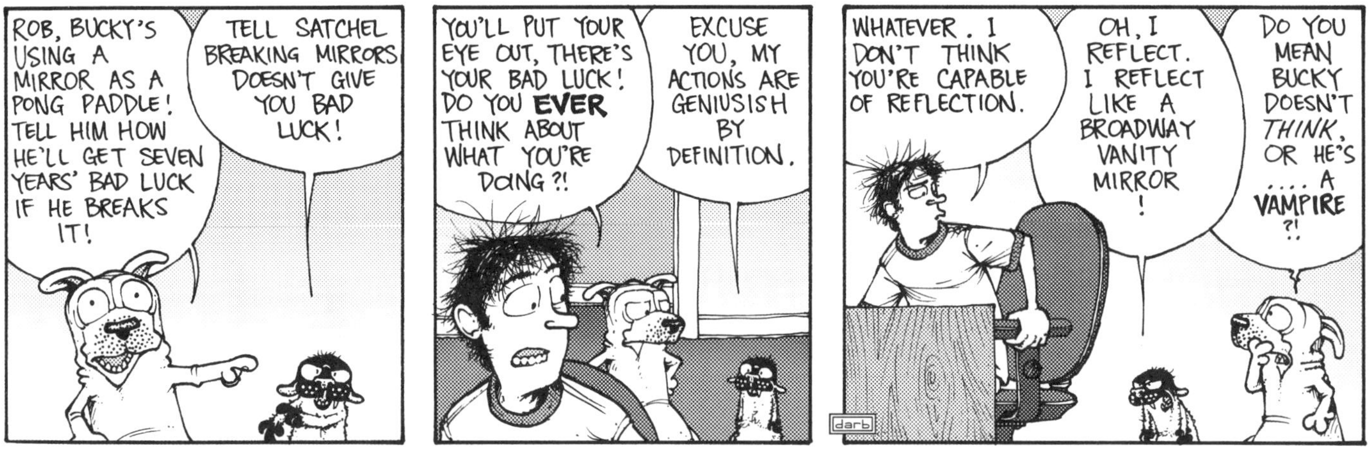
ROB, BUCKY'S USING A MIRROR AS A PONG PADDLE! TELL HIM HOW HE'LL GET SEVEN YEARS' BAD LUCK IF HE BREAKS IT!
TELL SATCHEL BREAKING MIRRORS DOESN'T GIVE YOU BAD LUCK!
YOU'LL PUT YOUR EYE OUT, THERE'S YOUR BAD LUCK! DO YOU **EVER** THINK ABOUT WHAT YOU'RE DOING?!
EXCUSE YOU, MY ACTIONS ARE GENIUSISH BY DEFINITION.
WHATEVER. I DON'T THINK YOU'RE CAPABLE OF REFLECTION.
OH, I REFLECT. I REFLECT LIKE A BROADWAY VANITY MIRROR!
DO YOU MEAN BUCKY DOESN'T *THINK*, OR HE'S .... A **VAMPIRE**?!
darb

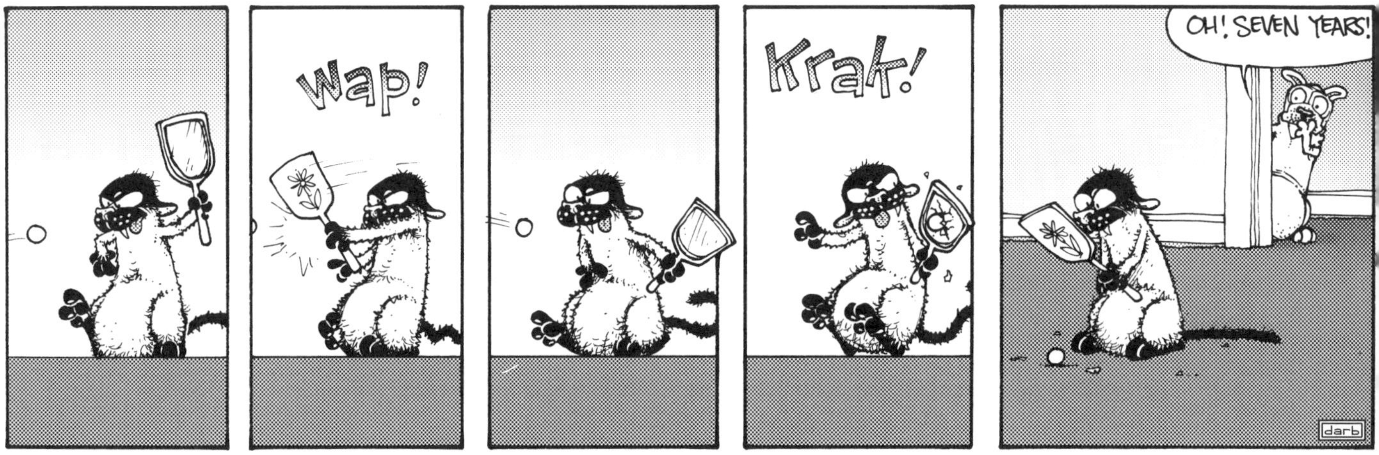
Wap!
Krak!
OH! SEVEN YEARS!
darb

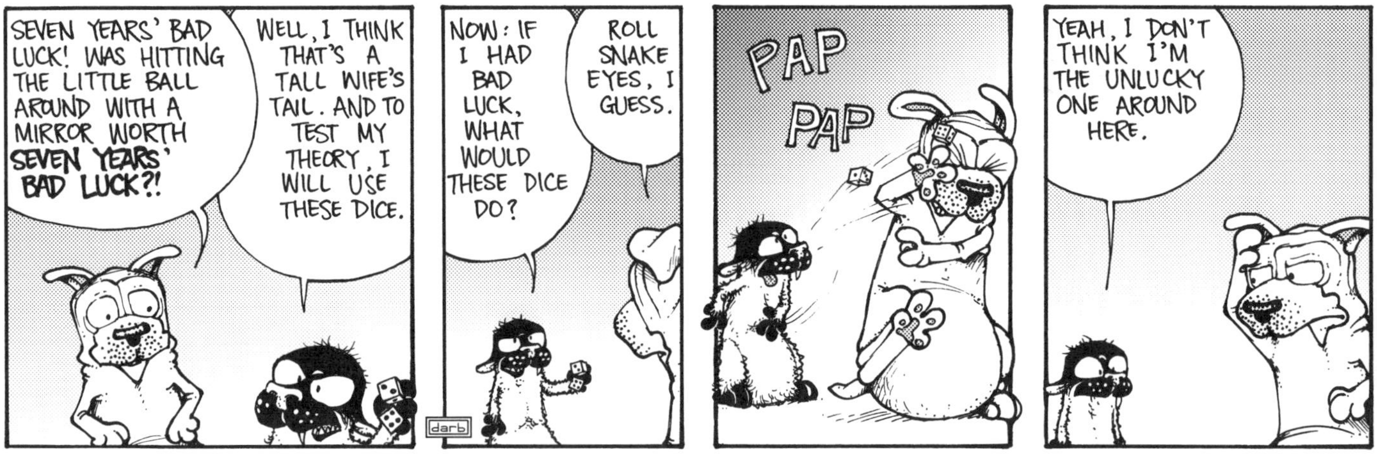
SEVEN YEARS' BAD LUCK! WAS HITTING THE LITTLE BALL AROUND WITH A MIRROR WORTH **SEVEN YEARS' BAD LUCK?!**
WELL, I THINK THAT'S A TALL WIFE'S TAIL. AND TO TEST MY THEORY, I WILL USE THESE DICE.
darb
NOW: IF I HAD BAD LUCK, WHAT WOULD THESE DICE DO?
ROLL SNAKE EYES, I GUESS.
PAP
PAP
YEAH, I DON'T THINK I'M THE UNLUCKY ONE AROUND HERE.

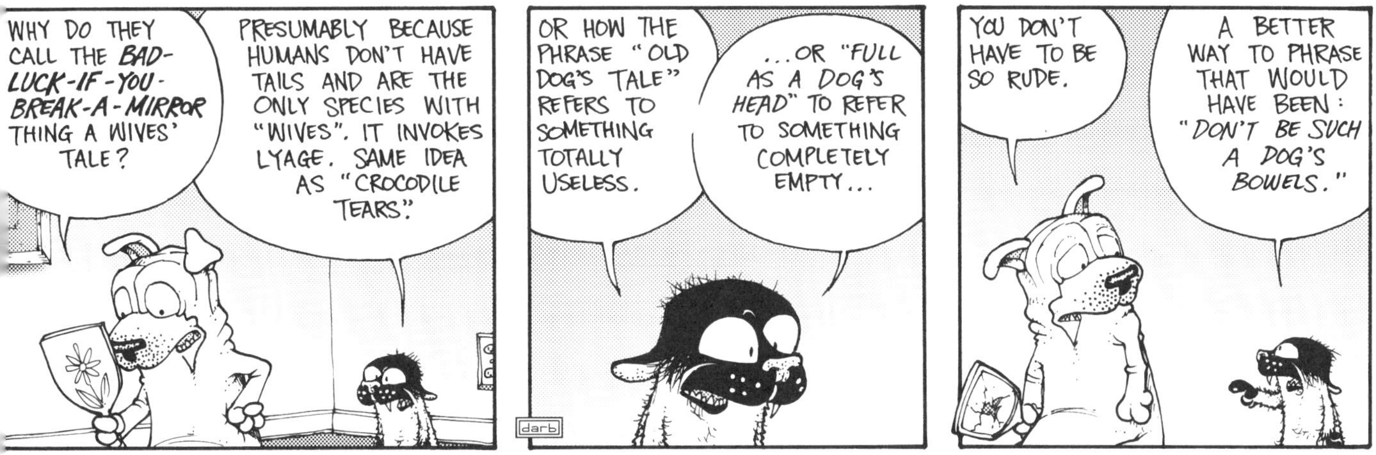
WHY DO THEY CALL THE *BAD-LUCK-IF-YOU-BREAK-A-MIRROR* THING A WIVES' TALE?
PRESUMABLY BECAUSE HUMANS DON'T HAVE TAILS AND ARE THE ONLY SPECIES WITH "WIVES". IT INVOKES LYAGE. SAME IDEA AS "CROCODILE TEARS."
OR HOW THE PHRASE "OLD DOG'S TALE" REFERS TO SOMETHING TOTALLY USELESS.
...OR "*FULL AS A DOG'S HEAD*" TO REFER TO SOMETHING COMPLETELY EMPTY...
darb
YOU DON'T HAVE TO BE SO RUDE.
A BETTER WAY TO PHRASE THAT WOULD HAVE BEEN: "*DON'T BE SUCH A DOG'S BOWELS.*"

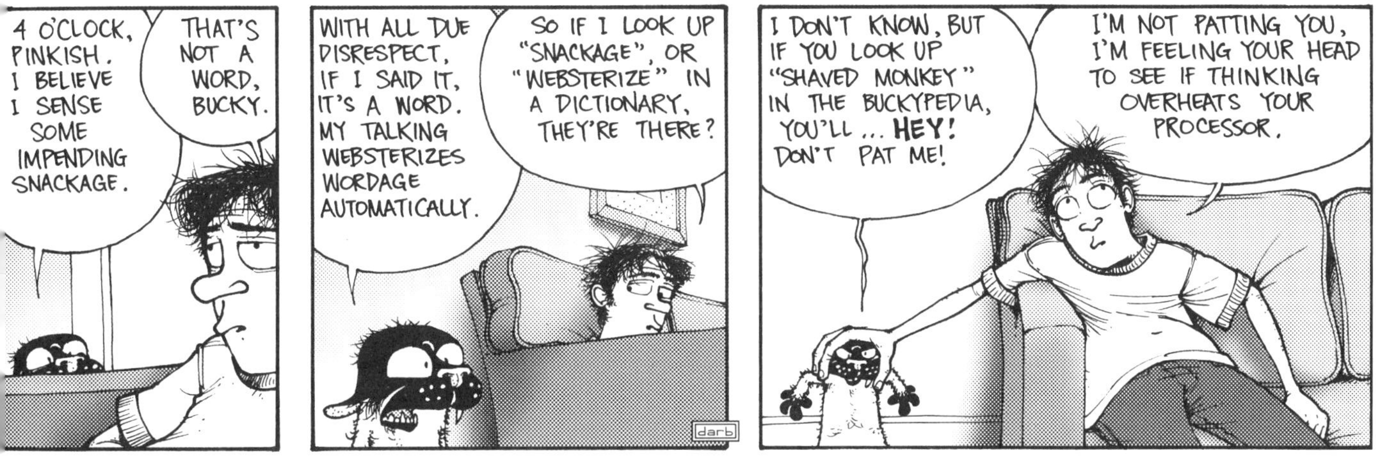
4 O'CLOCK, PINKISH. I BELIEVE I SENSE SOME IMPENDING SNACKAGE.
THAT'S NOT A WORD, BUCKY.
WITH ALL DUE DISRESPECT, IF I SAID IT, IT'S A WORD. MY TALKING WEBSTERIZES WORDAGE AUTOMATICALLY.
SO IF I LOOK UP "SNACKAGE", OR "WEBSTERIZE" IN A DICTIONARY, THEY'RE THERE?
darb
I DON'T KNOW, BUT IF YOU LOOK UP "SHAVED MONKEY" IN THE BUCKYPEDIA, YOU'LL... **HEY!** DON'T PAT ME!
I'M NOT PATTING YOU, I'M FEELING YOUR HEAD TO SEE IF THINKING OVERHEATS YOUR PROCESSOR.

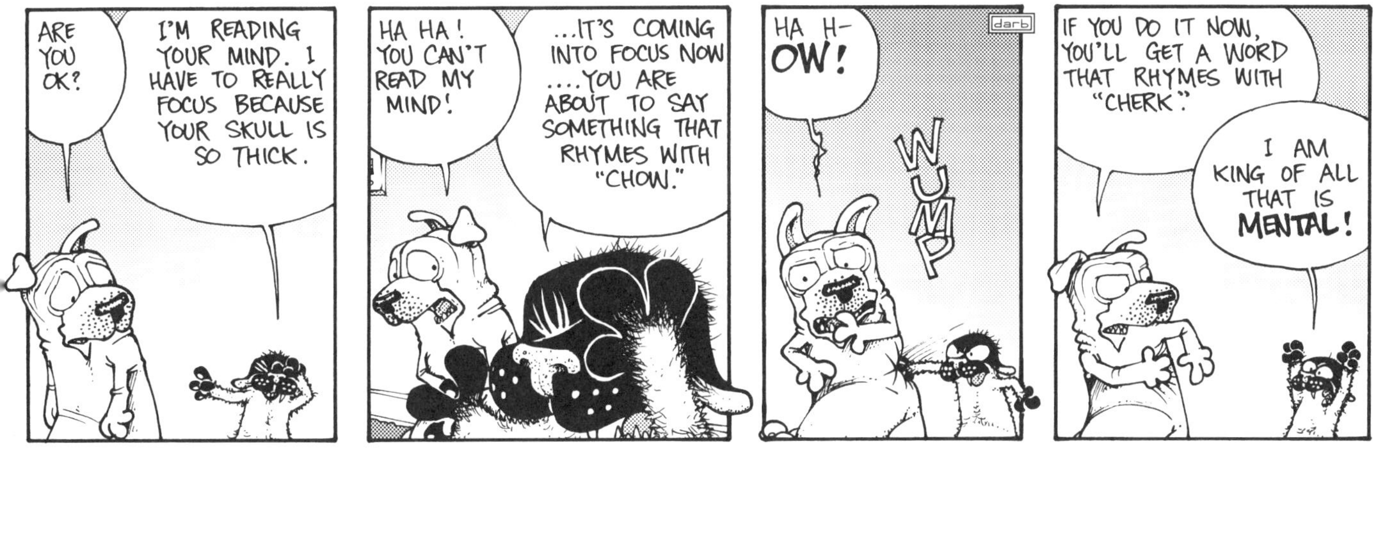
ARE YOU OK?
I'M READING YOUR MIND. I HAVE TO REALLY FOCUS BECAUSE YOUR SKULL IS SO THICK.
HA HA! YOU CAN'T READ MY MIND!
...IT'S COMING INTO FOCUS NOW ....YOU ARE ABOUT TO SAY SOMETHING THAT RHYMES WITH "CHOW."
HA H- **OW!**
WUMP
darb
IF YOU DO IT NOW, YOU'LL GET A WORD THAT RHYMES WITH "CHERK."
I AM KING OF ALL THAT IS **MENTAL!**

I'VE BEEN THINKIN' ABOUT THE WHOLE INFINITE MONKEY THING LATELY...

YOU LOST ME.

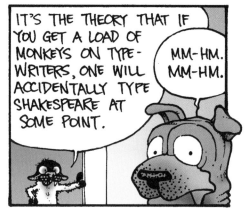

IT'S THE THEORY THAT IF YOU GET A LOAD OF MONKEYS ON TYPE-WRITERS, ONE WILL ACCIDENTALLY TYPE SHAKESPEARE AT SOME POINT.

MM-HM. MM-HM.

WELL, THE WHOLE THEORY IS FLAWED. "INFINITE" IS TOO MANY MONKEYS. OVER 8 MONKEYS AND YOU'RE RUNNING INTO DISCIPLINE AND HYGIENE ISSUES.

AND WHO'S GONNA READ INFINITE MONKEY SCRIPTS? SOME CHIMP COULD HAVE WRITTEN THE NEXT DA VINCI CODE, BUT *NEWSFLASH*: HE'S EATING THAT SCRIPT BEFORE YOU EVER SEE IT.

HERE'S WHAT YOU DO: YOU BUY A $2 BAG OF NUTS. YOU GO TRAP YOURSELF SOME SQUIRRELS...

YOU PUT THEM ON WORD PROCESSORS -- ***WITH SPELLCHECK*** -- AND YOU SHOOT FOR A "TWO AND A HALF MEN" SCRIPT...

YOU POCKET THE INFINITE MONKEY ALLOCATION MONEY, SELL THE SCRIPT, AND RETIRE TO HAWAII.

SO NOW IT'S FINITE SQUIRRELS AT WORD PROCESSORS? ...I'M STILL LOST.

NEVER MIND. YOU GOT TWO DOLLARS?

28

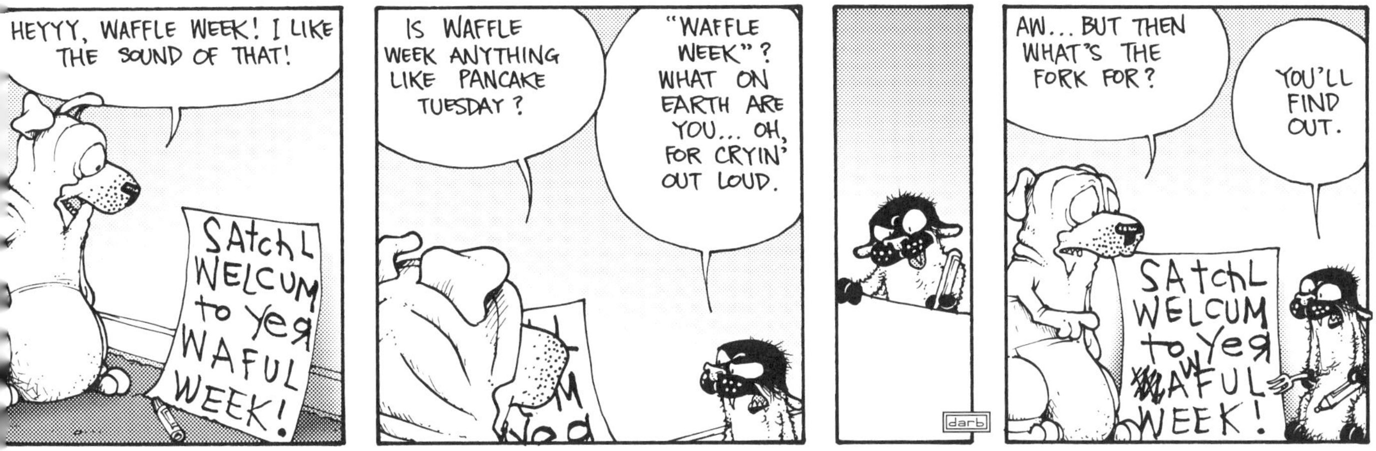
HEYYY, WAFFLE WEEK! I LIKE THE SOUND OF THAT!
SAtchL WELCUM to Yer WAFUL WEEK!
IS WAFFLE WEEK ANYTHING LIKE PANCAKE TUESDAY?
"WAFFLE WEEK"? WHAT ON EARTH ARE YOU... OH, FOR CRYIN' OUT LOUD.
AW... BUT THEN WHAT'S THE FORK FOR?
YOU'LL FIND OUT.
SAtchL WELCUM to Yer AWFUL WEEK!
darb

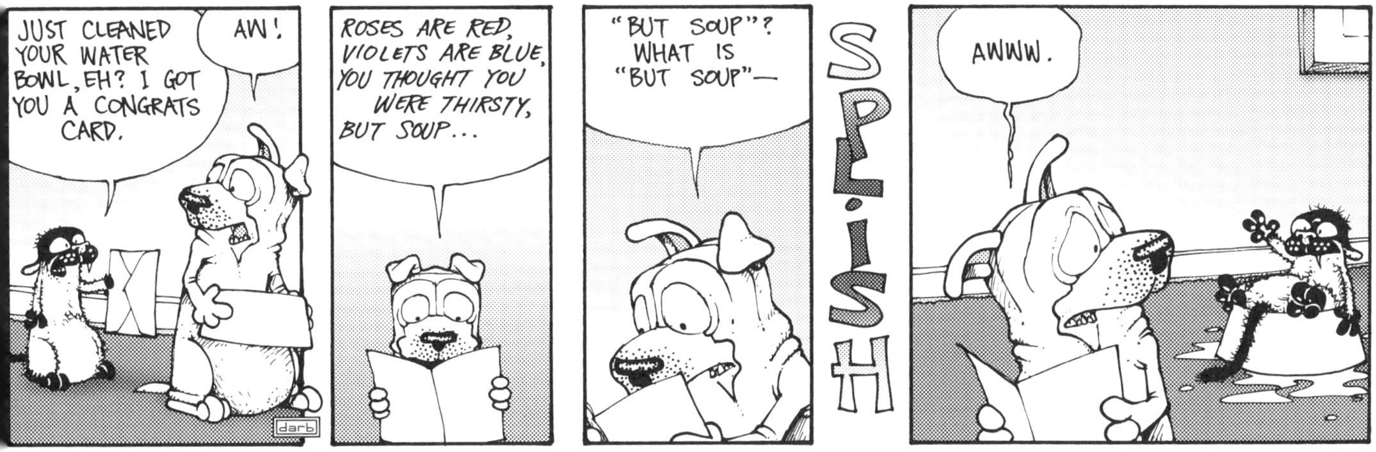
JUST CLEANED YOUR WATER BOWL, EH? I GOT YOU A CONGRATS CARD.
AW!
darb
ROSES ARE RED, VIOLETS ARE BLUE, YOU THOUGHT YOU WERE THIRSTY, BUT SOUP...
"BUT SOUP"? WHAT IS "BUT SOUP"—
SPLISH
AWWW.

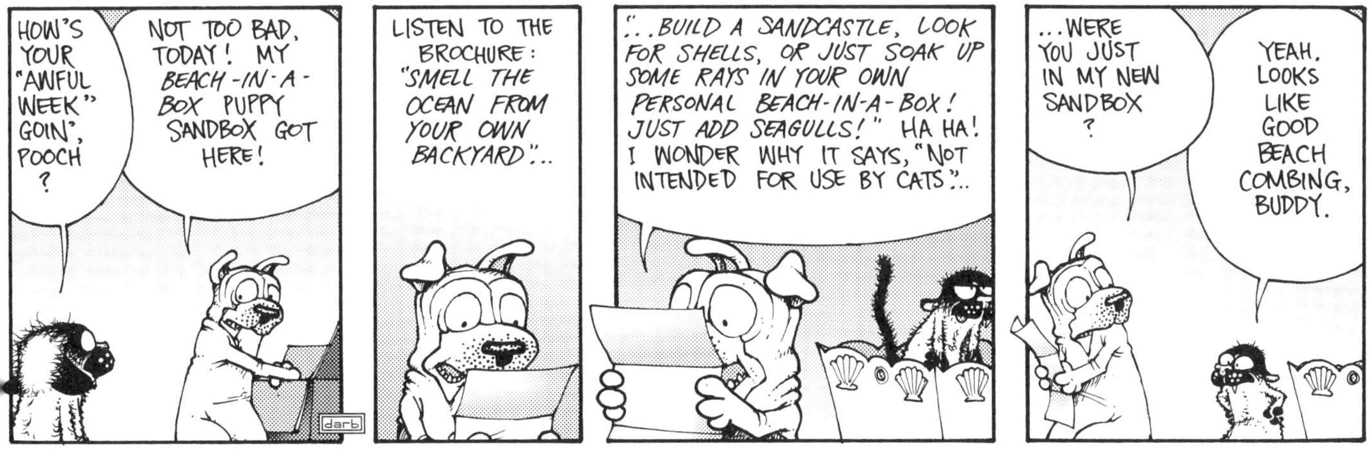
HOW'S YOUR "AWFUL WEEK" GOIN', POOCH?
NOT TOO BAD, TODAY! MY BEACH-IN-A-BOX PUPPY SANDBOX GOT HERE!
darb
LISTEN TO THE BROCHURE: "SMELL THE OCEAN FROM YOUR OWN BACKYARD"...
"...BUILD A SANDCASTLE, LOOK FOR SHELLS, OR JUST SOAK UP SOME RAYS IN YOUR OWN PERSONAL BEACH-IN-A-BOX! JUST ADD SEAGULLS!" HA HA! I WONDER WHY IT SAYS, "NOT INTENDED FOR USE BY CATS"...
...WERE YOU JUST IN MY NEW SANDBOX?
YEAH. LOOKS LIKE GOOD BEACH COMBING, BUDDY.

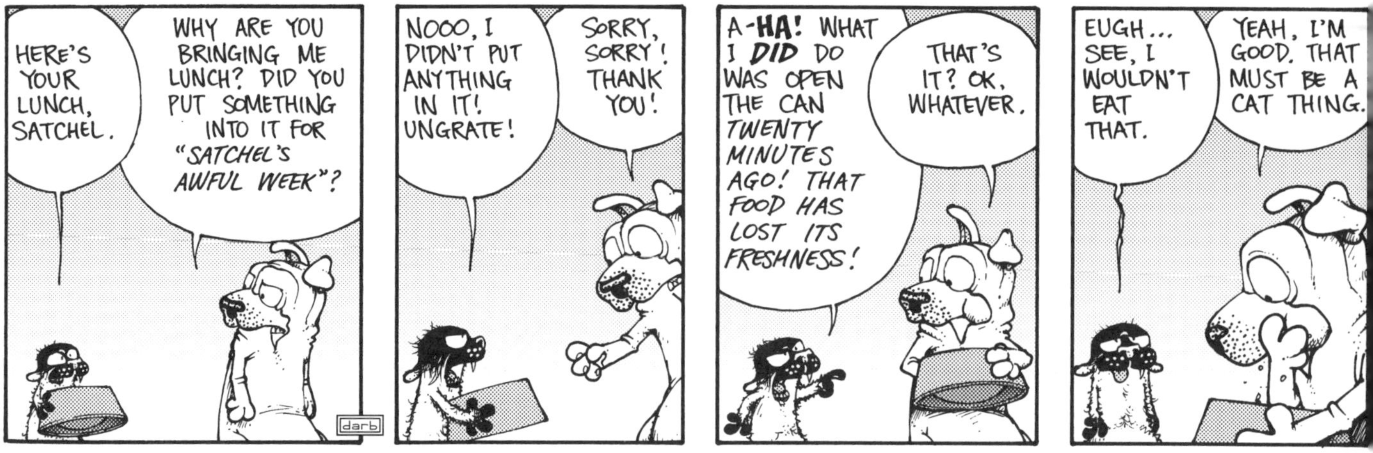
HERE'S YOUR LUNCH, SATCHEL.
WHY ARE YOU BRINGING ME LUNCH? DID YOU PUT SOMETHING INTO IT FOR "SATCHEL'S AWFUL WEEK"?
NOOO, I DIDN'T PUT ANYTHING IN IT! UNGRATE!
SORRY, SORRY! THANK YOU!
A-HA! WHAT I DID DO WAS OPEN THE CAN TWENTY MINUTES AGO! THAT FOOD HAS LOST ITS FRESHNESS!
THAT'S IT? OK, WHATEVER.
EUGH... SEE, I WOULDN'T EAT THAT.
YEAH, I'M GOOD. THAT MUST BE A CAT THING.
darb

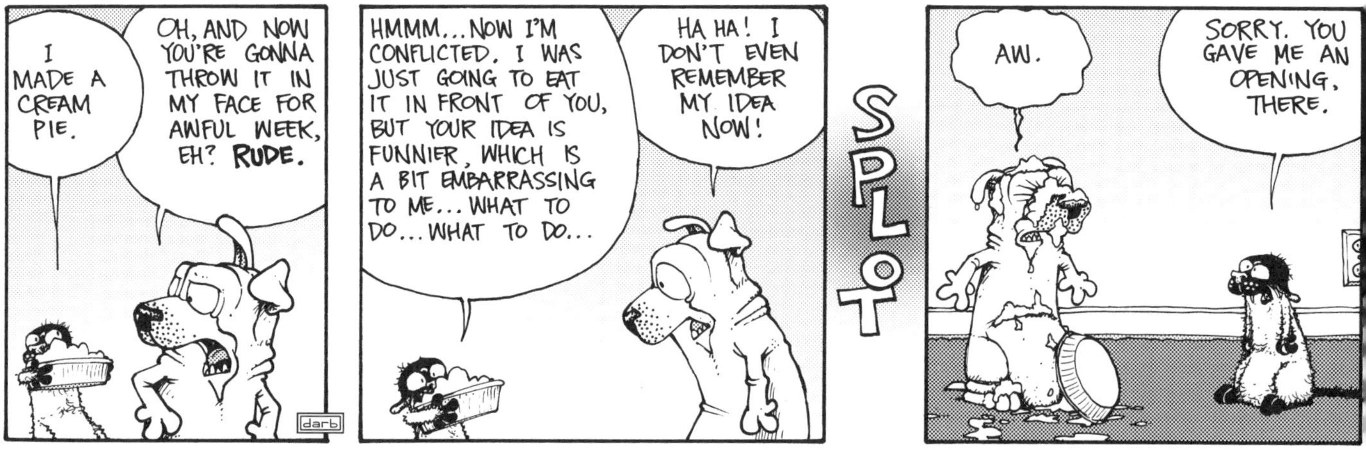
I MADE A CREAM PIE.
OH, AND NOW YOU'RE GONNA THROW IT IN MY FACE FOR AWFUL WEEK, EH? RUDE.
HMMM... NOW I'M CONFLICTED. I WAS JUST GOING TO EAT IT IN FRONT OF YOU, BUT YOUR IDEA IS FUNNIER, WHICH IS A BIT EMBARRASSING TO ME... WHAT TO DO... WHAT TO DO...
HA HA! I DON'T EVEN REMEMBER MY IDEA NOW!
SPLOT
AW.
SORRY. YOU GAVE ME AN OPENING, THERE.
darb

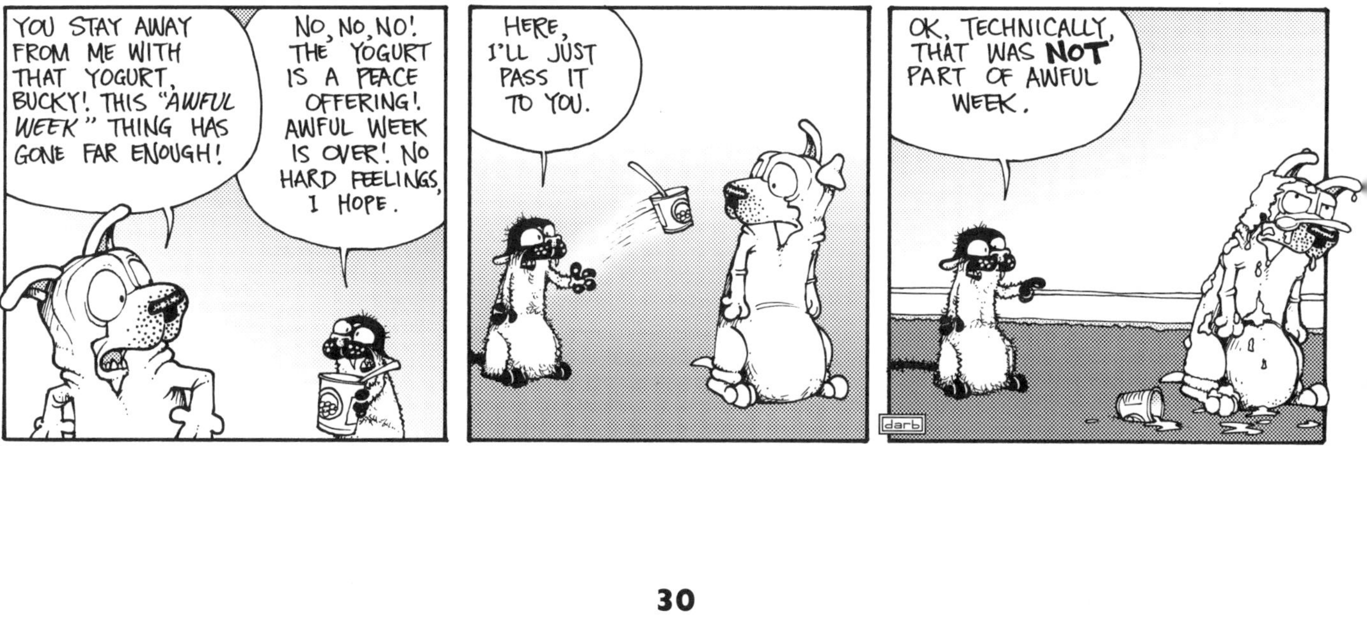
YOU STAY AWAY FROM ME WITH THAT YOGURT, BUCKY! THIS "AWFUL WEEK" THING HAS GONE FAR ENOUGH!
NO, NO, NO! THE YOGURT IS A PEACE OFFERING! AWFUL WEEK IS OVER! NO HARD FEELINGS, I HOPE.
HERE, I'LL JUST PASS IT TO YOU.
OK, TECHNICALLY, THAT WAS NOT PART OF AWFUL WEEK.
darb

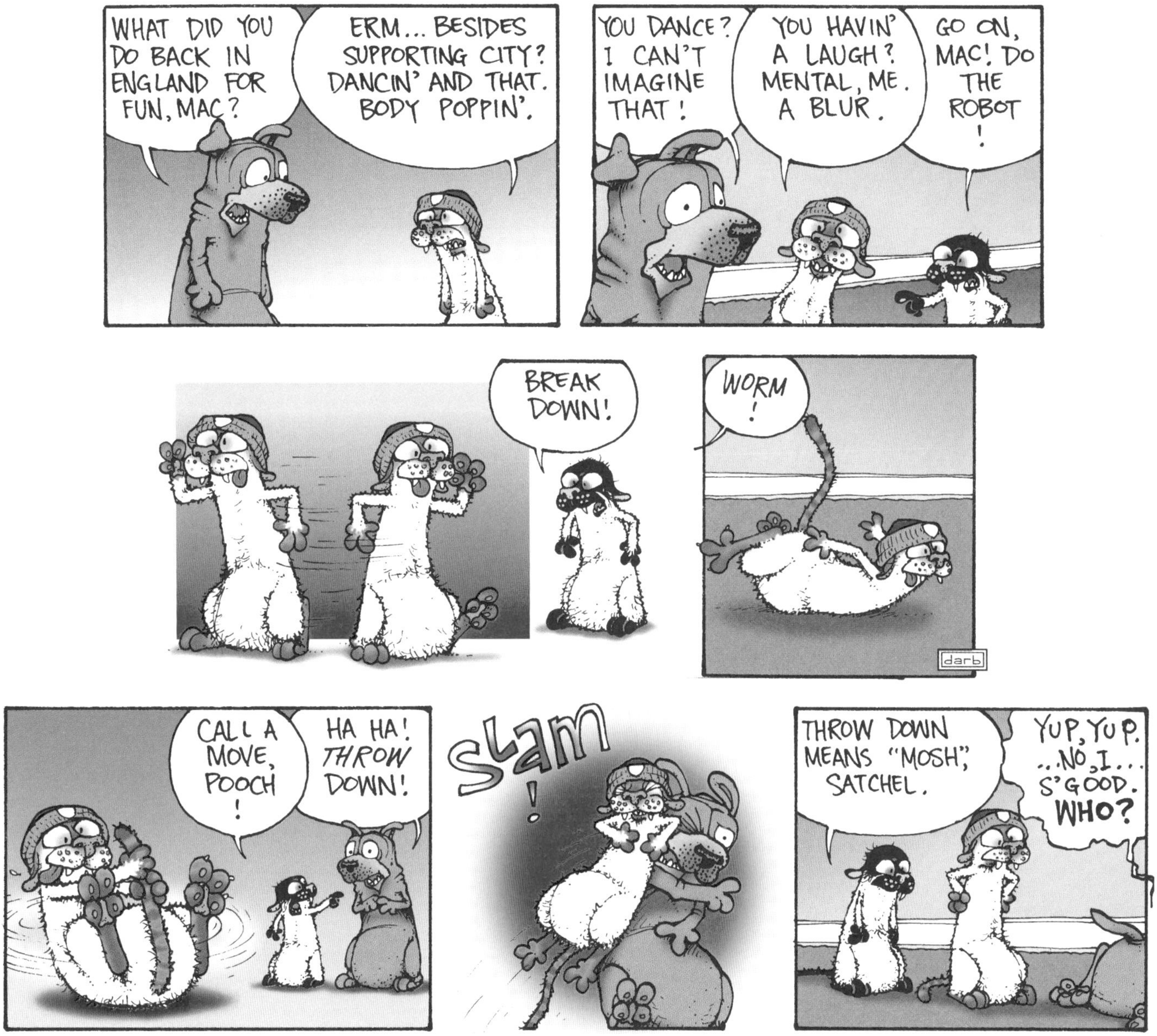
WHAT DID YOU DO BACK IN ENGLAND FOR FUN, MAC?
ERM... BESIDES SUPPORTING CITY? DANCIN' AND THAT. BODY POPPIN'.
YOU DANCE? I CAN'T IMAGINE THAT!
YOU HAVIN' A LAUGH? MENTAL, ME. A BLUR.
GO ON, MAC! DO THE ROBOT!
BREAK DOWN!
WORM!
darb
CALL A MOVE, POOCH!
HA HA! THROW DOWN!
SLAM!
THROW DOWN MEANS "MOSH," SATCHEL.
YUP, YUP. ...NO, I... S'GOOD. WHO?

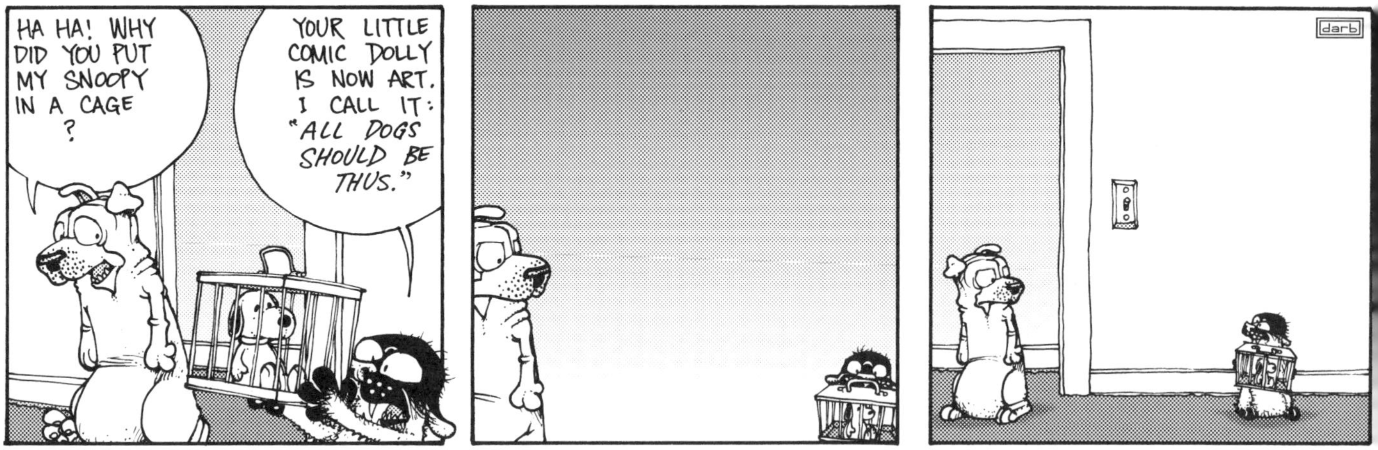
HA HA! WHY DID YOU PUT MY SNOOPY IN A CAGE ?
YOUR LITTLE COMIC DOLLY IS NOW ART. I CALL IT: "ALL DOGS SHOULD BE THUS."
darb

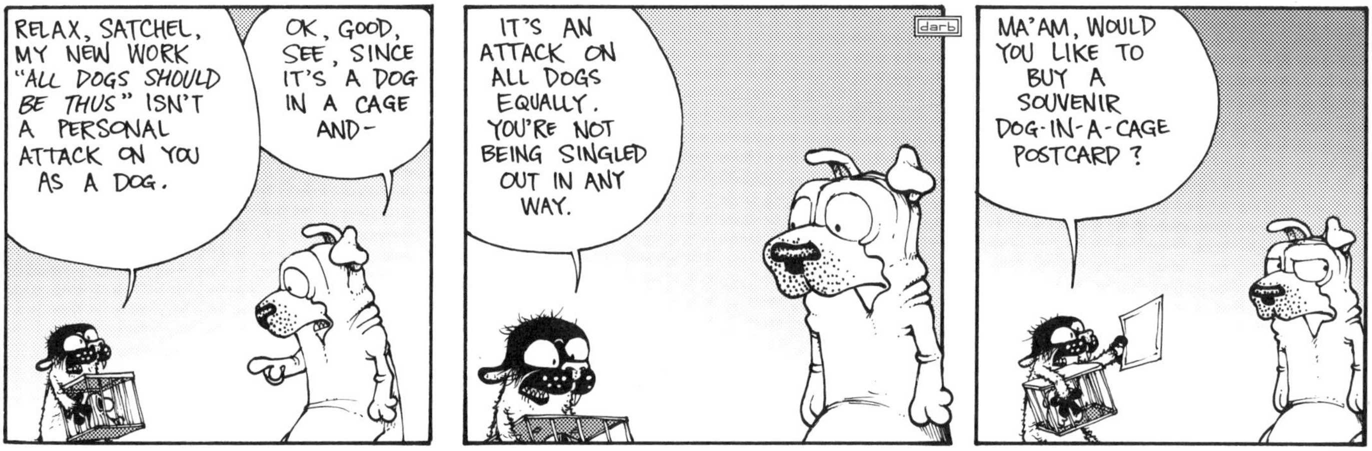
RELAX, SATCHEL, MY NEW WORK "ALL DOGS SHOULD BE THUS" ISN'T A PERSONAL ATTACK ON YOU AS A DOG.
OK, GOOD, SEE, SINCE IT'S A DOG IN A CAGE AND-
IT'S AN ATTACK ON ALL DOGS EQUALLY. YOU'RE NOT BEING SINGLED OUT IN ANY WAY.
darb
MA'AM, WOULD YOU LIKE TO BUY A SOUVENIR DOG-IN-A-CAGE POSTCARD ?

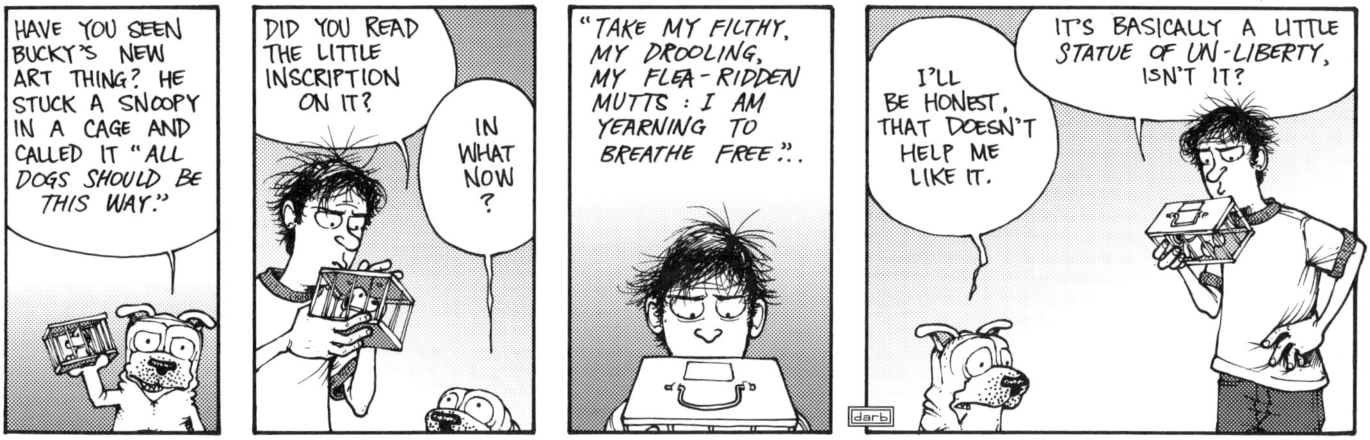
HAVE YOU SEEN BUCKY'S NEW ART THING? HE STUCK A SNOOPY IN A CAGE AND CALLED IT "ALL DOGS SHOULD BE THIS WAY."
DID YOU READ THE LITTLE INSCRIPTION ON IT?
IN WHAT NOW ?
"TAKE MY FILTHY, MY DROOLING, MY FLEA-RIDDEN MUTTS : I AM YEARNING TO BREATHE FREE."...
darb
IT'S BASICALLY A LITTLE STATUE OF UN-LIBERTY, ISN'T IT?
I'LL BE HONEST, THAT DOESN'T HELP ME LIKE IT.

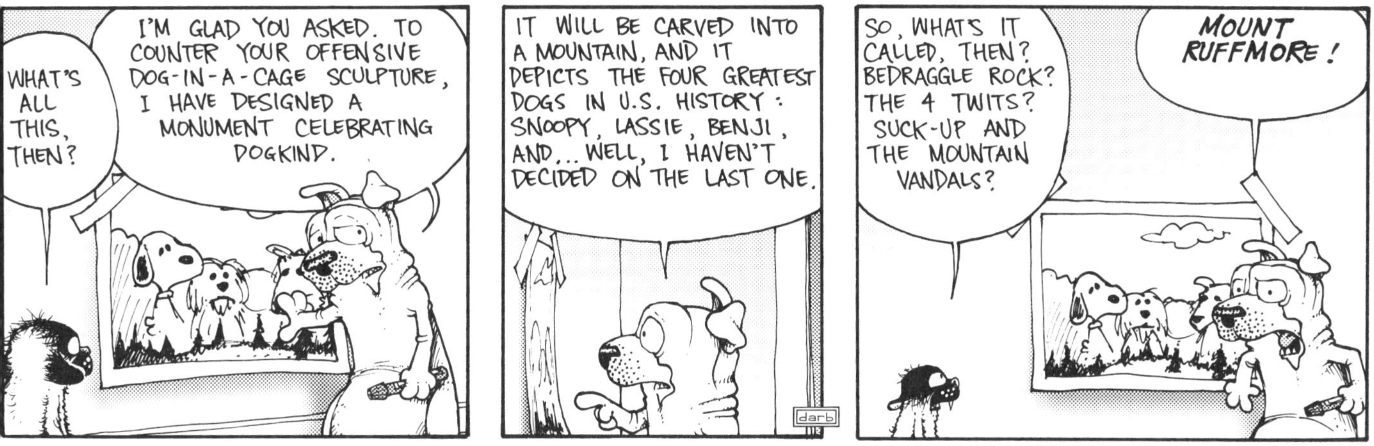
WHAT'S ALL THIS, THEN?
I'M GLAD YOU ASKED. TO COUNTER YOUR OFFENSIVE DOG-IN-A-CAGE SCULPTURE, I HAVE DESIGNED A MONUMENT CELEBRATING DOGKIND.
IT WILL BE CARVED INTO A MOUNTAIN, AND IT DEPICTS THE FOUR GREATEST DOGS IN U.S. HISTORY: SNOOPY, LASSIE, BENJI, AND... WELL, I HAVEN'T DECIDED ON THE LAST ONE.
darb
SO, WHAT'S IT CALLED, THEN? BEDRAGGLE ROCK? THE 4 TWITS? SUCK-UP AND THE MOUNTAIN VANDALS?
MOUNT RUFFMORE!

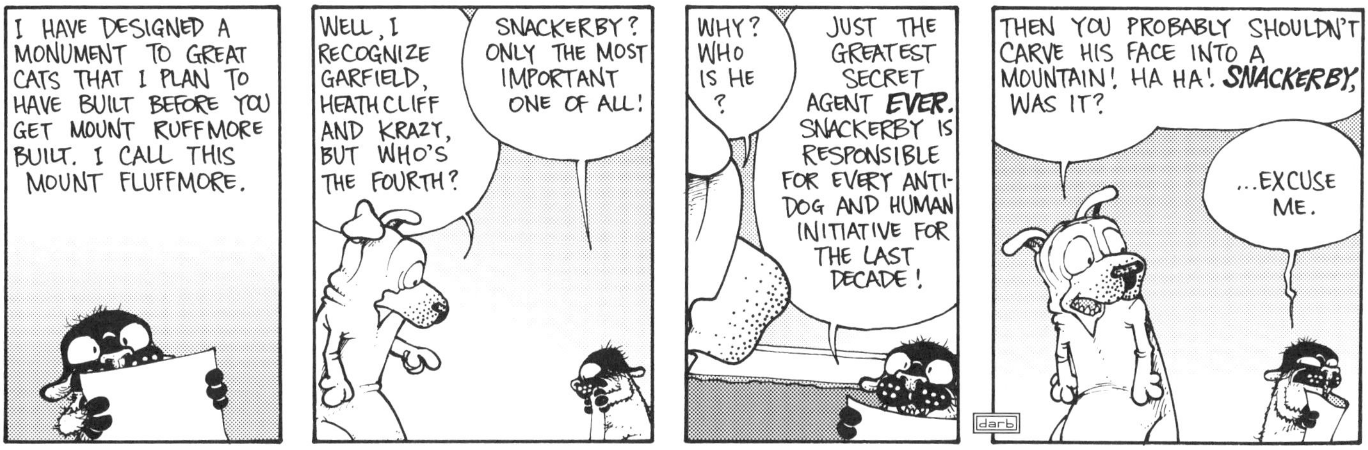
I HAVE DESIGNED A MONUMENT TO GREAT CATS THAT I PLAN TO HAVE BUILT BEFORE YOU GET MOUNT RUFFMORE BUILT. I CALL THIS MOUNT FLUFFMORE.
WELL, I RECOGNIZE GARFIELD, HEATHCLIFF AND KRAZY, BUT WHO'S THE FOURTH?
SNACKERBY? ONLY THE MOST IMPORTANT ONE OF ALL!
WHY? WHO IS HE?
JUST THE GREATEST SECRET AGENT EVER. SNACKERBY IS RESPONSIBLE FOR EVERY ANTI-DOG AND HUMAN INITIATIVE FOR THE LAST DECADE!
darb
THEN YOU PROBABLY SHOULDN'T CARVE HIS FACE INTO A MOUNTAIN! HA HA! SNACKERBY, WAS IT?
...EXCUSE ME.

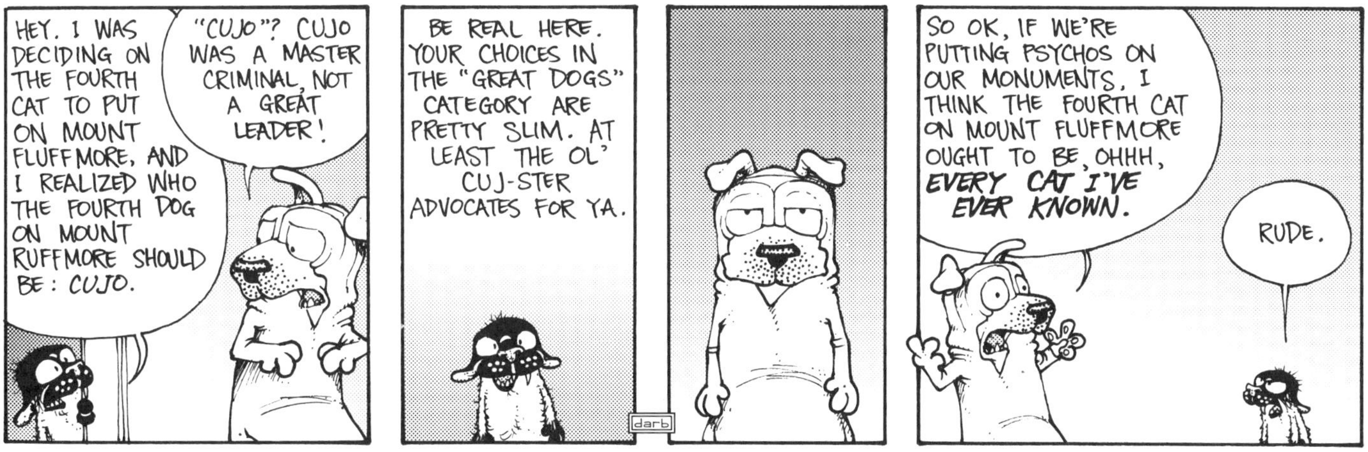
HEY. I WAS DECIDING ON THE FOURTH CAT TO PUT ON MOUNT FLUFFMORE, AND I REALIZED WHO THE FOURTH DOG ON RUFFMORE SHOULD BE: CUJO.
"CUJO"? CUJO WAS A MASTER CRIMINAL, NOT A GREAT LEADER!
BE REAL HERE. YOUR CHOICES IN THE "GREAT DOGS" CATEGORY ARE PRETTY SLIM. AT LEAST THE OL' CUJ-STER ADVOCATES FOR YA.
darb
SO OK, IF WE'RE PUTTING PSYCHOS ON OUR MONUMENTS, I THINK THE FOURTH CAT ON MOUNT FLUFFMORE OUGHT TO BE, OHHH, EVERY CAT I'VE EVER KNOWN.
RUDE.

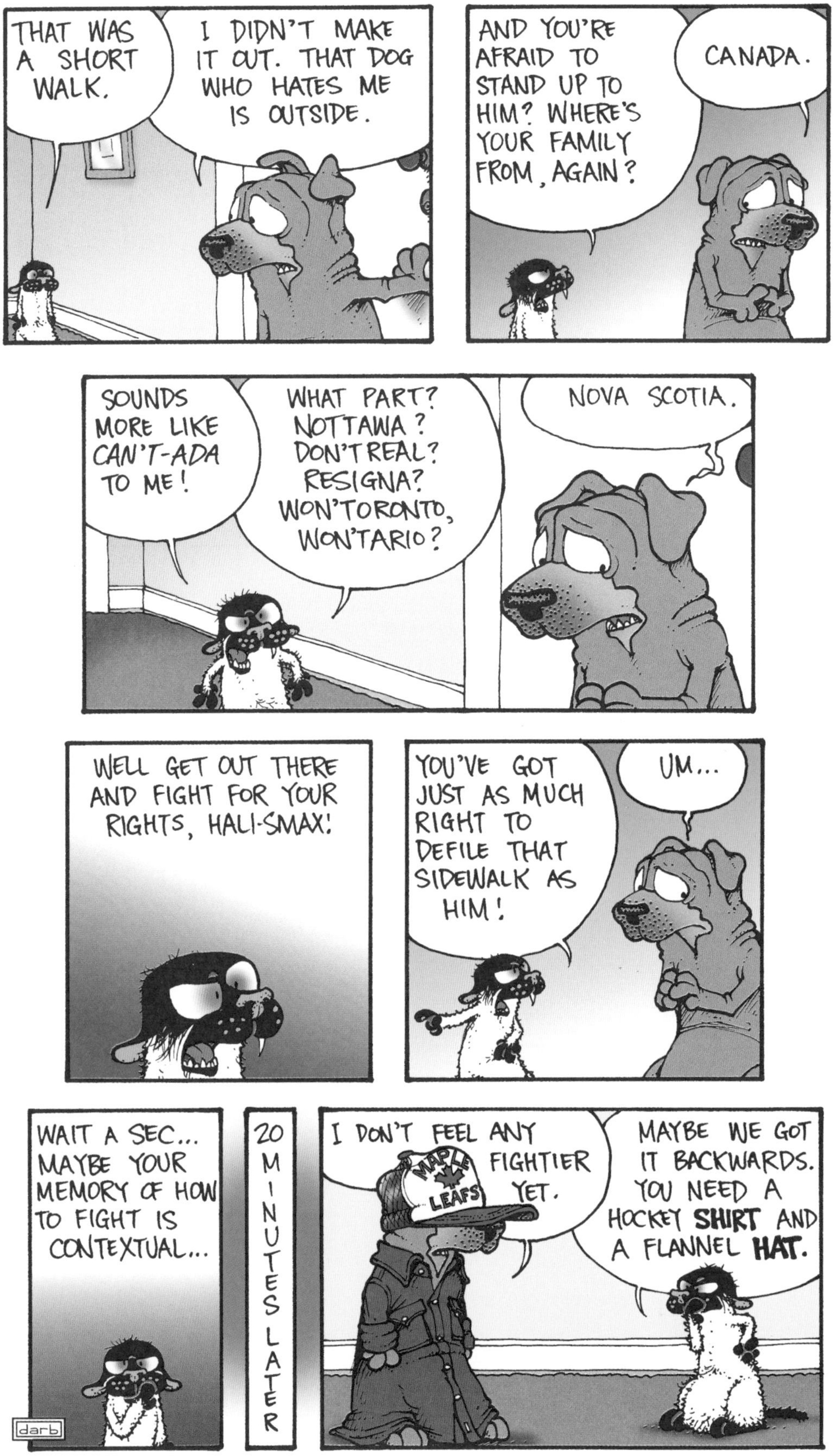
THAT WAS A SHORT WALK.
I DIDN'T MAKE IT OUT. THAT DOG WHO HATES ME IS OUTSIDE.
AND YOU'RE AFRAID TO STAND UP TO HIM? WHERE'S YOUR FAMILY FROM, AGAIN?
CANADA.
SOUNDS MORE LIKE CAN'T-ADA TO ME!
WHAT PART? NOTTAWA? DON'TREAL? RESIGNA? WON'TORONTO, WON'TARIO?
NOVA SCOTIA.
WELL GET OUT THERE AND FIGHT FOR YOUR RIGHTS, HALI-SMAX!
YOU'VE GOT JUST AS MUCH RIGHT TO DEFILE THAT SIDEWALK AS HIM!
UM...
WAIT A SEC... MAYBE YOUR MEMORY OF HOW TO FIGHT IS CONTEXTUAL...
darb
20 MINUTES LATER
I DON'T FEEL ANY FIGHTIER YET.
MAPLE LEAFS
MAYBE WE GOT IT BACKWARDS. YOU NEED A HOCKEY **SHIRT** AND A FLANNEL **HAT**.

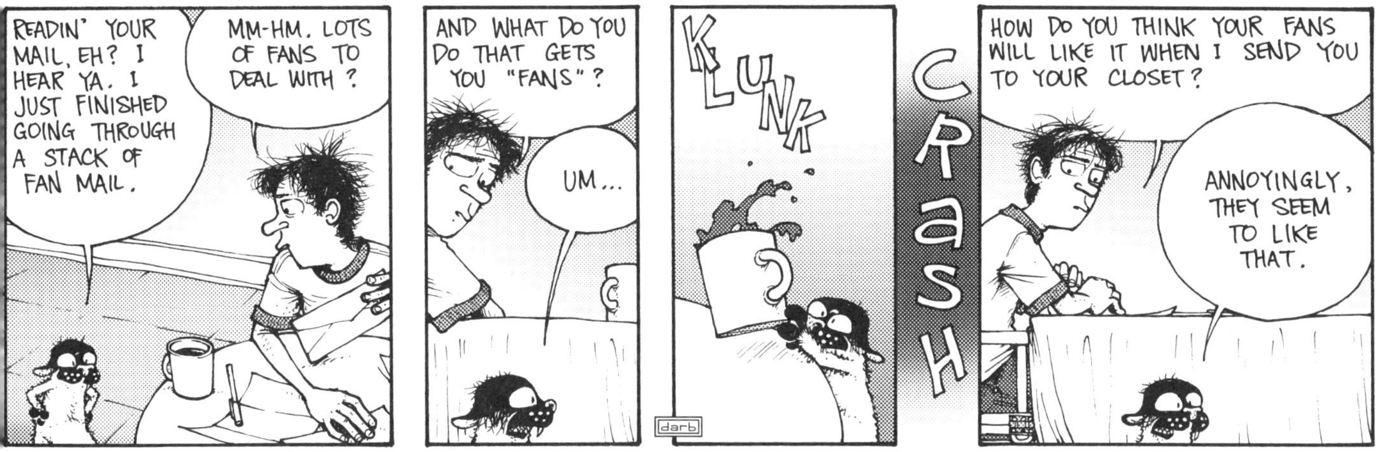
READIN' YOUR MAIL, EH? I HEAR YA. I JUST FINISHED GOING THROUGH A STACK OF FAN MAIL.
MM-HM. LOTS OF FANS TO DEAL WITH?
AND WHAT DO YOU DO THAT GETS YOU "FANS"?
UM...
KLUNK
darb
CRASH
HOW DO YOU THINK YOUR FANS WILL LIKE IT WHEN I SEND YOU TO YOUR CLOSET?
ANNOYINGLY, THEY SEEM TO LIKE THAT.

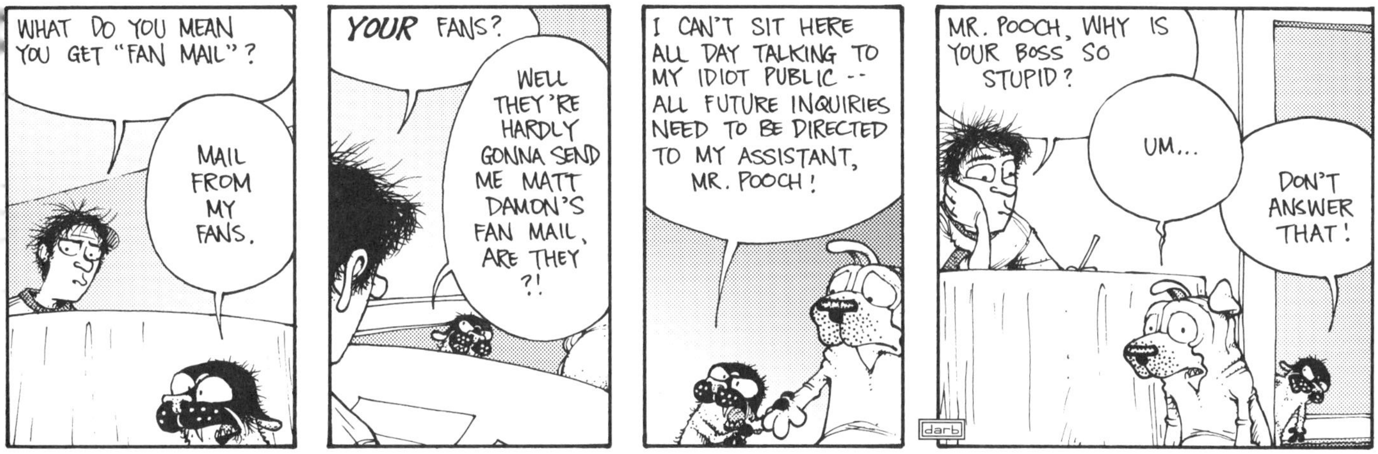
WHAT DO YOU MEAN YOU GET "FAN MAIL"?
MAIL FROM MY FANS.
YOUR FANS?
WELL THEY'RE HARDLY GONNA SEND ME MATT DAMON'S FAN MAIL, ARE THEY ?!
I CAN'T SIT HERE ALL DAY TALKING TO MY IDIOT PUBLIC -- ALL FUTURE INQUIRIES NEED TO BE DIRECTED TO MY ASSISTANT, MR. POOCH!
darb
MR. POOCH, WHY IS YOUR BOSS SO STUPID?
UM...
DON'T ANSWER THAT!

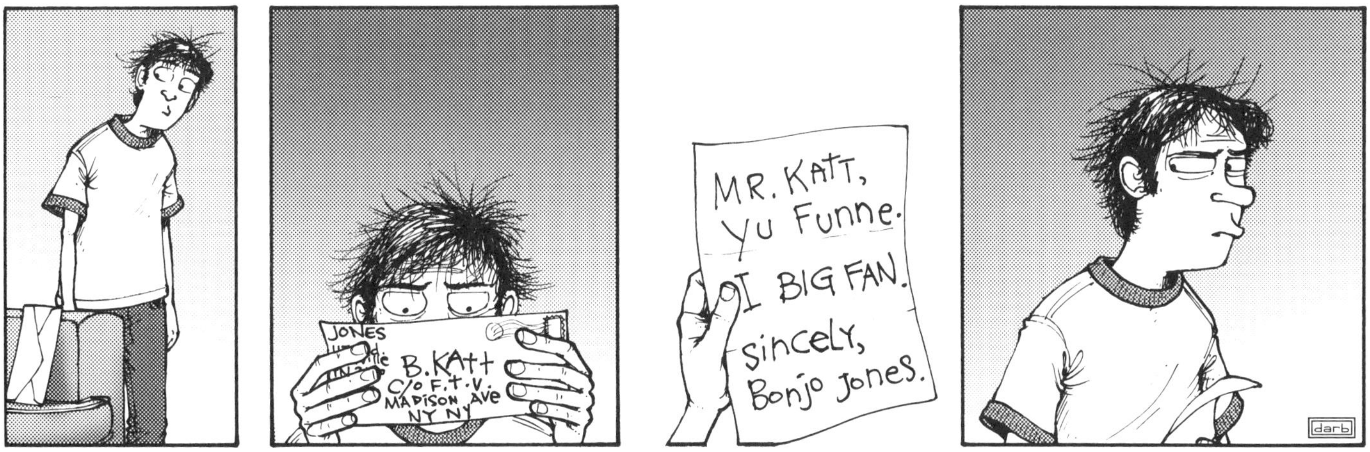
JONES
B. KAtt
C/o F.t.V.
MADISON Ave
NY NY
MR. KATT,
YU Funne.
I BIG FAN.
Sincely,
Bonjo Jones.
darb

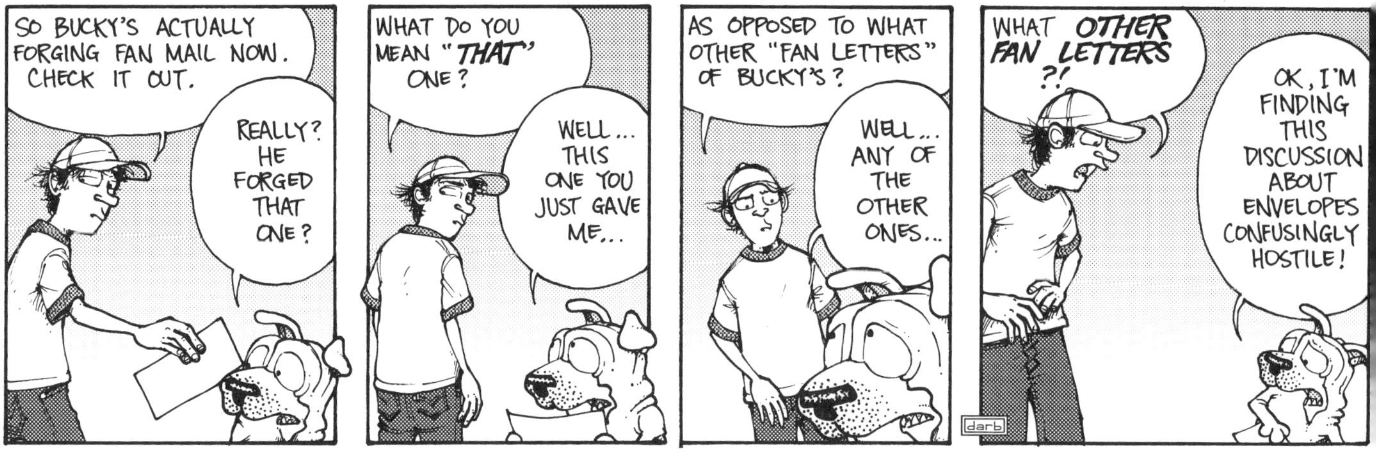
SO BUCKY'S ACTUALLY FORGING FAN MAIL NOW. CHECK IT OUT.
REALLY? HE FORGED THAT ONE?
WHAT DO YOU MEAN "THAT" ONE?
WELL... THIS ONE YOU JUST GAVE ME...
AS OPPOSED TO WHAT OTHER "FAN LETTERS" OF BUCKY'S?
WELL... ANY OF THE OTHER ONES...
WHAT OTHER FAN LETTERS ?!
OK, I'M FINDING THIS DISCUSSION ABOUT ENVELOPES CONFUSINGLY HOSTILE!
darb

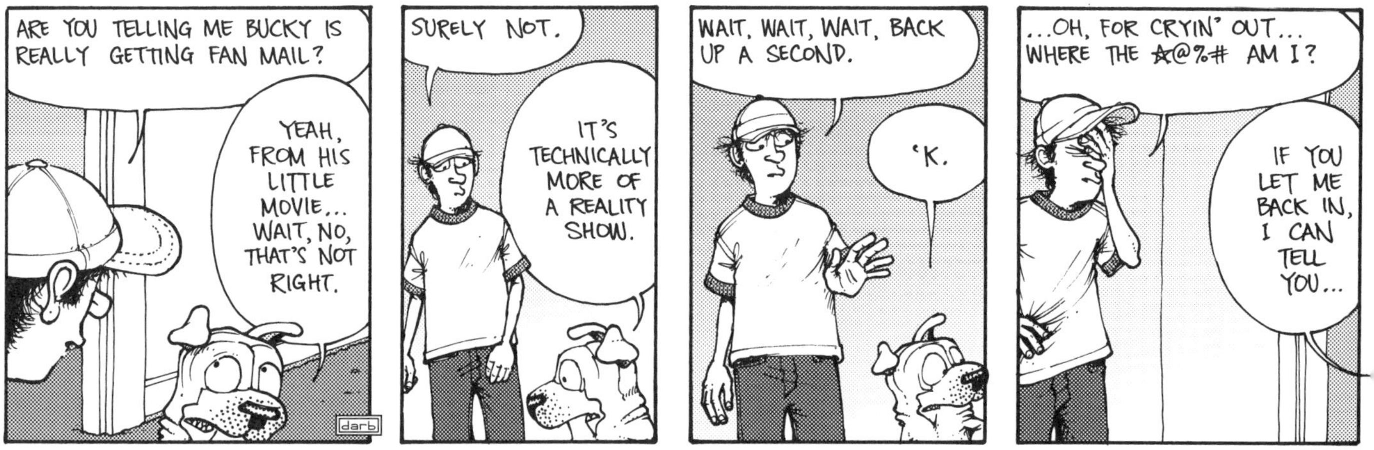
ARE YOU TELLING ME BUCKY IS REALLY GETTING FAN MAIL?
YEAH, FROM HIS LITTLE MOVIE... WAIT, NO, THAT'S NOT RIGHT.
darb
SURELY NOT.
IT'S TECHNICALLY MORE OF A REALITY SHOW.
WAIT, WAIT, WAIT, BACK UP A SECOND.
'K.
...OH, FOR CRYIN' OUT... WHERE THE ★@%# AM I?
IF YOU LET ME BACK IN, I CAN TELL YOU...

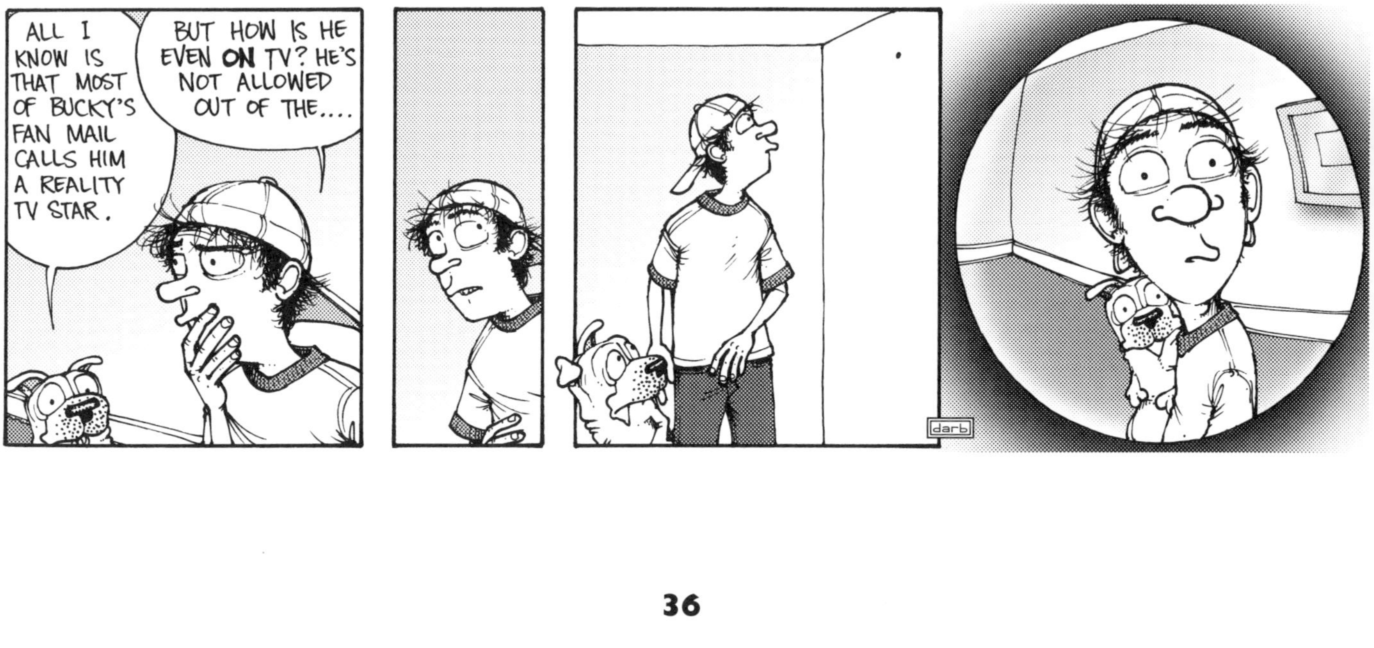
ALL I KNOW IS THAT MOST OF BUCKY'S FAN MAIL CALLS HIM A REALITY TV STAR.
BUT HOW IS HE EVEN ON TV? HE'S NOT ALLOWED OUT OF THE....
darb

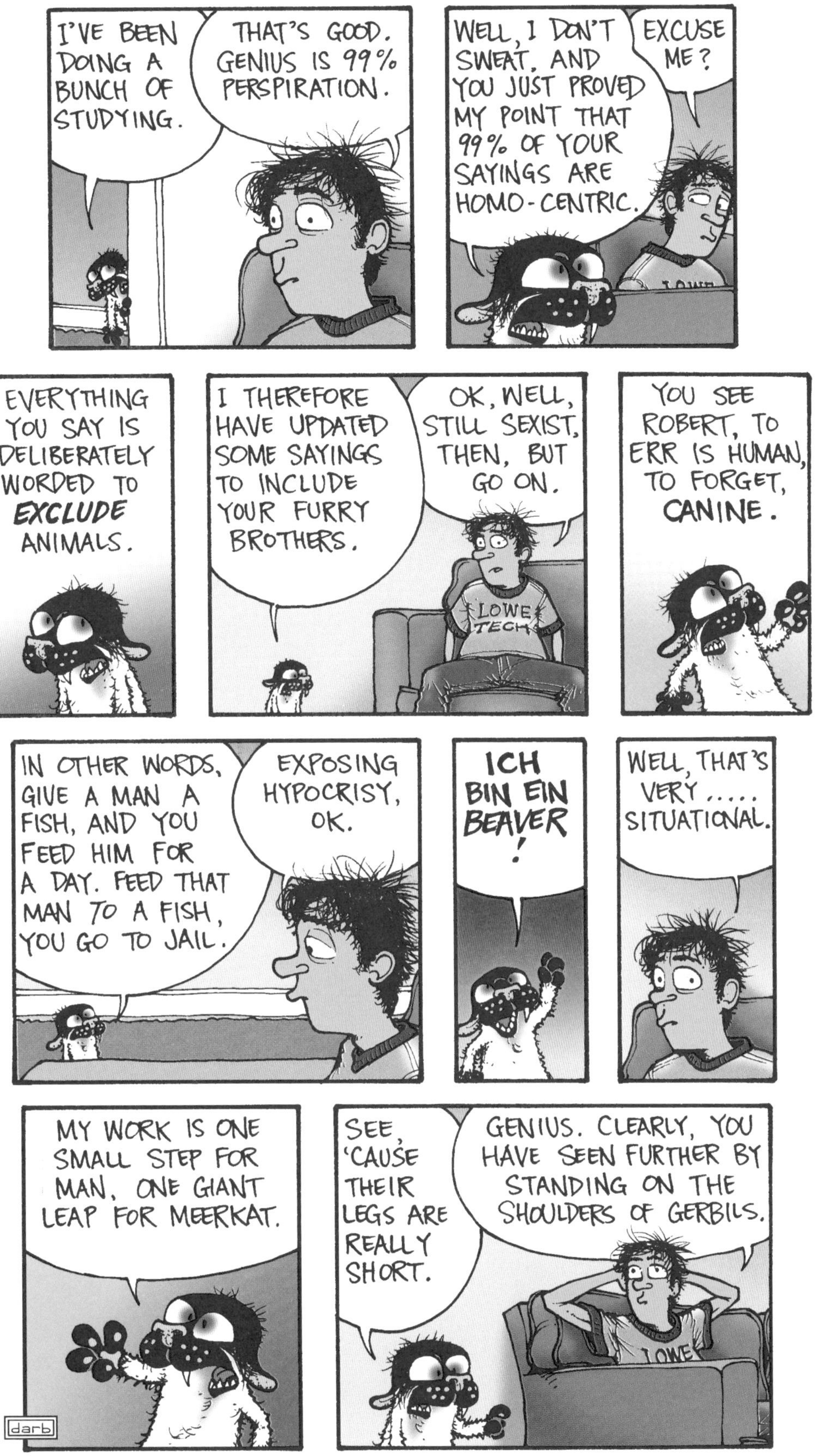
I'VE BEEN DOING A BUNCH OF STUDYING.
THAT'S GOOD. GENIUS IS 99% PERSPIRATION.
WELL, I DON'T SWEAT, AND YOU JUST PROVED MY POINT THAT 99% OF YOUR SAYINGS ARE HOMO-CENTRIC.
EXCUSE ME?
EVERYTHING YOU SAY IS DELIBERATELY WORDED TO EXCLUDE ANIMALS.
I THEREFORE HAVE UPDATED SOME SAYINGS TO INCLUDE YOUR FURRY BROTHERS.
OK, WELL, STILL SEXIST, THEN, BUT GO ON.
LOWE TECH
YOU SEE ROBERT, TO ERR IS HUMAN, TO FORGET, CANINE.
IN OTHER WORDS, GIVE A MAN A FISH, AND YOU FEED HIM FOR A DAY. FEED THAT MAN TO A FISH, YOU GO TO JAIL.
EXPOSING HYPOCRISY, OK.
ICH BIN EIN BEAVER!
WELL, THAT'S VERY..... SITUATIONAL.
MY WORK IS ONE SMALL STEP FOR MAN, ONE GIANT LEAP FOR MEERKAT.
darb
GENIUS. CLEARLY, YOU HAVE SEEN FURTHER BY STANDING ON THE SHOULDERS OF GERBILS.
SEE, 'CAUSE THEIR LEGS ARE REALLY SHORT.
LOWE

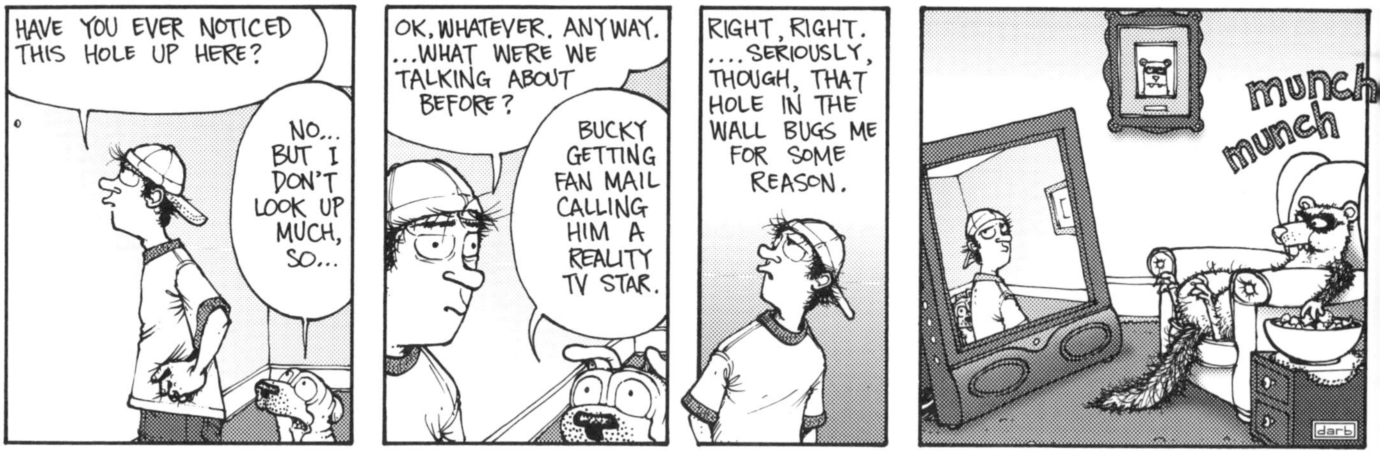
HAVE YOU EVER NOTICED THIS HOLE UP HERE?
NO... BUT I DON'T LOOK UP MUCH, SO...
OK, WHATEVER. ANYWAY. ...WHAT WERE WE TALKING ABOUT BEFORE?
BUCKY GETTING FAN MAIL CALLING HIM A REALITY TV STAR.
RIGHT, RIGHT. ....SERIOUSLY, THOUGH, THAT HOLE IN THE WALL BUGS ME FOR SOME REASON.
munch munch
darb

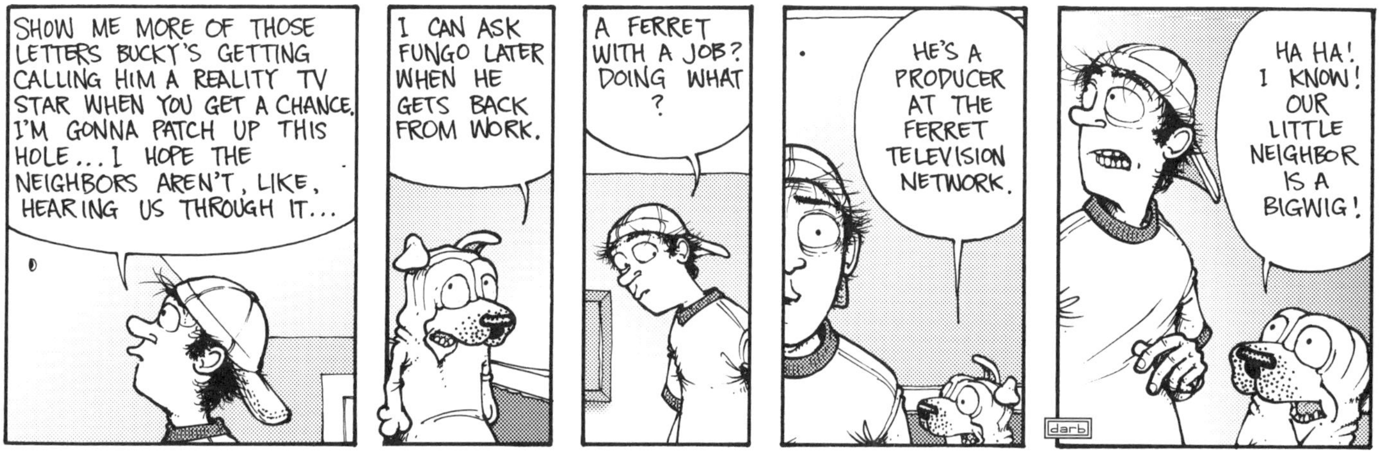
SHOW ME MORE OF THOSE LETTERS BUCKY'S GETTING CALLING HIM A REALITY TV STAR WHEN YOU GET A CHANCE. I'M GONNA PATCH UP THIS HOLE... I HOPE THE NEIGHBORS AREN'T, LIKE, HEARING US THROUGH IT...
I CAN ASK FUNGO LATER WHEN HE GETS BACK FROM WORK.
A FERRET WITH A JOB? DOING WHAT?
HE'S A PRODUCER AT THE FERRET TELEVISION NETWORK.
HA HA! I KNOW! OUR LITTLE NEIGHBOR IS A BIGWIG!
darb

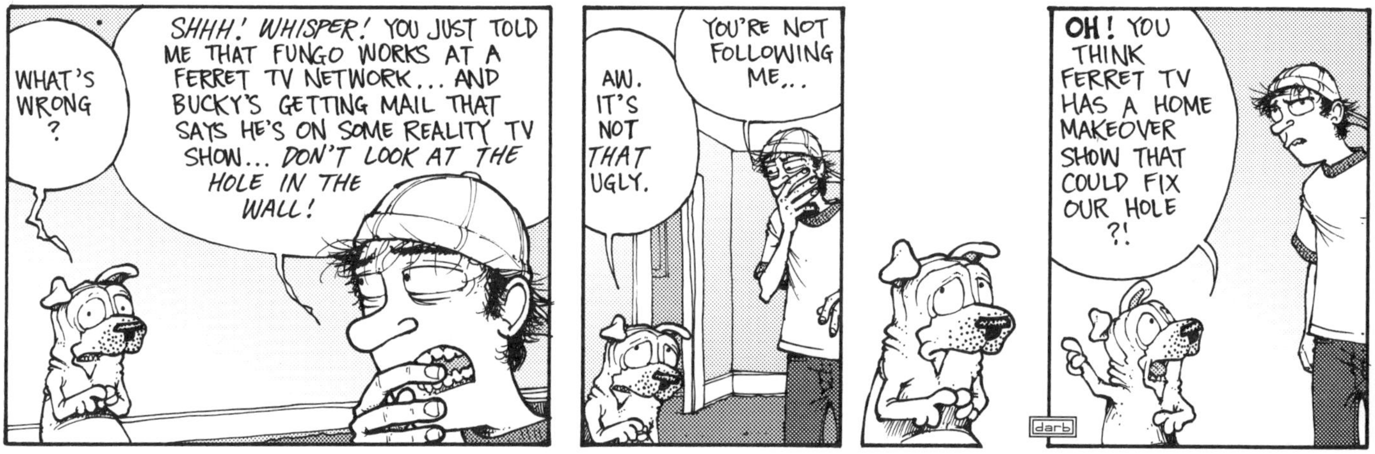
WHAT'S WRONG?
SHHH! WHISPER! YOU JUST TOLD ME THAT FUNGO WORKS AT A FERRET TV NETWORK... AND BUCKY'S GETTING MAIL THAT SAYS HE'S ON SOME REALITY TV SHOW... DON'T LOOK AT THE HOLE IN THE WALL!
AW. IT'S NOT THAT UGLY.
YOU'RE NOT FOLLOWING ME...
OH! YOU THINK FERRET TV HAS A HOME MAKEOVER SHOW THAT COULD FIX OUR HOLE ?!
darb

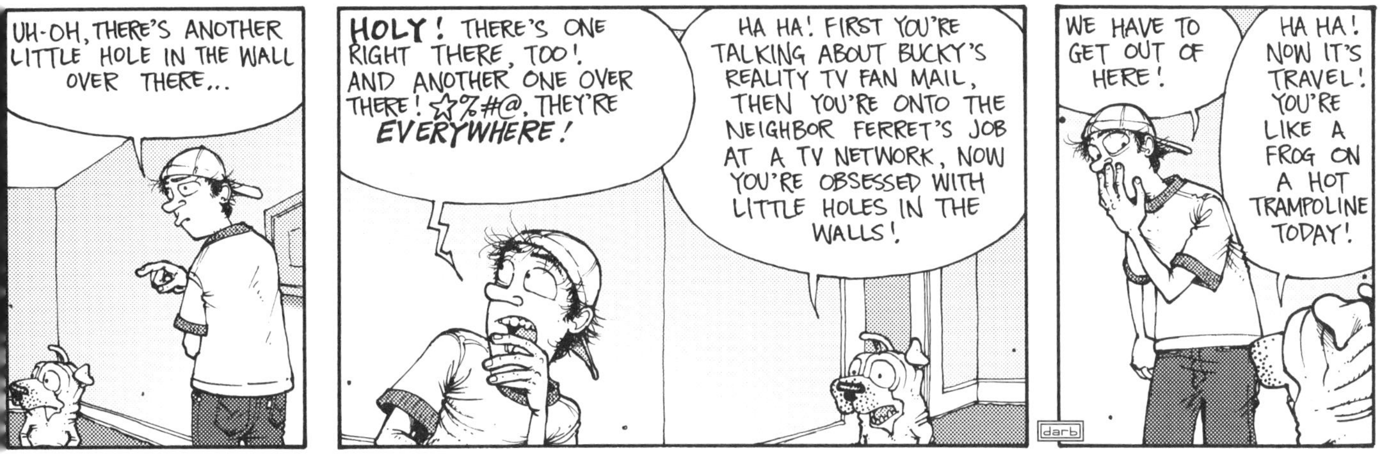
UH-OH, THERE'S ANOTHER LITTLE HOLE IN THE WALL OVER THERE...
HOLY! THERE'S ONE RIGHT THERE, TOO! AND ANOTHER ONE OVER THERE! ☆%#@, THEY'RE EVERYWHERE!
HA HA! FIRST YOU'RE TALKING ABOUT BUCKY'S REALITY TV FAN MAIL, THEN YOU'RE ONTO THE NEIGHBOR FERRET'S JOB AT A TV NETWORK, NOW YOU'RE OBSESSED WITH LITTLE HOLES IN THE WALLS!
WE HAVE TO GET OUT OF HERE!
HA HA! NOW IT'S TRAVEL! YOU'RE LIKE A FROG ON A HOT TRAMPOLINE TODAY!
darb

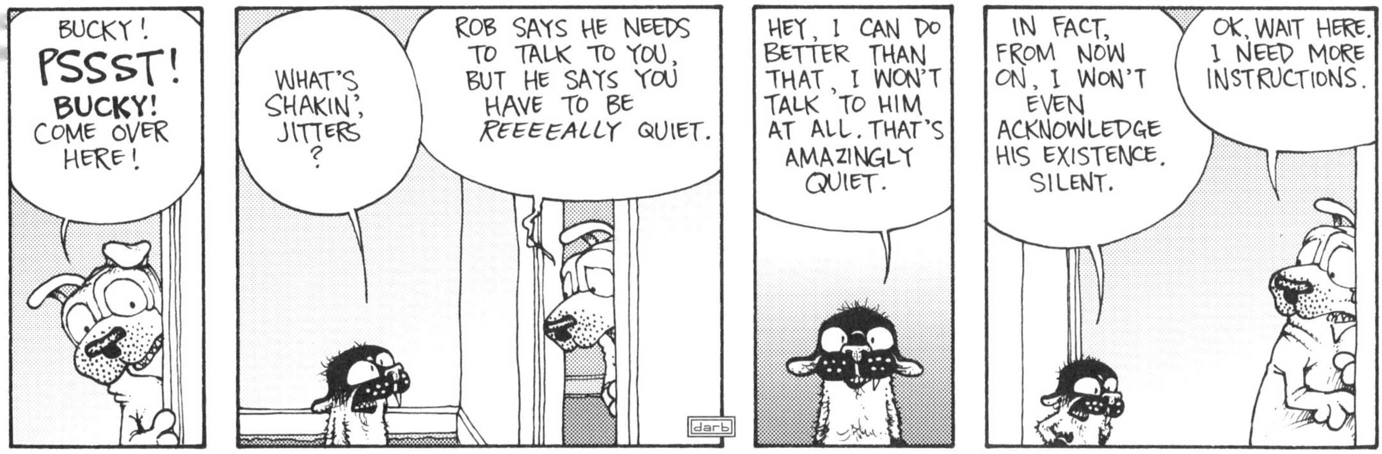
BUCKY! PSSST! BUCKY! COME OVER HERE!
WHAT'S SHAKIN', JITTERS?
ROB SAYS HE NEEDS TO TALK TO YOU, BUT HE SAYS YOU HAVE TO BE REEEEALLY QUIET.
darb
HEY, I CAN DO BETTER THAN THAT, I WON'T TALK TO HIM AT ALL. THAT'S AMAZINGLY QUIET.
IN FACT, FROM NOW ON, I WON'T EVEN ACKNOWLEDGE HIS EXISTENCE. SILENT.
OK, WAIT HERE. I NEED MORE INSTRUCTIONS.

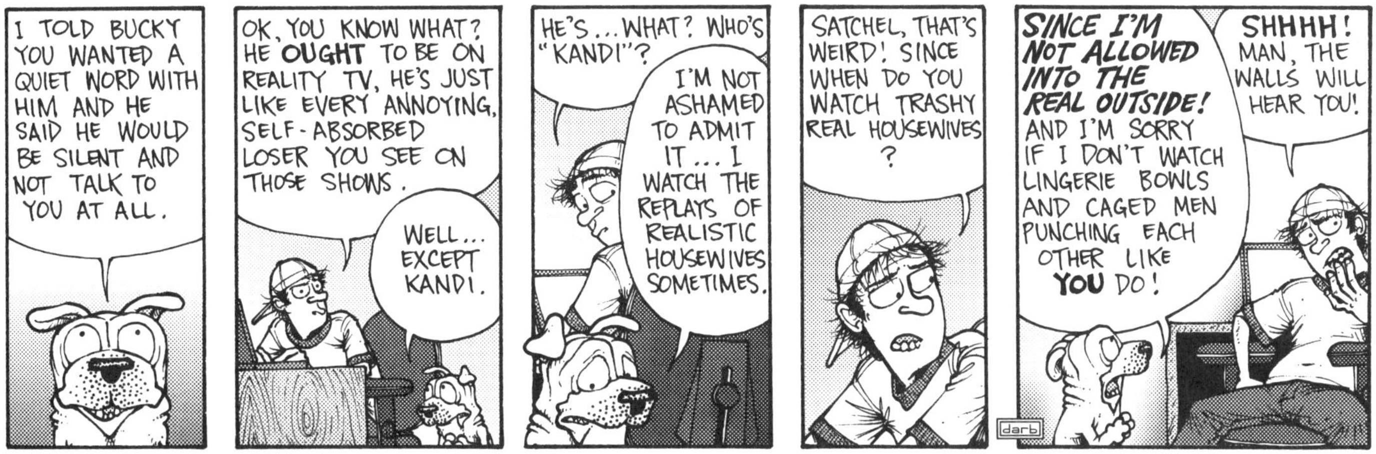
I TOLD BUCKY YOU WANTED A QUIET WORD WITH HIM AND HE SAID HE WOULD BE SILENT AND NOT TALK TO YOU AT ALL.
OK, YOU KNOW WHAT? HE OUGHT TO BE ON REALITY TV, HE'S JUST LIKE EVERY ANNOYING, SELF-ABSORBED LOSER YOU SEE ON THOSE SHOWS.
WELL... EXCEPT KANDI.
HE'S... WHAT? WHO'S "KANDI"?
I'M NOT ASHAMED TO ADMIT IT... I WATCH THE REPLAYS OF REALISTIC HOUSEWIVES SOMETIMES.
SATCHEL, THAT'S WEIRD! SINCE WHEN DO YOU WATCH TRASHY REAL HOUSEWIVES?
darb
SINCE I'M NOT ALLOWED INTO THE REAL OUTSIDE! AND I'M SORRY IF I DON'T WATCH LINGERIE BOWLS AND CAGED MEN PUNCHING EACH OTHER LIKE YOU DO!
SHHHH! MAN, THE WALLS WILL HEAR YOU!

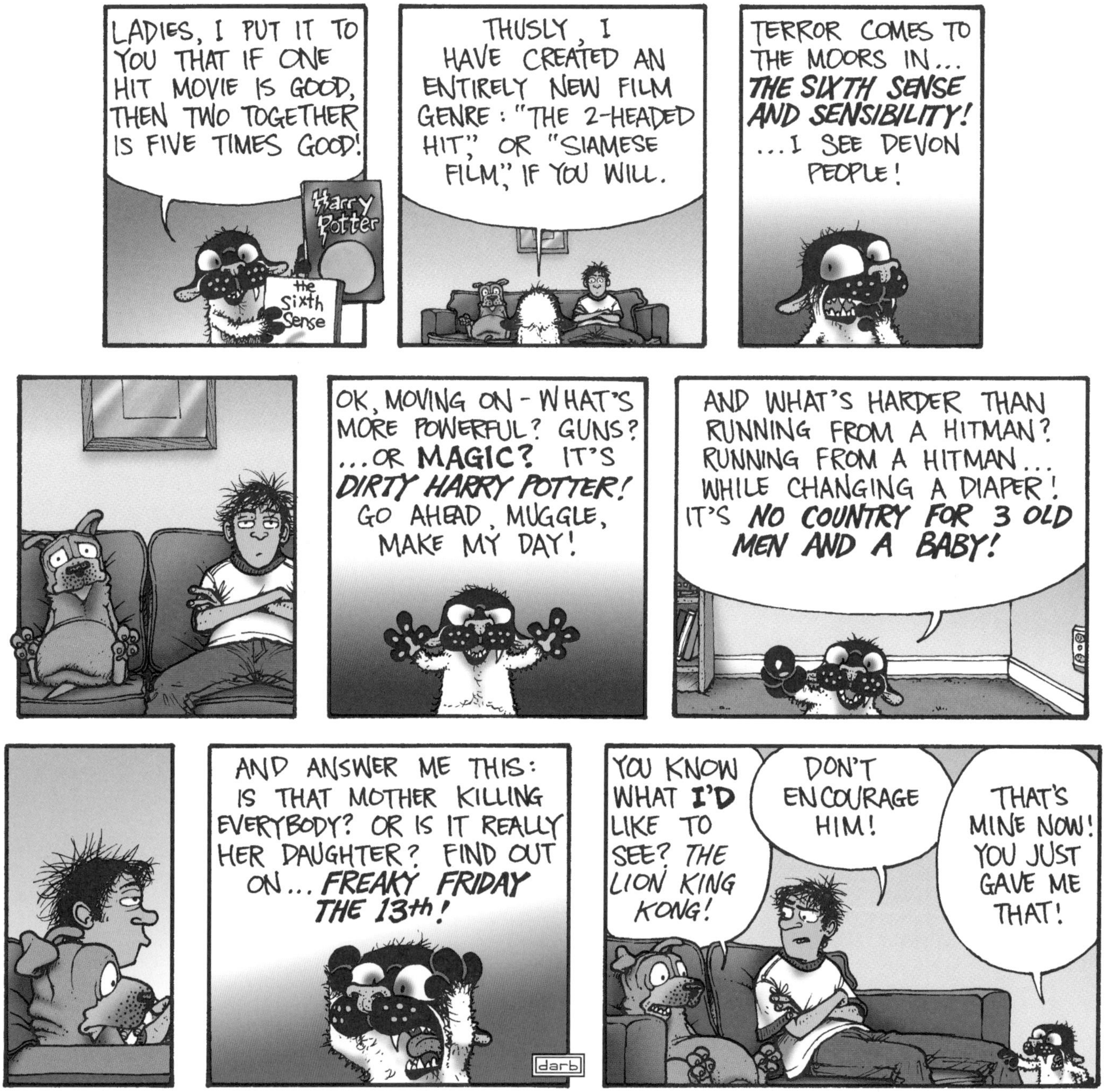
LADIES, I PUT IT TO YOU THAT IF ONE HIT MOVIE IS GOOD, THEN TWO TOGETHER IS FIVE TIMES GOOD!
Harry Potter
the Sixth Sense
THUSLY, I HAVE CREATED AN ENTIRELY NEW FILM GENRE: "THE 2-HEADED HIT," OR "SIAMESE FILM," IF YOU WILL.
TERROR COMES TO THE MOORS IN... THE SIXTH SENSE AND SENSIBILITY! ...I SEE DEVON PEOPLE!
OK, MOVING ON - WHAT'S MORE POWERFUL? GUNS? ...OR MAGIC? IT'S DIRTY HARRY POTTER! GO AHEAD, MUGGLE, MAKE MY DAY!
AND WHAT'S HARDER THAN RUNNING FROM A HITMAN? RUNNING FROM A HITMAN... WHILE CHANGING A DIAPER! IT'S NO COUNTRY FOR 3 OLD MEN AND A BABY!
AND ANSWER ME THIS: IS THAT MOTHER KILLING EVERYBODY? OR IS IT REALLY HER DAUGHTER? FIND OUT ON... FREAKY FRIDAY THE 13th!
darb
YOU KNOW WHAT I'D LIKE TO SEE? THE LION KING KONG!
DON'T ENCOURAGE HIM!
THAT'S MINE NOW! YOU JUST GAVE ME THAT!

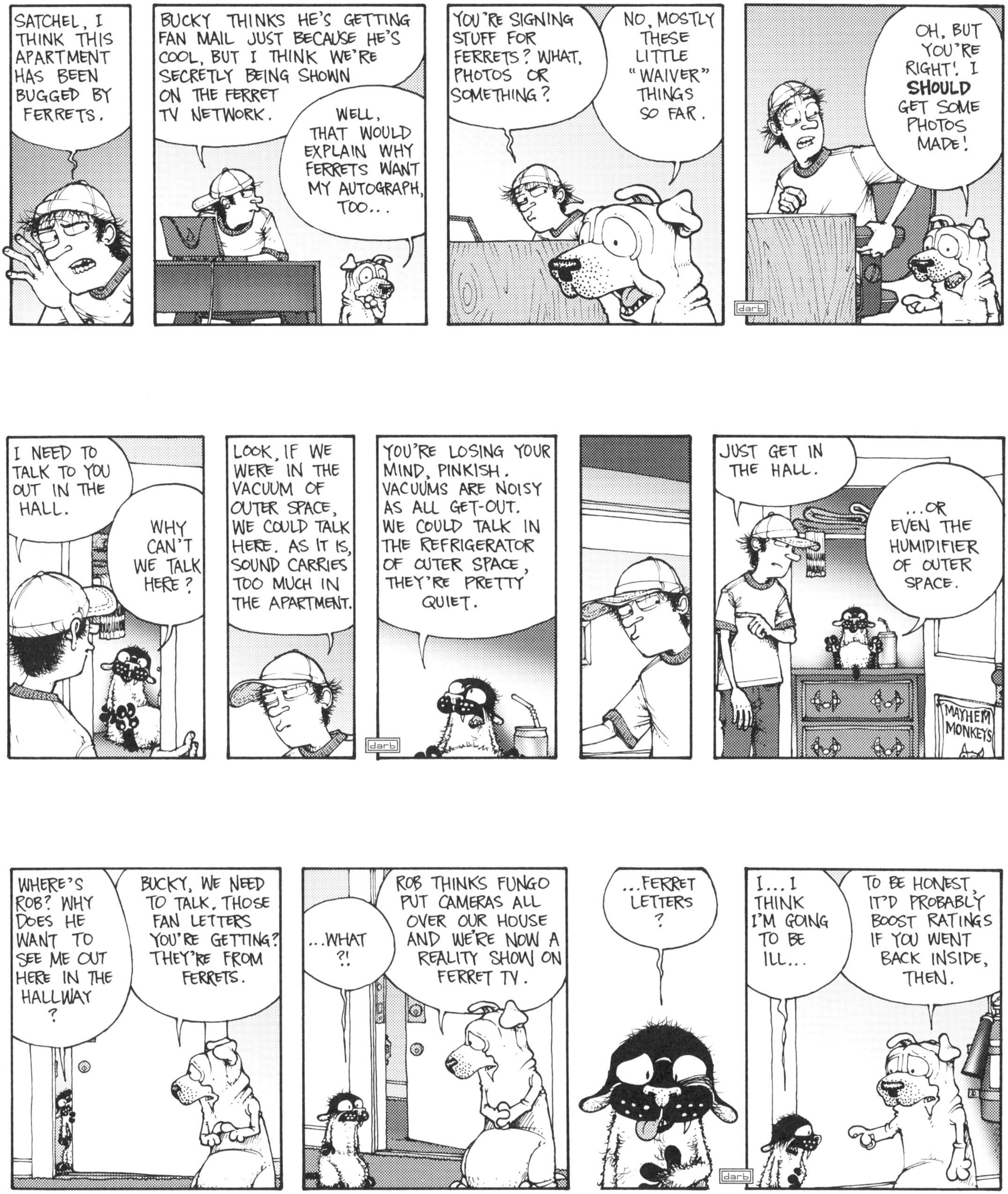
SATCHEL, I THINK THIS APARTMENT HAS BEEN BUGGED BY FERRETS.
BUCKY THINKS HE'S GETTING FAN MAIL JUST BECAUSE HE'S COOL, BUT I THINK WE'RE SECRETLY BEING SHOWN ON THE FERRET TV NETWORK.
WELL, THAT WOULD EXPLAIN WHY FERRETS WANT MY AUTOGRAPH, TOO...
YOU'RE SIGNING STUFF FOR FERRETS? WHAT, PHOTOS OR SOMETHING?
NO, MOSTLY THESE LITTLE "WAIVER" THINGS SO FAR.
OH, BUT YOU'RE RIGHT! I **SHOULD** GET SOME PHOTOS MADE!
darb
I NEED TO TALK TO YOU OUT IN THE HALL.
WHY CAN'T WE TALK HERE?
LOOK, IF WE WERE IN THE VACUUM OF OUTER SPACE, WE COULD TALK HERE. AS IT IS, SOUND CARRIES TOO MUCH IN THE APARTMENT.
darb
YOU'RE LOSING YOUR MIND, PINKISH. VACUUMS ARE NOISY AS ALL GET-OUT. WE COULD TALK IN THE REFRIGERATOR OF OUTER SPACE, THEY'RE PRETTY QUIET.
JUST GET IN THE HALL.
...OR EVEN THE HUMIDIFIER OF OUTER SPACE.
MAYHEM MONKEYS
WHERE'S ROB? WHY DOES HE WANT TO SEE ME OUT HERE IN THE HALLWAY?
BUCKY, WE NEED TO TALK. THOSE FAN LETTERS YOU'RE GETTING? THEY'RE FROM FERRETS.
...WHAT?!
ROB THINKS FUNGO PUT CAMERAS ALL OVER OUR HOUSE AND WE'RE NOW A REALITY SHOW ON FERRET TV.
...FERRET LETTERS?
darb
I... I THINK I'M GOING TO BE ILL...
TO BE HONEST, IT'D PROBABLY BOOST RATINGS IF YOU WENT BACK INSIDE, THEN.

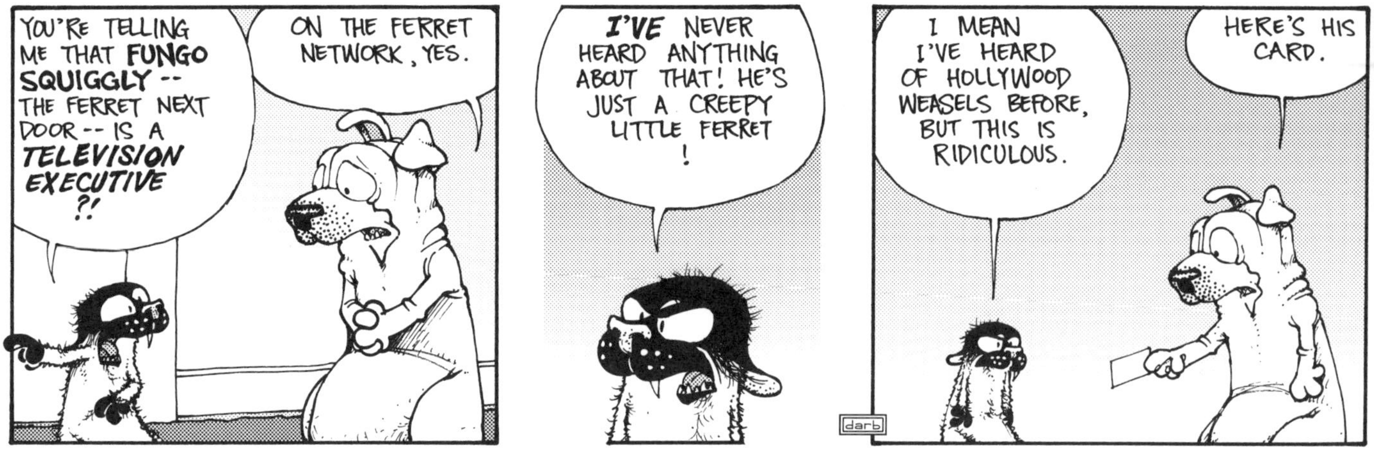
YOU'RE TELLING ME THAT **FUNGO SQUIGGLY** -- THE FERRET NEXT DOOR -- IS A ***TELEVISION EXECUTIVE*** ?!
ON THE FERRET NETWORK, YES.
I'VE NEVER HEARD ANYTHING ABOUT THAT! HE'S JUST A CREEPY LITTLE FERRET!
I MEAN I'VE HEARD OF HOLLYWOOD WEASELS BEFORE, BUT THIS IS RIDICULOUS.
HERE'S HIS CARD.
darb

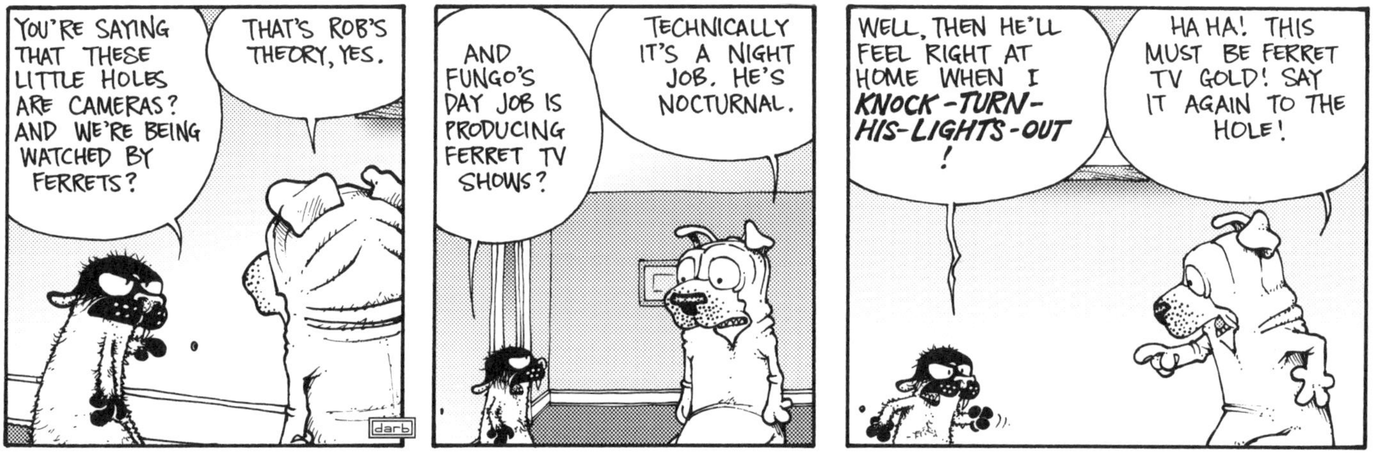
YOU'RE SAYING THAT THESE LITTLE HOLES ARE CAMERAS? AND WE'RE BEING WATCHED BY FERRETS?
THAT'S ROB'S THEORY, YES.
darb
AND FUNGO'S DAY JOB IS PRODUCING FERRET TV SHOWS?
TECHNICALLY IT'S A NIGHT JOB. HE'S NOCTURNAL.
WELL, THEN HE'LL FEEL RIGHT AT HOME WHEN I ***KNOCK-TURN-HIS-LIGHTS-OUT*** !
HA HA! THIS MUST BE FERRET TV GOLD! SAY IT AGAIN TO THE HOLE!

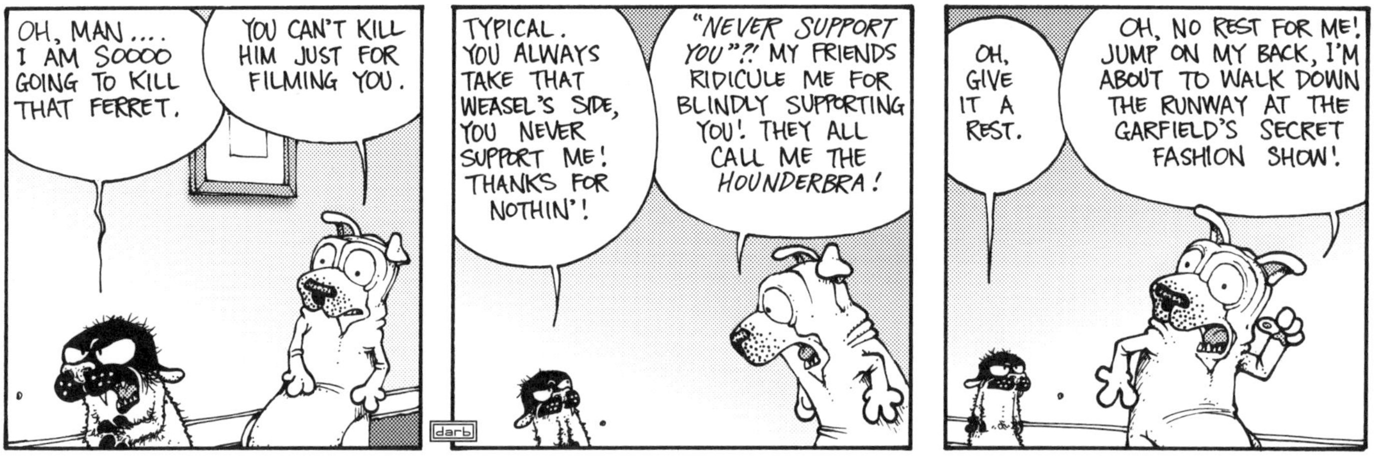
OH, MAN.... I AM SOOOO GOING TO KILL THAT FERRET.
YOU CAN'T KILL HIM JUST FOR FILMING YOU.
darb
TYPICAL. YOU ALWAYS TAKE THAT WEASEL'S SIDE, YOU NEVER SUPPORT ME! THANKS FOR NOTHIN'!
"NEVER SUPPORT YOU"?! MY FRIENDS RIDICULE ME FOR BLINDLY SUPPORTING YOU! THEY ALL CALL ME THE *HOUNDERBRA*!
OH, GIVE IT A REST.
OH, NO REST FOR ME! JUMP ON MY BACK, I'M ABOUT TO WALK DOWN THE RUNWAY AT THE GARFIELD'S SECRET FASHION SHOW!

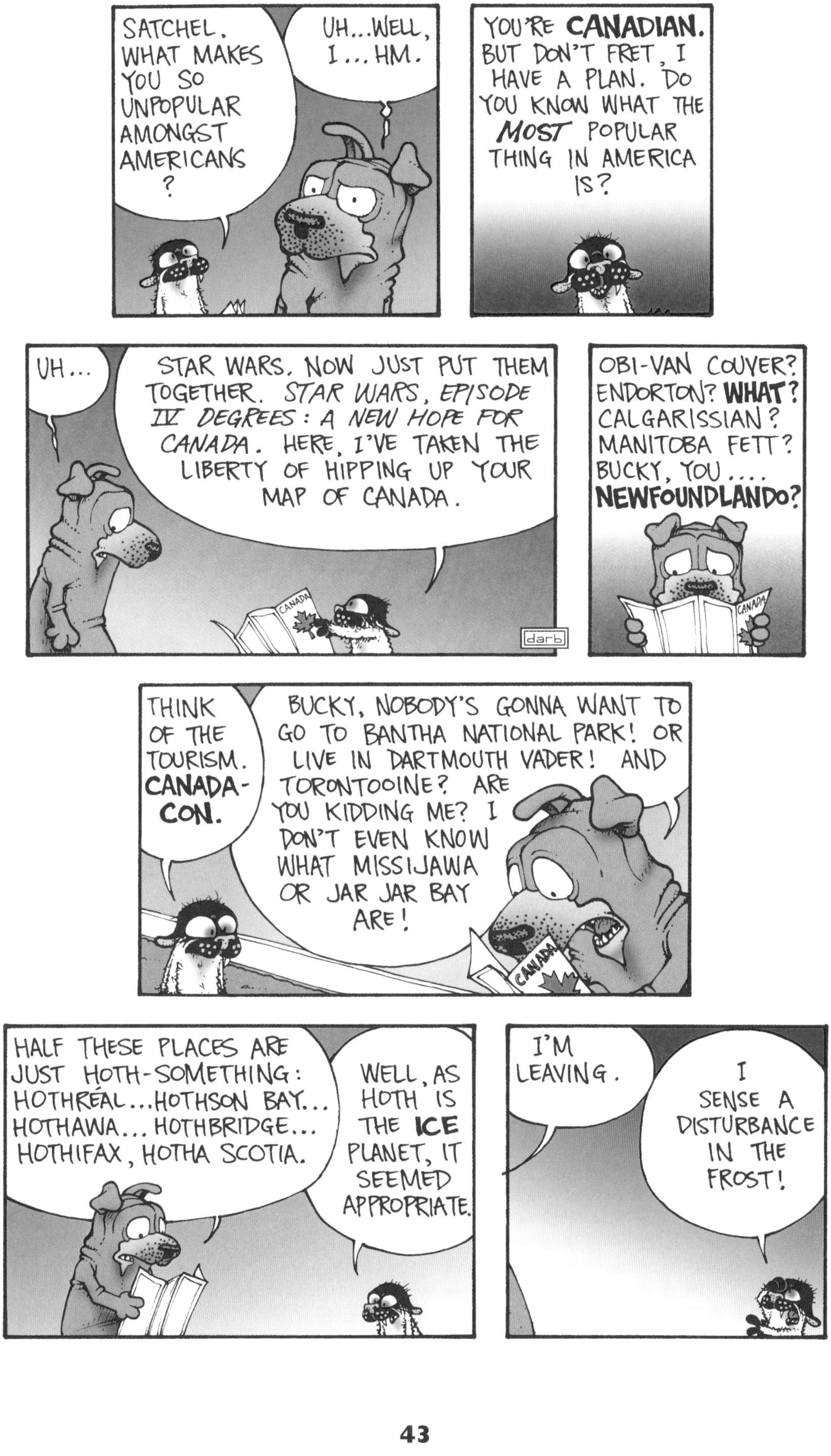
SATCHEL. WHAT MAKES YOU SO UNPOPULAR AMONGST AMERICANS ?
UH...WELL, I... HM.
YOU'RE **CANADIAN.** BUT DON'T FRET, I HAVE A PLAN. DO YOU KNOW WHAT THE ***MOST*** POPULAR THING IN AMERICA IS?
UH...
STAR WARS. NOW JUST PUT THEM TOGETHER. *STAR WARS, EPISODE IV DEGREES: A NEW HOPE FOR CANADA.* HERE, I'VE TAKEN THE LIBERTY OF HIPPING UP YOUR MAP OF CANADA.
CANADA
darb
OBI-VAN COUVER? ENDORTON? **WHAT**? CALGARISSIAN? MANITOBA FETT? BUCKY, YOU.... **NEWFOUNDLANDO**?
CANADA
THINK OF THE TOURISM. **CANADA-CON.**
BUCKY, NOBODY'S GONNA WANT TO GO TO BANTHA NATIONAL PARK! OR LIVE IN DARTMOUTH VADER! AND TORONTOOINE? ARE YOU KIDDING ME? I DON'T EVEN KNOW WHAT MISSIJAWA OR JAR JAR BAY ARE!
CANADA
HALF THESE PLACES ARE JUST HOTH-SOMETHING: HOTHRÉAL...HOTHSON BAY... HOTHAWA... HOTHBRIDGE... HOTHIFAX, HOTHA SCOTIA.
WELL, AS HOTH IS THE **ICE** PLANET, IT SEEMED APPROPRIATE.
I'M LEAVING.
I SENSE A DISTURBANCE IN THE FROST!

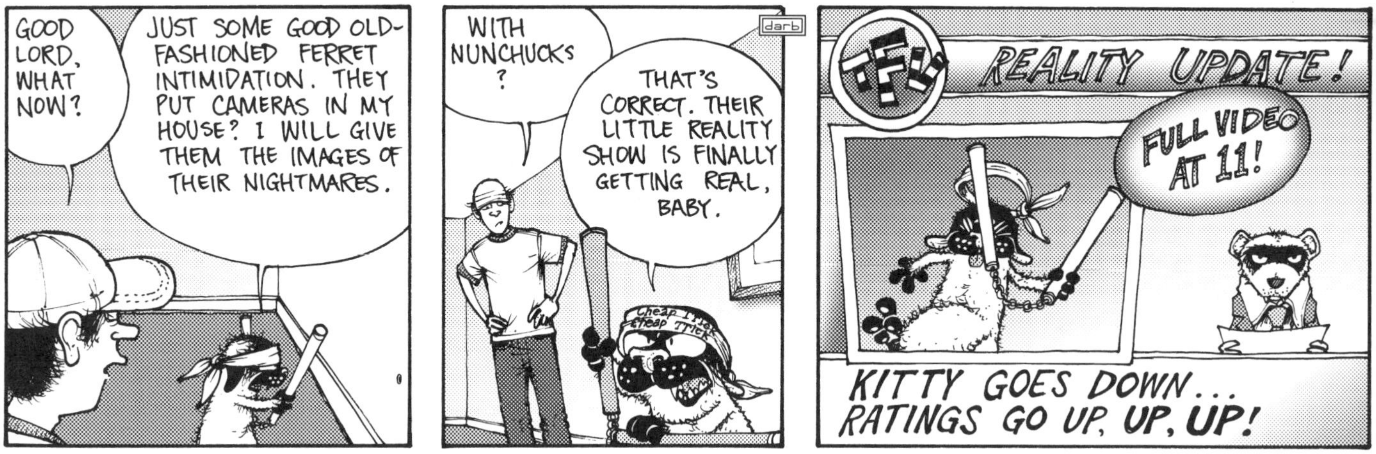
GOOD LORD, WHAT NOW?
JUST SOME GOOD OLD-FASHIONED FERRET INTIMIDATION. THEY PUT CAMERAS IN MY HOUSE? I WILL GIVE THEM THE IMAGES OF THEIR NIGHTMARES.
WITH NUNCHUCKS?
THAT'S CORRECT. THEIR LITTLE REALITY SHOW IS FINALLY GETTING REAL, BABY.
REALITY UPDATE!
FULL VIDEO AT 11!
KITTY GOES DOWN... RATINGS GO UP, UP, UP!

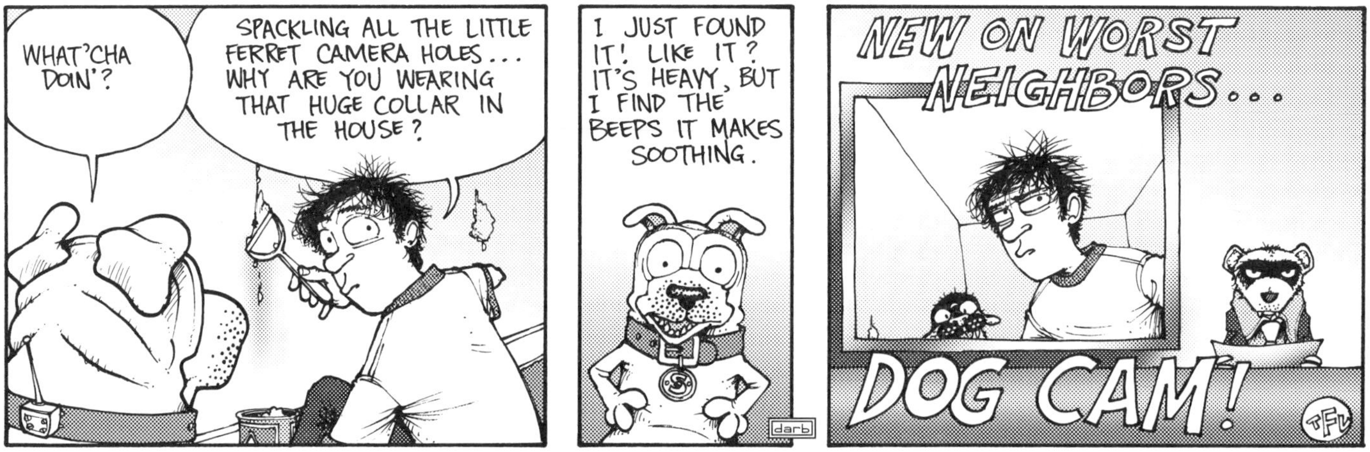
WHAT'CHA DOIN'?
SPACKLING ALL THE LITTLE FERRET CAMERA HOLES... WHY ARE YOU WEARING THAT HUGE COLLAR IN THE HOUSE?
I JUST FOUND IT! LIKE IT? IT'S HEAVY, BUT I FIND THE BEEPS IT MAKES SOOTHING.
NEW ON WORST NEIGHBORS...
DOG CAM!

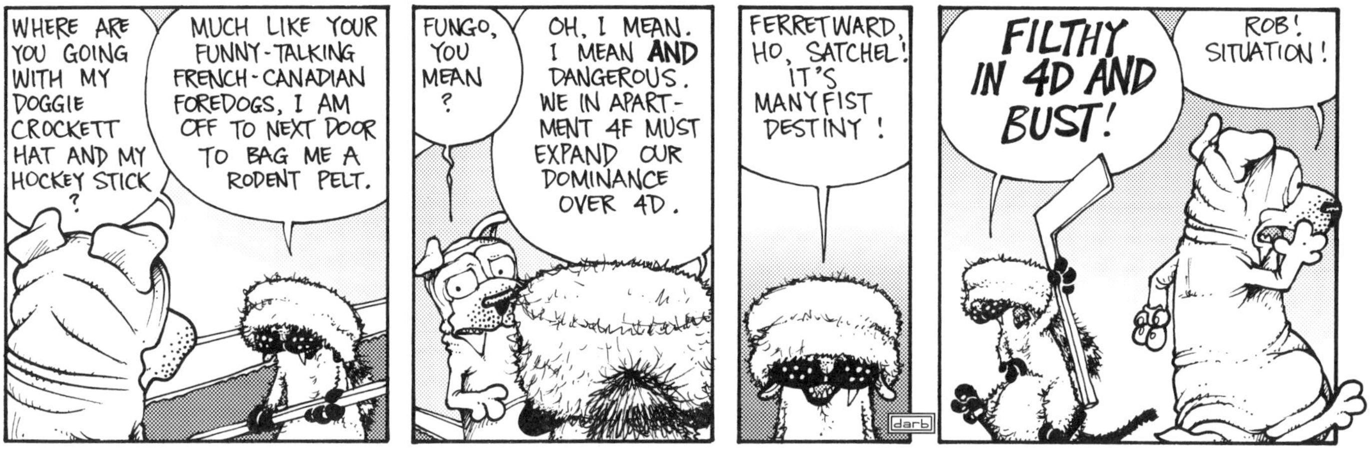
WHERE ARE YOU GOING WITH MY DOGGIE CROCKETT HAT AND MY HOCKEY STICK?
MUCH LIKE YOUR FUNNY-TALKING FRENCH-CANADIAN FOREDOGS, I AM OFF TO NEXT DOOR TO BAG ME A RODENT PELT.
FUNGO, YOU MEAN?
OH, I MEAN. I MEAN AND DANGEROUS. WE IN APARTMENT 4F MUST EXPAND OUR DOMINANCE OVER 4D.
FERRETWARD, HO, SATCHEL! IT'S MANYFIST DESTINY!
FILTHY IN 4D AND BUST!
ROB! SITUATION!

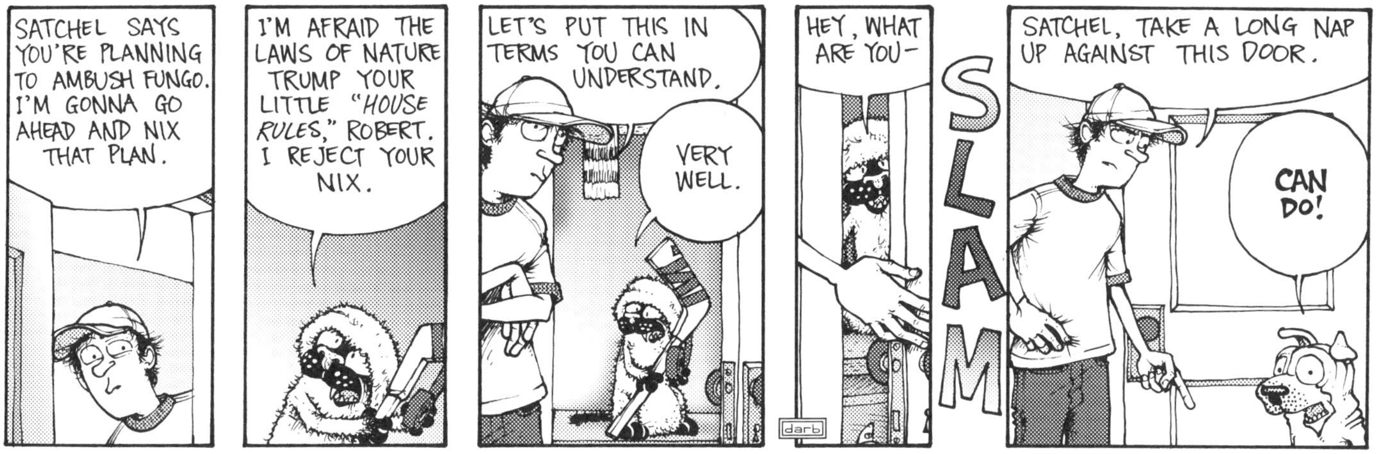
SATCHEL SAYS YOU'RE PLANNING TO AMBUSH FUNGO. I'M GONNA GO AHEAD AND NIX THAT PLAN.
I'M AFRAID THE LAWS OF NATURE TRUMP YOUR LITTLE "HOUSE RULES," ROBERT. I REJECT YOUR NIX.
LET'S PUT THIS IN TERMS YOU CAN UNDERSTAND.
VERY WELL.
HEY, WHAT ARE YOU-
SLAM
SATCHEL, TAKE A LONG NAP UP AGAINST THIS DOOR.
CAN DO!

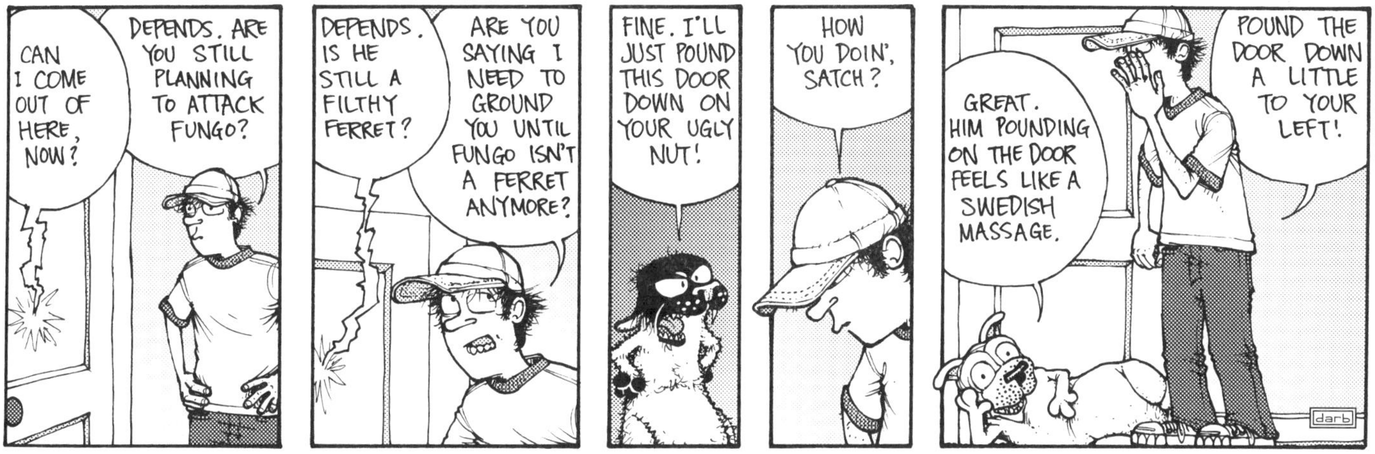
CAN I COME OUT OF HERE, NOW?
DEPENDS. ARE YOU STILL PLANNING TO ATTACK FUNGO?
DEPENDS. IS HE STILL A FILTHY FERRET?
ARE YOU SAYING I NEED TO GROUND YOU UNTIL FUNGO ISN'T A FERRET ANYMORE?
FINE. I'LL JUST POUND THIS DOOR DOWN ON YOUR UGLY NUT!
HOW YOU DOIN', SATCH?
GREAT. HIM POUNDING ON THE DOOR FEELS LIKE A SWEDISH MASSAGE.
POUND THE DOOR DOWN A LITTLE TO YOUR LEFT!

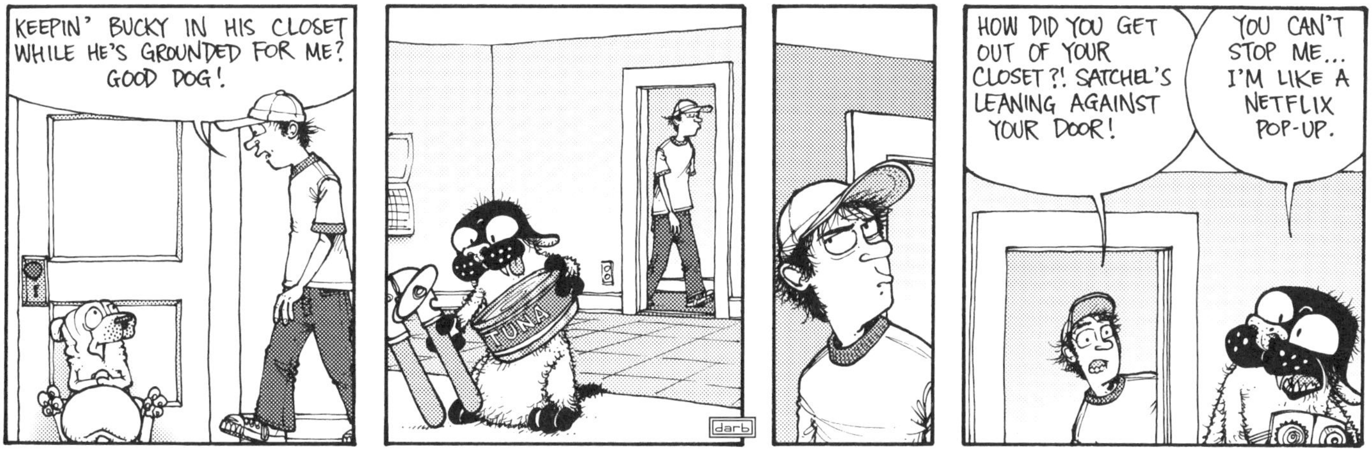
KEEPIN' BUCKY IN HIS CLOSET WHILE HE'S GROUNDED FOR ME? GOOD DOG!
TUNA
HOW DID YOU GET OUT OF YOUR CLOSET?! SATCHEL'S LEANING AGAINST YOUR DOOR!
YOU CAN'T STOP ME... I'M LIKE A NETFLIX POP-UP.

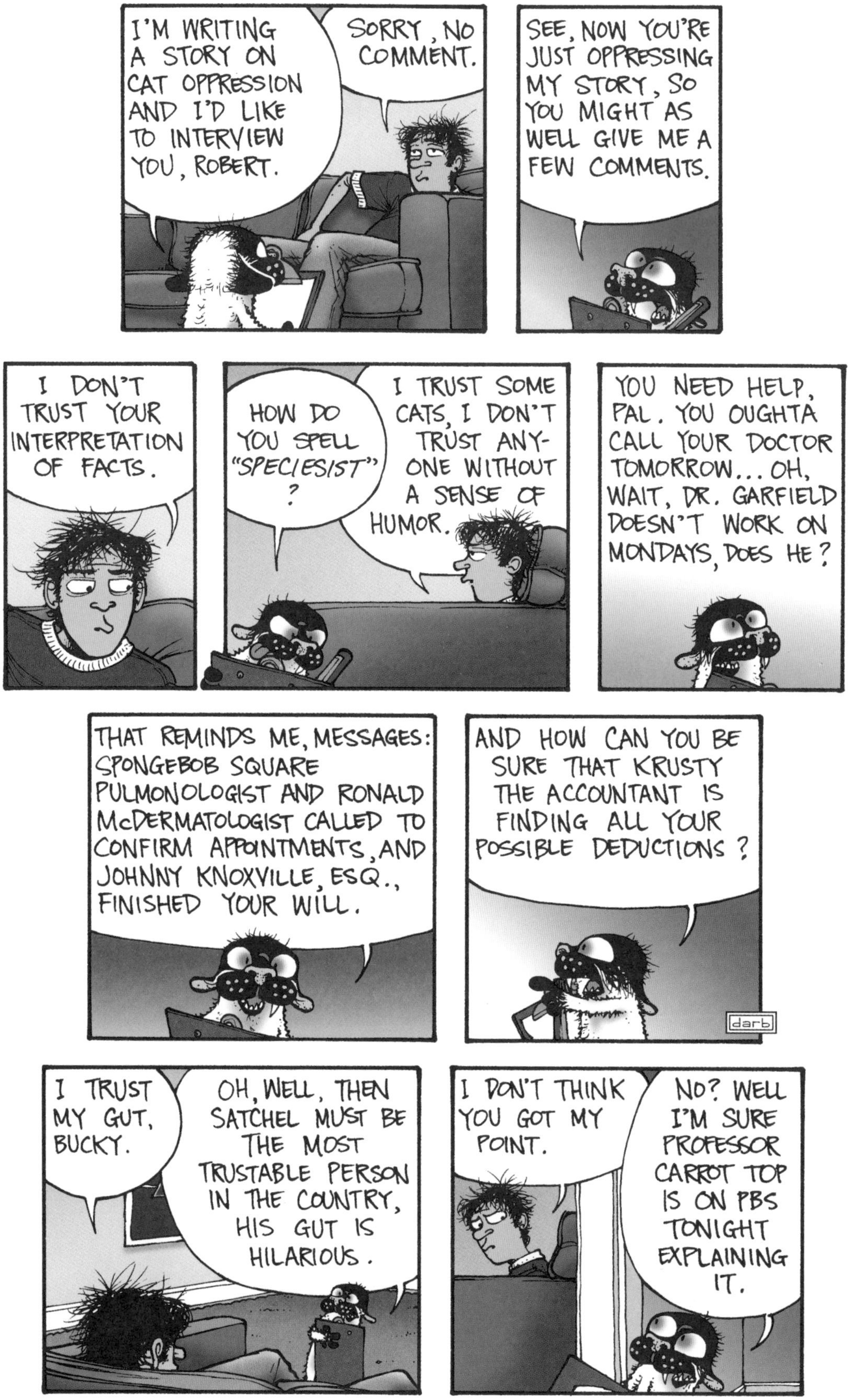
I'M WRITING A STORY ON CAT OPPRESSION AND I'D LIKE TO INTERVIEW YOU, ROBERT.
SORRY, NO COMMENT.
SEE, NOW YOU'RE JUST OPPRESSING MY STORY, SO YOU MIGHT AS WELL GIVE ME A FEW COMMENTS.
I DON'T TRUST YOUR INTERPRETATION OF FACTS.
HOW DO YOU SPELL "SPECIESIST"?
I TRUST SOME CATS, I DON'T TRUST ANYONE WITHOUT A SENSE OF HUMOR.
YOU NEED HELP, PAL. YOU OUGHTA CALL YOUR DOCTOR TOMORROW... OH, WAIT, DR. GARFIELD DOESN'T WORK ON MONDAYS, DOES HE?
THAT REMINDS ME, MESSAGES: SPONGEBOB SQUARE PULMONOLOGIST AND RONALD McDERMATOLOGIST CALLED TO CONFIRM APPOINTMENTS, AND JOHNNY KNOXVILLE, ESQ., FINISHED YOUR WILL.
AND HOW CAN YOU BE SURE THAT KRUSTY THE ACCOUNTANT IS FINDING ALL YOUR POSSIBLE DEDUCTIONS?
darb
I TRUST MY GUT, BUCKY.
OH, WELL, THEN SATCHEL MUST BE THE MOST TRUSTABLE PERSON IN THE COUNTRY, HIS GUT IS HILARIOUS.
I DON'T THINK YOU GOT MY POINT.
NO? WELL I'M SURE PROFESSOR CARROT TOP IS ON PBS TONIGHT EXPLAINING IT.

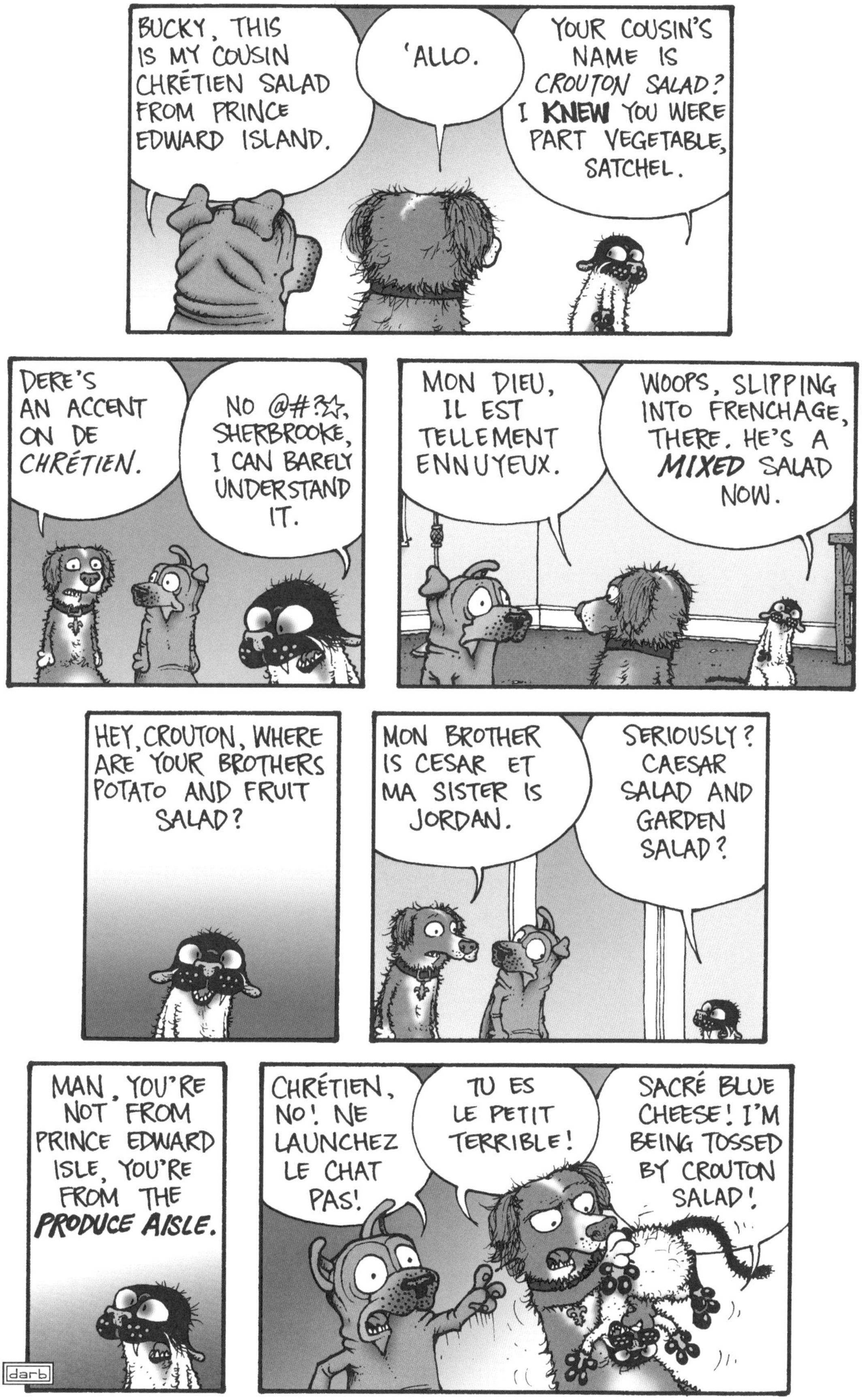
BUCKY, THIS IS MY COUSIN CHRÉTIEN SALAD FROM PRINCE EDWARD ISLAND.
'ALLO.
YOUR COUSIN'S NAME IS CROUTON SALAD? I KNEW YOU WERE PART VEGETABLE, SATCHEL.
DERE'S AN ACCENT ON DE CHRÉTIEN.
NO @#?☆, SHERBROOKE, I CAN BARELY UNDERSTAND IT.
MON DIEU, IL EST TELLEMENT ENNUYEUX.
WOOPS, SLIPPING INTO FRENCHAGE, THERE. HE'S A MIXED SALAD NOW.
HEY, CROUTON, WHERE ARE YOUR BROTHERS POTATO AND FRUIT SALAD?
MON BROTHER IS CESAR ET MA SISTER IS JORDAN.
SERIOUSLY? CAESAR SALAD AND GARDEN SALAD?
MAN, YOU'RE NOT FROM PRINCE EDWARD ISLE, YOU'RE FROM THE PRODUCE AISLE.
darb
CHRÉTIEN, NO! NE LAUNCHEZ LE CHAT PAS!
TU ES LE PETIT TERRIBLE!
SACRÉ BLUE CHEESE! I'M BEING TOSSED BY CROUTON SALAD!

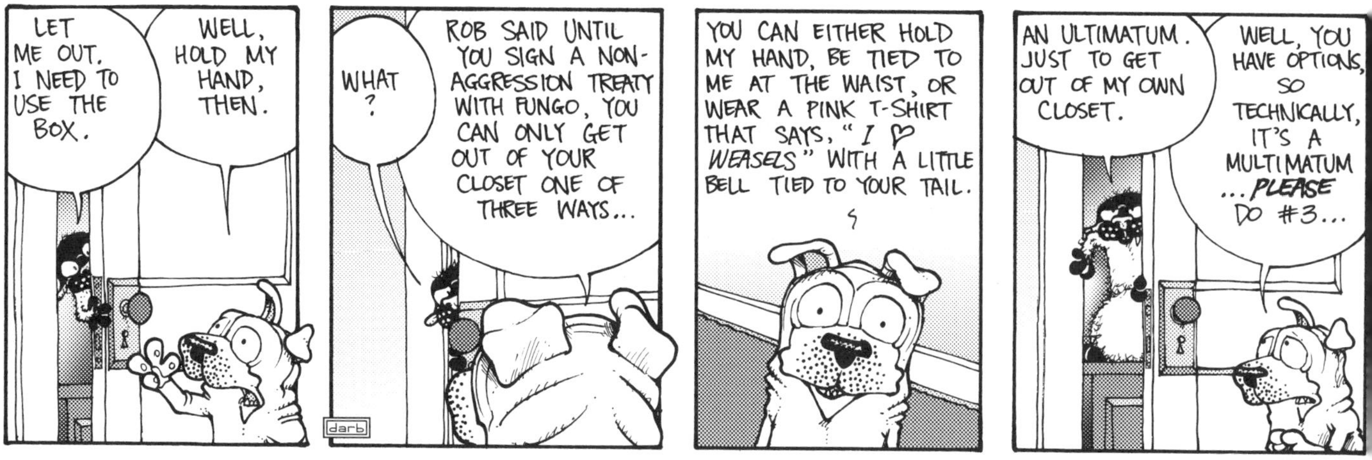
LET ME OUT. I NEED TO USE THE BOX.
WELL, HOLD MY HAND, THEN.
WHAT?
ROB SAID UNTIL YOU SIGN A NON-AGGRESSION TREATY WITH FUNGO, YOU CAN ONLY GET OUT OF YOUR CLOSET ONE OF THREE WAYS...
YOU CAN EITHER HOLD MY HAND, BE TIED TO ME AT THE WAIST, OR WEAR A PINK T-SHIRT THAT SAYS, "I ♥ WEASELS" WITH A LITTLE BELL TIED TO YOUR TAIL.
AN ULTIMATUM. JUST TO GET OUT OF MY OWN CLOSET.
WELL, YOU HAVE OPTIONS, SO TECHNICALLY, IT'S A MULTIMATUM ...PLEASE DO #3...
darb

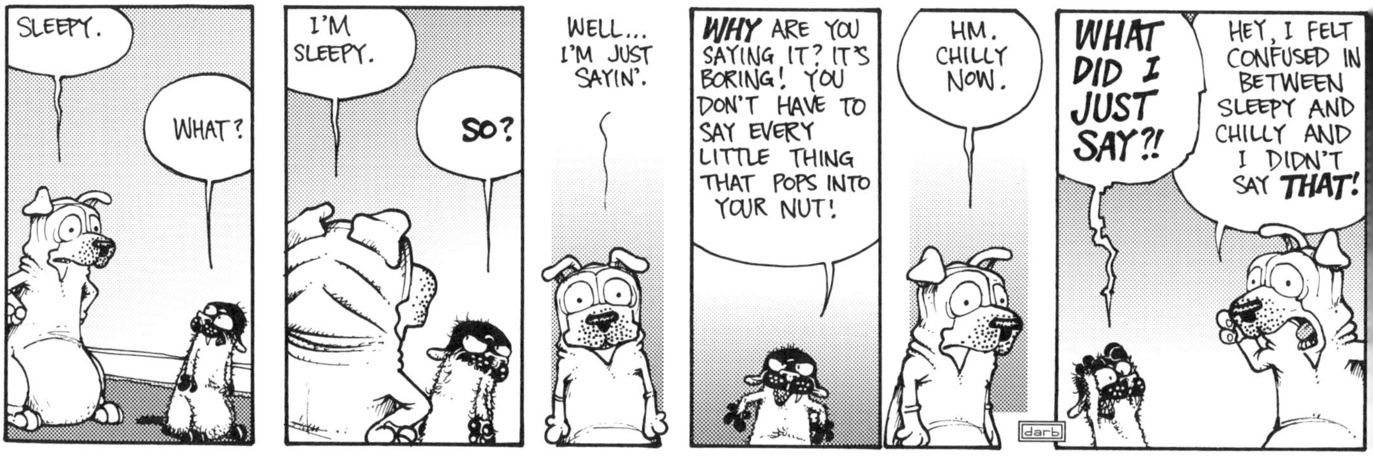
SLEEPY.
WHAT?
I'M SLEEPY.
SO?
WELL... I'M JUST SAYIN'.
WHY ARE YOU SAYING IT? IT'S BORING! YOU DON'T HAVE TO SAY EVERY LITTLE THING THAT POPS INTO YOUR NUT!
HM. CHILLY NOW.
WHAT DID I JUST SAY?!
HEY, I FELT CONFUSED IN BETWEEN SLEEPY AND CHILLY AND I DIDN'T SAY THAT!
darb

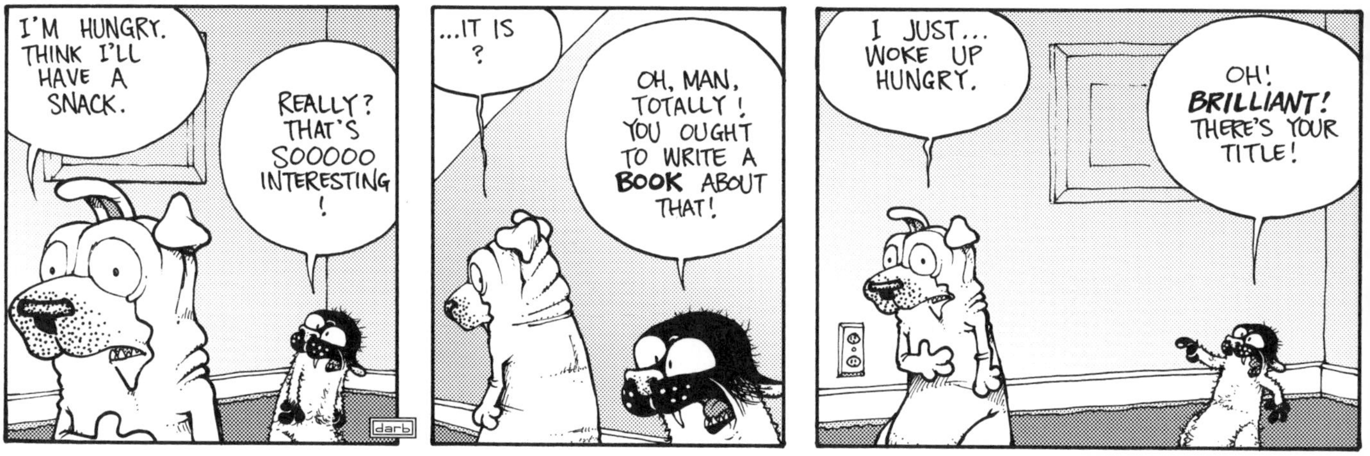
I'M HUNGRY. THINK I'LL HAVE A SNACK.
REALLY? THAT'S SOOOOO INTERESTING!
...IT IS?
OH, MAN, TOTALLY! YOU OUGHT TO WRITE A BOOK ABOUT THAT!
I JUST... WOKE UP HUNGRY.
OH! BRILLIANT! THERE'S YOUR TITLE!
darb

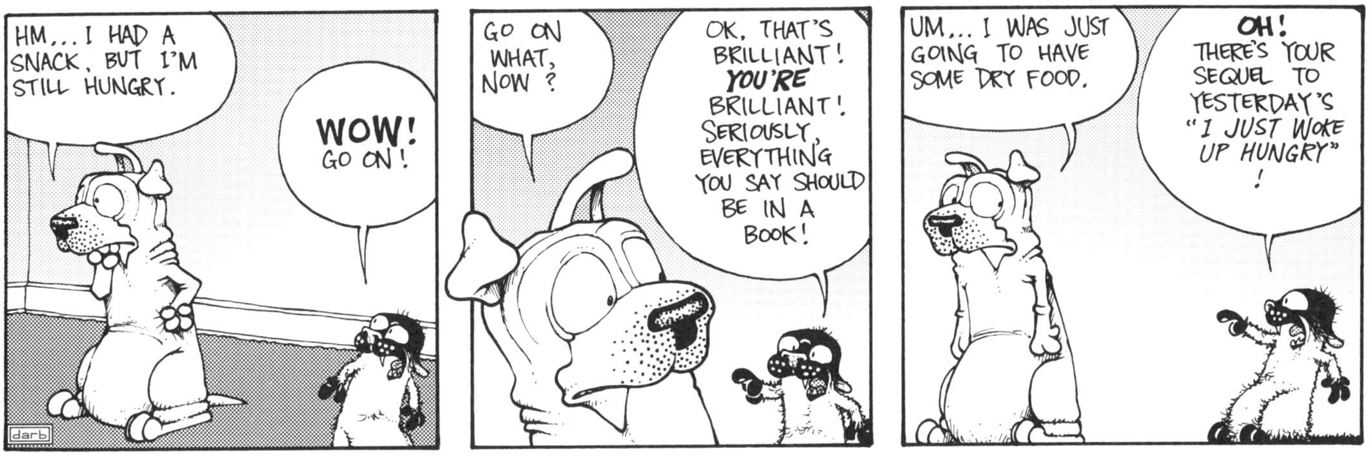
HM... I HAD A SNACK, BUT I'M STILL HUNGRY.
WOW! GO ON!
GO ON WHAT, NOW?
OK, THAT'S BRILLIANT! YOU'RE BRILLIANT! SERIOUSLY, EVERYTHING YOU SAY SHOULD BE IN A BOOK!
UM... I WAS JUST GOING TO HAVE SOME DRY FOOD.
OH! THERE'S YOUR SEQUEL TO YESTERDAY'S "I JUST WOKE UP HUNGRY"!
darb

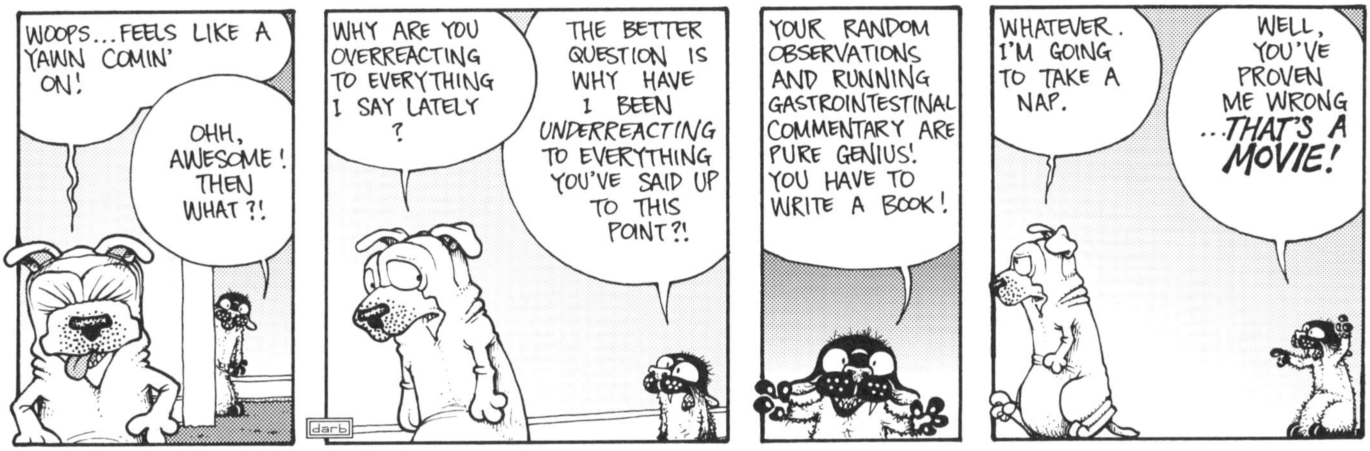
WOOPS... FEELS LIKE A YAWN COMIN' ON!
OHH, AWESOME! THEN WHAT?!
WHY ARE YOU OVERREACTING TO EVERYTHING I SAY LATELY?
THE BETTER QUESTION IS WHY HAVE I BEEN UNDERREACTING TO EVERYTHING YOU'VE SAID UP TO THIS POINT?!
YOUR RANDOM OBSERVATIONS AND RUNNING GASTROINTESTINAL COMMENTARY ARE PURE GENIUS! YOU HAVE TO WRITE A BOOK!
WHATEVER. I'M GOING TO TAKE A NAP.
WELL, YOU'VE PROVEN ME WRONG ...THAT'S A MOVIE!
darb

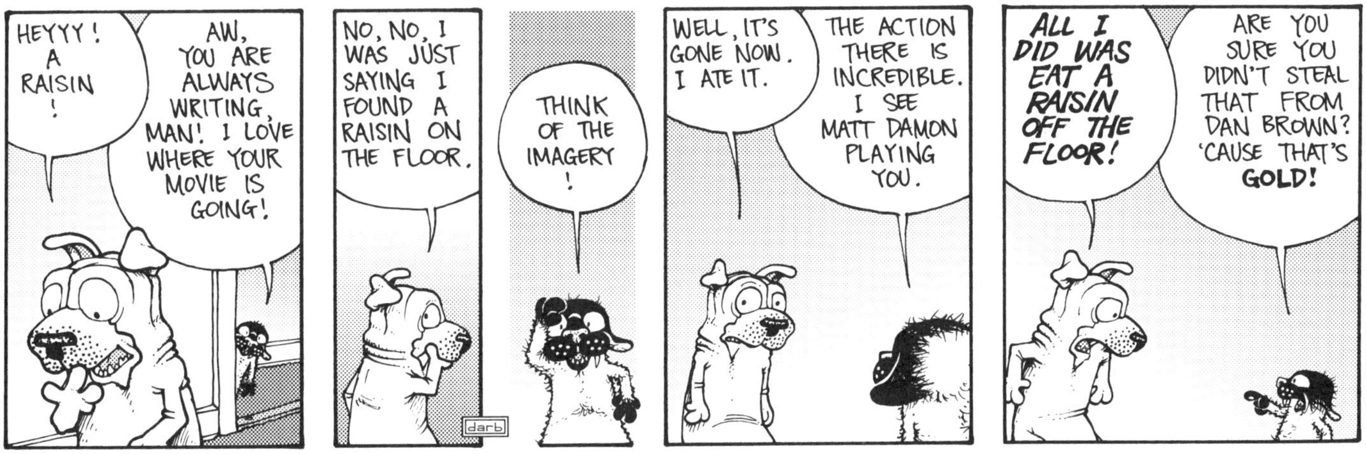
HEYYY! A RAISIN!
AW, YOU ARE ALWAYS WRITING, MAN! I LOVE WHERE YOUR MOVIE IS GOING!
NO, NO, I WAS JUST SAYING I FOUND A RAISIN ON THE FLOOR.
THINK OF THE IMAGERY!
WELL, IT'S GONE NOW. I ATE IT.
THE ACTION THERE IS INCREDIBLE. I SEE MATT DAMON PLAYING YOU.
ALL I DID WAS EAT A RAISIN OFF THE FLOOR!
ARE YOU SURE YOU DIDN'T STEAL THAT FROM DAN BROWN? 'CAUSE THAT'S GOLD!
darb

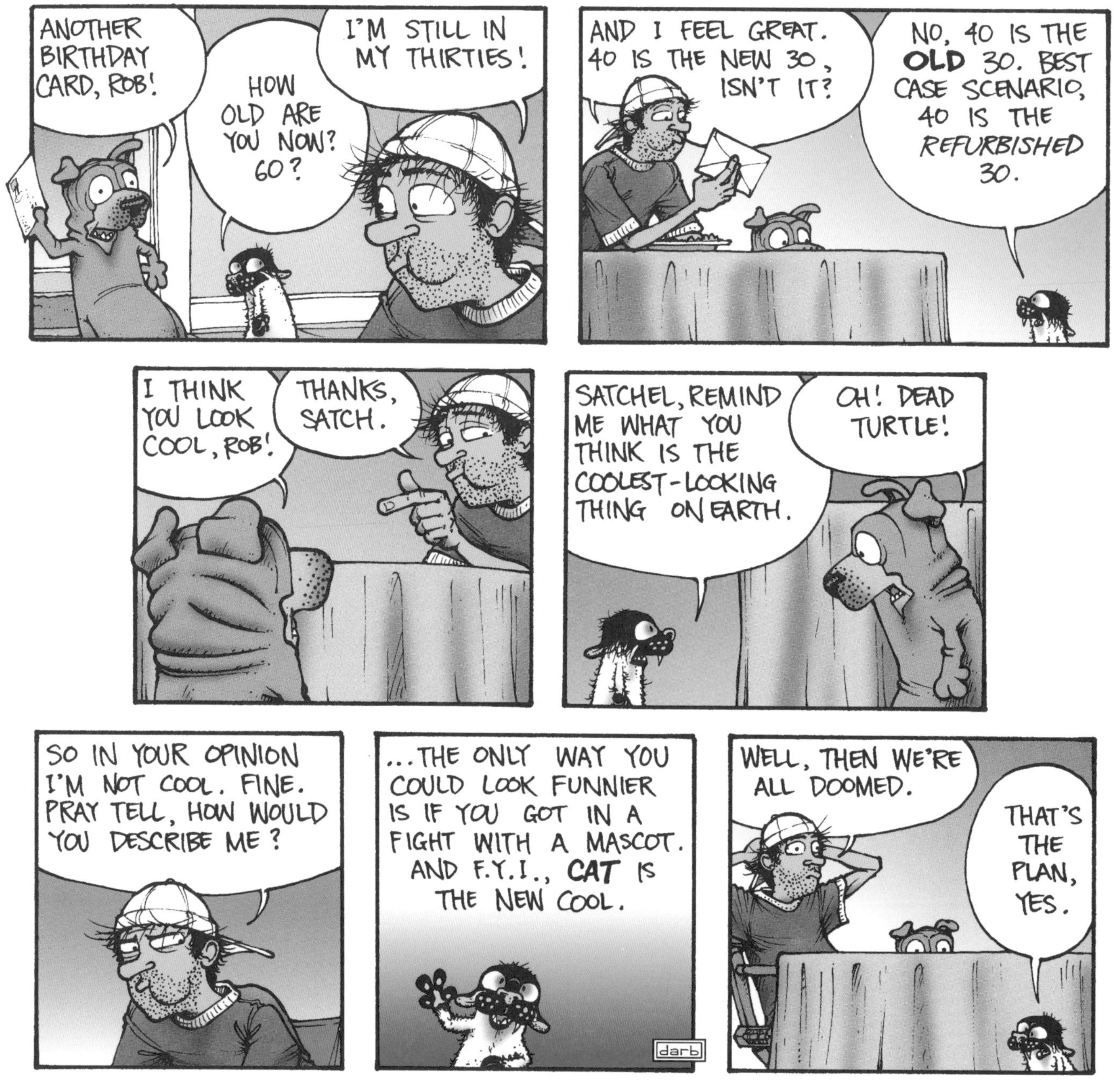
ANOTHER BIRTHDAY CARD, ROB!
HOW OLD ARE YOU NOW? 60?
I'M STILL IN MY THIRTIES!
AND I FEEL GREAT. 40 IS THE NEW 30, ISN'T IT?
NO, 40 IS THE OLD 30. BEST CASE SCENARIO, 40 IS THE REFURBISHED 30.
I THINK YOU LOOK COOL, ROB!
THANKS, SATCH.
SATCHEL, REMIND ME WHAT YOU THINK IS THE COOLEST-LOOKING THING ON EARTH.
OH! DEAD TURTLE!
SO IN YOUR OPINION I'M NOT COOL. FINE. PRAY TELL, HOW WOULD YOU DESCRIBE ME?
...THE ONLY WAY YOU COULD LOOK FUNNIER IS IF YOU GOT IN A FIGHT WITH A MASCOT. AND F.Y.I., CAT IS THE NEW COOL.
darb
WELL, THEN WE'RE ALL DOOMED.
THAT'S THE PLAN, YES.

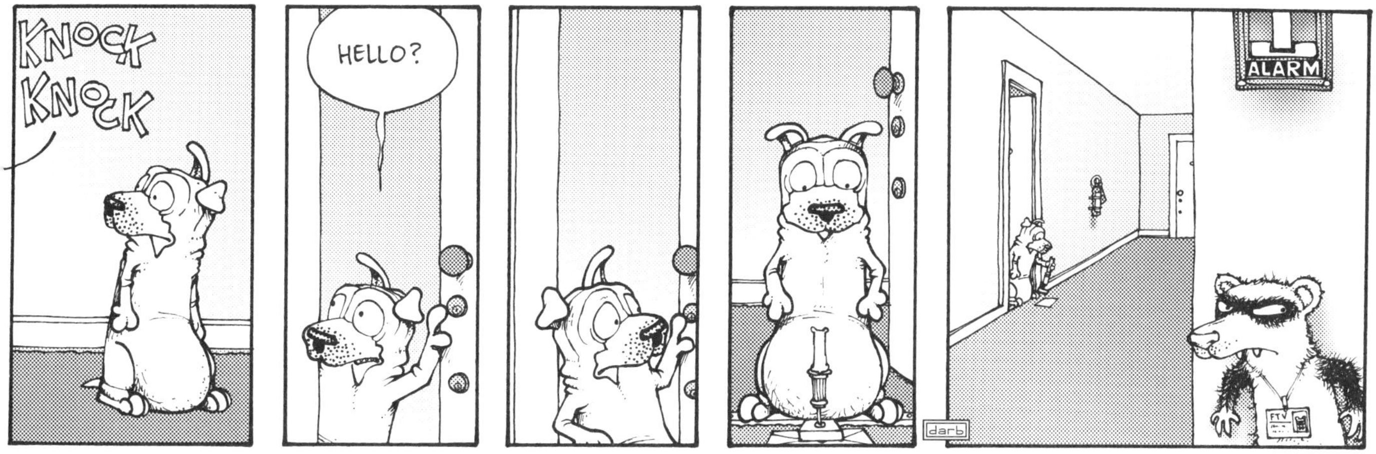
KNOCK KNOCK
HELLO?
ALARM

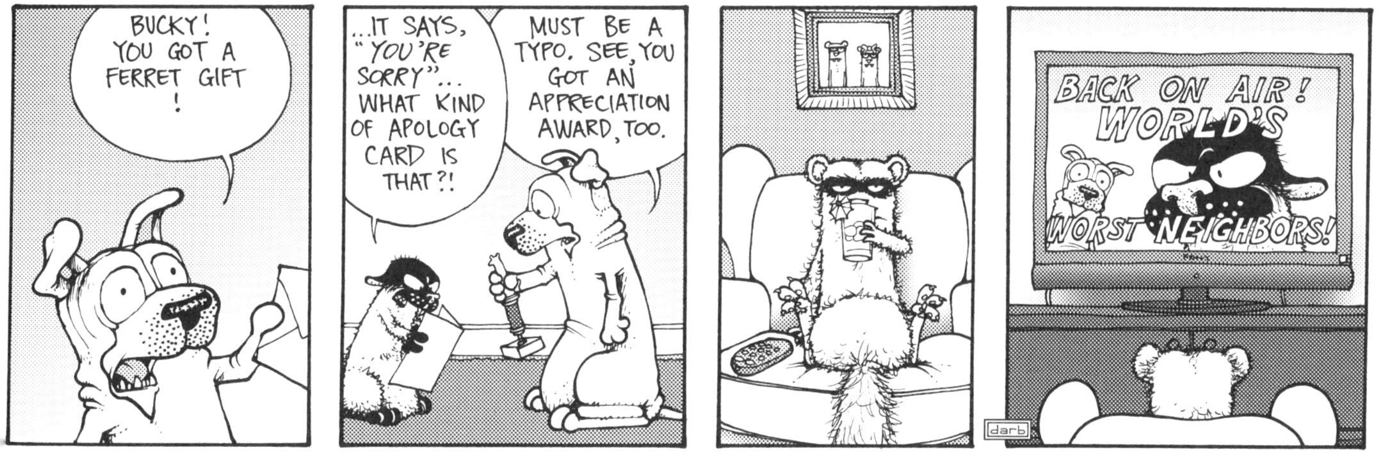
BUCKY! YOU GOT A FERRET GIFT!
...IT SAYS, "YOU'RE SORRY"... WHAT KIND OF APOLOGY CARD IS THAT?!
MUST BE A TYPO. SEE, YOU GOT AN APPRECIATION AWARD, TOO.
BACK ON AIR! WORLD'S WORST NEIGHBORS!

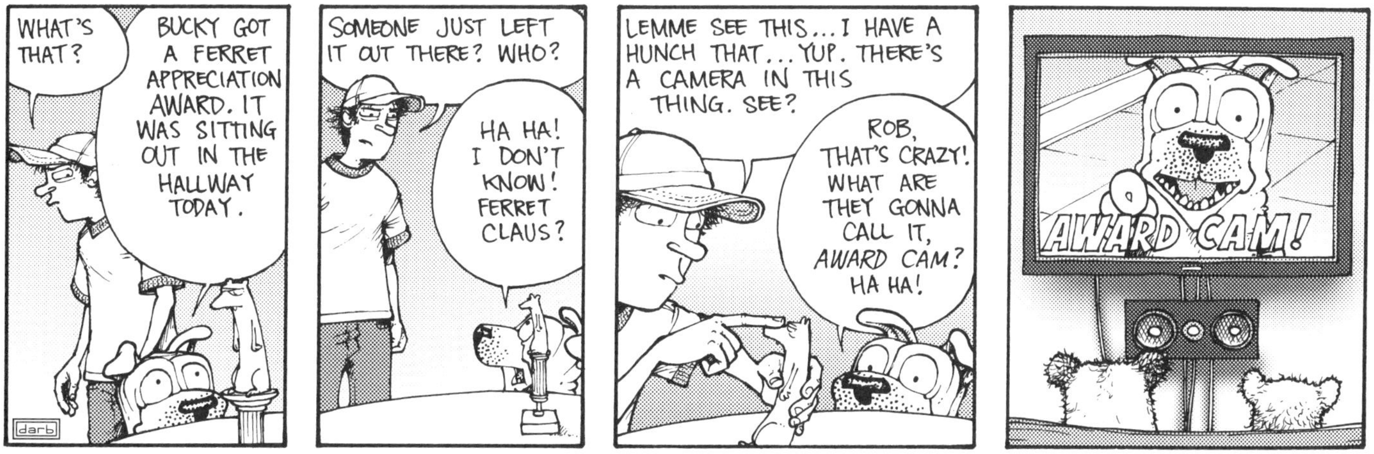
WHAT'S THAT?
BUCKY GOT A FERRET APPRECIATION AWARD. IT WAS SITTING OUT IN THE HALLWAY TODAY.
SOMEONE JUST LEFT IT OUT THERE? WHO?
HA HA! I DON'T KNOW! FERRET CLAUS?
LEMME SEE THIS... I HAVE A HUNCH THAT... YUP. THERE'S A CAMERA IN THIS THING. SEE?
ROB, THAT'S CRAZY! WHAT ARE THEY GONNA CALL IT, AWARD CAM? HA HA!
AWARD CAM!

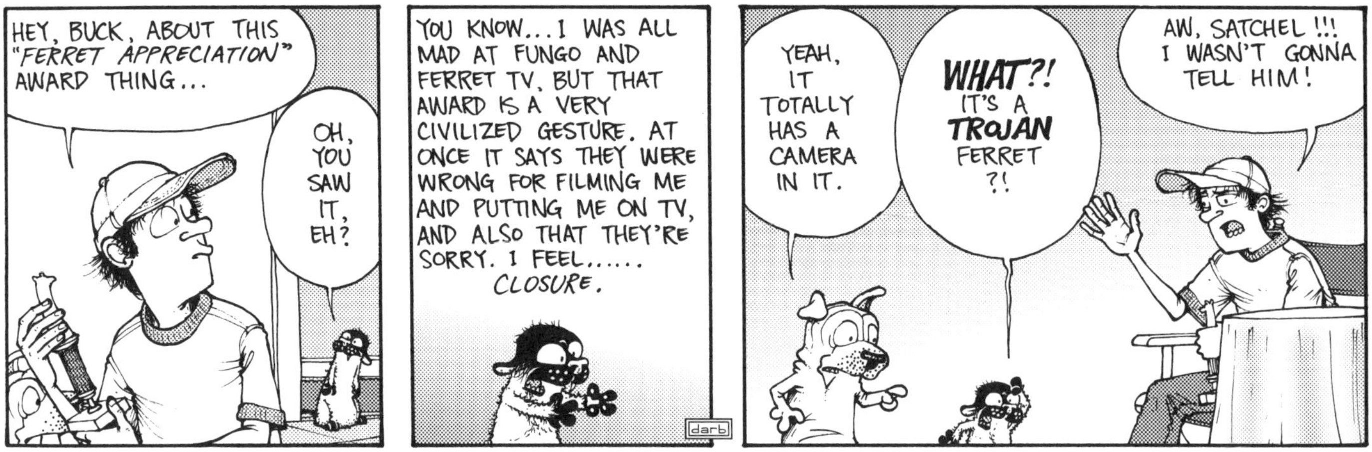
HEY, BUCK, ABOUT THIS "FERRET APPRECIATION" AWARD THING...
OH, YOU SAW IT, EH?
YOU KNOW... I WAS ALL MAD AT FUNGO AND FERRET TV, BUT THAT AWARD IS A VERY CIVILIZED GESTURE. AT ONCE IT SAYS THEY WERE WRONG FOR FILMING ME AND PUTTING ME ON TV, AND ALSO THAT THEY'RE SORRY. I FEEL...... CLOSURE.
darb
YEAH, IT TOTALLY HAS A CAMERA IN IT.
WHAT?! IT'S A TROJAN FERRET ?!
AW, SATCHEL !!! I WASN'T GONNA TELL HIM!

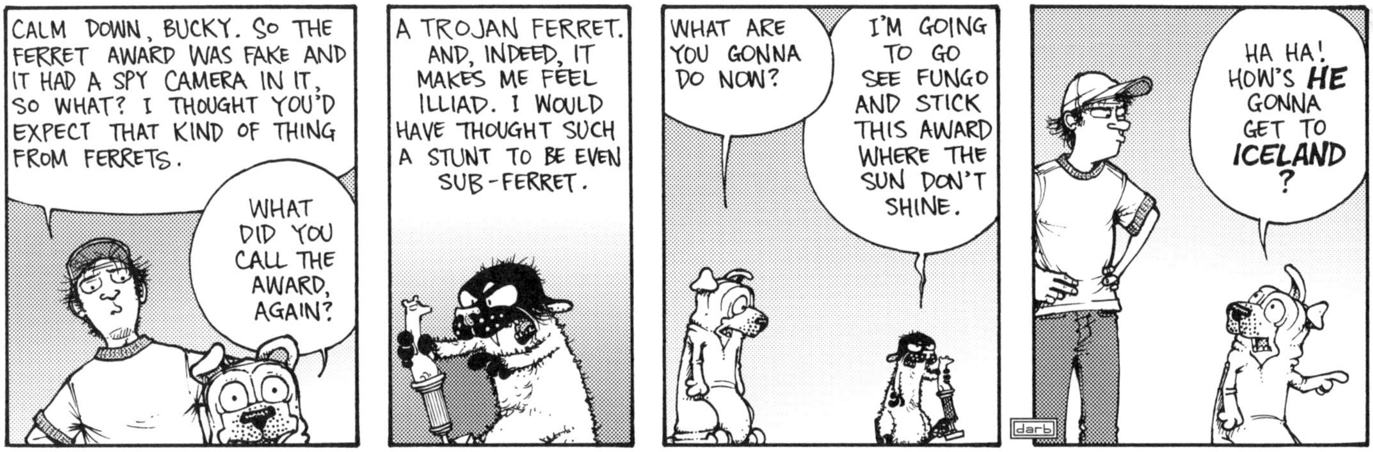
CALM DOWN, BUCKY. SO THE FERRET AWARD WAS FAKE AND IT HAD A SPY CAMERA IN IT, SO WHAT? I THOUGHT YOU'D EXPECT THAT KIND OF THING FROM FERRETS.
WHAT DID YOU CALL THE AWARD, AGAIN?
A TROJAN FERRET. AND, INDEED, IT MAKES ME FEEL ILLIAD. I WOULD HAVE THOUGHT SUCH A STUNT TO BE EVEN SUB-FERRET.
WHAT ARE YOU GONNA DO NOW?
I'M GOING TO GO SEE FUNGO AND STICK THIS AWARD WHERE THE SUN DON'T SHINE.
darb
HA HA! HOW'S HE GONNA GET TO ICELAND ?

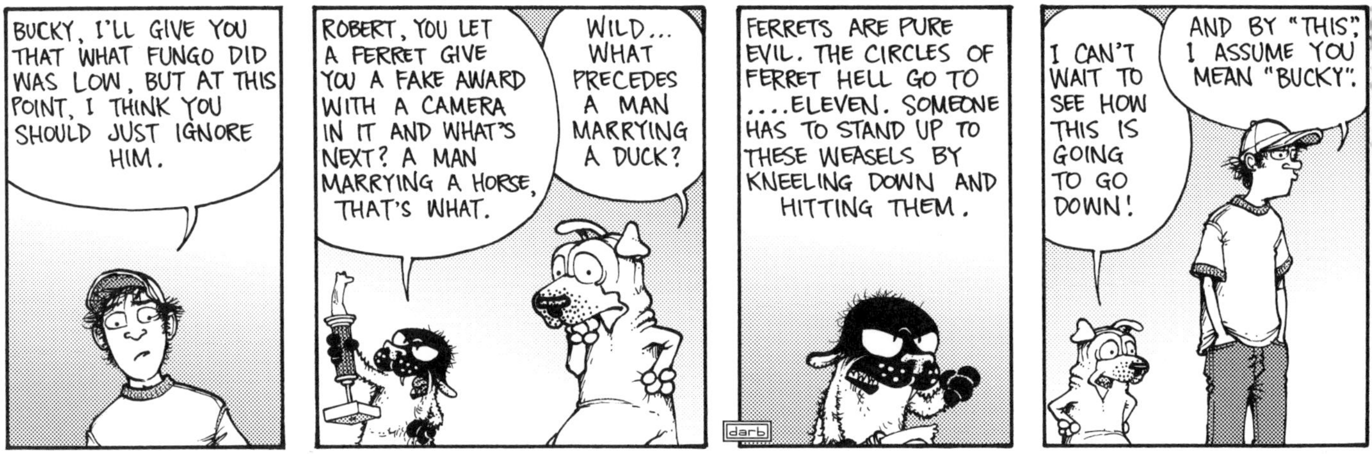
BUCKY, I'LL GIVE YOU THAT WHAT FUNGO DID WAS LOW, BUT AT THIS POINT, I THINK YOU SHOULD JUST IGNORE HIM.
ROBERT, YOU LET A FERRET GIVE YOU A FAKE AWARD WITH A CAMERA IN IT AND WHAT'S NEXT? A MAN MARRYING A HORSE, THAT'S WHAT.
WILD... WHAT PRECEDES A MAN MARRYING A DUCK?
darb
FERRETS ARE PURE EVIL. THE CIRCLES OF FERRET HELL GO TO ....ELEVEN. SOMEONE HAS TO STAND UP TO THESE WEASELS BY KNEELING DOWN AND HITTING THEM.
I CAN'T WAIT TO SEE HOW THIS IS GOING TO GO DOWN!
AND BY "THIS", I ASSUME YOU MEAN "BUCKY".

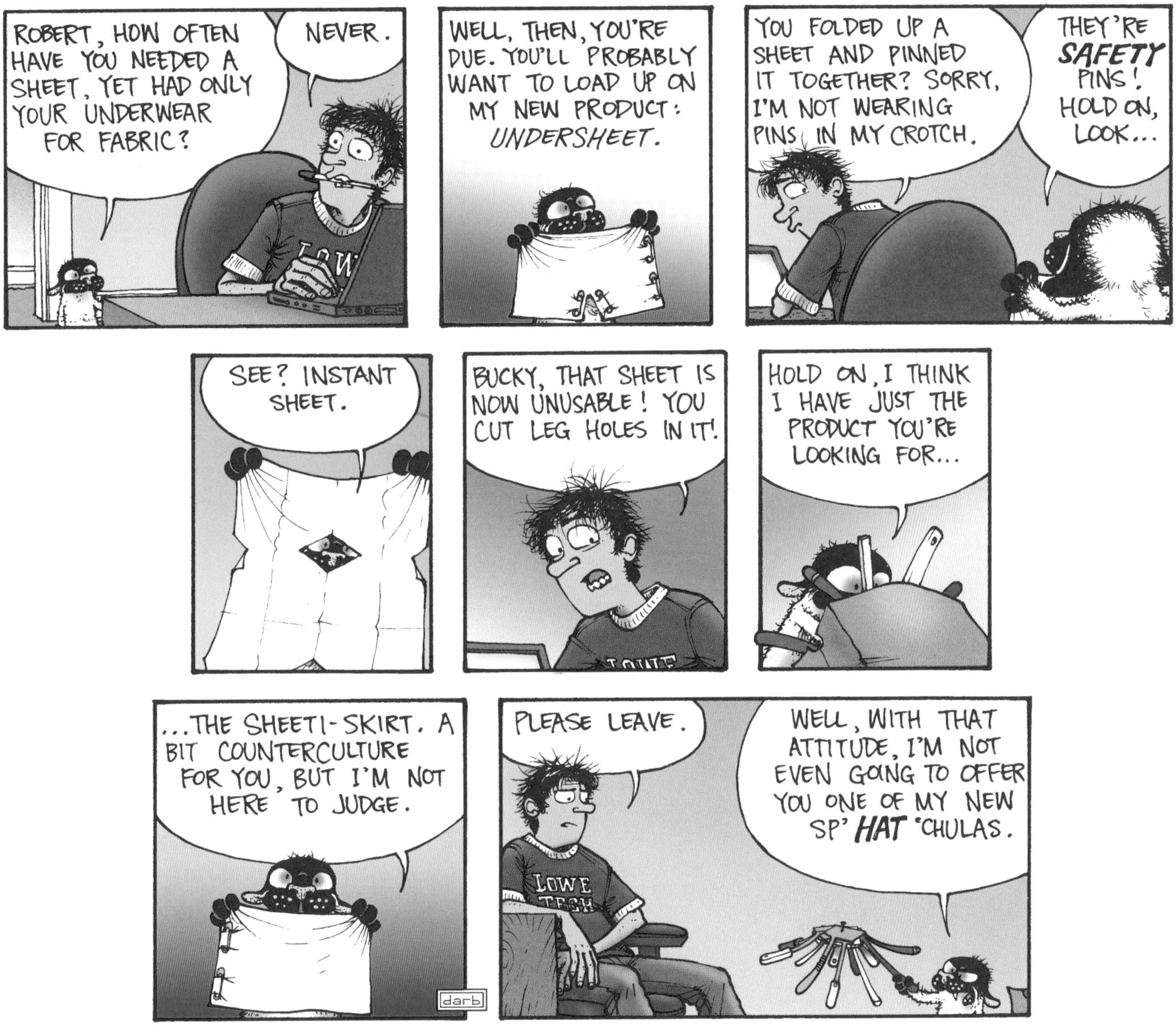
ROBERT, HOW OFTEN HAVE YOU NEEDED A SHEET, YET HAD ONLY YOUR UNDERWEAR FOR FABRIC?
NEVER.
WELL, THEN, YOU'RE DUE. YOU'LL PROBABLY WANT TO LOAD UP ON MY NEW PRODUCT: UNDERSHEET.
YOU FOLDED UP A SHEET AND PINNED IT TOGETHER? SORRY, I'M NOT WEARING PINS IN MY CROTCH.
THEY'RE SAFETY PINS! HOLD ON, LOOK...
SEE? INSTANT SHEET.
BUCKY, THAT SHEET IS NOW UNUSABLE! YOU CUT LEG HOLES IN IT!
HOLD ON, I THINK I HAVE JUST THE PRODUCT YOU'RE LOOKING FOR...
...THE SHEETI-SKIRT. A BIT COUNTERCULTURE FOR YOU, BUT I'M NOT HERE TO JUDGE.
darb
PLEASE LEAVE.
WELL, WITH THAT ATTITUDE, I'M NOT EVEN GOING TO OFFER YOU ONE OF MY NEW SP'HAT'CHULAS.

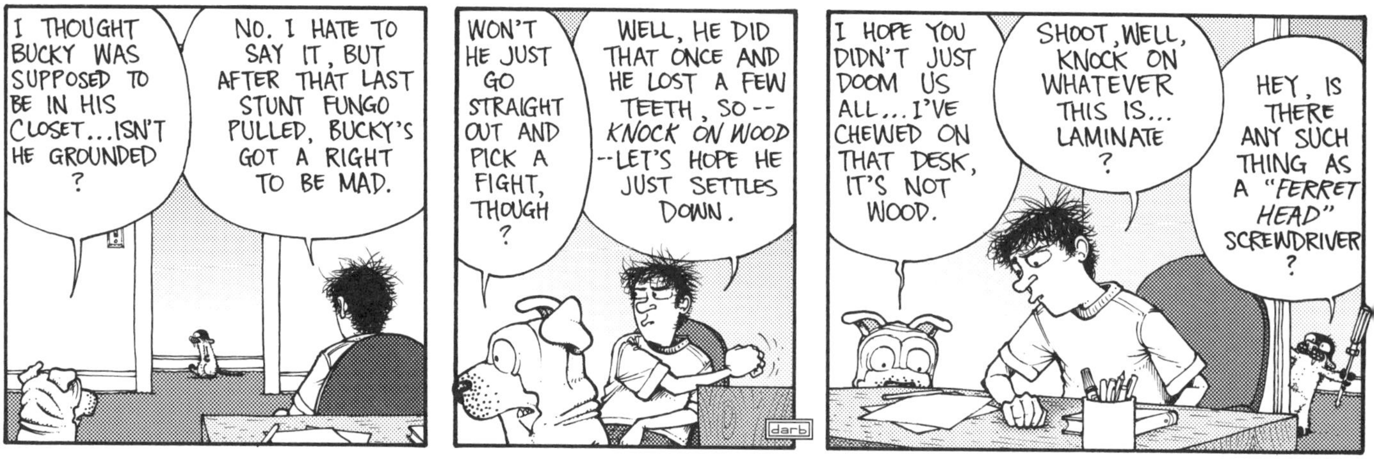
I THOUGHT BUCKY WAS SUPPOSED TO BE IN HIS CLOSET...ISN'T HE GROUNDED ?
NO. I HATE TO SAY IT, BUT AFTER THAT LAST STUNT FUNGO PULLED, BUCKY'S GOT A RIGHT TO BE MAD.
WON'T HE JUST GO STRAIGHT OUT AND PICK A FIGHT, THOUGH ?
WELL, HE DID THAT ONCE AND HE LOST A FEW TEETH, SO-- *KNOCK ON WOOD* --LET'S HOPE HE JUST SETTLES DOWN.
darb
I HOPE YOU DIDN'T JUST DOOM US ALL... I'VE CHEWED ON THAT DESK, IT'S NOT WOOD.
SHOOT, WELL, KNOCK ON WHATEVER THIS IS... LAMINATE ?
HEY, IS THERE ANY SUCH THING AS A "*FERRET HEAD*" SCREWDRIVER ?

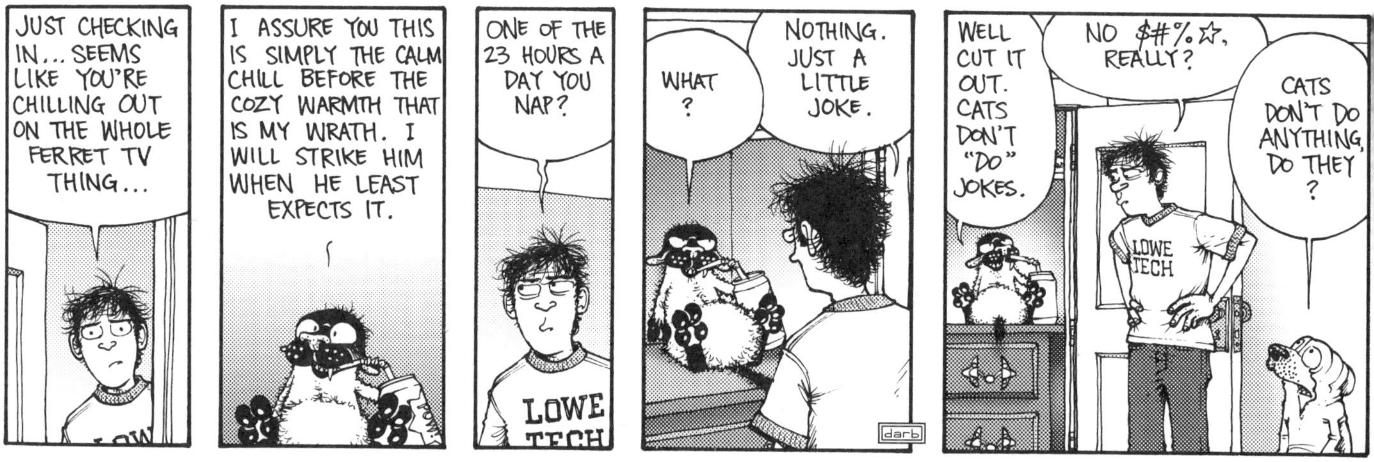
JUST CHECKING IN... SEEMS LIKE YOU'RE CHILLING OUT ON THE WHOLE FERRET TV THING...
I ASSURE YOU THIS IS SIMPLY THE CALM CHILL BEFORE THE COZY WARMTH THAT IS MY WRATH. I WILL STRIKE HIM WHEN HE LEAST EXPECTS IT.
ONE OF THE 23 HOURS A DAY YOU NAP?
LOWE TECH
WHAT ?
NOTHING. JUST A LITTLE JOKE.
darb
WELL CUT IT OUT. CATS DON'T "DO" JOKES.
NO $#%☆, REALLY?
CATS DON'T DO ANYTHING, DO THEY ?
LOWE TECH

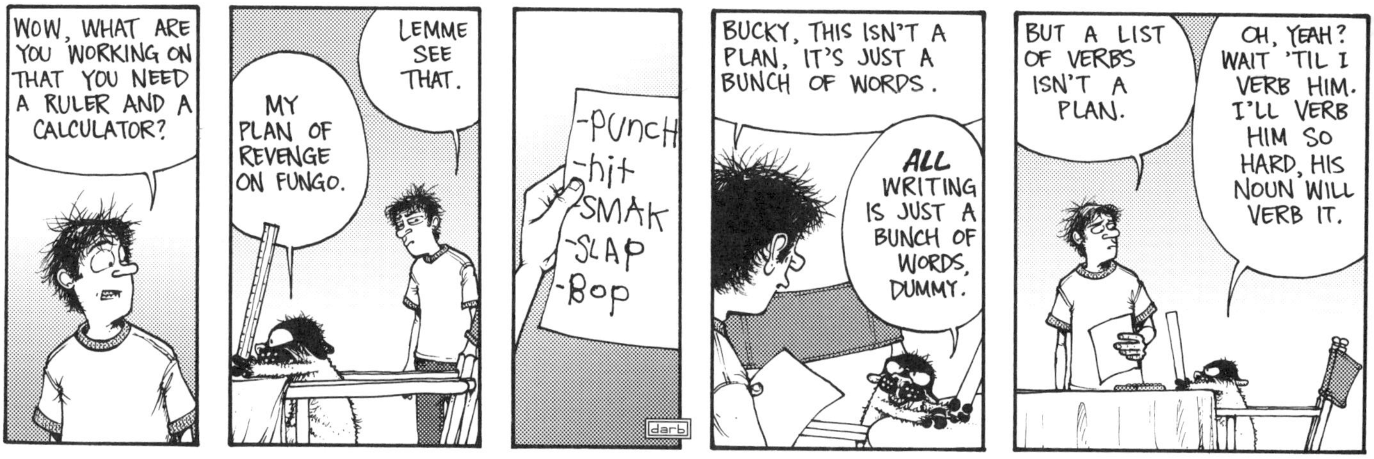
WOW, WHAT ARE YOU WORKING ON THAT YOU NEED A RULER AND A CALCULATOR?
MY PLAN OF REVENGE ON FUNGO.
LEMME SEE THAT.
-punch
-hit
-SMAK
-SLAP
-Bop
darb
BUCKY, THIS ISN'T A PLAN, IT'S JUST A BUNCH OF WORDS.
ALL WRITING IS JUST A BUNCH OF WORDS, DUMMY.
BUT A LIST OF VERBS ISN'T A PLAN.
OH, YEAH? WAIT 'TIL I VERB HIM. I'LL VERB HIM SO HARD, HIS NOUN WILL VERB IT.

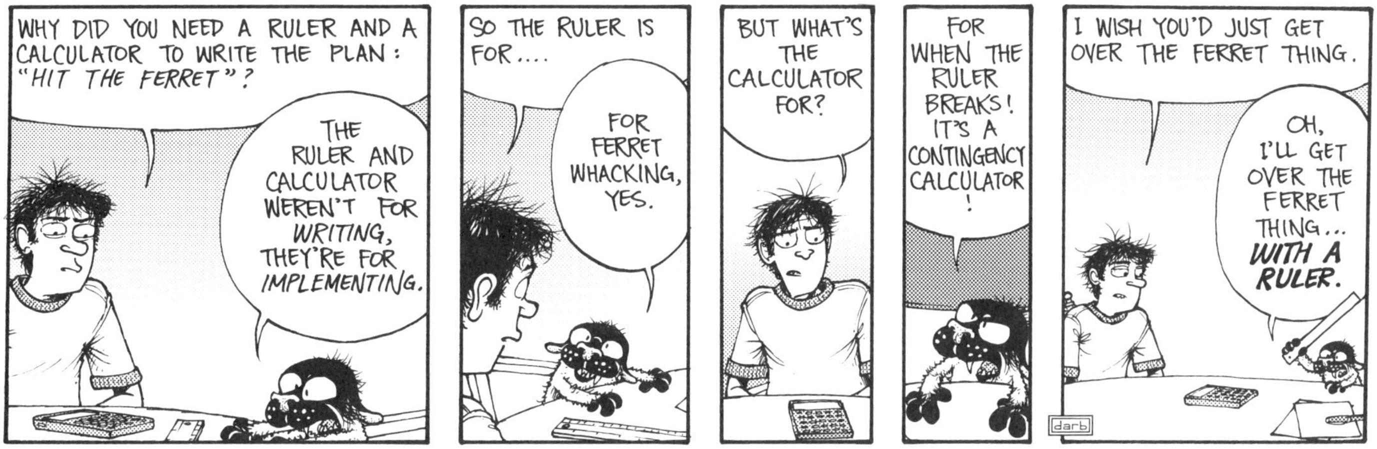
WHY DID YOU NEED A RULER AND A CALCULATOR TO WRITE THE PLAN: "*HIT THE FERRET*"?
THE RULER AND CALCULATOR WEREN'T FOR *WRITING*, THEY'RE FOR *IMPLEMENTING*.
SO THE RULER IS FOR....
FOR FERRET WHACKING, YES.
BUT WHAT'S THE CALCULATOR FOR?
FOR WHEN THE RULER BREAKS! IT'S A CONTINGENCY CALCULATOR!
I WISH YOU'D JUST GET OVER THE FERRET THING.
OH, I'LL GET OVER THE FERRET THING... ***WITH A RULER.***
darb

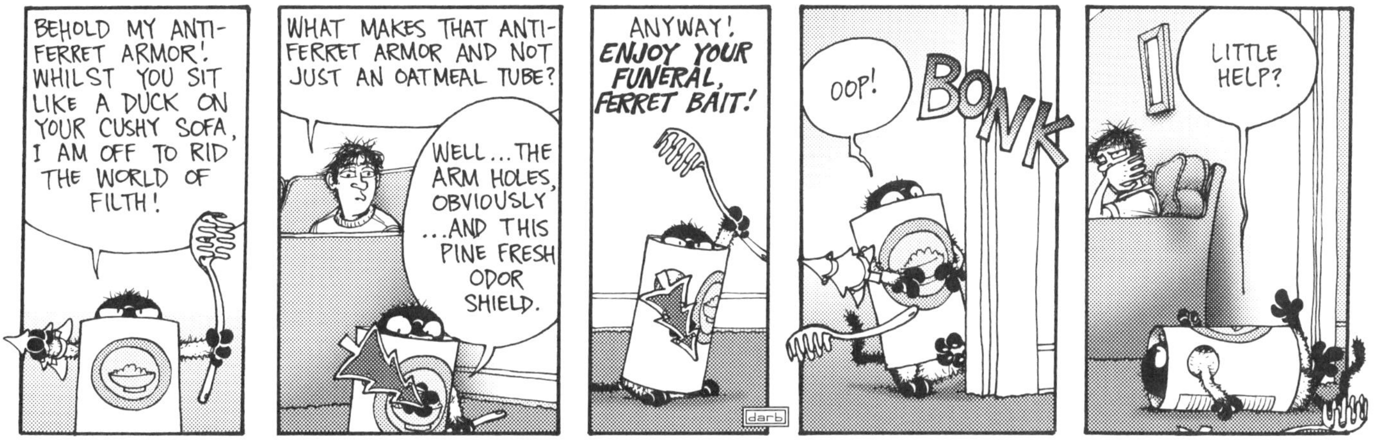
BEHOLD MY ANTI-FERRET ARMOR! WHILST YOU SIT LIKE A DUCK ON YOUR CUSHY SOFA, I AM OFF TO RID THE WORLD OF FILTH!
WHAT MAKES THAT ANTI-FERRET ARMOR AND NOT JUST AN OATMEAL TUBE?
WELL... THE ARM HOLES, OBVIOUSLY ...AND THIS PINE FRESH ODOR SHIELD.
ANYWAY! ***ENJOY YOUR FUNERAL, FERRET BAIT!***
darb
OOP!
BONK
LITTLE HELP?

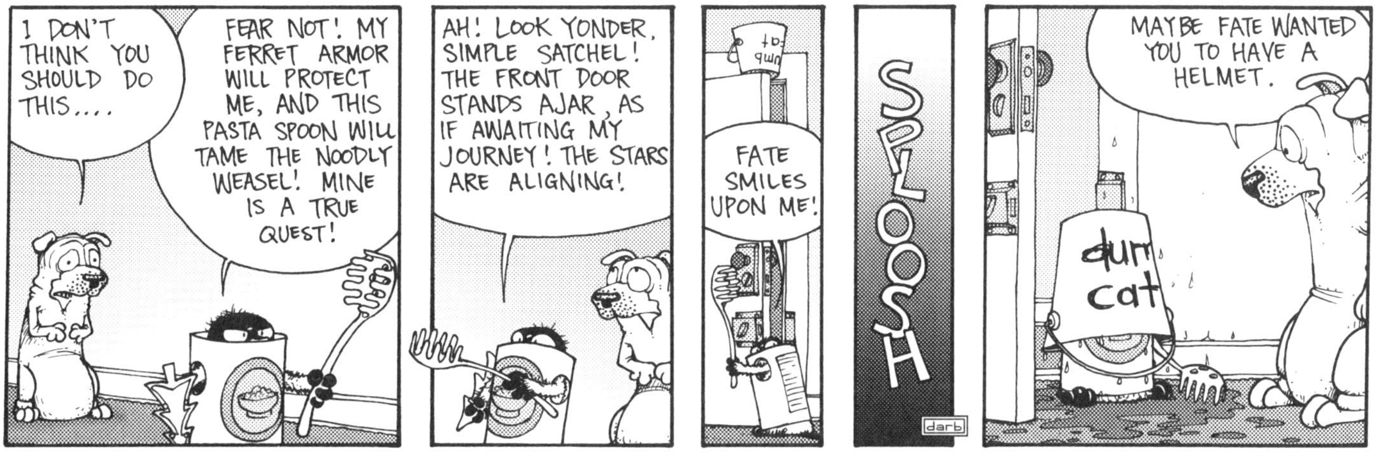
I DON'T THINK YOU SHOULD DO THIS....
FEAR NOT! MY FERRET ARMOR WILL PROTECT ME, AND THIS PASTA SPOON WILL TAME THE NOODLY WEASEL! MINE IS A TRUE QUEST!
AH! LOOK YONDER, SIMPLE SATCHEL! THE FRONT DOOR STANDS AJAR, AS IF AWAITING MY JOURNEY! THE STARS ARE ALIGNING!
FATE SMILES UPON ME!
SPLOOSH
darb
MAYBE FATE WANTED YOU TO HAVE A HELMET.

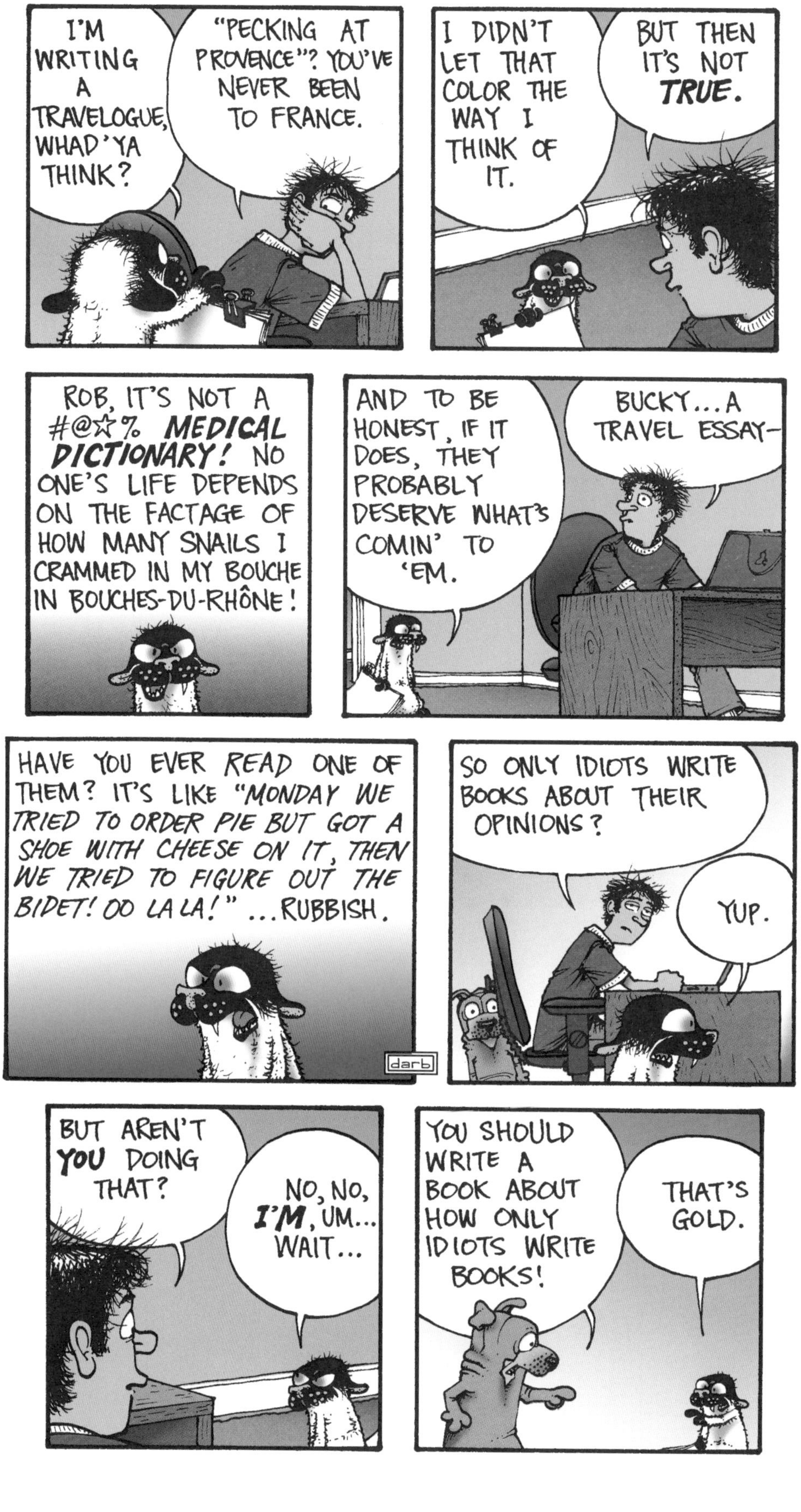
I'M WRITING A TRAVELOGUE, WHAD'YA THINK?
"PECKING AT PROVENCE"? YOU'VE NEVER BEEN TO FRANCE.
I DIDN'T LET THAT COLOR THE WAY I THINK OF IT.
BUT THEN IT'S NOT TRUE.
ROB, IT'S NOT A #@☆% MEDICAL DICTIONARY! NO ONE'S LIFE DEPENDS ON THE FACTAGE OF HOW MANY SNAILS I CRAMMED IN MY BOUCHE IN BOUCHES-DU-RHÔNE!
AND TO BE HONEST, IF IT DOES, THEY PROBABLY DESERVE WHAT'S COMIN' TO 'EM.
BUCKY... A TRAVEL ESSAY-
HAVE YOU EVER READ ONE OF THEM? IT'S LIKE "MONDAY WE TRIED TO ORDER PIE BUT GOT A SHOE WITH CHEESE ON IT, THEN WE TRIED TO FIGURE OUT THE BIDET! OO LA LA!" ...RUBBISH.
darb
SO ONLY IDIOTS WRITE BOOKS ABOUT THEIR OPINIONS?
YUP.
BUT AREN'T YOU DOING THAT?
NO, NO, I'M, UM... WAIT...
YOU SHOULD WRITE A BOOK ABOUT HOW ONLY IDIOTS WRITE BOOKS!
THAT'S GOLD.

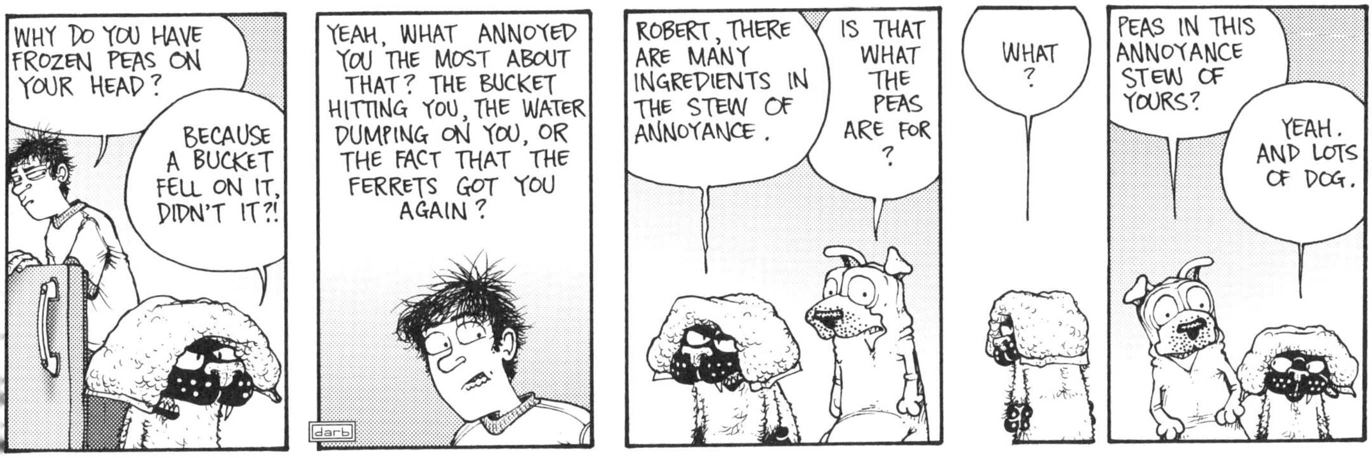
WHY DO YOU HAVE FROZEN PEAS ON YOUR HEAD?
BECAUSE A BUCKET FELL ON IT, DIDN'T IT?!
YEAH, WHAT ANNOYED YOU THE MOST ABOUT THAT? THE BUCKET HITTING YOU, THE WATER DUMPING ON YOU, OR THE FACT THAT THE FERRETS GOT YOU AGAIN?
darb
ROBERT, THERE ARE MANY INGREDIENTS IN THE STEW OF ANNOYANCE.
IS THAT WHAT THE PEAS ARE FOR?
WHAT?
PEAS IN THIS ANNOYANCE STEW OF YOURS?
YEAH. AND LOTS OF DOG.

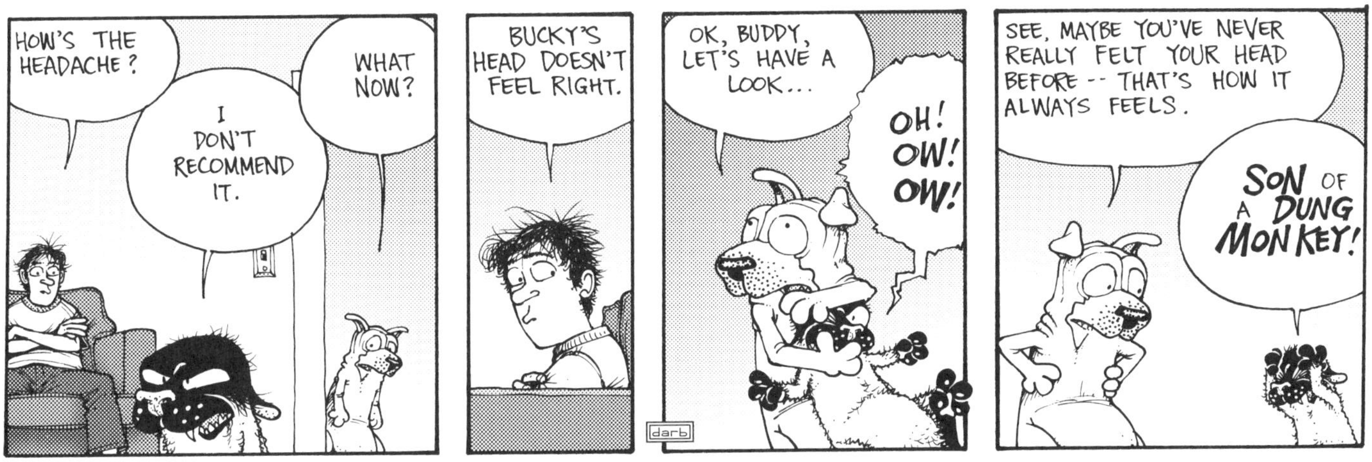
HOW'S THE HEADACHE?
I DON'T RECOMMEND IT.
WHAT NOW?
BUCKY'S HEAD DOESN'T FEEL RIGHT.
darb
OK, BUDDY, LET'S HAVE A LOOK...
OH! OW! OW!
SEE, MAYBE YOU'VE NEVER REALLY FELT YOUR HEAD BEFORE -- THAT'S HOW IT ALWAYS FEELS.
SON OF A DUNG MONKEY!

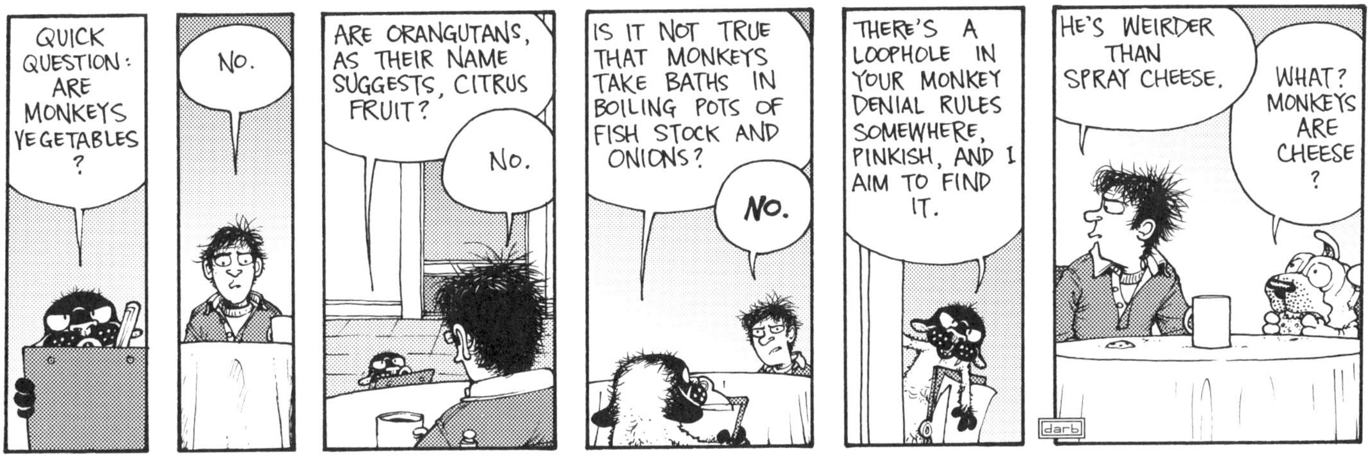
QUICK QUESTION: ARE MONKEYS VEGETABLES?
NO.
ARE ORANGUTANS, AS THEIR NAME SUGGESTS, CITRUS FRUIT?
NO.
IS IT NOT TRUE THAT MONKEYS TAKE BATHS IN BOILING POTS OF FISH STOCK AND ONIONS?
NO.
THERE'S A LOOPHOLE IN YOUR MONKEY DENIAL RULES SOMEWHERE, PINKISH, AND I AIM TO FIND IT.
HE'S WEIRDER THAN SPRAY CHEESE.
WHAT? MONKEYS ARE CHEESE?
darb

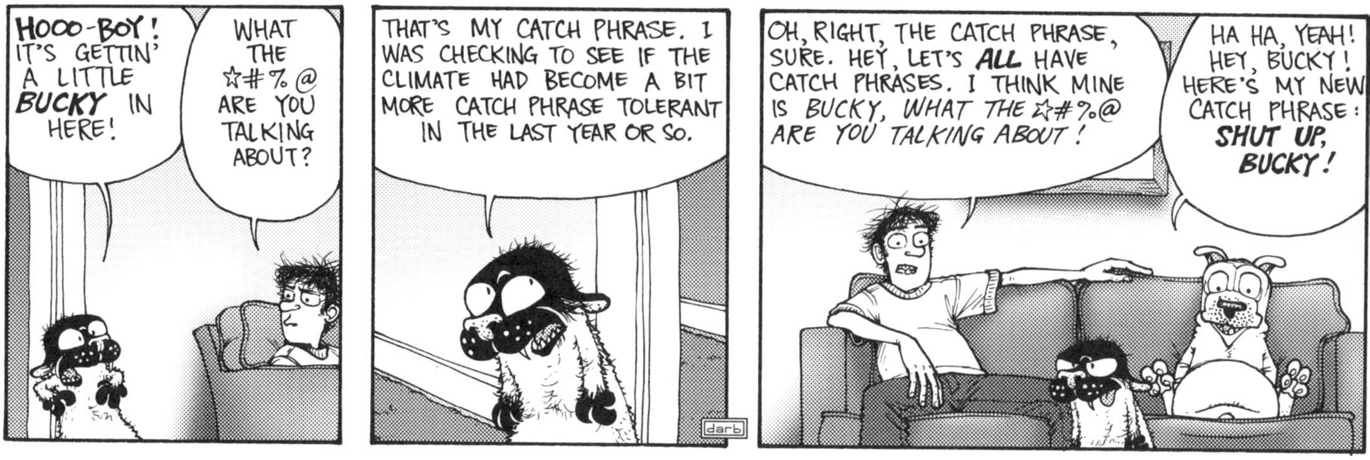
HOOO-BOY! IT'S GETTIN' A LITTLE BUCKY IN HERE!
WHAT THE ☆#%@ ARE YOU TALKING ABOUT?
THAT'S MY CATCH PHRASE. I WAS CHECKING TO SEE IF THE CLIMATE HAD BECOME A BIT MORE CATCH PHRASE TOLERANT IN THE LAST YEAR OR SO.
OH, RIGHT, THE CATCH PHRASE, SURE. HEY, LET'S ALL HAVE CATCH PHRASES. I THINK MINE IS BUCKY, WHAT THE ☆#%@ ARE YOU TALKING ABOUT!
HA HA, YEAH! HEY, BUCKY! HERE'S MY NEW CATCH PHRASE: SHUT UP, BUCKY!

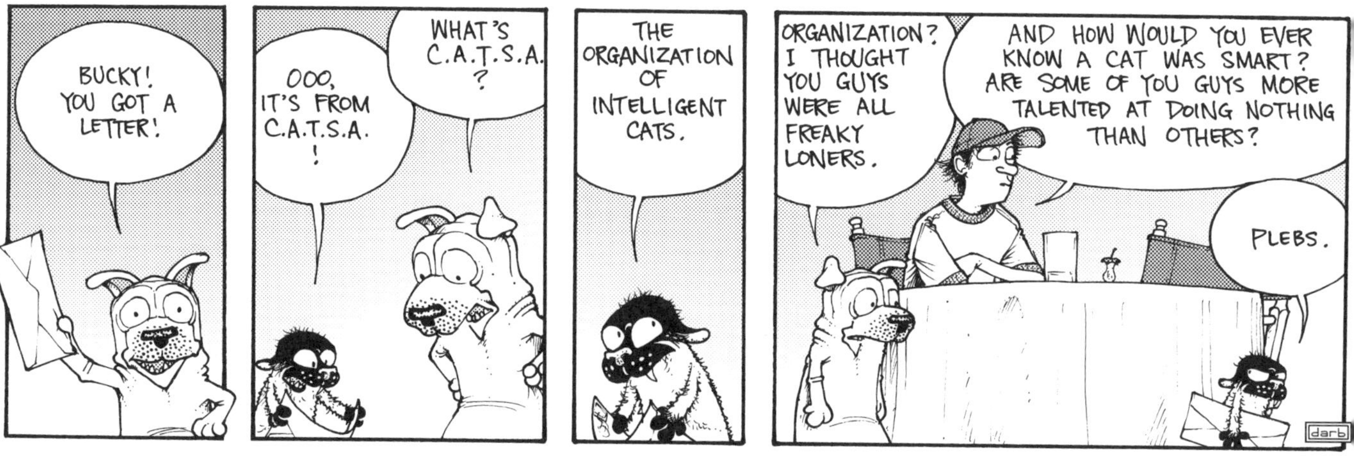
BUCKY! YOU GOT A LETTER!
OOO, IT'S FROM C.A.T.S.A.!
WHAT'S C.A.T.S.A.?
THE ORGANIZATION OF INTELLIGENT CATS.
ORGANIZATION? I THOUGHT YOU GUYS WERE ALL FREAKY LONERS.
AND HOW WOULD YOU EVER KNOW A CAT WAS SMART? ARE SOME OF YOU GUYS MORE TALENTED AT DOING NOTHING THAN OTHERS?
PLEBS.

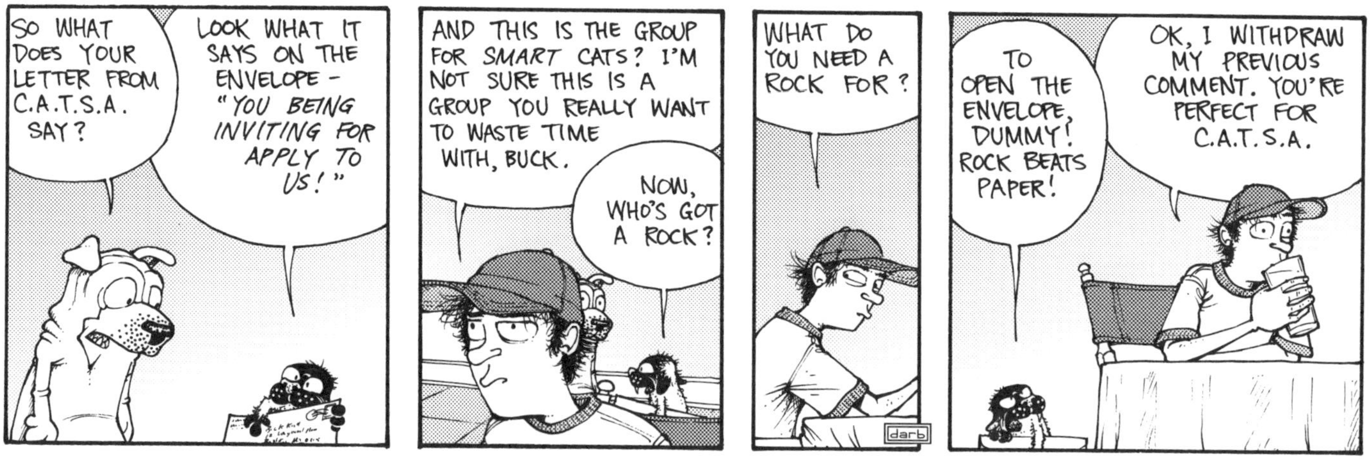
SO WHAT DOES YOUR LETTER FROM C.A.T.S.A. SAY?
LOOK WHAT IT SAYS ON THE ENVELOPE - "YOU BEING INVITING FOR APPLY TO US!"
AND THIS IS THE GROUP FOR SMART CATS? I'M NOT SURE THIS IS A GROUP YOU REALLY WANT TO WASTE TIME WITH, BUCK.
NOW, WHO'S GOT A ROCK?
WHAT DO YOU NEED A ROCK FOR?
TO OPEN THE ENVELOPE, DUMMY! ROCK BEATS PAPER!
OK, I WITHDRAW MY PREVIOUS COMMENT. YOU'RE PERFECT FOR C.A.T.S.A.

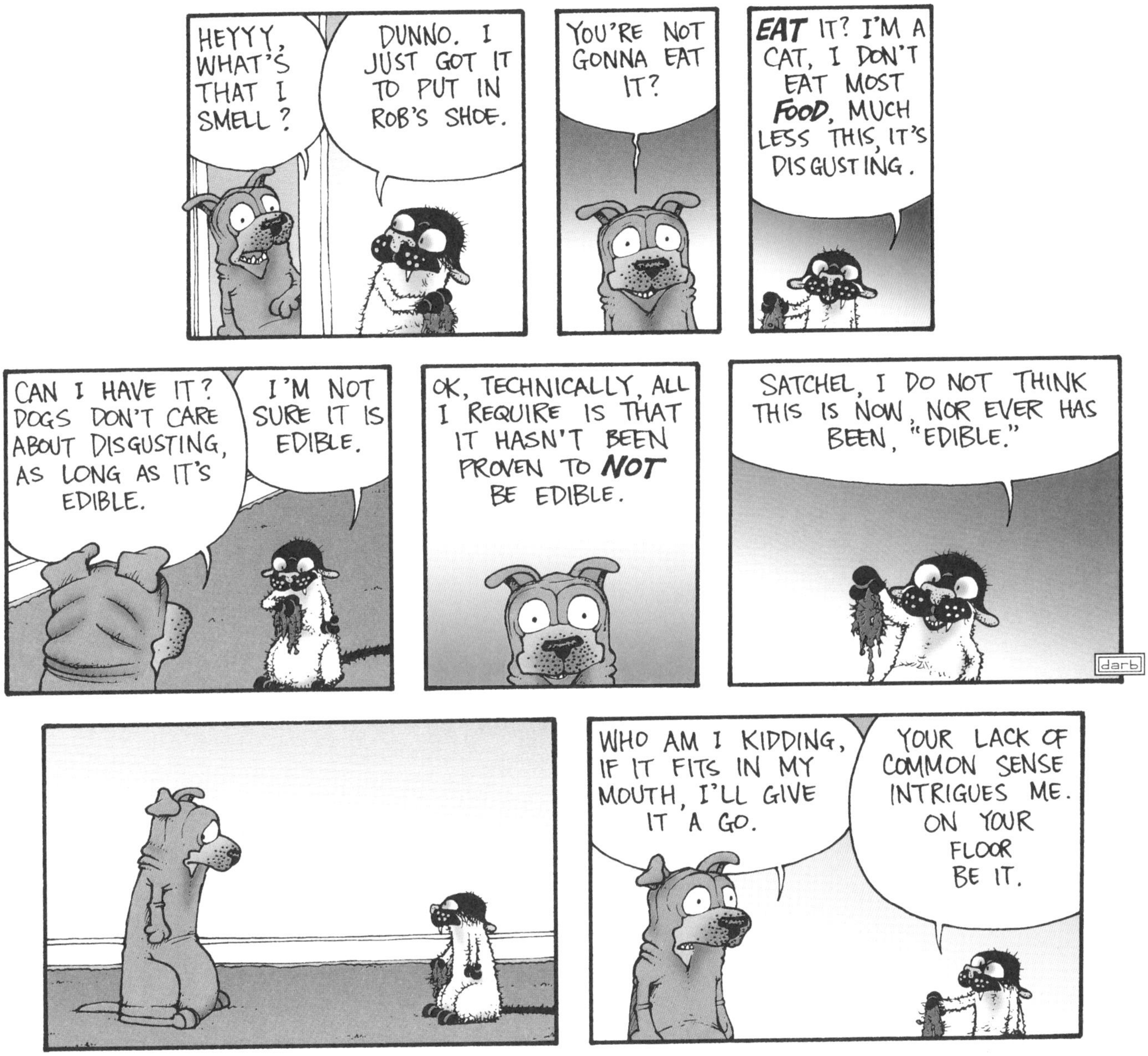
HEYYY, WHAT'S THAT I SMELL?
DUNNO. I JUST GOT IT TO PUT IN ROB'S SHOE.
YOU'RE NOT GONNA EAT IT?
EAT IT? I'M A CAT, I DON'T EAT MOST FOOD, MUCH LESS THIS, IT'S DISGUSTING.
CAN I HAVE IT? DOGS DON'T CARE ABOUT DISGUSTING, AS LONG AS IT'S EDIBLE.
I'M NOT SURE IT IS EDIBLE.
OK, TECHNICALLY, ALL I REQUIRE IS THAT IT HASN'T BEEN PROVEN TO NOT BE EDIBLE.
SATCHEL, I DO NOT THINK THIS IS NOW, NOR EVER HAS BEEN, "EDIBLE."
darb
WHO AM I KIDDING, IF IT FITS IN MY MOUTH, I'LL GIVE IT A GO.
YOUR LACK OF COMMON SENSE INTRIGUES ME. ON YOUR FLOOR BE IT.

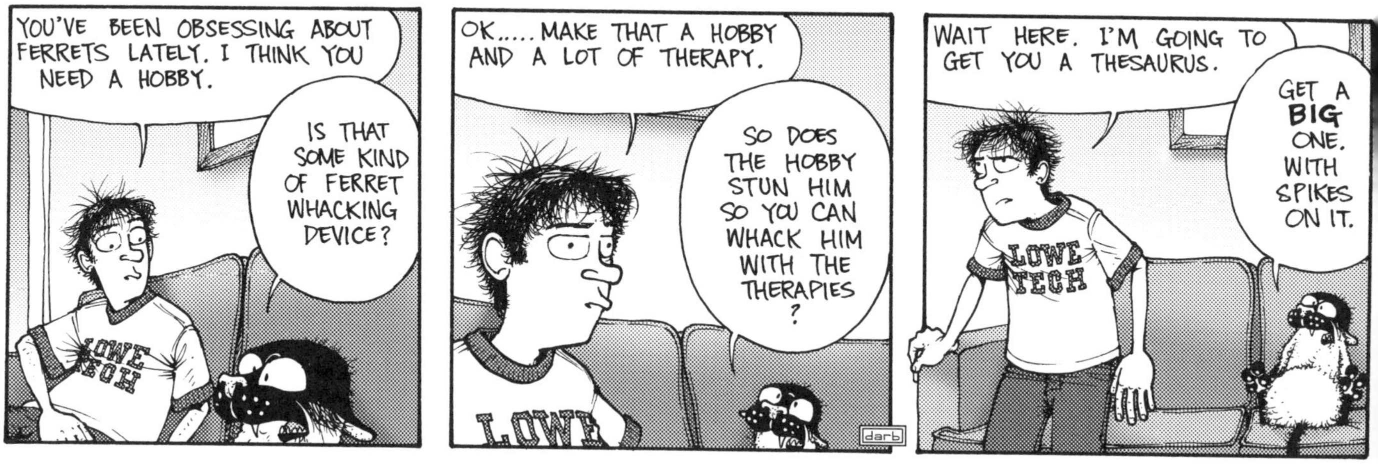
YOU'VE BEEN OBSESSING ABOUT FERRETS LATELY. I THINK YOU NEED A HOBBY.
IS THAT SOME KIND OF FERRET WHACKING DEVICE?
OK..... MAKE THAT A HOBBY AND A LOT OF THERAPY.
SO DOES THE HOBBY STUN HIM SO YOU CAN WHACK HIM WITH THE THERAPIES ?
WAIT HERE. I'M GOING TO GET YOU A THESAURUS.
GET A **BIG** ONE. WITH SPIKES ON IT.

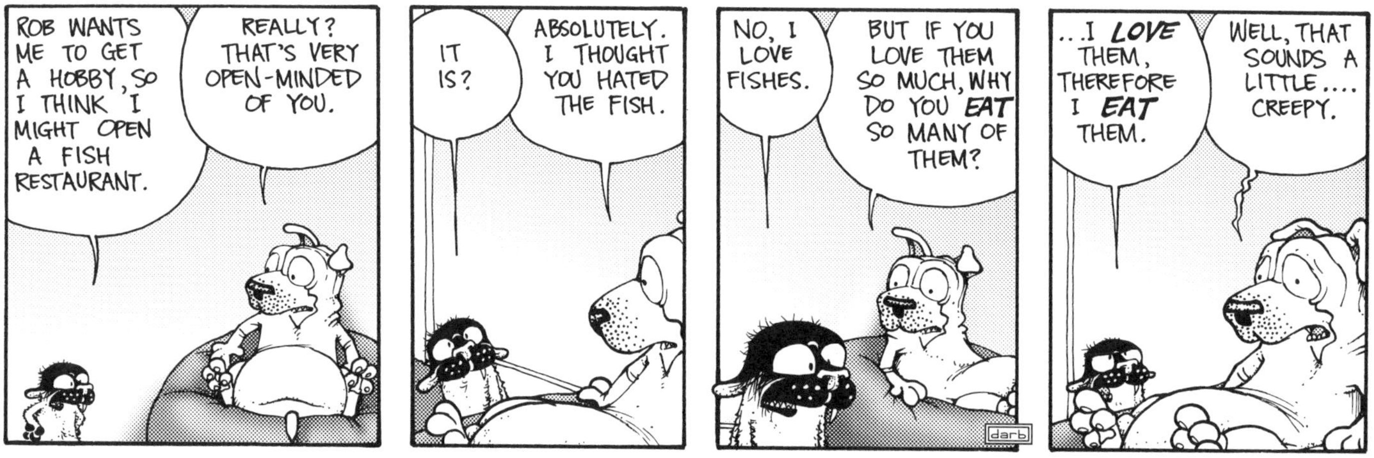
ROB WANTS ME TO GET A HOBBY, SO I THINK I MIGHT OPEN A FISH RESTAURANT.
REALLY? THAT'S VERY OPEN-MINDED OF YOU.
IT IS?
ABSOLUTELY. I THOUGHT YOU HATED THE FISH.
NO, I LOVE FISHES.
BUT IF YOU LOVE THEM SO MUCH, WHY DO YOU *EAT* SO MANY OF THEM?
...I *LOVE* THEM, THEREFORE I *EAT* THEM.
WELL, THAT SOUNDS A LITTLE.... CREEPY.

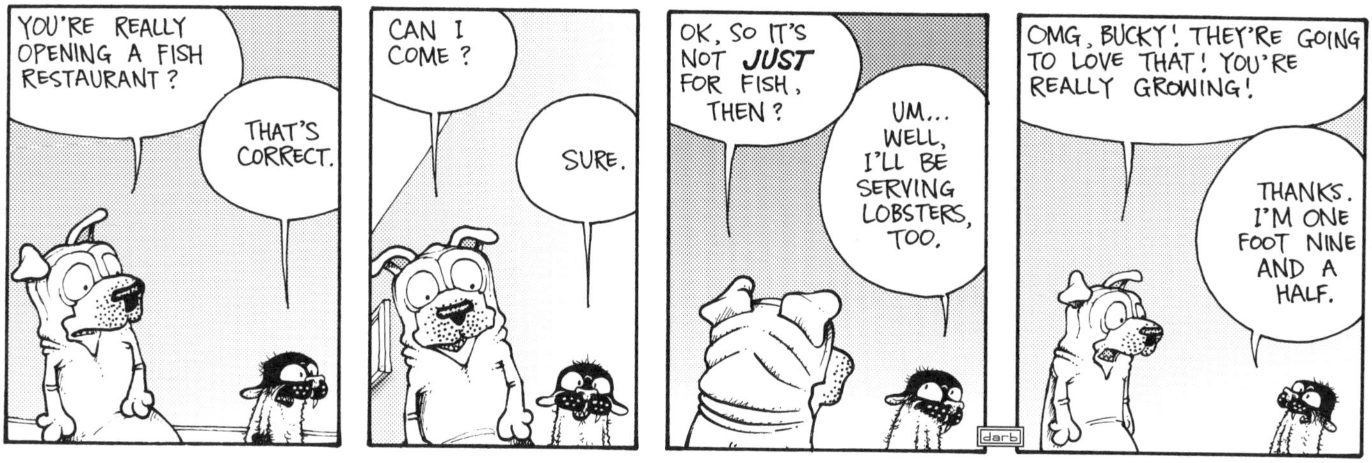
YOU'RE REALLY OPENING A FISH RESTAURANT?
THAT'S CORRECT.
CAN I COME ?
SURE.
OK, SO IT'S NOT *JUST* FOR FISH, THEN?
UM... WELL, I'LL BE SERVING LOBSTERS, TOO.
OMG, BUCKY! THEY'RE GOING TO LOVE THAT! YOU'RE REALLY GROWING!
THANKS. I'M ONE FOOT NINE AND A HALF.

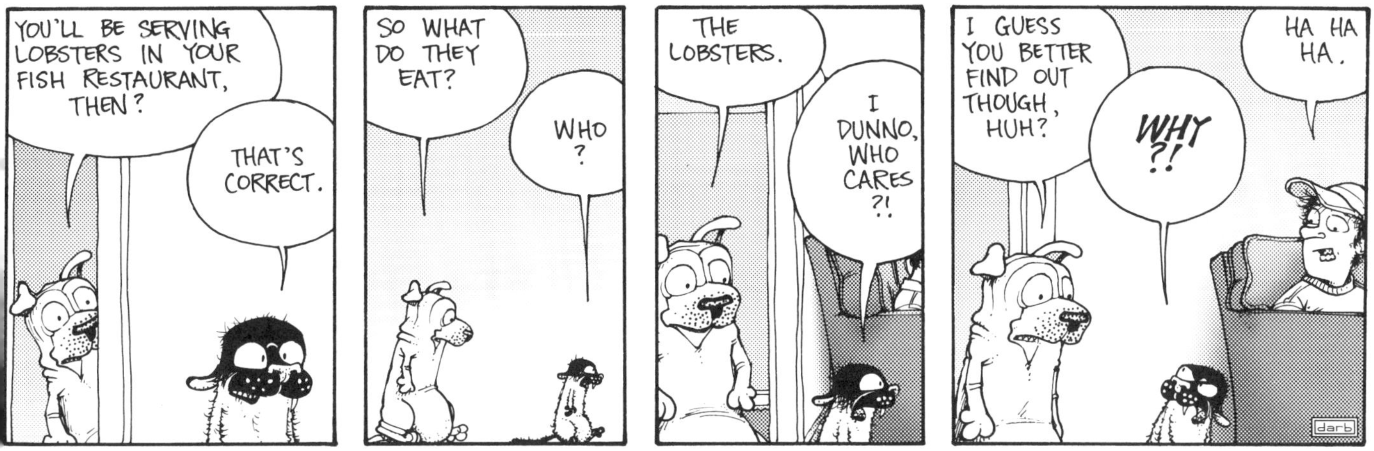
YOU'LL BE SERVING LOBSTERS IN YOUR FISH RESTAURANT, THEN?
THAT'S CORRECT.
SO WHAT DO THEY EAT?
WHO?
THE LOBSTERS.
I DUNNO, WHO CARES ?!
I GUESS YOU BETTER FIND OUT THOUGH, HUH?
WHY ?!
HA HA HA.
darb

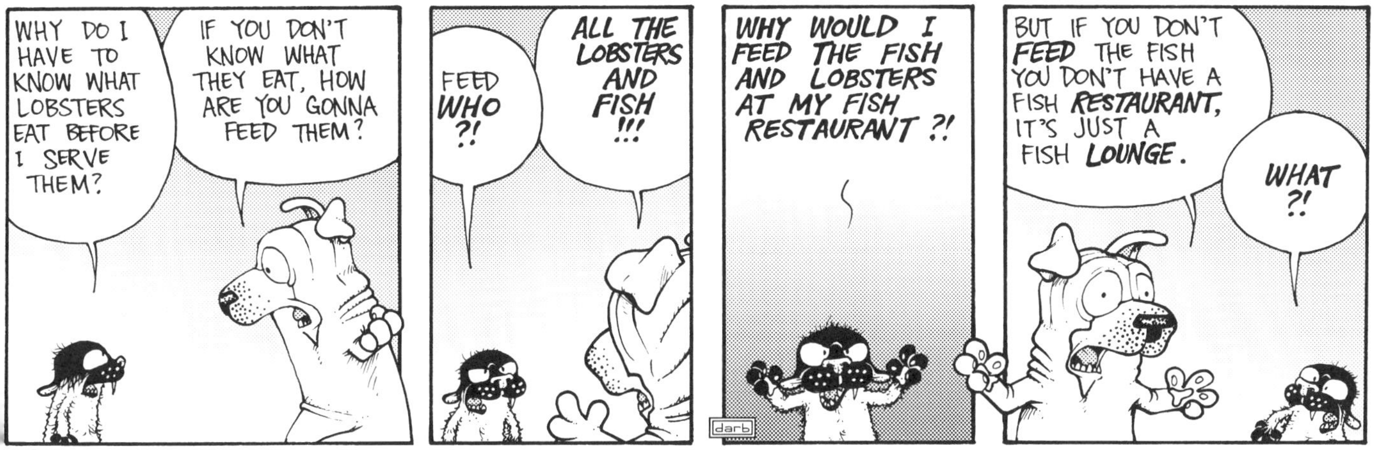
WHY DO I HAVE TO KNOW WHAT LOBSTERS EAT BEFORE I SERVE THEM?
IF YOU DON'T KNOW WHAT THEY EAT, HOW ARE YOU GONNA FEED THEM?
FEED WHO ?!
ALL THE LOBSTERS AND FISH !!!
WHY WOULD I FEED THE FISH AND LOBSTERS AT MY FISH RESTAURANT ?!
darb
BUT IF YOU DON'T FEED THE FISH YOU DON'T HAVE A FISH RESTAURANT, IT'S JUST A FISH LOUNGE.
WHAT ?!

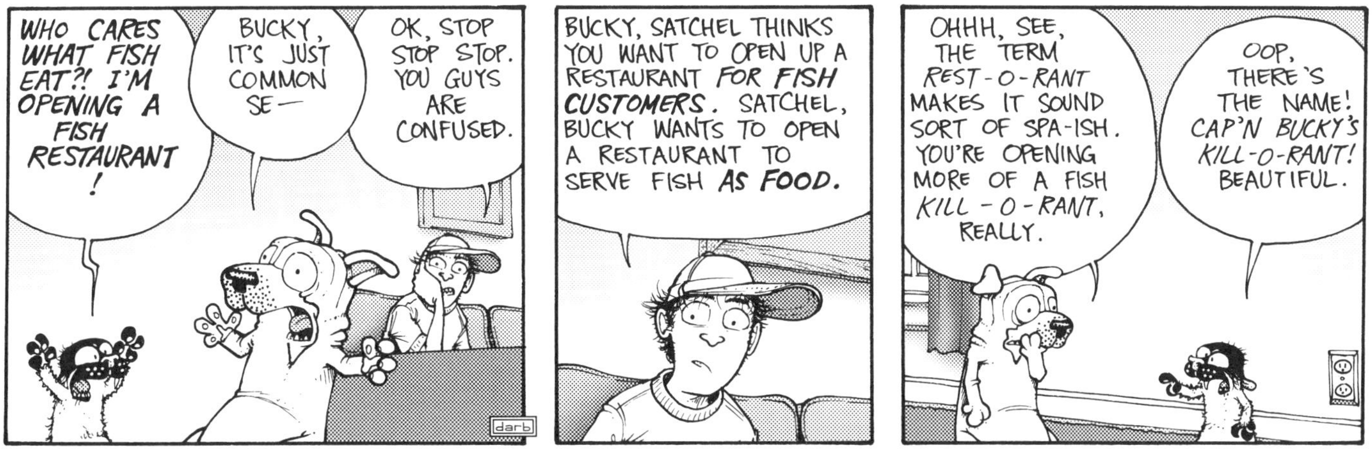
WHO CARES WHAT FISH EAT?! I'M OPENING A FISH RESTAURANT !
BUCKY, IT'S JUST COMMON SE—
OK, STOP STOP STOP. YOU GUYS ARE CONFUSED.
darb
BUCKY, SATCHEL THINKS YOU WANT TO OPEN UP A RESTAURANT FOR FISH CUSTOMERS. SATCHEL, BUCKY WANTS TO OPEN A RESTAURANT TO SERVE FISH AS FOOD.
OHHH, SEE, THE TERM REST-O-RANT MAKES IT SOUND SORT OF SPA-ISH. YOU'RE OPENING MORE OF A FISH KILL-O-RANT, REALLY.
OOP, THERE'S THE NAME! CAP'N BUCKY'S KILL-O-RANT! BEAUTIFUL.

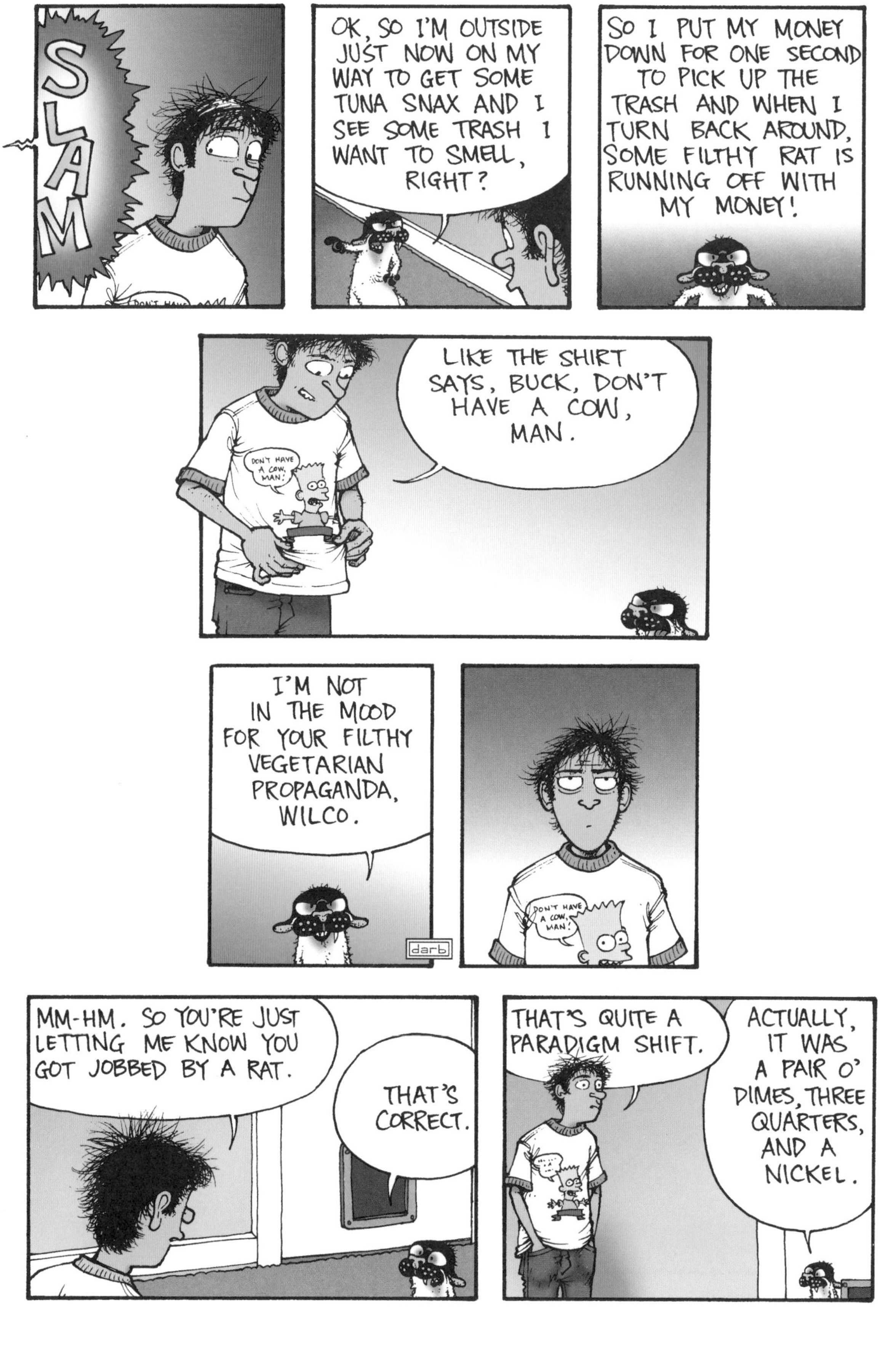
SLAM
OK, SO I'M OUTSIDE JUST NOW ON MY WAY TO GET SOME TUNA SNAX AND I SEE SOME TRASH I WANT TO SMELL, RIGHT?
SO I PUT MY MONEY DOWN FOR ONE SECOND TO PICK UP THE TRASH AND WHEN I TURN BACK AROUND, SOME FILTHY RAT IS RUNNING OFF WITH MY MONEY!
LIKE THE SHIRT SAYS, BUCK, DON'T HAVE A COW, MAN.
DON'T HAVE A COW, MAN!
I'M NOT IN THE MOOD FOR YOUR FILTHY VEGETARIAN PROPAGANDA, WILCO.
darb
DON'T HAVE A COW, MAN!
MM-HM. SO YOU'RE JUST LETTING ME KNOW YOU GOT JOBBED BY A RAT.
THAT'S CORRECT.
THAT'S QUITE A PARADIGM SHIFT.
ACTUALLY, IT WAS A PAIR O' DIMES, THREE QUARTERS, AND A NICKEL.

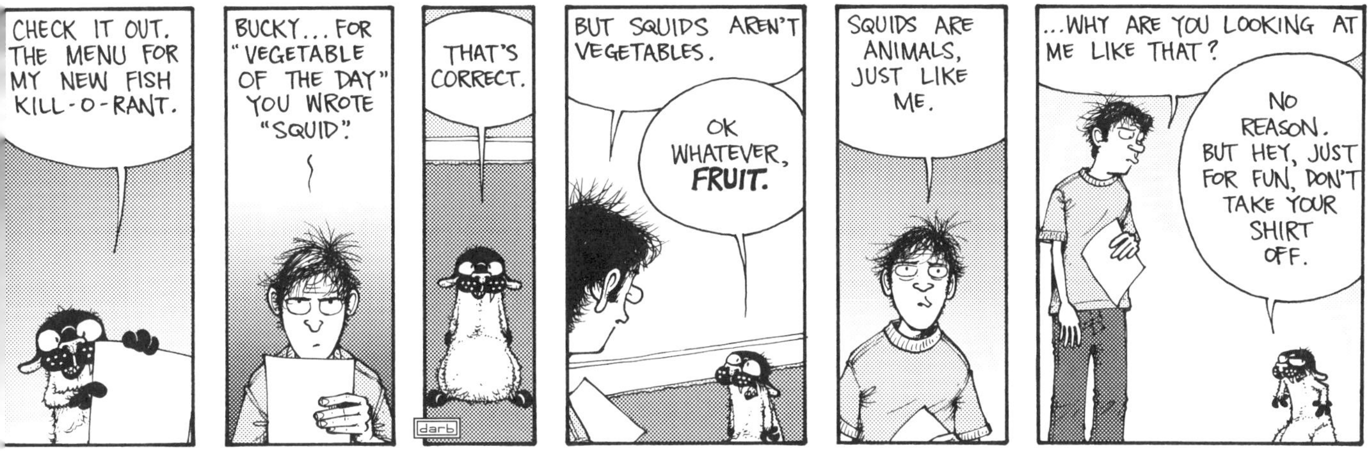
CHECK IT OUT. THE MENU FOR MY NEW FISH KILL-O-RANT.
BUCKY... FOR "VEGETABLE OF THE DAY" YOU WROTE "SQUID".
THAT'S CORRECT.
BUT SQUIDS AREN'T VEGETABLES.
OK WHATEVER, FRUIT.
SQUIDS ARE ANIMALS, JUST LIKE ME.
...WHY ARE YOU LOOKING AT ME LIKE THAT?
NO REASON. BUT HEY, JUST FOR FUN, DON'T TAKE YOUR SHIRT OFF.
darb

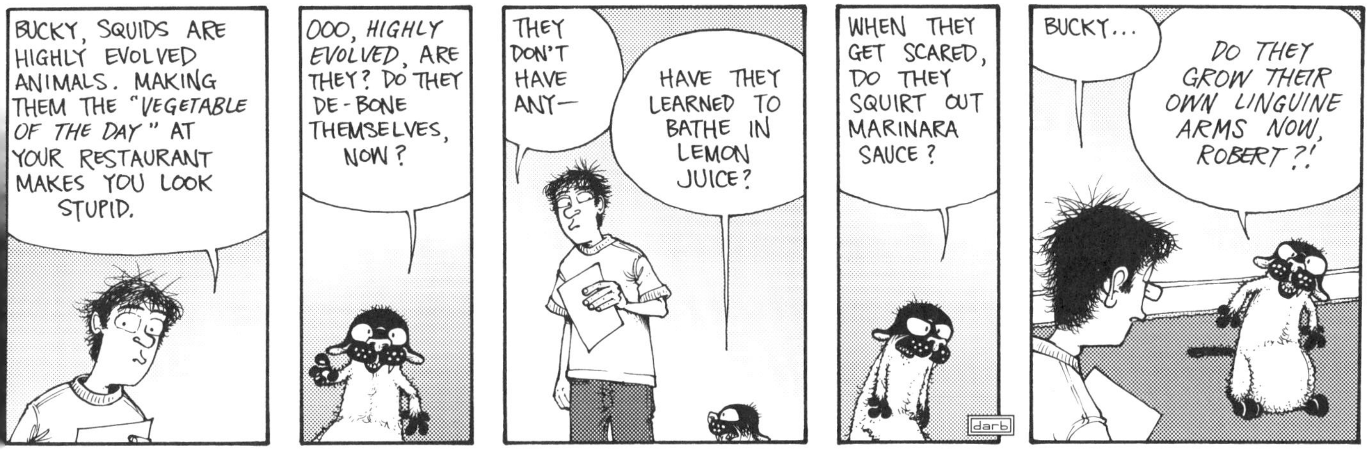
BUCKY, SQUIDS ARE HIGHLY EVOLVED ANIMALS. MAKING THEM THE "VEGETABLE OF THE DAY" AT YOUR RESTAURANT MAKES YOU LOOK STUPID.
OOO, HIGHLY EVOLVED, ARE THEY? DO THEY DE-BONE THEMSELVES, NOW?
THEY DON'T HAVE ANY—
HAVE THEY LEARNED TO BATHE IN LEMON JUICE?
WHEN THEY GET SCARED, DO THEY SQUIRT OUT MARINARA SAUCE?
BUCKY...
DO THEY GROW THEIR OWN LINGUINE ARMS NOW, ROBERT?!
darb

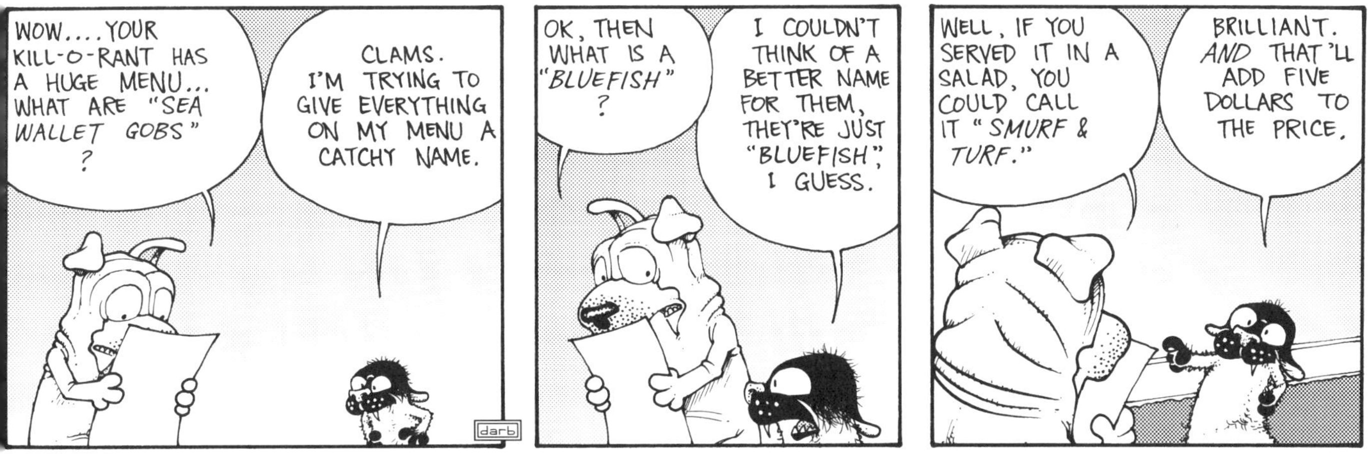
WOW.... YOUR KILL-O-RANT HAS A HUGE MENU... WHAT ARE "SEA WALLET GOBS"?
CLAMS. I'M TRYING TO GIVE EVERYTHING ON MY MENU A CATCHY NAME.
OK, THEN WHAT IS A "BLUEFISH"?
I COULDN'T THINK OF A BETTER NAME FOR THEM, THEY'RE JUST "BLUEFISH", I GUESS.
WELL, IF YOU SERVED IT IN A SALAD, YOU COULD CALL IT "SMURF & TURF."
BRILLIANT. AND THAT'LL ADD FIVE DOLLARS TO THE PRICE.
darb

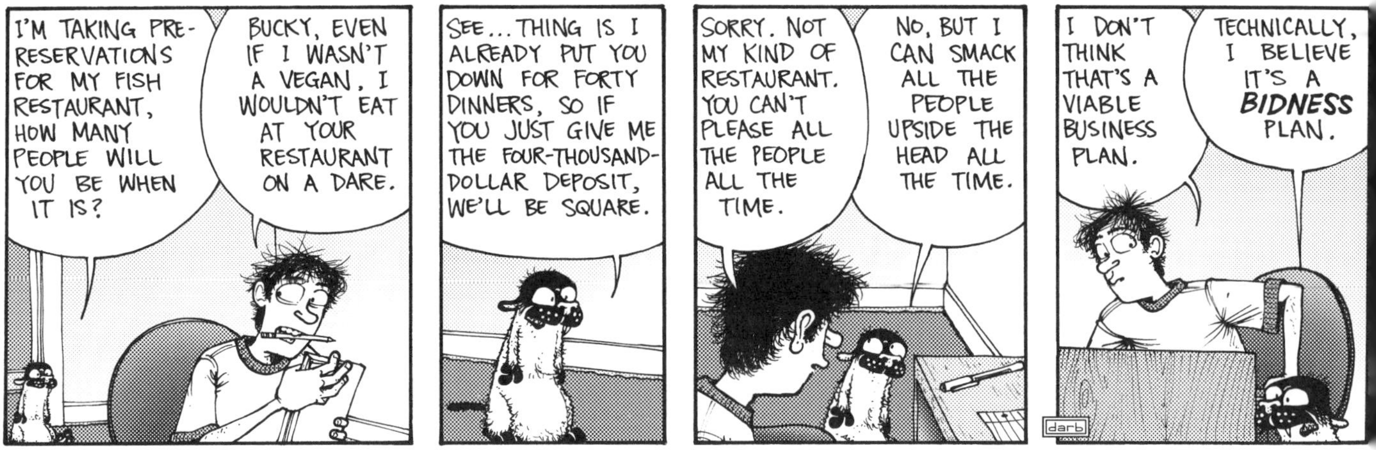
I'M TAKING PRE-RESERVATIONS FOR MY FISH RESTAURANT. HOW MANY PEOPLE WILL YOU BE WHEN IT IS?
BUCKY, EVEN IF I WASN'T A VEGAN, I WOULDN'T EAT AT YOUR RESTAURANT ON A DARE.
SEE... THING IS I ALREADY PUT YOU DOWN FOR FORTY DINNERS, SO IF YOU JUST GIVE ME THE FOUR-THOUSAND-DOLLAR DEPOSIT, WE'LL BE SQUARE.
SORRY. NOT MY KIND OF RESTAURANT. YOU CAN'T PLEASE ALL THE PEOPLE ALL THE TIME.
NO, BUT I CAN SMACK ALL THE PEOPLE UPSIDE THE HEAD ALL THE TIME.
I DON'T THINK THAT'S A VIABLE BUSINESS PLAN.
TECHNICALLY, I BELIEVE IT'S A BIDNESS PLAN.
darb

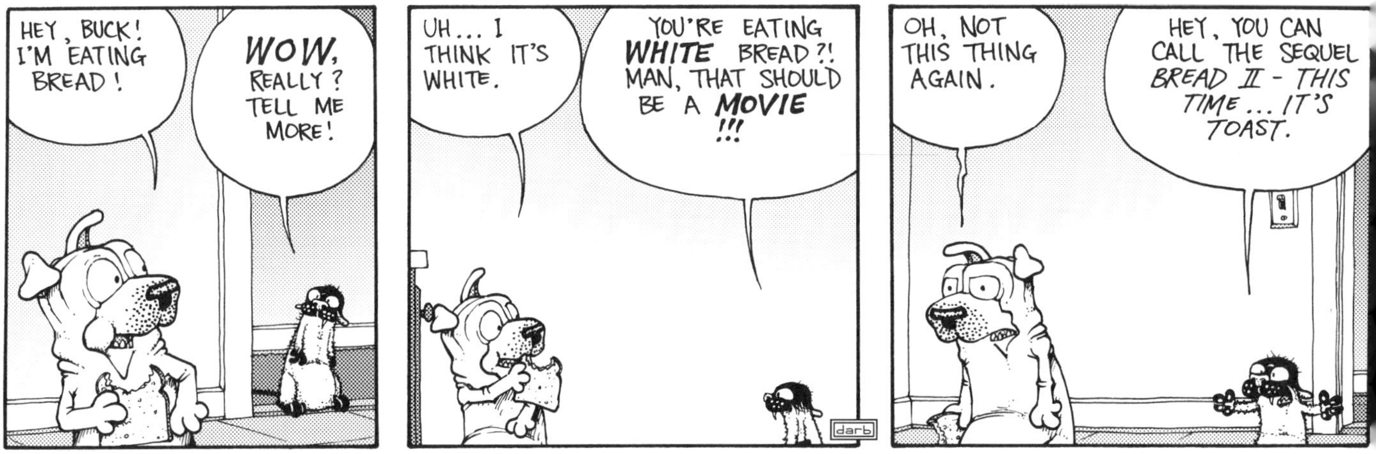
HEY, BUCK! I'M EATING BREAD!
WOW, REALLY? TELL ME MORE!
UH... I THINK IT'S WHITE.
YOU'RE EATING WHITE BREAD?! MAN, THAT SHOULD BE A MOVIE !!!
darb
OH, NOT THIS THING AGAIN.
HEY, YOU CAN CALL THE SEQUEL BREAD II - THIS TIME... IT'S TOAST.

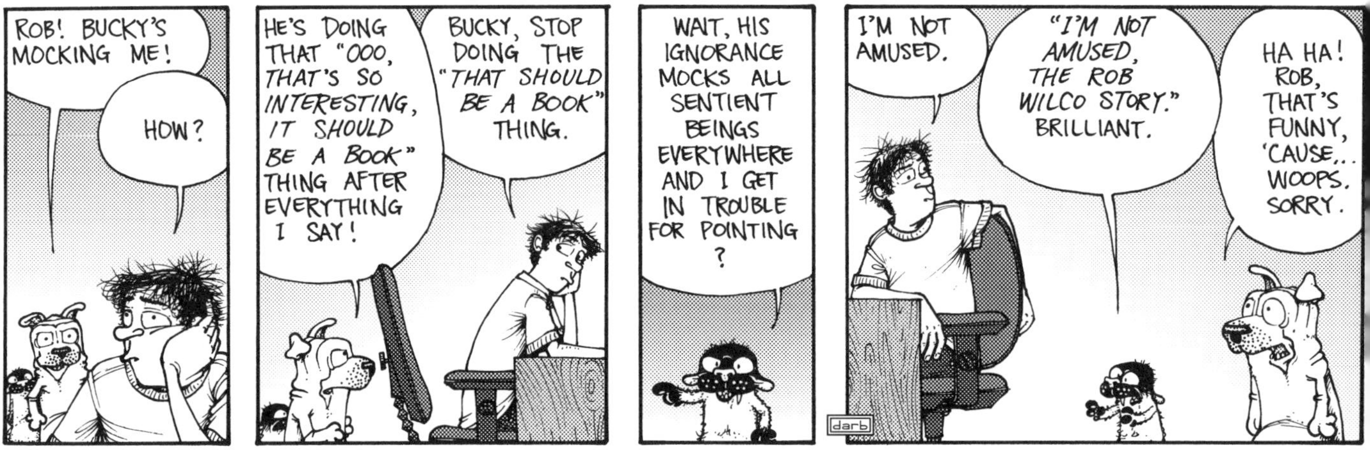
ROB! BUCKY'S MOCKING ME!
HOW?
HE'S DOING THAT "OOO, THAT'S SO INTERESTING, IT SHOULD BE A BOOK" THING AFTER EVERYTHING I SAY!
BUCKY, STOP DOING THE "THAT SHOULD BE A BOOK" THING.
WAIT, HIS IGNORANCE MOCKS ALL SENTIENT BEINGS EVERYWHERE AND I GET IN TROUBLE FOR POINTING?
darb
I'M NOT AMUSED.
"I'M NOT AMUSED, THE ROB WILCO STORY." BRILLIANT.
HA HA! ROB, THAT'S FUNNY, 'CAUSE... WOOPS. SORRY.

THESE GUYS NEED TO START MOVING NORTH-SOUTH, DUDE. TOO MUCH EAST-WEST GOIN' ON HERE.

YOU WANT THEM TO GET THERE, RIGHT? THAT **IS** WEST.

EAST-WEST MEANS SIDE-TO-SIDE, NOT GOAL-TO-GOAL.

THAT'S STUPID. LOOK AT THE SUN, THE GOAL **IS** WEST.

IT'S JUST AN EXPRESSION, DON'T LOSE ANY OF YOUR 22 HOURS OF SLEEP ON IT.

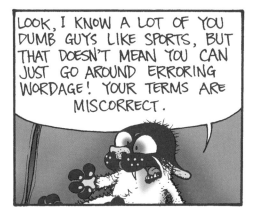

LOOK, I KNOW A LOT OF YOU DUMB GUYS LIKE SPORTS, BUT THAT DOESN'T MEAN YOU CAN JUST GO AROUND ERRORING WORDAGE! YOUR TERMS ARE MISCORRECT.

SUCH AS?

WELL, RIGHT HERE IN YOUR SILLY RUGBY, WHAT ARE THE SCORES CALLED, AGAIN?

YOU MEAN "TRIES"?

RIGHT, THAT'S STUPID. DID HE OR DID HE NOT SCORE? DON'T GIVE POINTS FOR A "TRY", GIVE 'EM FOR A "DO."

AND WHAT'S WITH "BALLS AND STRIKES"? NEVER SEEN A PITCHER THROW ANYTHING BUT BALLS.

NEVER MIND.

THROW SOMETHIN' ELSE AND I'LL LET YOU MAKE NEW TERMS UP. LIKE "*WHOOPS! THERE'S A **SHOE** JUST OUTSIDE!*"

darb

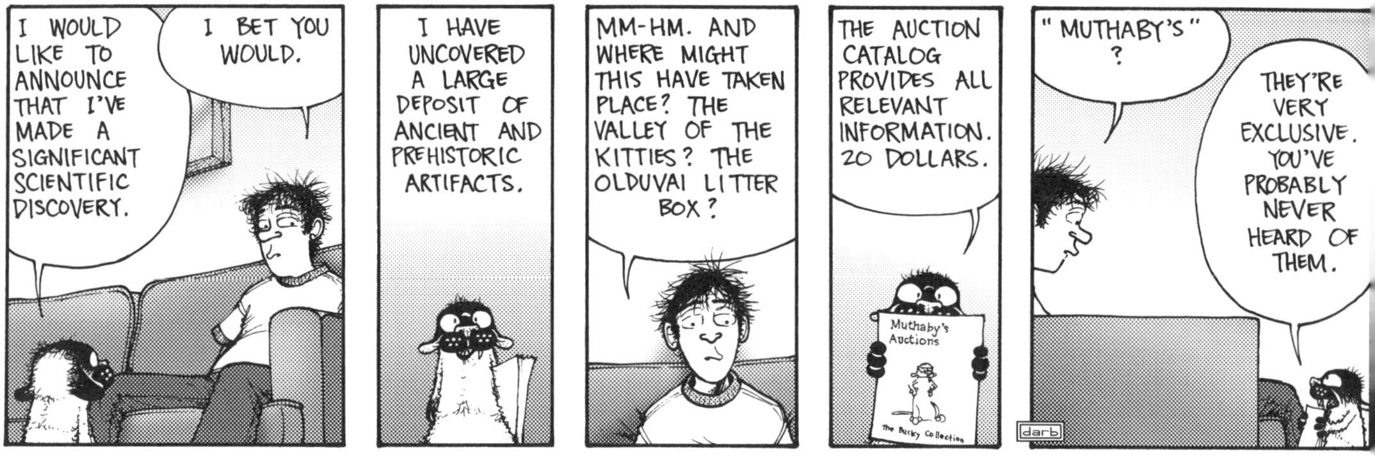
I WOULD LIKE TO ANNOUNCE THAT I'VE MADE A SIGNIFICANT SCIENTIFIC DISCOVERY.
I BET YOU WOULD.
I HAVE UNCOVERED A LARGE DEPOSIT OF ANCIENT AND PREHISTORIC ARTIFACTS.
MM-HM. AND WHERE MIGHT THIS HAVE TAKEN PLACE? THE VALLEY OF THE KITTIES? THE OLDUVAI LITTER BOX?
THE AUCTION CATALOG PROVIDES ALL RELEVANT INFORMATION. 20 DOLLARS.
Muthaby's Auctions
The Bucky Collection
"MUTHABY'S"?
THEY'RE VERY EXCLUSIVE. YOU'VE PROBABLY NEVER HEARD OF THEM.
darb

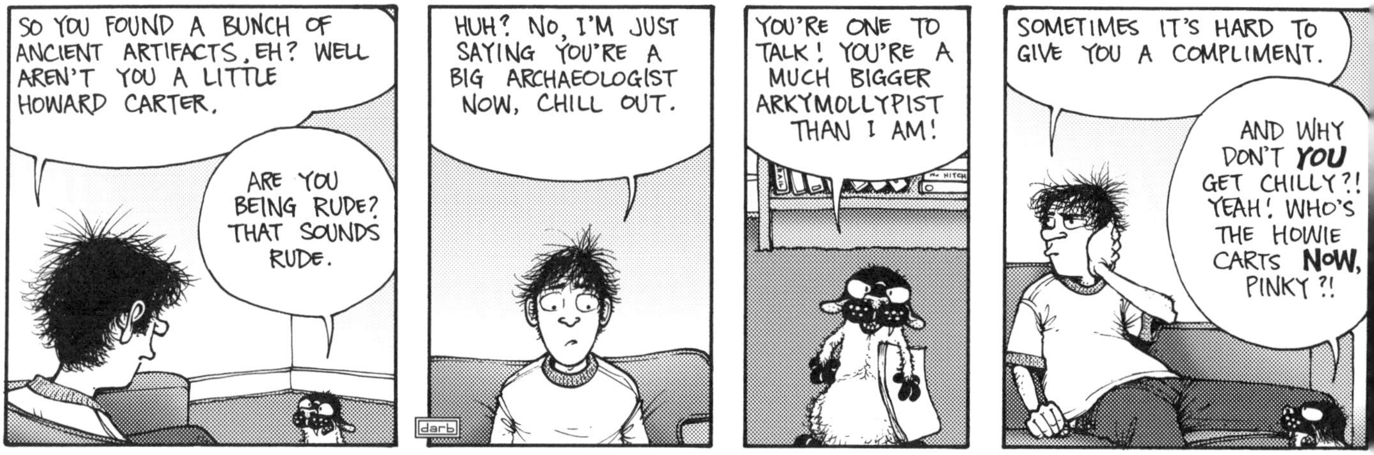
SO YOU FOUND A BUNCH OF ANCIENT ARTIFACTS, EH? WELL AREN'T YOU A LITTLE HOWARD CARTER.
ARE YOU BEING RUDE? THAT SOUNDS RUDE.
darb
HUH? NO, I'M JUST SAYING YOU'RE A BIG ARCHAEOLOGIST NOW, CHILL OUT.
YOU'RE ONE TO TALK! YOU'RE A MUCH BIGGER ARKYMOLLYPIST THAN I AM!
SOMETIMES IT'S HARD TO GIVE YOU A COMPLIMENT.
AND WHY DON'T YOU GET CHILLY?! YEAH! WHO'S THE HOWIE CARTS NOW, PINKY?!

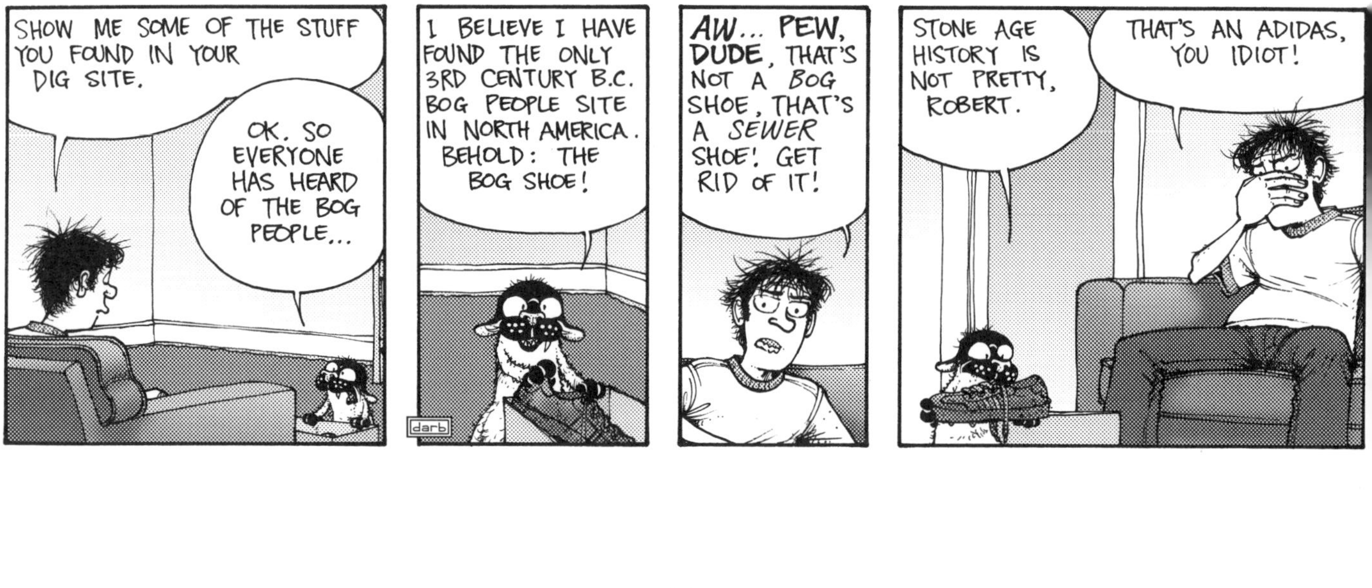
SHOW ME SOME OF THE STUFF YOU FOUND IN YOUR DIG SITE.
OK. SO EVERYONE HAS HEARD OF THE BOG PEOPLE...
darb
I BELIEVE I HAVE FOUND THE ONLY 3RD CENTURY B.C. BOG PEOPLE SITE IN NORTH AMERICA. BEHOLD: THE BOG SHOE!
AW... PEW, DUDE, THAT'S NOT A BOG SHOE, THAT'S A SEWER SHOE! GET RID OF IT!
STONE AGE HISTORY IS NOT PRETTY, ROBERT.
THAT'S AN ADIDAS, YOU IDIOT!

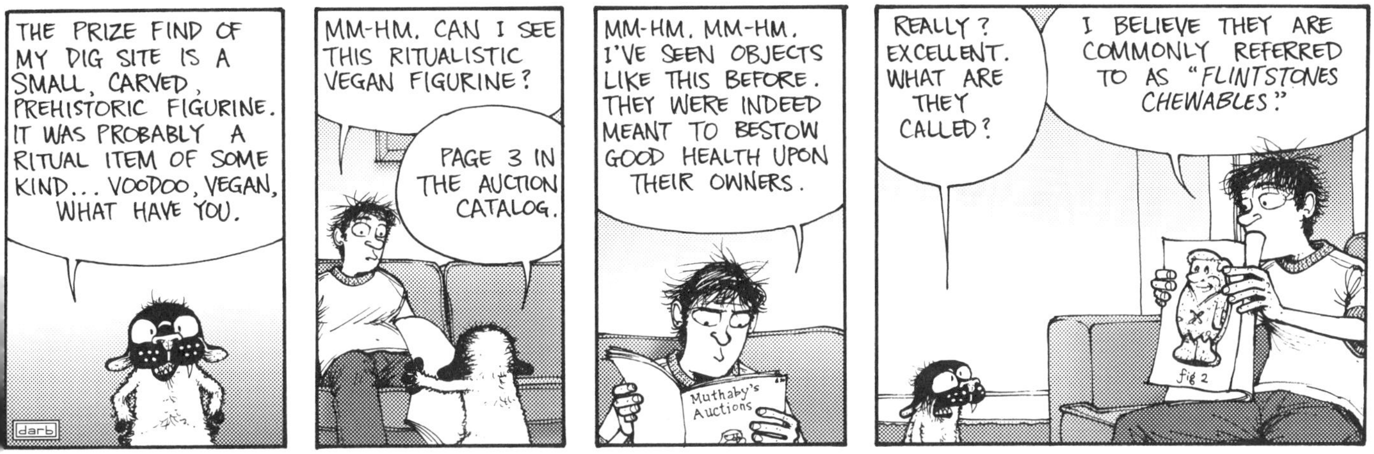
THE PRIZE FIND OF MY DIG SITE IS A SMALL, CARVED, PREHISTORIC FIGURINE. IT WAS PROBABLY A RITUAL ITEM OF SOME KIND... VOODOO, VEGAN, WHAT HAVE YOU.
darb
MM-HM. CAN I SEE THIS RITUALISTIC VEGAN FIGURINE?
PAGE 3 IN THE AUCTION CATALOG.
MM-HM. MM-HM. I'VE SEEN OBJECTS LIKE THIS BEFORE. THEY WERE INDEED MEANT TO BESTOW GOOD HEALTH UPON THEIR OWNERS.
Muthaby's Auctions
REALLY? EXCELLENT. WHAT ARE THEY CALLED?
I BELIEVE THEY ARE COMMONLY REFERRED TO AS "FLINTSTONES CHEWABLES."
fig 2

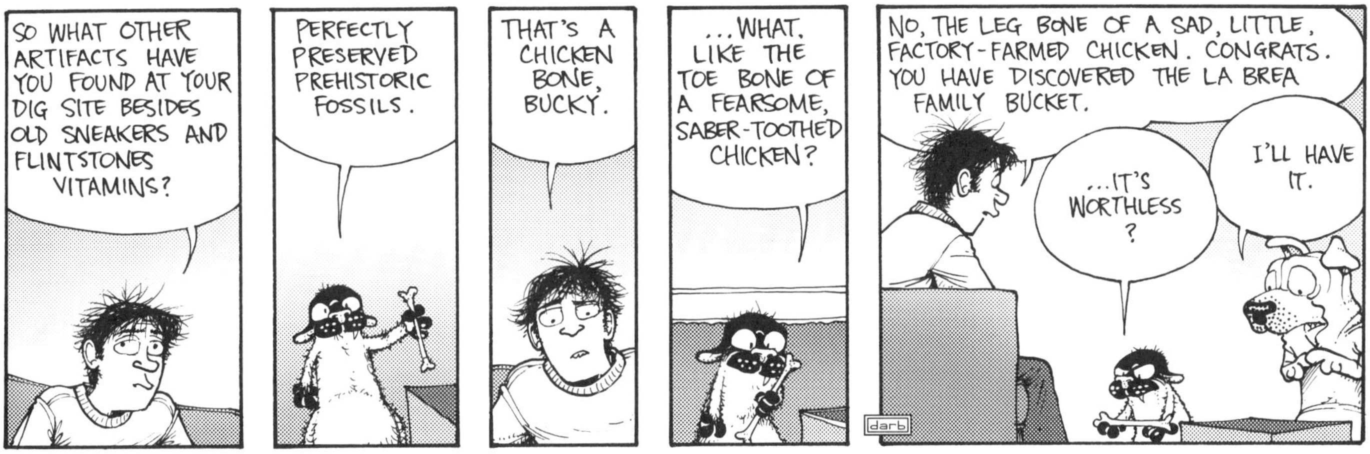
SO WHAT OTHER ARTIFACTS HAVE YOU FOUND AT YOUR DIG SITE BESIDES OLD SNEAKERS AND FLINTSTONES VITAMINS?
PERFECTLY PRESERVED PREHISTORIC FOSSILS.
THAT'S A CHICKEN BONE, BUCKY.
...WHAT. LIKE THE TOE BONE OF A FEARSOME, SABER-TOOTHED CHICKEN?
NO, THE LEG BONE OF A SAD, LITTLE, FACTORY-FARMED CHICKEN. CONGRATS. YOU HAVE DISCOVERED THE LA BREA FAMILY BUCKET.
...IT'S WORTHLESS?
I'LL HAVE IT.
darb

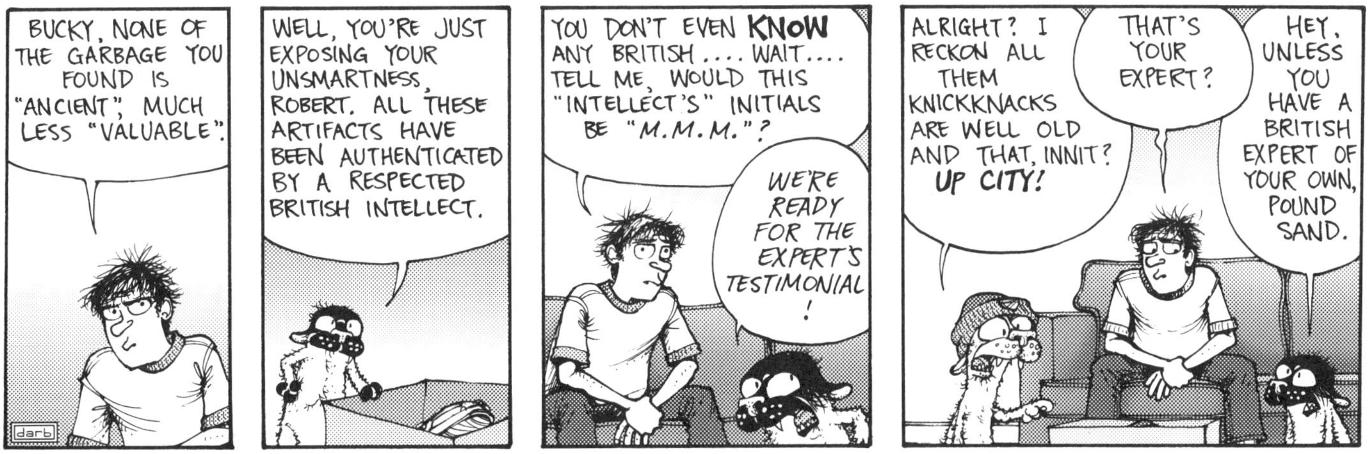
BUCKY, NONE OF THE GARBAGE YOU FOUND IS "ANCIENT," MUCH LESS "VALUABLE."
darb
WELL, YOU'RE JUST EXPOSING YOUR UNSMARTNESS, ROBERT. ALL THESE ARTIFACTS HAVE BEEN AUTHENTICATED BY A RESPECTED BRITISH INTELLECT.
YOU DON'T EVEN KNOW ANY BRITISH.... WAIT.... TELL ME, WOULD THIS "INTELLECT'S" INITIALS BE "M.M.M."?
WE'RE READY FOR THE EXPERT'S TESTIMONIAL!
ALRIGHT? I RECKON ALL THEM KNICKKNACKS ARE WELL OLD AND THAT, INNIT? UP CITY!
THAT'S YOUR EXPERT?
HEY, UNLESS YOU HAVE A BRITISH EXPERT OF YOUR OWN, POUND SAND.

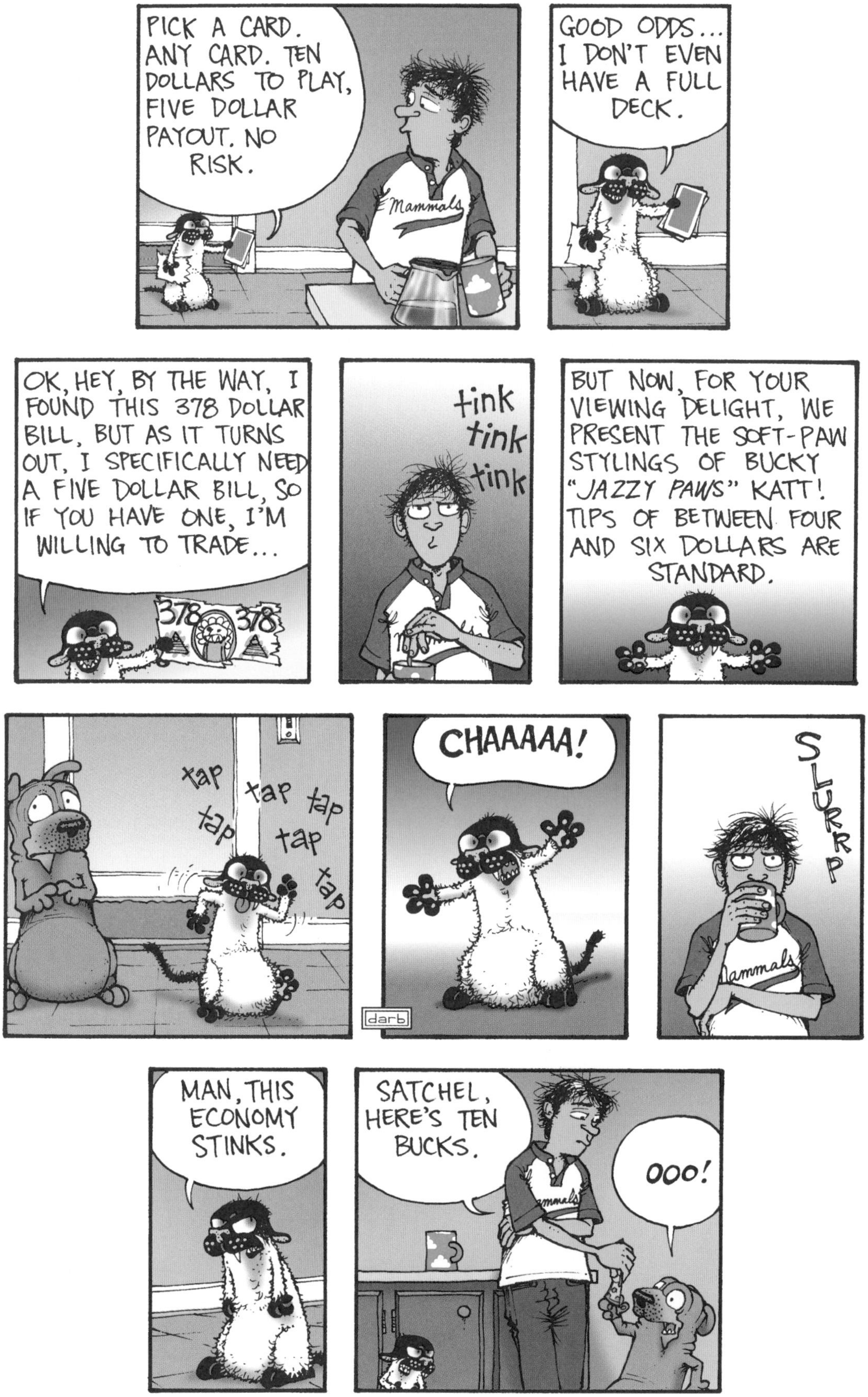
PICK A CARD. ANY CARD. TEN DOLLARS TO PLAY, FIVE DOLLAR PAYOUT. NO RISK.
Mammals
GOOD ODDS... I DON'T EVEN HAVE A FULL DECK.
OK, HEY, BY THE WAY, I FOUND THIS 378 DOLLAR BILL, BUT AS IT TURNS OUT, I SPECIFICALLY NEED A FIVE DOLLAR BILL, SO IF YOU HAVE ONE, I'M WILLING TO TRADE...
378 378
tink tink tink
BUT NOW, FOR YOUR VIEWING DELIGHT, WE PRESENT THE SOFT-PAW STYLINGS OF BUCKY "JAZZY PAWS" KATT! TIPS OF BETWEEN FOUR AND SIX DOLLARS ARE STANDARD.
tap tap tap tap tap tap
CHAAAAA!
darb
SLURRP
Mammals
MAN, THIS ECONOMY STINKS.
SATCHEL, HERE'S TEN BUCKS.
OOO!

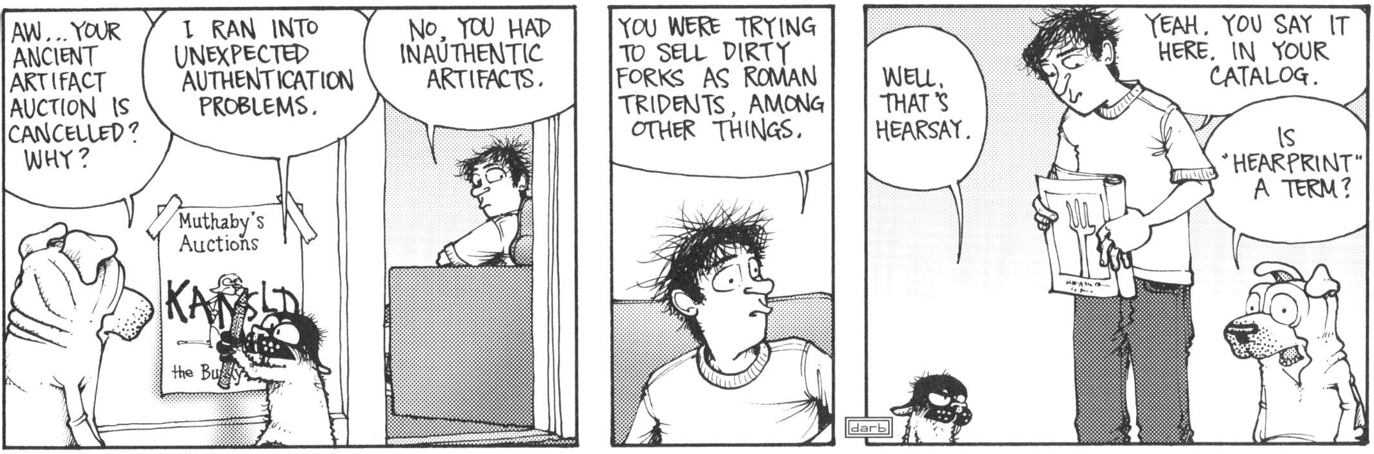
AW... YOUR ANCIENT ARTIFACT AUCTION IS CANCELLED? WHY?
I RAN INTO UNEXPECTED AUTHENTICATION PROBLEMS.
Muthaby's Auctions
NO, YOU HAD INAUTHENTIC ARTIFACTS.
YOU WERE TRYING TO SELL DIRTY FORKS AS ROMAN TRIDENTS, AMONG OTHER THINGS.
WELL, THAT'S HEARSAY.
YEAH. YOU SAY IT HERE. IN YOUR CATALOG.
IS "HEARPRINT" A TERM?
darb

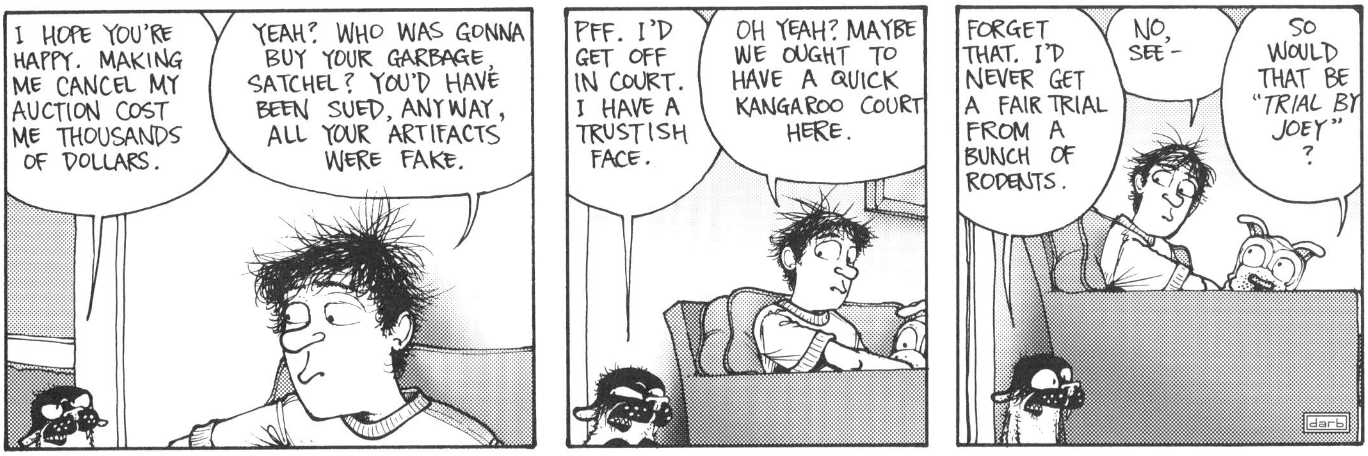
I HOPE YOU'RE HAPPY. MAKING ME CANCEL MY AUCTION COST ME THOUSANDS OF DOLLARS.
YEAH? WHO WAS GONNA BUY YOUR GARBAGE, SATCHEL? YOU'D HAVE BEEN SUED, ANYWAY, ALL YOUR ARTIFACTS WERE FAKE.
PFF. I'D GET OFF IN COURT. I HAVE A TRUSTISH FACE.
OH YEAH? MAYBE WE OUGHT TO HAVE A QUICK KANGAROO COURT HERE.
FORGET THAT. I'D NEVER GET A FAIR TRIAL FROM A BUNCH OF RODENTS.
NO, SEE-
SO WOULD THAT BE "TRIAL BY JOEY"?
darb

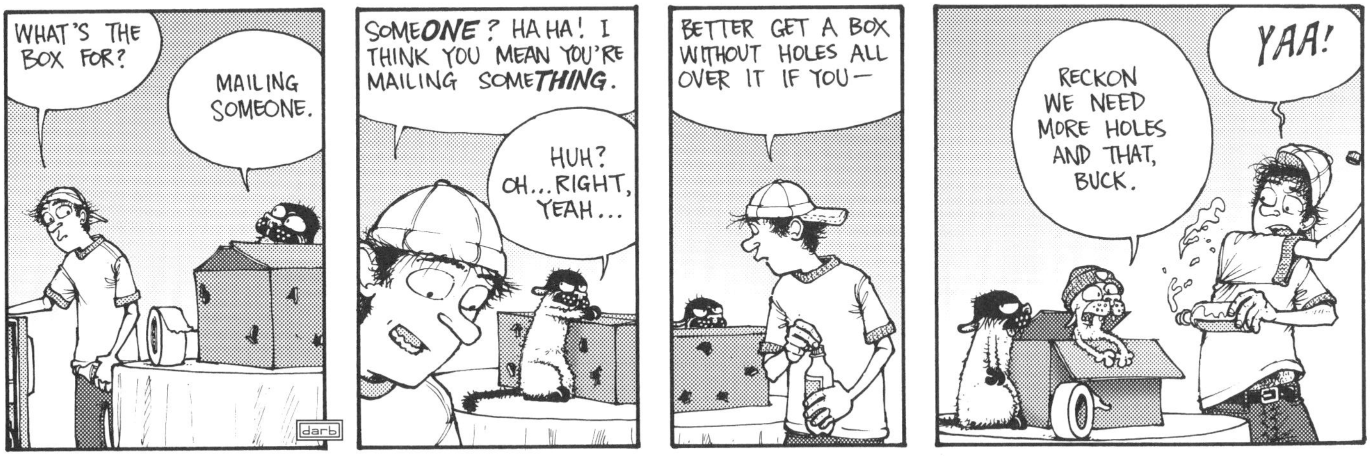
WHAT'S THE BOX FOR?
MAILING SOMEONE.
darb
SOMEONE? HA HA! I THINK YOU MEAN YOU'RE MAILING SOMETHING.
HUH? OH... RIGHT, YEAH...
BETTER GET A BOX WITHOUT HOLES ALL OVER IT IF YOU—
RECKON WE NEED MORE HOLES AND THAT, BUCK.
YAA!

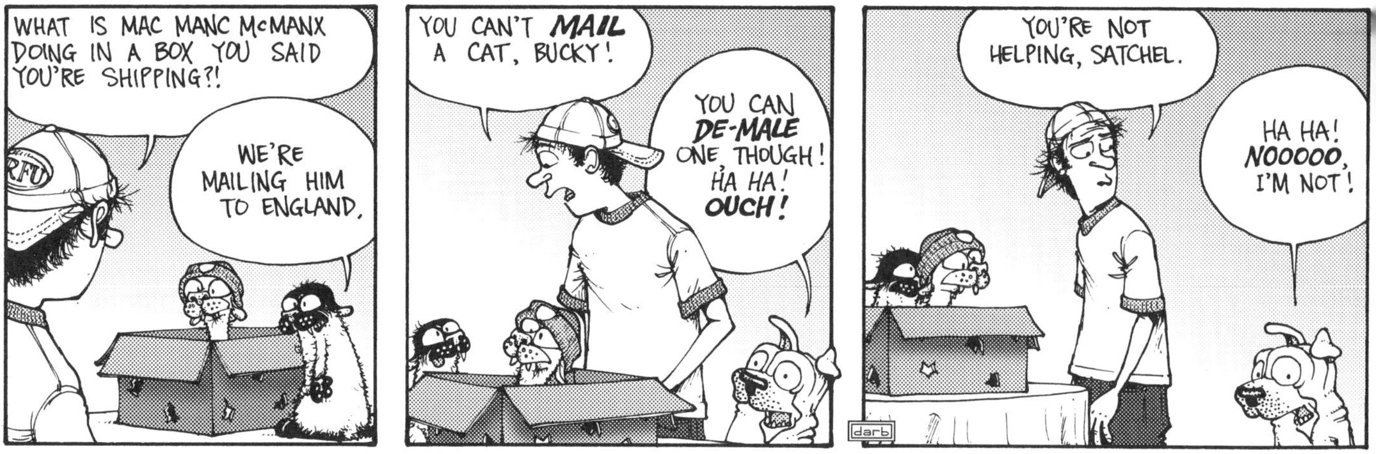
WHAT IS MAC MANC McMANX DOING IN A BOX YOU SAID YOU'RE SHIPPING?!
WE'RE MAILING HIM TO ENGLAND.
YOU CAN'T **MAIL** A CAT, BUCKY!
YOU CAN **DE-MALE** ONE THOUGH! HA HA! **OUCH!**
YOU'RE NOT HELPING, SATCHEL.
HA HA! **NOOOOO,** I'M NOT!
darb

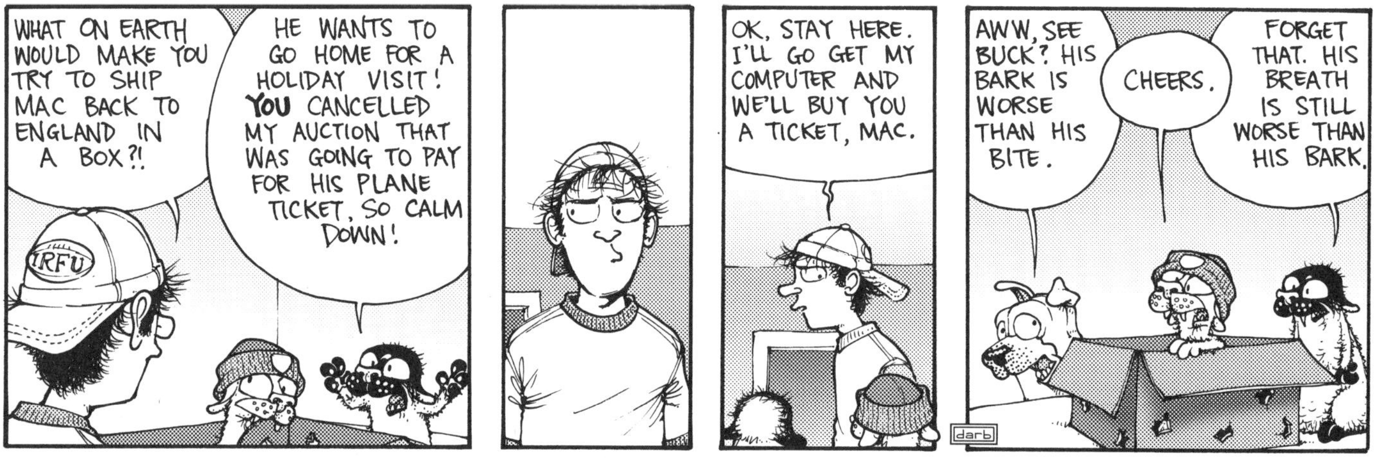
WHAT ON EARTH WOULD MAKE YOU TRY TO SHIP MAC BACK TO ENGLAND IN A BOX?!
HE WANTS TO GO HOME FOR A HOLIDAY VISIT! **YOU** CANCELLED MY AUCTION THAT WAS GOING TO PAY FOR HIS PLANE TICKET, SO CALM DOWN!
OK, STAY HERE. I'LL GO GET MY COMPUTER AND WE'LL BUY YOU A TICKET, MAC.
AWW, SEE BUCK? HIS BARK IS WORSE THAN HIS BITE.
CHEERS.
FORGET THAT. HIS BREATH IS STILL WORSE THAN HIS BARK.
darb

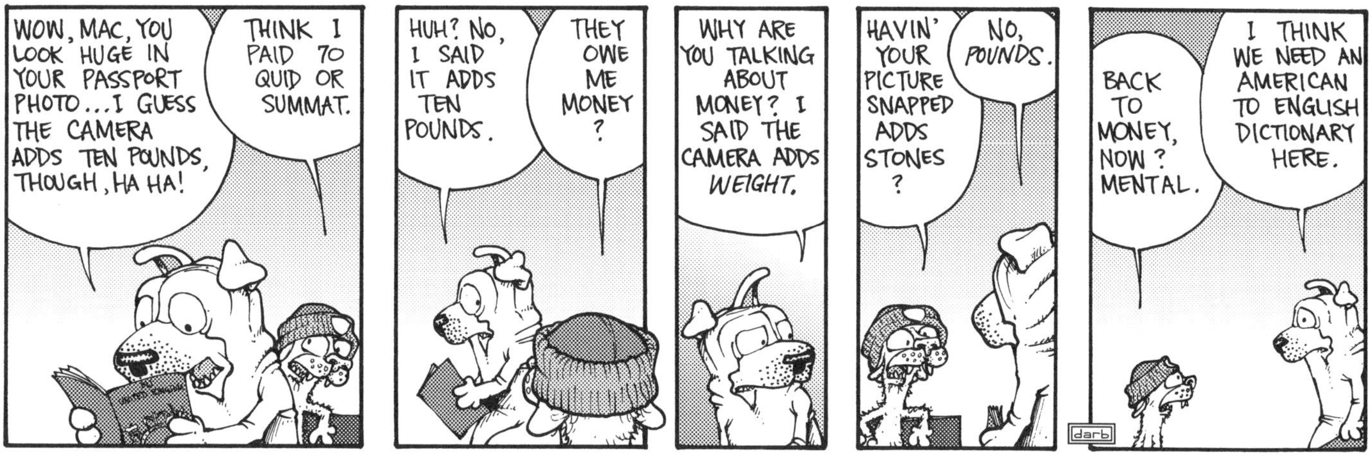
WOW, MAC, YOU LOOK HUGE IN YOUR PASSPORT PHOTO... I GUESS THE CAMERA ADDS TEN POUNDS, THOUGH, HA HA!
THINK I PAID 70 QUID OR SUMMAT.
HUH? NO, I SAID IT ADDS TEN POUNDS.
THEY OWE ME MONEY?
WHY ARE YOU TALKING ABOUT MONEY? I SAID THE CAMERA ADDS *WEIGHT.*
HAVIN' YOUR PICTURE SNAPPED ADDS STONES?
NO, *POUNDS.*
BACK TO MONEY, NOW? MENTAL.
I THINK WE NEED AN AMERICAN TO ENGLISH DICTIONARY HERE.
darb

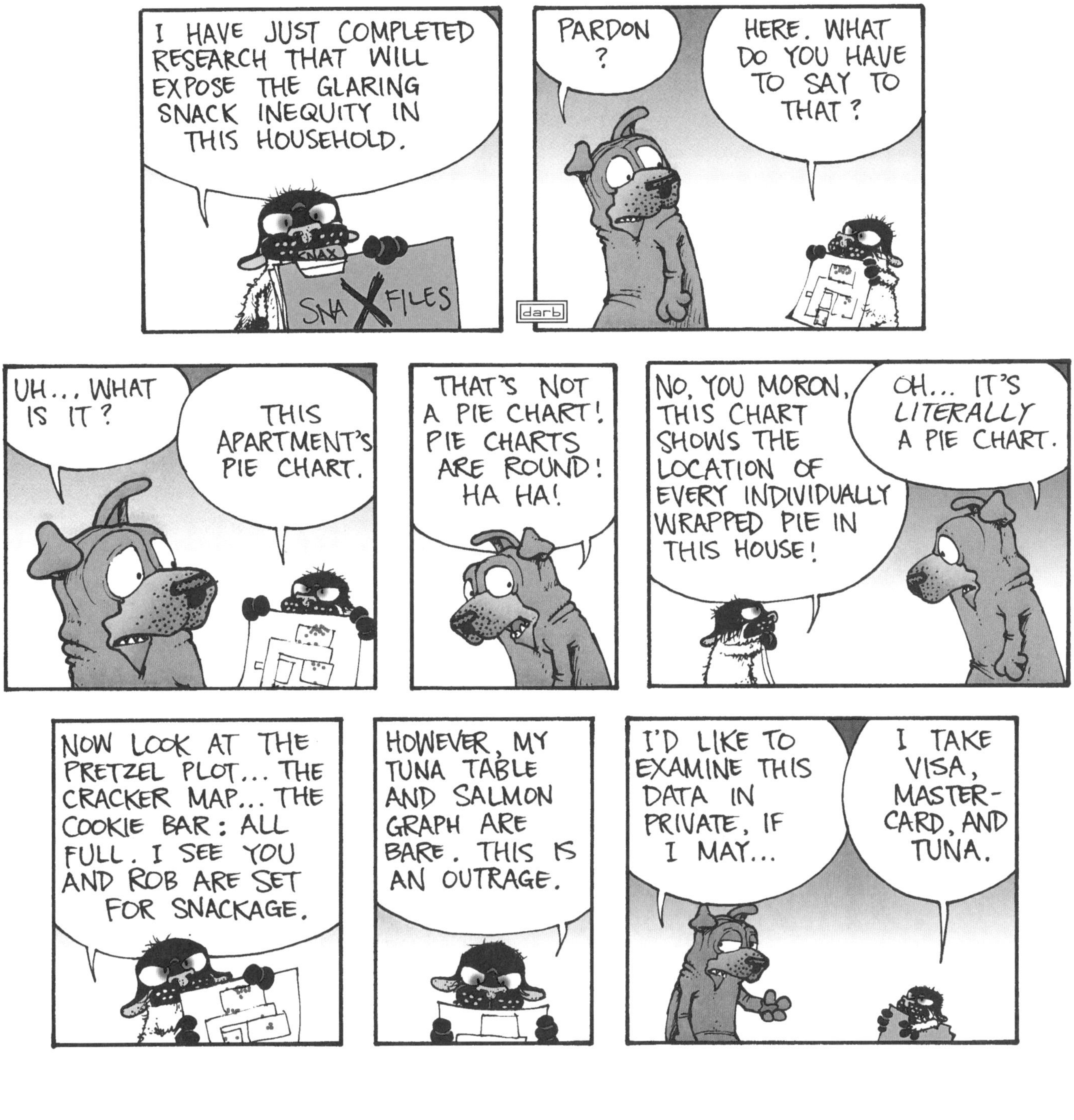
I HAVE JUST COMPLETED RESEARCH THAT WILL EXPOSE THE GLARING SNACK INEQUITY IN THIS HOUSEHOLD.
SNAX
SNAX FILES
PARDON ?
HERE. WHAT DO YOU HAVE TO SAY TO THAT ?
darb
UH... WHAT IS IT ?
THIS APARTMENT'S PIE CHART.
THAT'S NOT A PIE CHART! PIE CHARTS ARE ROUND! HA HA!
NO, YOU MORON, THIS CHART SHOWS THE LOCATION OF EVERY INDIVIDUALLY WRAPPED PIE IN THIS HOUSE!
OH... IT'S *LITERALLY* A PIE CHART.
NOW LOOK AT THE PRETZEL PLOT... THE CRACKER MAP... THE COOKIE BAR: ALL FULL. I SEE YOU AND ROB ARE SET FOR SNACKAGE.
HOWEVER, MY TUNA TABLE AND SALMON GRAPH ARE BARE. THIS IS AN OUTRAGE.
I'D LIKE TO EXAMINE THIS DATA IN PRIVATE, IF I MAY...
I TAKE VISA, MASTER-CARD, AND TUNA.

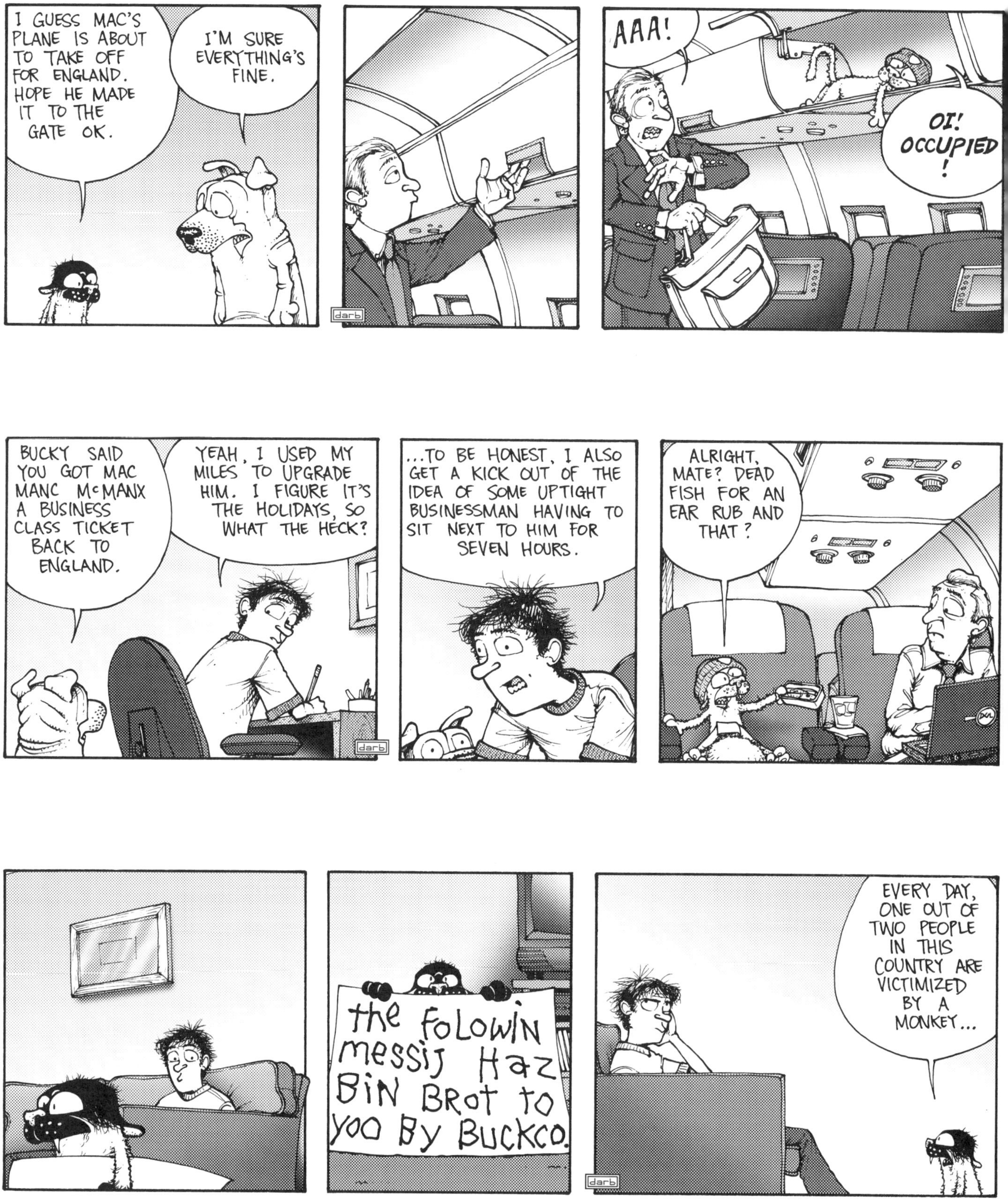
I GUESS MAC'S PLANE IS ABOUT TO TAKE OFF FOR ENGLAND. HOPE HE MADE IT TO THE GATE OK.
I'M SURE EVERYTHING'S FINE.
darb
AAA!
OI! OCCUPIED!
BUCKY SAID YOU GOT MAC MANC McMANX A BUSINESS CLASS TICKET BACK TO ENGLAND.
YEAH, I USED MY MILES TO UPGRADE HIM. I FIGURE IT'S THE HOLIDAYS, SO WHAT THE HECK?
darb
...TO BE HONEST, I ALSO GET A KICK OUT OF THE IDEA OF SOME UPTIGHT BUSINESSMAN HAVING TO SIT NEXT TO HIM FOR SEVEN HOURS.
ALRIGHT, MATE? DEAD FISH FOR AN EAR RUB AND THAT?
the Folowin messij Haz Bin Brot to yoo By Buckco.
darb
EVERY DAY, ONE OUT OF TWO PEOPLE IN THIS COUNTRY ARE VICTIMIZED BY A MONKEY...

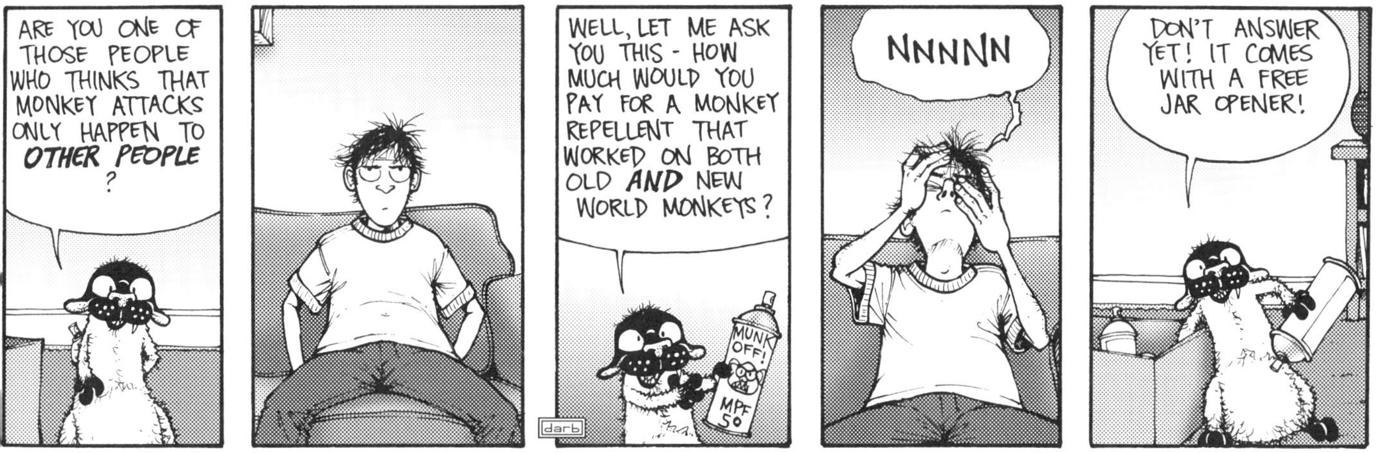
ARE YOU ONE OF THOSE PEOPLE WHO THINKS THAT MONKEY ATTACKS ONLY HAPPEN TO **OTHER PEOPLE** ?
WELL, LET ME ASK YOU THIS - HOW MUCH WOULD YOU PAY FOR A MONKEY REPELLENT THAT WORKED ON BOTH OLD **AND** NEW WORLD MONKEYS?
MUNK OFF! MPF 50
darb
NNNNN
DON'T ANSWER YET! IT COMES WITH A FREE JAR OPENER!

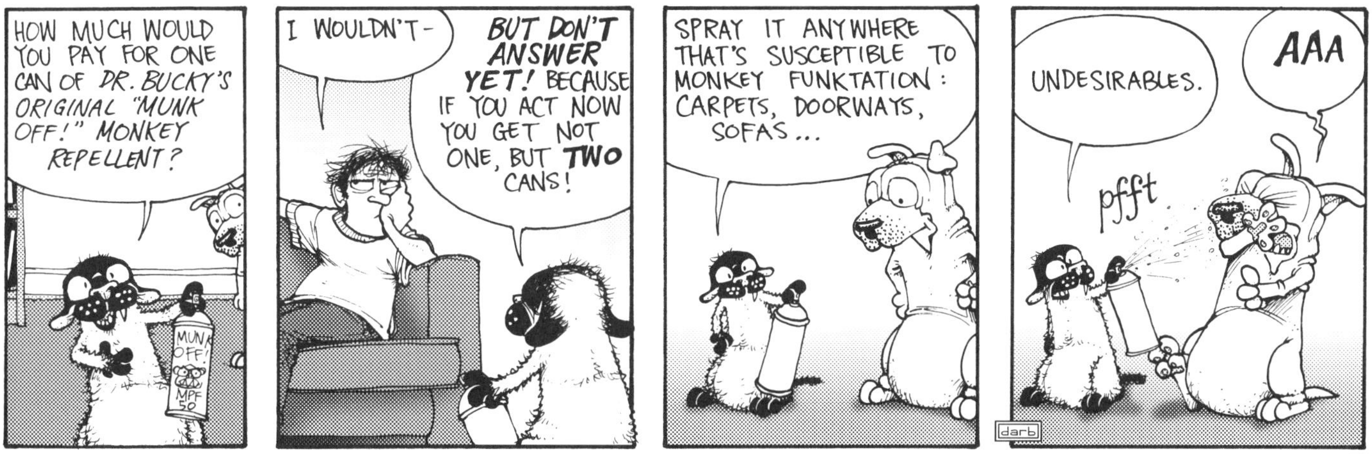
HOW MUCH WOULD YOU PAY FOR ONE CAN OF *DR. BUCKY'S ORIGINAL "MUNK OFF!" MONKEY REPELLENT?*
MUNK OFF! MPF 50
I WOULDN'T-
BUT DON'T ANSWER YET! BECAUSE IF YOU ACT NOW YOU GET NOT ONE, BUT **TWO** CANS!
SPRAY IT ANYWHERE THAT'S SUSCEPTIBLE TO MONKEY FUNKTATION: CARPETS, DOORWAYS, SOFAS...
UNDESIRABLES.
AAA
pfft
darb

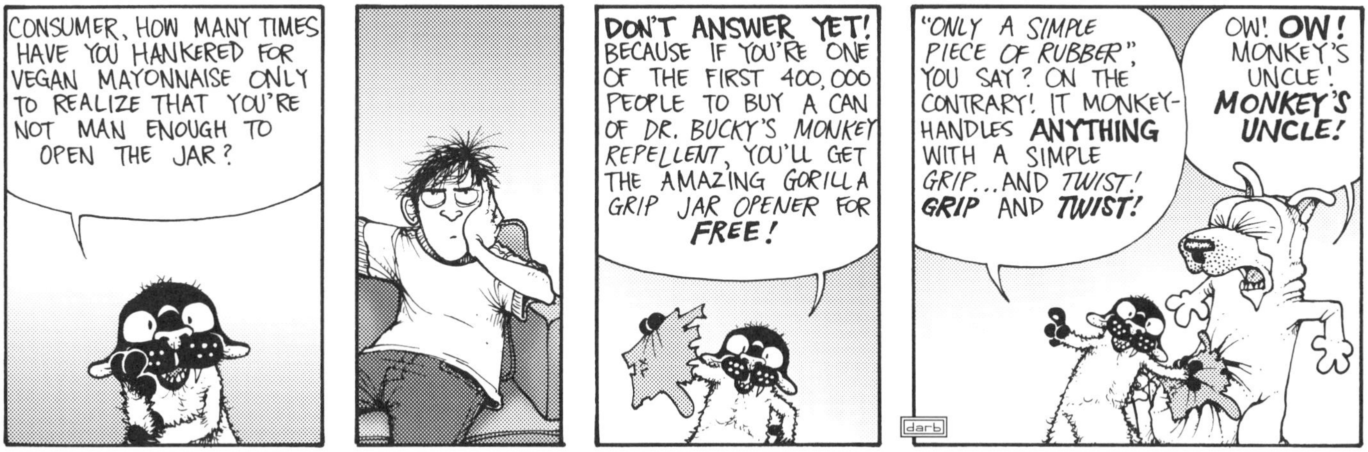
CONSUMER, HOW MANY TIMES HAVE YOU HANKERED FOR VEGAN MAYONNAISE ONLY TO REALIZE THAT YOU'RE NOT MAN ENOUGH TO OPEN THE JAR?
DON'T ANSWER YET! BECAUSE IF YOU'RE ONE OF THE FIRST 400,000 PEOPLE TO BUY A CAN OF *DR. BUCKY'S MONKEY REPELLENT*, YOU'LL GET THE AMAZING GORILLA GRIP JAR OPENER FOR ***FREE!***
"ONLY A SIMPLE PIECE OF RUBBER", YOU SAY? ON THE CONTRARY! IT MONKEY-HANDLES **ANYTHING** WITH A SIMPLE *GRIP... AND TWIST!* ***GRIP*** AND ***TWIST!***
OW! **OW!** MONKEY'S UNCLE! ***MONKEY'S UNCLE!***
darb

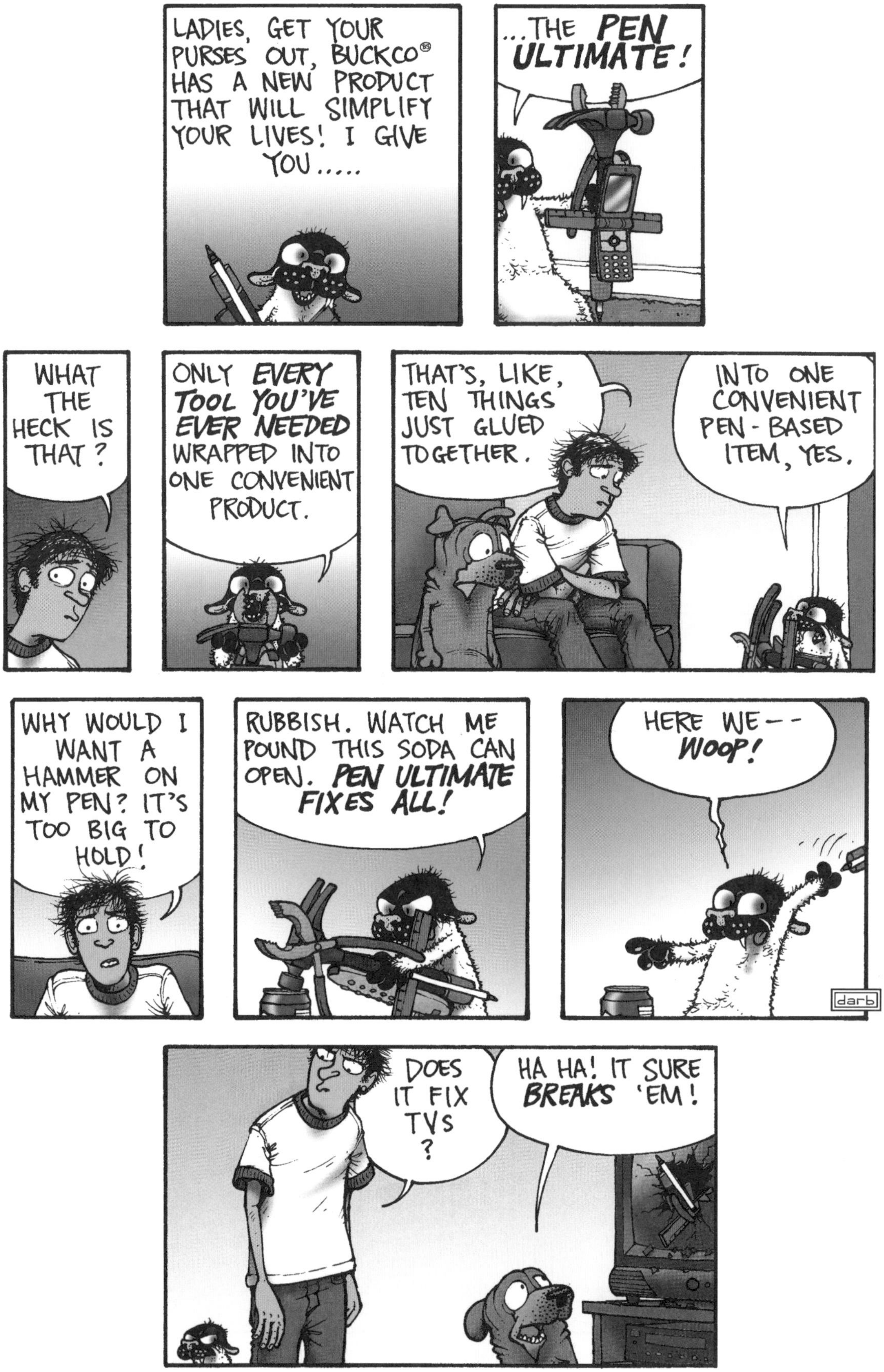
LADIES, GET YOUR PURSES OUT, BUCKCO® HAS A NEW PRODUCT THAT WILL SIMPLIFY YOUR LIVES! I GIVE YOU.....
...THE PEN ULTIMATE!
WHAT THE HECK IS THAT?
ONLY EVERY TOOL YOU'VE EVER NEEDED WRAPPED INTO ONE CONVENIENT PRODUCT.
THAT'S, LIKE, TEN THINGS JUST GLUED TOGETHER.
INTO ONE CONVENIENT PEN-BASED ITEM, YES.
WHY WOULD I WANT A HAMMER ON MY PEN? IT'S TOO BIG TO HOLD!
RUBBISH. WATCH ME POUND THIS SODA CAN OPEN. PEN ULTIMATE FIXES ALL!
HERE WE--
WOOP!
darb
DOES IT FIX TVS?
HA HA! IT SURE BREAKS 'EM!

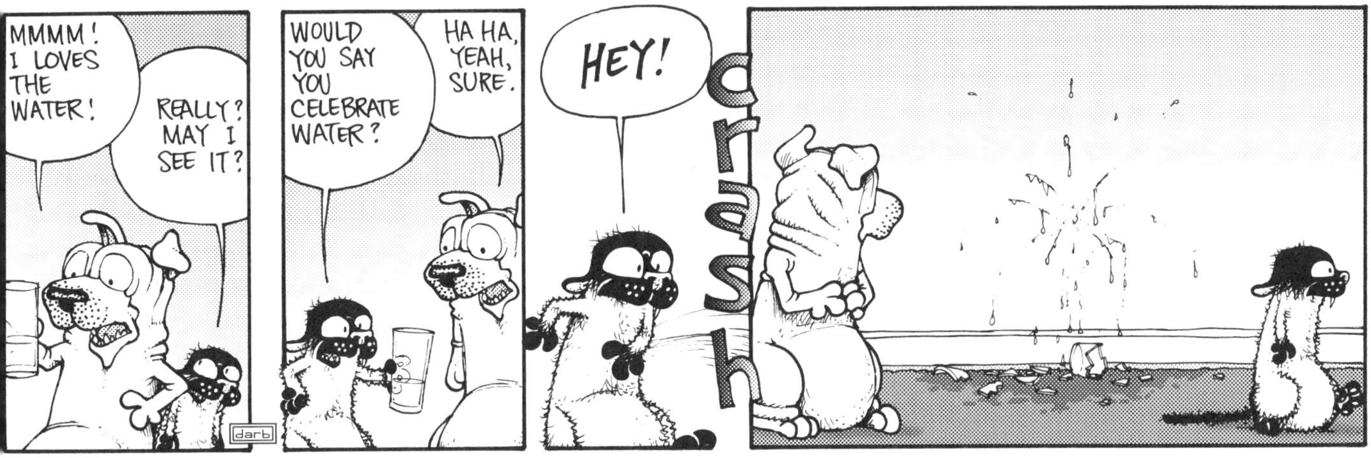
MMMM! I LOVES THE WATER!
REALLY? MAY I SEE IT?
darb
WOULD YOU SAY YOU CELEBRATE WATER?
HA HA, YEAH, SURE.
HEY!
crash

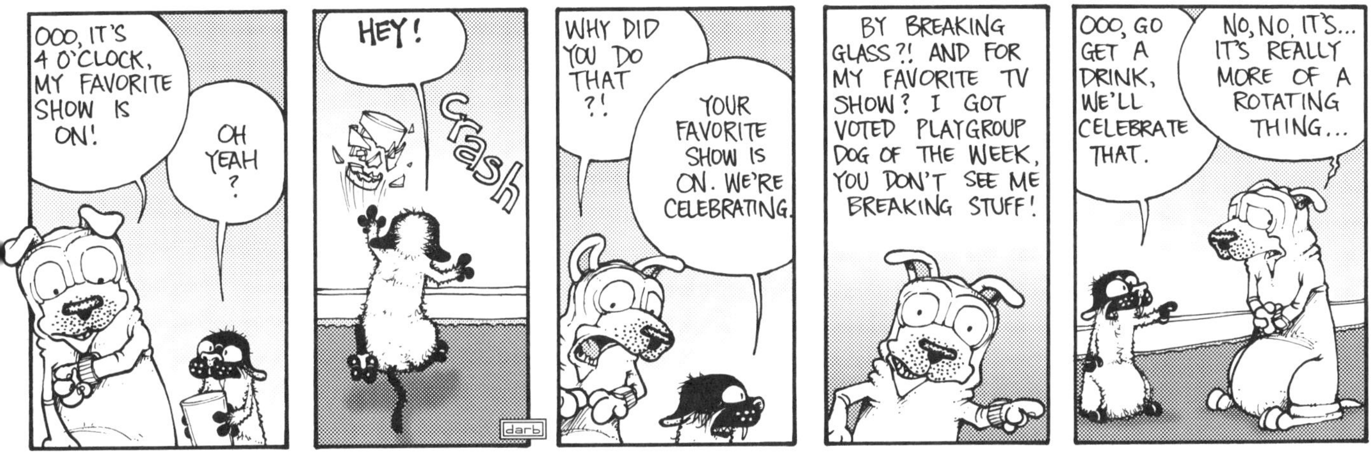
OOO, IT'S 4 O'CLOCK, MY FAVORITE SHOW IS ON!
OH YEAH?
HEY!
crash
darb
WHY DID YOU DO THAT?!
YOUR FAVORITE SHOW IS ON. WE'RE CELEBRATING.
BY BREAKING GLASS?! AND FOR MY FAVORITE TV SHOW? I GOT VOTED PLAYGROUP DOG OF THE WEEK, YOU DON'T SEE ME BREAKING STUFF!
OOO, GO GET A DRINK, WE'LL CELEBRATE THAT.
NO, NO, IT'S... IT'S REALLY MORE OF A ROTATING THING...

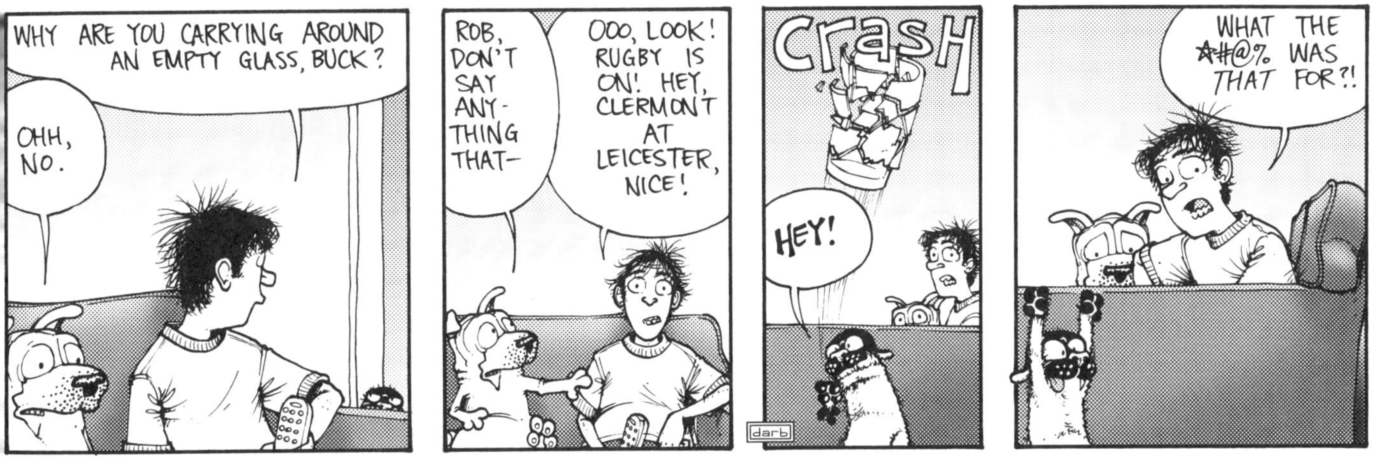
WHY ARE YOU CARRYING AROUND AN EMPTY GLASS, BUCK?
OHH, NO.
ROB, DON'T SAY ANY-THING THAT-
OOO, LOOK! RUGBY IS ON! HEY, CLERMONT AT LEICESTER, NICE!
CRASH
HEY!
darb
WHAT THE *#@% WAS THAT FOR?!

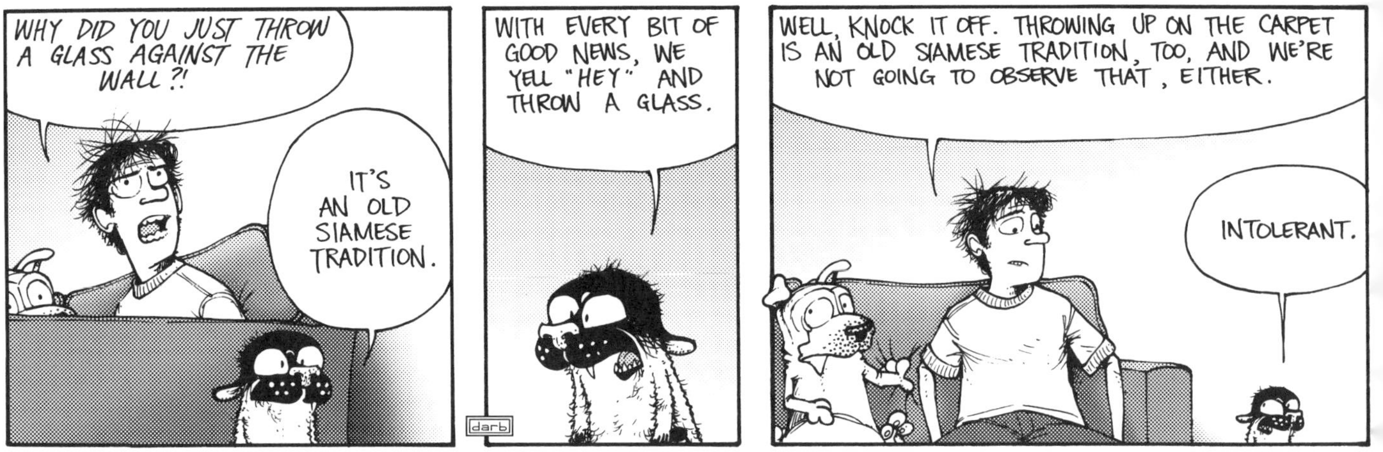
WHY DID YOU JUST THROW A GLASS AGAINST THE WALL?!
IT'S AN OLD SIAMESE TRADITION.
WITH EVERY BIT OF GOOD NEWS, WE YELL "HEY" AND THROW A GLASS.
WELL, KNOCK IT OFF. THROWING UP ON THE CARPET IS AN OLD SIAMESE TRADITION, TOO, AND WE'RE NOT GOING TO OBSERVE THAT, EITHER.
INTOLERANT.

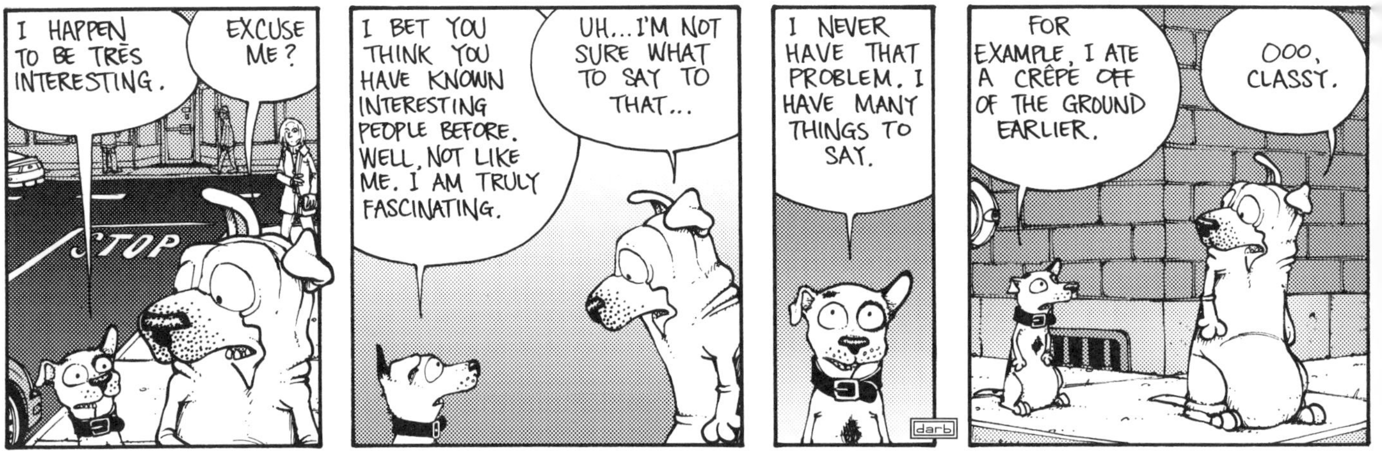
I HAPPEN TO BE TRÈS INTERESTING.
EXCUSE ME?
STOP
I BET YOU THINK YOU HAVE KNOWN INTERESTING PEOPLE BEFORE. WELL, NOT LIKE ME. I AM TRULY FASCINATING.
UH... I'M NOT SURE WHAT TO SAY TO THAT...
I NEVER HAVE THAT PROBLEM. I HAVE MANY THINGS TO SAY.
FOR EXAMPLE, I ATE A CRÊPE OFF OF THE GROUND EARLIER.
OOO, CLASSY.

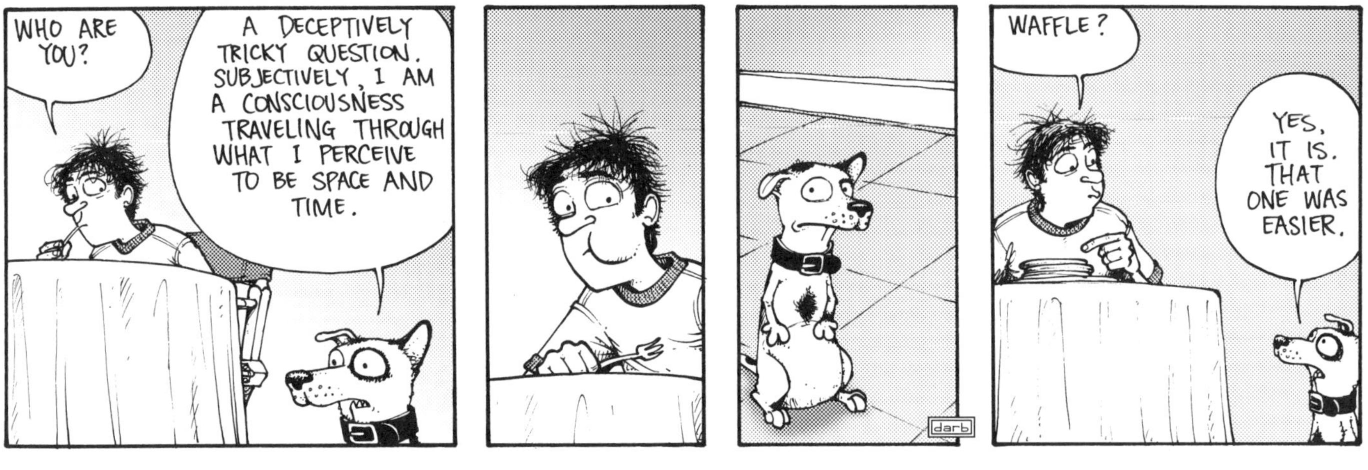
WHO ARE YOU?
A DECEPTIVELY TRICKY QUESTION. SUBJECTIVELY, I AM A CONSCIOUSNESS TRAVELING THROUGH WHAT I PERCEIVE TO BE SPACE AND TIME.
WAFFLE?
YES, IT IS. THAT ONE WAS EASIER.

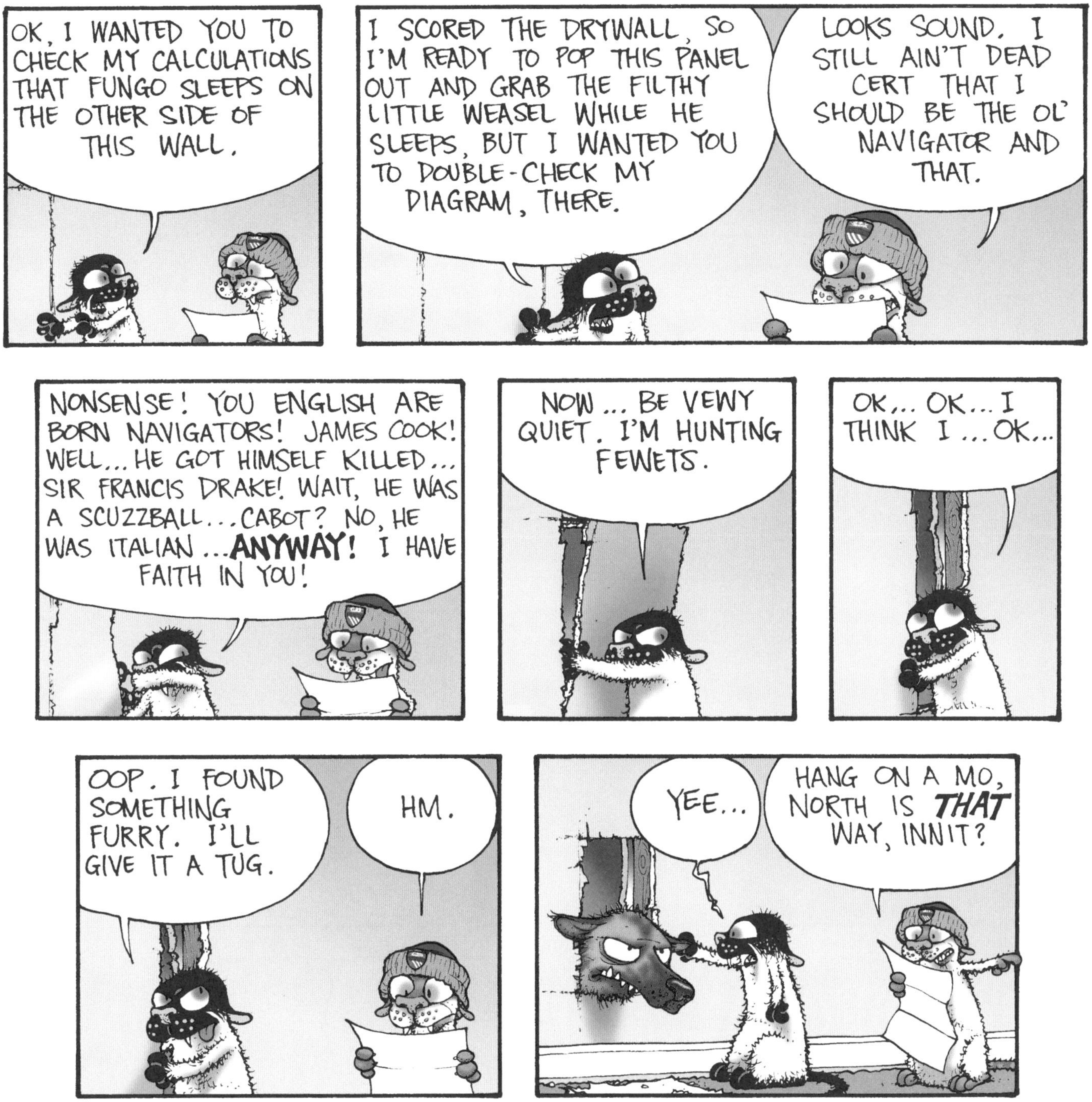
OK, I WANTED YOU TO CHECK MY CALCULATIONS THAT FUNGO SLEEPS ON THE OTHER SIDE OF THIS WALL.
I SCORED THE DRYWALL, SO I'M READY TO POP THIS PANEL OUT AND GRAB THE FILTHY LITTLE WEASEL WHILE HE SLEEPS, BUT I WANTED YOU TO DOUBLE-CHECK MY DIAGRAM, THERE.
LOOKS SOUND. I STILL AIN'T DEAD CERT THAT I SHOULD BE THE OL' NAVIGATOR AND THAT.
NONSENSE! YOU ENGLISH ARE BORN NAVIGATORS! JAMES COOK! WELL... HE GOT HIMSELF KILLED... SIR FRANCIS DRAKE! WAIT, HE WAS A SCUZZBALL... CABOT? NO, HE WAS ITALIAN... **ANYWAY!** I HAVE FAITH IN YOU!
NOW... BE VEWY QUIET. I'M HUNTING FEWETS.
OK,... OK... I THINK I... OK...
OOP. I FOUND SOMETHING FURRY. I'LL GIVE IT A TUG.
HM.
YEE...
HANG ON A MO, NORTH IS ***THAT*** WAY, INNIT?

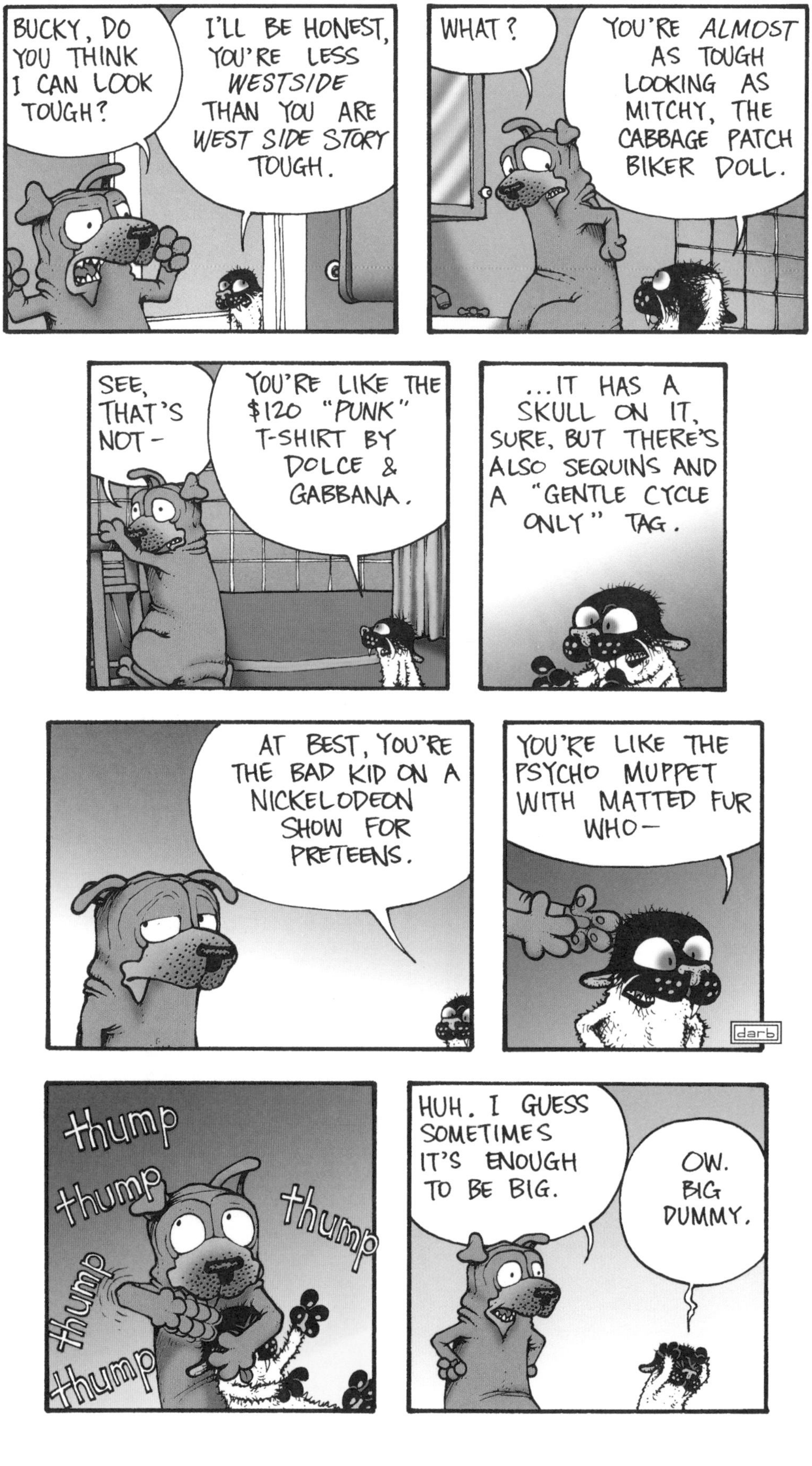
BUCKY, DO YOU THINK I CAN LOOK TOUGH?
I'LL BE HONEST, YOU'RE LESS *WESTSIDE* THAN YOU ARE *WEST SIDE STORY* TOUGH.
WHAT?
YOU'RE *ALMOST* AS TOUGH LOOKING AS MITCHY, THE CABBAGE PATCH BIKER DOLL.
SEE, THAT'S NOT-
YOU'RE LIKE THE $120 "*PUNK*" T-SHIRT BY DOLCE & GABBANA.
...IT HAS A SKULL ON IT, SURE, BUT THERE'S ALSO SEQUINS AND A "GENTLE CYCLE ONLY" TAG.
AT BEST, YOU'RE THE BAD KID ON A NICKELODEON SHOW FOR PRETEENS.
YOU'RE LIKE THE PSYCHO MUPPET WITH MATTED FUR WHO—
darb
thump
thump
thump
thump
thump
HUH. I GUESS SOMETIMES IT'S ENOUGH TO BE BIG.
OW. BIG DUMMY.

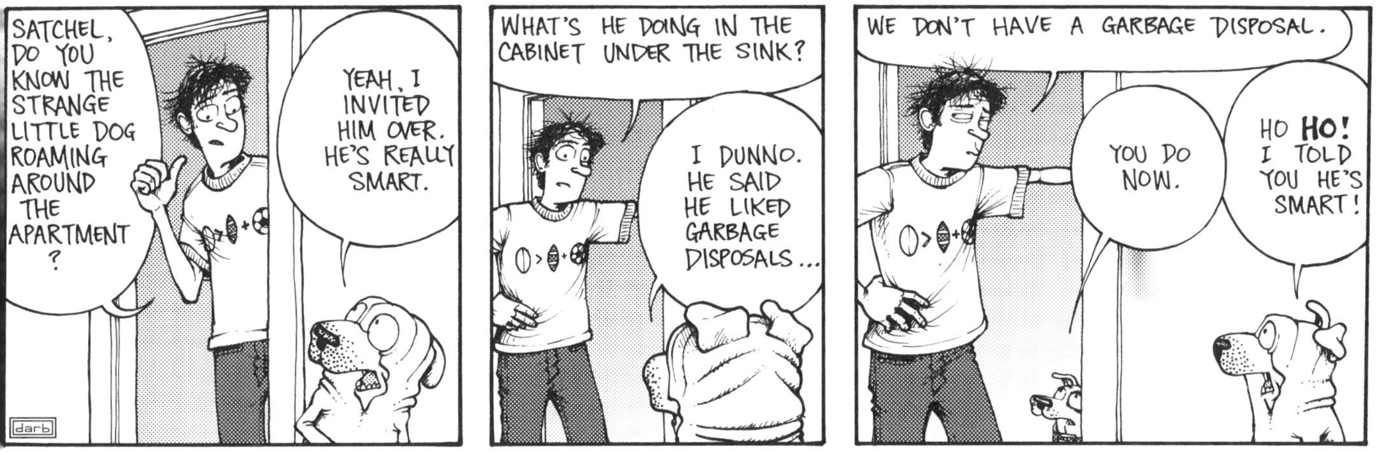
SATCHEL, DO YOU KNOW THE STRANGE LITTLE DOG ROAMING AROUND THE APARTMENT?
YEAH, I INVITED HIM OVER. HE'S REALLY SMART.
darb
WHAT'S HE DOING IN THE CABINET UNDER THE SINK?
I DUNNO. HE SAID HE LIKED GARBAGE DISPOSALS...
WE DON'T HAVE A GARBAGE DISPOSAL.
YOU DO NOW.
HO HO! I TOLD YOU HE'S SMART!

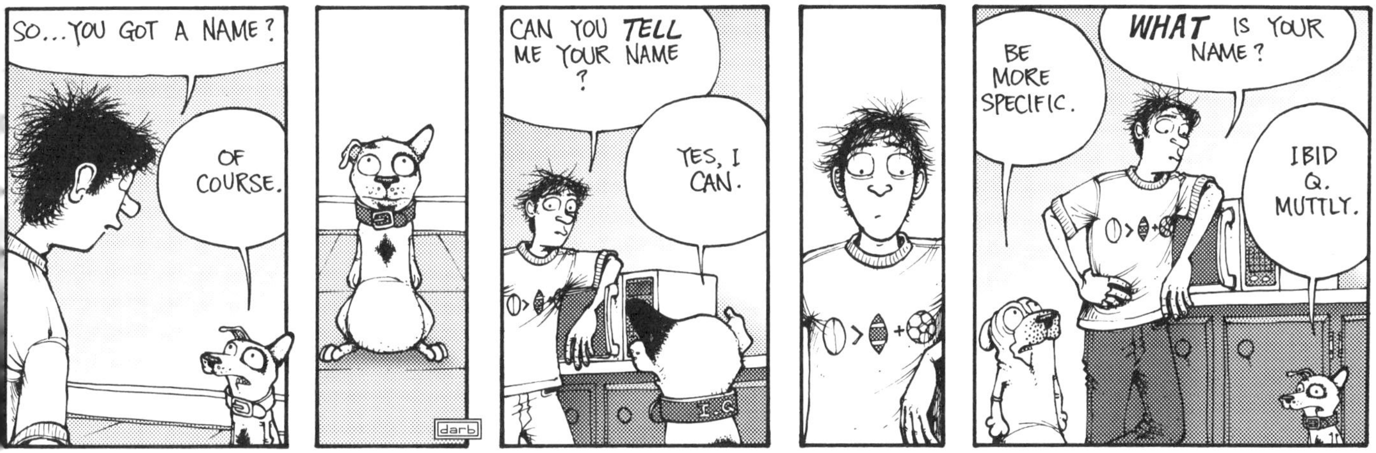
SO... YOU GOT A NAME?
OF COURSE.
darb
CAN YOU TELL ME YOUR NAME?
YES, I CAN.
BE MORE SPECIFIC.
WHAT IS YOUR NAME?
IBID Q. MUTTLY.

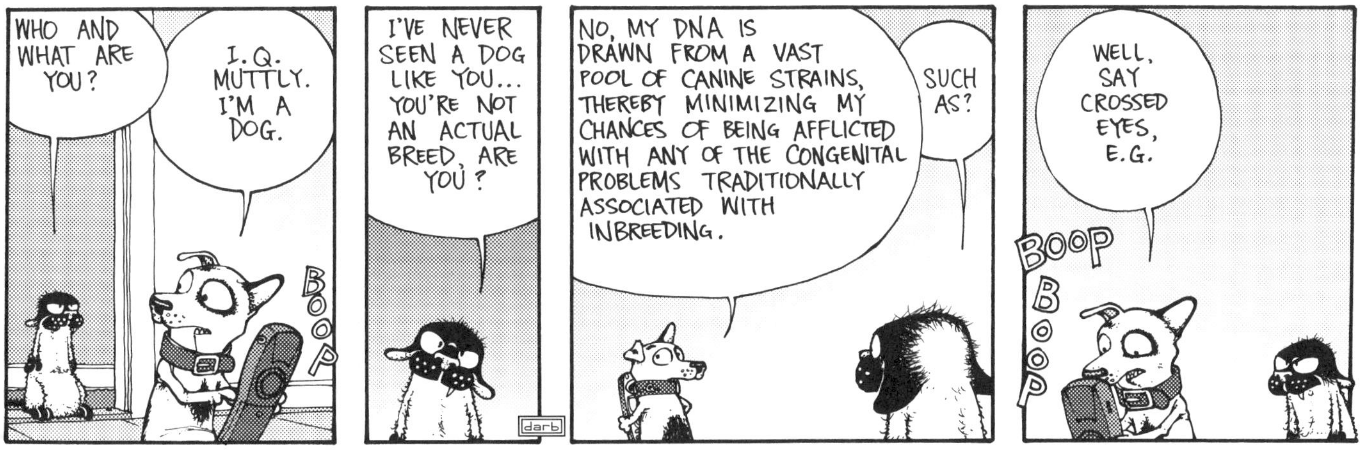
WHO AND WHAT ARE YOU?
I.Q. MUTTLY. I'M A DOG.
BOOP
I'VE NEVER SEEN A DOG LIKE YOU... YOU'RE NOT AN ACTUAL BREED, ARE YOU?
darb
NO, MY DNA IS DRAWN FROM A VAST POOL OF CANINE STRAINS, THEREBY MINIMIZING MY CHANCES OF BEING AFFLICTED WITH ANY OF THE CONGENITAL PROBLEMS TRADITIONALLY ASSOCIATED WITH INBREEDING.
SUCH AS?
BOOP
BOOP
WELL, SAY CROSSED EYES, E.G.

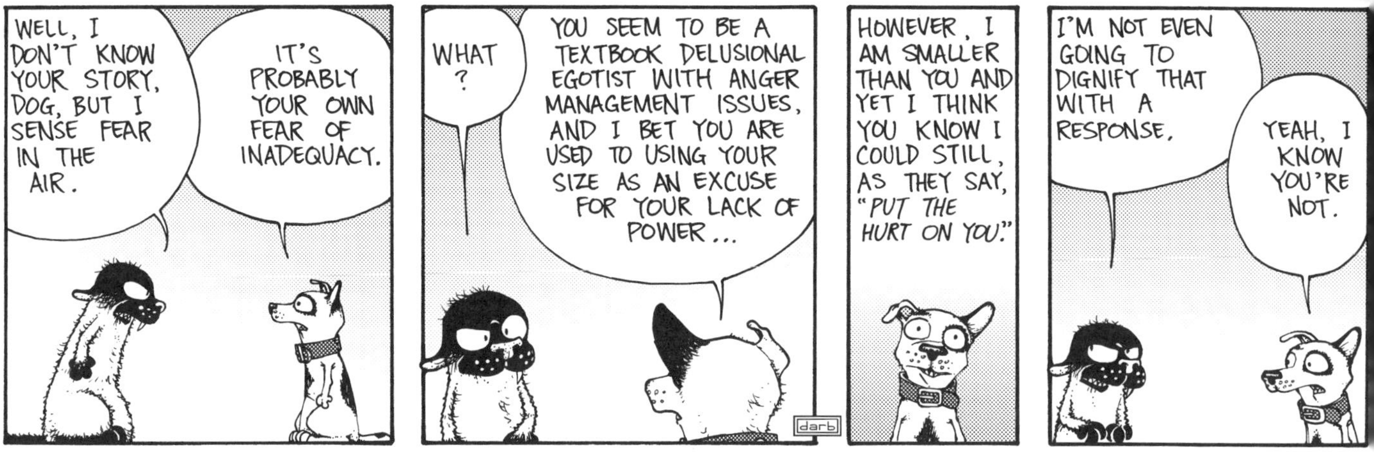
WELL, I DON'T KNOW YOUR STORY, DOG, BUT I SENSE FEAR IN THE AIR.
IT'S PROBABLY YOUR OWN FEAR OF INADEQUACY.
WHAT?
YOU SEEM TO BE A TEXTBOOK DELUSIONAL EGOTIST WITH ANGER MANAGEMENT ISSUES, AND I BET YOU ARE USED TO USING YOUR SIZE AS AN EXCUSE FOR YOUR LACK OF POWER...
darb
HOWEVER, I AM SMALLER THAN YOU AND YET I THINK YOU KNOW I COULD STILL, AS THEY SAY, "PUT THE HURT ON YOU."
I'M NOT EVEN GOING TO DIGNIFY THAT WITH A RESPONSE.
YEAH, I KNOW YOU'RE NOT.

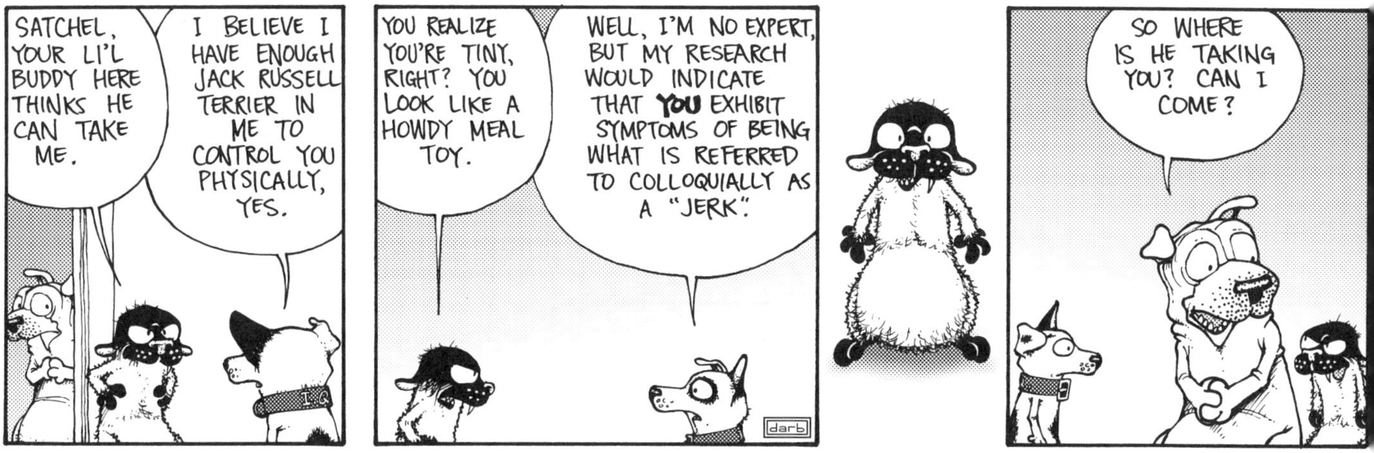
SATCHEL, YOUR LI'L BUDDY HERE THINKS HE CAN TAKE ME.
I BELIEVE I HAVE ENOUGH JACK RUSSELL TERRIER IN ME TO CONTROL YOU PHYSICALLY, YES.
YOU REALIZE YOU'RE TINY, RIGHT? YOU LOOK LIKE A HOWDY MEAL TOY.
WELL, I'M NO EXPERT, BUT MY RESEARCH WOULD INDICATE THAT **YOU** EXHIBIT SYMPTOMS OF BEING WHAT IS REFERRED TO COLLOQUIALLY AS A "JERK."
darb
SO WHERE IS HE TAKING YOU? CAN I COME?

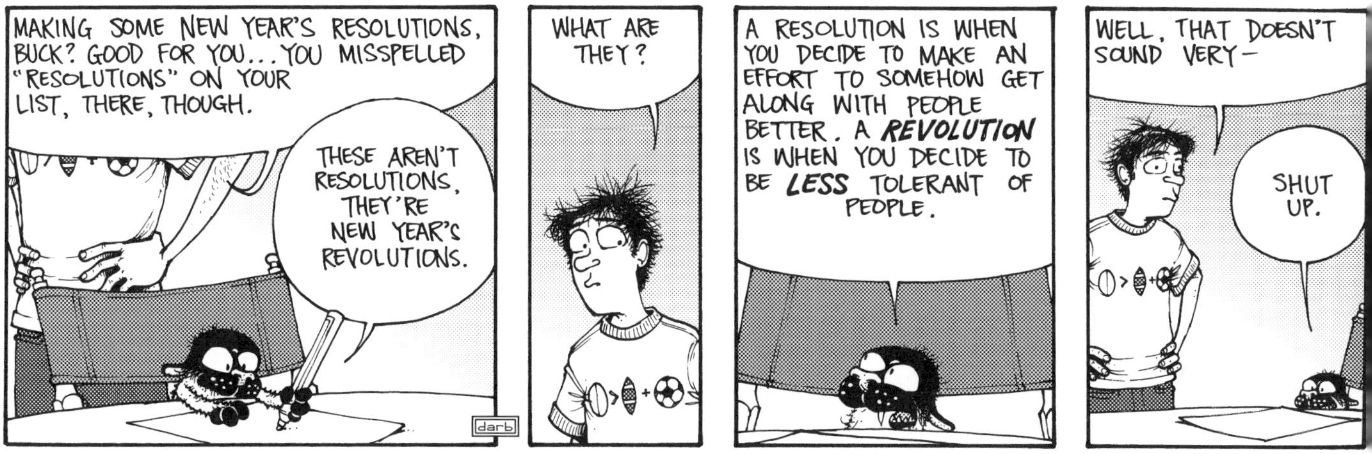
MAKING SOME NEW YEAR'S RESOLUTIONS, BUCK? GOOD FOR YOU... YOU MISSPELLED "RESOLUTIONS" ON YOUR LIST, THERE, THOUGH.
THESE AREN'T RESOLUTIONS, THEY'RE NEW YEAR'S REVOLUTIONS.
darb
WHAT ARE THEY?
A RESOLUTION IS WHEN YOU DECIDE TO MAKE AN EFFORT TO SOMEHOW GET ALONG WITH PEOPLE BETTER. A ***REVOLUTION*** IS WHEN YOU DECIDE TO BE ***LESS*** TOLERANT OF PEOPLE.
WELL, THAT DOESN'T SOUND VERY—
SHUT UP.

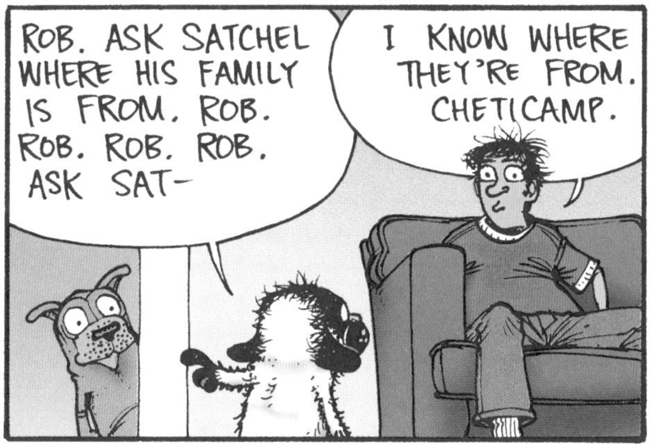
ROB. ASK SATCHEL WHERE HIS FAMILY IS FROM. ROB. ROB. ROB. ROB. ASK SAT-
I KNOW WHERE THEY'RE FROM. CHETICAMP.

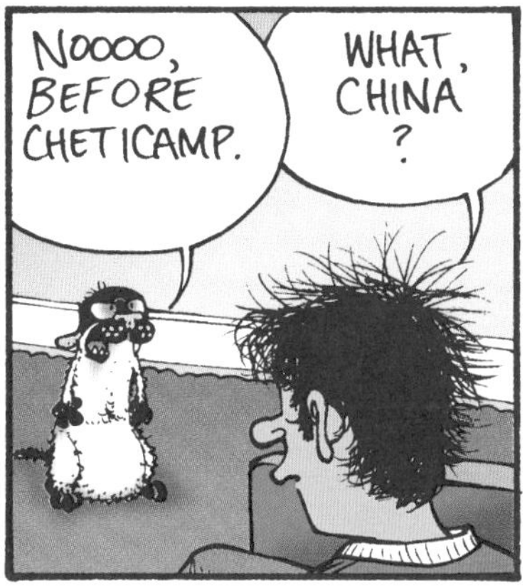
NOOOO, BEFORE CHETICAMP.
WHAT, CHINA ?

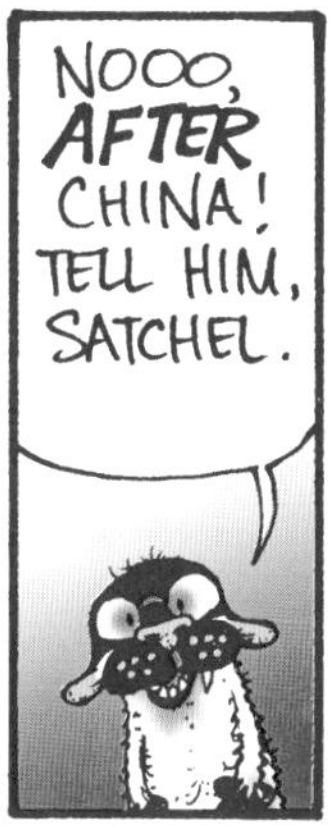
NOOO, AFTER CHINA! TELL HIM, SATCHEL.

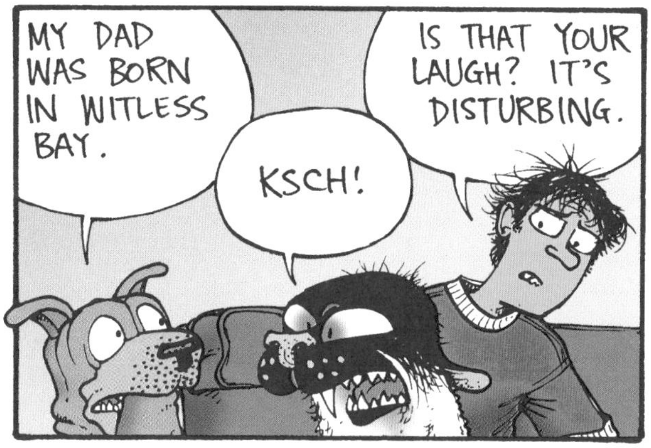
MY DAD WAS BORN IN WITLESS BAY.
KSCH!
IS THAT YOUR LAUGH? IT'S DISTURBING.

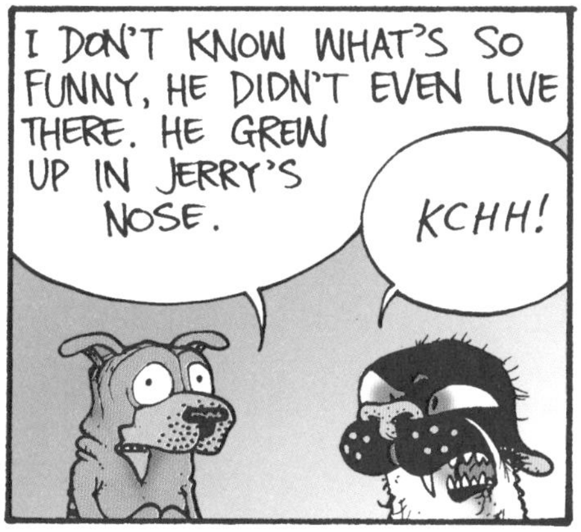
I DON'T KNOW WHAT'S SO FUNNY, HE DIDN'T EVEN LIVE THERE. HE GREW UP IN JERRY'S NOSE.
KCHH!

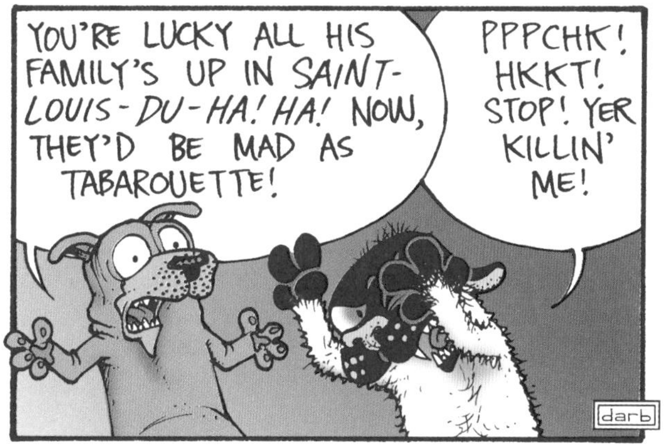
YOU'RE LUCKY ALL HIS FAMILY'S UP IN SAINT-LOUIS-DU-HA! HA! NOW, THEY'D BE MAD AS TABAROUETTE!
PPPCHK! HKKT! STOP! YER KILLIN' ME!
darb

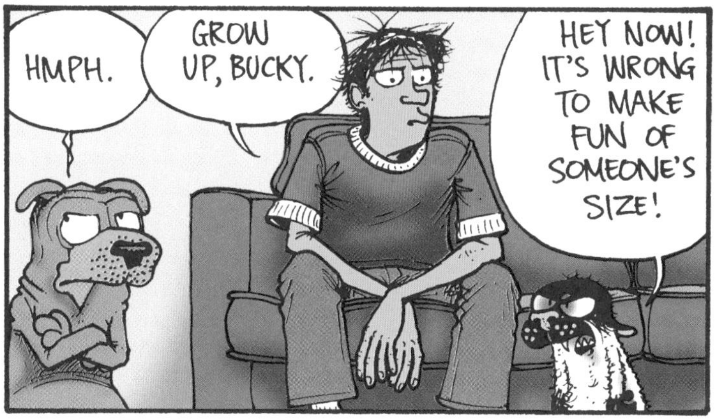
HMPH.
GROW UP, BUCKY.
HEY NOW! IT'S WRONG TO MAKE FUN OF SOMEONE'S SIZE!

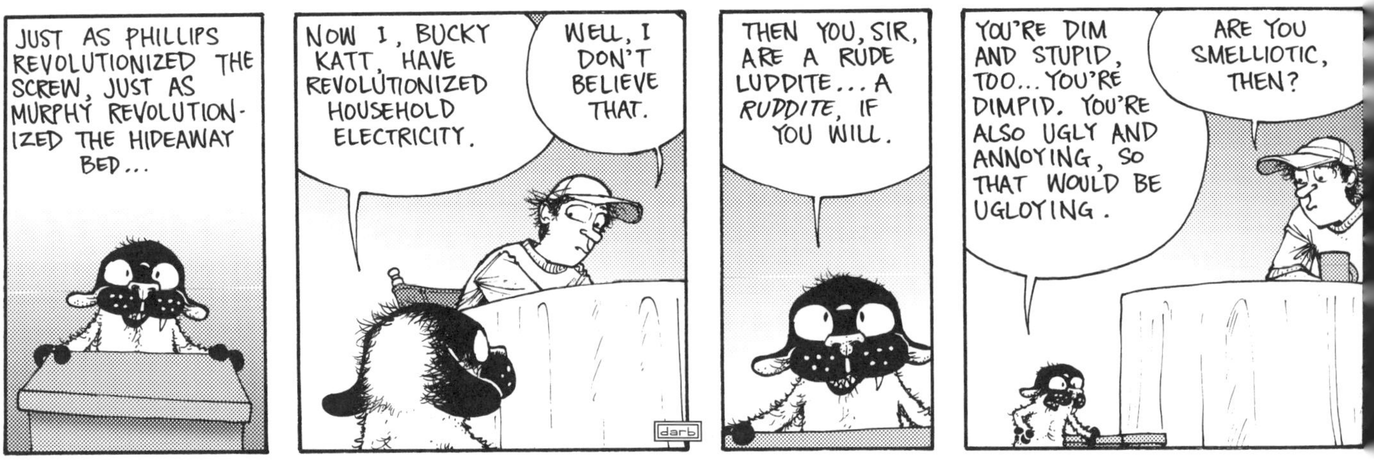
JUST AS PHILLIPS REVOLUTIONIZED THE SCREW, JUST AS MURPHY REVOLUTIONIZED THE HIDEAWAY BED...
NOW I, BUCKY KATT, HAVE REVOLUTIONIZED HOUSEHOLD ELECTRICITY.
WELL, I DON'T BELIEVE THAT.
THEN YOU, SIR, ARE A RUDE LUDDITE... A RUDDITE, IF YOU WILL.
YOU'RE DIM AND STUPID, TOO... YOU'RE DIMPID. YOU'RE ALSO UGLY AND ANNOYING, SO THAT WOULD BE UGLOYING.
ARE YOU SMELLIOTIC, THEN?

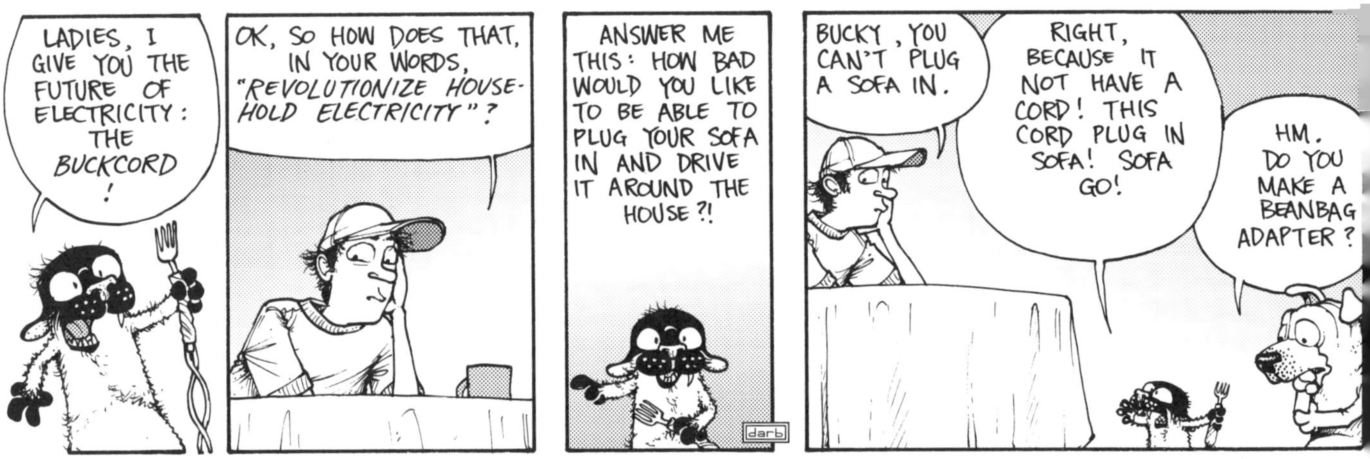
LADIES, I GIVE YOU THE FUTURE OF ELECTRICITY: THE BUCKCORD!
OK, SO HOW DOES THAT, IN YOUR WORDS, "REVOLUTIONIZE HOUSEHOLD ELECTRICITY"?
ANSWER ME THIS: HOW BAD WOULD YOU LIKE TO BE ABLE TO PLUG YOUR SOFA IN AND DRIVE IT AROUND THE HOUSE?!
BUCKY, YOU CAN'T PLUG A SOFA IN.
RIGHT, BECAUSE IT NOT HAVE A CORD! THIS CORD PLUG IN SOFA! SOFA GO!
HM. DO YOU MAKE A BEANBAG ADAPTER?

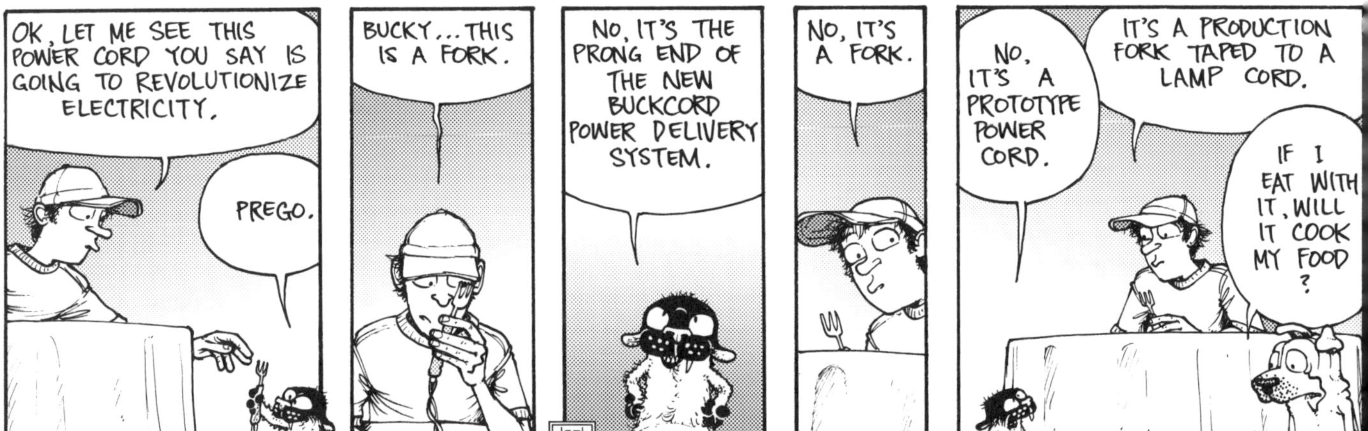
OK, LET ME SEE THIS POWER CORD YOU SAY IS GOING TO REVOLUTIONIZE ELECTRICITY.
PREGO.
BUCKY... THIS IS A FORK.
NO, IT'S THE PRONG END OF THE NEW BUCKCORD POWER DELIVERY SYSTEM.
NO, IT'S A FORK.
NO, IT'S A PROTOTYPE POWER CORD.
IT'S A PRODUCTION FORK TAPED TO A LAMP CORD.
IF I EAT WITH IT, WILL IT COOK MY FOOD?

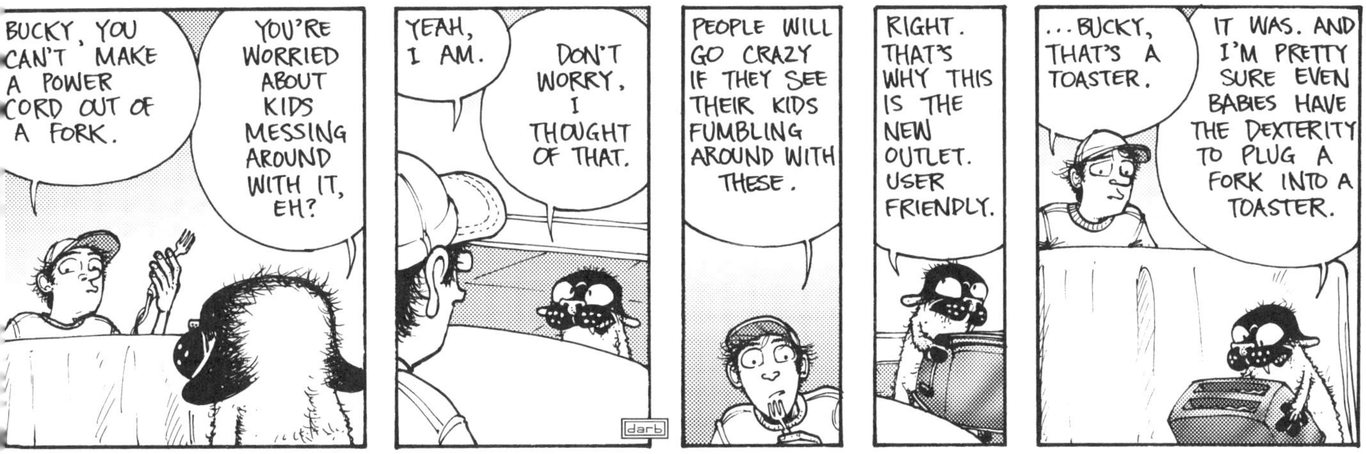
BUCKY, YOU CAN'T MAKE A POWER CORD OUT OF A FORK.
YOU'RE WORRIED ABOUT KIDS MESSING AROUND WITH IT, EH?
YEAH, I AM.
DON'T WORRY, I THOUGHT OF THAT.
PEOPLE WILL GO CRAZY IF THEY SEE THEIR KIDS FUMBLING AROUND WITH THESE.
RIGHT. THAT'S WHY THIS IS THE NEW OUTLET. USER FRIENDLY.
...BUCKY, THAT'S A TOASTER.
IT WAS. AND I'M PRETTY SURE EVEN BABIES HAVE THE DEXTERITY TO PLUG A FORK INTO A TOASTER.
darb

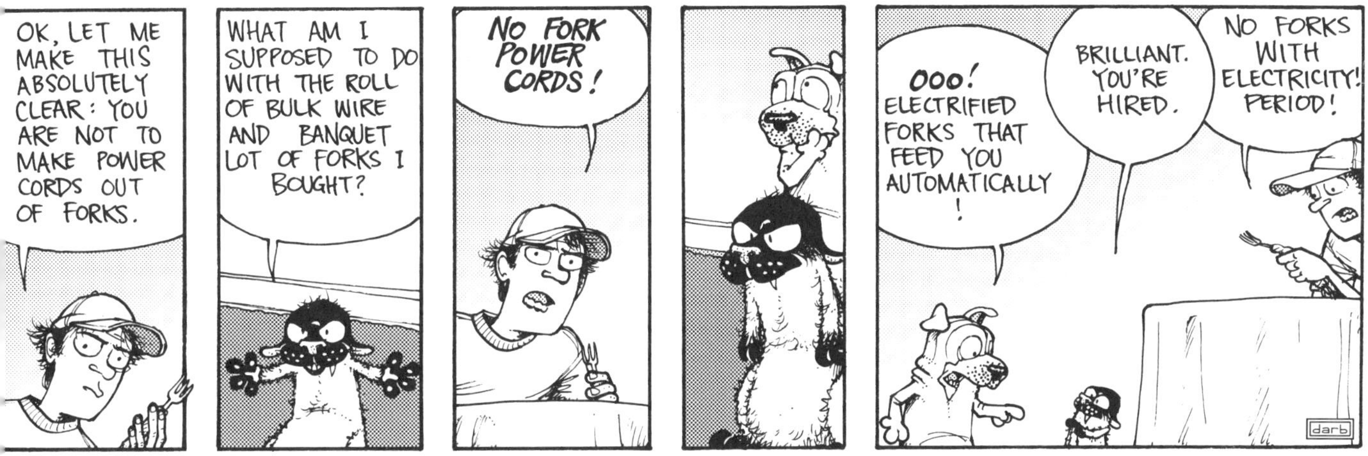
OK, LET ME MAKE THIS ABSOLUTELY CLEAR: YOU ARE NOT TO MAKE POWER CORDS OUT OF FORKS.
WHAT AM I SUPPOSED TO DO WITH THE ROLL OF BULK WIRE AND BANQUET LOT OF FORKS I BOUGHT?
NO FORK POWER CORDS!
OOO! ELECTRIFIED FORKS THAT FEED YOU AUTOMATICALLY!
BRILLIANT. YOU'RE HIRED.
NO FORKS WITH ELECTRICITY! PERIOD!
darb

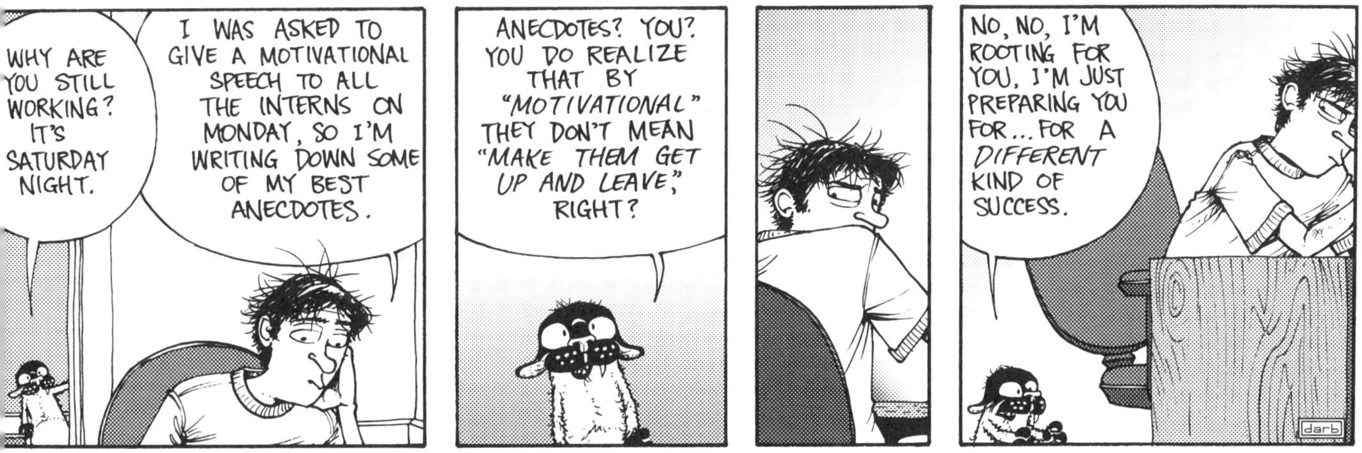
WHY ARE YOU STILL WORKING? IT'S SATURDAY NIGHT.
I WAS ASKED TO GIVE A MOTIVATIONAL SPEECH TO ALL THE INTERNS ON MONDAY, SO I'M WRITING DOWN SOME OF MY BEST ANECDOTES.
ANECDOTES? YOU? YOU DO REALIZE THAT BY "MOTIVATIONAL" THEY DON'T MEAN "MAKE THEM GET UP AND LEAVE," RIGHT?
NO, NO, I'M ROOTING FOR YOU, I'M JUST PREPARING YOU FOR... FOR A DIFFERENT KIND OF SUCCESS.
darb

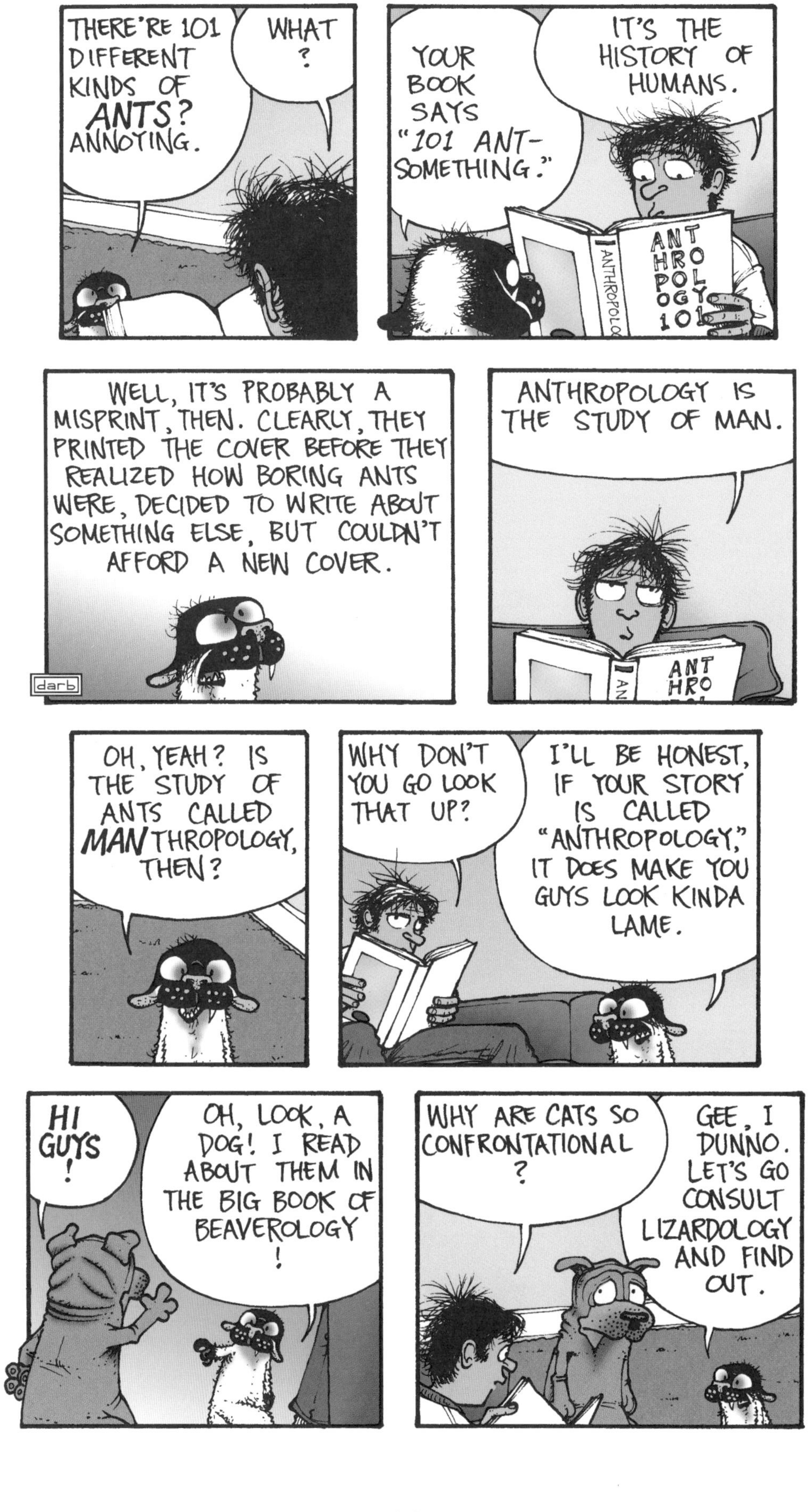
THERE'RE 101 DIFFERENT KINDS OF ANTS? ANNOYING.
WHAT?
YOUR BOOK SAYS "101 ANT-SOMETHING."
IT'S THE HISTORY OF HUMANS.
WELL, IT'S PROBABLY A MISPRINT, THEN. CLEARLY, THEY PRINTED THE COVER BEFORE THEY REALIZED HOW BORING ANTS WERE, DECIDED TO WRITE ABOUT SOMETHING ELSE, BUT COULDN'T AFFORD A NEW COVER.
ANTHROPOLOGY IS THE STUDY OF MAN.
OH, YEAH? IS THE STUDY OF ANTS CALLED MANTHROPOLOGY, THEN?
WHY DON'T YOU GO LOOK THAT UP?
I'LL BE HONEST, IF YOUR STORY IS CALLED "ANTHROPOLOGY," IT DOES MAKE YOU GUYS LOOK KINDA LAME.
HI GUYS!
OH, LOOK, A DOG! I READ ABOUT THEM IN THE BIG BOOK OF BEAVEROLOGY!
WHY ARE CATS SO CONFRONTATIONAL?
GEE, I DUNNO. LET'S GO CONSULT LIZARDOLOGY AND FIND OUT.

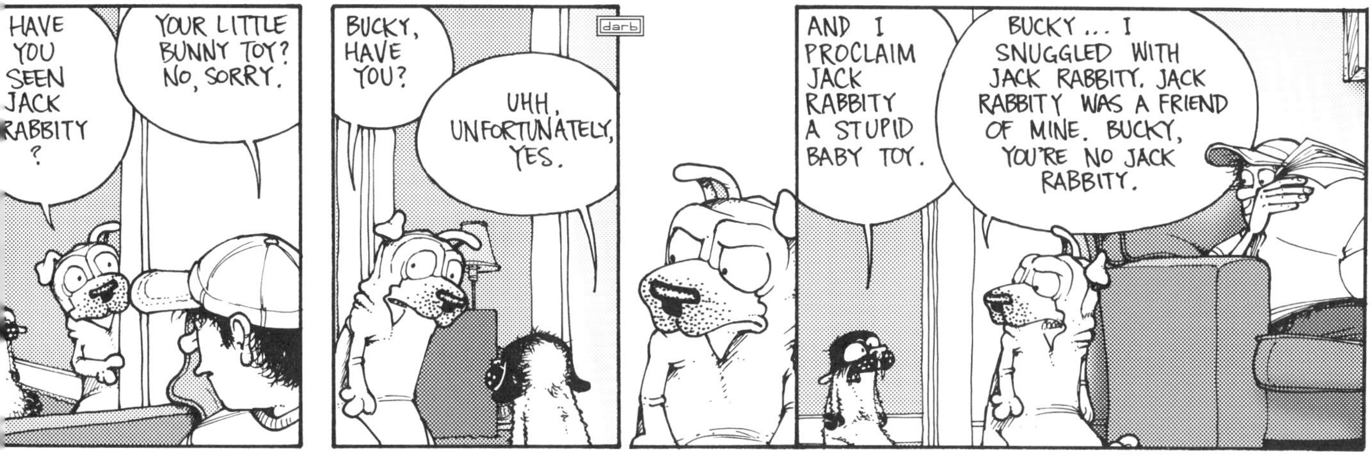
HAVE YOU SEEN JACK RABBITY ?
YOUR LITTLE BUNNY TOY? NO, SORRY.
darb
BUCKY, HAVE YOU?
UHH, UNFORTUNATELY, YES.
AND I PROCLAIM JACK RABBITY A STUPID BABY TOY.
BUCKY... I SNUGGLED WITH JACK RABBITY. JACK RABBITY WAS A FRIEND OF MINE. BUCKY, YOU'RE NO JACK RABBITY.

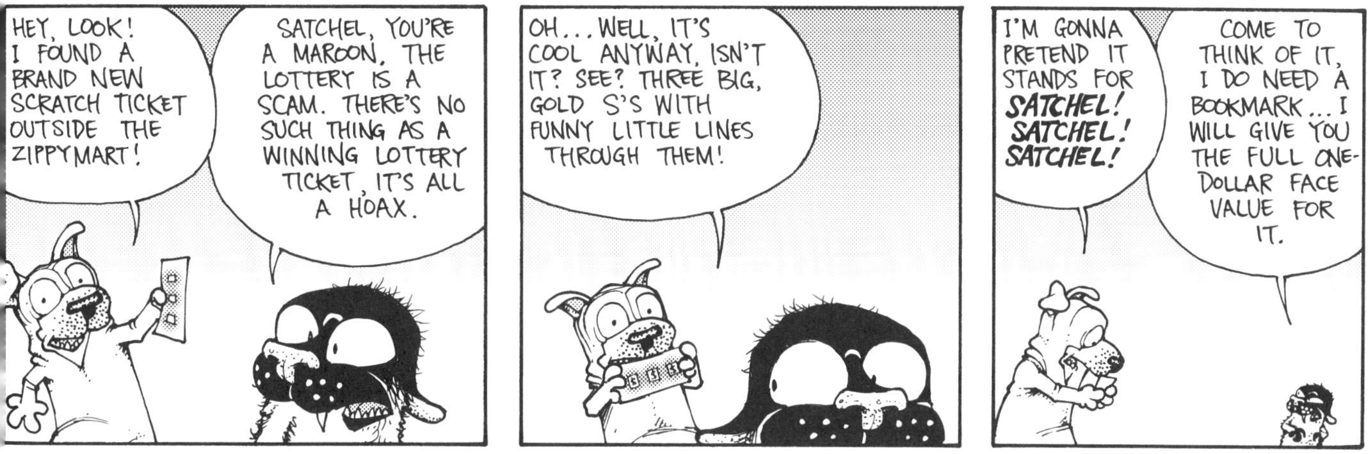
HEY, LOOK! I FOUND A BRAND NEW SCRATCH TICKET OUTSIDE THE ZIPPYMART!
SATCHEL, YOU'RE A MAROON. THE LOTTERY IS A SCAM. THERE'S NO SUCH THING AS A WINNING LOTTERY TICKET. IT'S ALL A HOAX.
OH... WELL, IT'S COOL ANYWAY, ISN'T IT? SEE? THREE BIG, GOLD S'S WITH FUNNY LITTLE LINES THROUGH THEM!
I'M GONNA PRETEND IT STANDS FOR SATCHEL! SATCHEL! SATCHEL!
COME TO THINK OF IT, I DO NEED A BOOKMARK... I WILL GIVE YOU THE FULL ONE-DOLLAR FACE VALUE FOR IT.

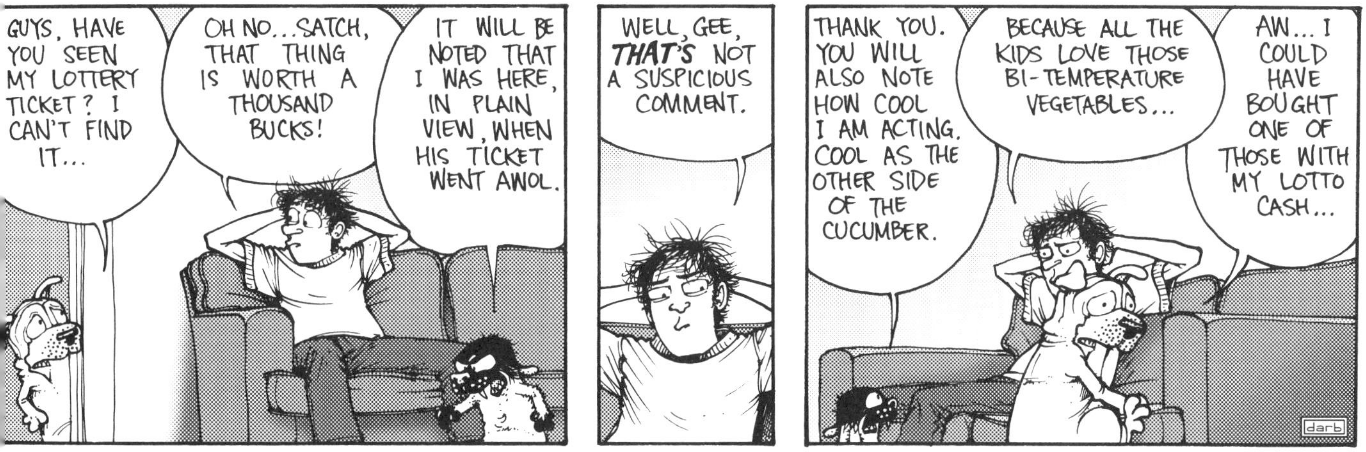
GUYS, HAVE YOU SEEN MY LOTTERY TICKET? I CAN'T FIND IT...
OH NO... SATCH, THAT THING IS WORTH A THOUSAND BUCKS!
IT WILL BE NOTED THAT I WAS HERE, IN PLAIN VIEW, WHEN HIS TICKET WENT AWOL.
WELL, GEE, THAT'S NOT A SUSPICIOUS COMMENT.
THANK YOU. YOU WILL ALSO NOTE HOW COOL I AM ACTING. COOL AS THE OTHER SIDE OF THE CUCUMBER.
BECAUSE ALL THE KIDS LOVE THOSE BI-TEMPERATURE VEGETABLES...
AW... I COULD HAVE BOUGHT ONE OF THOSE WITH MY LOTTO CASH...
darb

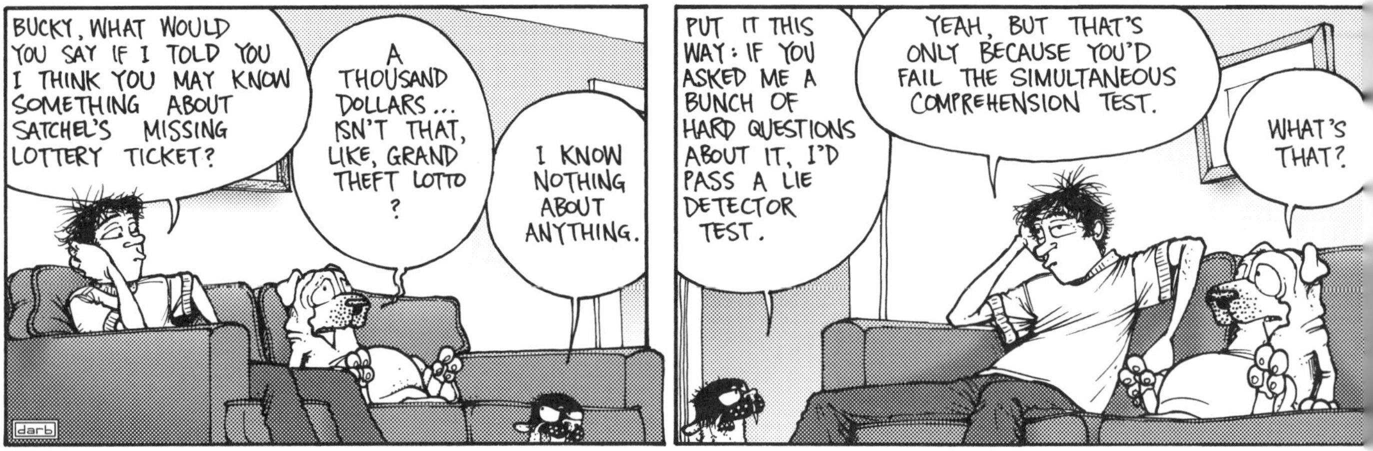
BUCKY, WHAT WOULD YOU SAY IF I TOLD YOU I THINK YOU MAY KNOW SOMETHING ABOUT SATCHEL'S MISSING LOTTERY TICKET?
A THOUSAND DOLLARS... ISN'T THAT, LIKE, GRAND THEFT LOTTO?
I KNOW NOTHING ABOUT ANYTHING.
PUT IT THIS WAY: IF YOU ASKED ME A BUNCH OF HARD QUESTIONS ABOUT IT, I'D PASS A LIE DETECTOR TEST.
YEAH, BUT THAT'S ONLY BECAUSE YOU'D FAIL THE SIMULTANEOUS COMPREHENSION TEST.
WHAT'S THAT?
darb

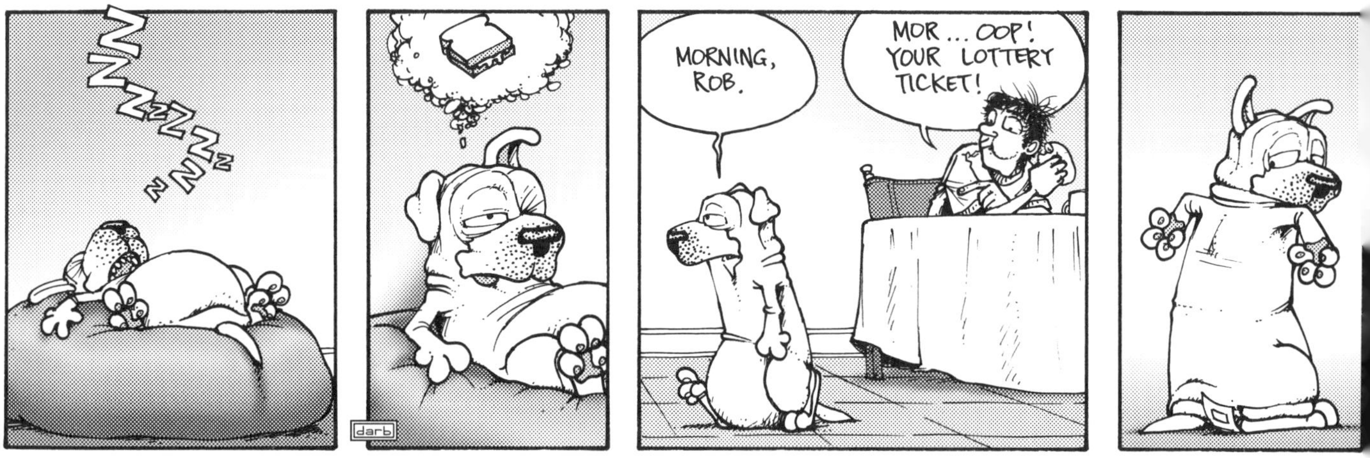
ZZZZZZZZ
darb
MORNING, ROB.
MOR... OOP! YOUR LOTTERY TICKET!

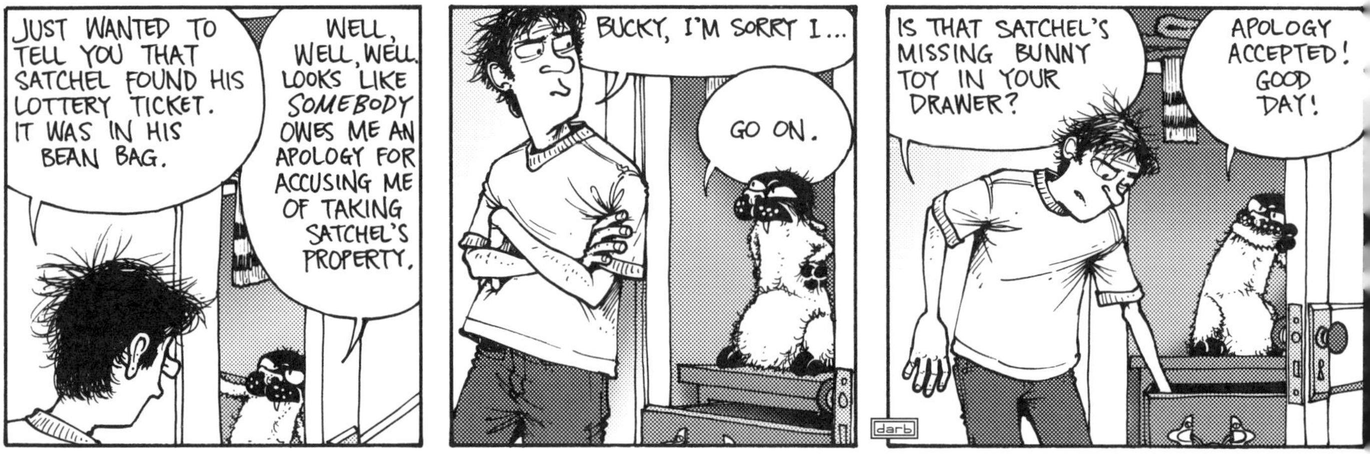
JUST WANTED TO TELL YOU THAT SATCHEL FOUND HIS LOTTERY TICKET. IT WAS IN HIS BEAN BAG.
WELL, WELL, WELL. LOOKS LIKE *SOMEBODY* OWES ME AN APOLOGY FOR ACCUSING ME OF TAKING SATCHEL'S PROPERTY.
BUCKY, I'M SORRY I...
GO ON.
IS THAT SATCHEL'S MISSING BUNNY TOY IN YOUR DRAWER?
APOLOGY ACCEPTED! GOOD DAY!
darb

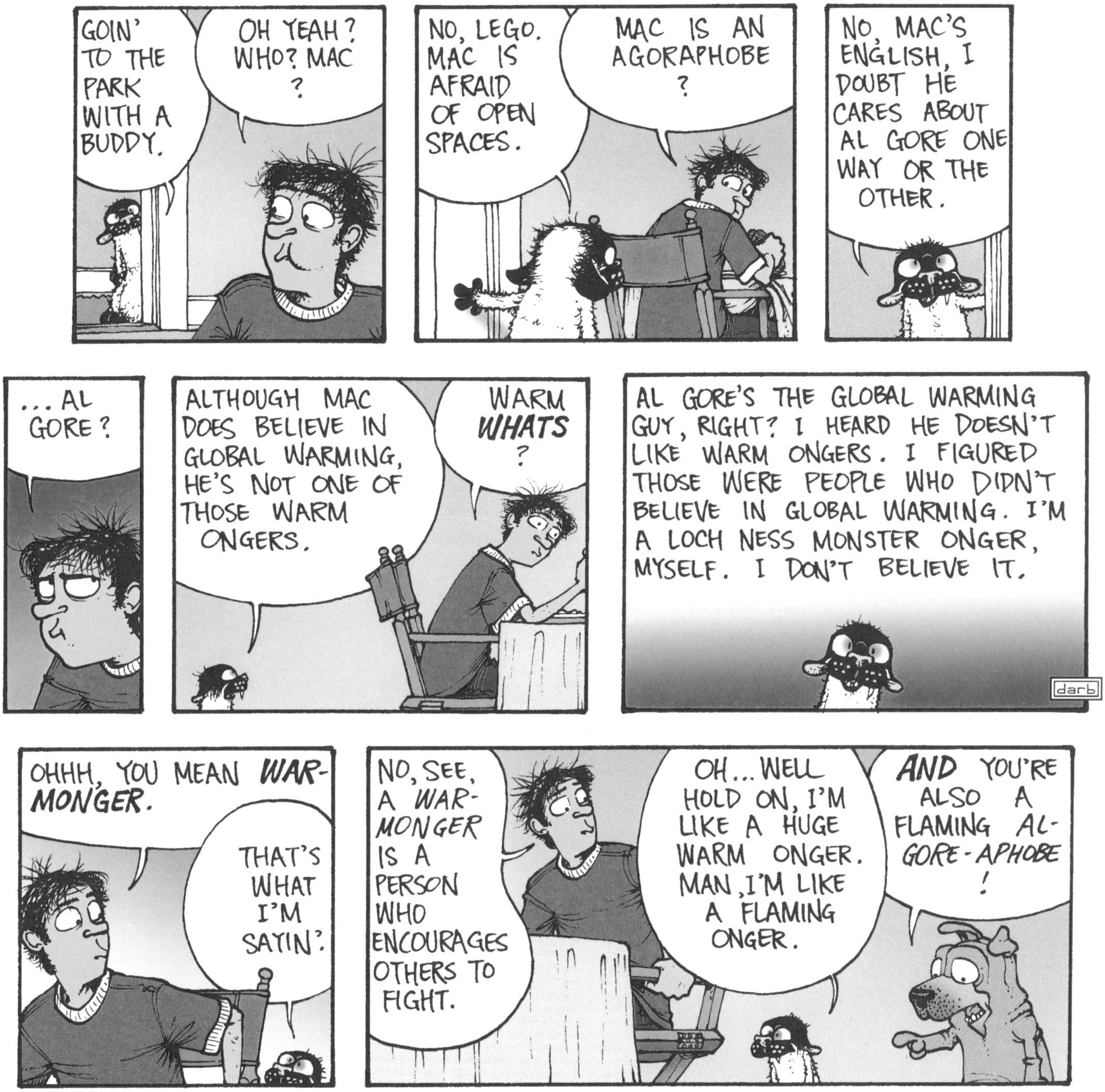
GOIN' TO THE PARK WITH A BUDDY.
OH YEAH? WHO? MAC?
NO, LEGO. MAC IS AFRAID OF OPEN SPACES.
MAC IS AN AGORAPHOBE?
NO, MAC'S ENGLISH, I DOUBT HE CARES ABOUT AL GORE ONE WAY OR THE OTHER.
... AL GORE?
ALTHOUGH MAC DOES BELIEVE IN GLOBAL WARMING, HE'S NOT ONE OF THOSE WARM ONGERS.
WARM **WHATS**?
AL GORE'S THE GLOBAL WARMING GUY, RIGHT? I HEARD HE DOESN'T LIKE WARM ONGERS. I FIGURED THOSE WERE PEOPLE WHO DIDN'T BELIEVE IN GLOBAL WARMING. I'M A LOCH NESS MONSTER ONGER, MYSELF. I DON'T BELIEVE IT.
darb
OHHH, YOU MEAN **WAR-MONGER**.
THAT'S WHAT I'M SAYIN'.
NO, SEE, A *WAR-MONGER* IS A PERSON WHO ENCOURAGES OTHERS TO FIGHT.
OH... WELL HOLD ON, I'M LIKE A HUGE WARM ONGER. MAN, I'M LIKE A FLAMING ONGER.
AND YOU'RE ALSO A FLAMING *AL-GORE-APHOBE*!

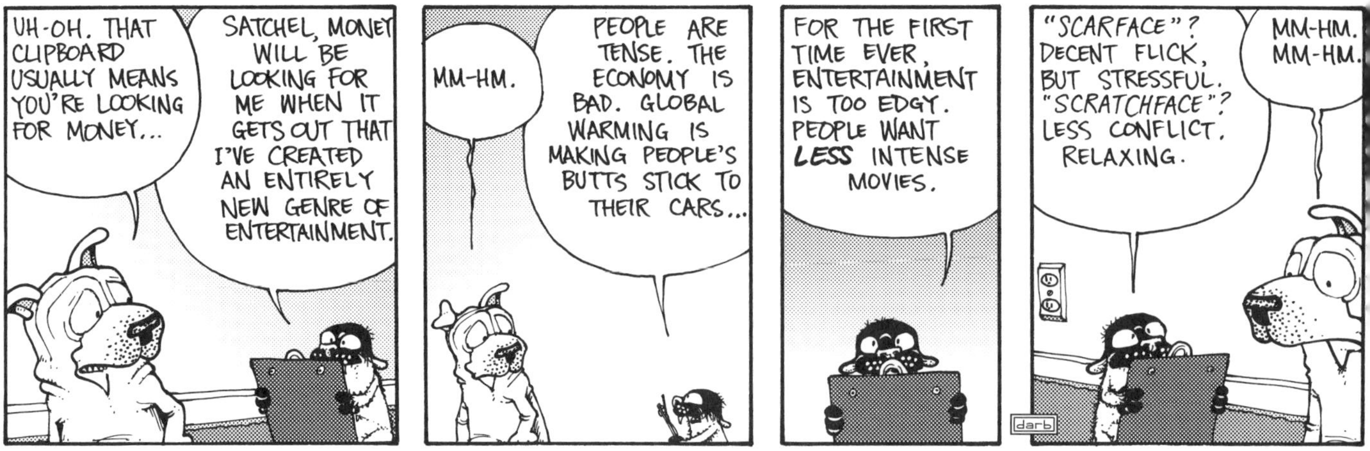
UH-OH. THAT CLIPBOARD USUALLY MEANS YOU'RE LOOKING FOR MONEY...
SATCHEL, MONEY WILL BE LOOKING FOR ME WHEN IT GETS OUT THAT I'VE CREATED AN ENTIRELY NEW GENRE OF ENTERTAINMENT.
MM-HM.
PEOPLE ARE TENSE. THE ECONOMY IS BAD. GLOBAL WARMING IS MAKING PEOPLE'S BUTTS STICK TO THEIR CARS...
FOR THE FIRST TIME EVER, ENTERTAINMENT IS TOO EDGY. PEOPLE WANT **LESS** INTENSE MOVIES.
"SCARFACE"? DECENT FLICK, BUT STRESSFUL. "SCRATCHFACE"? LESS CONFLICT. RELAXING.
MM-HM. MM-HM.
darb

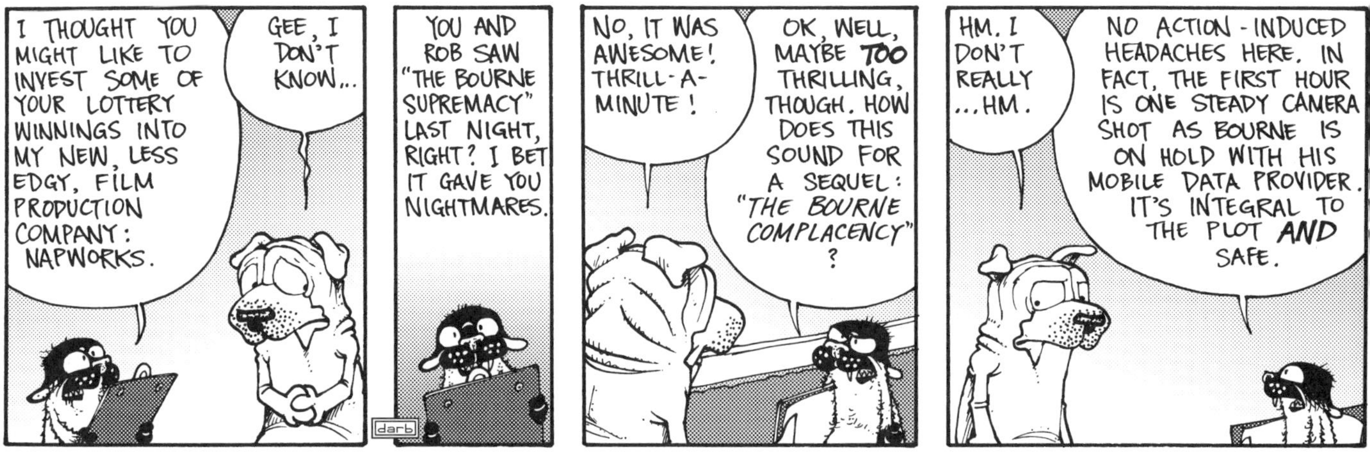
I THOUGHT YOU MIGHT LIKE TO INVEST SOME OF YOUR LOTTERY WINNINGS INTO MY NEW, LESS EDGY, FILM PRODUCTION COMPANY: NAPWORKS.
GEE, I DON'T KNOW...
YOU AND ROB SAW "THE BOURNE SUPREMACY" LAST NIGHT, RIGHT? I BET IT GAVE YOU NIGHTMARES.
darb
NO, IT WAS AWESOME! THRILL-A-MINUTE!
OK, WELL, MAYBE **TOO** THRILLING, THOUGH. HOW DOES THIS SOUND FOR A SEQUEL: *"THE BOURNE COMPLACENCY"*?
HM. I DON'T REALLY ...HM.
NO ACTION-INDUCED HEADACHES HERE. IN FACT, THE FIRST HOUR IS ONE STEADY CAMERA SHOT AS BOURNE IS ON HOLD WITH HIS MOBILE DATA PROVIDER. IT'S INTEGRAL TO THE PLOT **AND** SAFE.

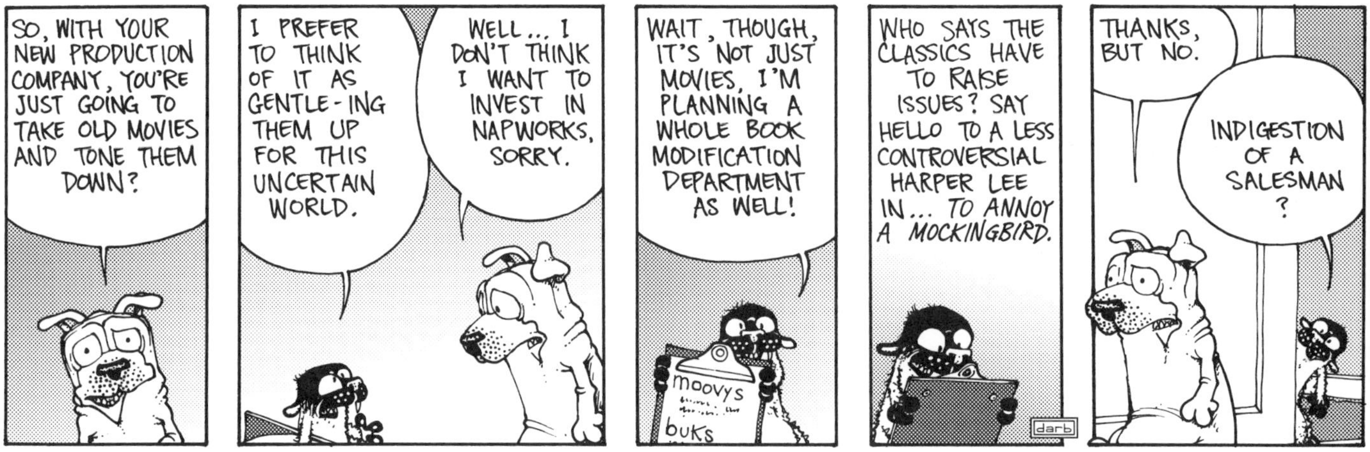
SO, WITH YOUR NEW PRODUCTION COMPANY, YOU'RE JUST GOING TO TAKE OLD MOVIES AND TONE THEM DOWN?
I PREFER TO THINK OF IT AS GENTLE-ING THEM UP FOR THIS UNCERTAIN WORLD.
WELL... I DON'T THINK I WANT TO INVEST IN NAPWORKS. SORRY.
WAIT, THOUGH, IT'S NOT JUST MOVIES. I'M PLANNING A WHOLE BOOK MODIFICATION DEPARTMENT AS WELL!
moovys
buks
WHO SAYS THE CLASSICS HAVE TO RAISE ISSUES? SAY HELLO TO A LESS CONTROVERSIAL HARPER LEE IN... *TO ANNOY A MOCKINGBIRD.*
darb
THANKS, BUT NO.
INDIGESTION OF A SALESMAN?

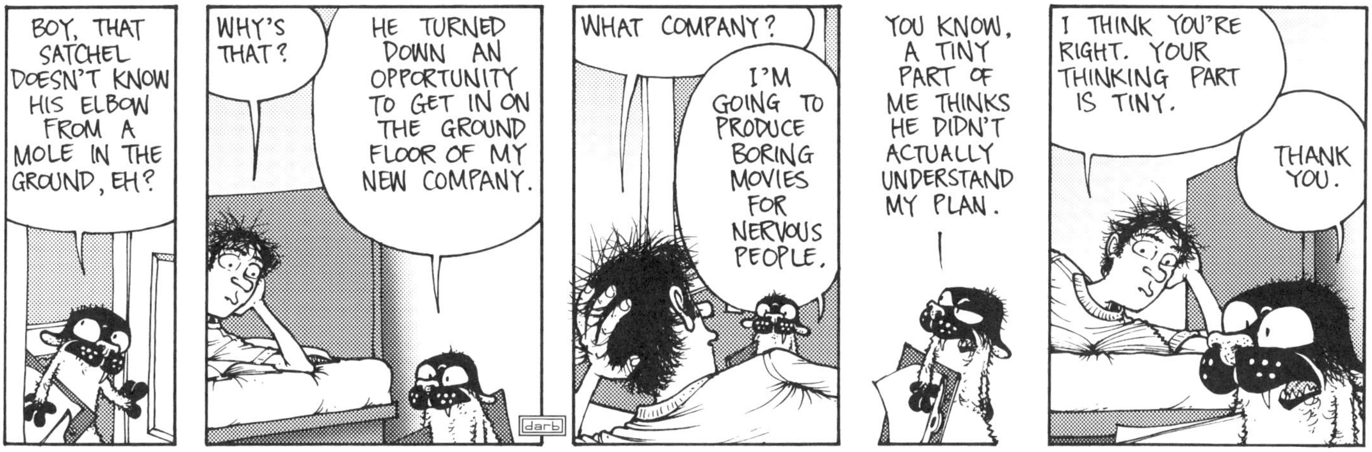
BOY, THAT SATCHEL DOESN'T KNOW HIS ELBOW FROM A MOLE IN THE GROUND, EH?
WHY'S THAT?
HE TURNED DOWN AN OPPORTUNITY TO GET IN ON THE GROUND FLOOR OF MY NEW COMPANY.
WHAT COMPANY?
I'M GOING TO PRODUCE BORING MOVIES FOR NERVOUS PEOPLE.
YOU KNOW, A TINY PART OF ME THINKS HE DIDN'T ACTUALLY UNDERSTAND MY PLAN.
I THINK YOU'RE RIGHT. YOUR THINKING PART IS TINY.
THANK YOU.

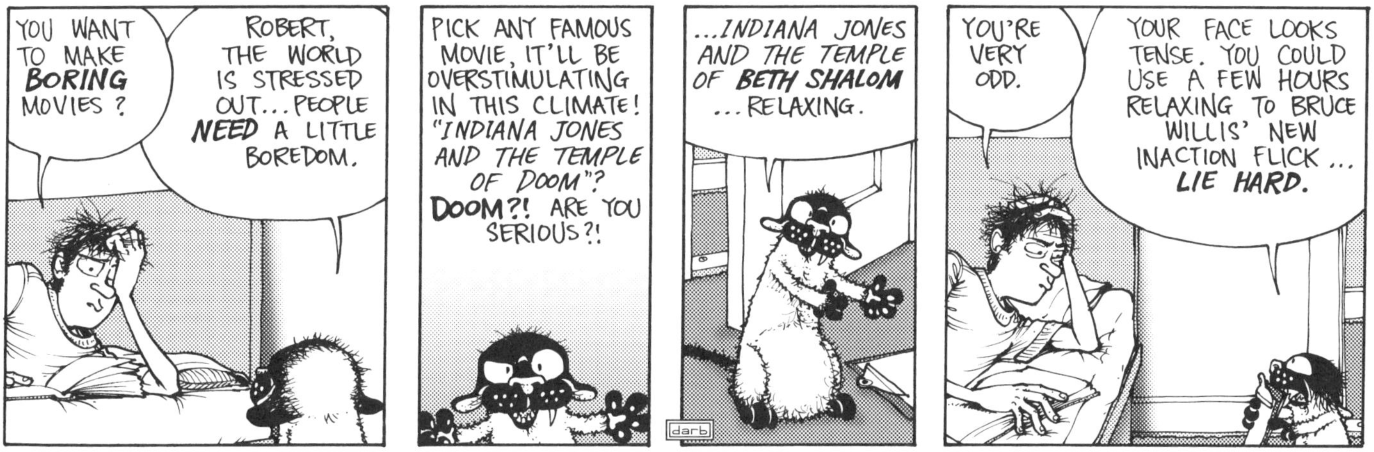
YOU WANT TO MAKE **BORING** MOVIES?
ROBERT, THE WORLD IS STRESSED OUT... PEOPLE **NEED** A LITTLE BOREDOM.
PICK ANY FAMOUS MOVIE, IT'LL BE OVERSTIMULATING IN THIS CLIMATE! "*INDIANA JONES AND THE TEMPLE OF DOOM*"? **DOOM?!** ARE YOU SERIOUS?!
...*INDIANA JONES AND THE TEMPLE OF* ***BETH SHALOM*** ...RELAXING.
YOU'RE VERY ODD.
YOUR FACE LOOKS TENSE. YOU COULD USE A FEW HOURS RELAXING TO BRUCE WILLIS' NEW INACTION FLICK... **LIE HARD.**

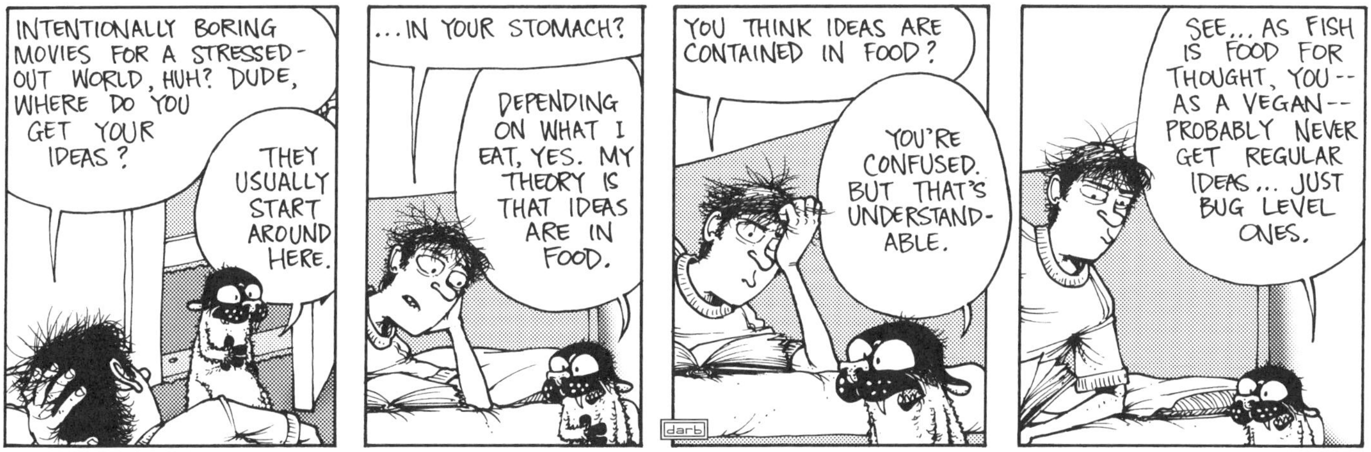
INTENTIONALLY BORING MOVIES FOR A STRESSED-OUT WORLD, HUH? DUDE, WHERE DO YOU GET YOUR IDEAS?
THEY USUALLY START AROUND HERE.
...IN YOUR STOMACH?
DEPENDING ON WHAT I EAT, YES. MY THEORY IS THAT IDEAS ARE IN FOOD.
YOU THINK IDEAS ARE CONTAINED IN FOOD?
YOU'RE CONFUSED. BUT THAT'S UNDERSTANDABLE.
SEE... AS FISH IS FOOD FOR THOUGHT, YOU--AS A VEGAN--PROBABLY NEVER GET REGULAR IDEAS... JUST BUG LEVEL ONES.

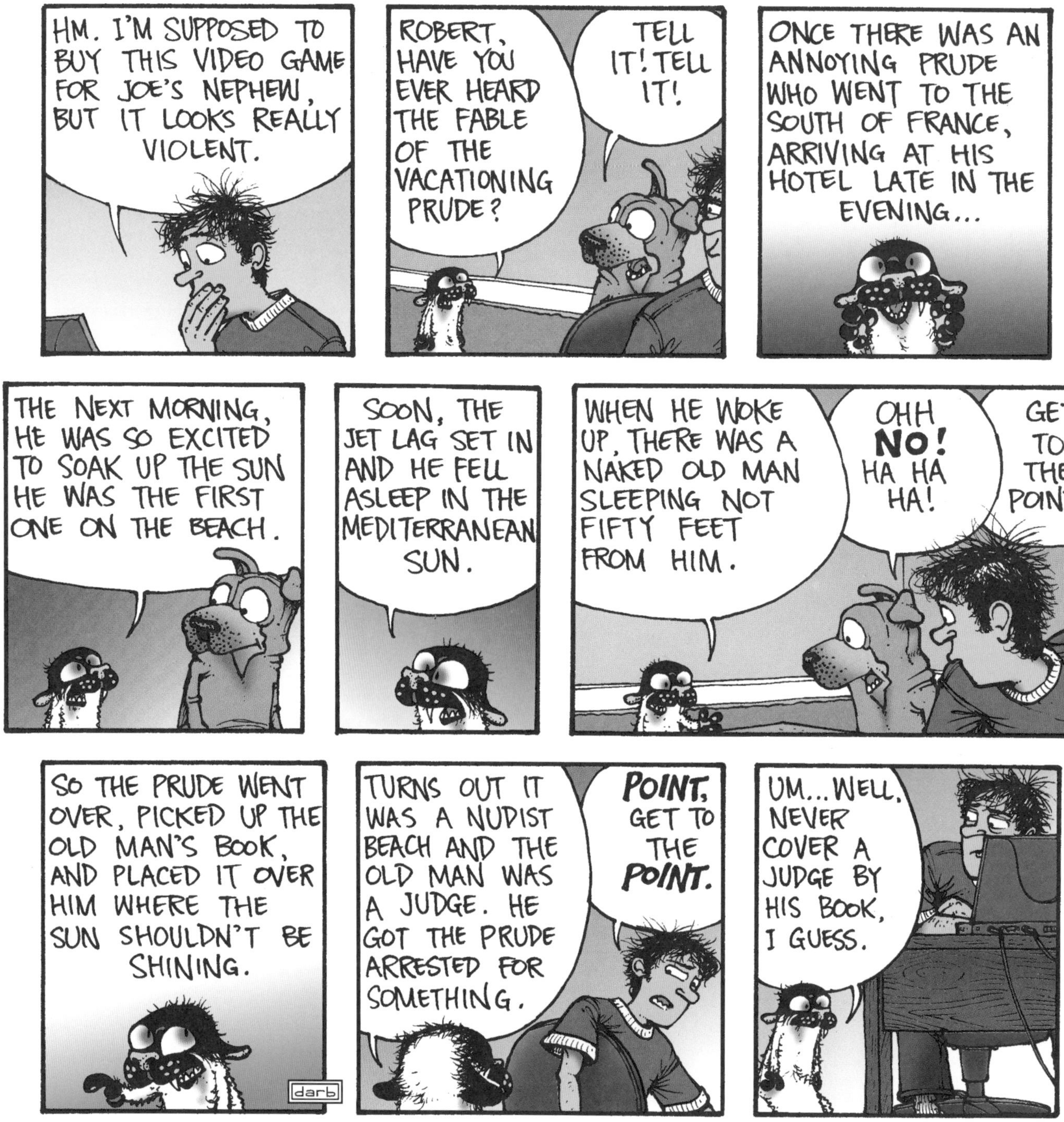
HM. I'M SUPPOSED TO BUY THIS VIDEO GAME FOR JOE'S NEPHEW, BUT IT LOOKS REALLY VIOLENT.
ROBERT, HAVE YOU EVER HEARD THE FABLE OF THE VACATIONING PRUDE?
TELL IT! TELL IT!
ONCE THERE WAS AN ANNOYING PRUDE WHO WENT TO THE SOUTH OF FRANCE, ARRIVING AT HIS HOTEL LATE IN THE EVENING...
THE NEXT MORNING, HE WAS SO EXCITED TO SOAK UP THE SUN HE WAS THE FIRST ONE ON THE BEACH.
SOON, THE JET LAG SET IN AND HE FELL ASLEEP IN THE MEDITERRANEAN SUN.
WHEN HE WOKE UP, THERE WAS A NAKED OLD MAN SLEEPING NOT FIFTY FEET FROM HIM.
OHH NO! HA HA HA!
GET TO THE POINT.
SO THE PRUDE WENT OVER, PICKED UP THE OLD MAN'S BOOK, AND PLACED IT OVER HIM WHERE THE SUN SHOULDN'T BE SHINING.
darb
TURNS OUT IT WAS A NUDIST BEACH AND THE OLD MAN WAS A JUDGE. HE GOT THE PRUDE ARRESTED FOR SOMETHING.
POINT, GET TO THE POINT.
UM... WELL, NEVER COVER A JUDGE BY HIS BOOK, I GUESS.

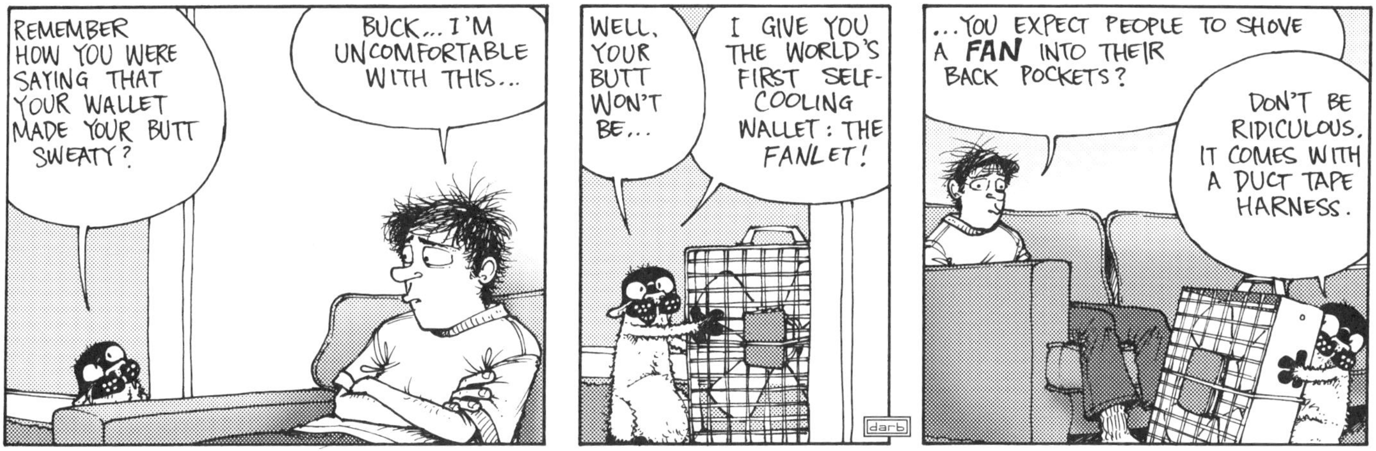
REMEMBER HOW YOU WERE SAYING THAT YOUR WALLET MADE YOUR BUTT SWEATY?
BUCK... I'M UNCOMFORTABLE WITH THIS...
WELL, YOUR BUTT WON'T BE...
I GIVE YOU THE WORLD'S FIRST SELF-COOLING WALLET: THE FANLET!
darb
...YOU EXPECT PEOPLE TO SHOVE A FAN INTO THEIR BACK POCKETS?
DON'T BE RIDICULOUS. IT COMES WITH A DUCT TAPE HARNESS.

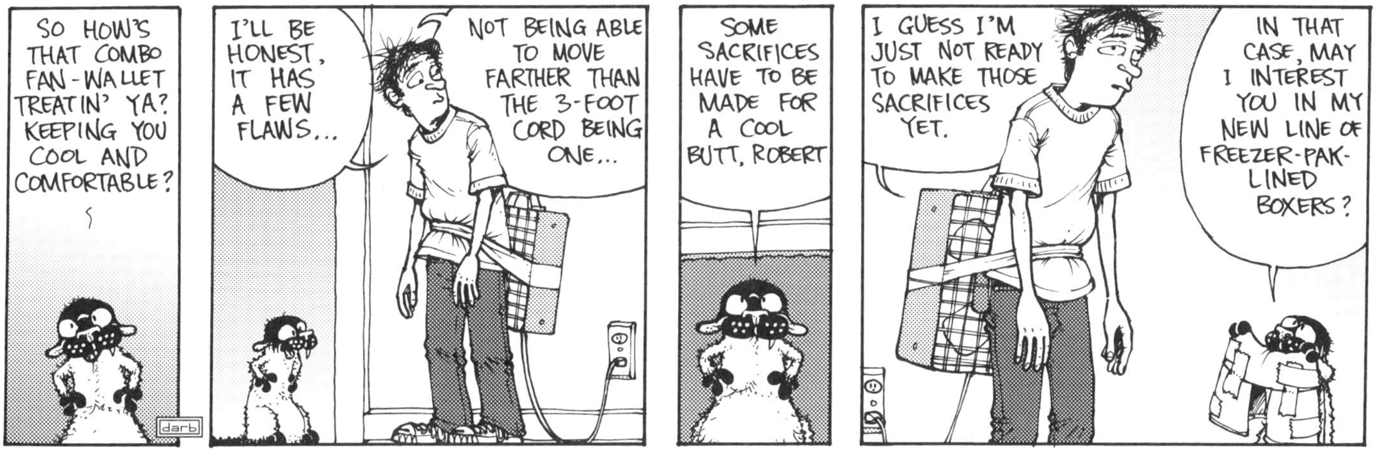
SO HOW'S THAT COMBO FAN-WALLET TREATIN' YA? KEEPING YOU COOL AND COMFORTABLE?
darb
I'LL BE HONEST, IT HAS A FEW FLAWS...
NOT BEING ABLE TO MOVE FARTHER THAN THE 3-FOOT CORD BEING ONE...
SOME SACRIFICES HAVE TO BE MADE FOR A COOL BUTT, ROBERT
I GUESS I'M JUST NOT READY TO MAKE THOSE SACRIFICES YET.
IN THAT CASE, MAY I INTEREST YOU IN MY NEW LINE OF FREEZER-PAK-LINED BOXERS?

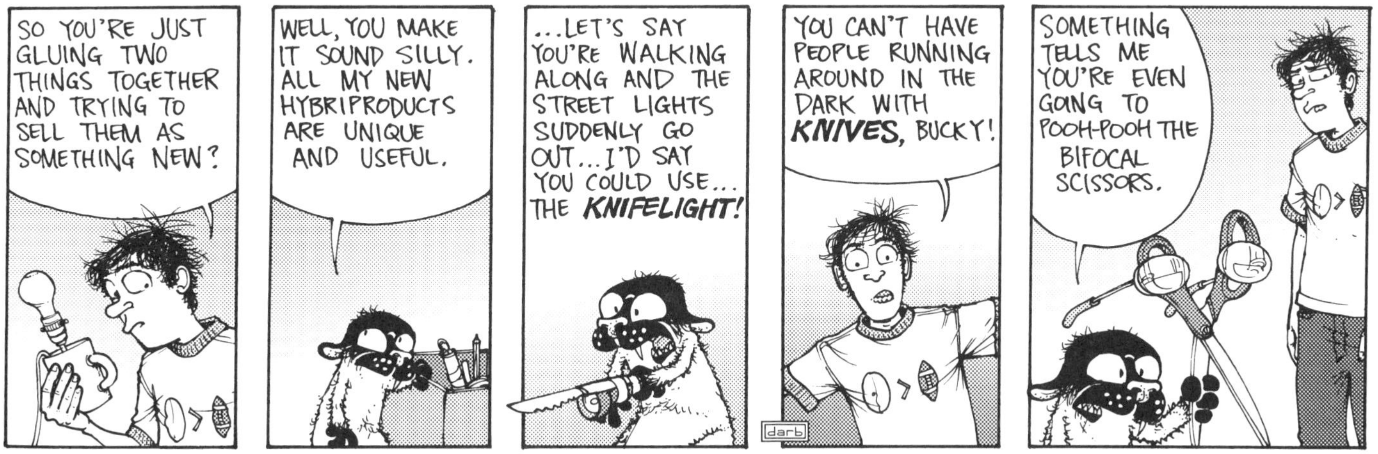
SO YOU'RE JUST GLUING TWO THINGS TOGETHER AND TRYING TO SELL THEM AS SOMETHING NEW?
WELL, YOU MAKE IT SOUND SILLY. ALL MY NEW HYBRIPRODUCTS ARE UNIQUE AND USEFUL.
...LET'S SAY YOU'RE WALKING ALONG AND THE STREET LIGHTS SUDDENLY GO OUT... I'D SAY YOU COULD USE... THE KNIFELIGHT!
darb
YOU CAN'T HAVE PEOPLE RUNNING AROUND IN THE DARK WITH KNIVES, BUCKY!
SOMETHING TELLS ME YOU'RE EVEN GOING TO POOH-POOH THE BIFOCAL SCISSORS.

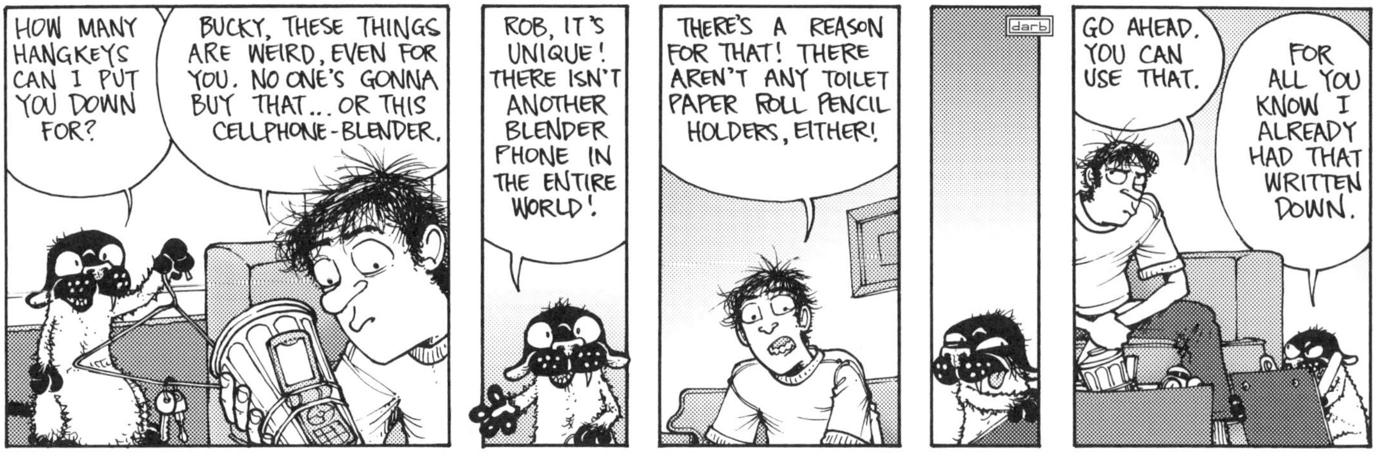
HOW MANY HANGKEYS CAN I PUT YOU DOWN FOR?
BUCKY, THESE THINGS ARE WEIRD, EVEN FOR YOU. NO ONE'S GONNA BUY THAT... OR THIS CELLPHONE-BLENDER.
ROB, IT'S UNIQUE! THERE ISN'T ANOTHER BLENDER PHONE IN THE ENTIRE WORLD!
THERE'S A REASON FOR THAT! THERE AREN'T ANY TOILET PAPER ROLL PENCIL HOLDERS, EITHER!
darb
GO AHEAD. YOU CAN USE THAT.
FOR ALL YOU KNOW I ALREADY HAD THAT WRITTEN DOWN.

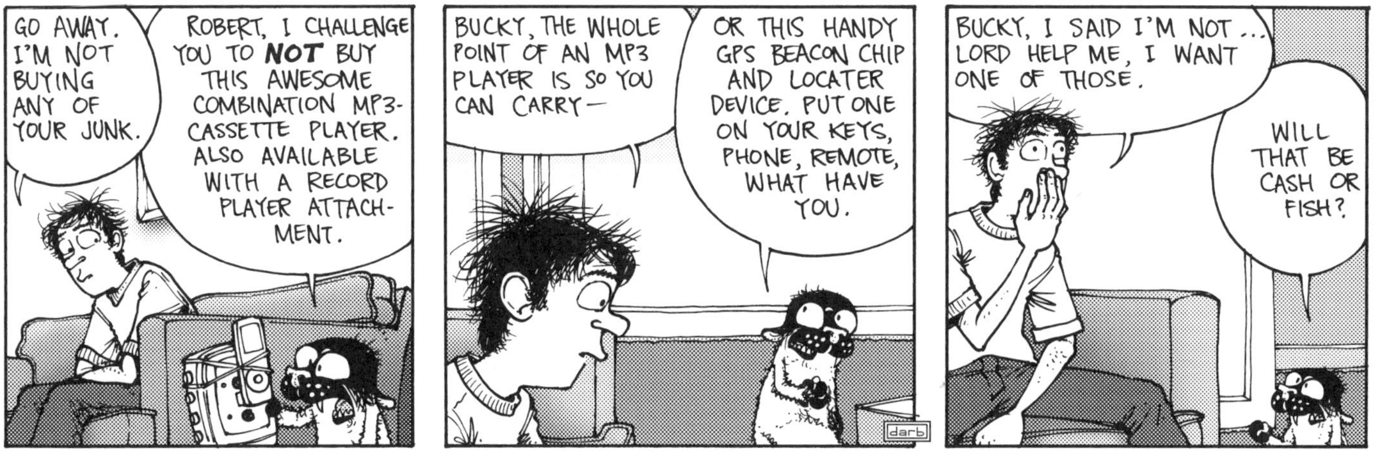
GO AWAY. I'M NOT BUYING ANY OF YOUR JUNK.
ROBERT, I CHALLENGE YOU TO **NOT** BUY THIS AWESOME COMBINATION MP3-CASSETTE PLAYER. ALSO AVAILABLE WITH A RECORD PLAYER ATTACHMENT.
BUCKY, THE WHOLE POINT OF AN MP3 PLAYER IS SO YOU CAN CARRY—
OR THIS HANDY GPS BEACON CHIP AND LOCATER DEVICE. PUT ONE ON YOUR KEYS, PHONE, REMOTE, WHAT HAVE YOU.
darb
BUCKY, I SAID I'M NOT... LORD HELP ME, I WANT ONE OF THOSE.
WILL THAT BE CASH OR FISH?

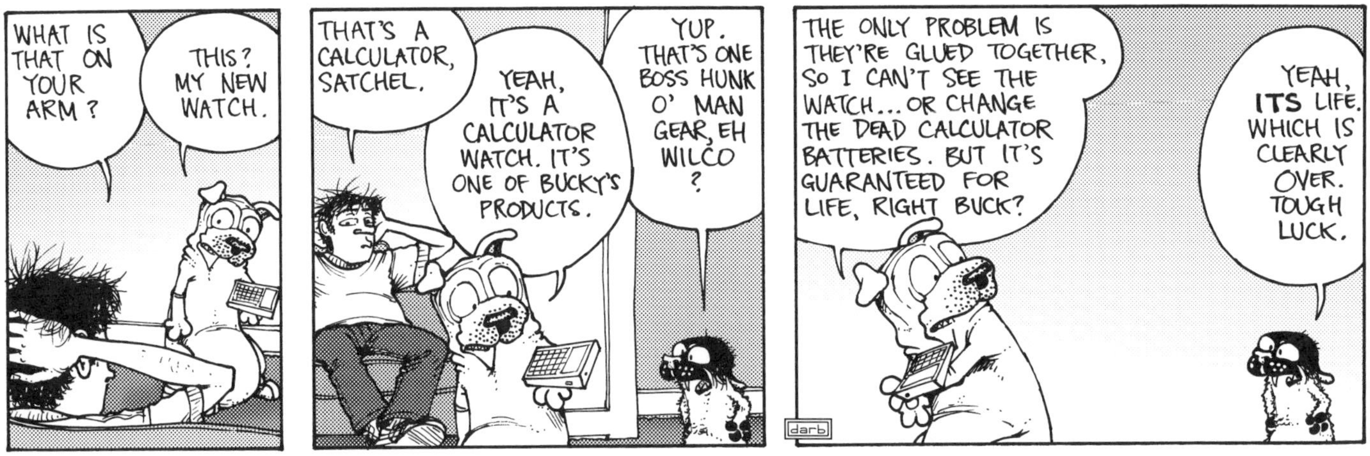
WHAT IS THAT ON YOUR ARM?
THIS? MY NEW WATCH.
THAT'S A CALCULATOR, SATCHEL.
YEAH, IT'S A CALCULATOR WATCH. IT'S ONE OF BUCKY'S PRODUCTS.
YUP. THAT'S ONE BOSS HUNK O' MAN GEAR, EH WILCO?
darb
THE ONLY PROBLEM IS THEY'RE GLUED TOGETHER, SO I CAN'T SEE THE WATCH... OR CHANGE THE DEAD CALCULATOR BATTERIES. BUT IT'S GUARANTEED FOR LIFE, RIGHT BUCK?
YEAH, **ITS** LIFE. WHICH IS CLEARLY OVER. TOUGH LUCK.

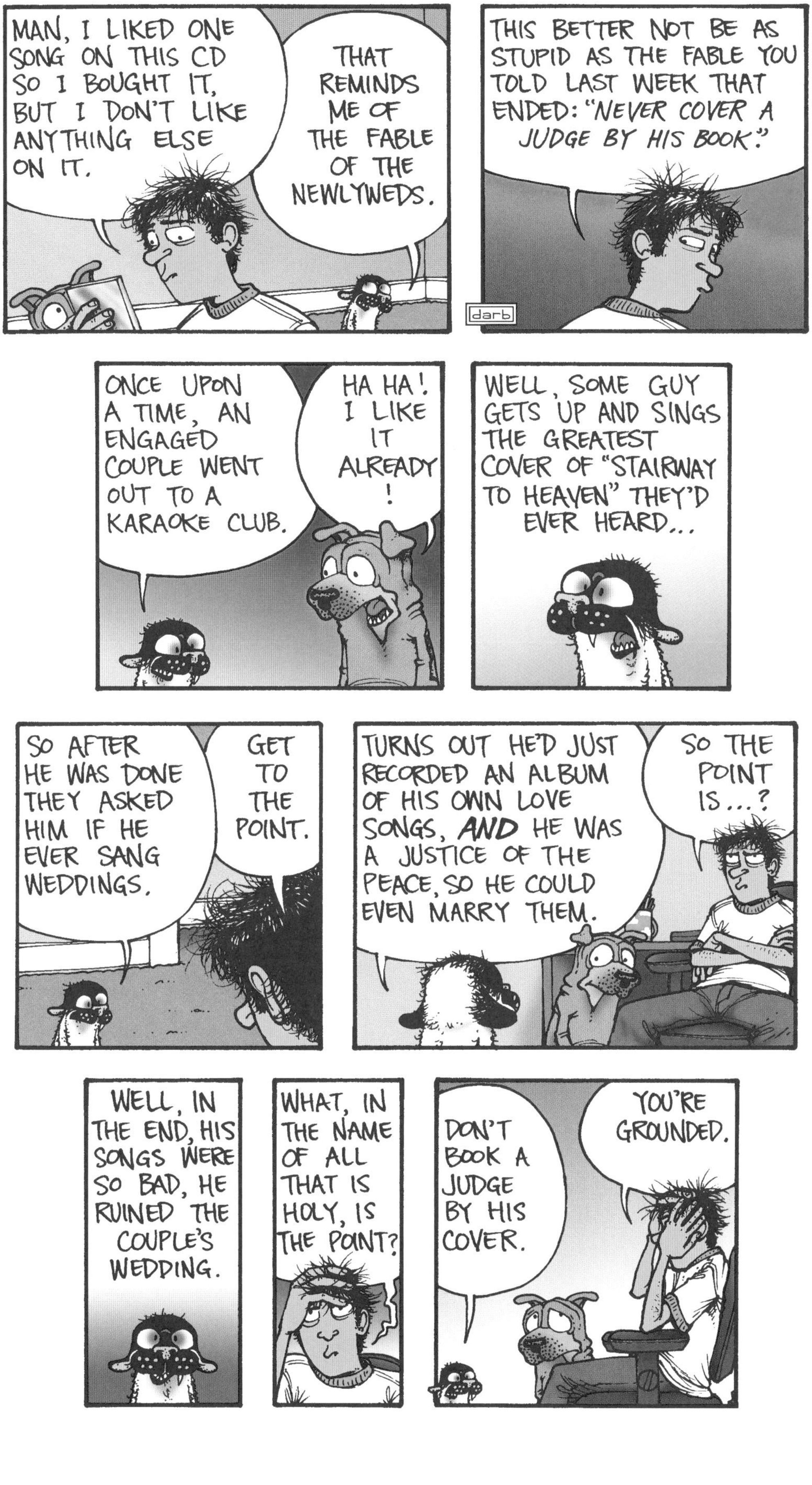
MAN, I LIKED ONE SONG ON THIS CD SO I BOUGHT IT, BUT I DON'T LIKE ANYTHING ELSE ON IT.
THAT REMINDS ME OF THE FABLE OF THE NEWLYWEDS.
darb
THIS BETTER NOT BE AS STUPID AS THE FABLE YOU TOLD LAST WEEK THAT ENDED: "NEVER COVER A JUDGE BY HIS BOOK."
ONCE UPON A TIME, AN ENGAGED COUPLE WENT OUT TO A KARAOKE CLUB.
HA HA! I LIKE IT ALREADY!
WELL, SOME GUY GETS UP AND SINGS THE GREATEST COVER OF "STAIRWAY TO HEAVEN" THEY'D EVER HEARD...
SO AFTER HE WAS DONE THEY ASKED HIM IF HE EVER SANG WEDDINGS.
GET TO THE POINT.
TURNS OUT HE'D JUST RECORDED AN ALBUM OF HIS OWN LOVE SONGS, AND HE WAS A JUSTICE OF THE PEACE, SO HE COULD EVEN MARRY THEM.
SO THE POINT IS...?
WELL, IN THE END, HIS SONGS WERE SO BAD, HE RUINED THE COUPLE'S WEDDING.
WHAT, IN THE NAME OF ALL THAT IS HOLY, IS THE POINT?
DON'T BOOK A JUDGE BY HIS COVER.
YOU'RE GROUNDED.

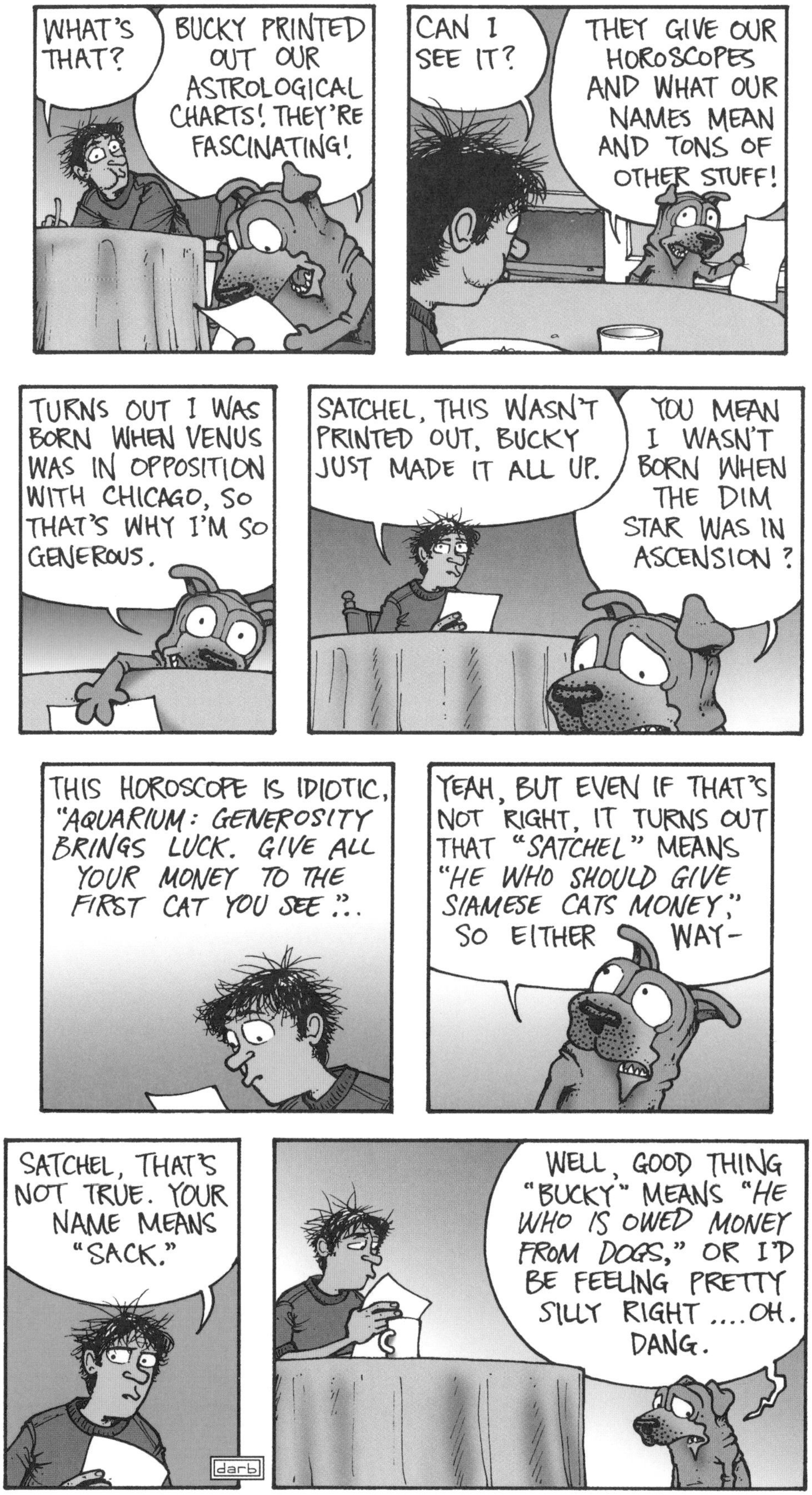
WHAT'S THAT?
BUCKY PRINTED OUT OUR ASTROLOGICAL CHARTS! THEY'RE FASCINATING!
CAN I SEE IT?
THEY GIVE OUR HOROSCOPES AND WHAT OUR NAMES MEAN AND TONS OF OTHER STUFF!
TURNS OUT I WAS BORN WHEN VENUS WAS IN OPPOSITION WITH CHICAGO, SO THAT'S WHY I'M SO GENEROUS.
SATCHEL, THIS WASN'T PRINTED OUT. BUCKY JUST MADE IT ALL UP.
YOU MEAN I WASN'T BORN WHEN THE DIM STAR WAS IN ASCENSION?
THIS HOROSCOPE IS IDIOTIC, "AQUARIUM: GENEROSITY BRINGS LUCK. GIVE ALL YOUR MONEY TO THE FIRST CAT YOU SEE."...
YEAH, BUT EVEN IF THAT'S NOT RIGHT, IT TURNS OUT THAT "SATCHEL" MEANS "HE WHO SHOULD GIVE SIAMESE CATS MONEY," SO EITHER WAY-
SATCHEL, THAT'S NOT TRUE. YOUR NAME MEANS "SACK."
darb
WELL, GOOD THING "BUCKY" MEANS "HE WHO IS OWED MONEY FROM DOGS," OR I'D BE FEELING PRETTY SILLY RIGHT ....OH. DANG.

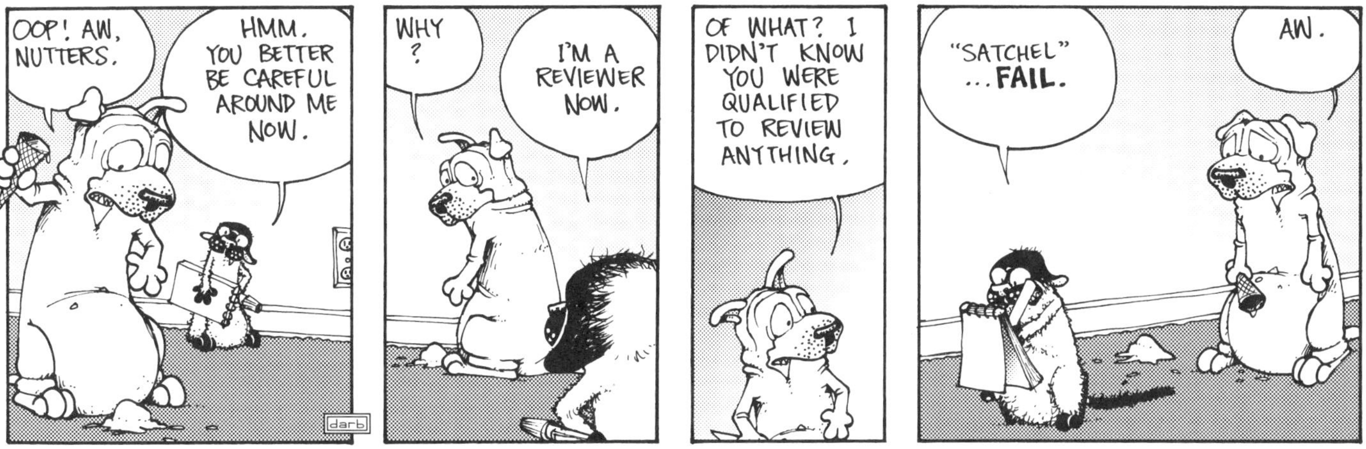
OOP! AW, NUTTERS.
HMM. YOU BETTER BE CAREFUL AROUND ME NOW.
WHY?
I'M A REVIEWER NOW.
OF WHAT? I DIDN'T KNOW YOU WERE QUALIFIED TO REVIEW ANYTHING.
"SATCHEL" ...**FAIL.**
AW.

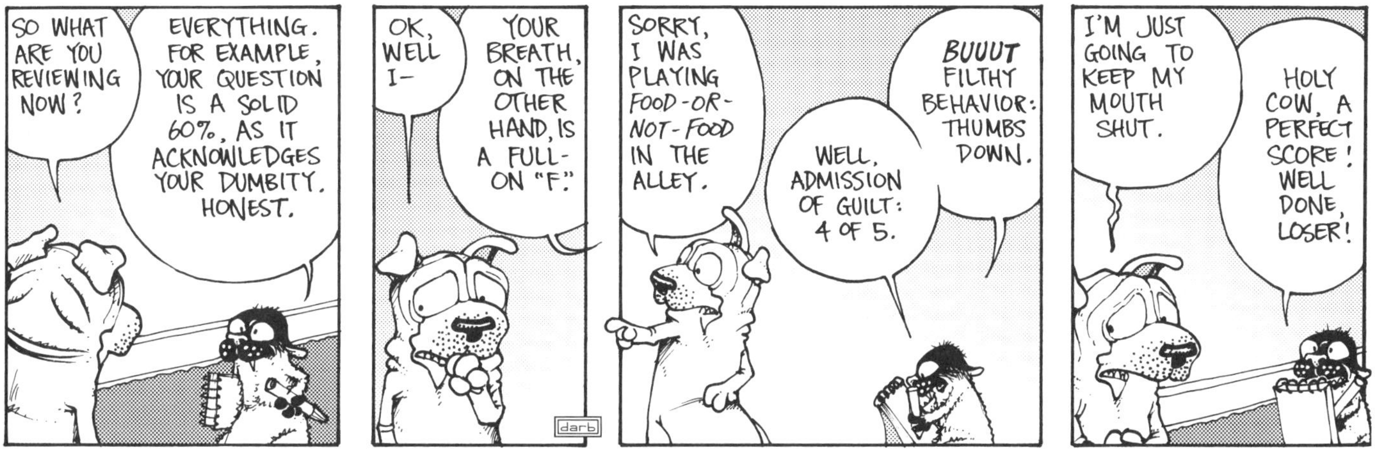
SO WHAT ARE YOU REVIEWING NOW?
EVERYTHING. FOR EXAMPLE, YOUR QUESTION IS A SOLID 60%, AS IT ACKNOWLEDGES YOUR DUMBITY. HONEST.
OK, WELL I—
YOUR BREATH, ON THE OTHER HAND, IS A FULL-ON "F."
SORRY, I WAS PLAYING *FOOD-OR-NOT-FOOD* IN THE ALLEY.
WELL. ADMISSION OF GUILT: 4 OF 5.
BUUUT FILTHY BEHAVIOR: THUMBS DOWN.
I'M JUST GOING TO KEEP MY MOUTH SHUT.
HOLY COW, A PERFECT SCORE! WELL DONE, LOSER!

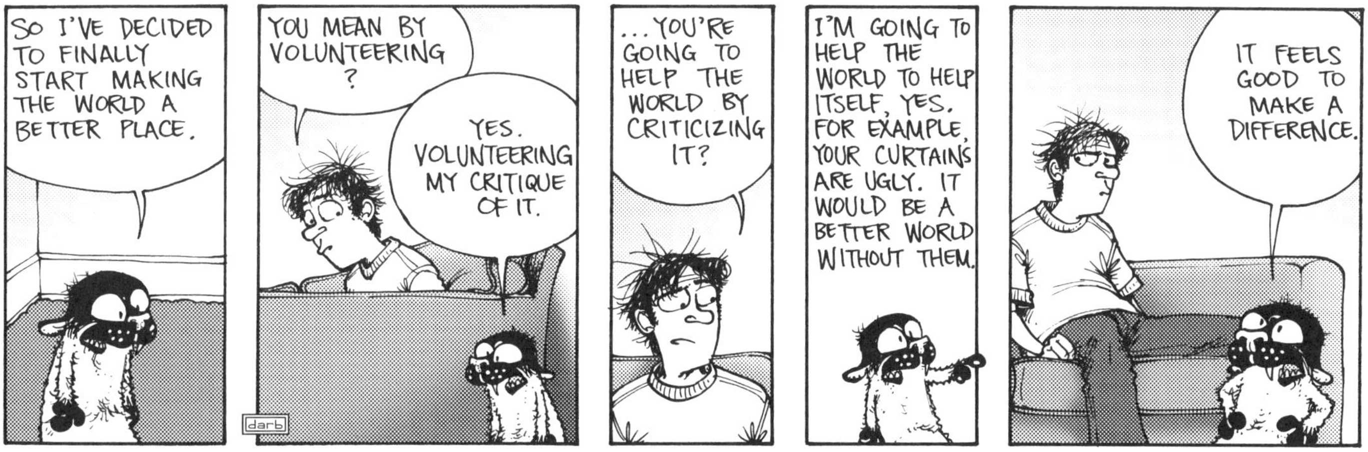
SO I'VE DECIDED TO FINALLY START MAKING THE WORLD A BETTER PLACE.
YOU MEAN BY VOLUNTEERING?
YES. VOLUNTEERING MY CRITIQUE OF IT.
...YOU'RE GOING TO HELP THE WORLD BY CRITICIZING IT?
I'M GOING TO HELP THE WORLD TO HELP ITSELF, YES. FOR EXAMPLE, YOUR CURTAINS ARE UGLY. IT WOULD BE A BETTER WORLD WITHOUT THEM.
IT FEELS GOOD TO MAKE A DIFFERENCE.

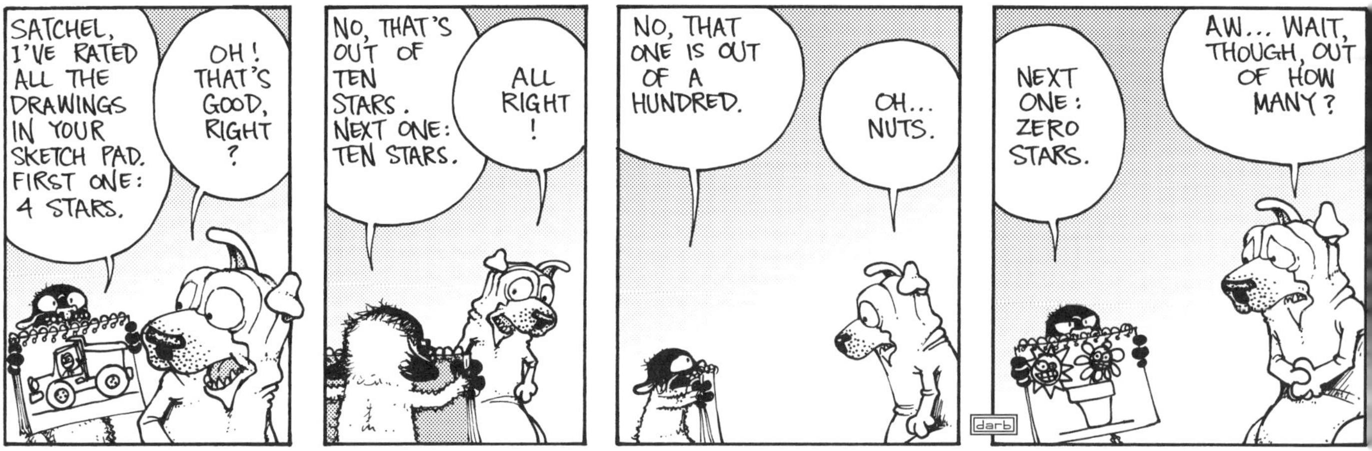
SATCHEL, I'VE RATED ALL THE DRAWINGS IN YOUR SKETCH PAD. FIRST ONE: 4 STARS.
OH! THAT'S GOOD, RIGHT?
NO, THAT'S OUT OF TEN STARS. NEXT ONE: TEN STARS.
ALL RIGHT!
NO, THAT ONE IS OUT OF A HUNDRED.
OH... NUTS.
NEXT ONE: ZERO STARS.
AW... WAIT, THOUGH, OUT OF HOW MANY?
darb

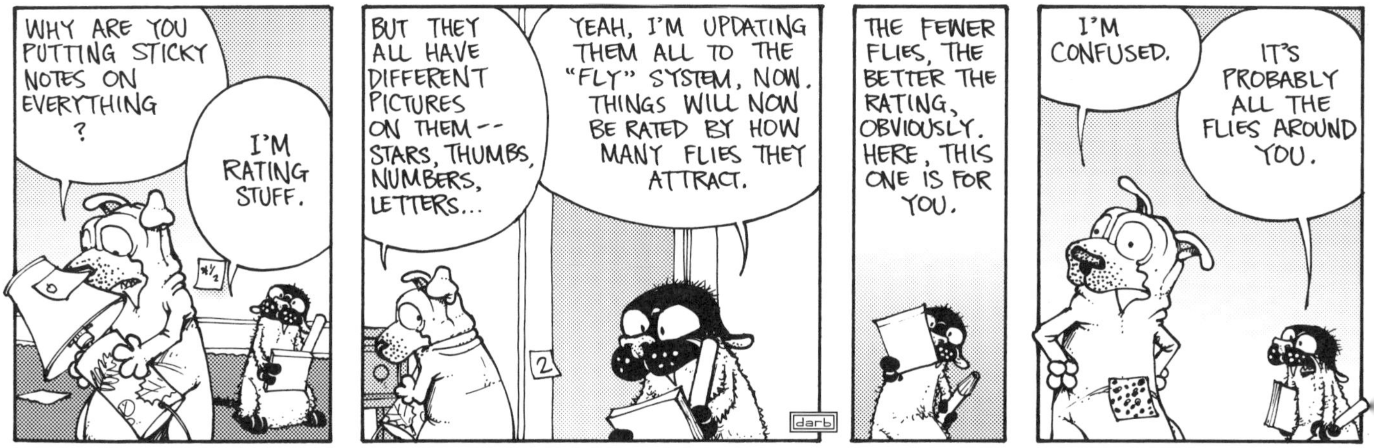
WHY ARE YOU PUTTING STICKY NOTES ON EVERYTHING?
I'M RATING STUFF.
BUT THEY ALL HAVE DIFFERENT PICTURES ON THEM -- STARS, THUMBS, NUMBERS, LETTERS...
YEAH, I'M UPDATING THEM ALL TO THE "FLY" SYSTEM, NOW. THINGS WILL NOW BE RATED BY HOW MANY FLIES THEY ATTRACT.
2
darb
THE FEWER FLIES, THE BETTER THE RATING, OBVIOUSLY. HERE, THIS ONE IS FOR YOU.
I'M CONFUSED.
IT'S PROBABLY ALL THE FLIES AROUND YOU.

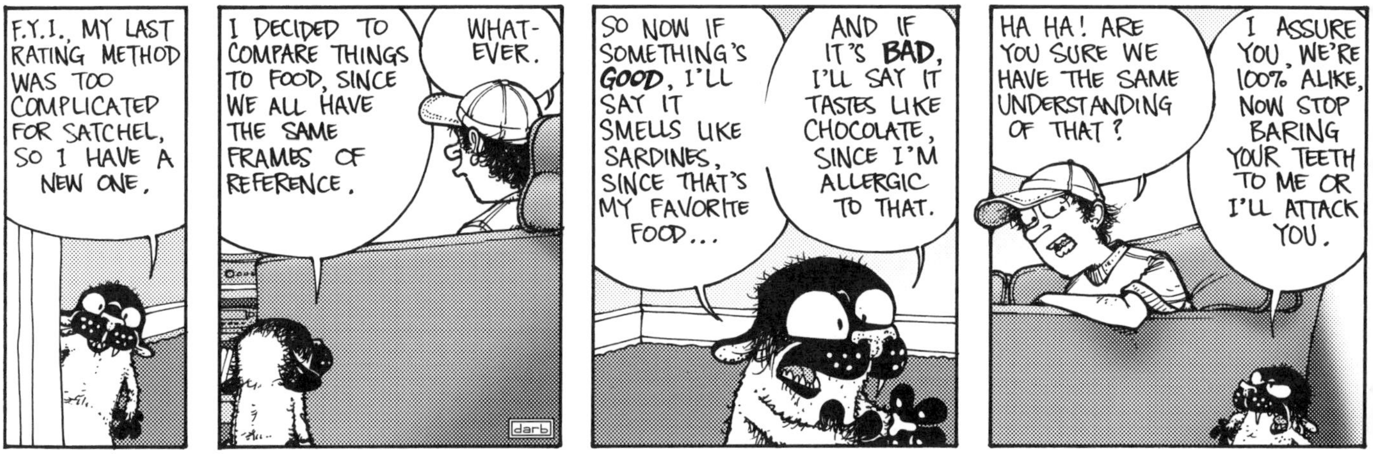
F.Y.I., MY LAST RATING METHOD WAS TOO COMPLICATED FOR SATCHEL, SO I HAVE A NEW ONE.
I DECIDED TO COMPARE THINGS TO FOOD, SINCE WE ALL HAVE THE SAME FRAMES OF REFERENCE.
WHAT-EVER.
darb
SO NOW IF SOMETHING'S GOOD, I'LL SAY IT SMELLS LIKE SARDINES, SINCE THAT'S MY FAVORITE FOOD...
AND IF IT'S BAD, I'LL SAY IT TASTES LIKE CHOCOLATE, SINCE I'M ALLERGIC TO THAT.
HA HA! ARE YOU SURE WE HAVE THE SAME UNDERSTANDING OF THAT?
I ASSURE YOU, WE'RE 100% ALIKE, NOW STOP BARING YOUR TEETH TO ME OR I'LL ATTACK YOU.

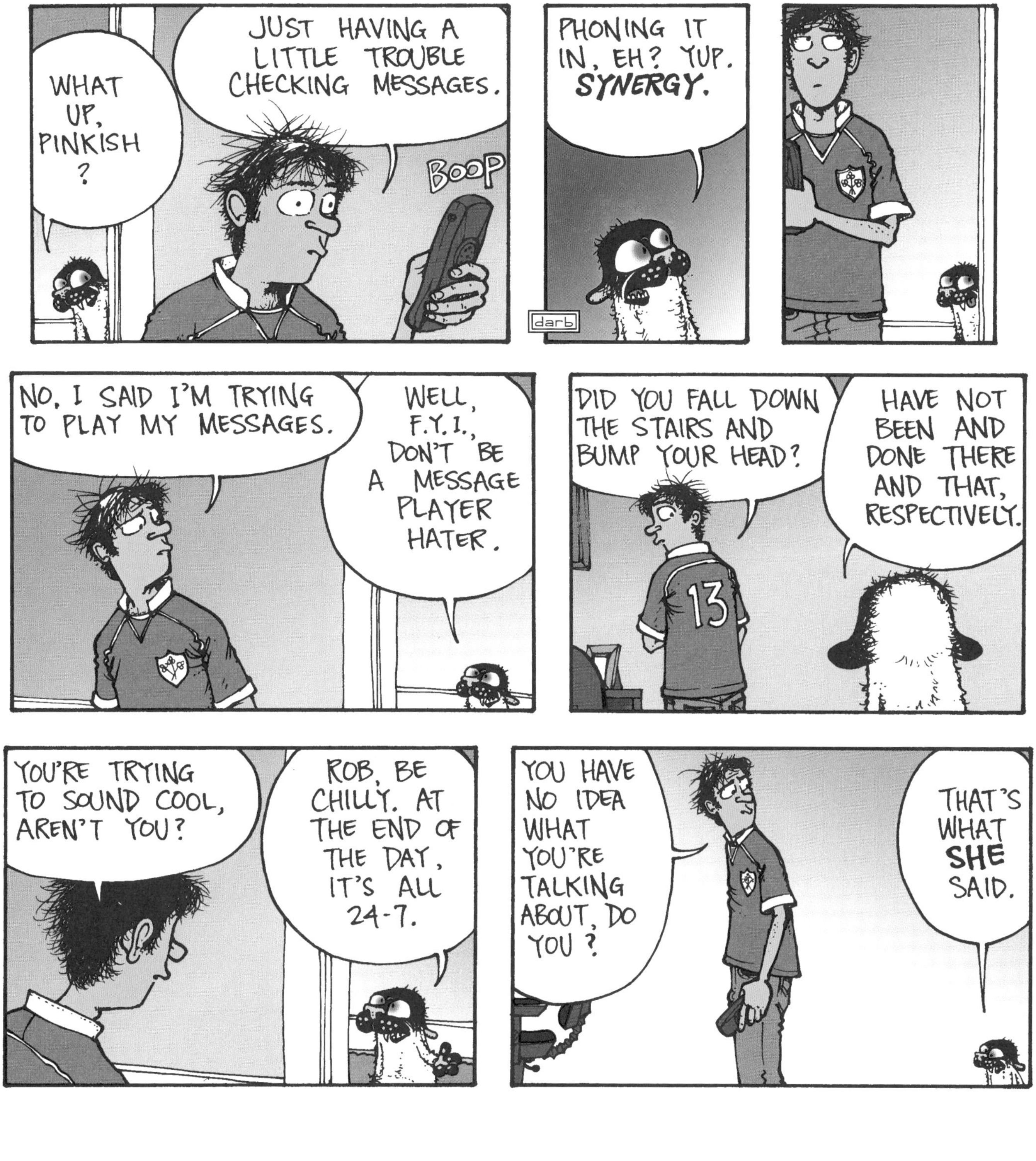
WHAT UP, PINKISH ?
JUST HAVING A LITTLE TROUBLE CHECKING MESSAGES.
BOOP
PHONING IT IN, EH? YUP. **SYNERGY.**
darb
NO, I SAID I'M TRYING TO PLAY MY MESSAGES.
WELL, F.Y.I., DON'T BE A MESSAGE PLAYER HATER.
DID YOU FALL DOWN THE STAIRS AND BUMP YOUR HEAD?
HAVE NOT BEEN AND DONE THERE AND THAT, RESPECTIVELY.
13
YOU'RE TRYING TO SOUND COOL, AREN'T YOU?
ROB, BE CHILLY. AT THE END OF THE DAY, IT'S ALL 24-7.
YOU HAVE NO IDEA WHAT YOU'RE TALKING ABOUT, DO YOU ?
THAT'S WHAT **SHE** SAID.

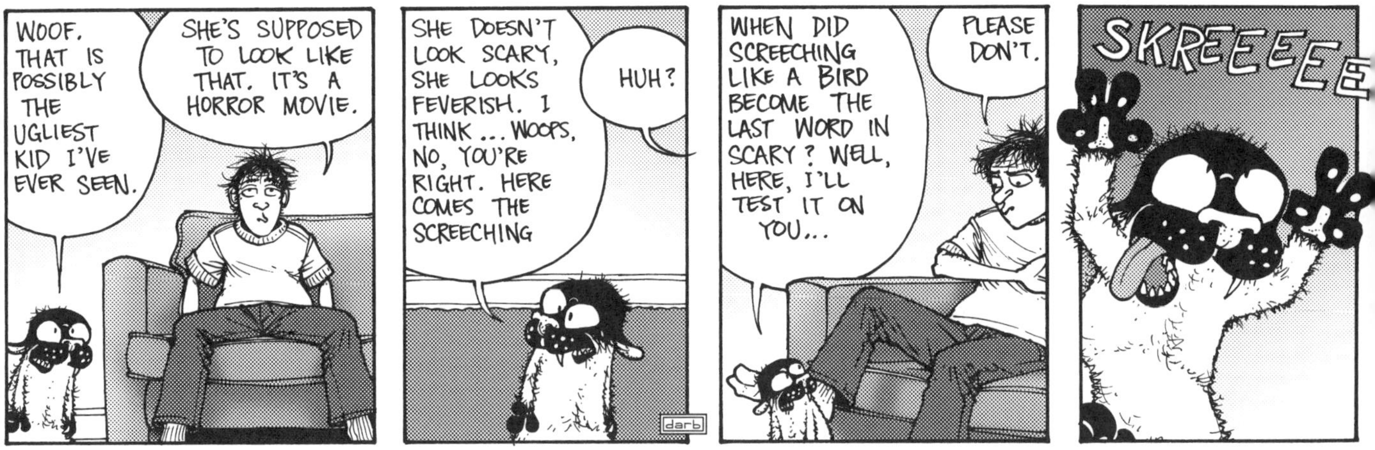
WOOF. THAT IS POSSIBLY THE UGLIEST KID I'VE EVER SEEN.
SHE'S SUPPOSED TO LOOK LIKE THAT. IT'S A HORROR MOVIE.
SHE DOESN'T LOOK SCARY, SHE LOOKS FEVERISH. I THINK ... WOOPS, NO, YOU'RE RIGHT. HERE COMES THE SCREECHING
HUH?
darb
WHEN DID SCREECHING LIKE A BIRD BECOME THE LAST WORD IN SCARY? WELL, HERE, I'LL TEST IT ON YOU...
PLEASE DON'T.
SKREEEEE

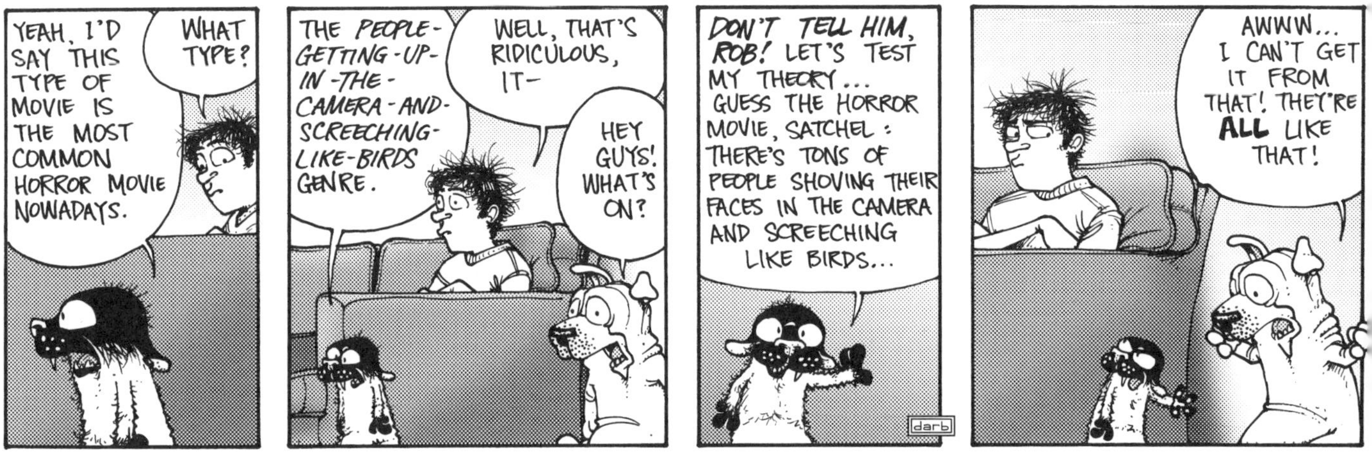
YEAH, I'D SAY THIS TYPE OF MOVIE IS THE MOST COMMON HORROR MOVIE NOWADAYS.
WHAT TYPE?
THE *PEOPLE-GETTING-UP-IN-THE-CAMERA-AND-SCREECHING-LIKE-BIRDS* GENRE.
WELL, THAT'S RIDICULOUS, IT—
HEY GUYS! WHAT'S ON?
DON'T TELL HIM, ROB! LET'S TEST MY THEORY... GUESS THE HORROR MOVIE, SATCHEL: THERE'S TONS OF PEOPLE SHOVING THEIR FACES IN THE CAMERA AND SCREECHING LIKE BIRDS...
darb
AWWW... I CAN'T GET IT FROM THAT! THEY'RE **ALL** LIKE THAT!

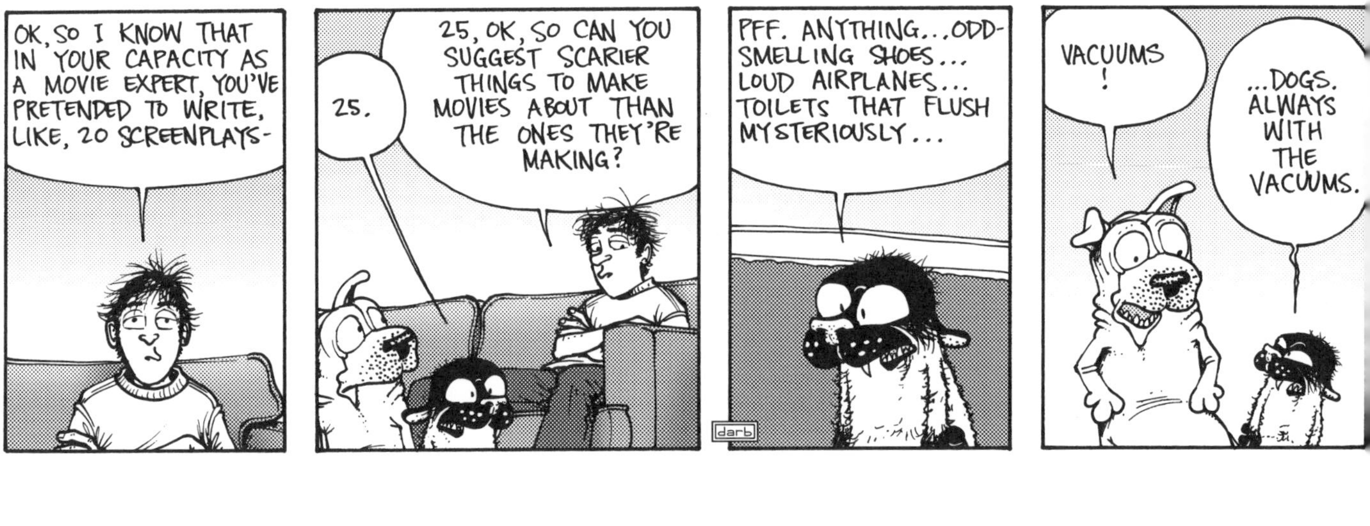
OK, SO I KNOW THAT IN YOUR CAPACITY AS A MOVIE EXPERT, YOU'VE PRETENDED TO WRITE, LIKE, 20 SCREENPLAYS-
25.
25, OK, SO CAN YOU SUGGEST SCARIER THINGS TO MAKE MOVIES ABOUT THAN THE ONES THEY'RE MAKING?
darb
PFF. ANYTHING...ODD-SMELLING SHOES... LOUD AIRPLANES... TOILETS THAT FLUSH MYSTERIOUSLY...
VACUUMS!
...DOGS. ALWAYS WITH THE VACUUMS.

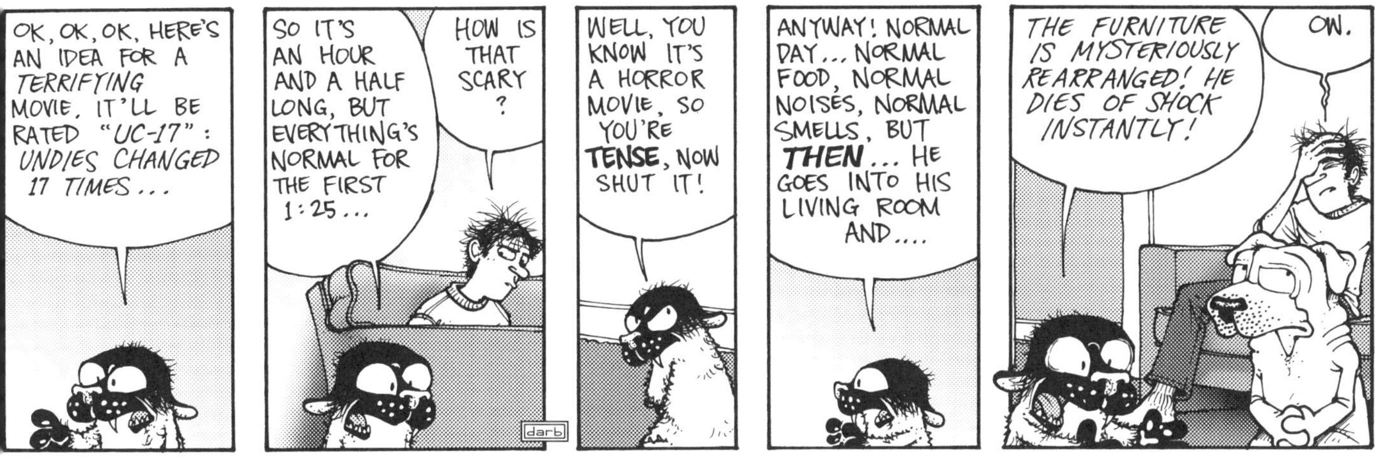
OK, OK, OK, HERE'S AN IDEA FOR A *TERRIFYING* MOVIE. IT'LL BE RATED "*UC-17*": *UNDIES CHANGED 17 TIMES*...
SO IT'S AN HOUR AND A HALF LONG, BUT EVERYTHING'S NORMAL FOR THE FIRST 1:25...
HOW IS THAT SCARY?
WELL, YOU KNOW IT'S A HORROR MOVIE, SO YOU'RE **TENSE**, NOW SHUT IT!
ANYWAY! NORMAL DAY... NORMAL FOOD, NORMAL NOISES, NORMAL SMELLS, BUT ***THEN***... HE GOES INTO HIS LIVING ROOM AND....
THE FURNITURE IS MYSTERIOUSLY REARRANGED! HE DIES OF SHOCK INSTANTLY!
OW.
darb

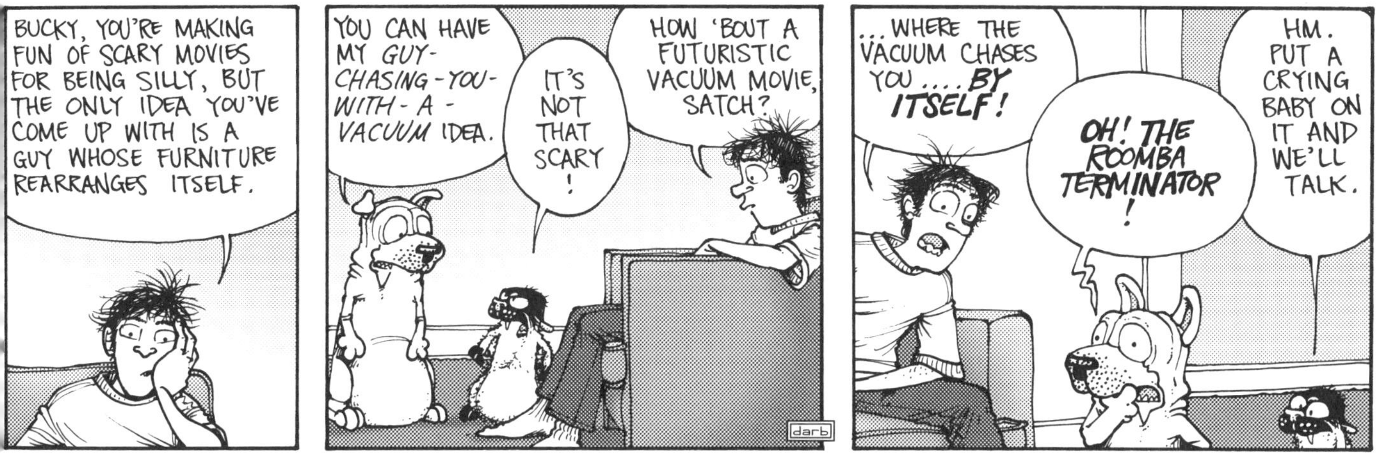
BUCKY, YOU'RE MAKING FUN OF SCARY MOVIES FOR BEING SILLY, BUT THE ONLY IDEA YOU'VE COME UP WITH IS A GUY WHOSE FURNITURE REARRANGES ITSELF.
YOU CAN HAVE MY *GUY-CHASING-YOU-WITH-A-VACUUM* IDEA.
IT'S NOT THAT SCARY!
HOW 'BOUT A FUTURISTIC VACUUM MOVIE, SATCH?
...WHERE THE VACUUM CHASES YOU.... ***BY ITSELF!***
OH! THE ROOMBA TERMINATOR!
HM. PUT A CRYING BABY ON IT AND WE'LL TALK.
darb

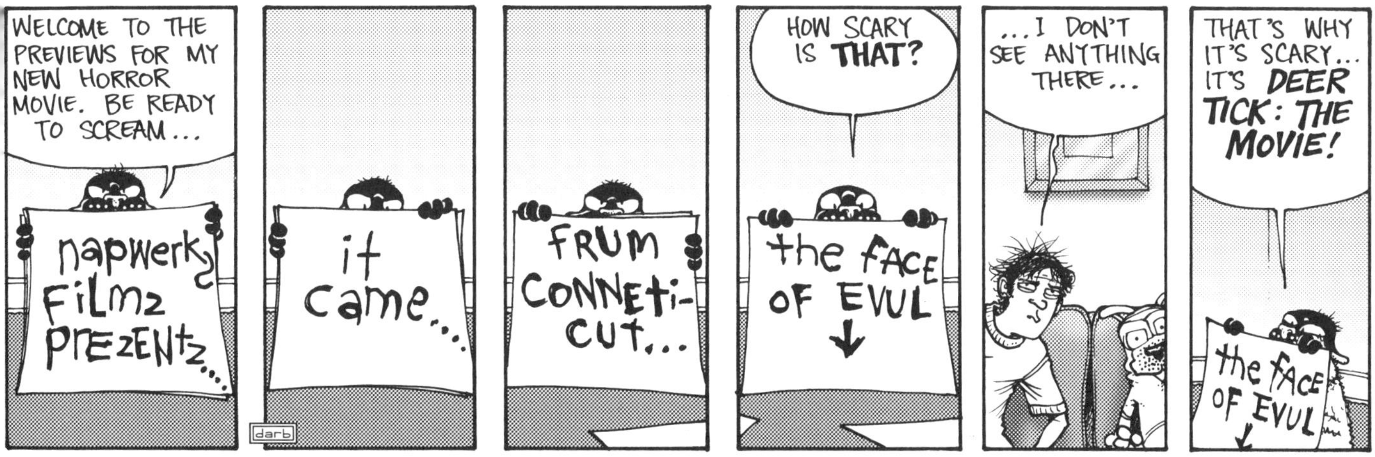
WELCOME TO THE PREVIEWS FOR MY NEW HORROR MOVIE. BE READY TO SCREAM...
napwerkz Filmz prezentz....
it came....
FRUM CONNETi-CUT...
HOW SCARY IS **THAT?**
the FACE OF EVUL
...I DON'T SEE ANYTHING THERE...
THAT'S WHY IT'S SCARY... IT'S ***DEER TICK: THE MOVIE!***
the FACE OF EVUL
darb

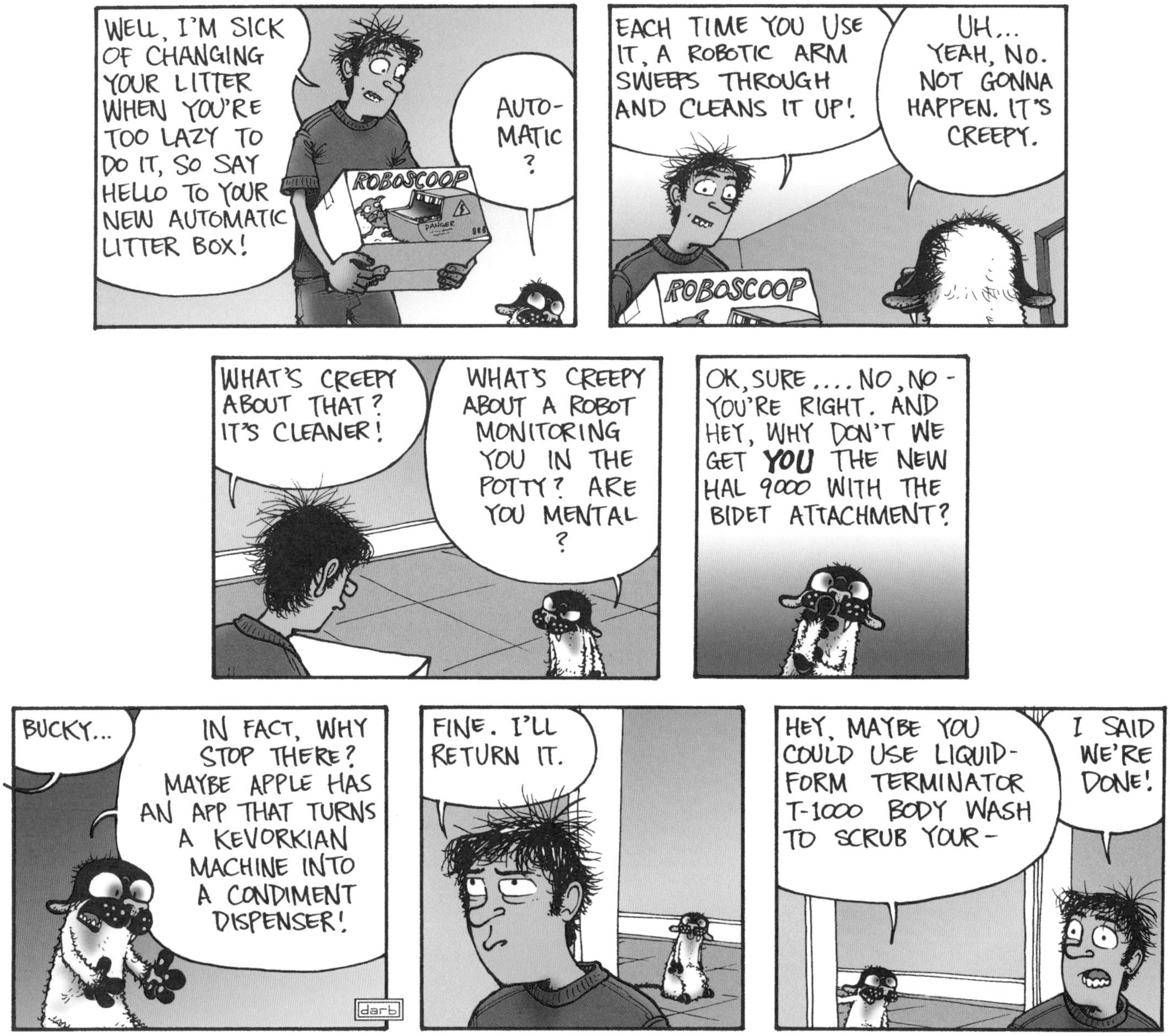
WELL, I'M SICK OF CHANGING YOUR LITTER WHEN YOU'RE TOO LAZY TO DO IT, SO SAY HELLO TO YOUR NEW AUTOMATIC LITTER BOX!
ROBOSCOOP
AUTO-MATIC?
EACH TIME YOU USE IT, A ROBOTIC ARM SWEEPS THROUGH AND CLEANS IT UP!
UH... YEAH, NO. NOT GONNA HAPPEN. IT'S CREEPY.
ROBOSCOOP
WHAT'S CREEPY ABOUT THAT? IT'S CLEANER!
WHAT'S CREEPY ABOUT A ROBOT MONITORING YOU IN THE POTTY? ARE YOU MENTAL?
OK, SURE.... NO, NO - YOU'RE RIGHT. AND HEY, WHY DON'T WE GET **YOU** THE NEW HAL 9000 WITH THE BIDET ATTACHMENT?
BUCKY...
IN FACT, WHY STOP THERE? MAYBE APPLE HAS AN APP THAT TURNS A KEVORKIAN MACHINE INTO A CONDIMENT DISPENSER!
darb
FINE. I'LL RETURN IT.
HEY, MAYBE YOU COULD USE LIQUID-FORM TERMINATOR T-1000 BODY WASH TO SCRUB YOUR-
I SAID WE'RE DONE!

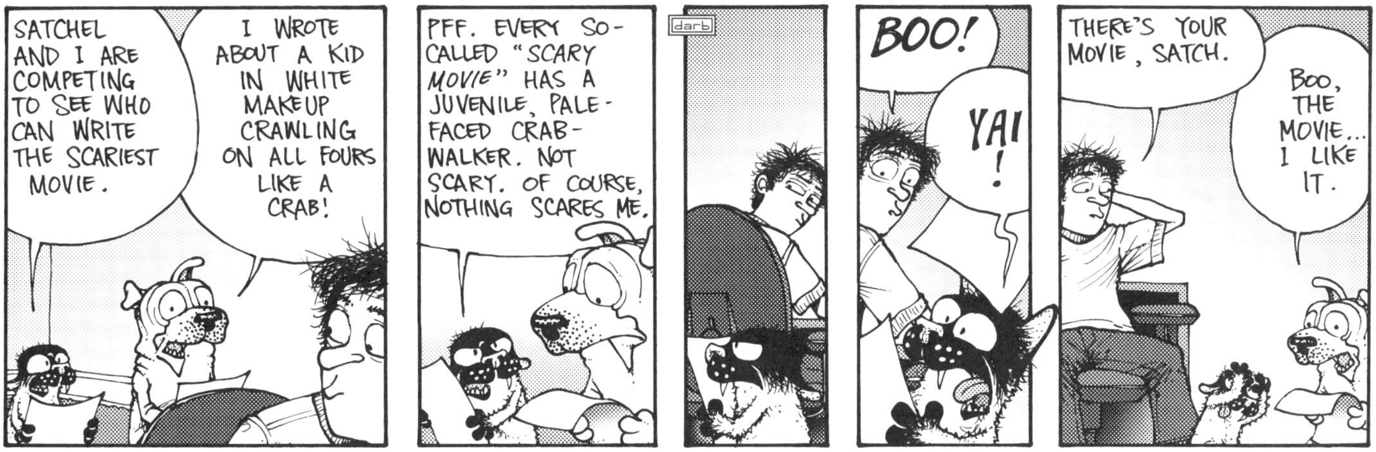
SATCHEL AND I ARE COMPETING TO SEE WHO CAN WRITE THE SCARIEST MOVIE.
I WROTE ABOUT A KID IN WHITE MAKEUP CRAWLING ON ALL FOURS LIKE A CRAB!
PFF. EVERY SO-CALLED "SCARY *MOVIE*" HAS A JUVENILE, PALE-FACED CRAB-WALKER. NOT SCARY. OF COURSE, NOTHING SCARES ME.
darb
BOO!
YAI!
THERE'S YOUR MOVIE, SATCH.
BOO, THE MOVIE... I LIKE IT.

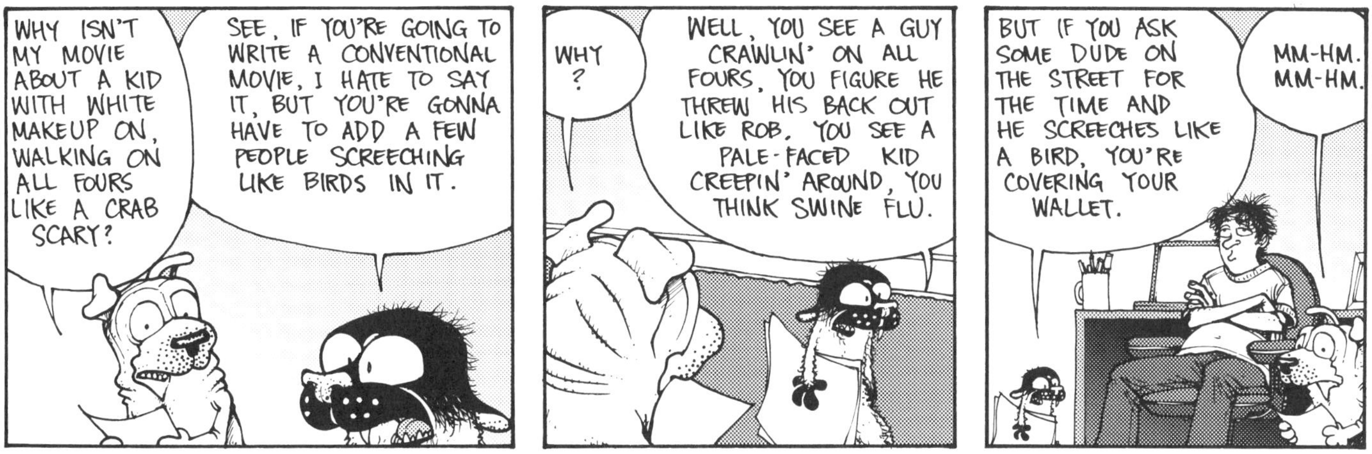
WHY ISN'T MY MOVIE ABOUT A KID WITH WHITE MAKEUP ON, WALKING ON ALL FOURS LIKE A CRAB SCARY?
SEE, IF YOU'RE GOING TO WRITE A CONVENTIONAL MOVIE, I HATE TO SAY IT, BUT YOU'RE GONNA HAVE TO ADD A FEW PEOPLE SCREECHING LIKE BIRDS IN IT.
WHY?
WELL, YOU SEE A GUY CRAWLIN' ON ALL FOURS, YOU FIGURE HE THREW HIS BACK OUT LIKE ROB. YOU SEE A PALE-FACED KID CREEPIN' AROUND, YOU THINK SWINE FLU.
BUT IF YOU ASK SOME DUDE ON THE STREET FOR THE TIME AND HE SCREECHES LIKE A BIRD, YOU'RE COVERING YOUR WALLET.
MM-HM. MM-HM.

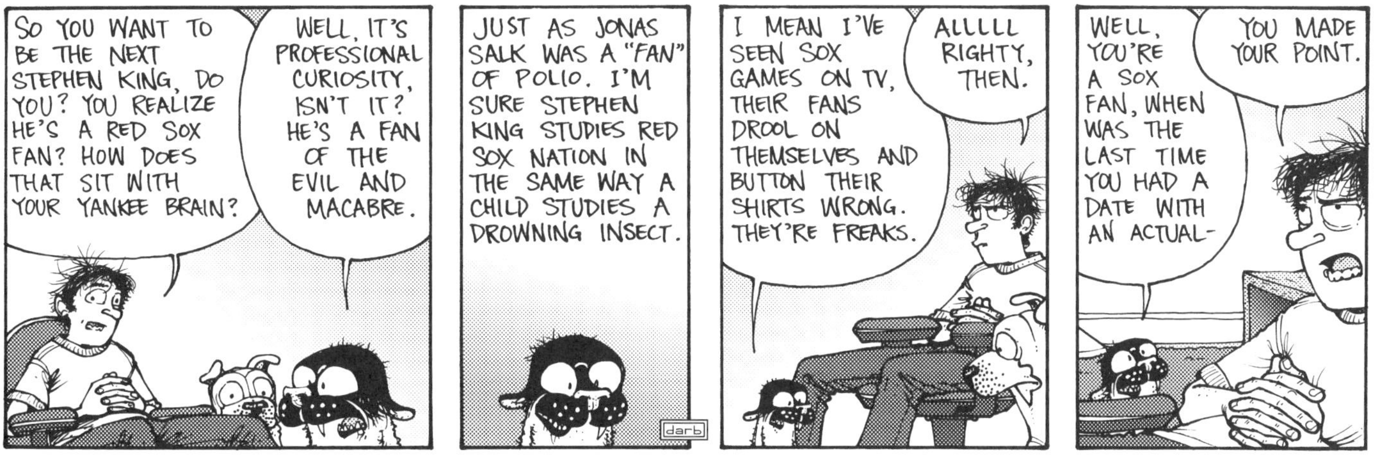
SO YOU WANT TO BE THE NEXT STEPHEN KING, DO YOU? YOU REALIZE HE'S A RED SOX FAN? HOW DOES THAT SIT WITH YOUR YANKEE BRAIN?
WELL, IT'S PROFESSIONAL CURIOSITY, ISN'T IT? HE'S A FAN OF THE EVIL AND MACABRE.
JUST AS JONAS SALK WAS A "FAN" OF POLIO. I'M SURE STEPHEN KING STUDIES RED SOX NATION IN THE SAME WAY A CHILD STUDIES A DROWNING INSECT.
darb
I MEAN I'VE SEEN SOX GAMES ON TV, THEIR FANS DROOL ON THEMSELVES AND BUTTON THEIR SHIRTS WRONG. THEY'RE FREAKS.
ALLLLL RIGHTY, THEN.
WELL, YOU'RE A SOX FAN, WHEN WAS THE LAST TIME YOU HAD A DATE WITH AN ACTUAL-
YOU MADE YOUR POINT.

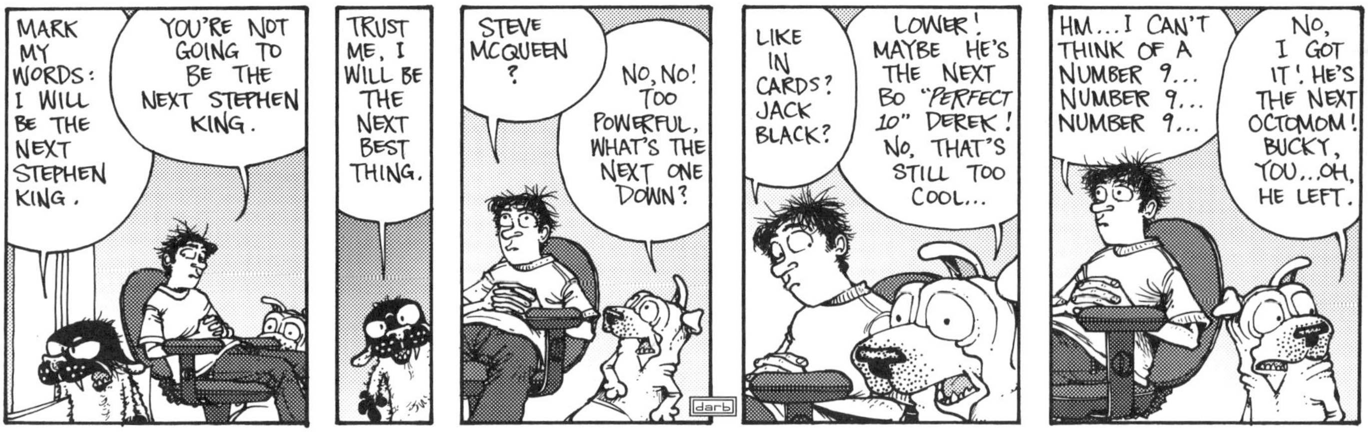
MARK MY WORDS: I WILL BE THE NEXT STEPHEN KING.
YOU'RE NOT GOING TO BE THE NEXT STEPHEN KING.
TRUST ME, I WILL BE THE NEXT BEST THING.
STEVE MCQUEEN?
NO, NO! TOO POWERFUL, WHAT'S THE NEXT ONE DOWN?
LIKE IN CARDS? JACK BLACK?
LOWER! MAYBE HE'S THE NEXT BO "PERFECT 10" DEREK! NO, THAT'S STILL TOO COOL...
HM... I CAN'T THINK OF A NUMBER 9... NUMBER 9... NUMBER 9...
NO, I GOT IT! HE'S THE NEXT OCTOMOM! BUCKY, YOU... OH, HE LEFT.

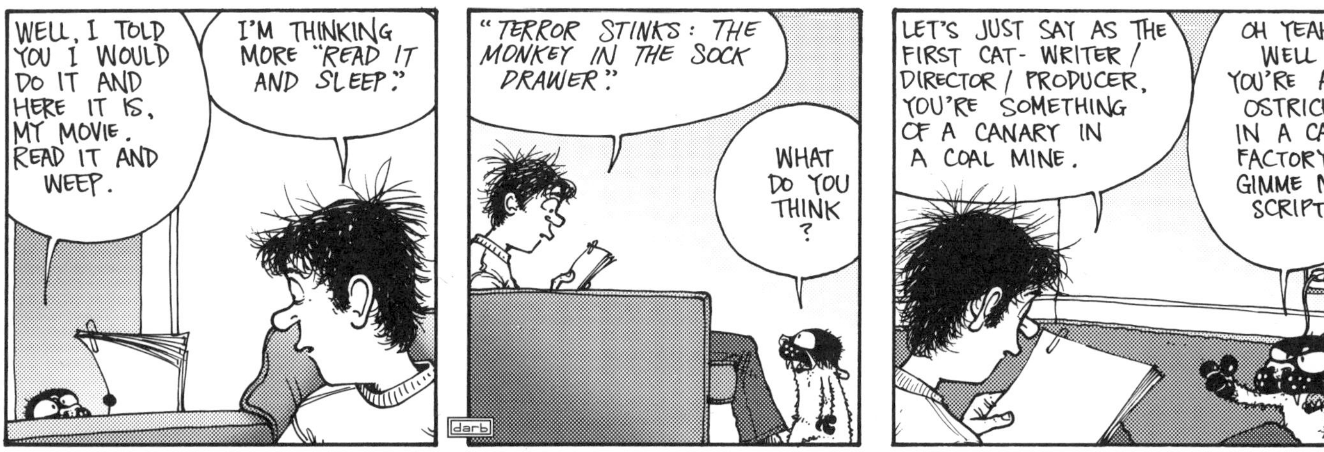
WELL, I TOLD YOU I WOULD DO IT AND HERE IT IS, MY MOVIE. READ IT AND WEEP.
I'M THINKING MORE "READ IT AND SLEEP."
"TERROR STINKS: THE MONKEY IN THE SOCK DRAWER."
WHAT DO YOU THINK?
LET'S JUST SAY AS THE FIRST CAT-WRITER/DIRECTOR/PRODUCER, YOU'RE SOMETHING OF A CANARY IN A COAL MINE.
OH YEAH? WELL YOU'RE AN OSTRICH IN A CAN FACTORY! GIMME MY SCRIPT!

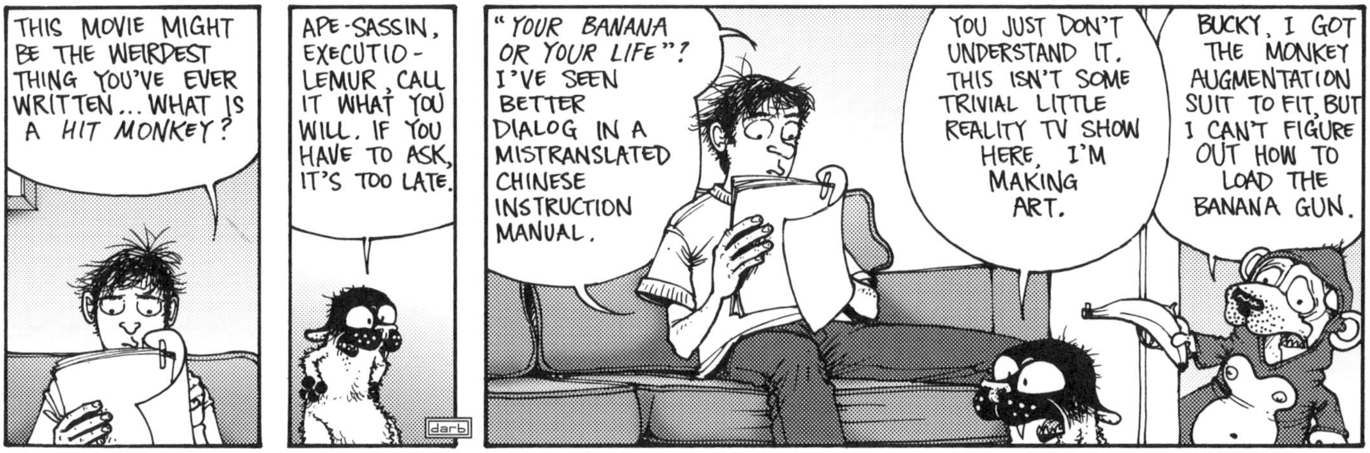
THIS MOVIE MIGHT BE THE WEIRDEST THING YOU'VE EVER WRITTEN... WHAT IS A HIT MONKEY?
APE-SASSIN, EXECUTIO-LEMUR, CALL IT WHAT YOU WILL. IF YOU HAVE TO ASK, IT'S TOO LATE.
"YOUR BANANA OR YOUR LIFE"? I'VE SEEN BETTER DIALOG IN A MISTRANSLATED CHINESE INSTRUCTION MANUAL.
YOU JUST DON'T UNDERSTAND IT. THIS ISN'T SOME TRIVIAL LITTLE REALITY TV SHOW HERE, I'M MAKING ART.
BUCKY, I GOT THE MONKEY AUGMENTATION SUIT TO FIT, BUT I CAN'T FIGURE OUT HOW TO LOAD THE BANANA GUN.

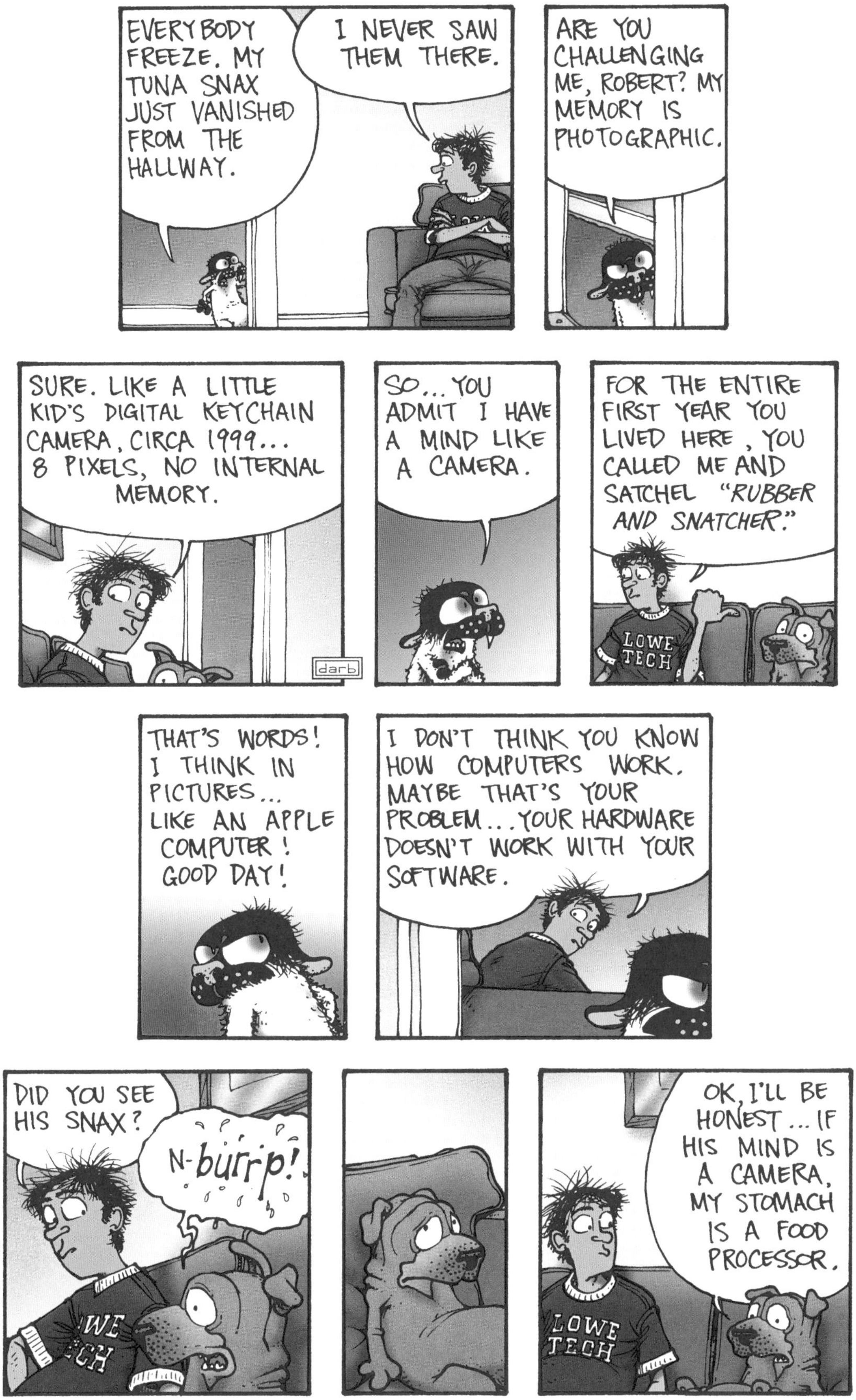
EVERYBODY FREEZE. MY TUNA SNAX JUST VANISHED FROM THE HALLWAY.
I NEVER SAW THEM THERE.
ARE YOU CHALLENGING ME, ROBERT? MY MEMORY IS PHOTOGRAPHIC.
SURE. LIKE A LITTLE KID'S DIGITAL KEYCHAIN CAMERA, CIRCA 1999... 8 PIXELS, NO INTERNAL MEMORY.
darb
SO... YOU ADMIT I HAVE A MIND LIKE A CAMERA.
FOR THE ENTIRE FIRST YEAR YOU LIVED HERE, YOU CALLED ME AND SATCHEL "RUBBER AND SNATCHER."
LOWE TECH
THAT'S WORDS! I THINK IN PICTURES... LIKE AN APPLE COMPUTER! GOOD DAY!
I DON'T THINK YOU KNOW HOW COMPUTERS WORK. MAYBE THAT'S YOUR PROBLEM... YOUR HARDWARE DOESN'T WORK WITH YOUR SOFTWARE.
DID YOU SEE HIS SNAX?
N-burrp!
OK, I'LL BE HONEST... IF HIS MIND IS A CAMERA, MY STOMACH IS A FOOD PROCESSOR.
LOWE TECH

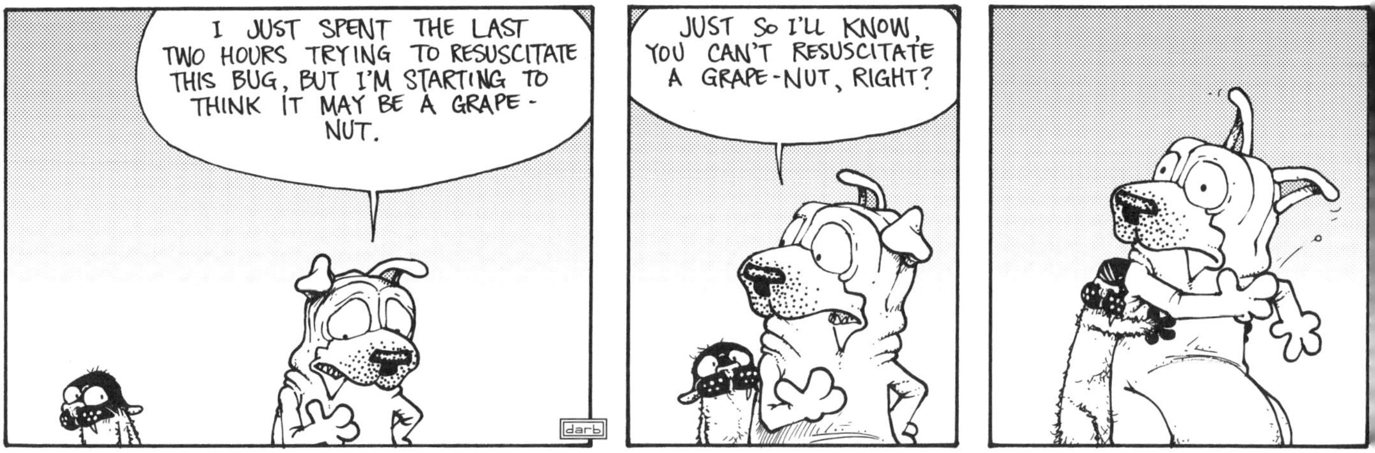
I JUST SPENT THE LAST TWO HOURS TRYING TO RESUSCITATE THIS BUG, BUT I'M STARTING TO THINK IT MAY BE A GRAPE-NUT.
JUST SO I'LL KNOW, YOU CAN'T RESUSCITATE A GRAPE-NUT, RIGHT?

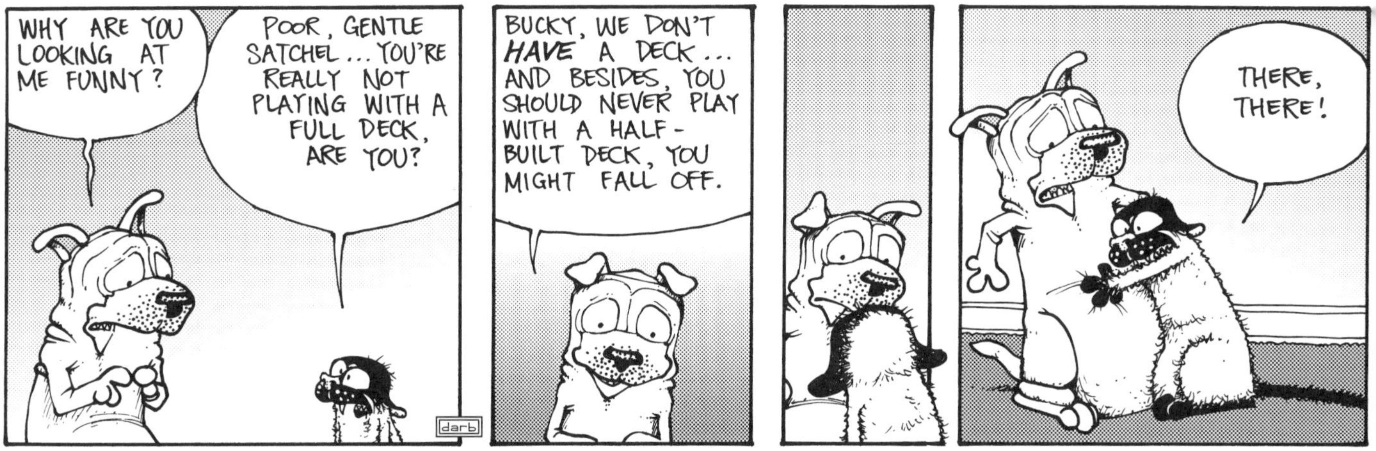
WHY ARE YOU LOOKING AT ME FUNNY?
POOR, GENTLE SATCHEL... YOU'RE REALLY NOT PLAYING WITH A FULL DECK, ARE YOU?
BUCKY, WE DON'T ***HAVE*** A DECK... AND BESIDES, YOU SHOULD NEVER PLAY WITH A HALF-BUILT DECK, YOU MIGHT FALL OFF.
THERE, THERE!

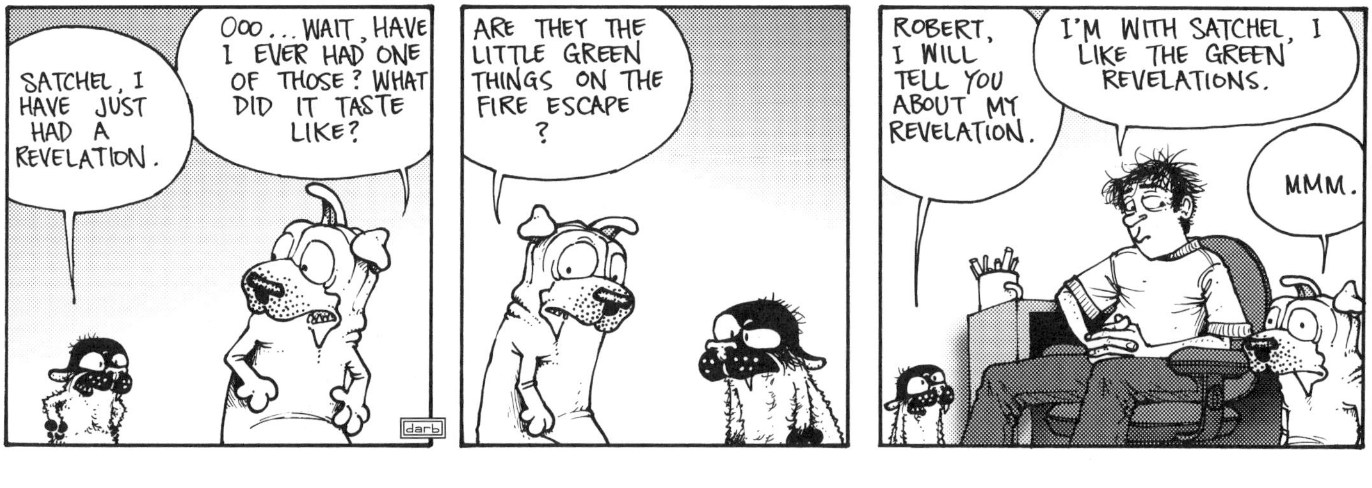
SATCHEL, I HAVE JUST HAD A REVELATION.
OOO... WAIT, HAVE I EVER HAD ONE OF THOSE? WHAT DID IT TASTE LIKE?
ARE THEY THE LITTLE GREEN THINGS ON THE FIRE ESCAPE ?
ROBERT, I WILL TELL YOU ABOUT MY REVELATION.
I'M WITH SATCHEL, I LIKE THE GREEN REVELATIONS.
MMM.

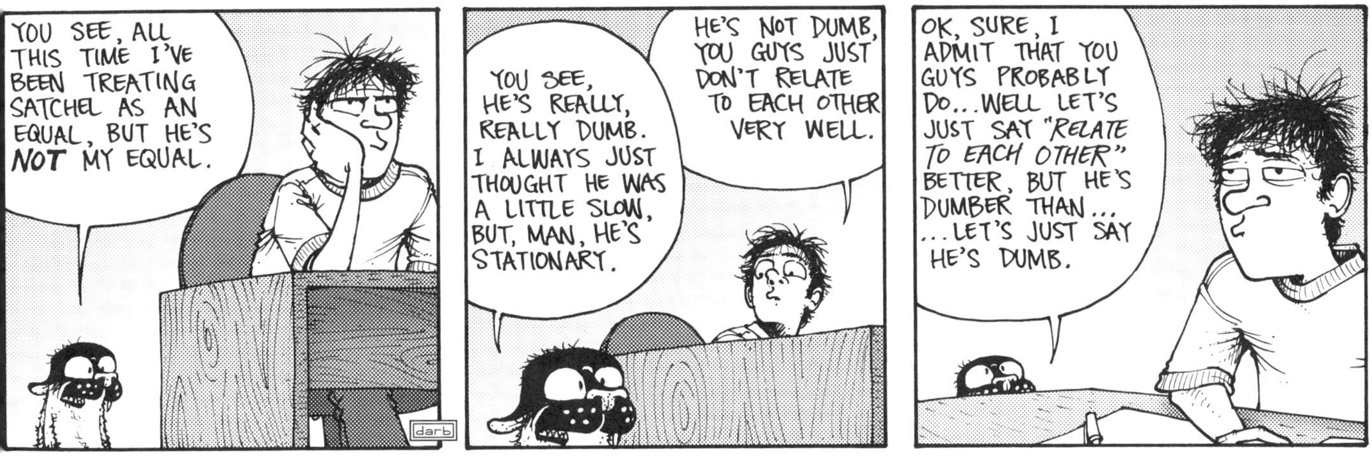
YOU SEE, ALL THIS TIME I'VE BEEN TREATING SATCHEL AS AN EQUAL, BUT HE'S **NOT** MY EQUAL.
YOU SEE, HE'S REALLY, REALLY DUMB. I ALWAYS JUST THOUGHT HE WAS A LITTLE SLOW, BUT, MAN, HE'S STATIONARY.
HE'S NOT DUMB, YOU GUYS JUST DON'T RELATE TO EACH OTHER VERY WELL.
OK, SURE, I ADMIT THAT YOU GUYS PROBABLY DO...WELL LET'S JUST SAY "*RELATE TO EACH OTHER*" BETTER, BUT HE'S DUMBER THAN... ...LET'S JUST SAY HE'S DUMB.
darb

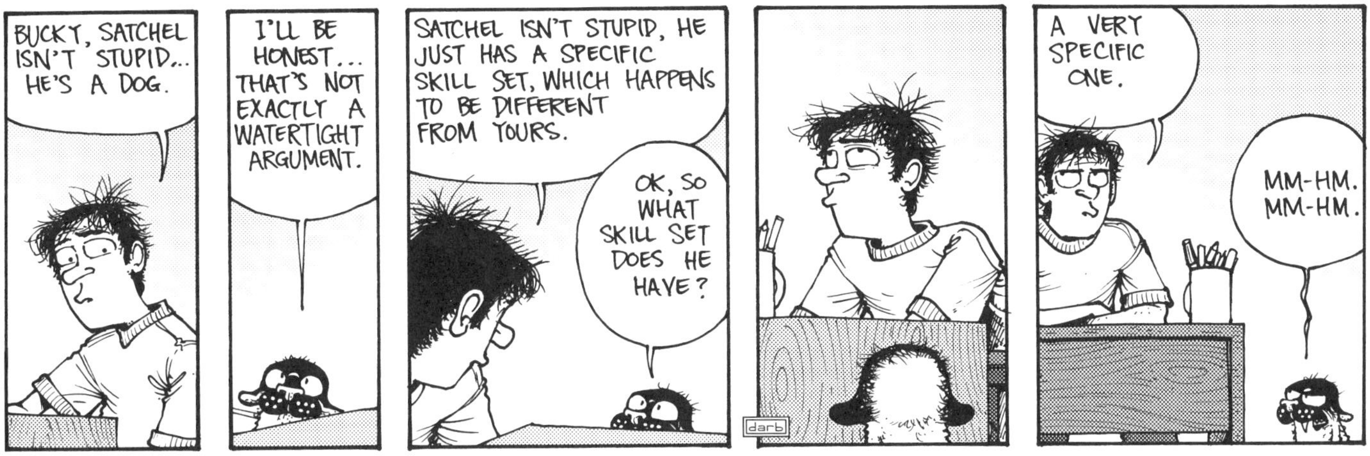
BUCKY, SATCHEL ISN'T STUPID... HE'S A DOG.
I'LL BE HONEST... THAT'S NOT EXACTLY A WATERTIGHT ARGUMENT.
SATCHEL ISN'T STUPID, HE JUST HAS A SPECIFIC SKILL SET, WHICH HAPPENS TO BE DIFFERENT FROM YOURS.
OK, SO WHAT SKILL SET DOES HE HAVE?
darb
A VERY SPECIFIC ONE.
MM-HM. MM-HM.

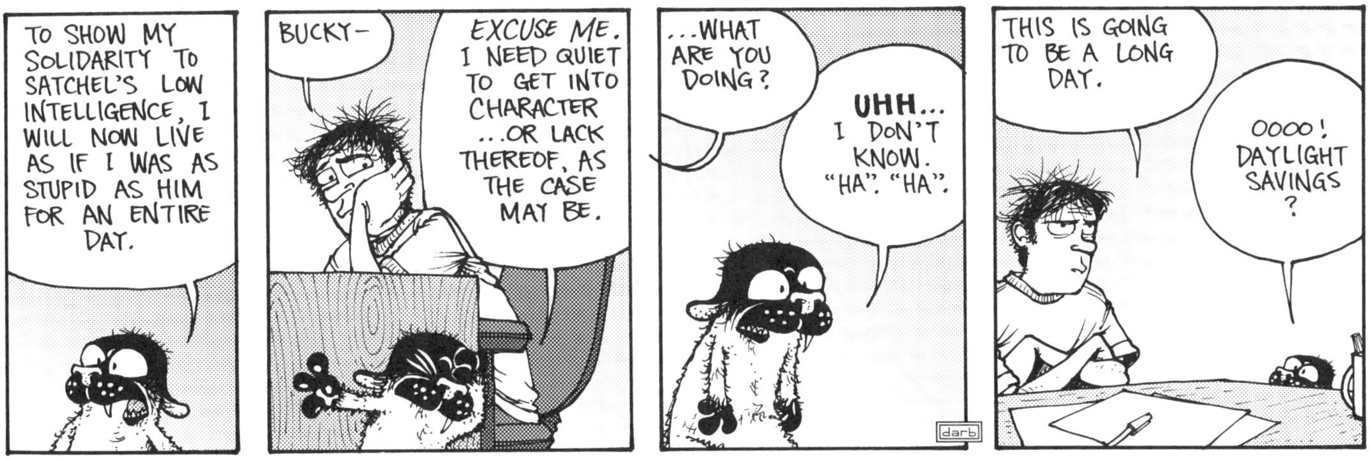
TO SHOW MY SOLIDARITY TO SATCHEL'S LOW INTELLIGENCE, I WILL NOW LIVE AS IF I WAS AS STUPID AS HIM FOR AN ENTIRE DAY.
BUCKY–
EXCUSE ME. I NEED QUIET TO GET INTO CHARACTER ...OR LACK THEREOF, AS THE CASE MAY BE.
...WHAT ARE YOU DOING?
UHH... I DON'T KNOW. "HA". "HA".
darb
THIS IS GOING TO BE A LONG DAY.
OOOO! DAYLIGHT SAVINGS ?

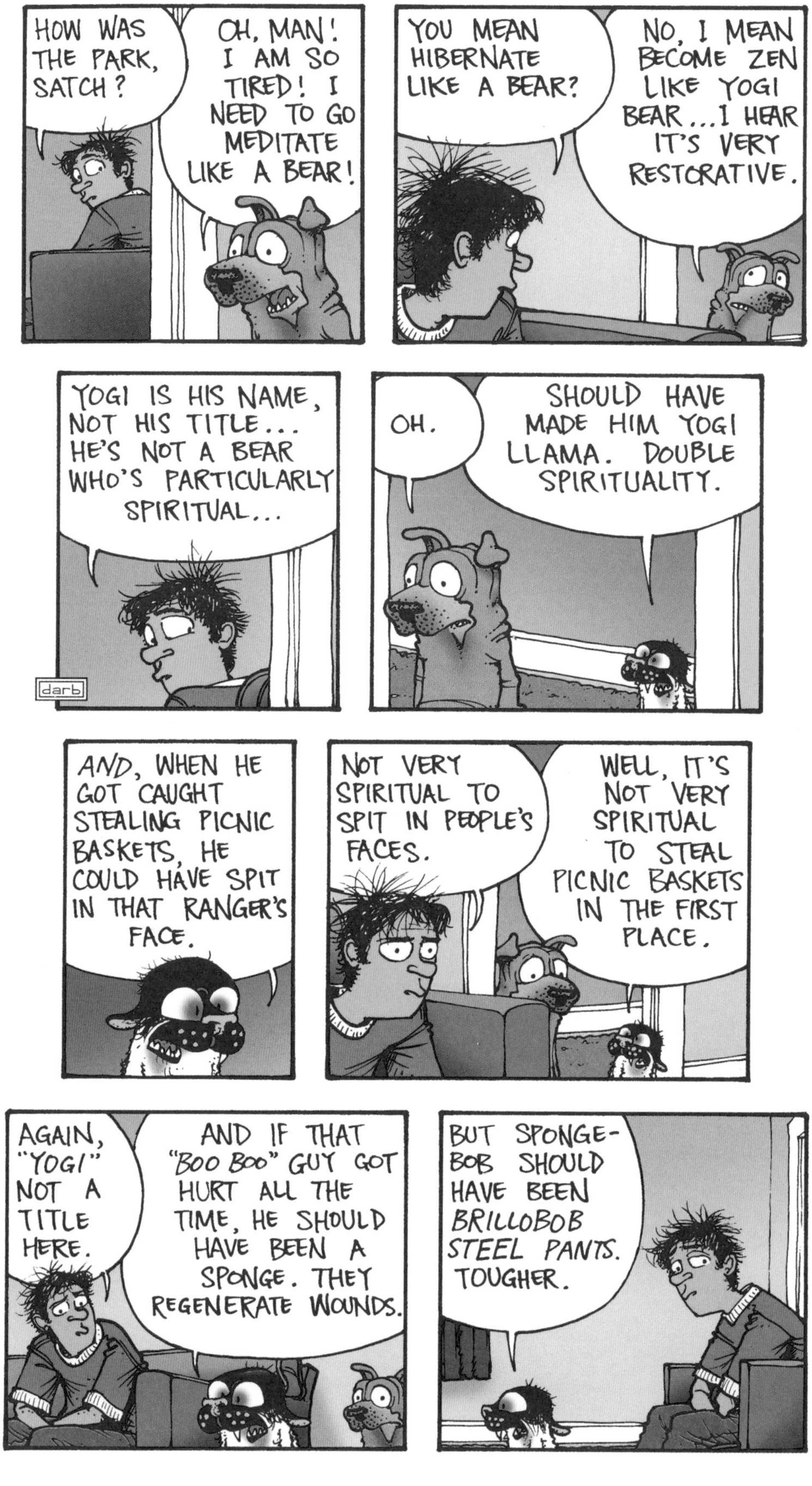
HOW WAS THE PARK, SATCH?
OH, MAN! I AM SO TIRED! I NEED TO GO MEDITATE LIKE A BEAR!
YOU MEAN HIBERNATE LIKE A BEAR?
NO, I MEAN BECOME ZEN LIKE YOGI BEAR... I HEAR IT'S VERY RESTORATIVE.
YOGI IS HIS NAME, NOT HIS TITLE... HE'S NOT A BEAR WHO'S PARTICULARLY SPIRITUAL...
darb
OH.
SHOULD HAVE MADE HIM YOGI LLAMA. DOUBLE SPIRITUALITY.
AND, WHEN HE GOT CAUGHT STEALING PICNIC BASKETS, HE COULD HAVE SPIT IN THAT RANGER'S FACE.
NOT VERY SPIRITUAL TO SPIT IN PEOPLE'S FACES.
WELL, IT'S NOT VERY SPIRITUAL TO STEAL PICNIC BASKETS IN THE FIRST PLACE.
AGAIN, "YOGI" NOT A TITLE HERE.
AND IF THAT "BOO BOO" GUY GOT HURT ALL THE TIME, HE SHOULD HAVE BEEN A SPONGE. THEY REGENERATE WOUNDS.
BUT SPONGE-BOB SHOULD HAVE BEEN BRILLOBOB STEEL PANTS. TOUGHER.

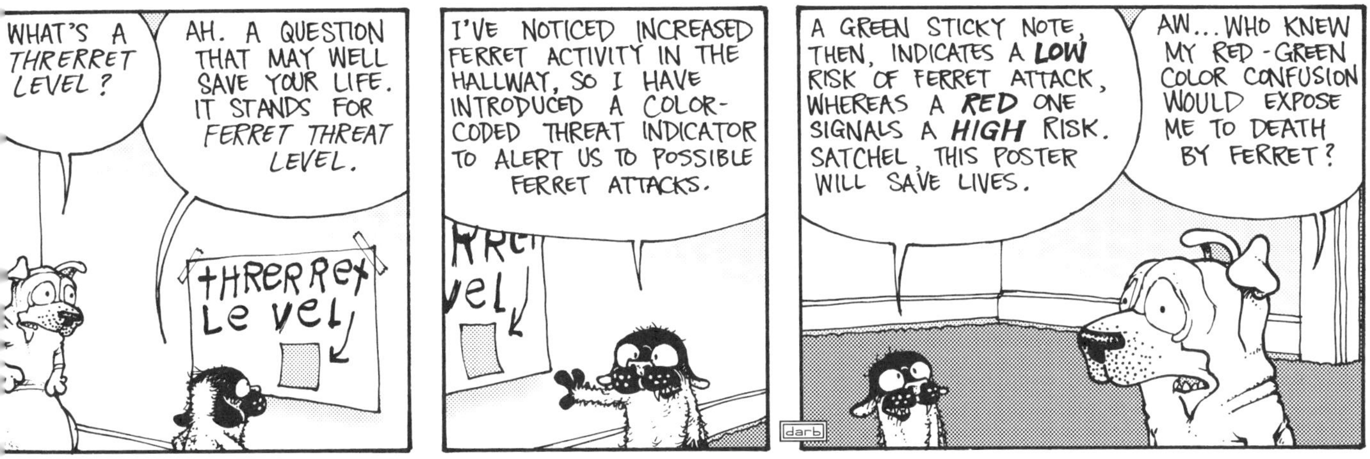
WHAT'S A *THRERRET LEVEL*?
AH. A QUESTION THAT MAY WELL SAVE YOUR LIFE. IT STANDS FOR *FERRET THREAT LEVEL*.
THRERRET LEVEL
I'VE NOTICED INCREASED FERRET ACTIVITY IN THE HALLWAY, SO I HAVE INTRODUCED A COLOR-CODED THREAT INDICATOR TO ALERT US TO POSSIBLE FERRET ATTACKS.
A GREEN STICKY NOTE, THEN, INDICATES A **LOW** RISK OF FERRET ATTACK, WHEREAS A **RED** ONE SIGNALS A **HIGH** RISK. SATCHEL, THIS POSTER WILL SAVE LIVES.
AW... WHO KNEW MY RED-GREEN COLOR CONFUSION WOULD EXPOSE ME TO DEATH BY FERRET?

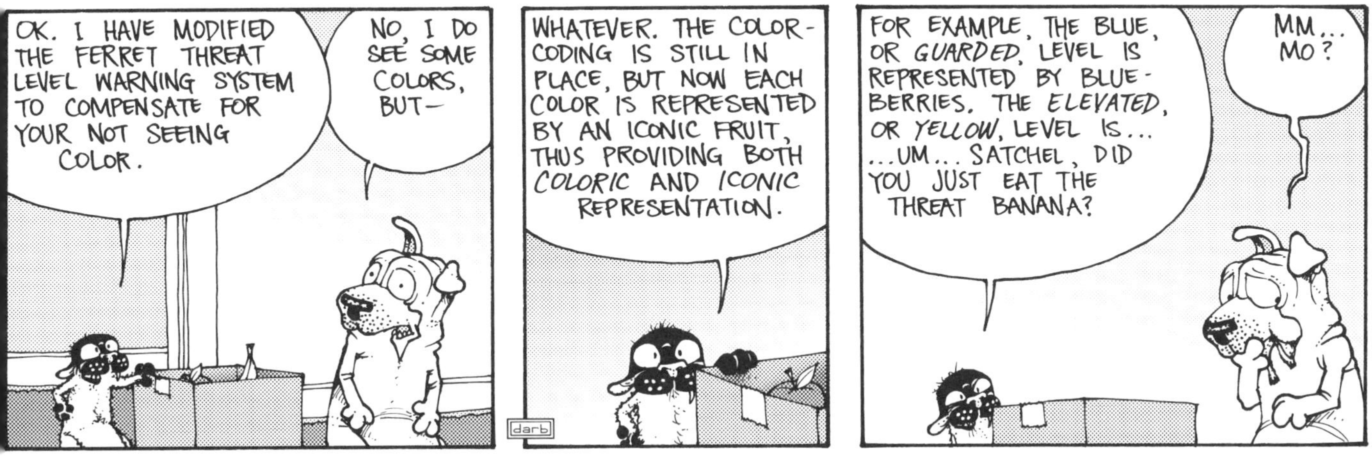
OK. I HAVE MODIFIED THE FERRET THREAT LEVEL WARNING SYSTEM TO COMPENSATE FOR YOUR NOT SEEING COLOR.
NO, I DO SEE SOME COLORS, BUT—
WHATEVER. THE COLOR-CODING IS STILL IN PLACE, BUT NOW EACH COLOR IS REPRESENTED BY AN ICONIC FRUIT, THUS PROVIDING BOTH *COLORIC* AND *ICONIC* REPRESENTATION.
FOR EXAMPLE, THE BLUE, OR *GUARDED*, LEVEL IS REPRESENTED BY BLUEBERRIES. THE *ELEVATED*, OR *YELLOW*, LEVEL IS... ...UM... SATCHEL, DID YOU JUST EAT THE THREAT BANANA?
MM... MO?

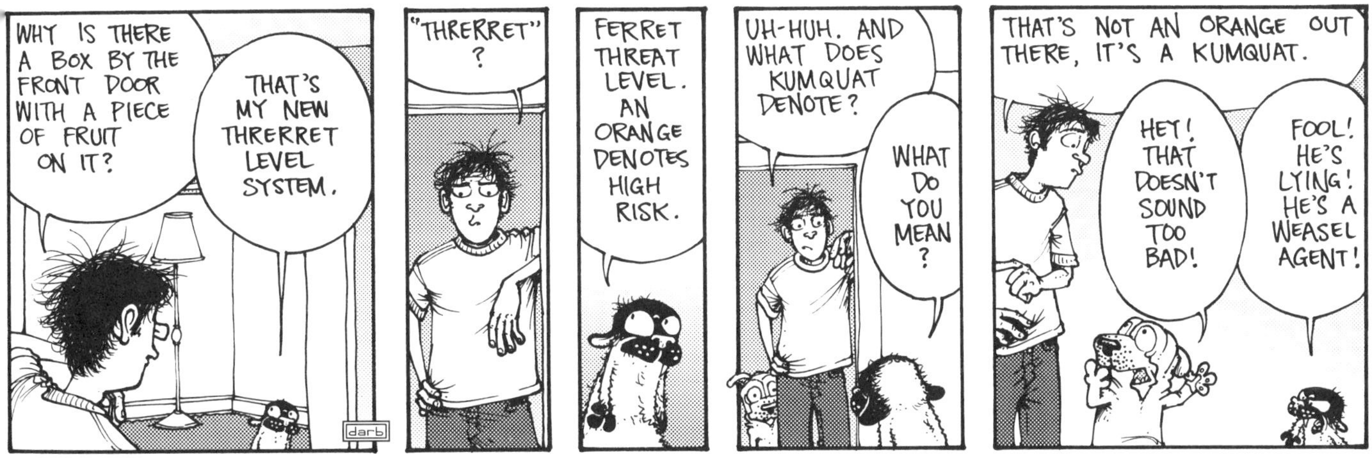
WHY IS THERE A BOX BY THE FRONT DOOR WITH A PIECE OF FRUIT ON IT?
THAT'S MY NEW THRERRET LEVEL SYSTEM.
"THRERRET"?
FERRET THREAT LEVEL. AN ORANGE DENOTES HIGH RISK.
UH-HUH. AND WHAT DOES KUMQUAT DENOTE?
WHAT DO YOU MEAN?
THAT'S NOT AN ORANGE OUT THERE, IT'S A KUMQUAT.
HEY! THAT DOESN'T SOUND TOO BAD!
FOOL! HE'S LYING! HE'S A WEASEL AGENT!

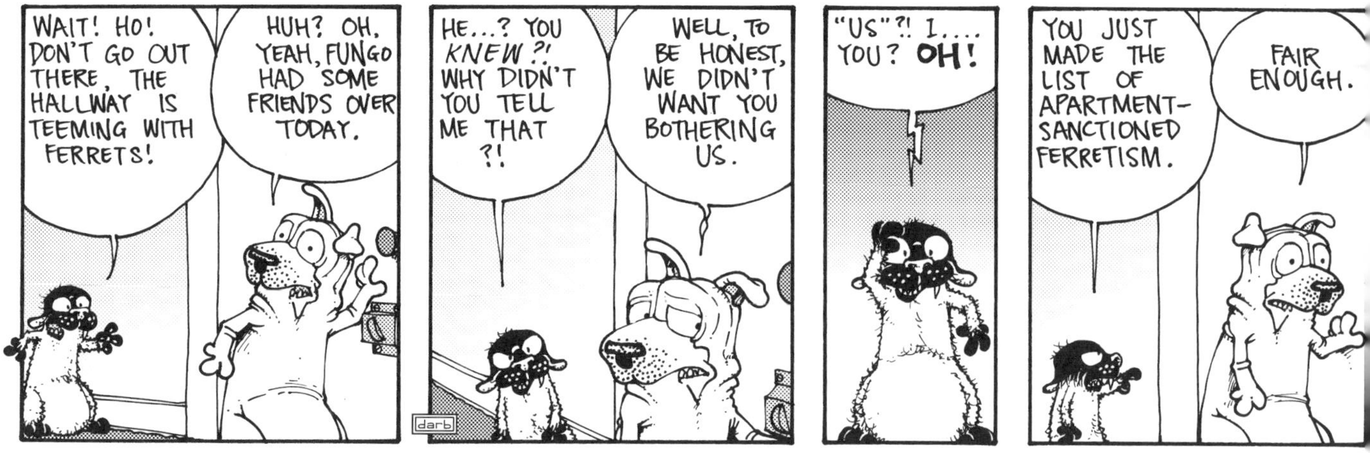
WAIT! HO! DON'T GO OUT THERE, THE HALLWAY IS TEEMING WITH FERRETS!
HUH? OH. YEAH, FUNGO HAD SOME FRIENDS OVER TODAY.
HE...? YOU *KNEW*?! WHY DIDN'T YOU TELL ME THAT ?!
WELL, TO BE HONEST, WE DIDN'T WANT YOU BOTHERING US.
"US"?! I.... YOU? **OH!**
YOU JUST MADE THE LIST OF APARTMENT-SANCTIONED FERRETISM.
FAIR ENOUGH.
darb

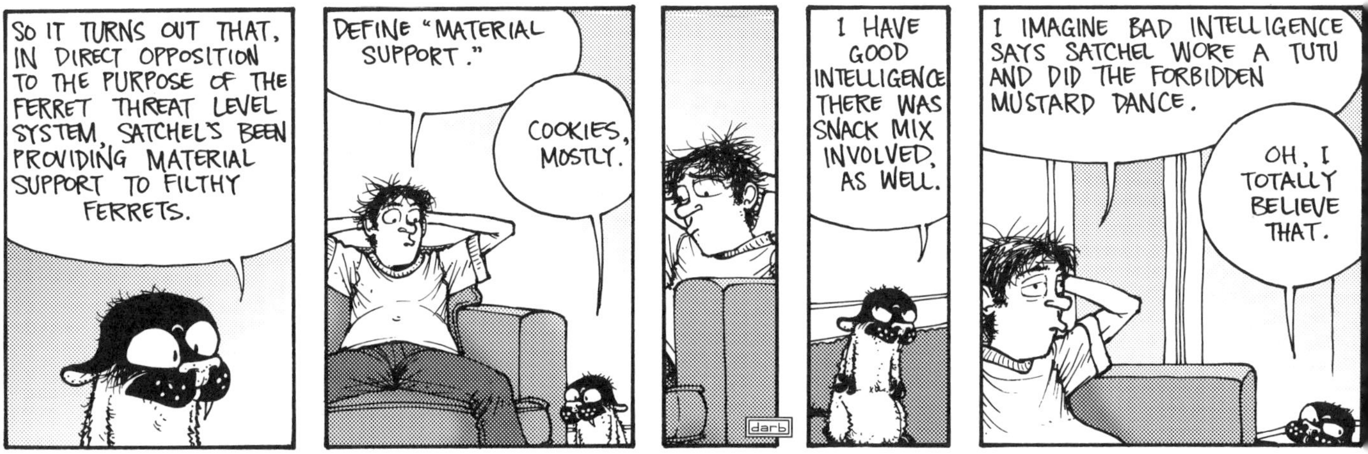
SO IT TURNS OUT THAT, IN DIRECT OPPOSITION TO THE PURPOSE OF THE FERRET THREAT LEVEL SYSTEM, SATCHEL'S BEEN PROVIDING MATERIAL SUPPORT TO FILTHY FERRETS.
DEFINE "MATERIAL SUPPORT."
COOKIES, MOSTLY.
I HAVE GOOD INTELLIGENCE THERE WAS SNACK MIX INVOLVED, AS WELL.
I IMAGINE BAD INTELLIGENCE SAYS SATCHEL WORE A TUTU AND DID THE FORBIDDEN MUSTARD DANCE.
OH, I TOTALLY BELIEVE THAT.
darb

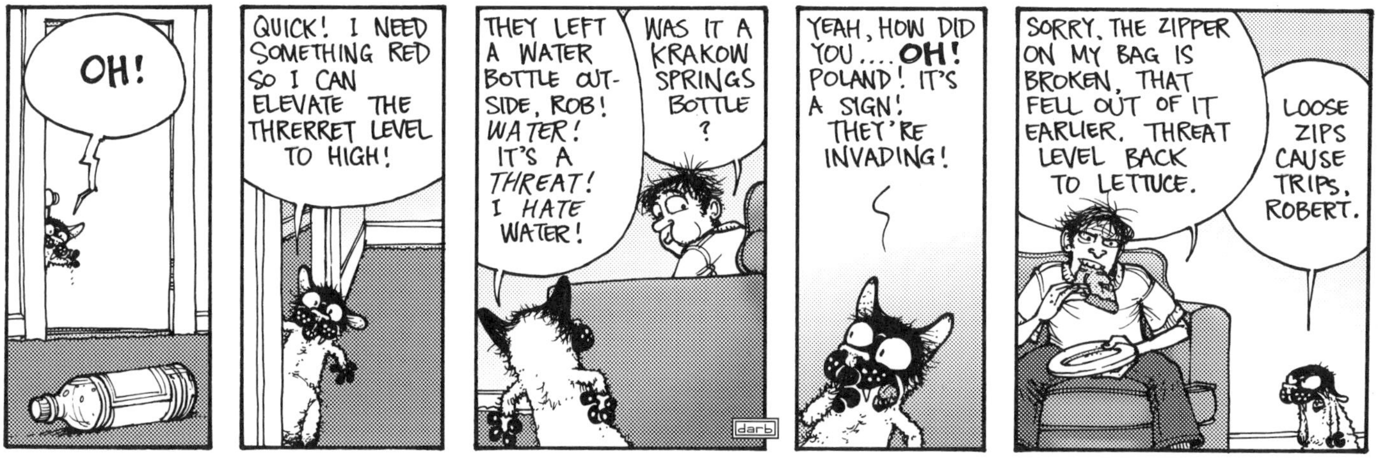
OH!
QUICK! I NEED SOMETHING RED SO I CAN ELEVATE THE THRERRET LEVEL TO HIGH!
THEY LEFT A WATER BOTTLE OUTSIDE, ROB! *WATER!* IT'S A *THREAT!* I HATE WATER!
WAS IT A KRAKOW SPRINGS BOTTLE ?
YEAH, HOW DID YOU.... **OH!** POLAND! IT'S A SIGN! THEY'RE INVADING!
SORRY. THE ZIPPER ON MY BAG IS BROKEN, THAT FELL OUT OF IT EARLIER. THREAT LEVEL BACK TO LETTUCE.
LOOSE ZIPS CAUSE TRIPS, ROBERT.
darb

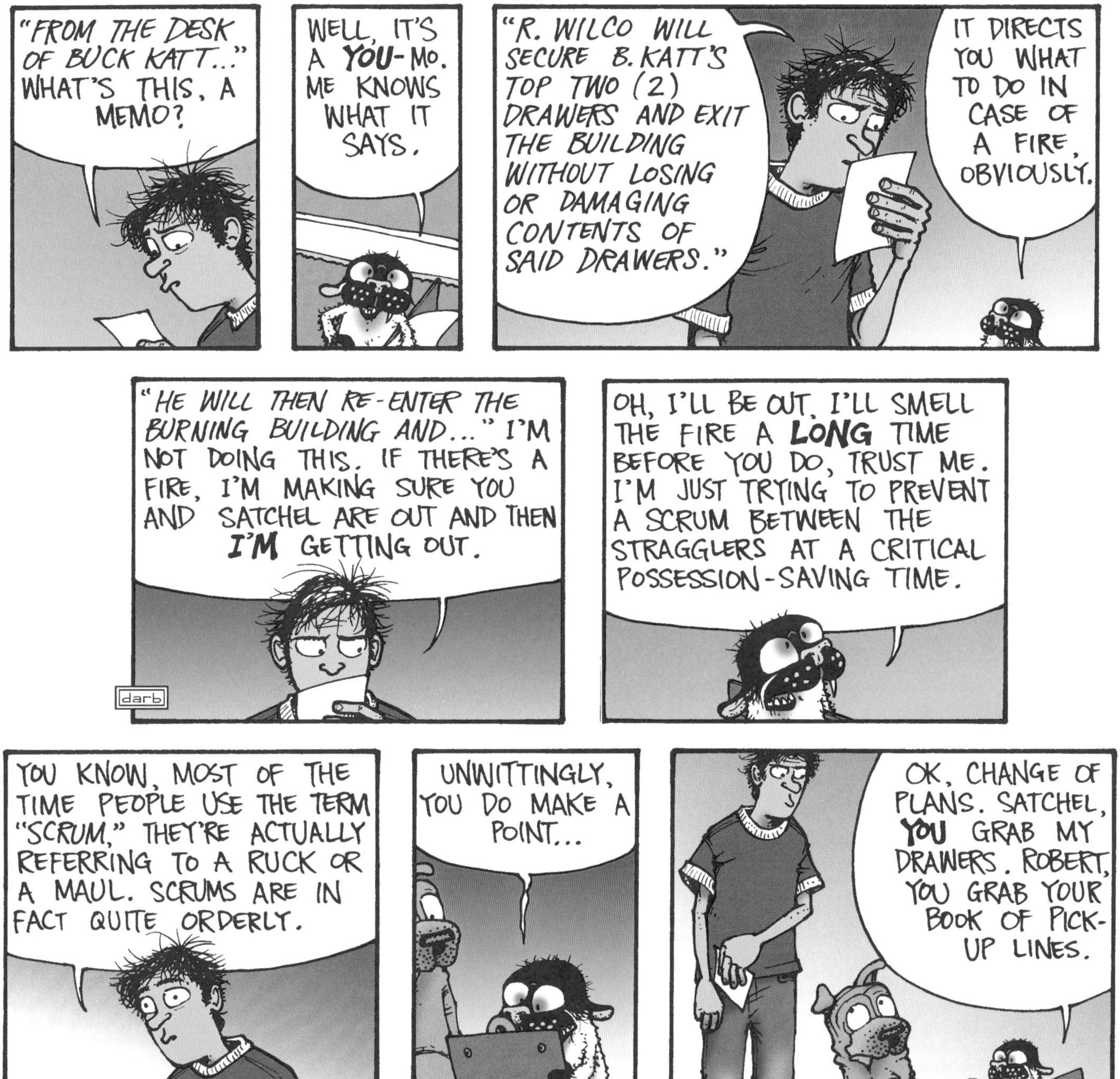
"FROM THE DESK OF BUCK KATT..." WHAT'S THIS, A MEMO?
WELL, IT'S A YOU-MO. ME KNOWS WHAT IT SAYS.
"R. WILCO WILL SECURE B. KATT'S TOP TWO (2) DRAWERS AND EXIT THE BUILDING WITHOUT LOSING OR DAMAGING CONTENTS OF SAID DRAWERS."
IT DIRECTS YOU WHAT TO DO IN CASE OF A FIRE, OBVIOUSLY.
"HE WILL THEN RE-ENTER THE BURNING BUILDING AND..." I'M NOT DOING THIS. IF THERE'S A FIRE, I'M MAKING SURE YOU AND SATCHEL ARE OUT AND THEN I'M GETTING OUT.
darb
OH, I'LL BE OUT. I'LL SMELL THE FIRE A LONG TIME BEFORE YOU DO, TRUST ME. I'M JUST TRYING TO PREVENT A SCRUM BETWEEN THE STRAGGLERS AT A CRITICAL POSSESSION-SAVING TIME.
YOU KNOW, MOST OF THE TIME PEOPLE USE THE TERM "SCRUM," THEY'RE ACTUALLY REFERRING TO A RUCK OR A MAUL. SCRUMS ARE IN FACT QUITE ORDERLY.
UNWITTINGLY, YOU DO MAKE A POINT...
OK, CHANGE OF PLANS. SATCHEL, YOU GRAB MY DRAWERS. ROBERT, YOU GRAB YOUR BOOK OF PICK-UP LINES.

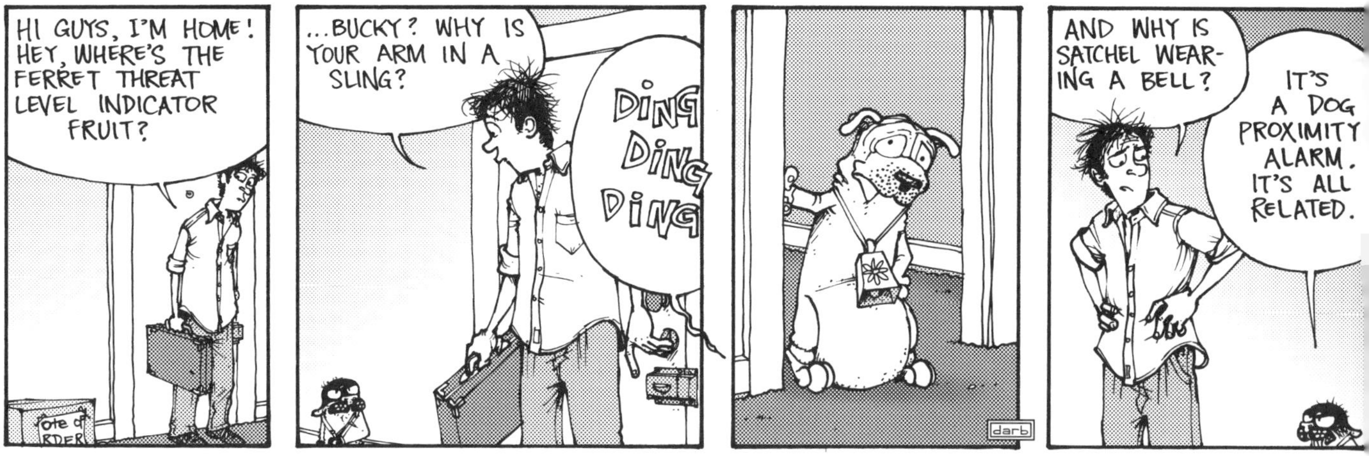
HI GUYS, I'M HOME! HEY, WHERE'S THE FERRET THREAT LEVEL INDICATOR FRUIT?
...BUCKY? WHY IS YOUR ARM IN A SLING?
DING DING DING
AND WHY IS SATCHEL WEAR-ING A BELL?
IT'S A DOG PROXIMITY ALARM. IT'S ALL RELATED.

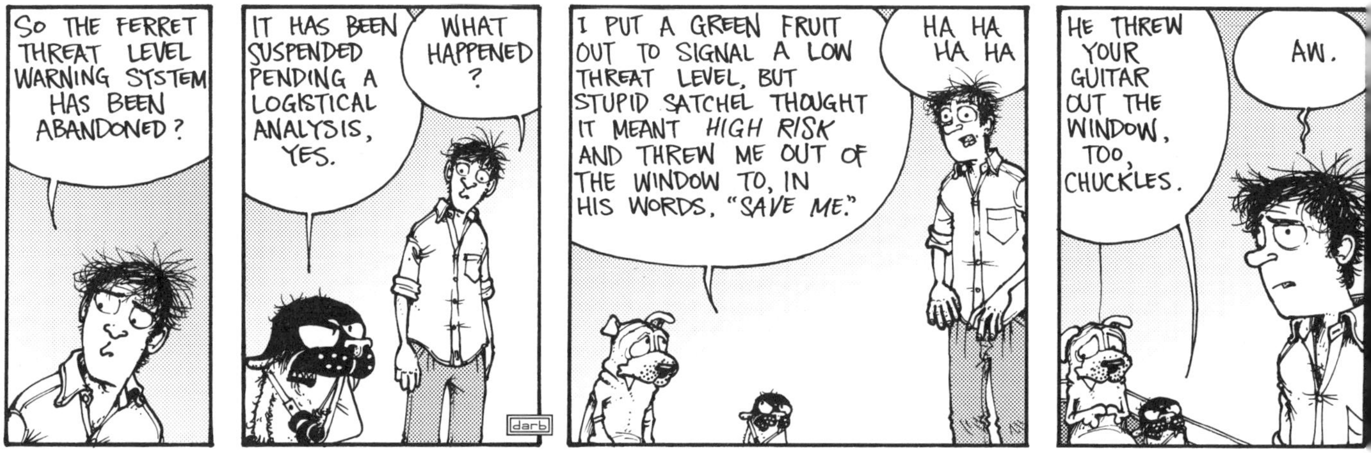
SO THE FERRET THREAT LEVEL WARNING SYSTEM HAS BEEN ABANDONED?
IT HAS BEEN SUSPENDED PENDING A LOGISTICAL ANALYSIS, YES.
WHAT HAPPENED?
I PUT A GREEN FRUIT OUT TO SIGNAL A LOW THREAT LEVEL, BUT STUPID SATCHEL THOUGHT IT MEANT *HIGH RISK* AND THREW ME OUT OF THE WINDOW TO, IN HIS WORDS, "*SAVE ME*."
HA HA HA HA
HE THREW YOUR GUITAR OUT THE WINDOW, TOO, CHUCKLES.
AW.

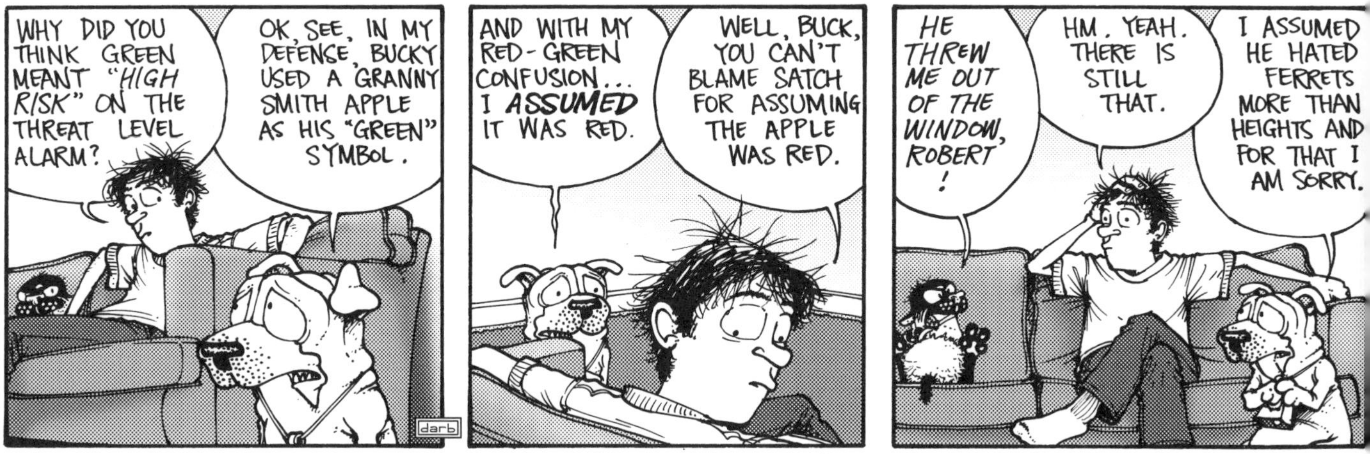
WHY DID YOU THINK GREEN MEANT "*HIGH RISK*" ON THE THREAT LEVEL ALARM?
OK, SEE, IN MY DEFENSE, BUCKY USED A GRANNY SMITH APPLE AS HIS "GREEN" SYMBOL.
AND WITH MY RED-GREEN CONFUSION... I ***ASSUMED*** IT WAS RED.
WELL, BUCK, YOU CAN'T BLAME SATCH FOR ASSUMING THE APPLE WAS RED.
HE THREW ME OUT OF THE WINDOW, ROBERT!
HM. YEAH. THERE IS STILL THAT.
I ASSUMED HE HATED FERRETS MORE THAN HEIGHTS AND FOR THAT I AM SORRY.

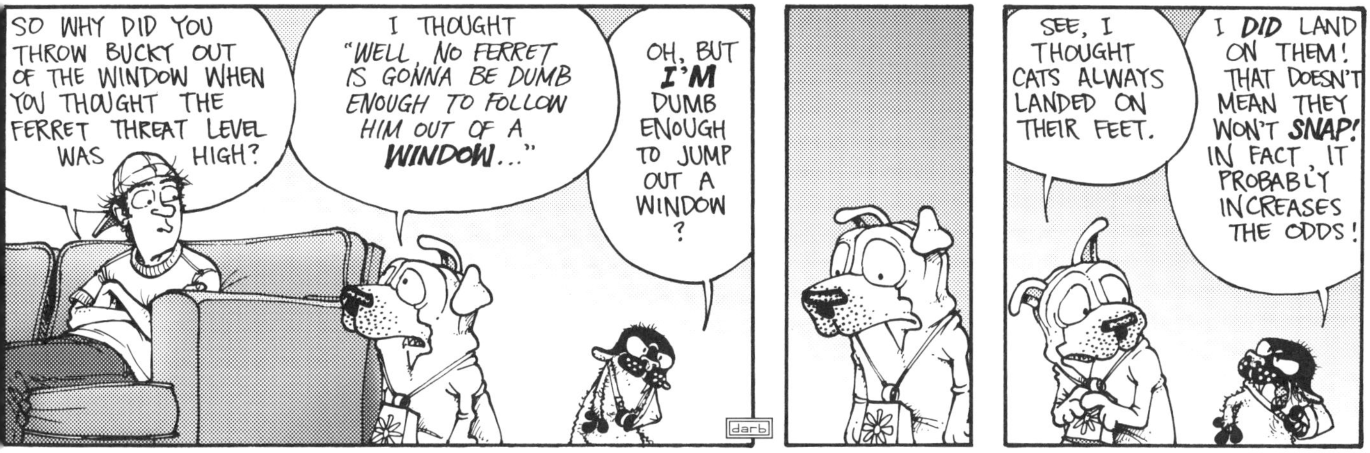
SO WHY DID YOU THROW BUCKY OUT OF THE WINDOW WHEN YOU THOUGHT THE FERRET THREAT LEVEL WAS HIGH?
I THOUGHT "WELL, NO FERRET IS GONNA BE DUMB ENOUGH TO FOLLOW HIM OUT OF A **WINDOW**..."
OH, BUT ***I'M*** DUMB ENOUGH TO JUMP OUT A WINDOW?
SEE, I THOUGHT CATS ALWAYS LANDED ON THEIR FEET.
I ***DID*** LAND ON THEM! THAT DOESN'T MEAN THEY WON'T ***SNAP!*** IN FACT, IT PROBABLY INCREASES THE ODDS!
darb

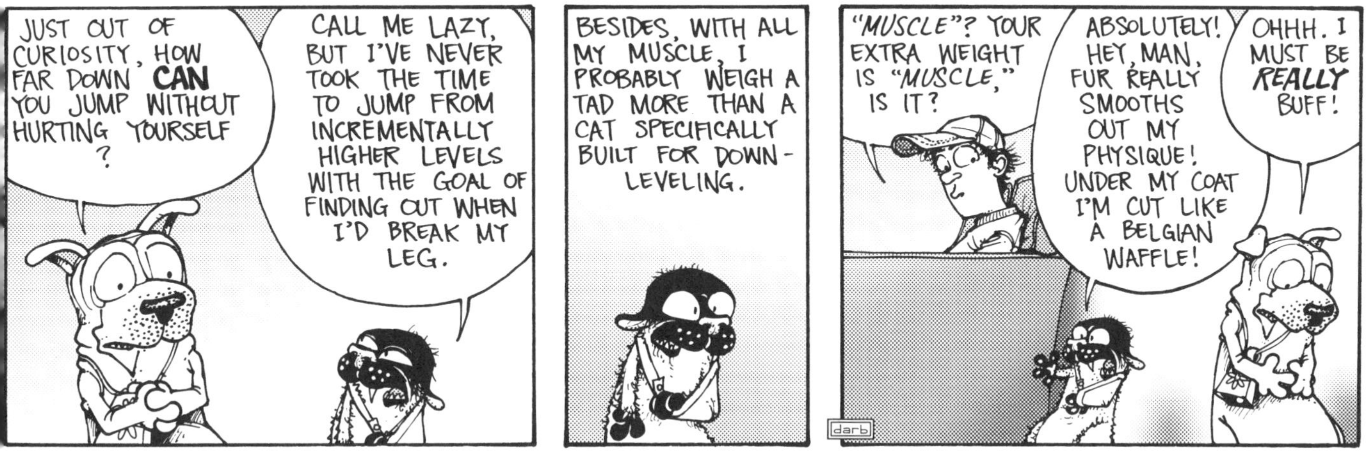
JUST OUT OF CURIOSITY, HOW FAR DOWN **CAN** YOU JUMP WITHOUT HURTING YOURSELF?
CALL ME LAZY, BUT I'VE NEVER TOOK THE TIME TO JUMP FROM INCREMENTALLY HIGHER LEVELS WITH THE GOAL OF FINDING OUT WHEN I'D BREAK MY LEG.
BESIDES, WITH ALL MY MUSCLE, I PROBABLY WEIGH A TAD MORE THAN A CAT SPECIFICALLY BUILT FOR DOWN-LEVELING.
"*MUSCLE*"? YOUR EXTRA WEIGHT IS "*MUSCLE*," IS IT?
ABSOLUTELY! HEY, MAN, FUR REALLY SMOOTHS OUT MY PHYSIQUE! UNDER MY COAT I'M CUT LIKE A BELGIAN WAFFLE!
OHHH. I MUST BE ***REALLY*** BUFF!
darb

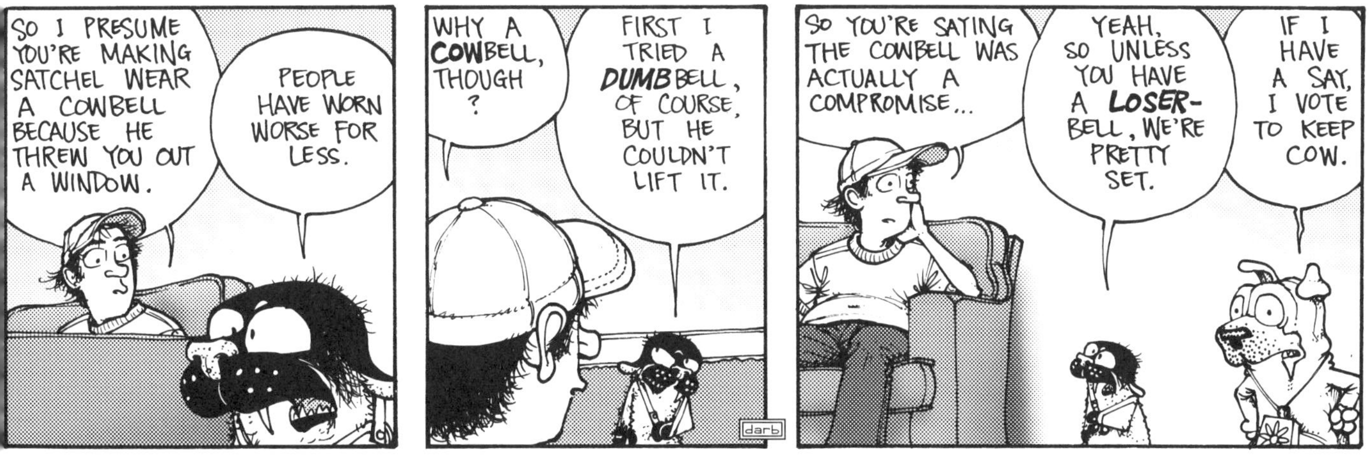
SO I PRESUME YOU'RE MAKING SATCHEL WEAR A COWBELL BECAUSE HE THREW YOU OUT A WINDOW.
PEOPLE HAVE WORN WORSE FOR LESS.
WHY A **COW**BELL, THOUGH?
FIRST I TRIED A ***DUMB***BELL, OF COURSE, BUT HE COULDN'T LIFT IT.
SO YOU'RE SAYING THE COWBELL WAS ACTUALLY A COMPROMISE...
YEAH, SO UNLESS YOU HAVE A **LOSER-**BELL, WE'RE PRETTY SET.
IF I HAVE A SAY, I VOTE TO KEEP COW.
darb

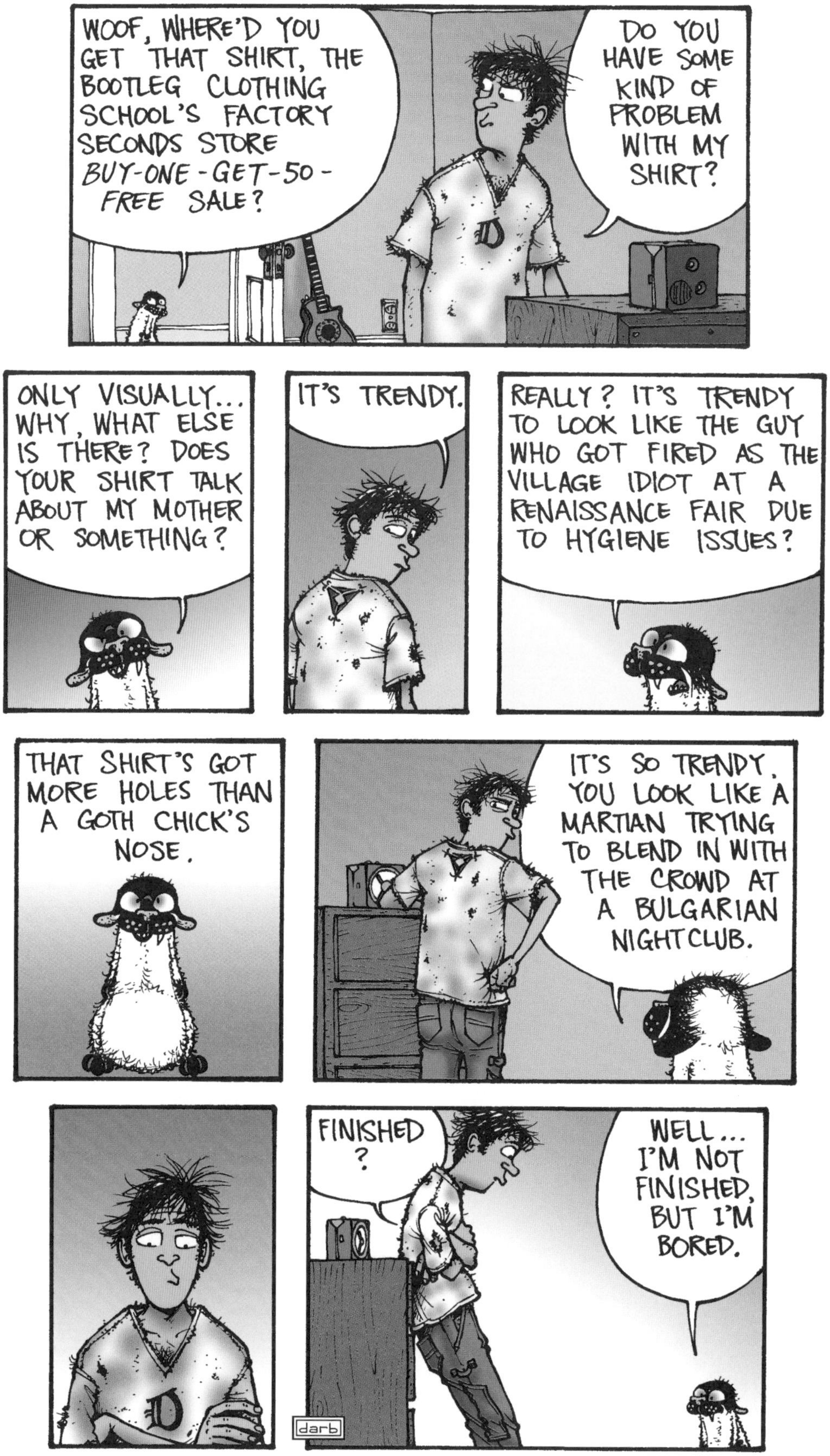
WOOF, WHERE'D YOU GET THAT SHIRT, THE BOOTLEG CLOTHING SCHOOL'S FACTORY SECONDS STORE *BUY-ONE-GET-50-FREE* SALE?
DO YOU HAVE SOME KIND OF PROBLEM WITH MY SHIRT?
ONLY VISUALLY... WHY, WHAT ELSE IS THERE? DOES YOUR SHIRT TALK ABOUT MY MOTHER OR SOMETHING?
IT'S TRENDY.
REALLY? IT'S TRENDY TO LOOK LIKE THE GUY WHO GOT FIRED AS THE VILLAGE IDIOT AT A RENAISSANCE FAIR DUE TO HYGIENE ISSUES?
THAT SHIRT'S GOT MORE HOLES THAN A GOTH CHICK'S NOSE.
IT'S SO TRENDY. YOU LOOK LIKE A MARTIAN TRYING TO BLEND IN WITH THE CROWD AT A BULGARIAN NIGHTCLUB.
FINISHED?
WELL... I'M NOT FINISHED, BUT I'M BORED.
darb

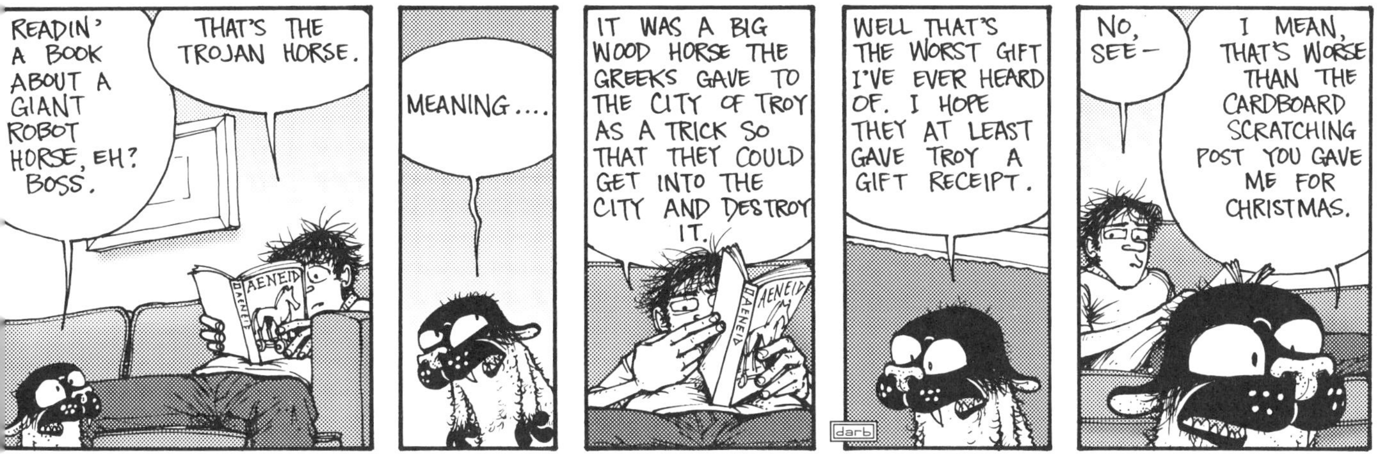
READIN' A BOOK ABOUT A GIANT ROBOT HORSE, EH? BOSS.
THAT'S THE TROJAN HORSE.
AENEID
MEANING....
IT WAS A BIG WOOD HORSE THE GREEKS GAVE TO THE CITY OF TROY AS A TRICK SO THAT THEY COULD GET INTO THE CITY AND DESTROY IT.
AENEID
WELL THAT'S THE WORST GIFT I'VE EVER HEARD OF. I HOPE THEY AT LEAST GAVE TROY A GIFT RECEIPT.
darb
NO, SEE-
I MEAN, THAT'S WORSE THAN THE CARDBOARD SCRATCHING POST YOU GAVE ME FOR CHRISTMAS.

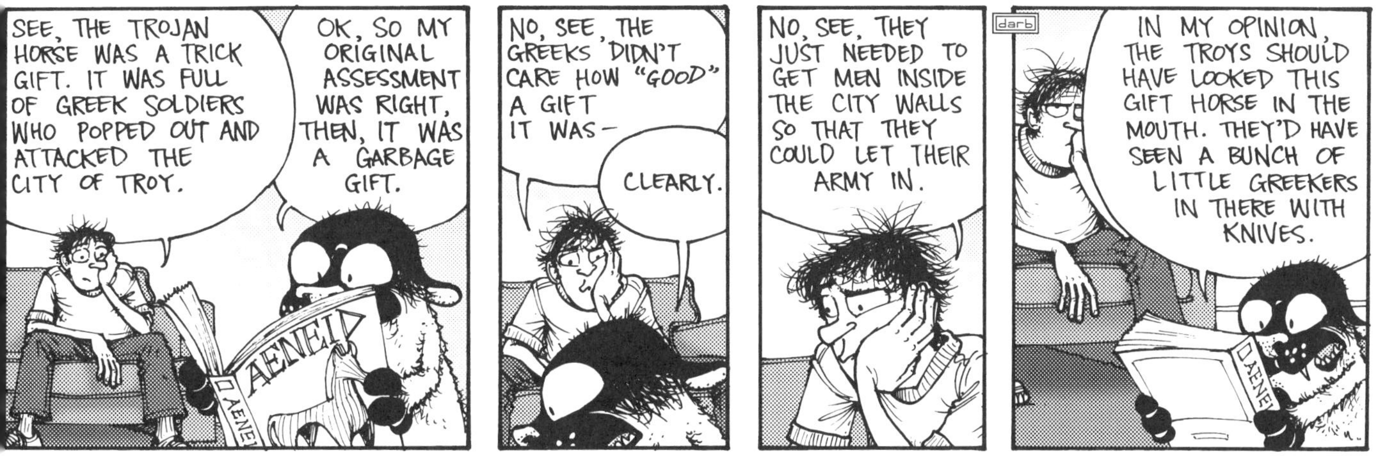
SEE, THE TROJAN HORSE WAS A TRICK GIFT. IT WAS FULL OF GREEK SOLDIERS WHO POPPED OUT AND ATTACKED THE CITY OF TROY.
OK, SO MY ORIGINAL ASSESSMENT WAS RIGHT, THEN, IT WAS A GARBAGE GIFT.
AENEID
NO, SEE, THE GREEKS DIDN'T CARE HOW "GOOD" A GIFT IT WAS-
CLEARLY.
NO, SEE, THEY JUST NEEDED TO GET MEN INSIDE THE CITY WALLS SO THAT THEY COULD LET THEIR ARMY IN.
darb
IN MY OPINION, THE TROYS SHOULD HAVE LOOKED THIS GIFT HORSE IN THE MOUTH. THEY'D HAVE SEEN A BUNCH OF LITTLE GREEKERS IN THERE WITH KNIVES.

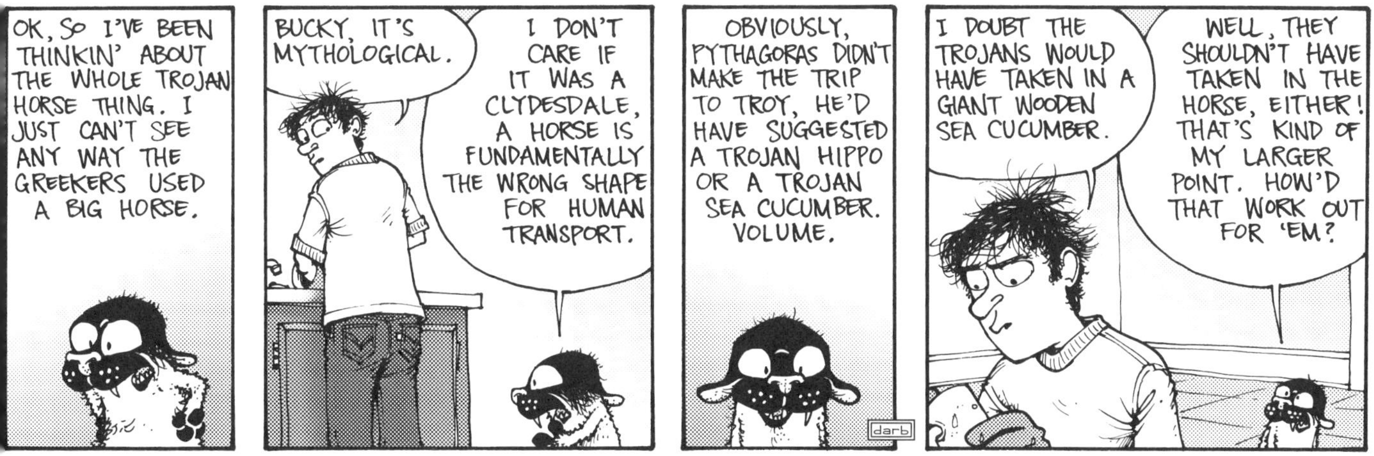
OK, SO I'VE BEEN THINKIN' ABOUT THE WHOLE TROJAN HORSE THING. I JUST CAN'T SEE ANY WAY THE GREEKERS USED A BIG HORSE.
BUCKY, IT'S MYTHOLOGICAL.
I DON'T CARE IF IT WAS A CLYDESDALE, A HORSE IS FUNDAMENTALLY THE WRONG SHAPE FOR HUMAN TRANSPORT.
OBVIOUSLY, PYTHAGORAS DIDN'T MAKE THE TRIP TO TROY, HE'D HAVE SUGGESTED A TROJAN HIPPO OR A TROJAN SEA CUCUMBER. VOLUME.
darb
I DOUBT THE TROJANS WOULD HAVE TAKEN IN A GIANT WOODEN SEA CUCUMBER.
WELL, THEY SHOULDN'T HAVE TAKEN IN THE HORSE, EITHER! THAT'S KIND OF MY LARGER POINT. HOW'D THAT WORK OUT FOR 'EM?

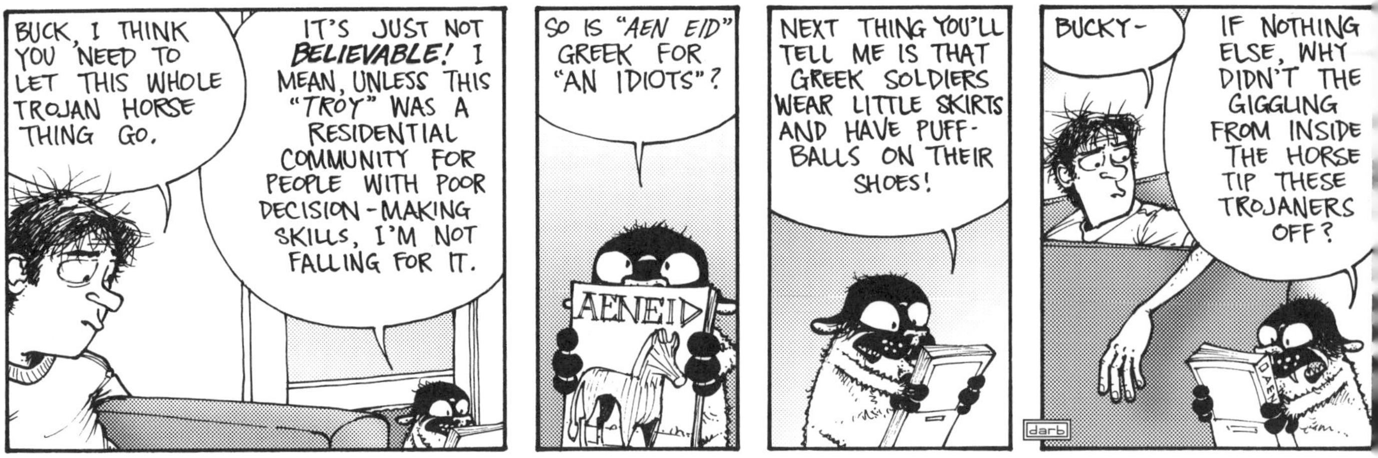
BUCK, I THINK YOU NEED TO LET THIS WHOLE TROJAN HORSE THING GO.
IT'S JUST NOT ***BELIEVABLE!*** I MEAN, UNLESS THIS "*TROY*" WAS A RESIDENTIAL COMMUNITY FOR PEOPLE WITH POOR DECISION-MAKING SKILLS, I'M NOT FALLING FOR IT.
AENEID
SO IS "*AEN EID*" GREEK FOR "AN IDIOTS"?
NEXT THING YOU'LL TELL ME IS THAT GREEK SOLDIERS WEAR LITTLE SKIRTS AND HAVE PUFF-BALLS ON THEIR SHOES!
BUCKY-
IF NOTHING ELSE, WHY DIDN'T THE GIGGLING FROM INSIDE THE HORSE TIP THESE TROJANERS OFF?
darb

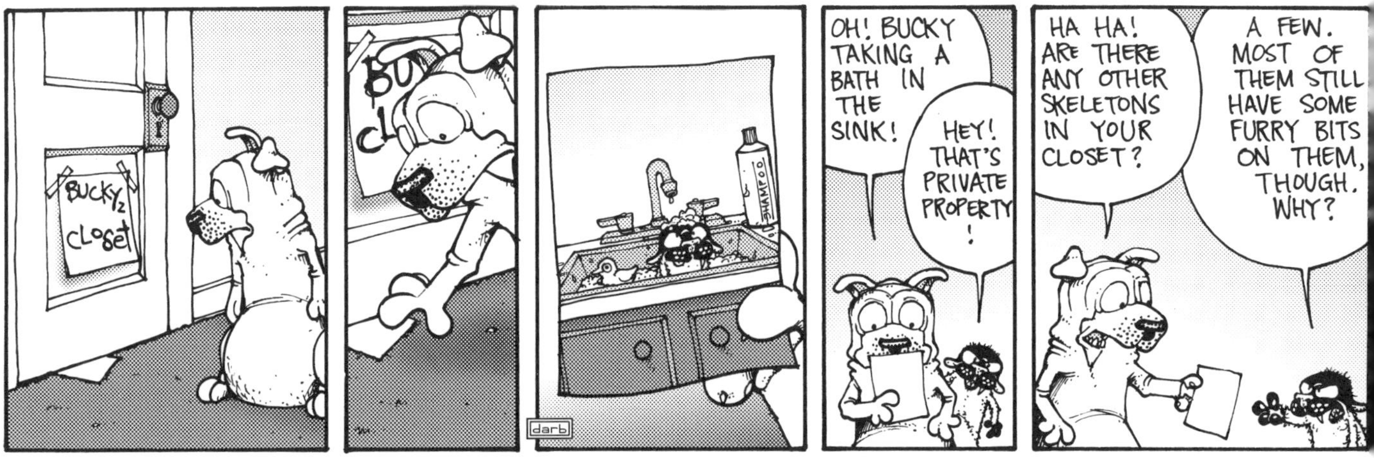
BUCKY'S CLOSET
darb
OH! BUCKY TAKING A BATH IN THE SINK!
HEY! THAT'S PRIVATE PROPERTY!
HA HA! ARE THERE ANY OTHER SKELETONS IN YOUR CLOSET?
A FEW. MOST OF THEM STILL HAVE SOME FURRY BITS ON THEM, THOUGH. WHY?

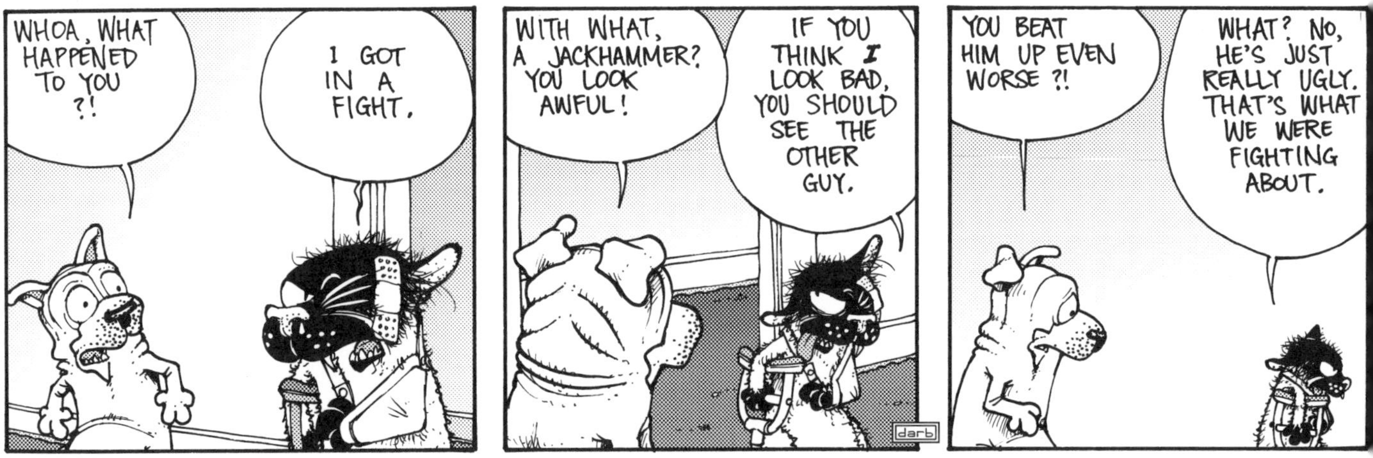
WHOA, WHAT HAPPENED TO YOU ?!
I GOT IN A FIGHT.
WITH WHAT, A JACKHAMMER? YOU LOOK AWFUL!
IF YOU THINK ***I*** LOOK BAD, YOU SHOULD SEE THE OTHER GUY.
darb
YOU BEAT HIM UP EVEN WORSE ?!
WHAT? NO, HE'S JUST REALLY UGLY. THAT'S WHAT WE WERE FIGHTING ABOUT.

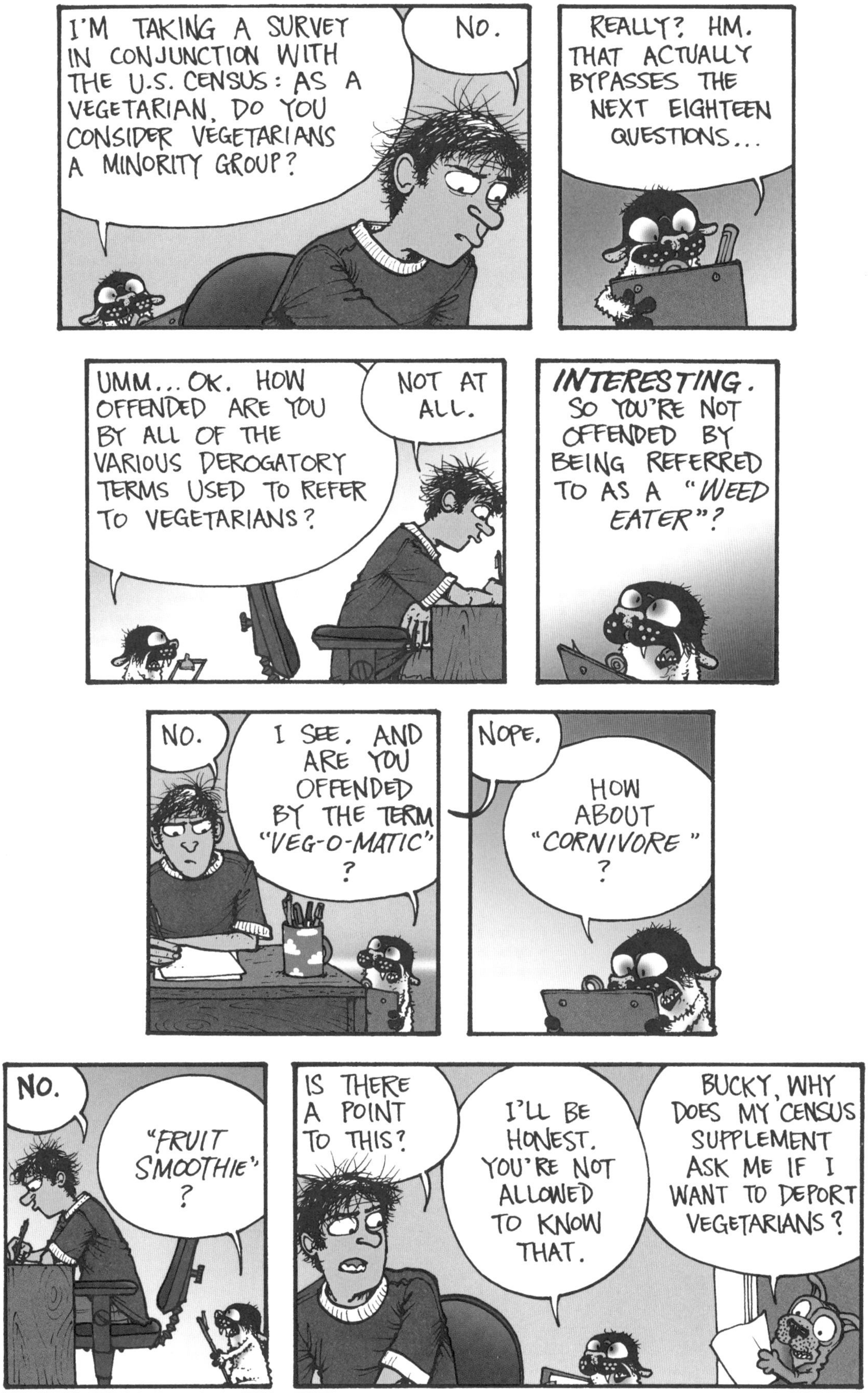
I'M TAKING A SURVEY IN CONJUNCTION WITH THE U.S. CENSUS: AS A VEGETARIAN, DO YOU CONSIDER VEGETARIANS A MINORITY GROUP?
NO.
REALLY? HM. THAT ACTUALLY BYPASSES THE NEXT EIGHTEEN QUESTIONS...
UMM... OK. HOW OFFENDED ARE YOU BY ALL OF THE VARIOUS DEROGATORY TERMS USED TO REFER TO VEGETARIANS?
NOT AT ALL.
INTERESTING. SO YOU'RE NOT OFFENDED BY BEING REFERRED TO AS A "WEED EATER"?
NO.
I SEE. AND ARE YOU OFFENDED BY THE TERM "VEG-O-MATIC"?
NOPE.
HOW ABOUT "CORNIVORE"?
NO.
"FRUIT SMOOTHIE"?
IS THERE A POINT TO THIS?
I'LL BE HONEST. YOU'RE NOT ALLOWED TO KNOW THAT.
BUCKY, WHY DOES MY CENSUS SUPPLEMENT ASK ME IF I WANT TO DEPORT VEGETARIANS?

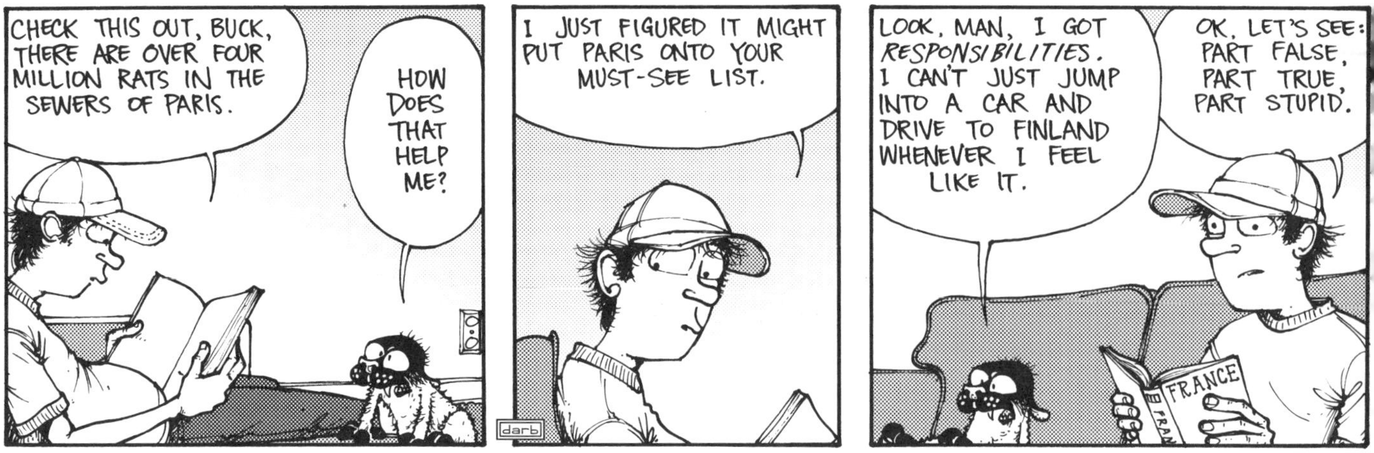
CHECK THIS OUT, BUCK, THERE ARE OVER FOUR MILLION RATS IN THE SEWERS OF PARIS.
HOW DOES THAT HELP ME?
I JUST FIGURED IT MIGHT PUT PARIS ONTO YOUR MUST-SEE LIST.
LOOK, MAN, I GOT RESPONSIBILITIES. I CAN'T JUST JUMP INTO A CAR AND DRIVE TO FINLAND WHENEVER I FEEL LIKE IT.
OK, LET'S SEE: PART FALSE, PART TRUE, PART STUPID.
FRANCE
darb

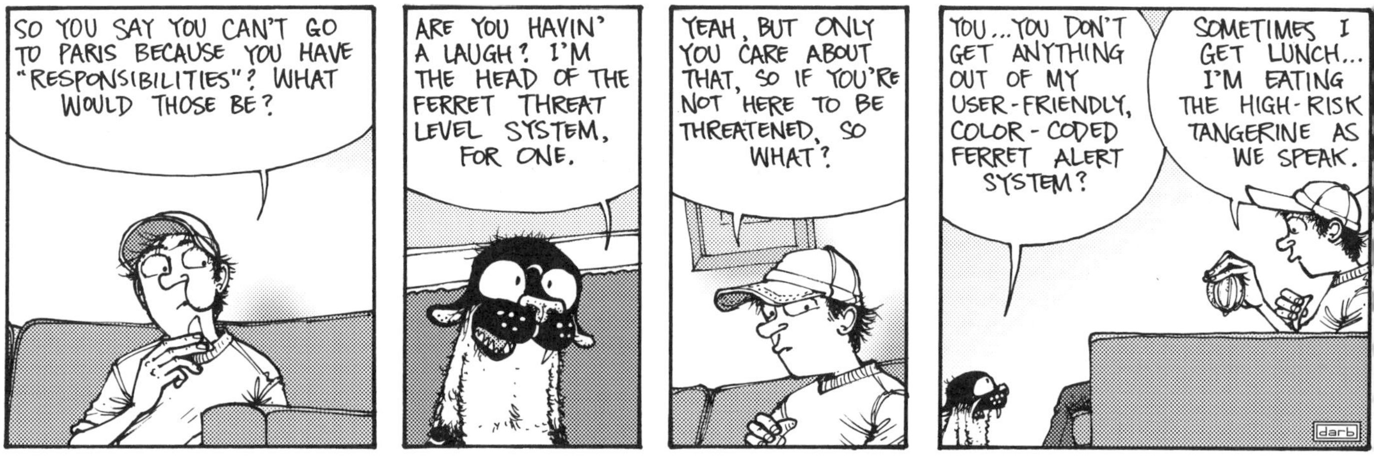
SO YOU SAY YOU CAN'T GO TO PARIS BECAUSE YOU HAVE "RESPONSIBILITIES"? WHAT WOULD THOSE BE?
ARE YOU HAVIN' A LAUGH? I'M THE HEAD OF THE FERRET THREAT LEVEL SYSTEM, FOR ONE.
YEAH, BUT ONLY YOU CARE ABOUT THAT, SO IF YOU'RE NOT HERE TO BE THREATENED, SO WHAT?
YOU...YOU DON'T GET ANYTHING OUT OF MY USER-FRIENDLY, COLOR-CODED FERRET ALERT SYSTEM?
SOMETIMES I GET LUNCH... I'M EATING THE HIGH-RISK TANGERINE AS WE SPEAK.
darb

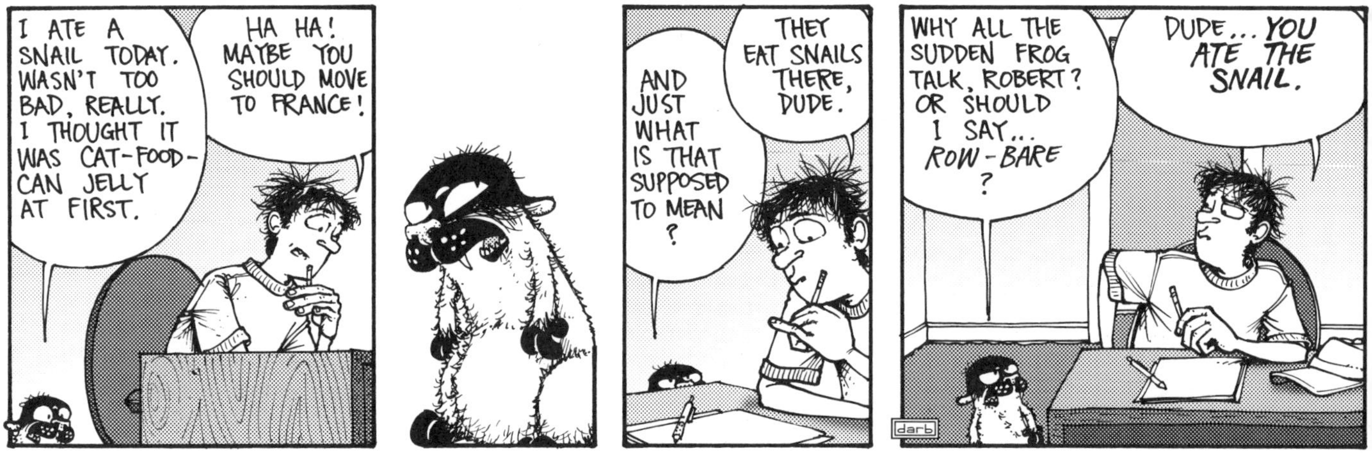
I ATE A SNAIL TODAY. WASN'T TOO BAD, REALLY. I THOUGHT IT WAS CAT-FOOD-CAN JELLY AT FIRST.
HA HA! MAYBE YOU SHOULD MOVE TO FRANCE!
THEY EAT SNAILS THERE, DUDE.
AND JUST WHAT IS THAT SUPPOSED TO MEAN?
WHY ALL THE SUDDEN FROG TALK, ROBERT? OR SHOULD I SAY... ROW-BARE?
DUDE... YOU ATE THE SNAIL.
darb

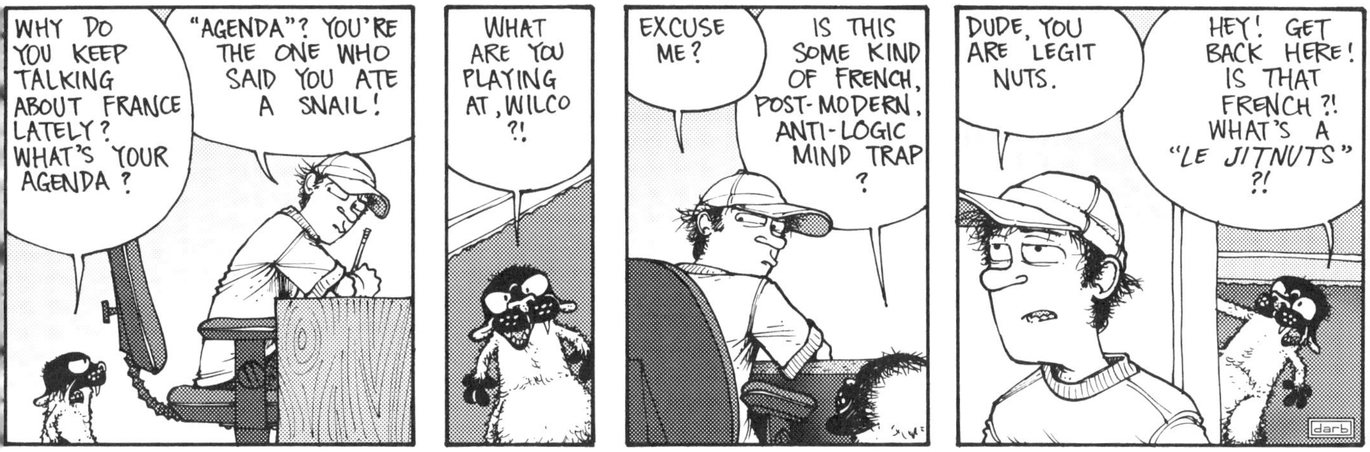
WHY DO YOU KEEP TALKING ABOUT FRANCE LATELY? WHAT'S YOUR AGENDA?
"AGENDA"? YOU'RE THE ONE WHO SAID YOU ATE A SNAIL!
WHAT ARE YOU PLAYING AT, WILCO ?!
EXCUSE ME?
IS THIS SOME KIND OF FRENCH, POST-MODERN, ANTI-LOGIC MIND TRAP ?
DUDE, YOU ARE LEGIT NUTS.
HEY! GET BACK HERE! IS THAT FRENCH ?! WHAT'S A "LE JITNUTS" ?!
darb

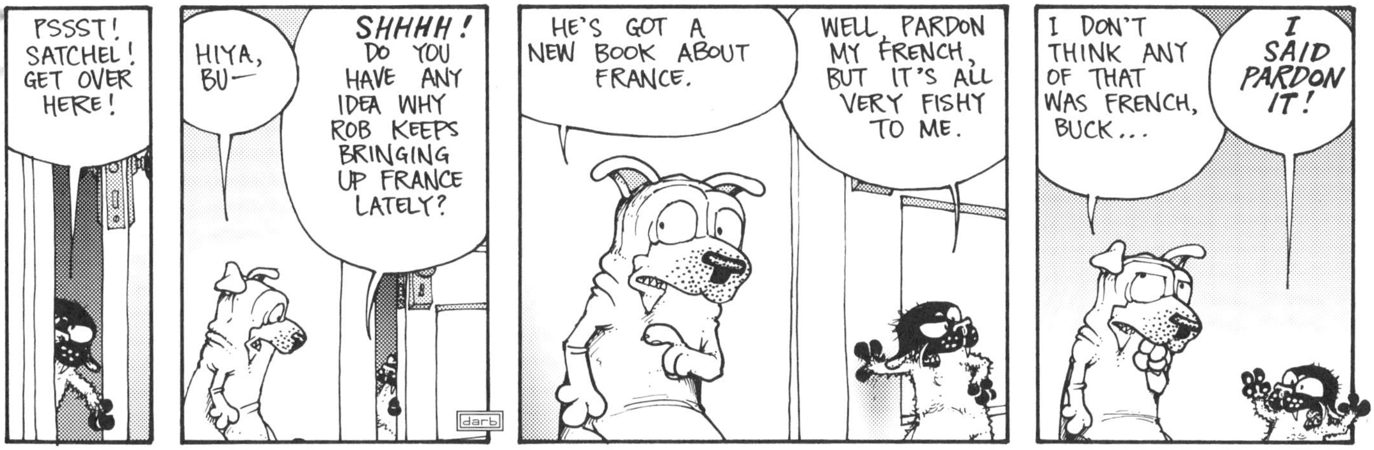
PSSST! SATCHEL! GET OVER HERE!
HIYA, BU—
SHHHH! DO YOU HAVE ANY IDEA WHY ROB KEEPS BRINGING UP FRANCE LATELY?
darb
HE'S GOT A NEW BOOK ABOUT FRANCE.
WELL, PARDON MY FRENCH, BUT IT'S ALL VERY FISHY TO ME.
I DON'T THINK ANY OF THAT WAS FRENCH, BUCK...
I SAID PARDON IT!

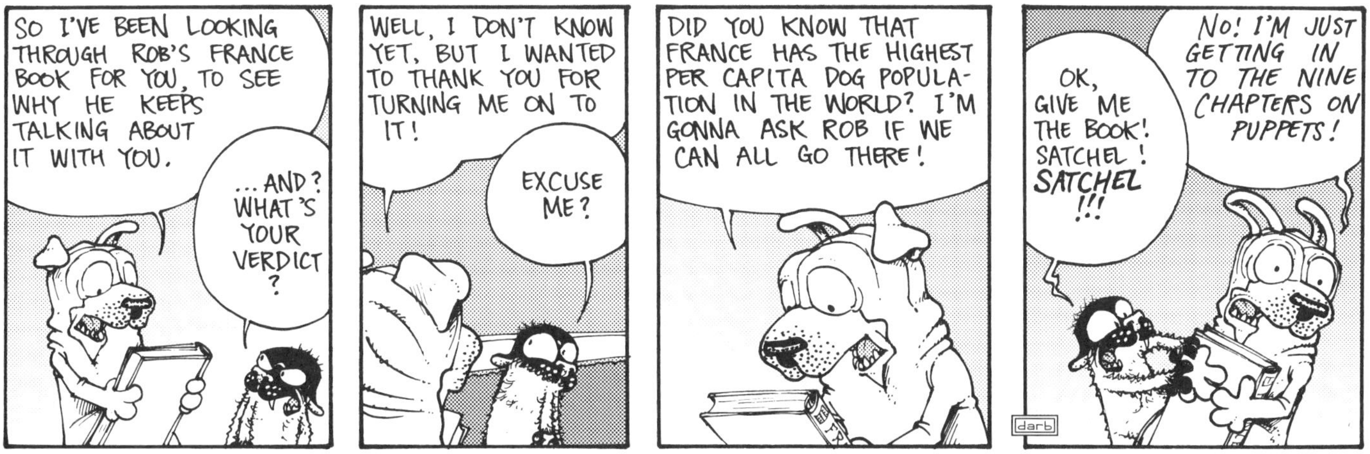
SO I'VE BEEN LOOKING THROUGH ROB'S FRANCE BOOK FOR YOU, TO SEE WHY HE KEEPS TALKING ABOUT IT WITH YOU.
...AND? WHAT'S YOUR VERDICT ?
WELL, I DON'T KNOW YET, BUT I WANTED TO THANK YOU FOR TURNING ME ON TO IT!
EXCUSE ME?
DID YOU KNOW THAT FRANCE HAS THE HIGHEST PER CAPITA DOG POPULATION IN THE WORLD? I'M GONNA ASK ROB IF WE CAN ALL GO THERE!
darb
OK, GIVE ME THE BOOK! SATCHEL! SATCHEL !!!
NO! I'M JUST GETTING IN TO THE NINE CHAPTERS ON PUPPETS!

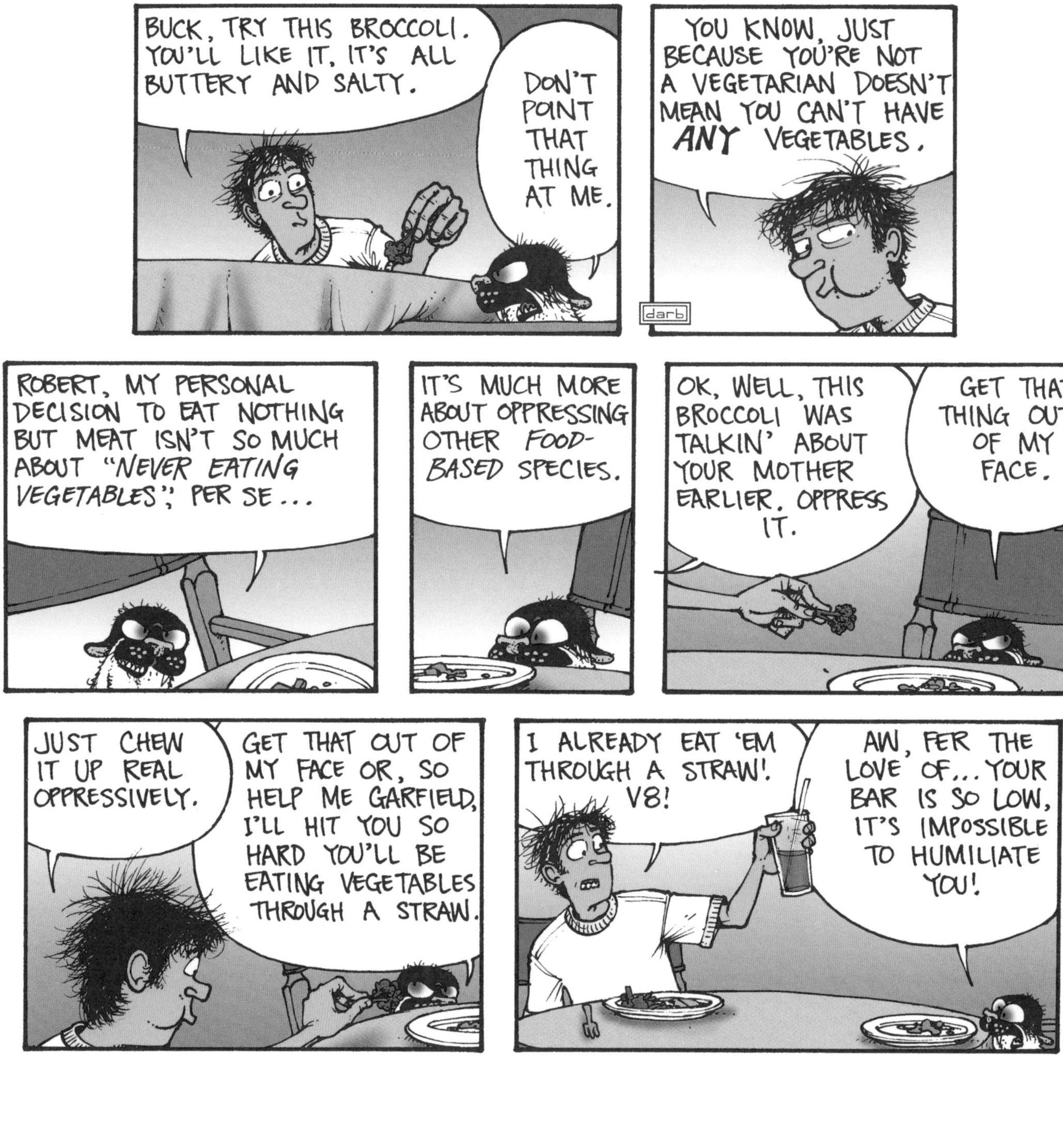
BUCK, TRY THIS BROCCOLI. YOU'LL LIKE IT, IT'S ALL BUTTERY AND SALTY.
DON'T POINT THAT THING AT ME.
YOU KNOW, JUST BECAUSE YOU'RE NOT A VEGETARIAN DOESN'T MEAN YOU CAN'T HAVE ANY VEGETABLES.
darb
ROBERT, MY PERSONAL DECISION TO EAT NOTHING BUT MEAT ISN'T SO MUCH ABOUT "NEVER EATING VEGETABLES" PER SE...
IT'S MUCH MORE ABOUT OPPRESSING OTHER FOOD-BASED SPECIES.
OK, WELL, THIS BROCCOLI WAS TALKIN' ABOUT YOUR MOTHER EARLIER. OPPRESS IT.
GET THAT THING OUT OF MY FACE.
JUST CHEW IT UP REAL OPPRESSIVELY.
GET THAT OUT OF MY FACE OR, SO HELP ME GARFIELD, I'LL HIT YOU SO HARD YOU'LL BE EATING VEGETABLES THROUGH A STRAW.
I ALREADY EAT 'EM THROUGH A STRAW! V8!
AW, FER THE LOVE OF... YOUR BAR IS SO LOW, IT'S IMPOSSIBLE TO HUMILIATE YOU!

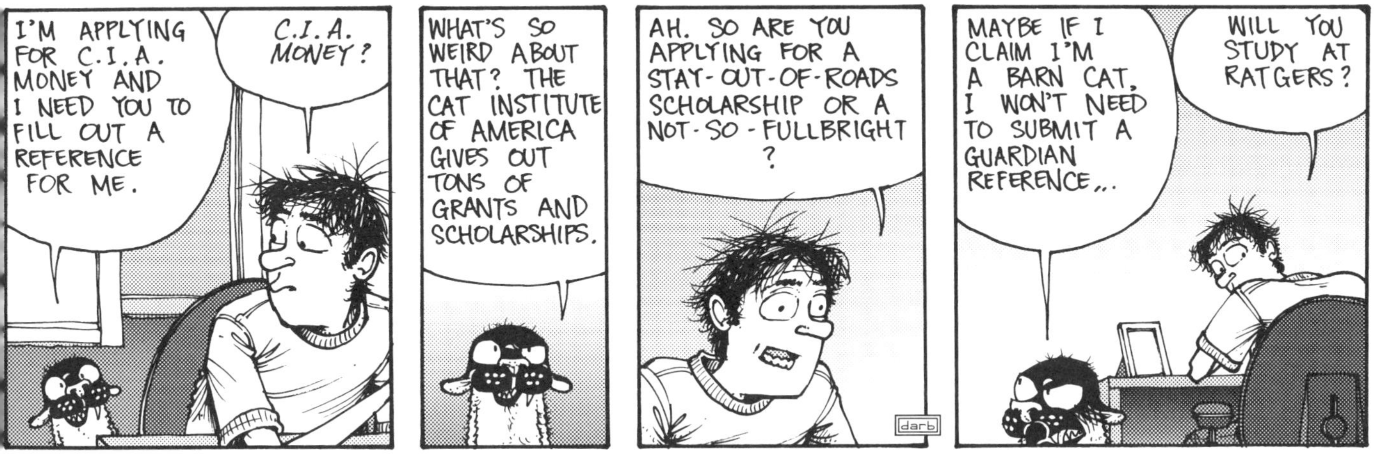
I'M APPLYING FOR C.I.A. MONEY AND I NEED YOU TO FILL OUT A REFERENCE FOR ME.
C.I.A. MONEY?
WHAT'S SO WEIRD ABOUT THAT? THE CAT INSTITUTE OF AMERICA GIVES OUT TONS OF GRANTS AND SCHOLARSHIPS.
AH. SO ARE YOU APPLYING FOR A STAY-OUT-OF-ROADS SCHOLARSHIP OR A NOT-SO-FULLBRIGHT?
MAYBE IF I CLAIM I'M A BARN CAT, I WON'T NEED TO SUBMIT A GUARDIAN REFERENCE...
WILL YOU STUDY AT RATGERS?

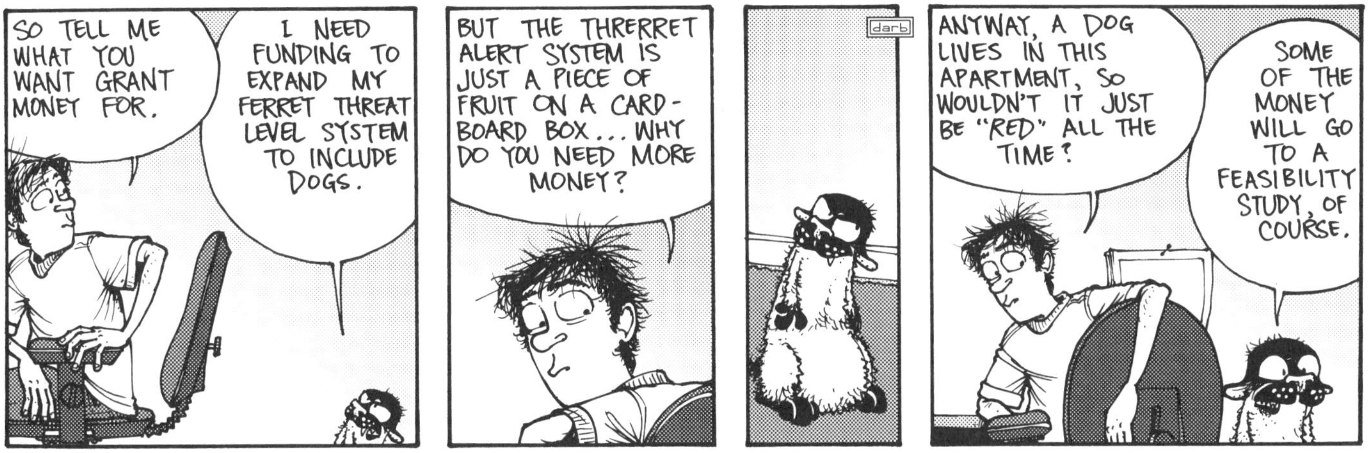
SO TELL ME WHAT YOU WANT GRANT MONEY FOR.
I NEED FUNDING TO EXPAND MY FERRET THREAT LEVEL SYSTEM TO INCLUDE DOGS.
BUT THE THRERRET ALERT SYSTEM IS JUST A PIECE OF FRUIT ON A CARDBOARD BOX... WHY DO YOU NEED MORE MONEY?
ANYWAY, A DOG LIVES IN THIS APARTMENT, SO WOULDN'T IT JUST BE "RED" ALL THE TIME?
SOME OF THE MONEY WILL GO TO A FEASIBILITY STUDY, OF COURSE.

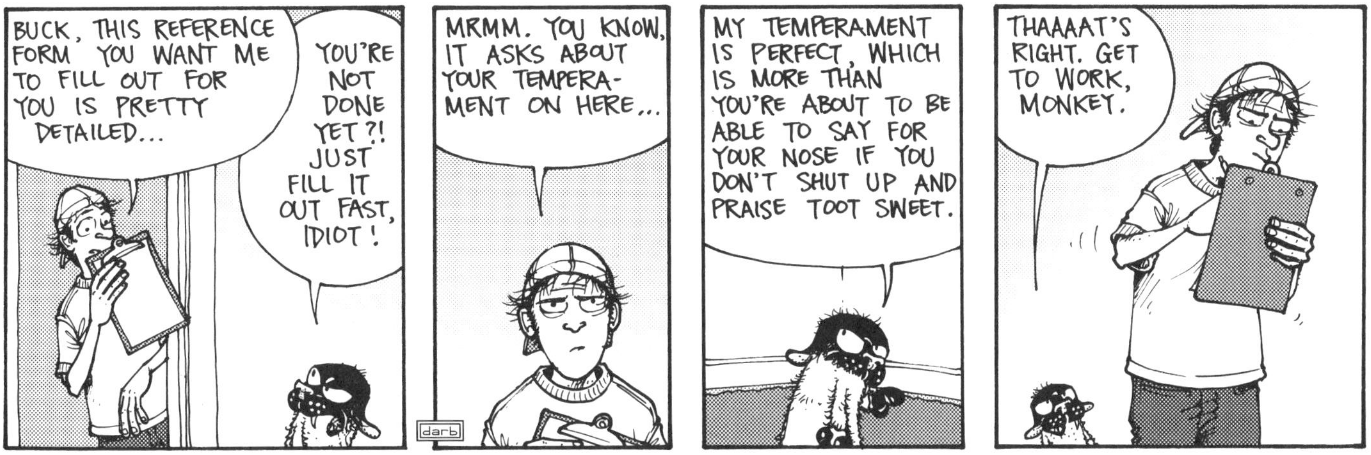
BUCK, THIS REFERENCE FORM YOU WANT ME TO FILL OUT FOR YOU IS PRETTY DETAILED...
YOU'RE NOT DONE YET?! JUST FILL IT OUT FAST, IDIOT!
MRMM. YOU KNOW, IT ASKS ABOUT YOUR TEMPERAMENT ON HERE...
MY TEMPERAMENT IS PERFECT, WHICH IS MORE THAN YOU'RE ABOUT TO BE ABLE TO SAY FOR YOUR NOSE IF YOU DON'T SHUT UP AND PRAISE TOOT SWEET.
THAAAAT'S RIGHT. GET TO WORK, MONKEY.

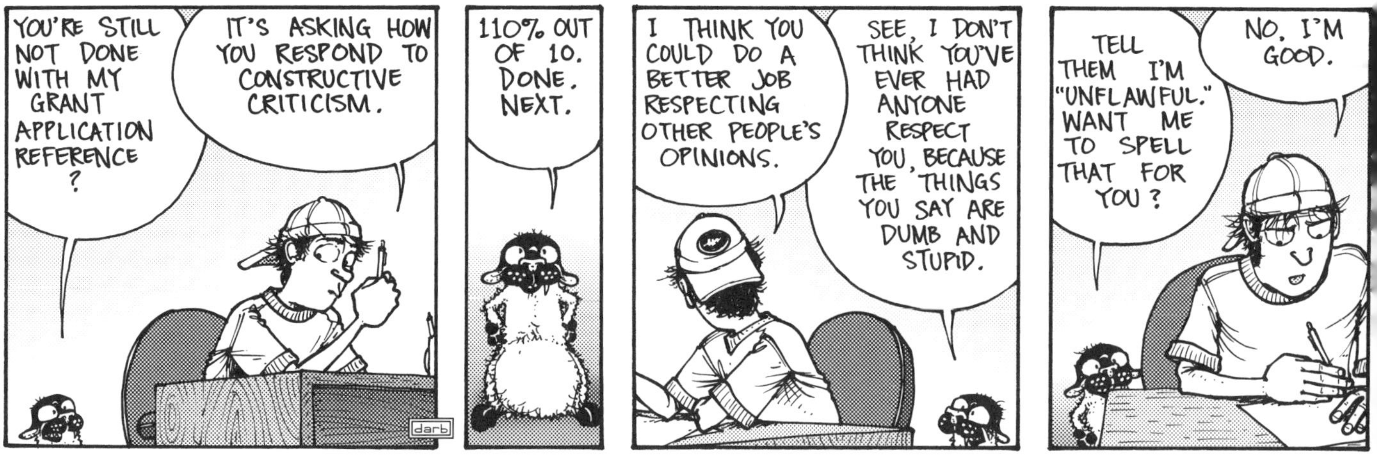
YOU'RE STILL NOT DONE WITH MY GRANT APPLICATION REFERENCE ?
IT'S ASKING HOW YOU RESPOND TO CONSTRUCTIVE CRITICISM.
110% OUT OF 10. DONE. NEXT.
I THINK YOU COULD DO A BETTER JOB RESPECTING OTHER PEOPLE'S OPINIONS.
SEE, I DON'T THINK YOU'VE EVER HAD ANYONE RESPECT YOU, BECAUSE THE THINGS YOU SAY ARE DUMB AND STUPID.
TELL THEM I'M "UNFLAWFUL." WANT ME TO SPELL THAT FOR YOU ?
NO, I'M GOOD.
darb

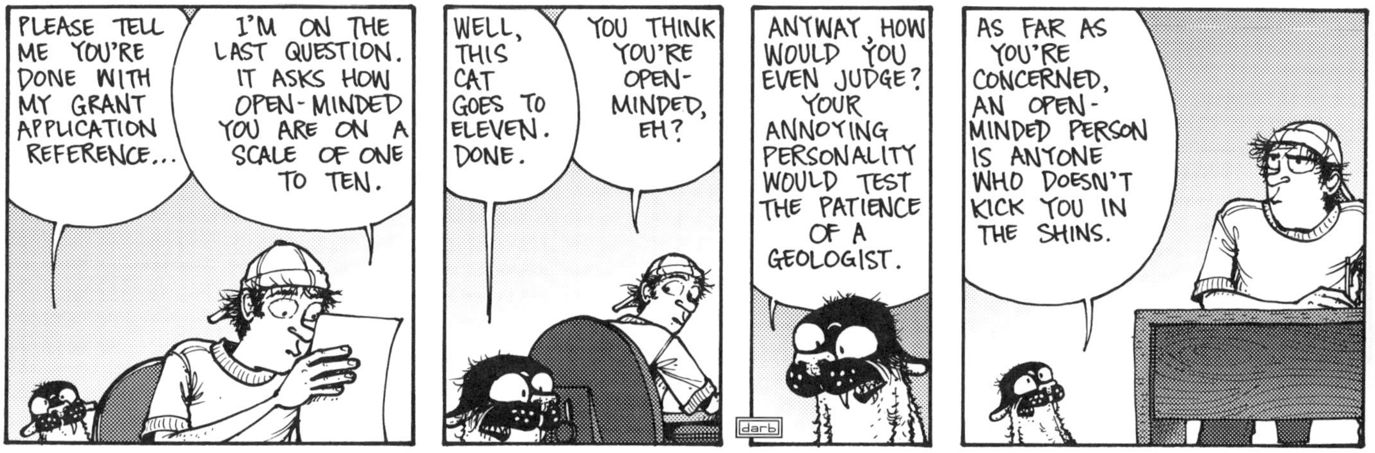
PLEASE TELL ME YOU'RE DONE WITH MY GRANT APPLICATION REFERENCE...
I'M ON THE LAST QUESTION. IT ASKS HOW OPEN-MINDED YOU ARE ON A SCALE OF ONE TO TEN.
WELL, THIS CAT GOES TO ELEVEN. DONE.
YOU THINK YOU'RE OPEN-MINDED, EH?
darb
ANYWAY, HOW WOULD YOU EVEN JUDGE? YOUR ANNOYING PERSONALITY WOULD TEST THE PATIENCE OF A GEOLOGIST.
AS FAR AS YOU'RE CONCERNED, AN OPEN-MINDED PERSON IS ANYONE WHO DOESN'T KICK YOU IN THE SHINS.

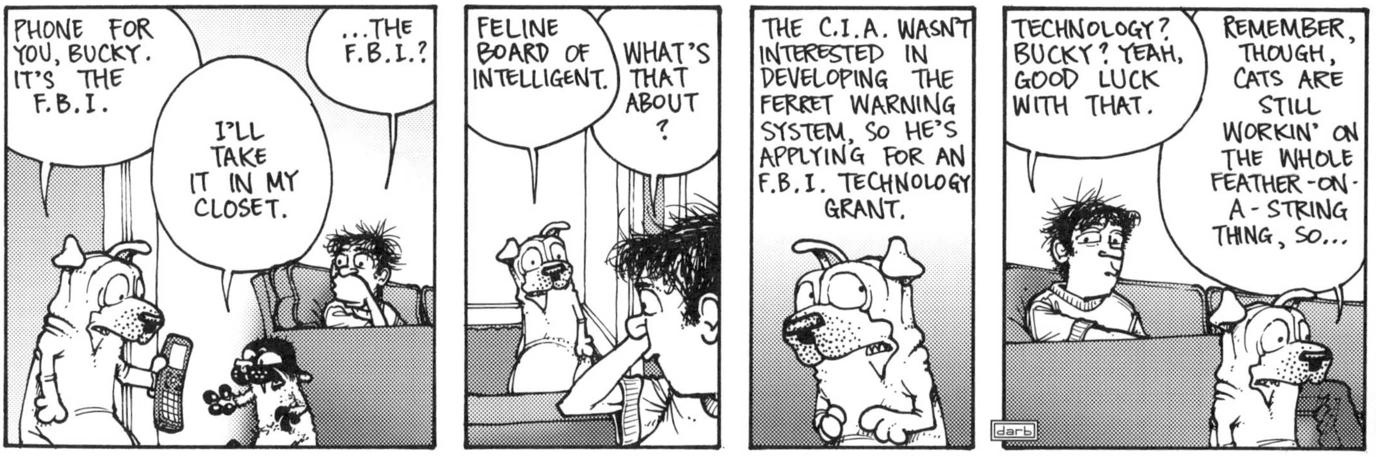
PHONE FOR YOU, BUCKY. IT'S THE F.B.I.
I'LL TAKE IT IN MY CLOSET.
...THE F.B.I.?
FELINE BOARD OF INTELLIGENT.
WHAT'S THAT ABOUT ?
THE C.I.A. WASN'T INTERESTED IN DEVELOPING THE FERRET WARNING SYSTEM, SO HE'S APPLYING FOR AN F.B.I. TECHNOLOGY GRANT.
TECHNOLOGY? BUCKY? YEAH, GOOD LUCK WITH THAT.
REMEMBER, THOUGH, CATS ARE STILL WORKIN' ON THE WHOLE FEATHER-ON-A-STRING THING, SO...
darb

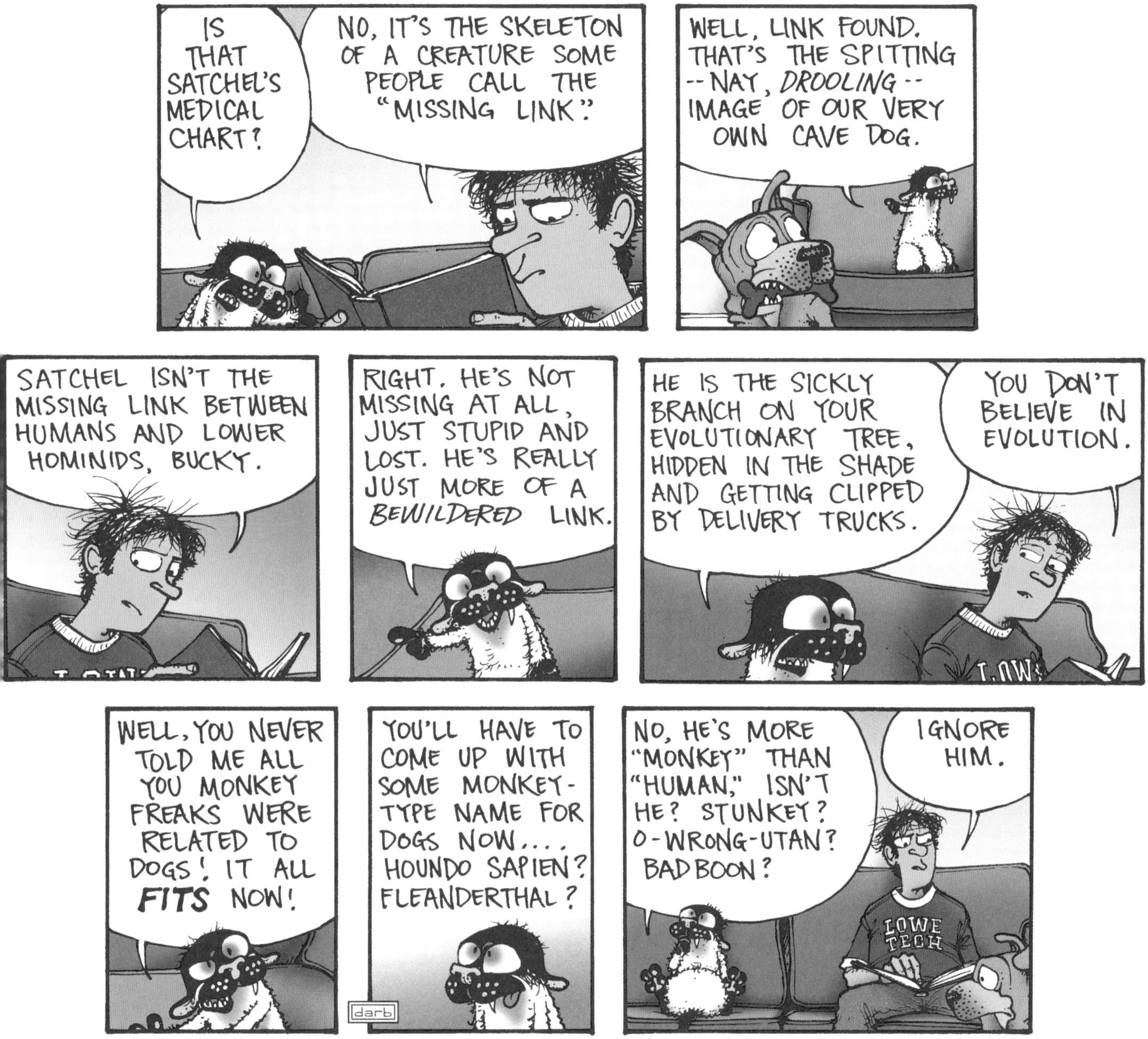
IS THAT SATCHEL'S MEDICAL CHART?
NO, IT'S THE SKELETON OF A CREATURE SOME PEOPLE CALL THE "MISSING LINK."
WELL, LINK FOUND. THAT'S THE SPITTING --NAY, DROOLING-- IMAGE OF OUR VERY OWN CAVE DOG.
SATCHEL ISN'T THE MISSING LINK BETWEEN HUMANS AND LOWER HOMINIDS, BUCKY.
RIGHT. HE'S NOT MISSING AT ALL, JUST STUPID AND LOST. HE'S REALLY JUST MORE OF A BEWILDERED LINK.
HE IS THE SICKLY BRANCH ON YOUR EVOLUTIONARY TREE, HIDDEN IN THE SHADE AND GETTING CLIPPED BY DELIVERY TRUCKS.
YOU DON'T BELIEVE IN EVOLUTION.
WELL, YOU NEVER TOLD ME ALL YOU MONKEY FREAKS WERE RELATED TO DOGS! IT ALL FITS NOW!
YOU'LL HAVE TO COME UP WITH SOME MONKEY-TYPE NAME FOR DOGS NOW.... HOUNDO SAPIEN? FLEANDERTHAL?
darb
NO, HE'S MORE "MONKEY" THAN "HUMAN," ISN'T HE? STUNKEY? O-WRONG-UTAN? BADBOON?
IGNORE HIM.
LOWE TECH

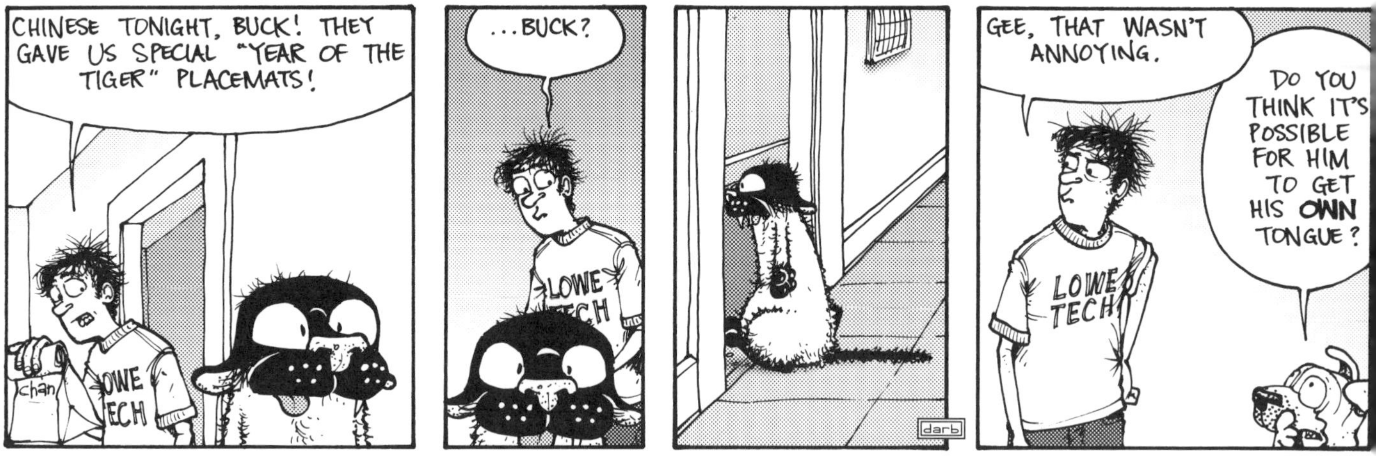
CHINESE TONIGHT, BUCK! THEY GAVE US SPECIAL "YEAR OF THE TIGER" PLACEMATS!
chan
LOWE TECH
...BUCK?
darb
GEE, THAT WASN'T ANNOYING.
DO YOU THINK IT'S POSSIBLE FOR HIM TO GET HIS **OWN** TONGUE?

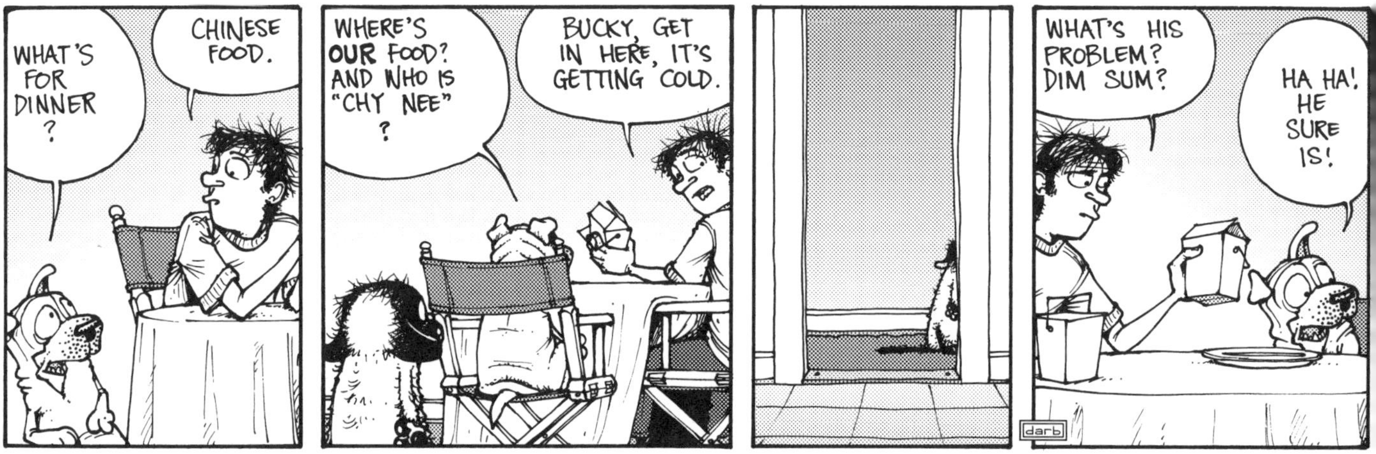
WHAT'S FOR DINNER?
CHINESE FOOD.
WHERE'S **OUR** FOOD? AND WHO IS "CHY NEE"?
BUCKY, GET IN HERE, IT'S GETTING COLD.
WHAT'S HIS PROBLEM? DIM SUM?
HA HA! HE SURE IS!
darb

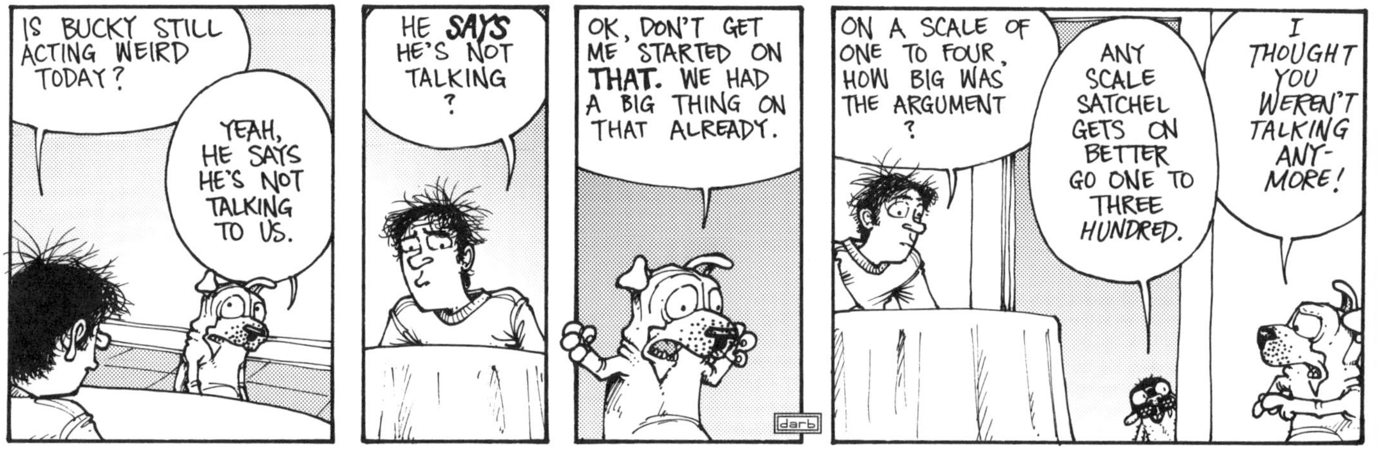
IS BUCKY STILL ACTING WEIRD TODAY?
YEAH, HE SAYS HE'S NOT TALKING TO US.
HE ***SAYS*** HE'S NOT TALKING?
OK, DON'T GET ME STARTED ON **THAT.** WE HAD A BIG THING ON THAT ALREADY.
darb
ON A SCALE OF ONE TO FOUR, HOW BIG WAS THE ARGUMENT?
ANY SCALE SATCHEL GETS ON BETTER GO ONE TO THREE *HUNDRED.*
I THOUGHT YOU WEREN'T TALKING ANY-MORE!

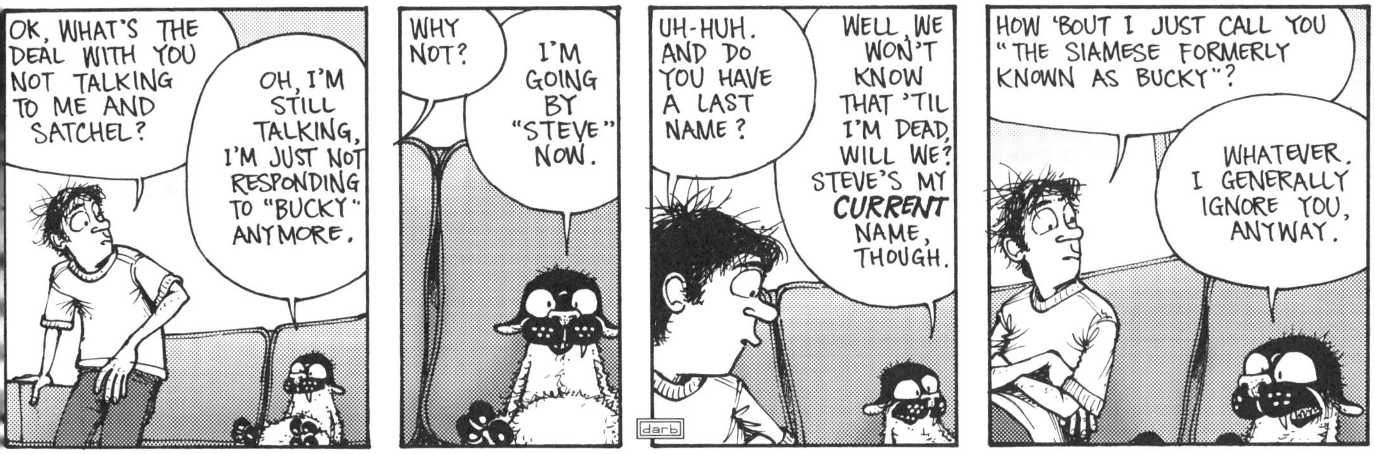
OK, WHAT'S THE DEAL WITH YOU NOT TALKING TO ME AND SATCHEL?
OH, I'M STILL TALKING, I'M JUST NOT RESPONDING TO "BUCKY" ANYMORE.
WHY NOT?
I'M GOING BY "STEVE" NOW.
UH-HUH. AND DO YOU HAVE A LAST NAME?
WELL, WE WON'T KNOW THAT 'TIL I'M DEAD, WILL WE? STEVE'S MY CURRENT NAME, THOUGH.
darb
HOW 'BOUT I JUST CALL YOU "THE SIAMESE FORMERLY KNOWN AS BUCKY"?
WHATEVER. I GENERALLY IGNORE YOU, ANYWAY.

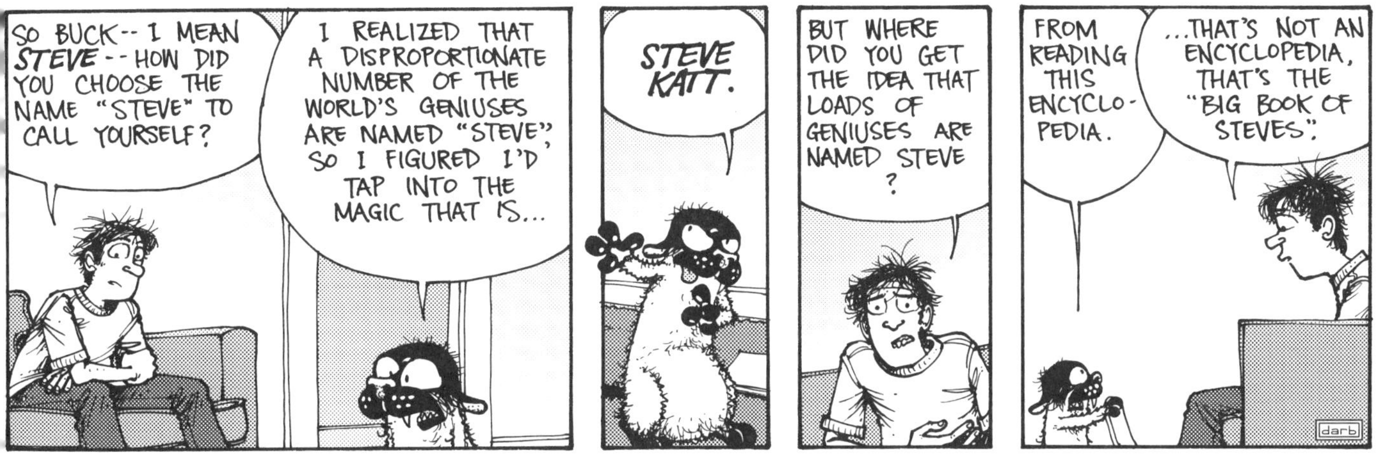
SO BUCK-- I MEAN STEVE--HOW DID YOU CHOOSE THE NAME "STEVE" TO CALL YOURSELF?
I REALIZED THAT A DISPROPORTIONATE NUMBER OF THE WORLD'S GENIUSES ARE NAMED "STEVE", SO I FIGURED I'D TAP INTO THE MAGIC THAT IS...
STEVE KATT.
BUT WHERE DID YOU GET THE IDEA THAT LOADS OF GENIUSES ARE NAMED STEVE?
FROM READING THIS ENCYCLOPEDIA.
...THAT'S NOT AN ENCYCLOPEDIA, THAT'S THE "BIG BOOK OF STEVES".
darb

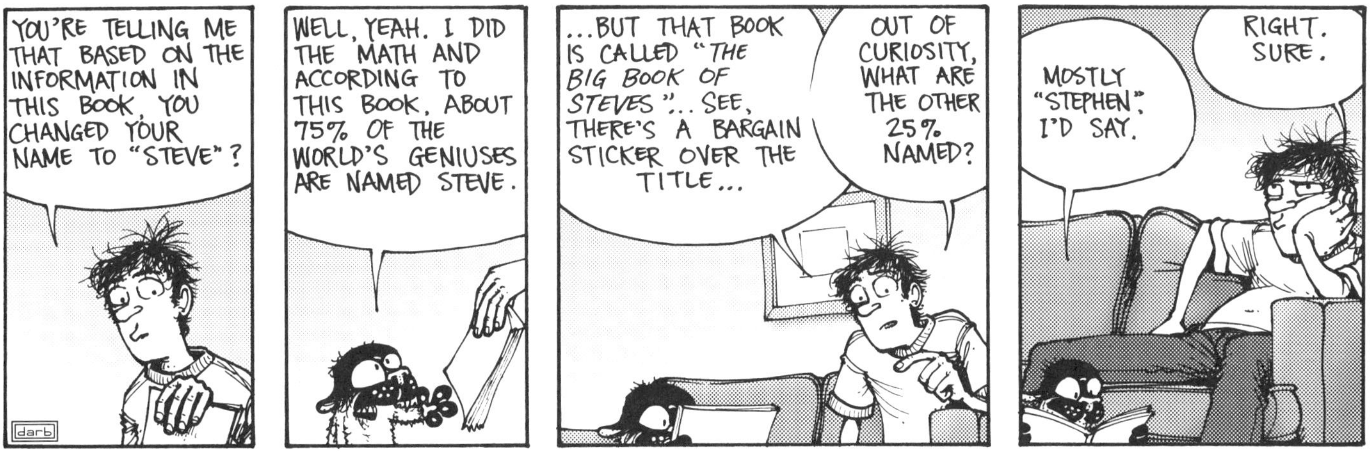
YOU'RE TELLING ME THAT BASED ON THE INFORMATION IN THIS BOOK, YOU CHANGED YOUR NAME TO "STEVE"?
darb
WELL, YEAH. I DID THE MATH AND ACCORDING TO THIS BOOK, ABOUT 75% OF THE WORLD'S GENIUSES ARE NAMED STEVE.
...BUT THAT BOOK IS CALLED "THE BIG BOOK OF STEVES"... SEE, THERE'S A BARGAIN STICKER OVER THE TITLE...
OUT OF CURIOSITY, WHAT ARE THE OTHER 25% NAMED?
MOSTLY "STEPHEN", I'D SAY.
RIGHT. SURE.

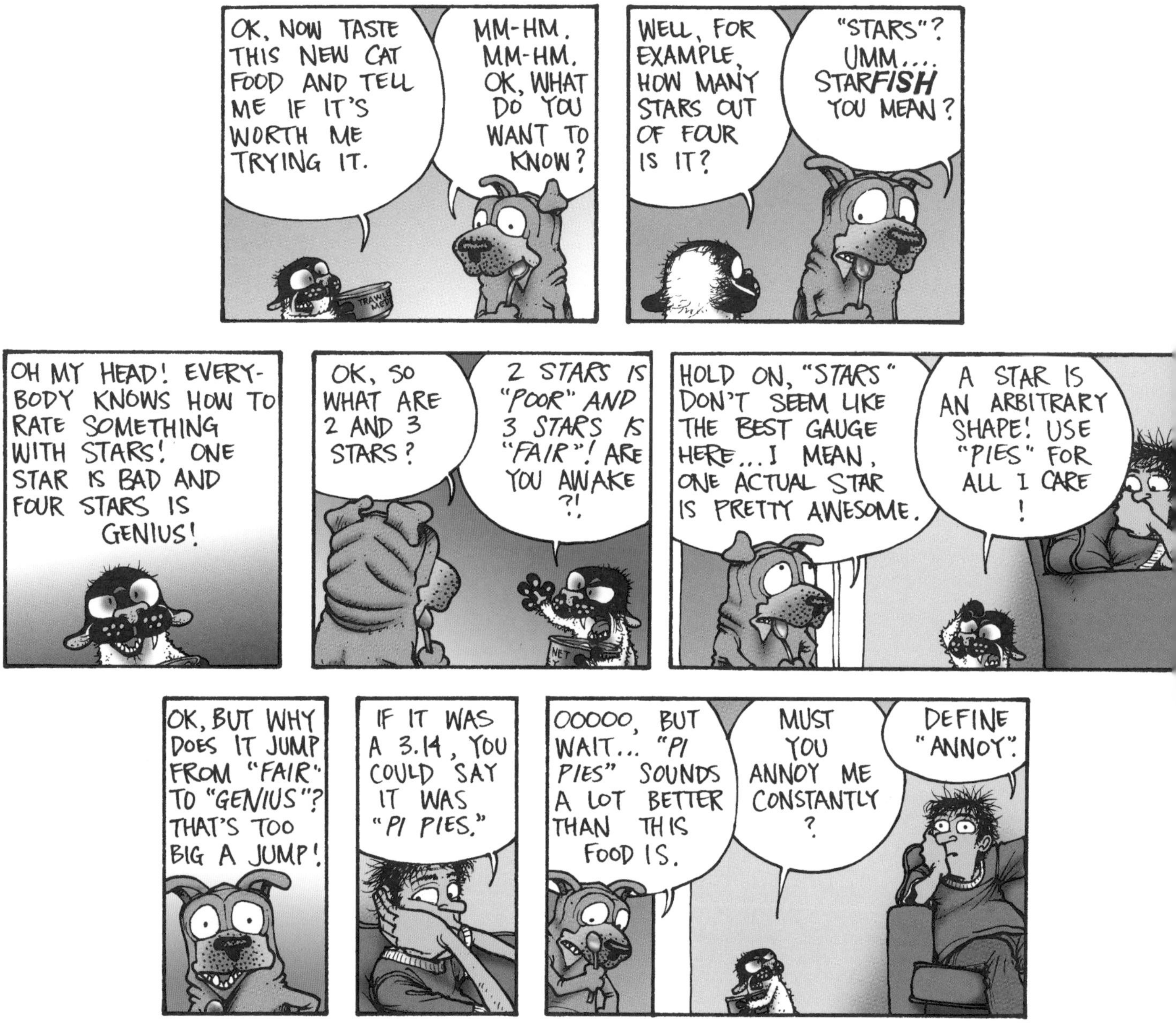

OK, NOW TASTE THIS NEW CAT FOOD AND TELL ME IF IT'S WORTH ME TRYING IT.
MM-HM. MM-HM. OK, WHAT DO YOU WANT TO KNOW?
WELL, FOR EXAMPLE, HOW MANY STARS OUT OF FOUR IS IT?
"STARS"? UMM.... STAR*FISH* YOU MEAN?
OH MY HEAD! EVERY-BODY KNOWS HOW TO RATE SOMETHING WITH STARS! ONE STAR IS BAD AND FOUR STARS IS GENIUS!
OK, SO WHAT ARE 2 AND 3 STARS?
2 STARS IS "POOR" AND 3 STARS IS "FAIR"! ARE YOU AWAKE ?!
HOLD ON, *"STARS"* DON'T SEEM LIKE THE BEST GAUGE HERE... I MEAN, ONE ACTUAL STAR IS PRETTY AWESOME.
A STAR IS AN ARBITRARY SHAPE! USE *"PIES"* FOR ALL I CARE!
OK, BUT WHY DOES IT JUMP FROM *"FAIR"* TO *"GENIUS"*? THAT'S TOO BIG A JUMP!
IF IT WAS A 3.14, YOU COULD SAY IT WAS *"PI PIES."*
OOOOO, BUT WAIT... *"PI PIES"* SOUNDS A LOT BETTER THAN THIS FOOD IS.
MUST YOU ANNOY ME CONSTANTLY?
DEFINE "ANNOY".

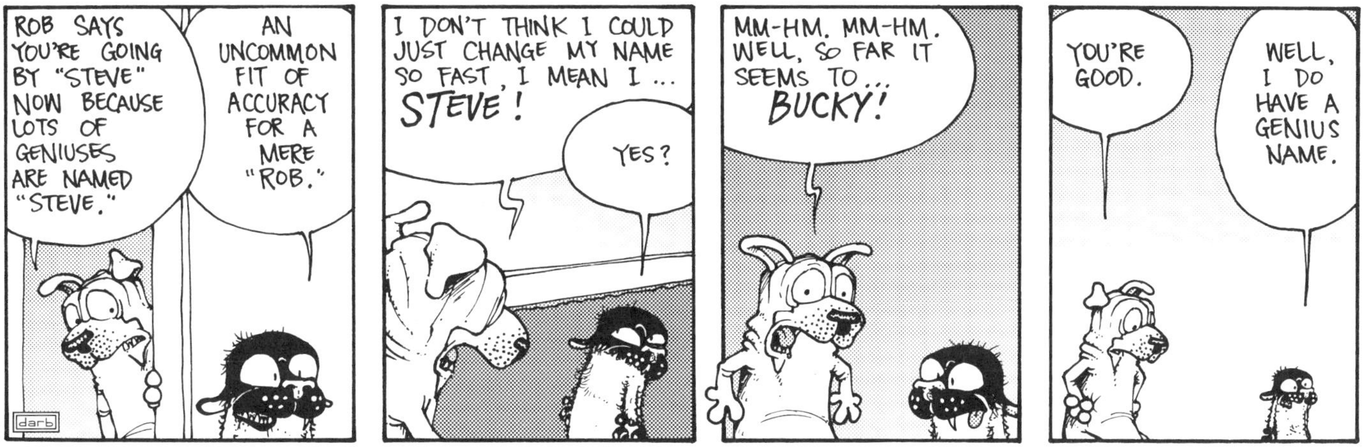
ROB SAYS YOU'RE GOING BY "STEVE" NOW BECAUSE LOTS OF GENIUSES ARE NAMED "STEVE."
AN UNCOMMON FIT OF ACCURACY FOR A MERE "ROB."
darb
I DON'T THINK I COULD JUST CHANGE MY NAME SO FAST, I MEAN I ... STEVE!
YES?
MM-HM. MM-HM. WELL, SO FAR IT SEEMS TO... BUCKY!
YOU'RE GOOD.
WELL, I DO HAVE A GENIUS NAME.

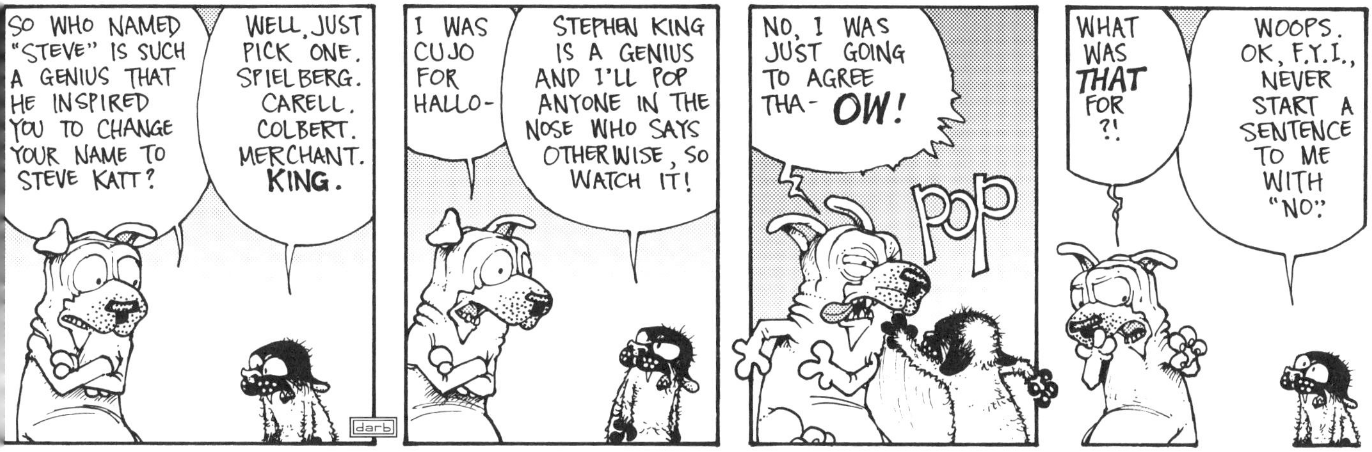
SO WHO NAMED "STEVE" IS SUCH A GENIUS THAT HE INSPIRED YOU TO CHANGE YOUR NAME TO STEVE KATT?
WELL, JUST PICK ONE. SPIELBERG. CARELL. COLBERT. MERCHANT. KING.
darb
I WAS CUJO FOR HALLO-
STEPHEN KING IS A GENIUS AND I'LL POP ANYONE IN THE NOSE WHO SAYS OTHERWISE, SO WATCH IT!
NO, I WAS JUST GOING TO AGREE THA- OW!
POP
WHAT WAS THAT FOR ?!
WOOPS. OK, F.Y.I., NEVER START A SENTENCE TO ME WITH "NO."

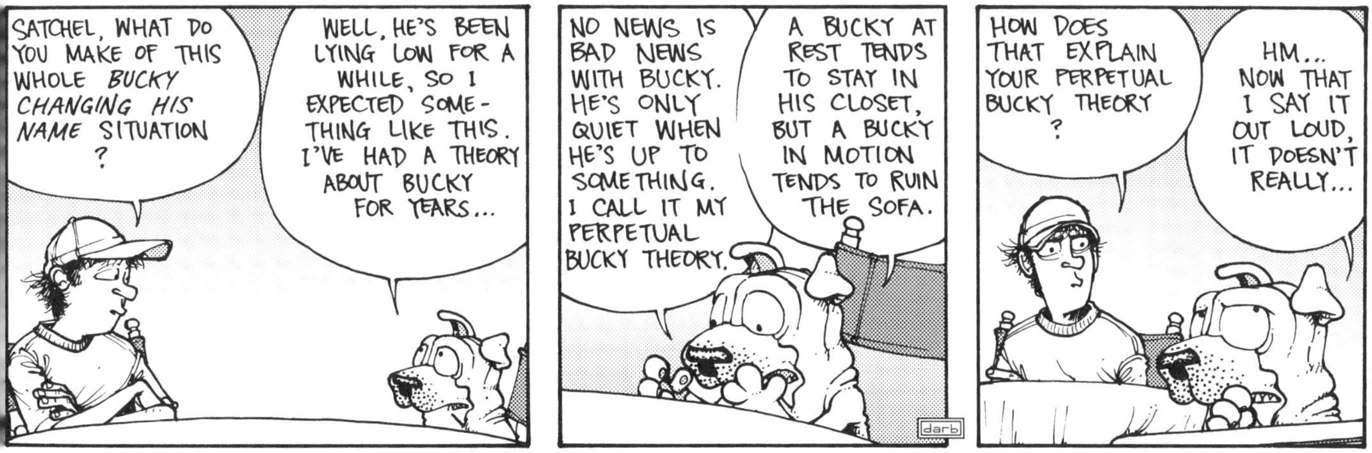
SATCHEL, WHAT DO YOU MAKE OF THIS WHOLE BUCKY CHANGING HIS NAME SITUATION ?
WELL, HE'S BEEN LYING LOW FOR A WHILE, SO I EXPECTED SOME-THING LIKE THIS. I'VE HAD A THEORY ABOUT BUCKY FOR YEARS...
NO NEWS IS BAD NEWS WITH BUCKY. HE'S ONLY QUIET WHEN HE'S UP TO SOMETHING. I CALL IT MY PERPETUAL BUCKY THEORY.
A BUCKY AT REST TENDS TO STAY IN HIS CLOSET, BUT A BUCKY IN MOTION TENDS TO RUIN THE SOFA.
darb
HOW DOES THAT EXPLAIN YOUR PERPETUAL BUCKY THEORY ?
HM... NOW THAT I SAY IT OUT LOUD, IT DOESN'T REALLY...

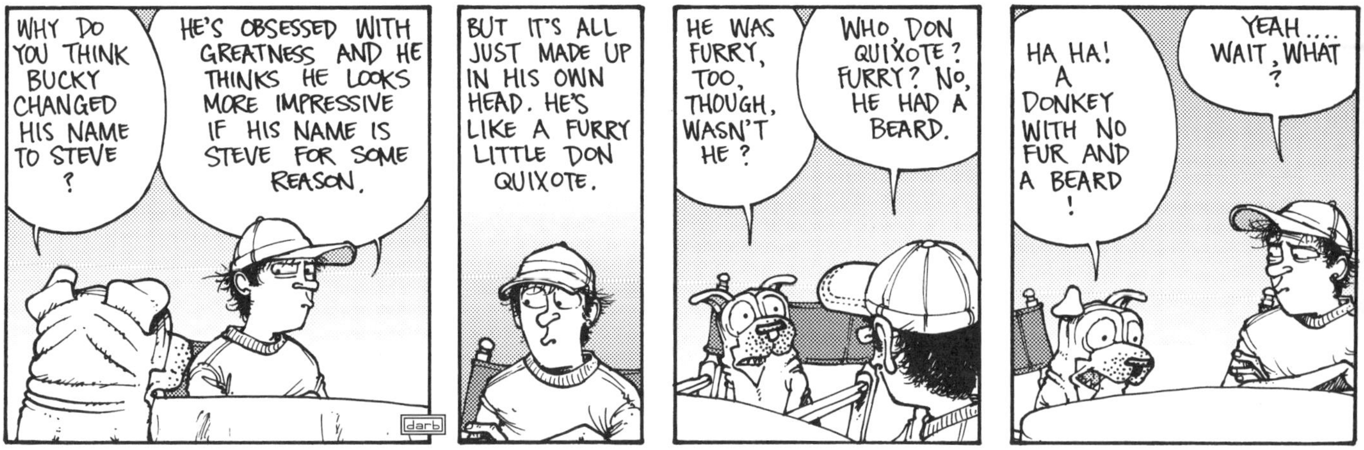
WHY DO YOU THINK BUCKY CHANGED HIS NAME TO STEVE ?
HE'S OBSESSED WITH GREATNESS AND HE THINKS HE LOOKS MORE IMPRESSIVE IF HIS NAME IS STEVE FOR SOME REASON.
BUT IT'S ALL JUST MADE UP IN HIS OWN HEAD. HE'S LIKE A FURRY LITTLE DON QUIXOTE.
HE WAS FURRY, TOO, THOUGH, WASN'T HE ?
WHO, DON QUIXOTE? FURRY? NO, HE HAD A BEARD.
HA HA! A DONKEY WITH NO FUR AND A BEARD !
YEAH.... WAIT, WHAT ?

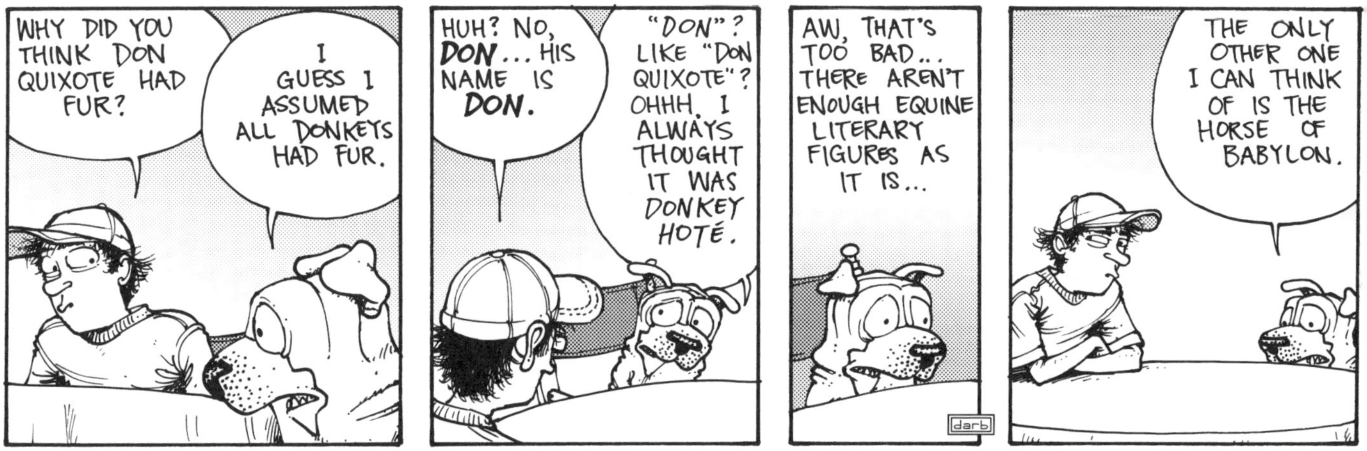
WHY DID YOU THINK DON QUIXOTE HAD FUR?
I GUESS I ASSUMED ALL DONKEYS HAD FUR.
HUH? NO, DON... HIS NAME IS DON.
"DON"? LIKE "DON QUIXOTE"? OHHH, I ALWAYS THOUGHT IT WAS DONKEY HOTÉ.
AW, THAT'S TOO BAD... THERE AREN'T ENOUGH EQUINE LITERARY FIGURES AS IT IS...
THE ONLY OTHER ONE I CAN THINK OF IS THE HORSE OF BABYLON.

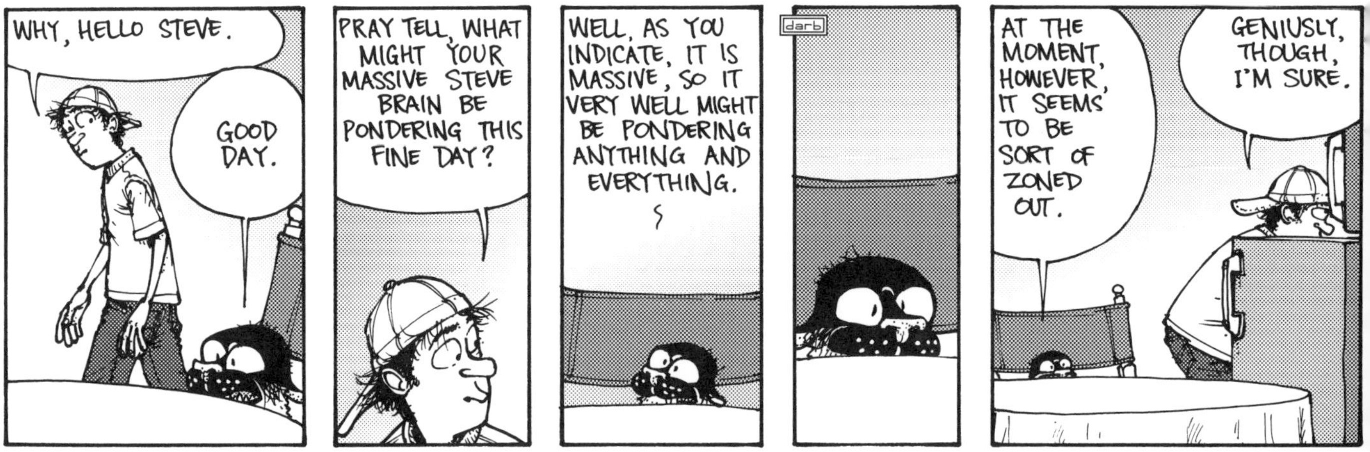
WHY, HELLO STEVE.
GOOD DAY.
PRAY TELL, WHAT MIGHT YOUR MASSIVE STEVE BRAIN BE PONDERING THIS FINE DAY?
WELL, AS YOU INDICATE, IT IS MASSIVE, SO IT VERY WELL MIGHT BE PONDERING ANYTHING AND EVERYTHING.
AT THE MOMENT, HOWEVER, IT SEEMS TO BE SORT OF ZONED OUT.
GENIUSLY, THOUGH, I'M SURE.

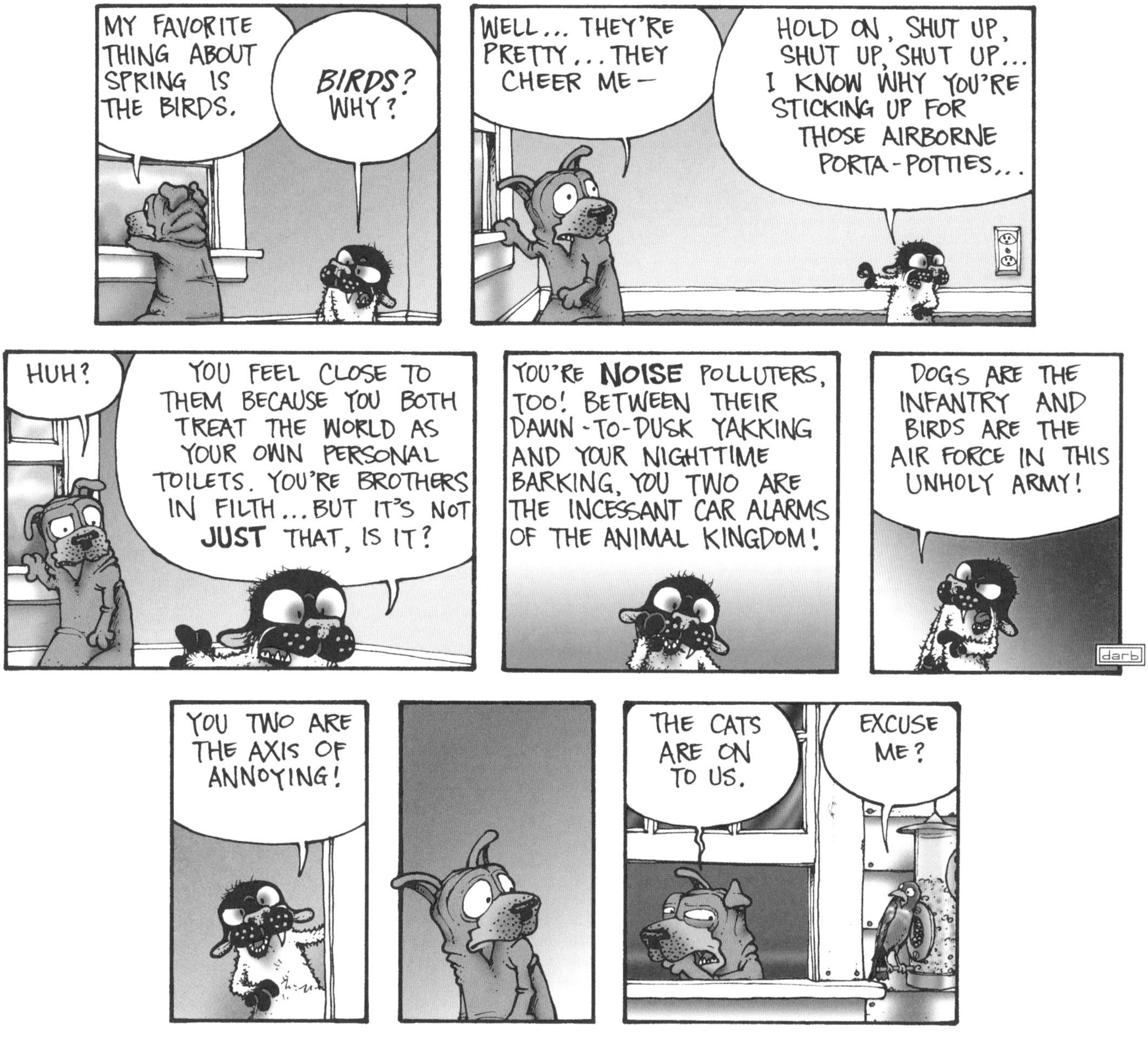
MY FAVORITE THING ABOUT SPRING IS THE BIRDS.
BIRDS? WHY?
WELL... THEY'RE PRETTY... THEY CHEER ME—
HOLD ON, SHUT UP, SHUT UP, SHUT UP... I KNOW WHY YOU'RE STICKING UP FOR THOSE AIRBORNE PORTA-POTTIES...
HUH?
YOU FEEL CLOSE TO THEM BECAUSE YOU BOTH TREAT THE WORLD AS YOUR OWN PERSONAL TOILETS. YOU'RE BROTHERS IN FILTH... BUT IT'S NOT JUST THAT, IS IT?
YOU'RE NOISE POLLUTERS, TOO! BETWEEN THEIR DAWN-TO-DUSK YAKKING AND YOUR NIGHTTIME BARKING, YOU TWO ARE THE INCESSANT CAR ALARMS OF THE ANIMAL KINGDOM!
DOGS ARE THE INFANTRY AND BIRDS ARE THE AIR FORCE IN THIS UNHOLY ARMY!
darb
YOU TWO ARE THE AXIS OF ANNOYING!
THE CATS ARE ON TO US.
EXCUSE ME?

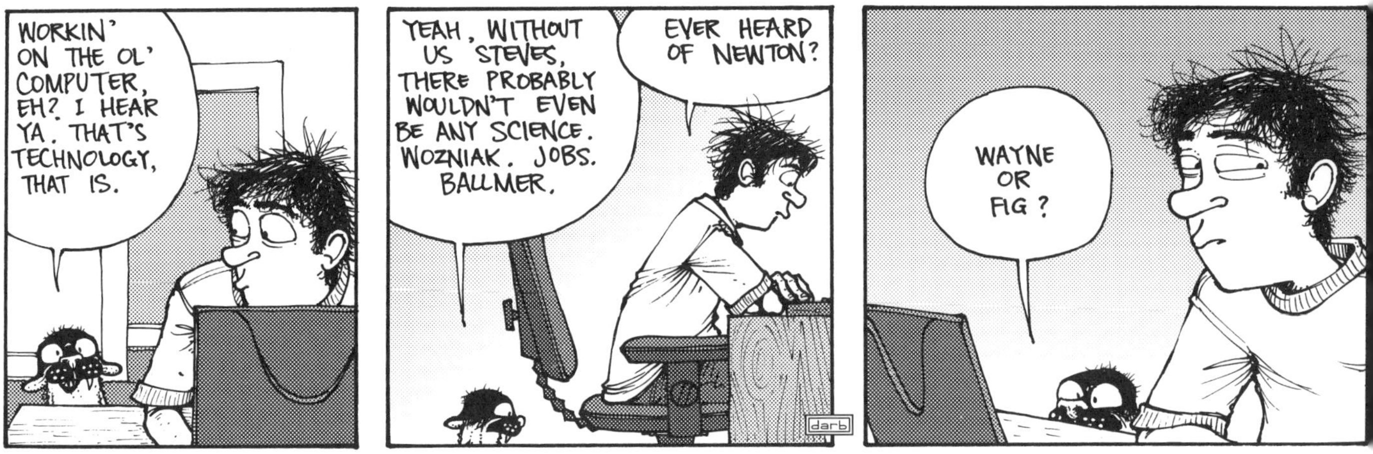
WORKIN' ON THE OL' COMPUTER, EH? I HEAR YA. THAT'S TECHNOLOGY, THAT IS.
YEAH, WITHOUT US STEVES, THERE PROBABLY WOULDN'T EVEN BE ANY SCIENCE. WOZNIAK. JOBS. BALLMER.
EVER HEARD OF NEWTON?
darb
WAYNE OR FIG?

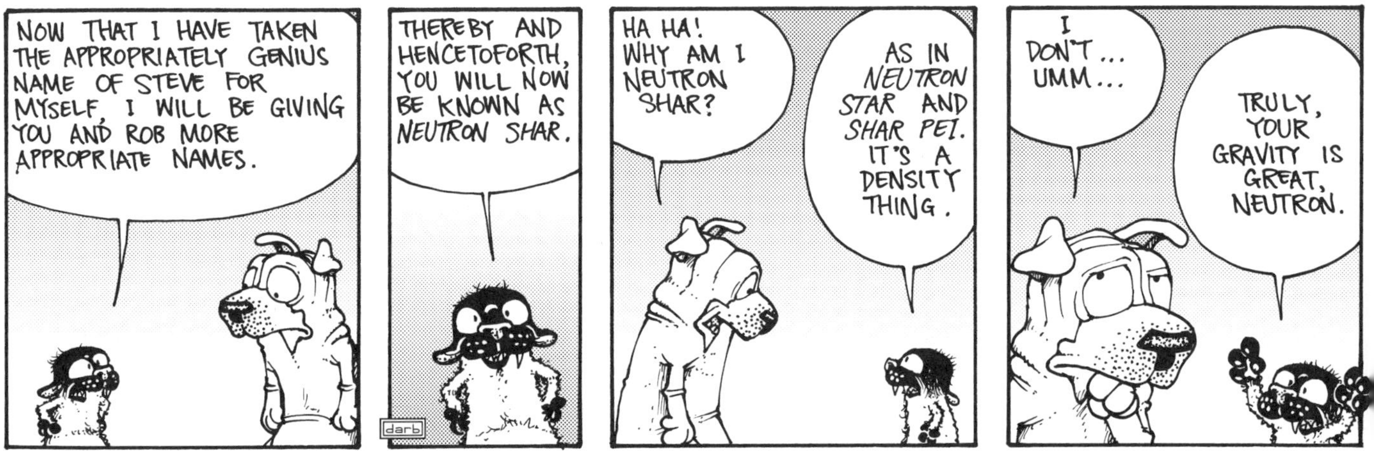
NOW THAT I HAVE TAKEN THE APPROPRIATELY GENIUS NAME OF STEVE FOR MYSELF, I WILL BE GIVING YOU AND ROB MORE APPROPRIATE NAMES.
THEREBY AND HENCETOFORTH, YOU WILL NOW BE KNOWN AS *NEUTRON SHAR*.
darb
HA HA! WHY AM I NEUTRON SHAR?
AS IN *NEUTRON STAR* AND *SHAR PEI*. IT'S A DENSITY THING.
I DON'T... UMM...
TRULY, YOUR GRAVITY IS GREAT, NEUTRON.

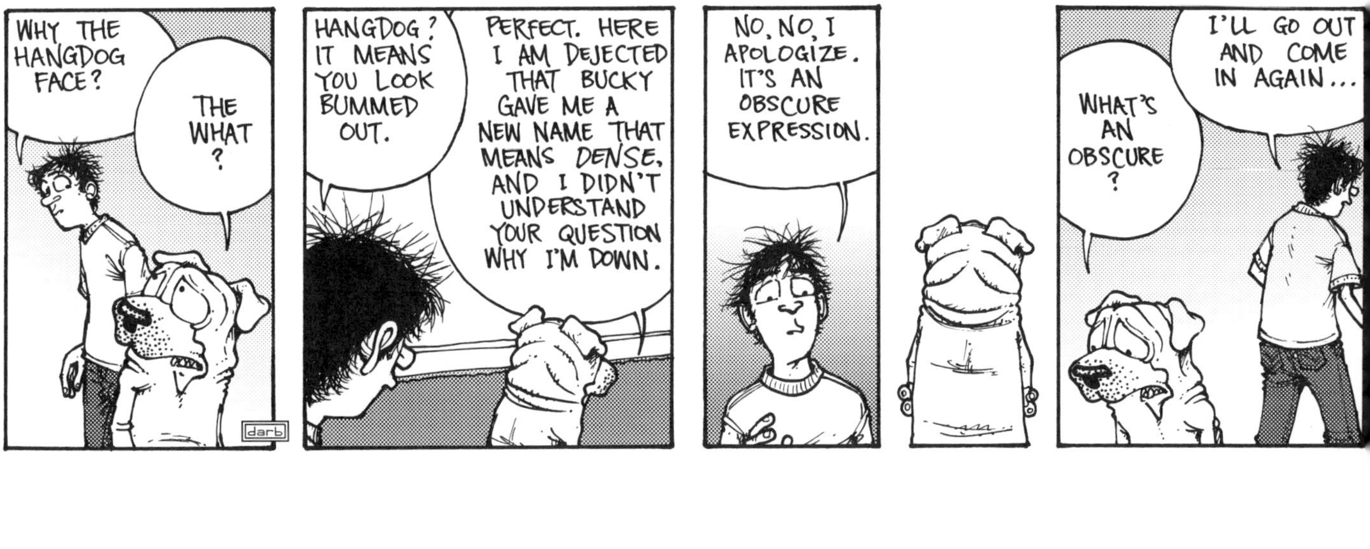
WHY THE HANGDOG FACE?
THE WHAT?
darb
HANGDOG? IT MEANS YOU LOOK BUMMED OUT.
PERFECT. HERE I AM DEJECTED THAT BUCKY GAVE ME A NEW NAME THAT MEANS *DENSE*, AND I DIDN'T UNDERSTAND YOUR QUESTION WHY I'M DOWN.
NO, NO, I APOLOGIZE. IT'S AN OBSCURE EXPRESSION.
WHAT'S AN OBSCURE?
I'LL GO OUT AND COME IN AGAIN...

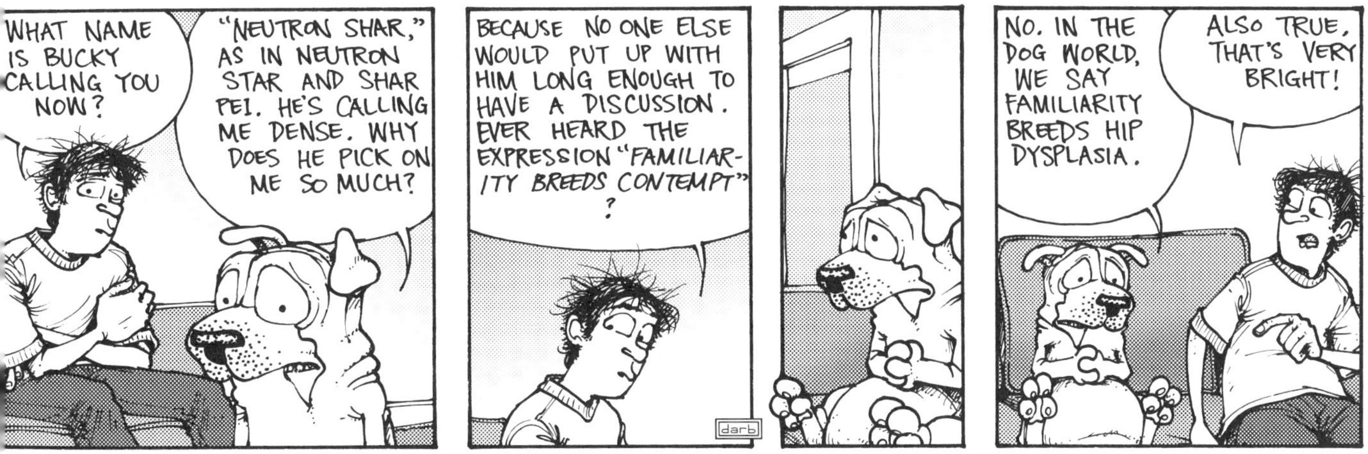
WHAT NAME IS BUCKY CALLING YOU NOW?
"NEUTRON SHAR," AS IN NEUTRON STAR AND SHAR PEI. HE'S CALLING ME DENSE. WHY DOES HE PICK ON ME SO MUCH?
BECAUSE NO ONE ELSE WOULD PUT UP WITH HIM LONG ENOUGH TO HAVE A DISCUSSION. EVER HEARD THE EXPRESSION "FAMILIARITY BREEDS CONTEMPT"?
darb
NO. IN THE DOG WORLD, WE SAY FAMILIARITY BREEDS HIP DYSPLASIA.
ALSO TRUE. THAT'S VERY BRIGHT!

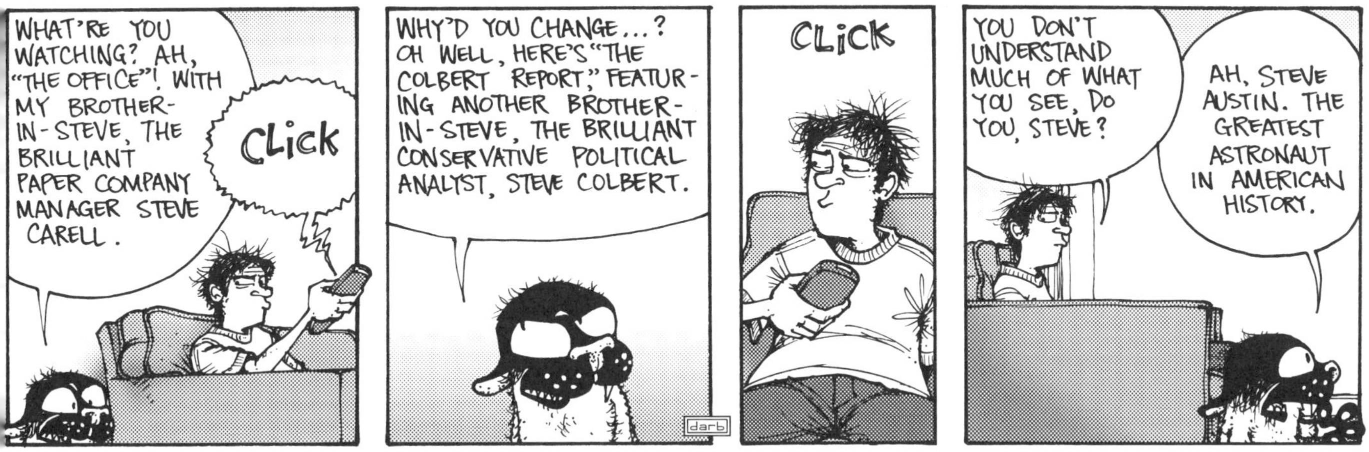
WHAT'RE YOU WATCHING? AH, "THE OFFICE"! WITH MY BROTHER-IN-STEVE, THE BRILLIANT PAPER COMPANY MANAGER STEVE CARELL.
CLICK
WHY'D YOU CHANGE...? OH WELL, HERE'S "THE COLBERT REPORT," FEATURING ANOTHER BROTHER-IN-STEVE, THE BRILLIANT CONSERVATIVE POLITICAL ANALYST, STEVE COLBERT.
darb
CLICK
YOU DON'T UNDERSTAND MUCH OF WHAT YOU SEE, DO YOU, STEVE?
AH, STEVE AUSTIN. THE GREATEST ASTRONAUT IN AMERICAN HISTORY.

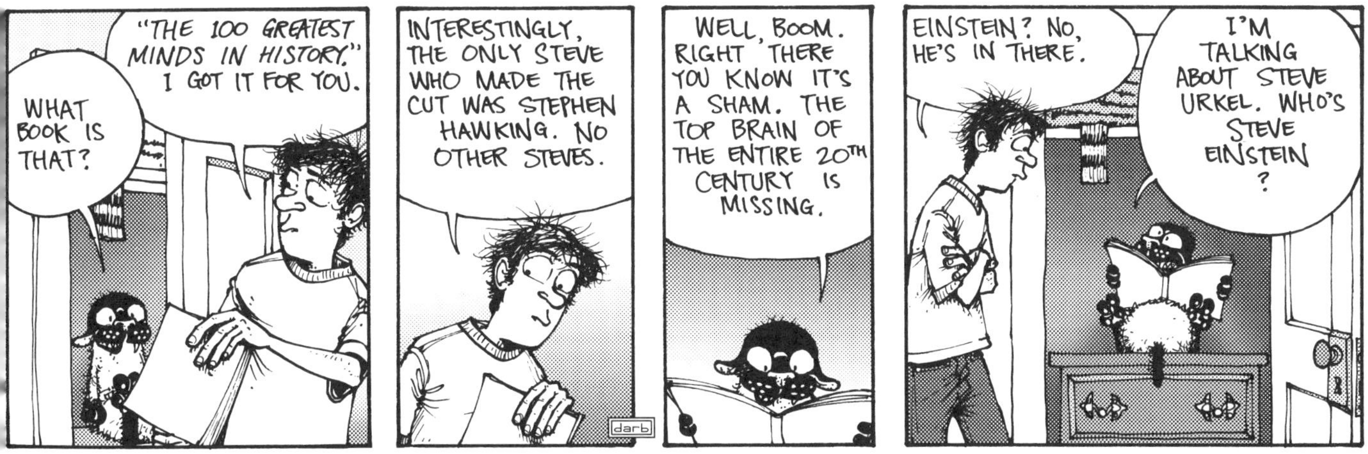
WHAT BOOK IS THAT?
"THE 100 GREATEST MINDS IN HISTORY." I GOT IT FOR YOU.
INTERESTINGLY, THE ONLY STEVE WHO MADE THE CUT WAS STEPHEN HAWKING. NO OTHER STEVES.
darb
WELL, BOOM. RIGHT THERE YOU KNOW IT'S A SHAM. THE TOP BRAIN OF THE ENTIRE 20TH CENTURY IS MISSING.
EINSTEIN? NO, HE'S IN THERE.
I'M TALKING ABOUT STEVE URKEL. WHO'S STEVE EINSTEIN?

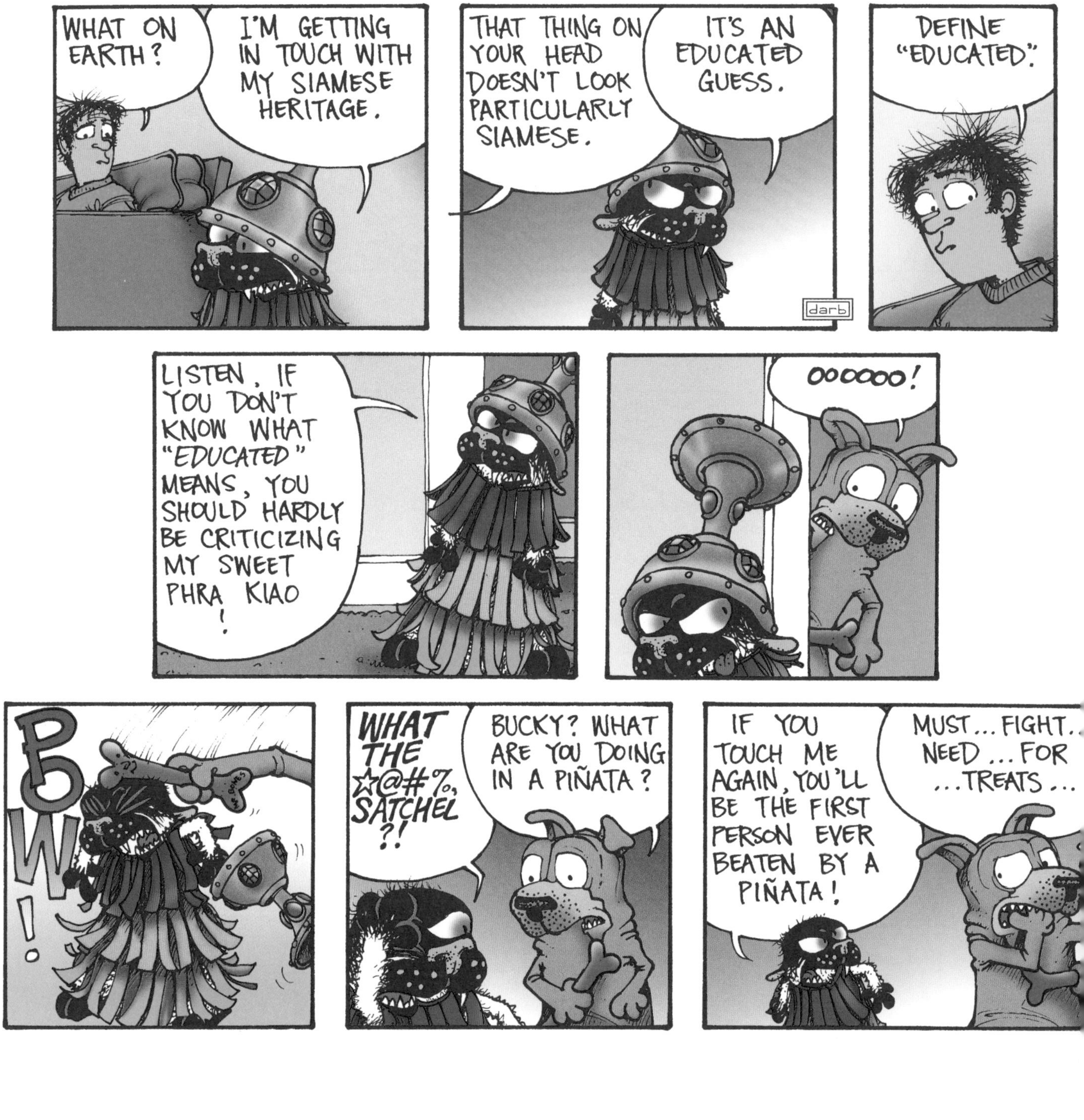
WHAT ON EARTH?
I'M GETTING IN TOUCH WITH MY SIAMESE HERITAGE.
THAT THING ON YOUR HEAD DOESN'T LOOK PARTICULARLY SIAMESE.
IT'S AN EDUCATED GUESS.
DEFINE "EDUCATED."
darb
LISTEN, IF YOU DON'T KNOW WHAT "EDUCATED" MEANS, YOU SHOULD HARDLY BE CRITICIZING MY SWEET PHRA KIAO!
OOOOOO!
POW!
WHAT THE ☆@#%, SATCHEL?!
BUCKY? WHAT ARE YOU DOING IN A PIÑATA?
IF YOU TOUCH ME AGAIN, YOU'LL BE THE FIRST PERSON EVER BEATEN BY A PIÑATA!
MUST... FIGHT... NEED... FOR ...TREATS...

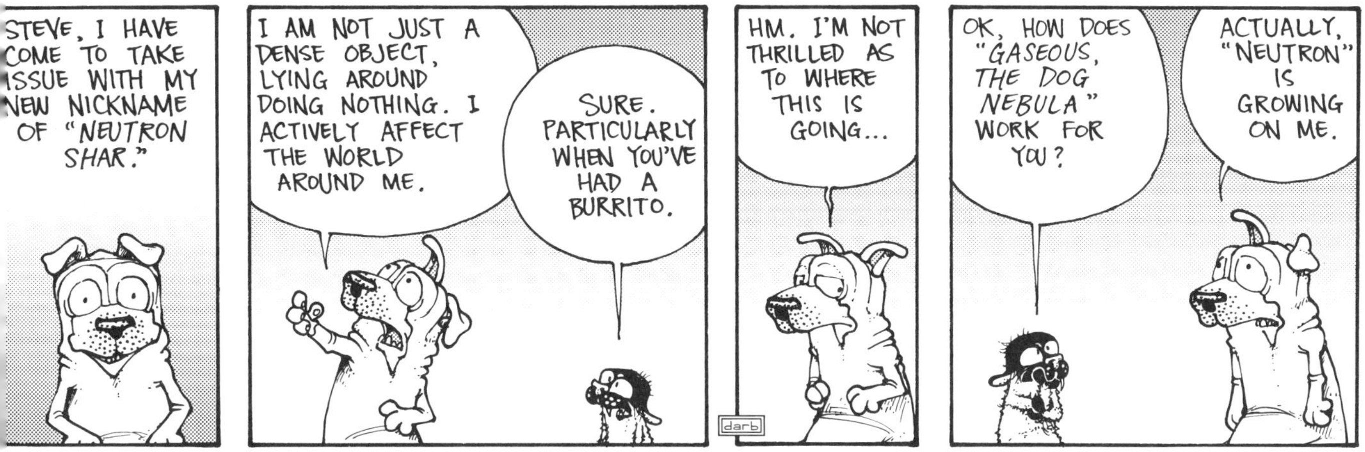
STEVE, I HAVE COME TO TAKE ISSUE WITH MY NEW NICKNAME OF "NEUTRON SHAR."
I AM NOT JUST A DENSE OBJECT, LYING AROUND DOING NOTHING. I ACTIVELY AFFECT THE WORLD AROUND ME.
SURE. PARTICULARLY WHEN YOU'VE HAD A BURRITO.
HM. I'M NOT THRILLED AS TO WHERE THIS IS GOING...
OK, HOW DOES "GASEOUS, THE DOG NEBULA" WORK FOR YOU?
ACTUALLY, "NEUTRON" IS GROWING ON ME.
darb

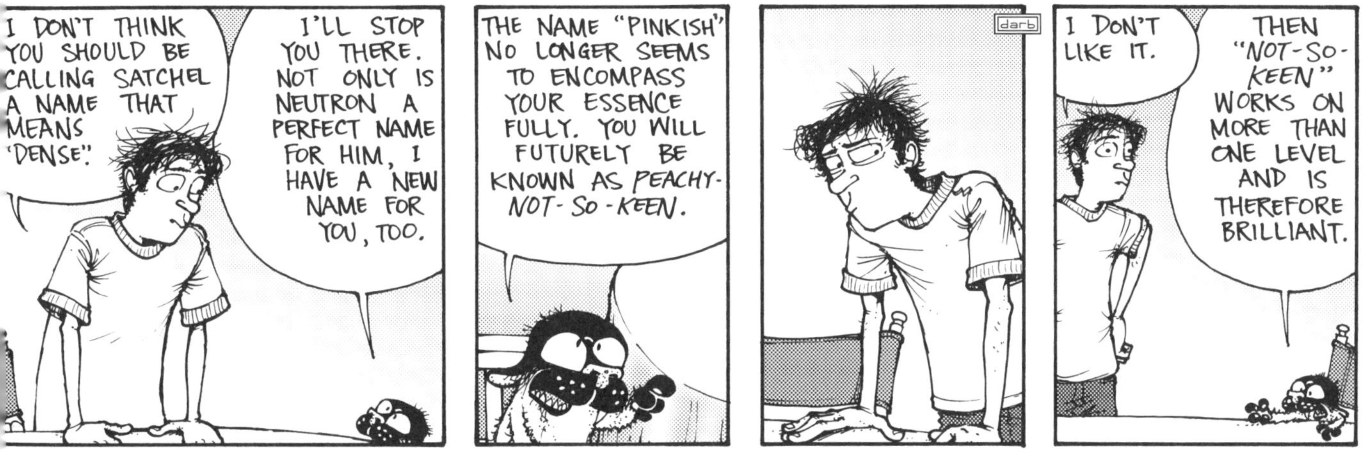
I DON'T THINK YOU SHOULD BE CALLING SATCHEL A NAME THAT MEANS 'DENSE.'
I'LL STOP YOU THERE. NOT ONLY IS NEUTRON A PERFECT NAME FOR HIM, I HAVE A NEW NAME FOR YOU, TOO.
THE NAME "PINKISH" NO LONGER SEEMS TO ENCOMPASS YOUR ESSENCE FULLY. YOU WILL FUTURELY BE KNOWN AS PEACHY-NOT-SO-KEEN.
darb
I DON'T LIKE IT.
THEN "NOT-SO-KEEN" WORKS ON MORE THAN ONE LEVEL AND IS THEREFORE BRILLIANT.

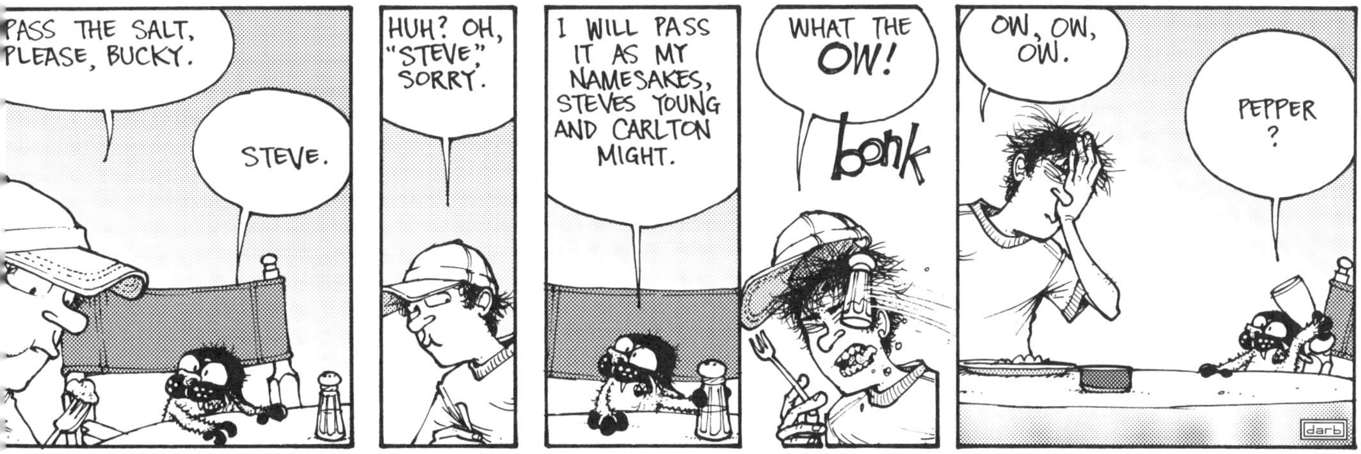
PASS THE SALT, PLEASE, BUCKY.
STEVE.
HUH? OH, "STEVE." SORRY.
I WILL PASS IT AS MY NAMESAKES, STEVES YOUNG AND CARLTON MIGHT.
WHAT THE OW!
bonk
OW, OW, OW.
PEPPER?
darb

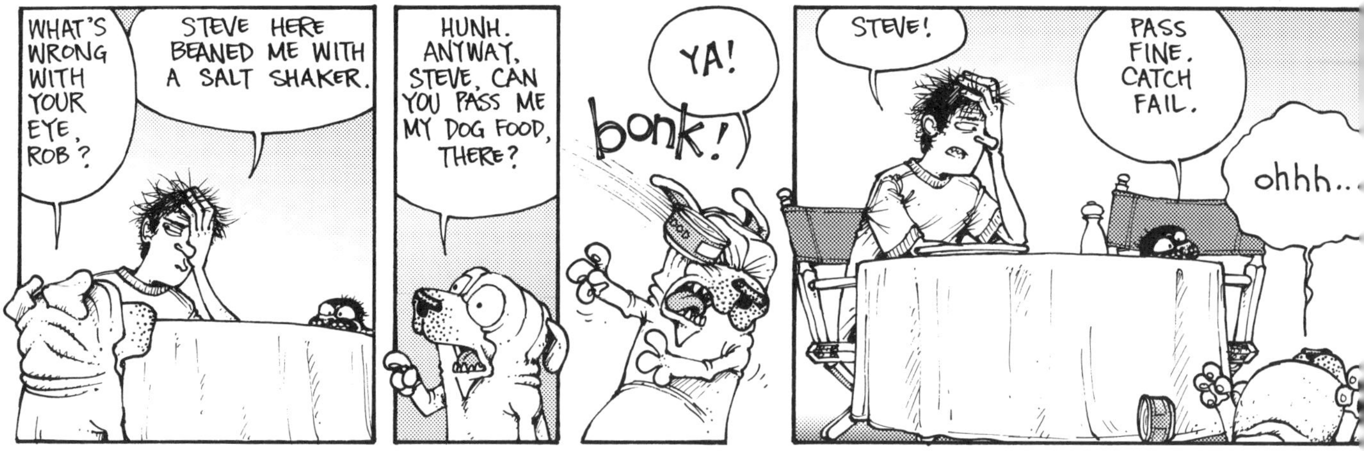
WHAT'S WRONG WITH YOUR EYE, ROB?
STEVE HERE BEANED ME WITH A SALT SHAKER.
HUNH. ANYWAY, STEVE, CAN YOU PASS ME MY DOG FOOD, THERE?
YA!
bonk!
STEVE!
PASS FINE. CATCH FAIL.
ohhh...

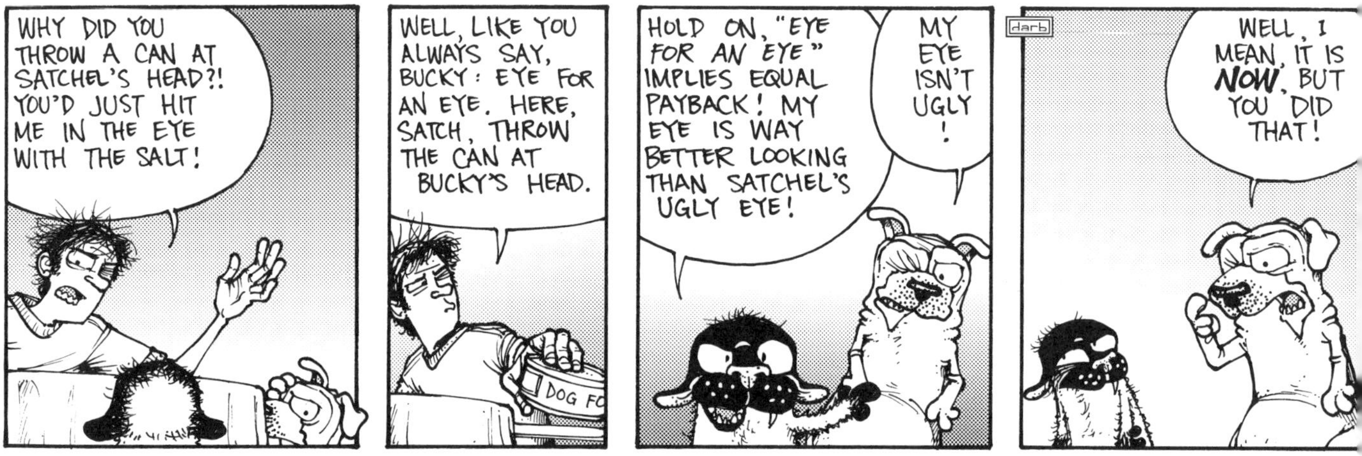
WHY DID YOU THROW A CAN AT SATCHEL'S HEAD?! YOU'D JUST HIT ME IN THE EYE WITH THE SALT!
WELL, LIKE YOU ALWAYS SAY, BUCKY: EYE FOR AN EYE. HERE, SATCH, THROW THE CAN AT BUCKY'S HEAD.
DOG FO
HOLD ON, "EYE FOR AN EYE" IMPLIES EQUAL PAYBACK! MY EYE IS WAY BETTER LOOKING THAN SATCHEL'S UGLY EYE!
MY EYE ISN'T UGLY!
darb
WELL, I MEAN, IT IS NOW, BUT YOU DID THAT!

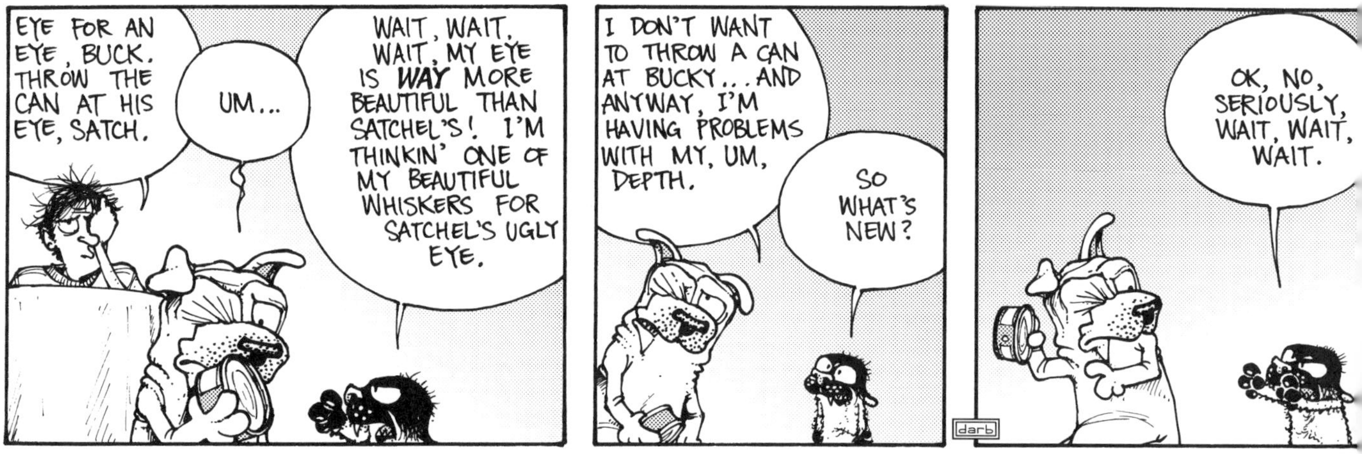
EYE FOR AN EYE, BUCK. THROW THE CAN AT HIS EYE, SATCH.
UM...
WAIT, WAIT, WAIT, MY EYE IS WAY MORE BEAUTIFUL THAN SATCHEL'S! I'M THINKIN' ONE OF MY BEAUTIFUL WHISKERS FOR SATCHEL'S UGLY EYE.
I DON'T WANT TO THROW A CAN AT BUCKY... AND ANYWAY, I'M HAVING PROBLEMS WITH MY, UM, DEPTH.
SO WHAT'S NEW?
darb
OK, NO, SERIOUSLY, WAIT, WAIT, WAIT.

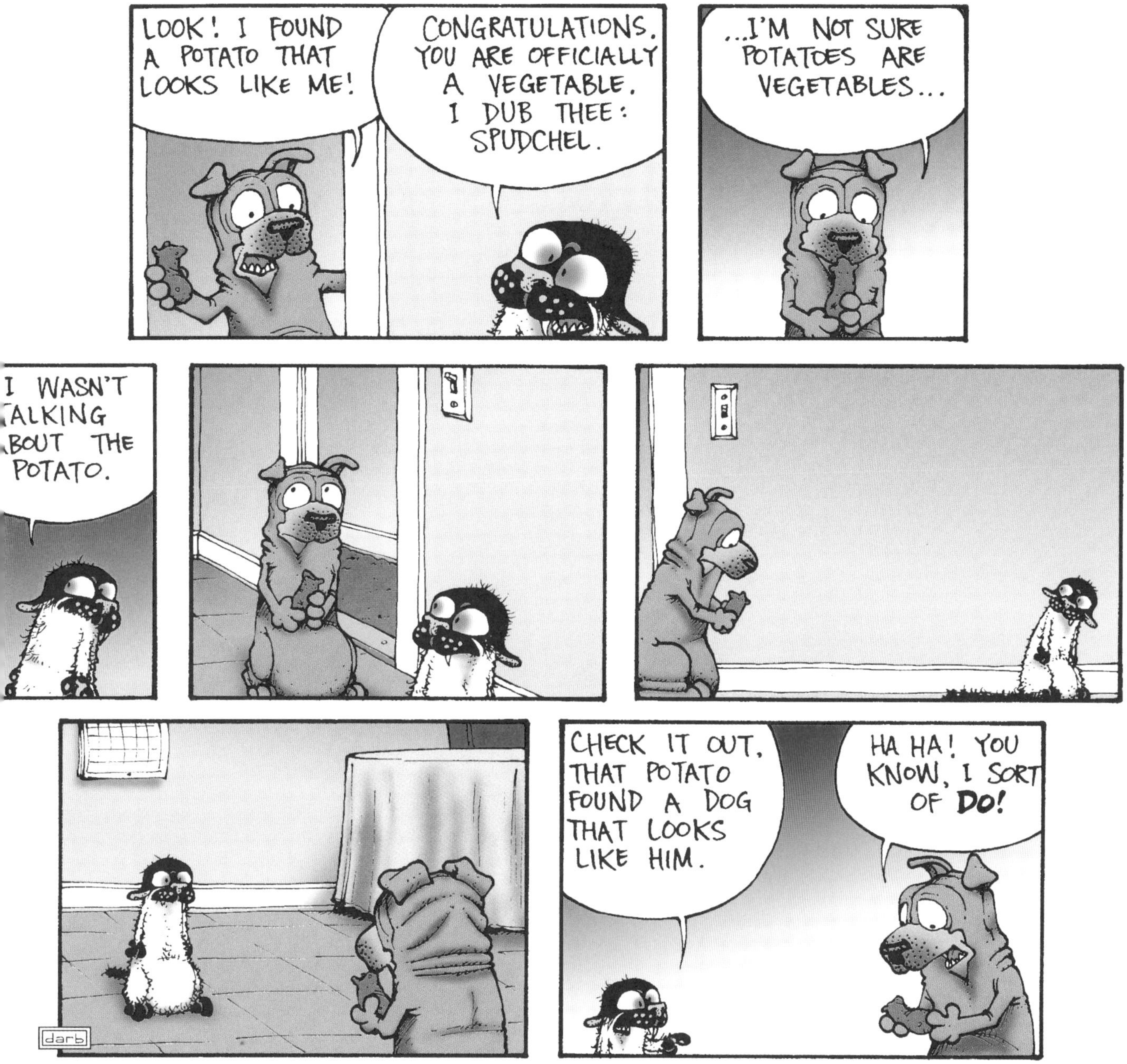
LOOK! I FOUND A POTATO THAT LOOKS LIKE ME!
CONGRATULATIONS. YOU ARE OFFICIALLY A VEGETABLE. I DUB THEE: SPUDCHEL.
...I'M NOT SURE POTATOES ARE VEGETABLES...
I WASN'T ALKING BOUT THE POTATO.
darb
CHECK IT OUT, THAT POTATO FOUND A DOG THAT LOOKS LIKE HIM.
HA HA! YOU KNOW, I SORT OF DO!

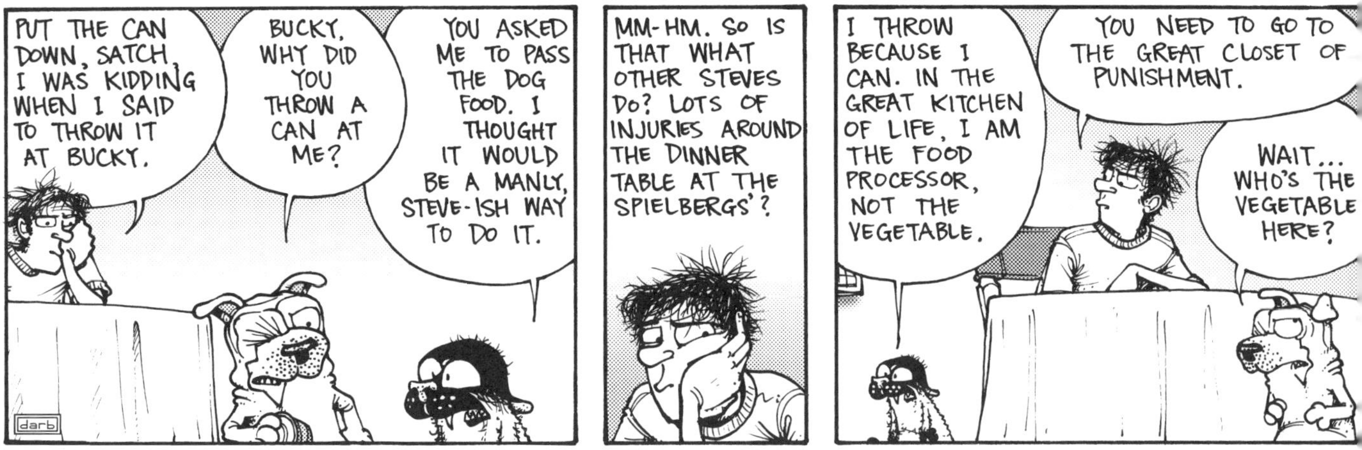
PUT THE CAN DOWN, SATCH. I WAS KIDDING WHEN I SAID TO THROW IT AT BUCKY.
BUCKY, WHY DID YOU THROW A CAN AT ME?
YOU ASKED ME TO PASS THE DOG FOOD. I THOUGHT IT WOULD BE A MANLY, STEVE-ISH WAY TO DO IT.
MM-HM. SO IS THAT WHAT OTHER STEVES DO? LOTS OF INJURIES AROUND THE DINNER TABLE AT THE SPIELBERGS'?
I THROW BECAUSE I CAN. IN THE GREAT KITCHEN OF LIFE, I AM THE FOOD PROCESSOR, NOT THE VEGETABLE.
YOU NEED TO GO TO THE GREAT CLOSET OF PUNISHMENT.
WAIT... WHO'S THE VEGETABLE HERE?

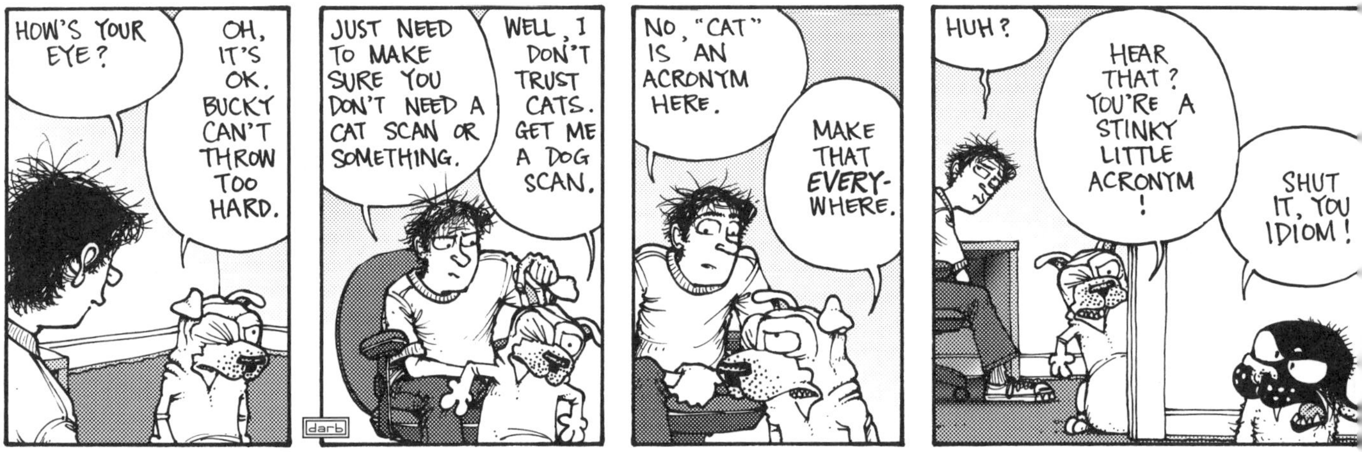
HOW'S YOUR EYE?
OH, IT'S OK. BUCKY CAN'T THROW TOO HARD.
JUST NEED TO MAKE SURE YOU DON'T NEED A CAT SCAN OR SOMETHING.
WELL, I DON'T TRUST CATS. GET ME A DOG SCAN.
NO, "CAT" IS AN ACRONYM HERE.
MAKE THAT EVERYWHERE.
HUH?
HEAR THAT? YOU'RE A STINKY LITTLE ACRONYM!
SHUT IT, YOU IDIOM!

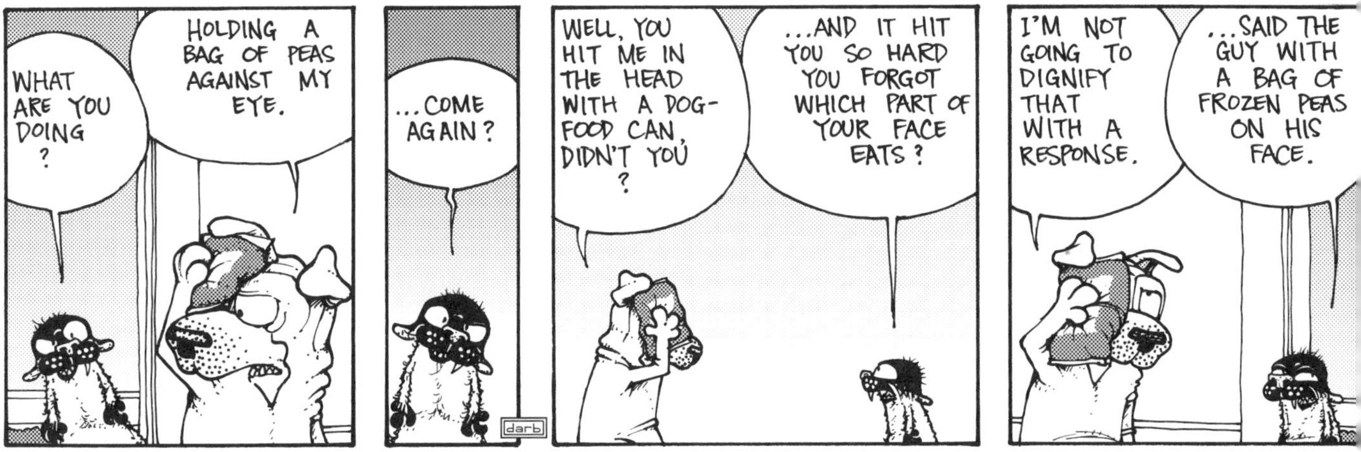
WHAT ARE YOU DOING?
HOLDING A BAG OF PEAS AGAINST MY EYE.
...COME AGAIN?
WELL, YOU HIT ME IN THE HEAD WITH A DOG-FOOD CAN, DIDN'T YOU?
...AND IT HIT YOU SO HARD YOU FORGOT WHICH PART OF YOUR FACE EATS?
I'M NOT GOING TO DIGNIFY THAT WITH A RESPONSE.
...SAID THE GUY WITH A BAG OF FROZEN PEAS ON HIS FACE.

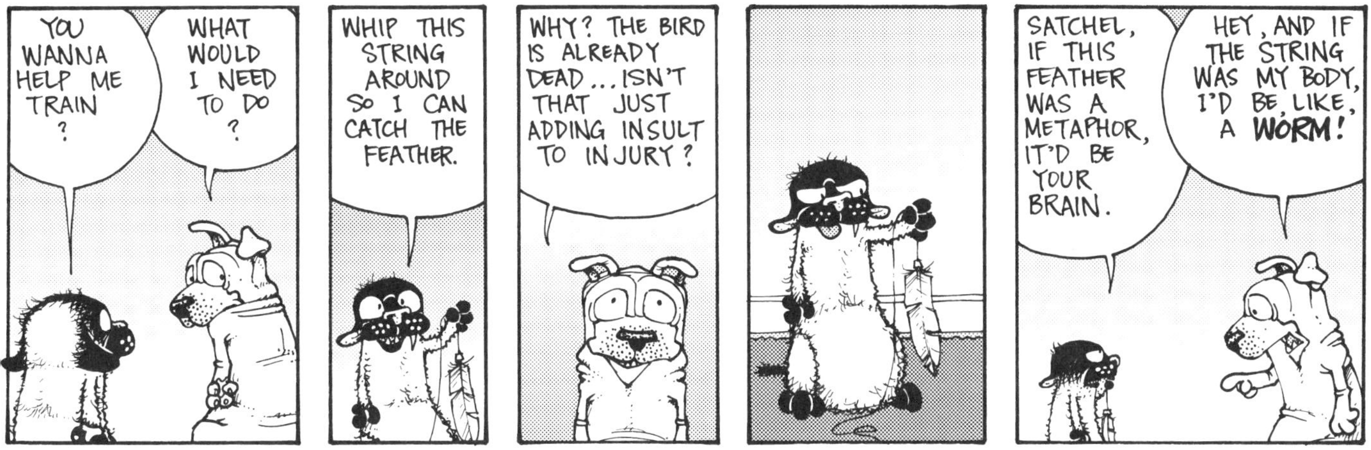
YOU WANNA HELP ME TRAIN ?
WHAT WOULD I NEED TO DO ?
WHIP THIS STRING AROUND SO I CAN CATCH THE FEATHER.
WHY? THE BIRD IS ALREADY DEAD... ISN'T THAT JUST ADDING INSULT TO INJURY ?
SATCHEL, IF THIS FEATHER WAS A METAPHOR, IT'D BE YOUR BRAIN.
HEY, AND IF THE STRING WAS MY BODY, I'D BE, LIKE, A **WORM!**

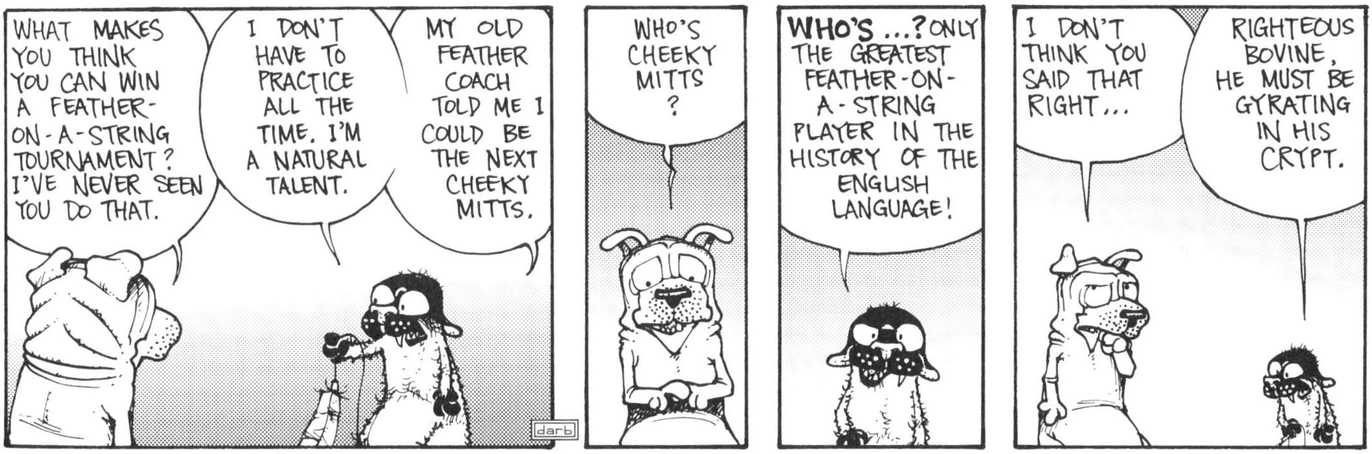
WHAT MAKES YOU THINK YOU CAN WIN A FEATHER-ON-A-STRING TOURNAMENT? I'VE NEVER SEEN YOU DO THAT.
I DON'T HAVE TO PRACTICE ALL THE TIME. I'M A NATURAL TALENT.
MY OLD FEATHER COACH TOLD ME I COULD BE THE NEXT CHEEKY MITTS.
WHO'S CHEEKY MITTS ?
WHO'S ...? ONLY THE GREATEST FEATHER-ON-A-STRING PLAYER IN THE HISTORY OF THE ENGLISH LANGUAGE!
I DON'T THINK YOU SAID THAT RIGHT...
RIGHTEOUS BOVINE, HE MUST BE GYRATING IN HIS CRYPT.

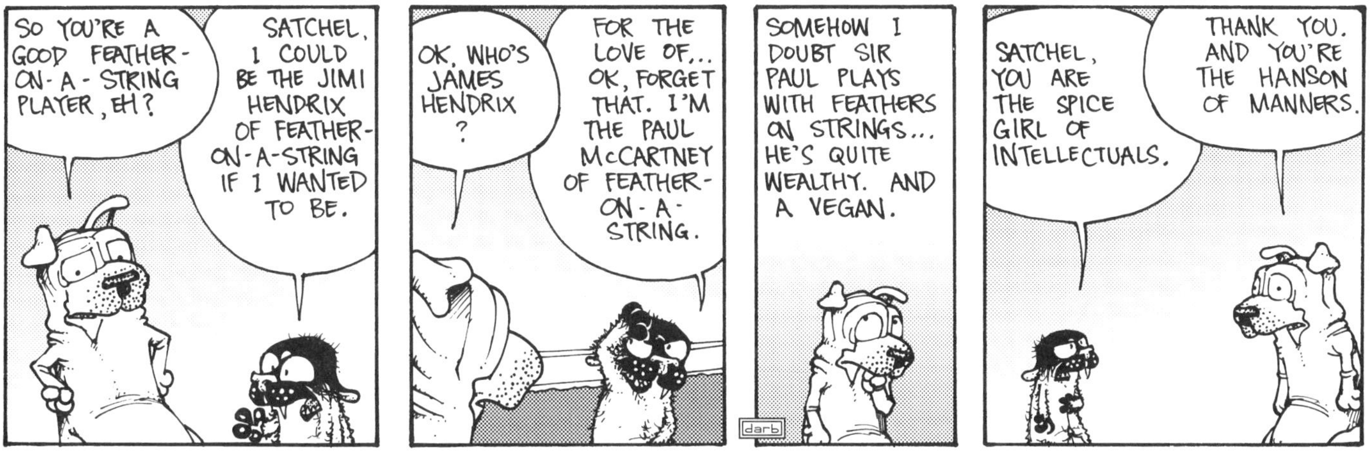
SO YOU'RE A GOOD FEATHER-ON-A-STRING PLAYER, EH?
SATCHEL, I COULD BE THE JIMI HENDRIX OF FEATHER-ON-A-STRING IF I WANTED TO BE.
OK, WHO'S JAMES HENDRIX ?
FOR THE LOVE OF... OK, FORGET THAT. I'M THE PAUL McCARTNEY OF FEATHER-ON-A-STRING.
SOMEHOW I DOUBT SIR PAUL PLAYS WITH FEATHERS ON STRINGS... HE'S QUITE WEALTHY. AND A VEGAN.
SATCHEL, YOU ARE THE SPICE GIRL OF INTELLECTUALS.
THANK YOU. AND YOU'RE THE HANSON OF MANNERS.

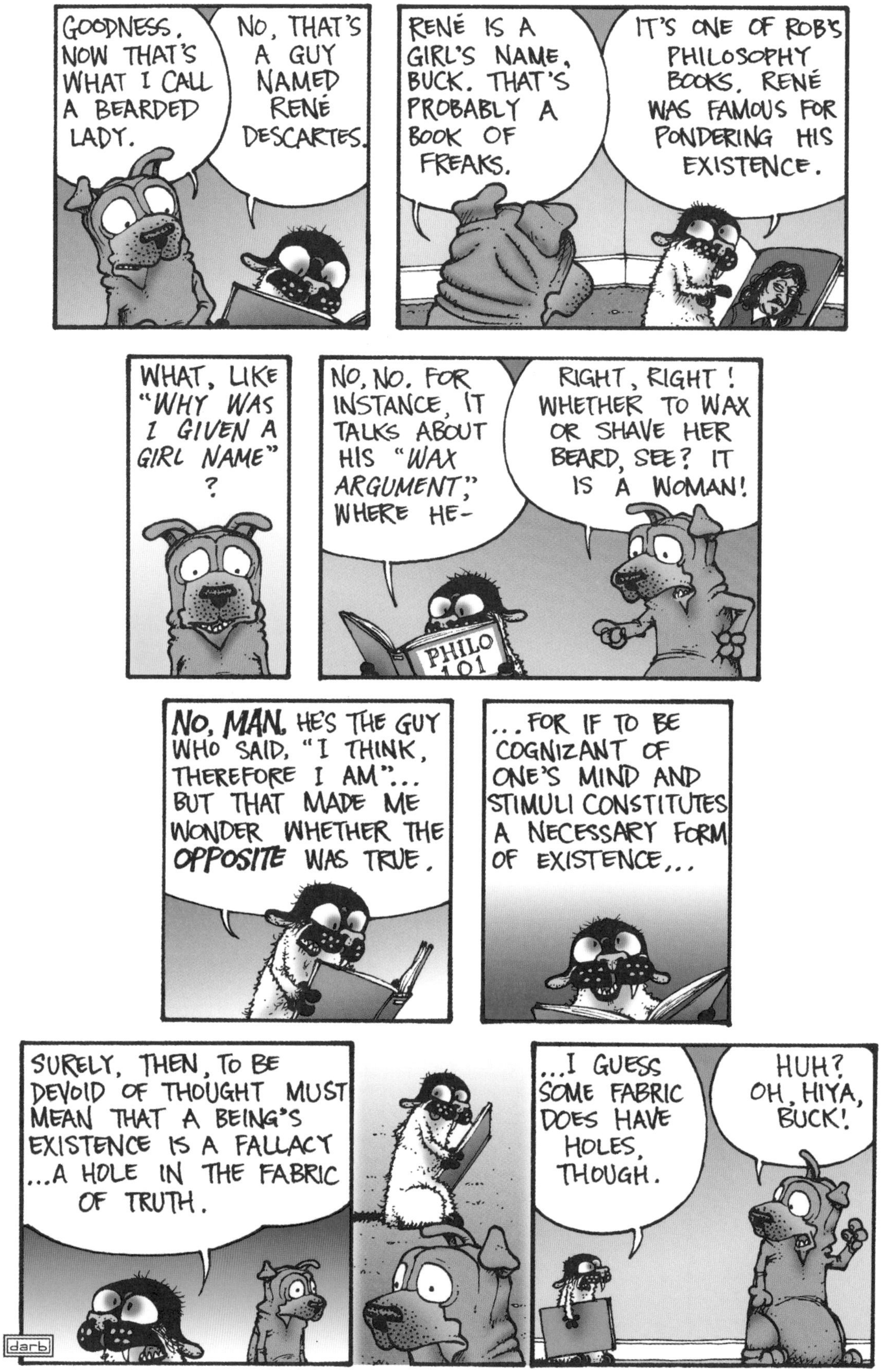
GOODNESS. NOW THAT'S WHAT I CALL A BEARDED LADY.
NO, THAT'S A GUY NAMED RENÉ DESCARTES.
RENÉ IS A GIRL'S NAME, BUCK. THAT'S PROBABLY A BOOK OF FREAKS.
IT'S ONE OF ROB'S PHILOSOPHY BOOKS. RENÉ WAS FAMOUS FOR PONDERING HIS EXISTENCE.
WHAT, LIKE "WHY WAS I GIVEN A GIRL NAME" ?
NO, NO. FOR INSTANCE, IT TALKS ABOUT HIS "WAX ARGUMENT," WHERE HE-
RIGHT, RIGHT! WHETHER TO WAX OR SHAVE HER BEARD, SEE? IT IS A WOMAN!
PHILO 101
NO, MAN. HE'S THE GUY WHO SAID, "I THINK, THEREFORE I AM"... BUT THAT MADE ME WONDER WHETHER THE OPPOSITE WAS TRUE.
...FOR IF TO BE COGNIZANT OF ONE'S MIND AND STIMULI CONSTITUTES A NECESSARY FORM OF EXISTENCE...
SURELY, THEN, TO BE DEVOID OF THOUGHT MUST MEAN THAT A BEING'S EXISTENCE IS A FALLACY ...A HOLE IN THE FABRIC OF TRUTH.
darb
...I GUESS SOME FABRIC DOES HAVE HOLES, THOUGH.
HUH? OH, HIYA, BUCK!

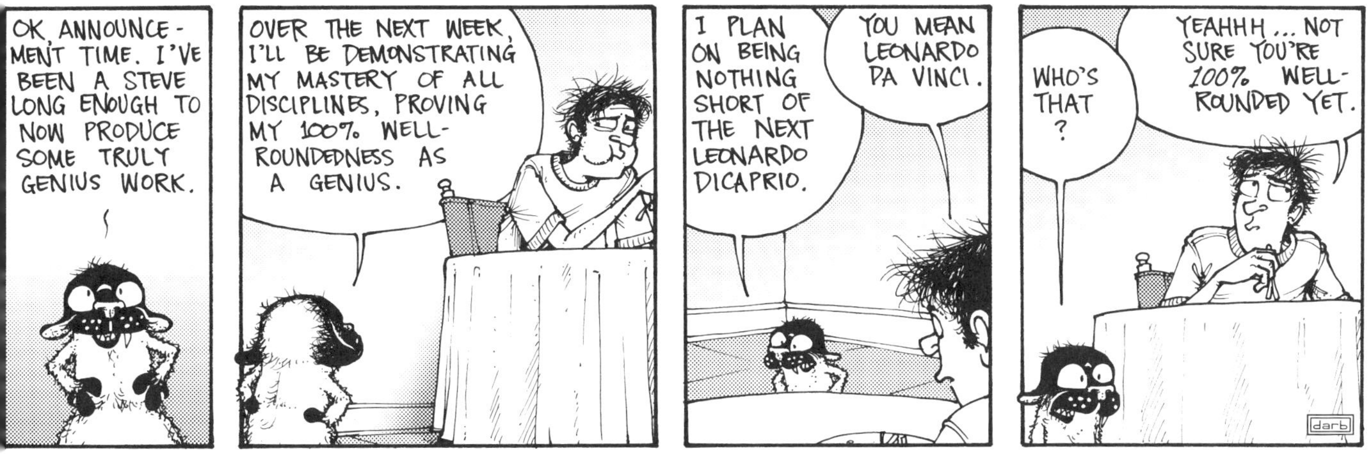
OK, ANNOUNCE-MENT TIME. I'VE BEEN A STEVE LONG ENOUGH TO NOW PRODUCE SOME TRULY GENIUS WORK.
OVER THE NEXT WEEK, I'LL BE DEMONSTRATING MY MASTERY OF ALL DISCIPLINES, PROVING MY 100% WELL-ROUNDEDNESS AS A GENIUS.
I PLAN ON BEING NOTHING SHORT OF THE NEXT LEONARDO DICAPRIO.
YOU MEAN LEONARDO DA VINCI.
WHO'S THAT?
YEAHHH... NOT SURE YOU'RE 100% WELL-ROUNDED YET.
darb

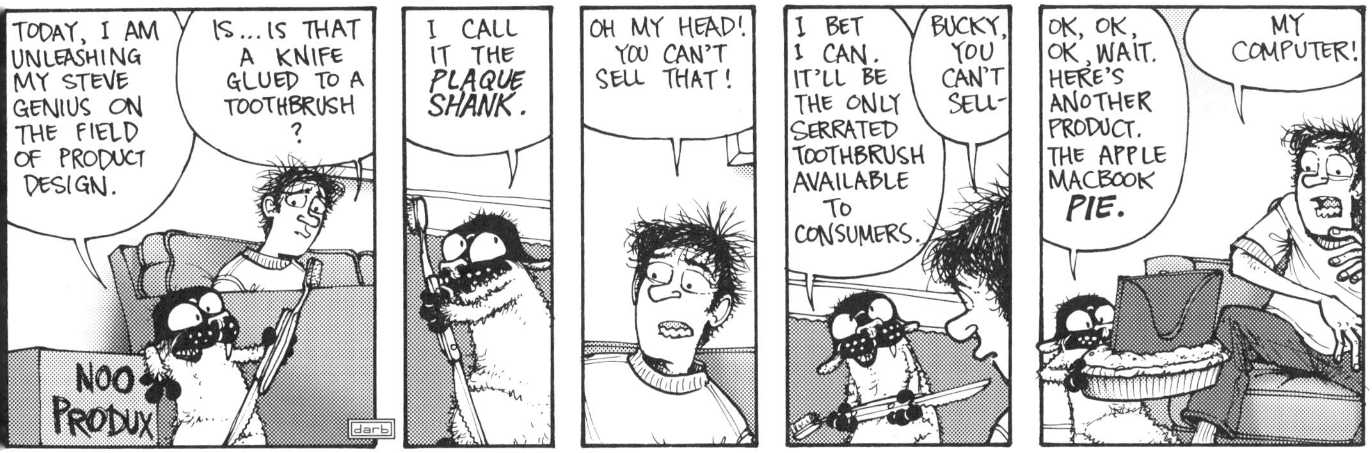
TODAY, I AM UNLEASHING MY STEVE GENIUS ON THE FIELD OF PRODUCT DESIGN.
IS... IS THAT A KNIFE GLUED TO A TOOTHBRUSH?
NOO PRODUX
darb
I CALL IT THE *PLAQUE SHANK*.
OH MY HEAD! YOU CAN'T SELL THAT!
I BET I CAN. IT'LL BE THE ONLY SERRATED TOOTHBRUSH AVAILABLE TO CONSUMERS.
BUCKY, YOU CAN'T SELL-
OK, OK, OK, WAIT. HERE'S ANOTHER PRODUCT. THE APPLE MACBOOK *PIE*.
MY COMPUTER!

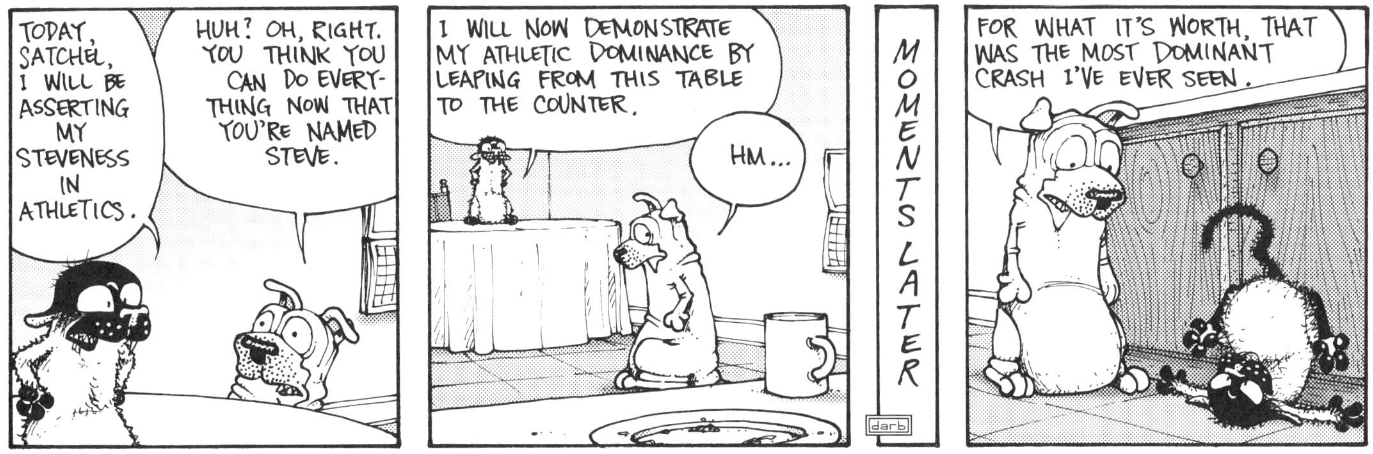
TODAY, SATCHEL, I WILL BE ASSERTING MY STEVENESS IN ATHLETICS.
HUH? OH, RIGHT. YOU THINK YOU CAN DO EVERYTHING NOW THAT YOU'RE NAMED STEVE.
I WILL NOW DEMONSTRATE MY ATHLETIC DOMINANCE BY LEAPING FROM THIS TABLE TO THE COUNTER.
HM...
darb
MOMENTS LATER
FOR WHAT IT'S WORTH, THAT WAS THE MOST DOMINANT CRASH I'VE EVER SEEN.

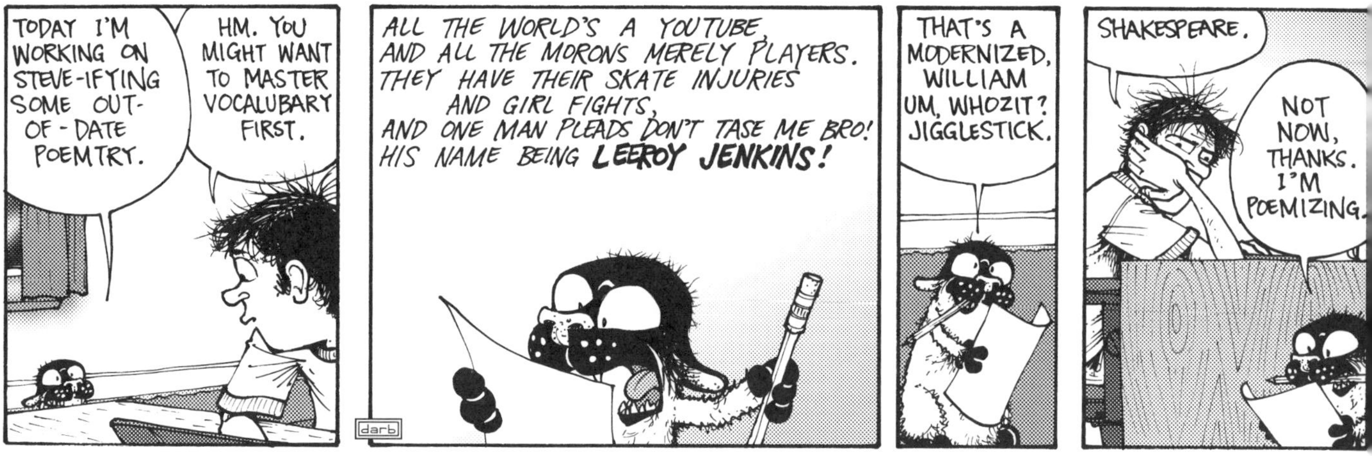
TODAY I'M WORKING ON STEVE-IFYING SOME OUT-OF-DATE POEMTRY.
HM. YOU MIGHT WANT TO MASTER VOCALUBARY FIRST.
ALL THE WORLD'S A YOUTUBE, AND ALL THE MORONS MERELY PLAYERS. THEY HAVE THEIR SKATE INJURIES AND GIRL FIGHTS, AND ONE MAN PLEADS DON'T TASE ME BRO! HIS NAME BEING LEEROY JENKINS!
darb
THAT'S A MODERNIZED, WILLIAM UM, WHOZIT? JIGGLESTICK.
SHAKESPEARE.
NOT NOW, THANKS. I'M POEMIZING.

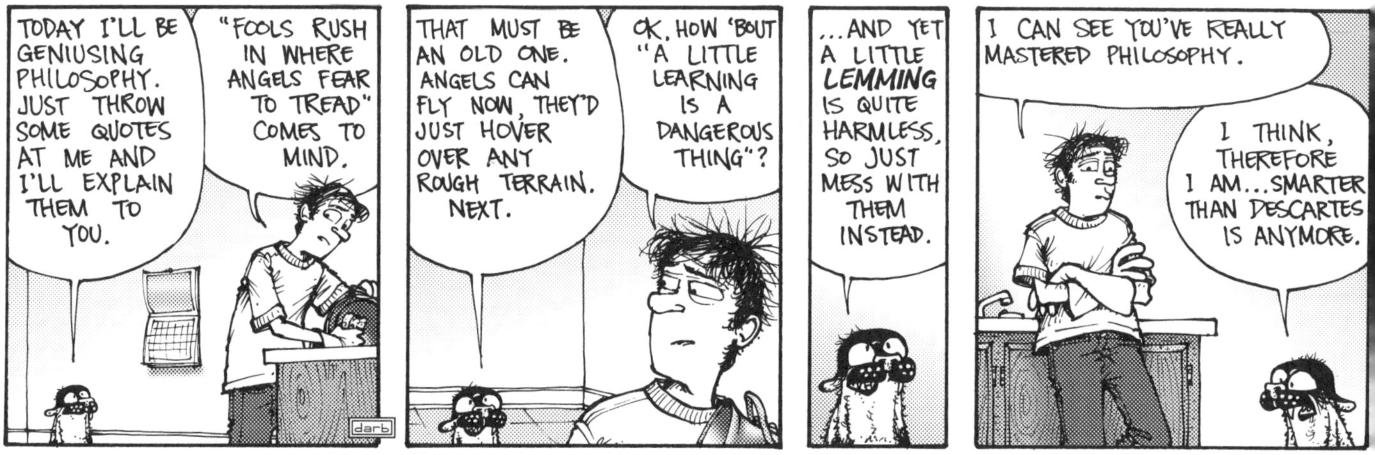
TODAY I'LL BE GENIUSING PHILOSOPHY. JUST THROW SOME QUOTES AT ME AND I'LL EXPLAIN THEM TO YOU.
"FOOLS RUSH IN WHERE ANGELS FEAR TO TREAD" COMES TO MIND.
darb
THAT MUST BE AN OLD ONE. ANGELS CAN FLY NOW, THEY'D JUST HOVER OVER ANY ROUGH TERRAIN. NEXT.
OK, HOW 'BOUT "A LITTLE LEARNING IS A DANGEROUS THING"?
...AND YET A LITTLE LEMMING IS QUITE HARMLESS, SO JUST MESS WITH THEM INSTEAD.
I CAN SEE YOU'VE REALLY MASTERED PHILOSOPHY.
I THINK, THEREFORE I AM...SMARTER THAN DESCARTES IS ANYMORE.

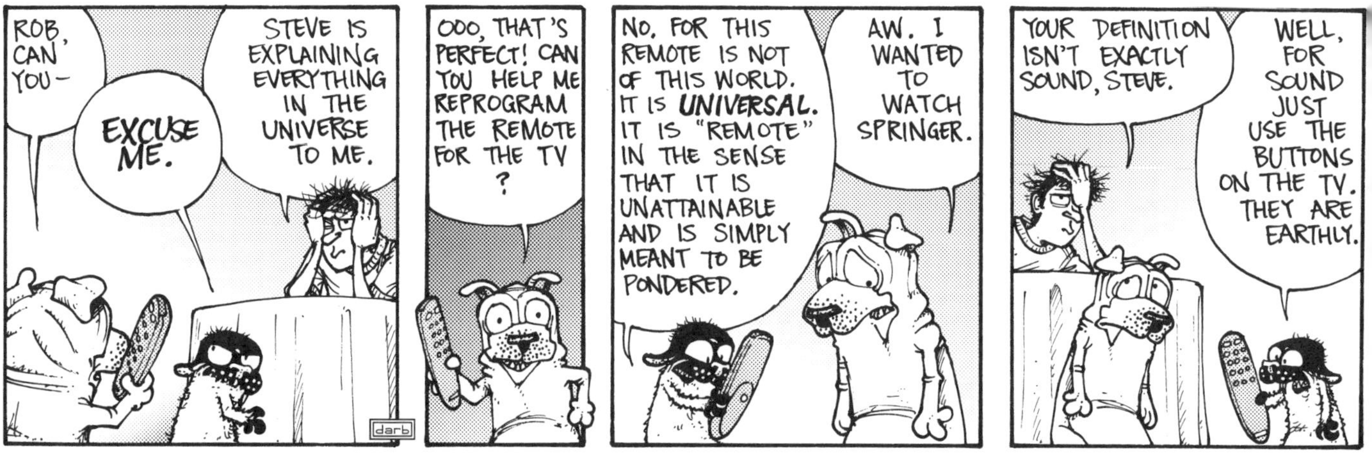
ROB, CAN YOU–
EXCUSE ME.
STEVE IS EXPLAINING EVERYTHING IN THE UNIVERSE TO ME.
darb
OOO, THAT'S PERFECT! CAN YOU HELP ME REPROGRAM THE REMOTE FOR THE TV ?
NO. FOR THIS REMOTE IS NOT OF THIS WORLD. IT IS UNIVERSAL. IT IS "REMOTE" IN THE SENSE THAT IT IS UNATTAINABLE AND IS SIMPLY MEANT TO BE PONDERED.
AW. I WANTED TO WATCH SPRINGER.
YOUR DEFINITION ISN'T EXACTLY SOUND, STEVE.
WELL, FOR SOUND JUST USE THE BUTTONS ON THE TV. THEY ARE EARTHLY.

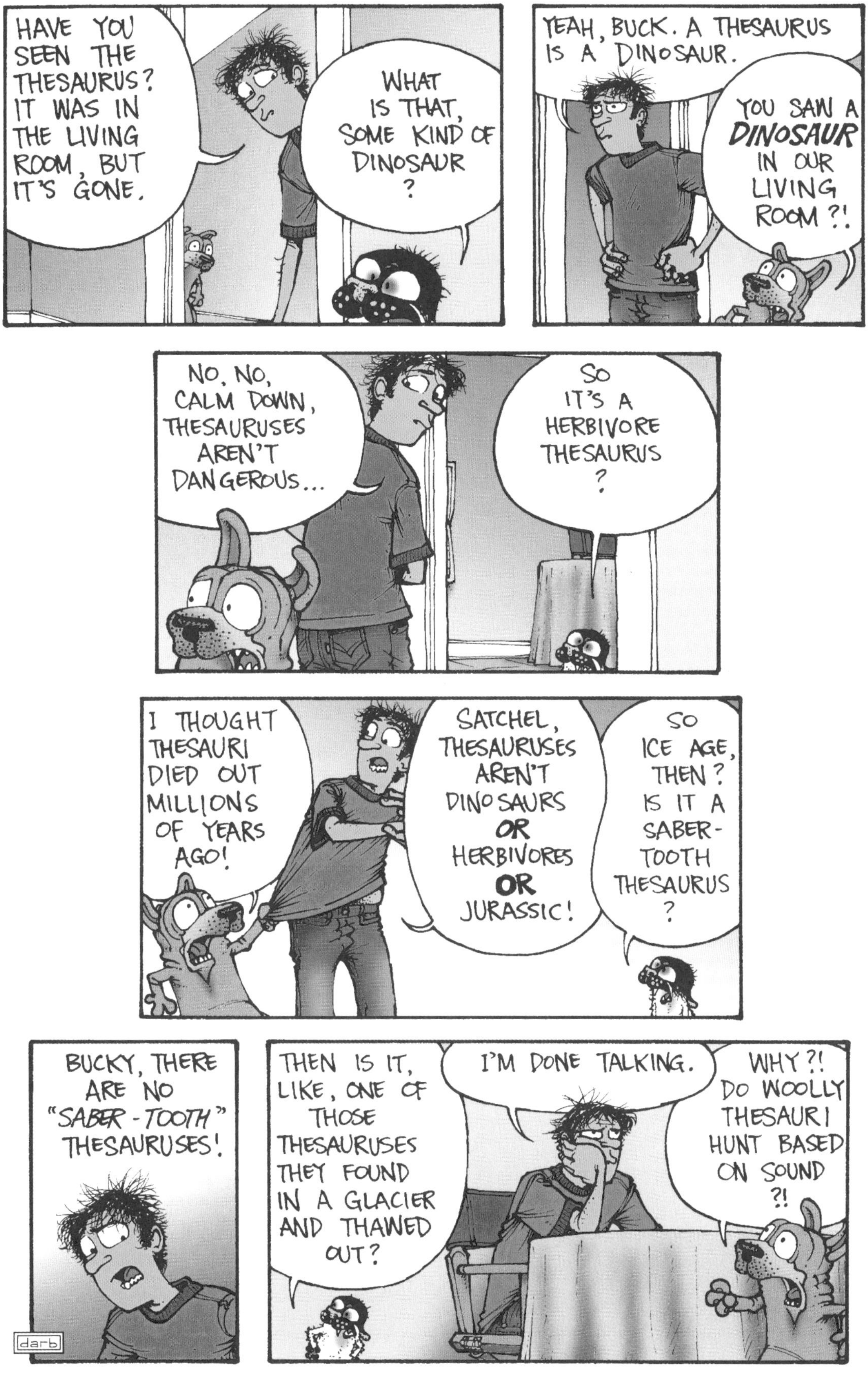
HAVE YOU SEEN THE THESAURUS? IT WAS IN THE LIVING ROOM, BUT IT'S GONE.
WHAT IS THAT, SOME KIND OF DINOSAUR?
YEAH, BUCK. A THESAURUS IS A DINOSAUR.
YOU SAW A DINOSAUR IN OUR LIVING ROOM?!
NO, NO, CALM DOWN, THESAURUSES AREN'T DANGEROUS...
SO IT'S A HERBIVORE THESAURUS?
I THOUGHT THESAURI DIED OUT MILLIONS OF YEARS AGO!
SATCHEL, THESAURUSES AREN'T DINOSAURS OR HERBIVORES OR JURASSIC!
SO ICE AGE, THEN? IS IT A SABER-TOOTH THESAURUS?
BUCKY, THERE ARE NO "SABER-TOOTH" THESAURUSES!
THEN IS IT, LIKE, ONE OF THOSE THESAURUSES THEY FOUND IN A GLACIER AND THAWED OUT?
I'M DONE TALKING.
WHY?! DO WOOLLY THESAURI HUNT BASED ON SOUND?!
darb

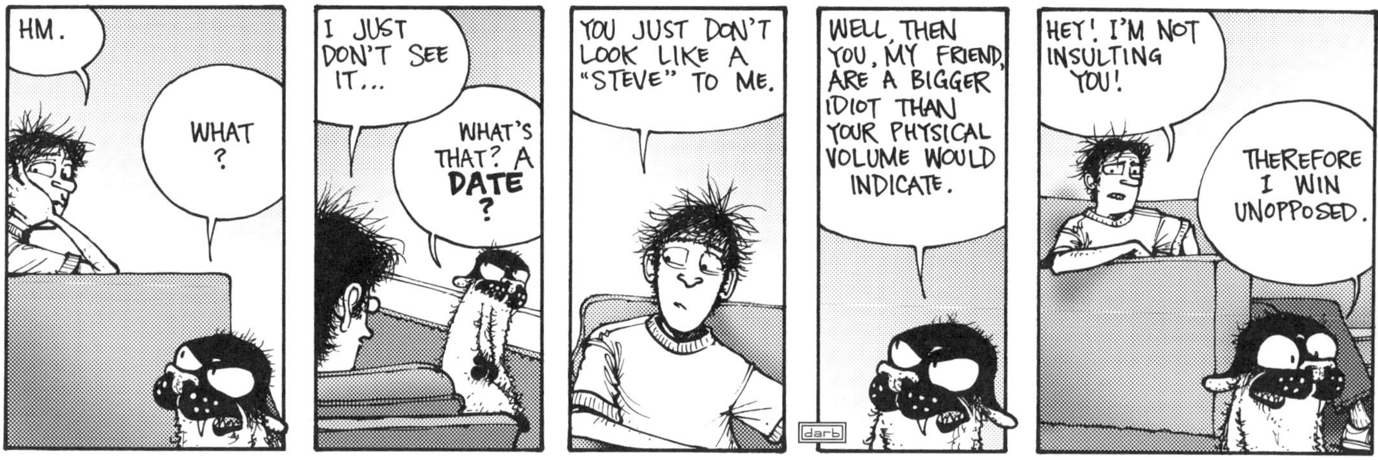
HM.
WHAT ?
I JUST DON'T SEE IT...
WHAT'S THAT? A **DATE** ?
YOU JUST DON'T LOOK LIKE A "STEVE" TO ME.
WELL, THEN YOU, MY FRIEND, ARE A BIGGER IDIOT THAN YOUR PHYSICAL VOLUME WOULD INDICATE.
darb
HEY! I'M NOT INSULTING YOU!
THEREFORE I WIN UNOPPOSED.

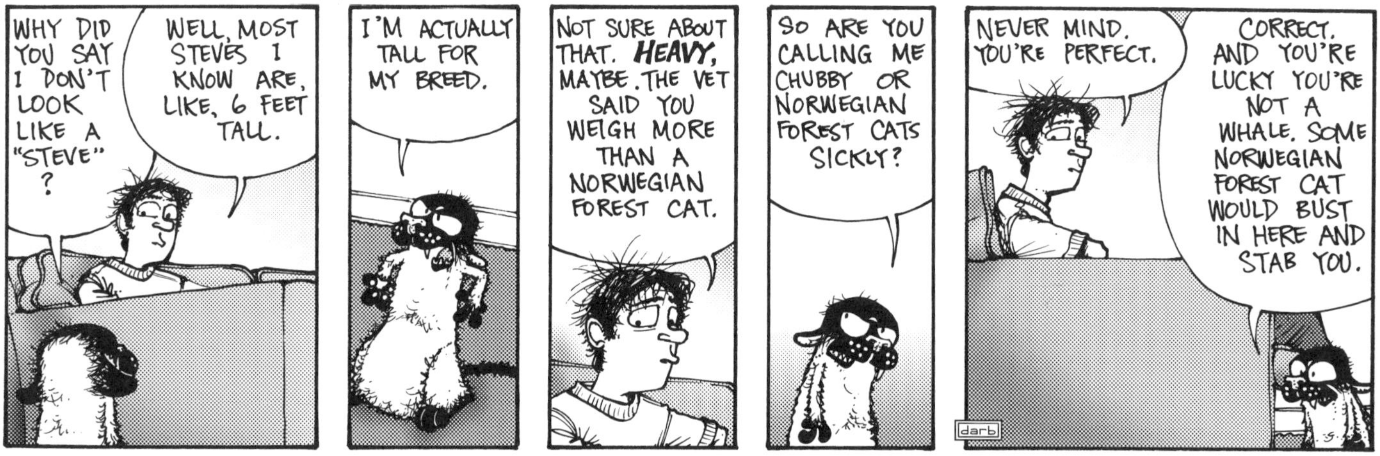
WHY DID YOU SAY I DON'T LOOK LIKE A "STEVE" ?
WELL, MOST STEVES I KNOW ARE, LIKE, 6 FEET TALL.
I'M ACTUALLY TALL FOR MY BREED.
NOT SURE ABOUT THAT. **HEAVY,** MAYBE. THE VET SAID YOU WEIGH MORE THAN A NORWEGIAN FOREST CAT.
SO ARE YOU CALLING ME CHUBBY OR NORWEGIAN FOREST CATS SICKLY?
darb
NEVER MIND. YOU'RE PERFECT.
CORRECT. AND YOU'RE LUCKY YOU'RE NOT A WHALE. SOME NORWEGIAN FOREST CAT WOULD BUST IN HERE AND STAB YOU.

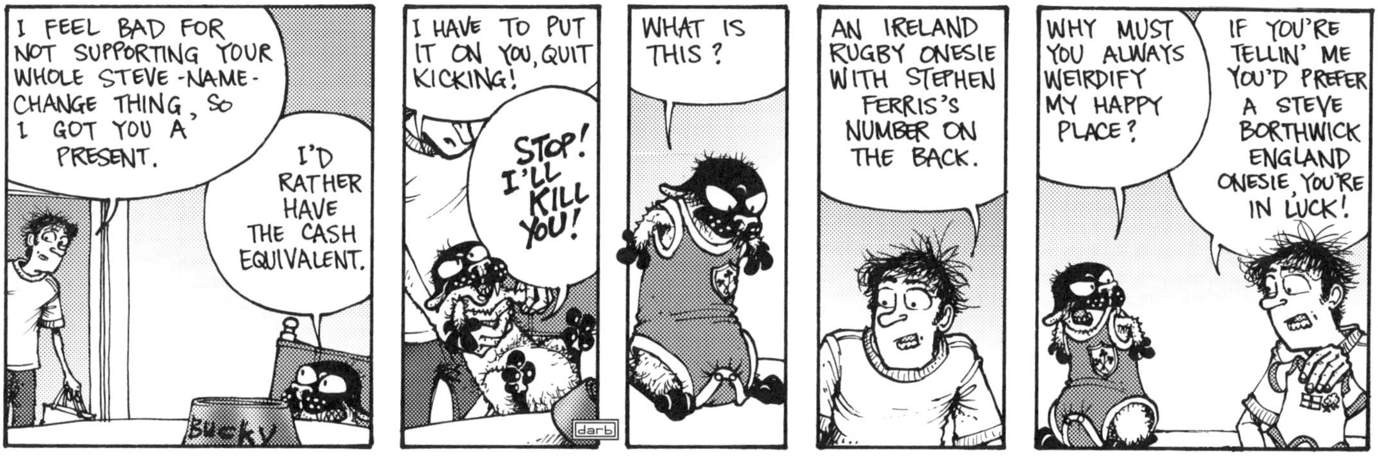
I FEEL BAD FOR NOT SUPPORTING YOUR WHOLE STEVE-NAME-CHANGE THING, SO I GOT YOU A PRESENT.
I'D RATHER HAVE THE CASH EQUIVALENT.
BUCKY
I HAVE TO PUT IT ON YOU, QUIT KICKING!
STOP! I'LL KILL YOU!
darb
WHAT IS THIS ?
AN IRELAND RUGBY ONESIE WITH STEPHEN FERRIS'S NUMBER ON THE BACK.
WHY MUST YOU ALWAYS WEIRDIFY MY HAPPY PLACE?
IF YOU'RE TELLIN' ME YOU'D PREFER A STEVE BORTHWICK ENGLAND ONESIE, YOU'RE IN LUCK!

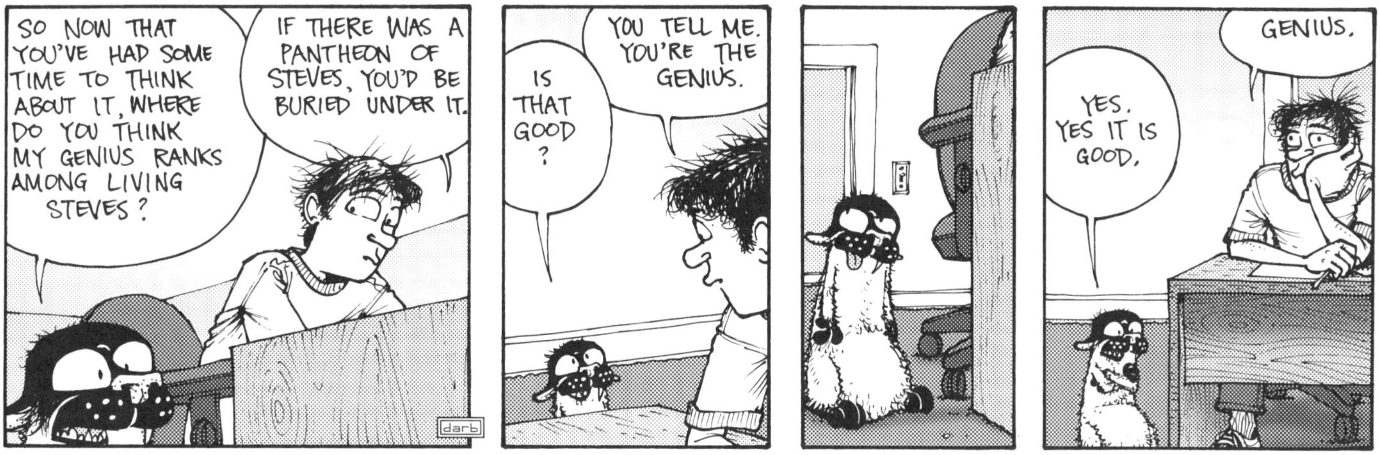
SO NOW THAT YOU'VE HAD SOME TIME TO THINK ABOUT IT, WHERE DO YOU THINK MY GENIUS RANKS AMONG LIVING STEVES?
IF THERE WAS A PANTHEON OF STEVES, YOU'D BE BURIED UNDER IT.
darb
IS THAT GOOD?
YOU TELL ME. YOU'RE THE GENIUS.
YES. YES IT IS GOOD.
GENIUS.

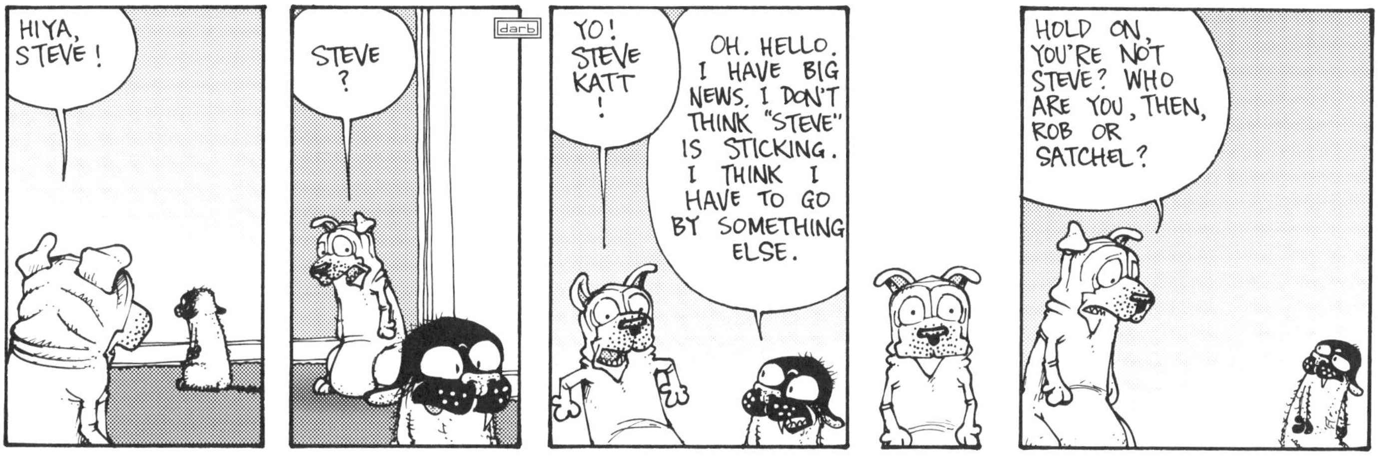
HIYA, STEVE!
STEVE?
darb
YO! STEVE KATT!
OH. HELLO. I HAVE BIG NEWS. I DON'T THINK "STEVE" IS STICKING. I THINK I HAVE TO GO BY SOMETHING ELSE.
HOLD ON, YOU'RE NOT STEVE? WHO ARE YOU, THEN, ROB OR SATCHEL?

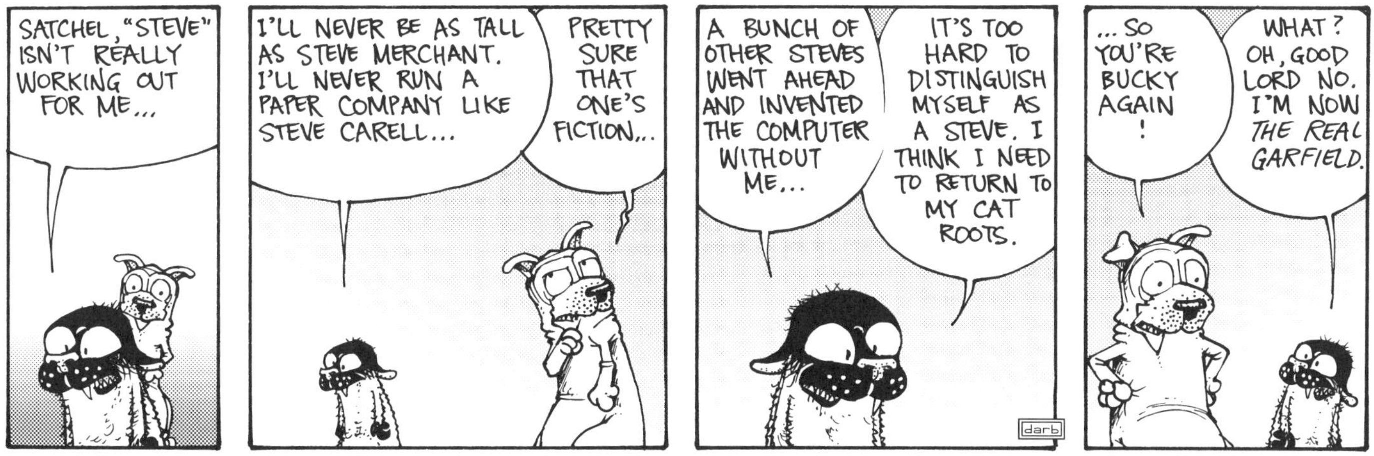
SATCHEL, "STEVE" ISN'T REALLY WORKING OUT FOR ME...
I'LL NEVER BE AS TALL AS STEVE MERCHANT. I'LL NEVER RUN A PAPER COMPANY LIKE STEVE CARELL...
PRETTY SURE THAT ONE'S FICTION...
A BUNCH OF OTHER STEVES WENT AHEAD AND INVENTED THE COMPUTER WITHOUT ME...
IT'S TOO HARD TO DISTINGUISH MYSELF AS A STEVE. I THINK I NEED TO RETURN TO MY CAT ROOTS.
darb
...SO YOU'RE BUCKY AGAIN!
WHAT? OH, GOOD LORD NO. I'M NOW THE REAL GARFIELD.

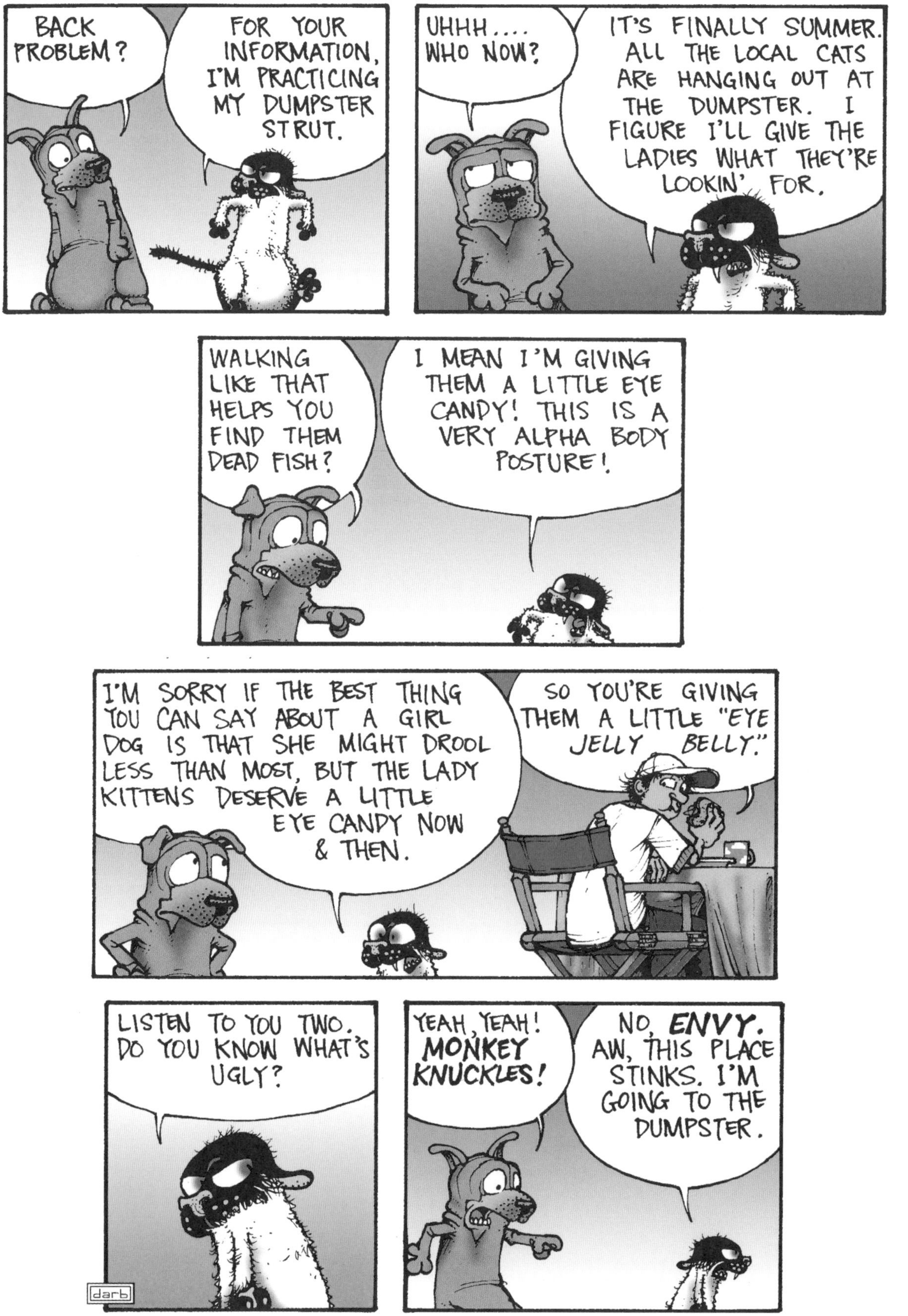
BACK PROBLEM?
FOR YOUR INFORMATION, I'M PRACTICING MY DUMPSTER STRUT.
UHHH.... WHO NOW?
IT'S FINALLY SUMMER. ALL THE LOCAL CATS ARE HANGING OUT AT THE DUMPSTER. I FIGURE I'LL GIVE THE LADIES WHAT THEY'RE LOOKIN' FOR.
WALKING LIKE THAT HELPS YOU FIND THEM DEAD FISH?
I MEAN I'M GIVING THEM A LITTLE EYE CANDY! THIS IS A VERY ALPHA BODY POSTURE!
I'M SORRY IF THE BEST THING YOU CAN SAY ABOUT A GIRL DOG IS THAT SHE MIGHT DROOL LESS THAN MOST, BUT THE LADY KITTENS DESERVE A LITTLE EYE CANDY NOW & THEN.
SO YOU'RE GIVING THEM A LITTLE "EYE JELLY BELLY."
LISTEN TO YOU TWO. DO YOU KNOW WHAT'S UGLY?
darb
YEAH, YEAH! MONKEY KNUCKLES!
NO, ENVY. AW, THIS PLACE STINKS. I'M GOING TO THE DUMPSTER.

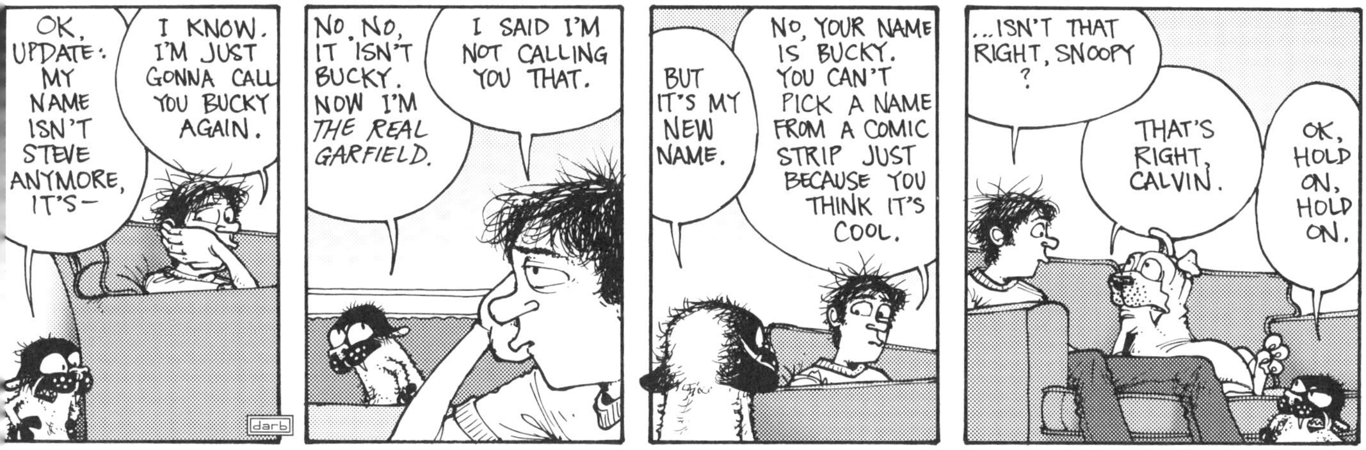
OK, UPDATE: MY NAME ISN'T STEVE ANYMORE, IT'S—
I KNOW. I'M JUST GONNA CALL YOU BUCKY AGAIN.
NO, NO, IT ISN'T BUCKY. NOW I'M *THE REAL GARFIELD.*
I SAID I'M NOT CALLING YOU THAT.
BUT IT'S MY NEW NAME.
NO, YOUR NAME IS BUCKY. YOU CAN'T PICK A NAME FROM A COMIC STRIP JUST BECAUSE YOU THINK IT'S COOL.
...ISN'T THAT RIGHT, SNOOPY?
THAT'S RIGHT, CALVIN.
OK, HOLD ON, HOLD ON.

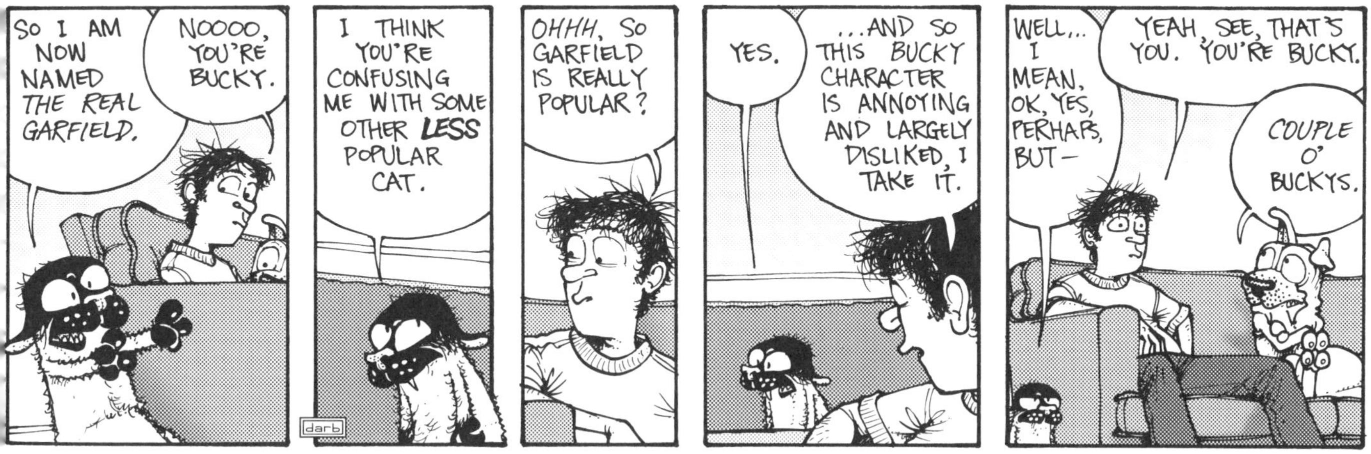
SO I AM NOW NAMED *THE REAL GARFIELD.*
NOOOO, YOU'RE BUCKY.
I THINK YOU'RE CONFUSING ME WITH SOME OTHER **LESS** POPULAR CAT.
OHHH, SO GARFIELD IS REALLY POPULAR?
YES.
...AND SO THIS BUCKY CHARACTER IS ANNOYING AND LARGELY DISLIKED, I TAKE IT.
WELL... I MEAN, OK, YES, PERHAPS, BUT—
YEAH, SEE, THAT'S YOU. YOU'RE BUCKY.
COUPLE O' BUCKYS.

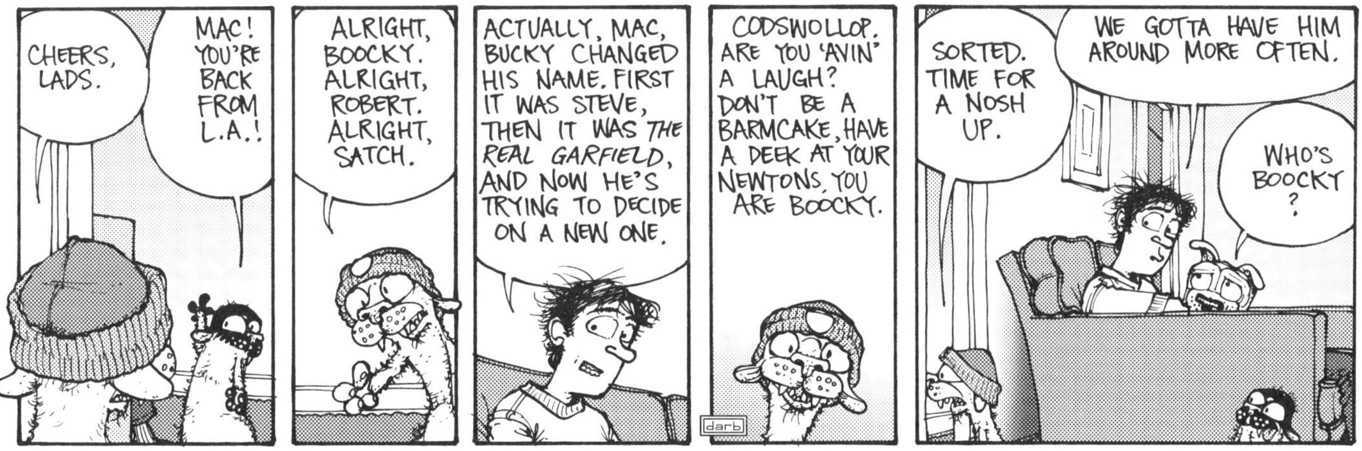
CHEERS, LADS.
MAC! YOU'RE BACK FROM L.A.!
ALRIGHT, BOOCKY. ALRIGHT, ROBERT. ALRIGHT, SATCH.
ACTUALLY, MAC, BUCKY CHANGED HIS NAME. FIRST IT WAS STEVE, THEN IT WAS *THE REAL GARFIELD*, AND NOW HE'S TRYING TO DECIDE ON A NEW ONE.
CODSWOLLOP. ARE YOU 'AVIN' A LAUGH? DON'T BE A BARMCAKE, HAVE A DEEK AT YOUR NEWTONS. YOU ARE BOOCKY.
SORTED. TIME FOR A NOSH UP.
WE GOTTA HAVE HIM AROUND MORE OFTEN.
WHO'S BOOCKY?

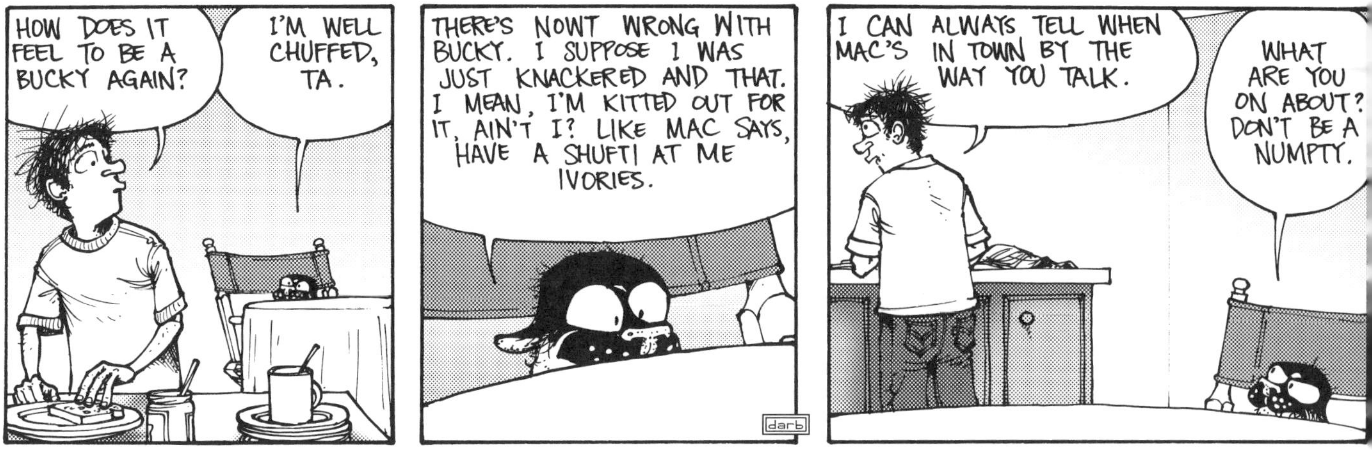
HOW DOES IT FEEL TO BE A BUCKY AGAIN?
I'M WELL CHUFFED, TA.
THERE'S NOWT WRONG WITH BUCKY. I SUPPOSE I WAS JUST KNACKERED AND THAT. I MEAN, I'M KITTED OUT FOR IT, AIN'T I? LIKE MAC SAYS, HAVE A SHUFTI AT ME IVORIES.
darb
I CAN ALWAYS TELL WHEN MAC'S IN TOWN BY THE WAY YOU TALK.
WHAT ARE YOU ON ABOUT? DON'T BE A NUMPTY.

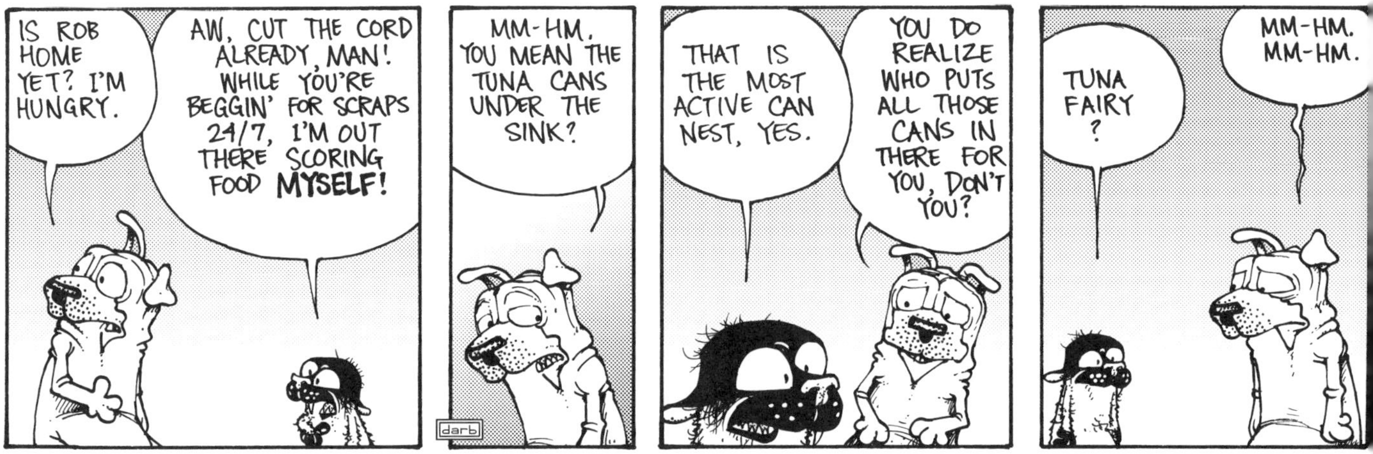
IS ROB HOME YET? I'M HUNGRY.
AW, CUT THE CORD ALREADY, MAN! WHILE YOU'RE BEGGIN' FOR SCRAPS 24/7, I'M OUT THERE SCORING FOOD MYSELF!
MM-HM. YOU MEAN THE TUNA CANS UNDER THE SINK?
darb
THAT IS THE MOST ACTIVE CAN NEST, YES.
YOU DO REALIZE WHO PUTS ALL THOSE CANS IN THERE FOR YOU, DON'T YOU?
TUNA FAIRY?
MM-HM. MM-HM.

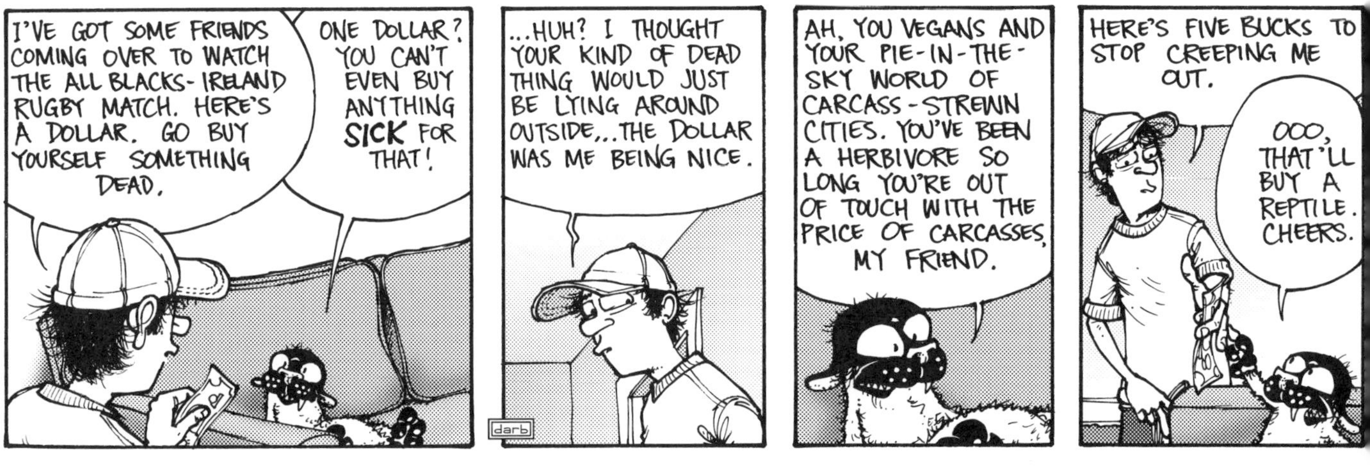
I'VE GOT SOME FRIENDS COMING OVER TO WATCH THE ALL BLACKS-IRELAND RUGBY MATCH. HERE'S A DOLLAR. GO BUY YOURSELF SOMETHING DEAD.
ONE DOLLAR? YOU CAN'T EVEN BUY ANYTHING SICK FOR THAT!
...HUH? I THOUGHT YOUR KIND OF DEAD THING WOULD JUST BE LYING AROUND OUTSIDE...THE DOLLAR WAS ME BEING NICE.
darb
AH, YOU VEGANS AND YOUR PIE-IN-THE-SKY WORLD OF CARCASS-STREWN CITIES. YOU'VE BEEN A HERBIVORE SO LONG YOU'RE OUT OF TOUCH WITH THE PRICE OF CARCASSES, MY FRIEND.
HERE'S FIVE BUCKS TO STOP CREEPING ME OUT.
OOO, THAT'LL BUY A REPTILE. CHEERS.

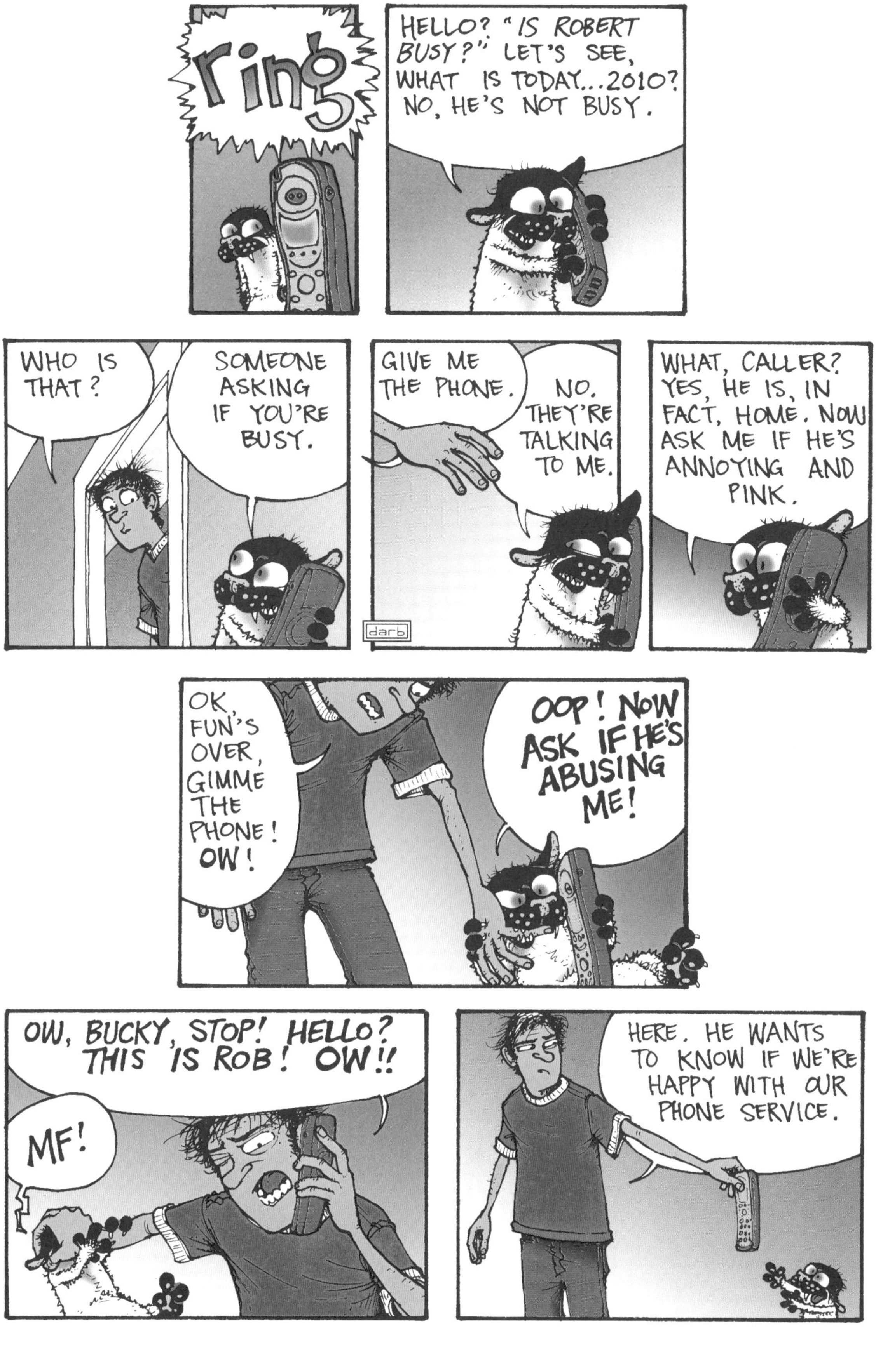
ring
HELLO? "IS ROBERT BUSY?" LET'S SEE, WHAT IS TODAY...2010? NO, HE'S NOT BUSY.
WHO IS THAT?
SOMEONE ASKING IF YOU'RE BUSY.
GIVE ME THE PHONE.
NO. THEY'RE TALKING TO ME.
darb
WHAT, CALLER? YES, HE IS, IN FACT, HOME. NOW ASK ME IF HE'S ANNOYING AND PINK.
OK, FUN'S OVER, GIMME THE PHONE! OW!
OOP! NOW ASK IF HE'S ABUSING ME!
OW, BUCKY, STOP! HELLO? THIS IS ROB! OW!!
MF!
HERE. HE WANTS TO KNOW IF WE'RE HAPPY WITH OUR PHONE SERVICE.

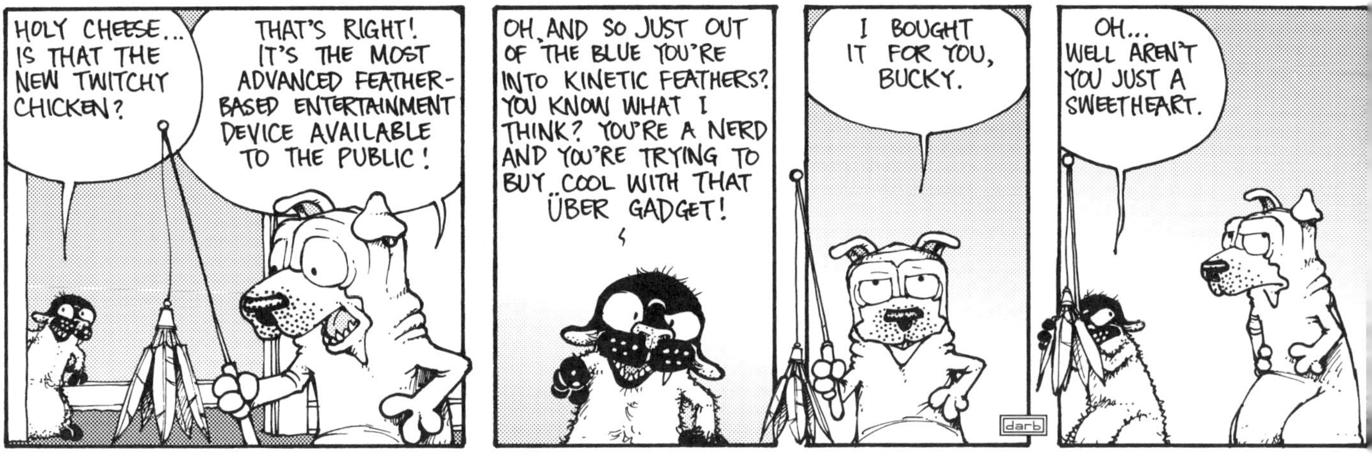
HOLY CHEESE... IS THAT THE NEW TWITCHY CHICKEN?
THAT'S RIGHT! IT'S THE MOST ADVANCED FEATHER-BASED ENTERTAINMENT DEVICE AVAILABLE TO THE PUBLIC!
OH, AND SO JUST OUT OF THE BLUE YOU'RE INTO KINETIC FEATHERS? YOU KNOW WHAT I THINK? YOU'RE A NERD AND YOU'RE TRYING TO BUY COOL WITH THAT ÜBER GADGET!
I BOUGHT IT FOR YOU, BUCKY.
OH... WELL AREN'T YOU JUST A SWEETHEART.

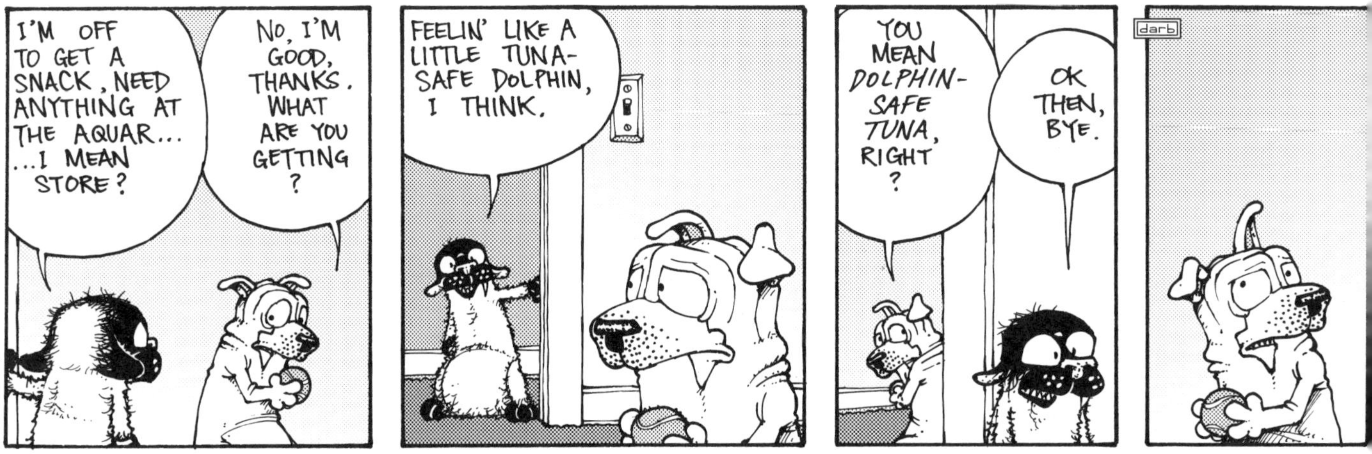
I'M OFF TO GET A SNACK, NEED ANYTHING AT THE AQUAR... ...I MEAN STORE?
NO, I'M GOOD, THANKS. WHAT ARE YOU GETTING?
FEELIN' LIKE A LITTLE TUNA-SAFE DOLPHIN, I THINK.
YOU MEAN *DOLPHIN-SAFE TUNA*, RIGHT?
OK THEN, BYE.

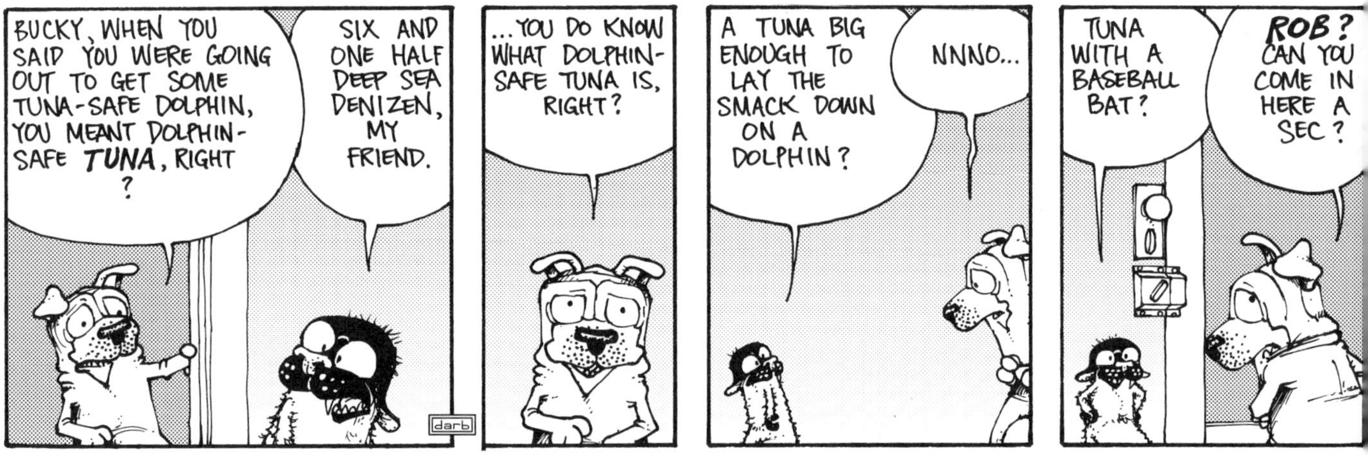
BUCKY, WHEN YOU SAID YOU WERE GOING OUT TO GET SOME TUNA-SAFE DOLPHIN, YOU MEANT DOLPHIN-SAFE **TUNA**, RIGHT?
SIX AND ONE HALF DEEP SEA DENIZEN, MY FRIEND.
...YOU DO KNOW WHAT DOLPHIN-SAFE TUNA IS, RIGHT?
A TUNA BIG ENOUGH TO LAY THE SMACK DOWN ON A DOLPHIN?
NNNO...
TUNA WITH A BASEBALL BAT?
ROB? CAN YOU COME IN HERE A SEC?

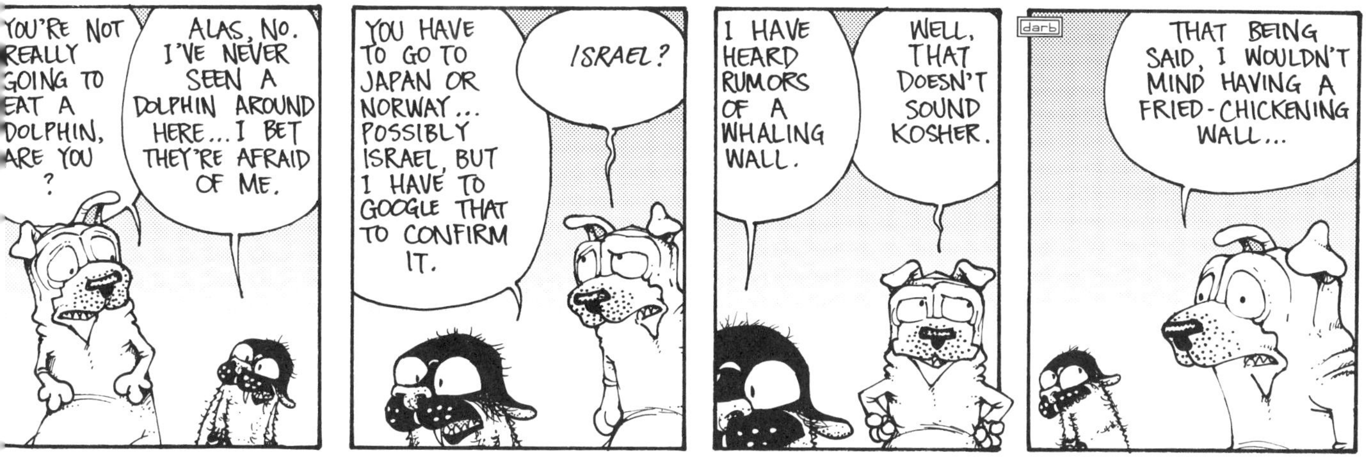
YOU'RE NOT REALLY GOING TO EAT A DOLPHIN, ARE YOU ?
ALAS, NO. I'VE NEVER SEEN A DOLPHIN AROUND HERE... I BET THEY'RE AFRAID OF ME.
YOU HAVE TO GO TO JAPAN OR NORWAY... POSSIBLY ISRAEL, BUT I HAVE TO GOOGLE THAT TO CONFIRM IT.
ISRAEL?
I HAVE HEARD RUMORS OF A WHALING WALL.
WELL, THAT DOESN'T SOUND KOSHER.
darb
THAT BEING SAID, I WOULDN'T MIND HAVING A FRIED-CHICKENING WALL...

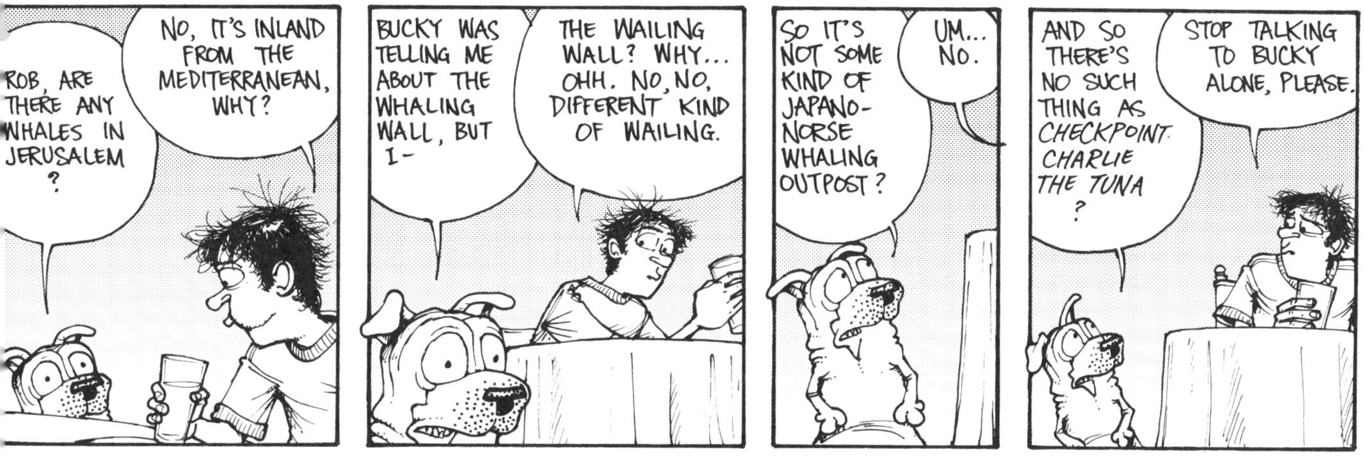
ROB, ARE THERE ANY WHALES IN JERUSALEM ?
NO, IT'S INLAND FROM THE MEDITERRANEAN, WHY?
BUCKY WAS TELLING ME ABOUT THE WHALING WALL, BUT I-
THE WAILING WALL? WHY... OHH. NO, NO, DIFFERENT KIND OF WAILING.
SO IT'S NOT SOME KIND OF JAPANO-NORSE WHALING OUTPOST?
UM... NO.
AND SO THERE'S NO SUCH THING AS CHECKPOINT CHARLIE THE TUNA ?
STOP TALKING TO BUCKY ALONE, PLEASE.

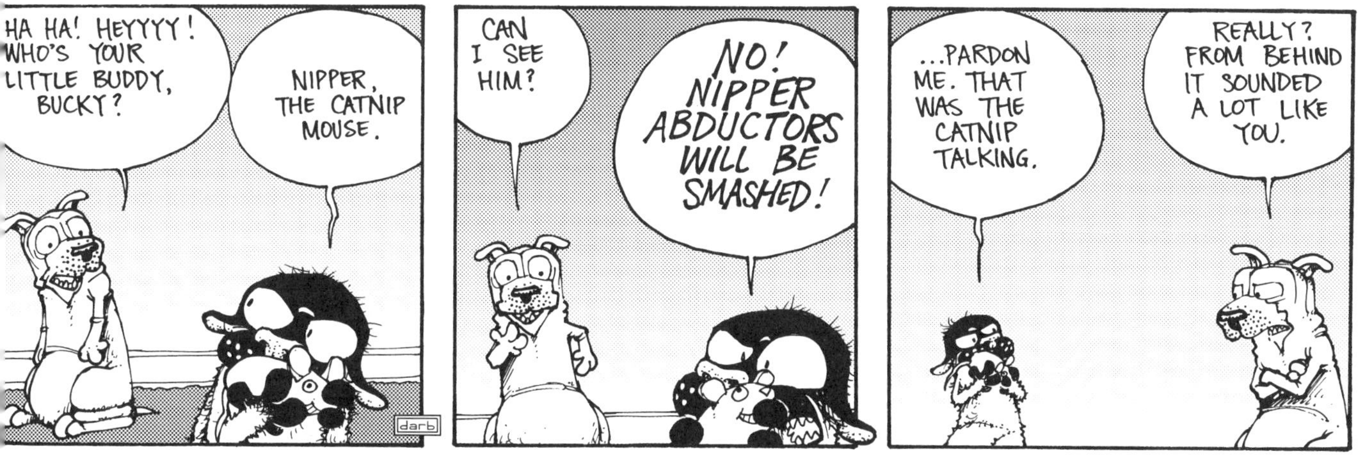
HA HA! HEYYYY! WHO'S YOUR LITTLE BUDDY, BUCKY?
NIPPER, THE CATNIP MOUSE.
darb
CAN I SEE HIM?
NO! NIPPER ABDUCTORS WILL BE SMASHED!
...PARDON ME. THAT WAS THE CATNIP TALKING.
REALLY? FROM BEHIND IT SOUNDED A LOT LIKE YOU.

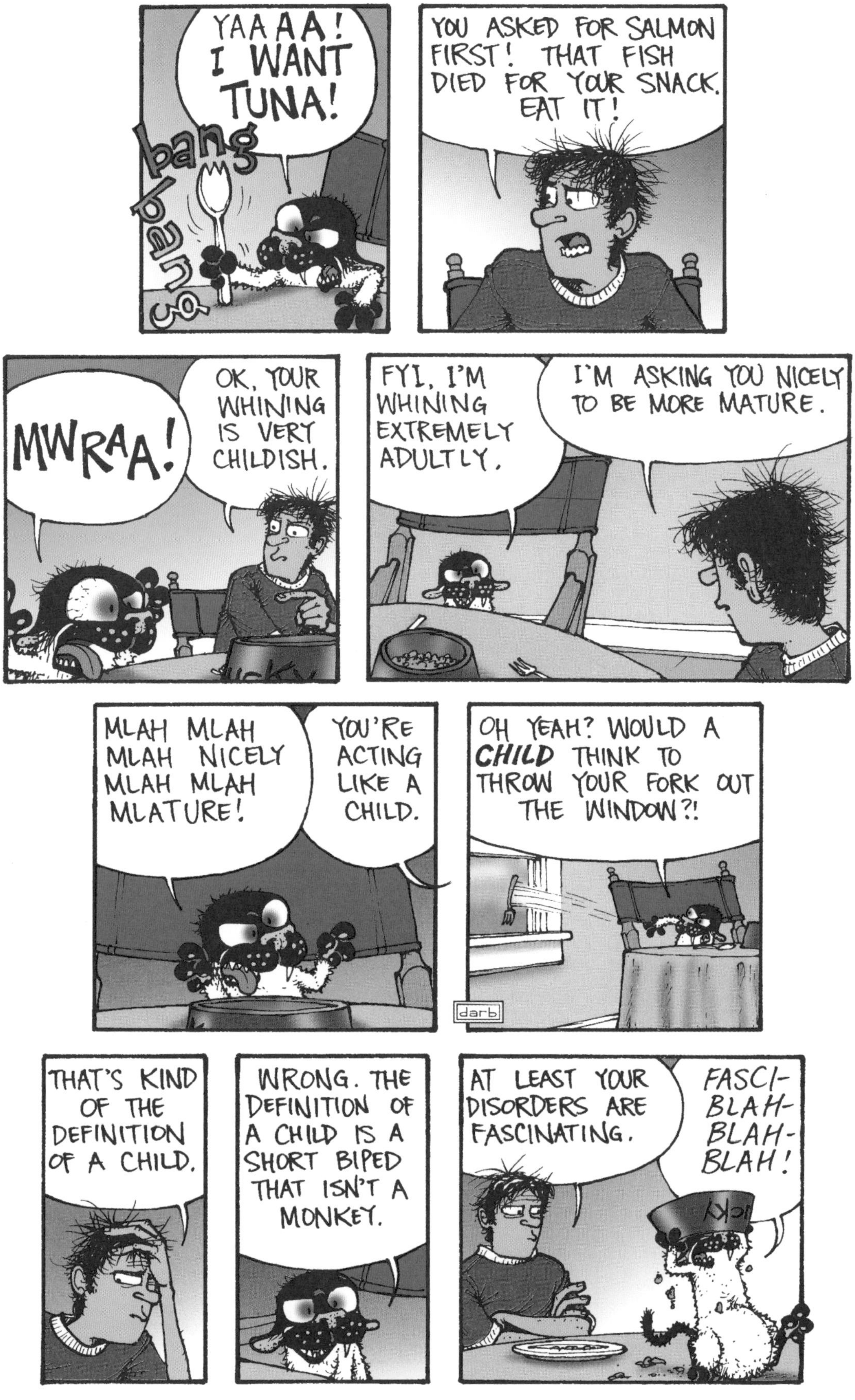
YAAAA! I WANT TUNA!
bang bang bang
YOU ASKED FOR SALMON FIRST! THAT FISH DIED FOR YOUR SNACK. EAT IT!
MWRAA!
OK, YOUR WHINING IS VERY CHILDISH.
FYI, I'M WHINING EXTREMELY ADULTLY.
I'M ASKING YOU NICELY TO BE MORE MATURE.
MLAH MLAH MLAH NICELY MLAH MLAH MLATURE!
YOU'RE ACTING LIKE A CHILD.
OH YEAH? WOULD A CHILD THINK TO THROW YOUR FORK OUT THE WINDOW?!
darb
THAT'S KIND OF THE DEFINITION OF A CHILD.
WRONG. THE DEFINITION OF A CHILD IS A SHORT BIPED THAT ISN'T A MONKEY.
AT LEAST YOUR DISORDERS ARE FASCINATING.
FASCI-BLAH-BLAH-BLAH!

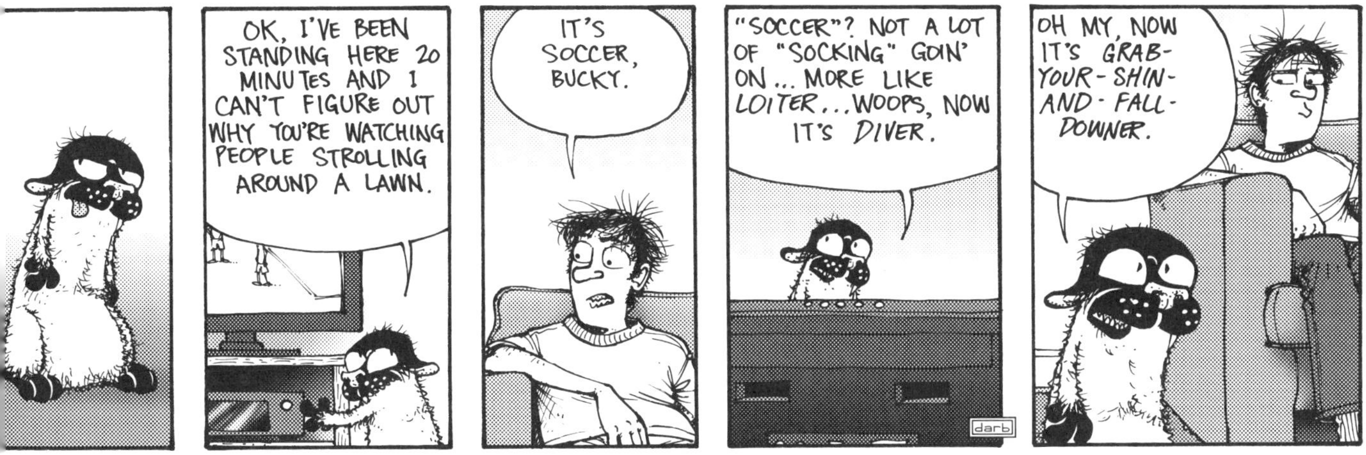
OK, I'VE BEEN STANDING HERE 20 MINUTES AND I CAN'T FIGURE OUT WHY YOU'RE WATCHING PEOPLE STROLLING AROUND A LAWN.
IT'S SOCCER, BUCKY.
"SOCCER"? NOT A LOT OF "SOCKING" GOIN' ON ... MORE LIKE *LOITER* ... WOOPS, NOW IT'S *DIVER*.
OH MY, NOW IT'S *GRAB-YOUR-SHIN-AND-FALL-DOWNER*.

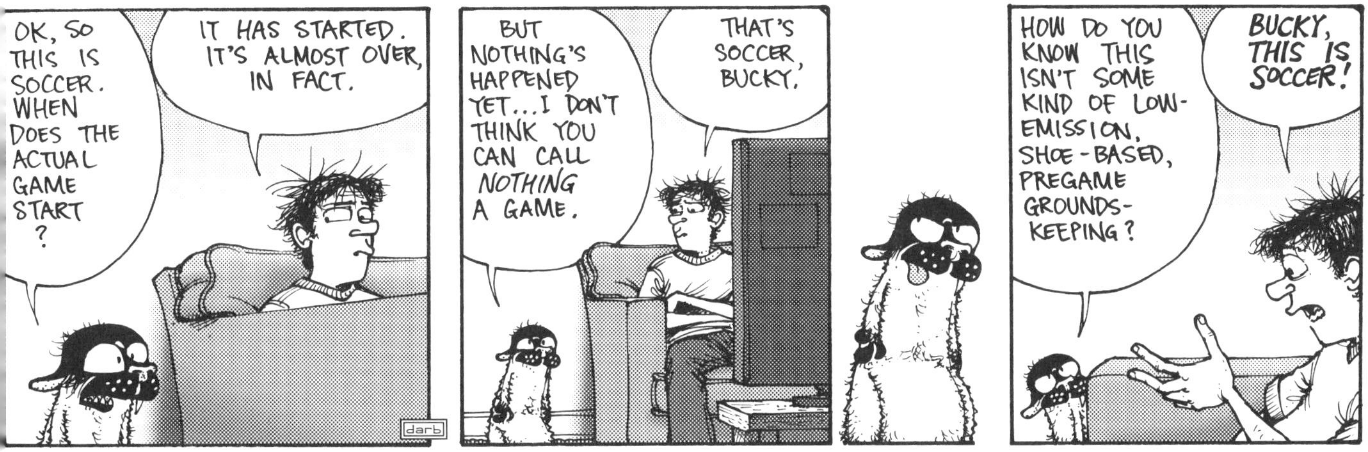
OK, SO THIS IS SOCCER. WHEN DOES THE ACTUAL GAME START?
IT HAS STARTED. IT'S ALMOST OVER, IN FACT.
BUT NOTHING'S HAPPENED YET... I DON'T THINK YOU CAN CALL *NOTHING* A GAME.
THAT'S SOCCER, BUCKY.
HOW DO YOU KNOW THIS ISN'T SOME KIND OF LOW-EMISSION, SHOE-BASED, PREGAME GROUNDSKEEPING?
BUCKY, THIS IS SOCCER!

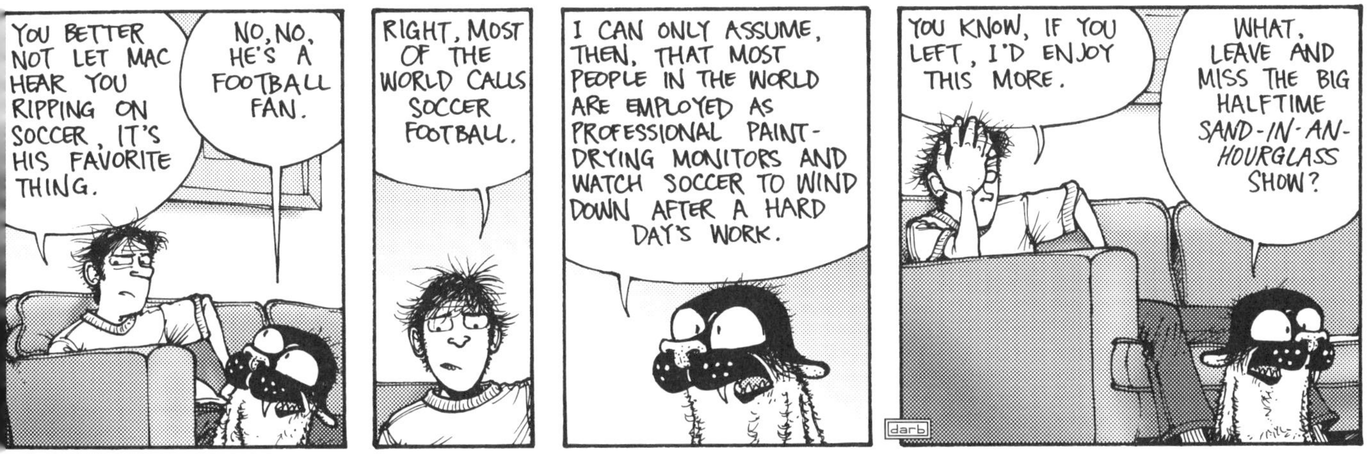
YOU BETTER NOT LET MAC HEAR YOU RIPPING ON SOCCER, IT'S HIS FAVORITE THING.
NO, NO, HE'S A FOOTBALL FAN.
RIGHT, MOST OF THE WORLD CALLS SOCCER FOOTBALL.
I CAN ONLY ASSUME, THEN, THAT MOST PEOPLE IN THE WORLD ARE EMPLOYED AS PROFESSIONAL PAINT-DRYING MONITORS AND WATCH SOCCER TO WIND DOWN AFTER A HARD DAY'S WORK.
YOU KNOW, IF YOU LEFT, I'D ENJOY THIS MORE.
WHAT, LEAVE AND MISS THE BIG HALFTIME *SAND-IN-AN-HOURGLASS* SHOW?

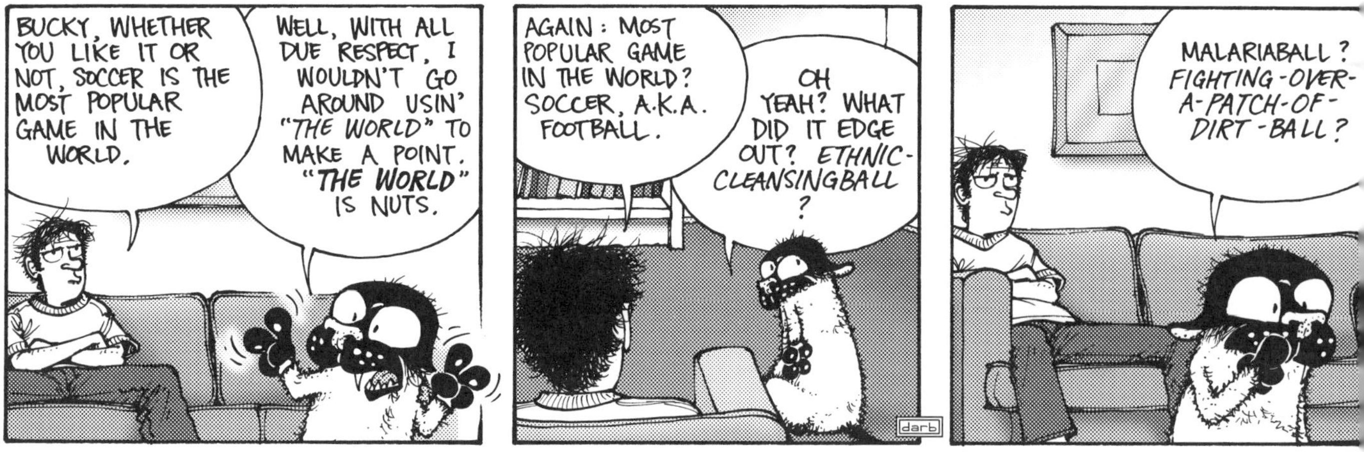
BUCKY, WHETHER YOU LIKE IT OR NOT, SOCCER IS THE MOST POPULAR GAME IN THE WORLD.
WELL, WITH ALL DUE RESPECT, I WOULDN'T GO AROUND USIN' "THE WORLD" TO MAKE A POINT. "THE WORLD" IS NUTS.
AGAIN: MOST POPULAR GAME IN THE WORLD? SOCCER, A.K.A. FOOTBALL.
OH YEAH? WHAT DID IT EDGE OUT? ETHNIC-CLEANSINGBALL ?
MALARIABALL? FIGHTING-OVER-A-PATCH-OF-DIRT-BALL?

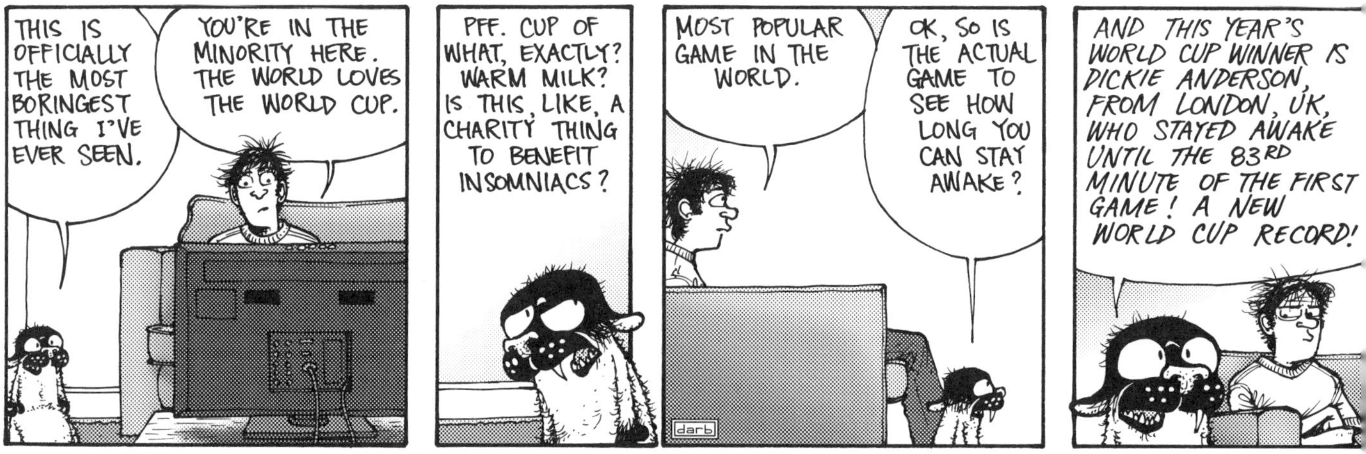
THIS IS OFFICIALLY THE MOST BORINGEST THING I'VE EVER SEEN.
YOU'RE IN THE MINORITY HERE. THE WORLD LOVES THE WORLD CUP.
PFF. CUP OF WHAT, EXACTLY? WARM MILK? IS THIS, LIKE, A CHARITY THING TO BENEFIT INSOMNIACS?
MOST POPULAR GAME IN THE WORLD.
OK, SO IS THE ACTUAL GAME TO SEE HOW LONG YOU CAN STAY AWAKE?
AND THIS YEAR'S WORLD CUP WINNER IS DICKIE ANDERSON, FROM LONDON, UK, WHO STAYED AWAKE UNTIL THE 83RD MINUTE OF THE FIRST GAME! A NEW WORLD CUP RECORD!

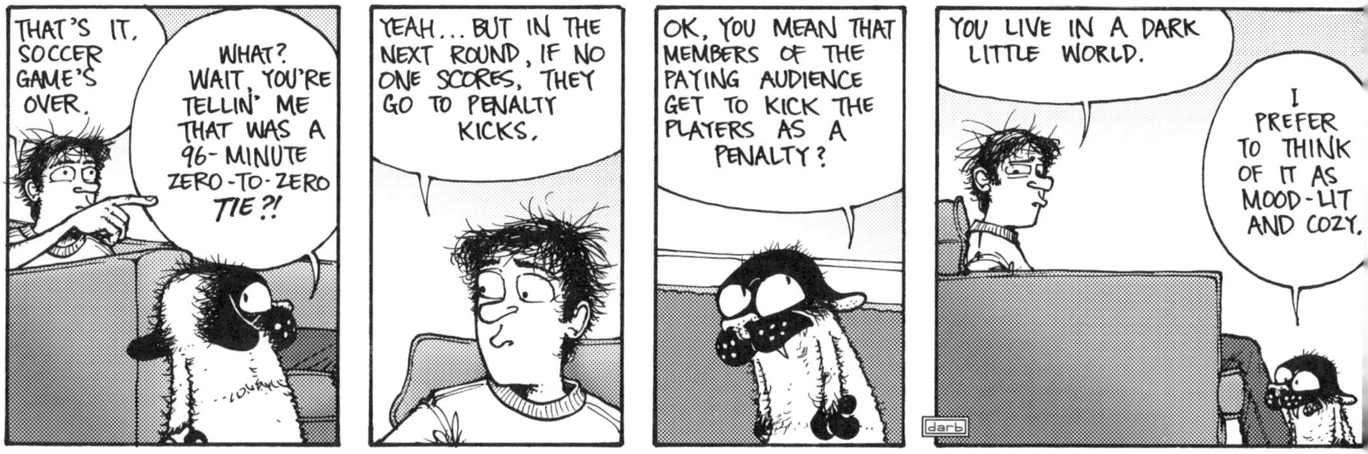
THAT'S IT. SOCCER GAME'S OVER.
WHAT? WAIT, YOU'RE TELLIN' ME THAT WAS A 96-MINUTE ZERO-TO-ZERO TIE?!
YEAH... BUT IN THE NEXT ROUND, IF NO ONE SCORES, THEY GO TO PENALTY KICKS.
OK, YOU MEAN THAT MEMBERS OF THE PAYING AUDIENCE GET TO KICK THE PLAYERS AS A PENALTY?
YOU LIVE IN A DARK LITTLE WORLD.
I PREFER TO THINK OF IT AS MOOD-LIT AND COZY.

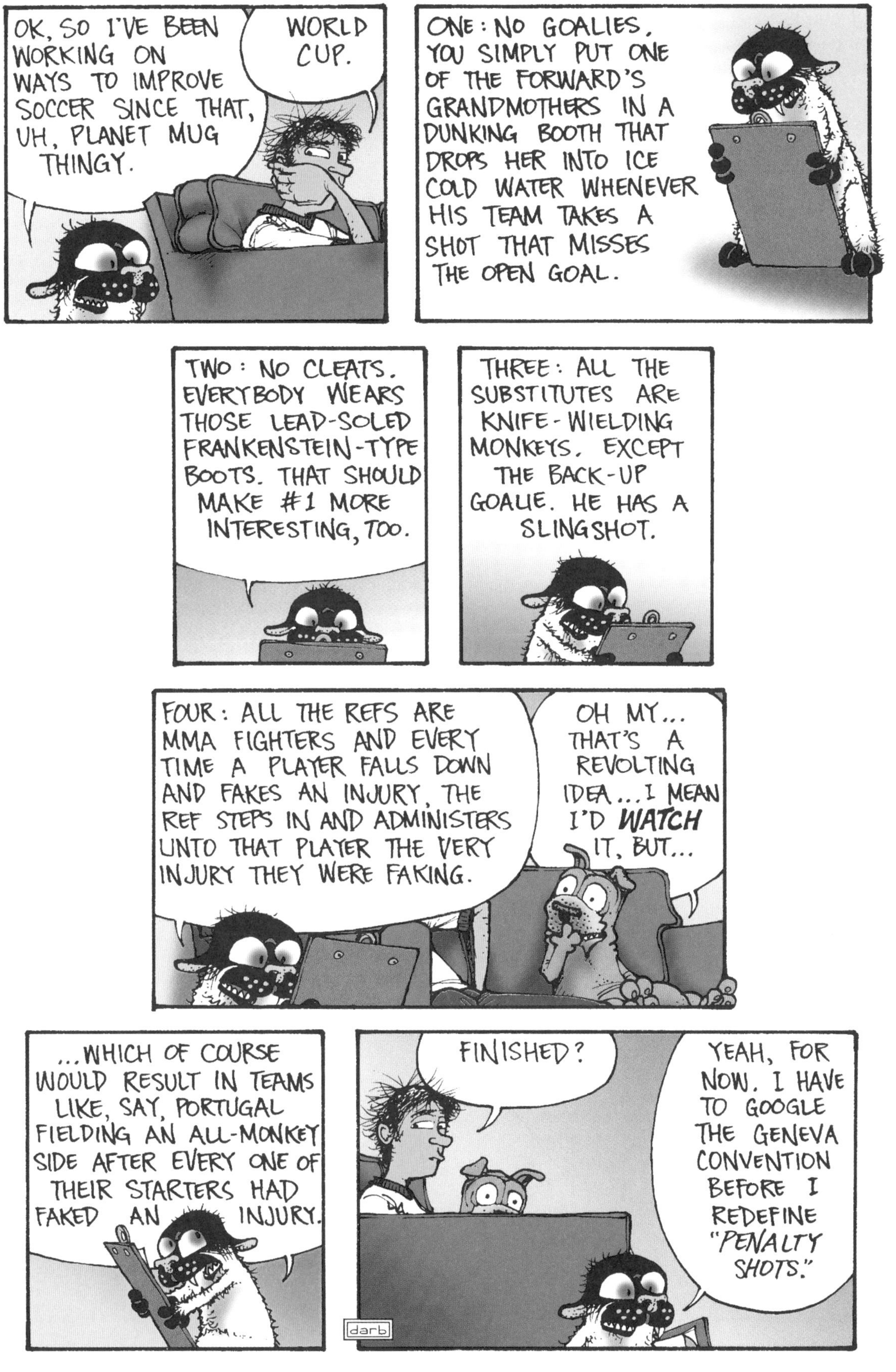
OK, SO I'VE BEEN WORKING ON WAYS TO IMPROVE SOCCER SINCE THAT, UH, PLANET MUG THINGY.
WORLD CUP.
ONE: NO GOALIES. YOU SIMPLY PUT ONE OF THE FORWARD'S GRANDMOTHERS IN A DUNKING BOOTH THAT DROPS HER INTO ICE COLD WATER WHENEVER HIS TEAM TAKES A SHOT THAT MISSES THE OPEN GOAL.
TWO: NO CLEATS. EVERYBODY WEARS THOSE LEAD-SOLED FRANKENSTEIN-TYPE BOOTS. THAT SHOULD MAKE #1 MORE INTERESTING, TOO.
THREE: ALL THE SUBSTITUTES ARE KNIFE-WIELDING MONKEYS. EXCEPT THE BACK-UP GOALIE. HE HAS A SLINGSHOT.
FOUR: ALL THE REFS ARE MMA FIGHTERS AND EVERY TIME A PLAYER FALLS DOWN AND FAKES AN INJURY, THE REF STEPS IN AND ADMINISTERS UNTO THAT PLAYER THE VERY INJURY THEY WERE FAKING.
OH MY... THAT'S A REVOLTING IDEA... I MEAN I'D WATCH IT, BUT...
...WHICH OF COURSE WOULD RESULT IN TEAMS LIKE, SAY, PORTUGAL FIELDING AN ALL-MONKEY SIDE AFTER EVERY ONE OF THEIR STARTERS HAD FAKED AN INJURY.
darb
FINISHED?
YEAH, FOR NOW. I HAVE TO GOOGLE THE GENEVA CONVENTION BEFORE I REDEFINE "PENALTY SHOTS."

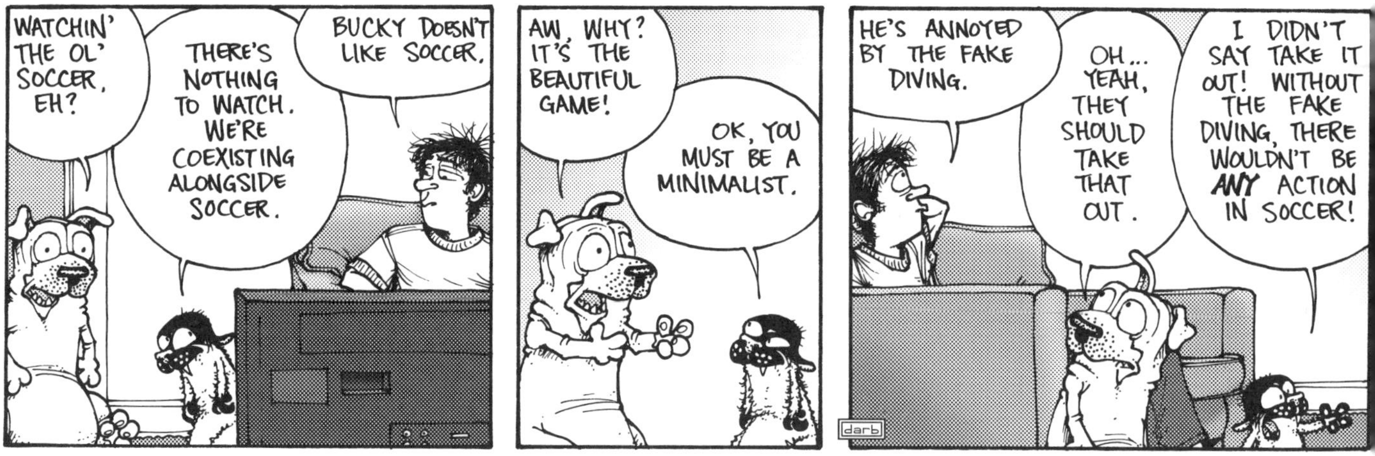
WATCHIN' THE OL' SOCCER, EH?
THERE'S NOTHING TO WATCH. WE'RE COEXISTING ALONGSIDE SOCCER.
BUCKY DOESN'T LIKE SOCCER.
AW, WHY? IT'S THE BEAUTIFUL GAME!
OK, YOU MUST BE A MINIMALIST.
HE'S ANNOYED BY THE FAKE DIVING.
OH... YEAH, THEY SHOULD TAKE THAT OUT.
I DIDN'T SAY TAKE IT OUT! WITHOUT THE FAKE DIVING, THERE WOULDN'T BE ANY ACTION IN SOCCER!
darb

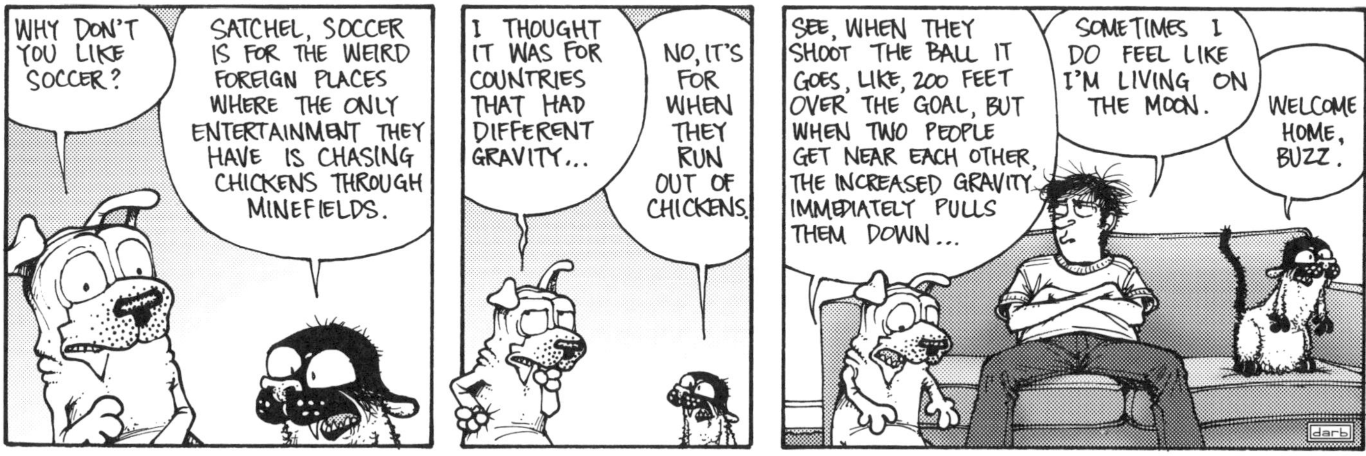
WHY DON'T YOU LIKE SOCCER?
SATCHEL, SOCCER IS FOR THE WEIRD FOREIGN PLACES WHERE THE ONLY ENTERTAINMENT THEY HAVE IS CHASING CHICKENS THROUGH MINEFIELDS.
I THOUGHT IT WAS FOR COUNTRIES THAT HAD DIFFERENT GRAVITY...
NO, IT'S FOR WHEN THEY RUN OUT OF CHICKENS.
SEE, WHEN THEY SHOOT THE BALL IT GOES, LIKE, 200 FEET OVER THE GOAL, BUT WHEN TWO PEOPLE GET NEAR EACH OTHER, THE INCREASED GRAVITY IMMEDIATELY PULLS THEM DOWN...
SOMETIMES I DO FEEL LIKE I'M LIVING ON THE MOON.
WELCOME HOME, BUZZ.
darb

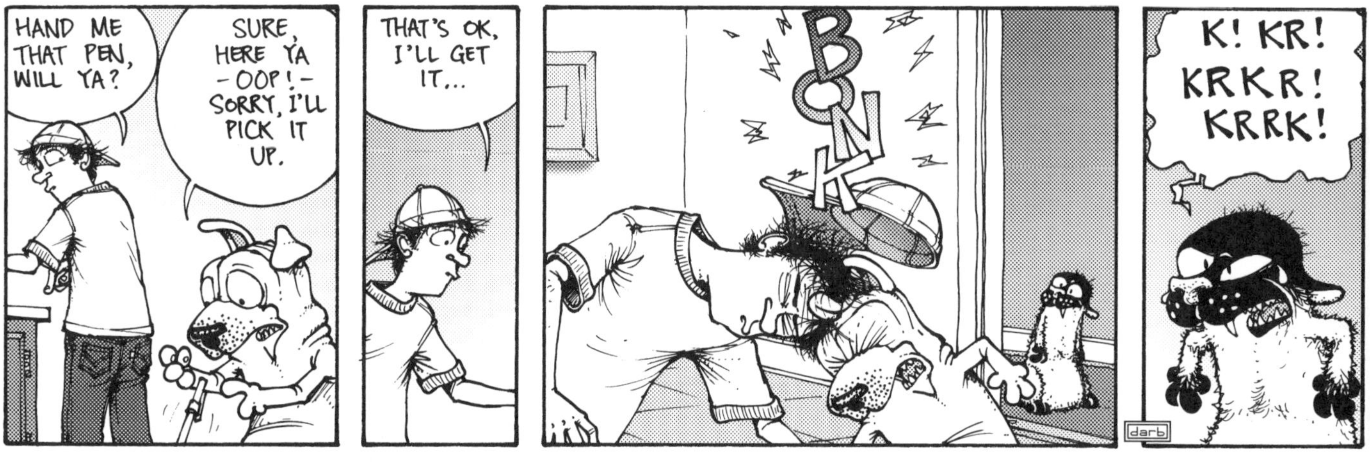
HAND ME THAT PEN, WILL YA?
SURE, HERE YA -OOP!- SORRY, I'LL PICK IT UP.
THAT'S OK, I'LL GET IT...
BONK
K! KR! KRKR! KRRK!
darb

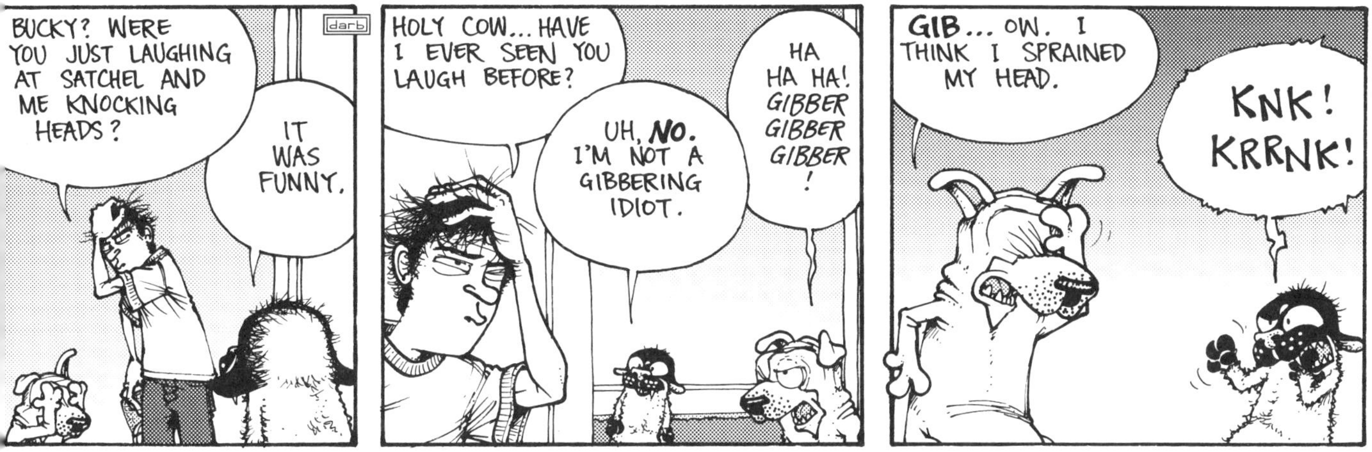
BUCKY? WERE YOU JUST LAUGHING AT SATCHEL AND ME KNOCKING HEADS?
IT WAS FUNNY.
darb
HOLY COW... HAVE I EVER SEEN YOU LAUGH BEFORE?
UH, NO. I'M NOT A GIBBERING IDIOT.
HA HA HA! GIBBER GIBBER GIBBER!
GIB... OW. I THINK I SPRAINED MY HEAD.
KNK! KRRNK!

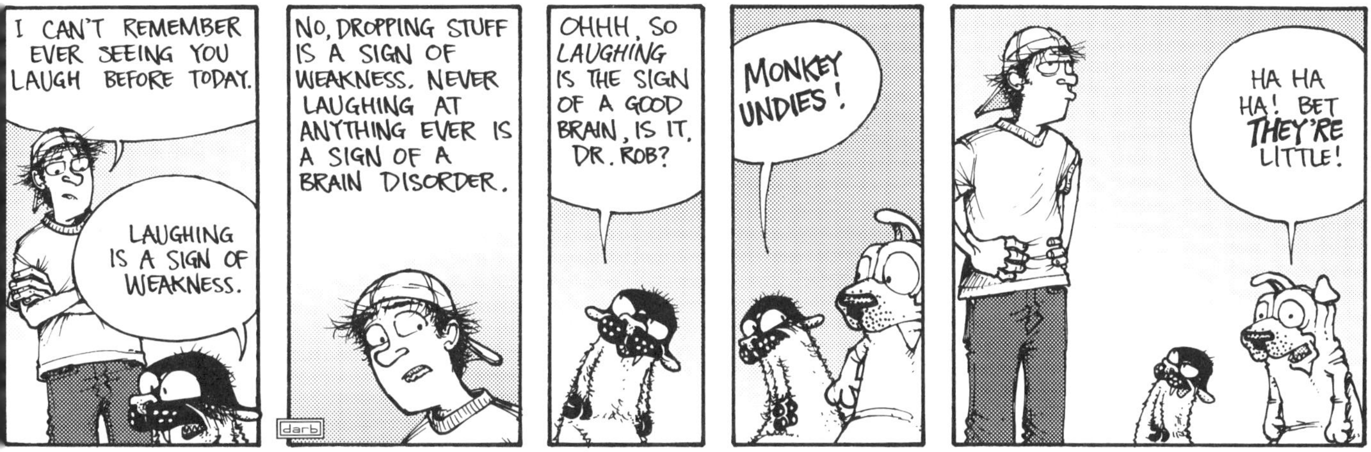
I CAN'T REMEMBER EVER SEEING YOU LAUGH BEFORE TODAY.
LAUGHING IS A SIGN OF WEAKNESS.
NO, DROPPING STUFF IS A SIGN OF WEAKNESS. NEVER LAUGHING AT ANYTHING EVER IS A SIGN OF A BRAIN DISORDER.
darb
OHHH, SO LAUGHING IS THE SIGN OF A GOOD BRAIN, IS IT, DR. ROB?
MONKEY UNDIES!
HA HA HA! BET THEY'RE LITTLE!

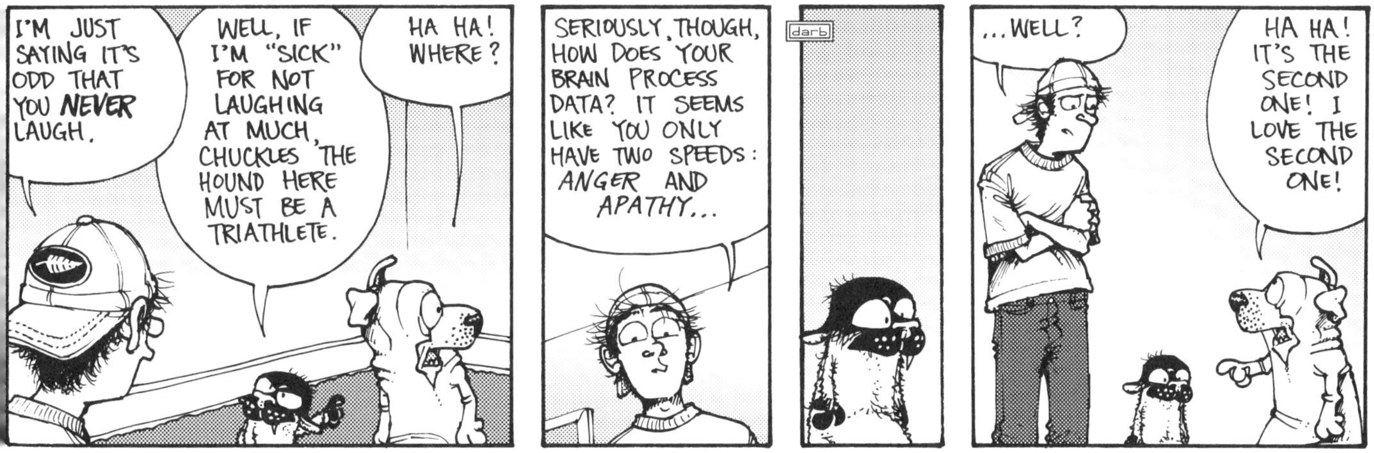
I'M JUST SAYING IT'S ODD THAT YOU NEVER LAUGH.
WELL, IF I'M "SICK" FOR NOT LAUGHING AT MUCH, CHUCKLES THE HOUND HERE MUST BE A TRIATHLETE.
HA HA! WHERE?
SERIOUSLY, THOUGH, HOW DOES YOUR BRAIN PROCESS DATA? IT SEEMS LIKE YOU ONLY HAVE TWO SPEEDS: ANGER AND APATHY...
darb
...WELL?
HA HA! IT'S THE SECOND ONE! I LOVE THE SECOND ONE!

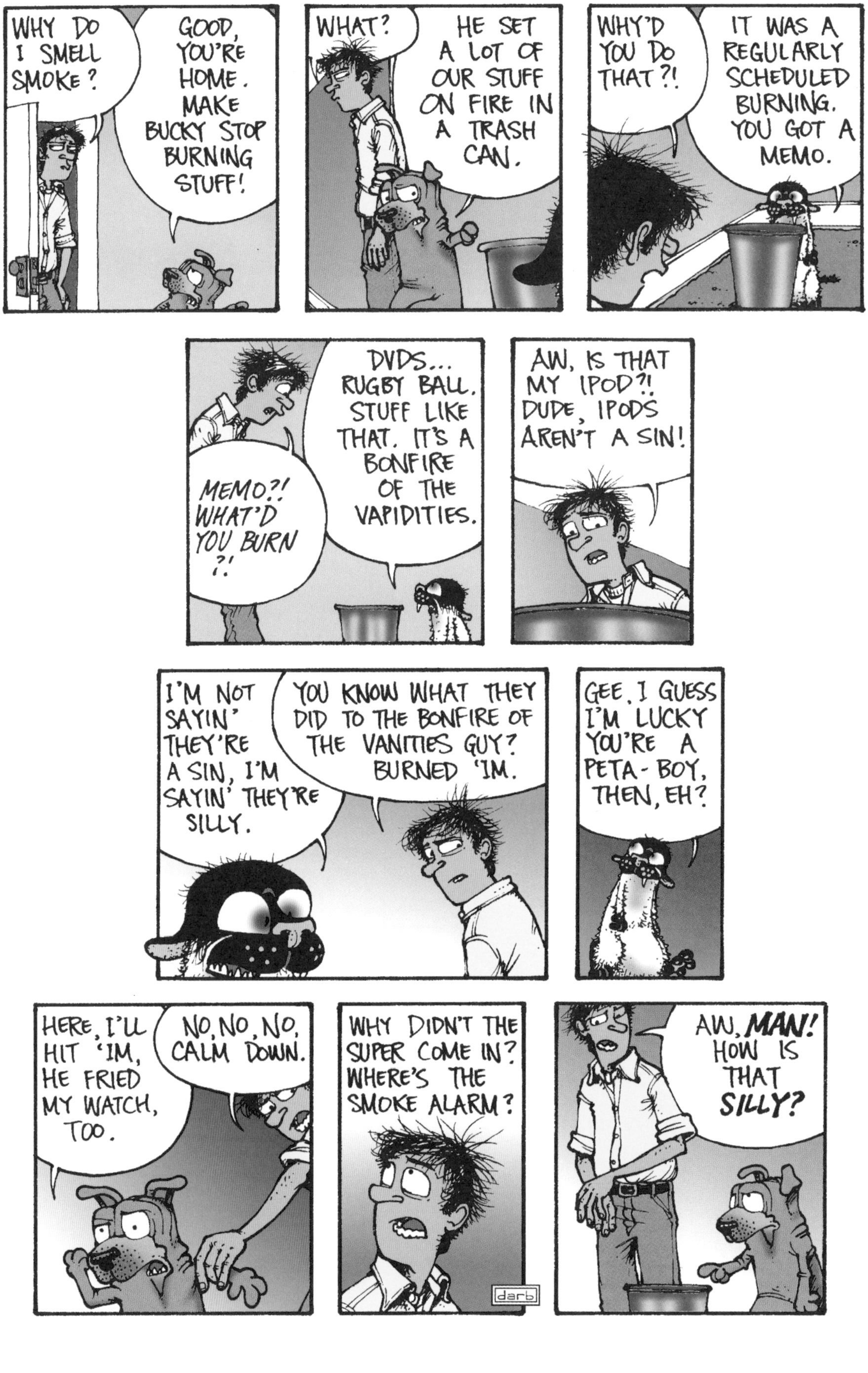

WHY DO I SMELL SMOKE?
GOOD, YOU'RE HOME. MAKE BUCKY STOP BURNING STUFF!
WHAT?
HE SET A LOT OF OUR STUFF ON FIRE IN A TRASH CAN.
WHY'D YOU DO THAT?!
IT WAS A REGULARLY SCHEDULED BURNING. YOU GOT A MEMO.
MEMO?! WHAT'D YOU BURN?!
DVDS... RUGBY BALL. STUFF LIKE THAT. IT'S A BONFIRE OF THE VAPIDITIES.
AW, IS THAT MY IPOD?! DUDE, IPODS AREN'T A SIN!
I'M NOT SAYIN' THEY'RE A SIN, I'M SAYIN' THEY'RE SILLY.
YOU KNOW WHAT THEY DID TO THE BONFIRE OF THE VANITIES GUY? BURNED 'IM.
GEE, I GUESS I'M LUCKY YOU'RE A PETA-BOY, THEN, EH?
HERE, I'LL HIT 'IM, HE FRIED MY WATCH, TOO.
NO, NO, NO, CALM DOWN.
WHY DIDN'T THE SUPER COME IN? WHERE'S THE SMOKE ALARM?
darb
AW, **MAN!** HOW IS THAT **SILLY?**

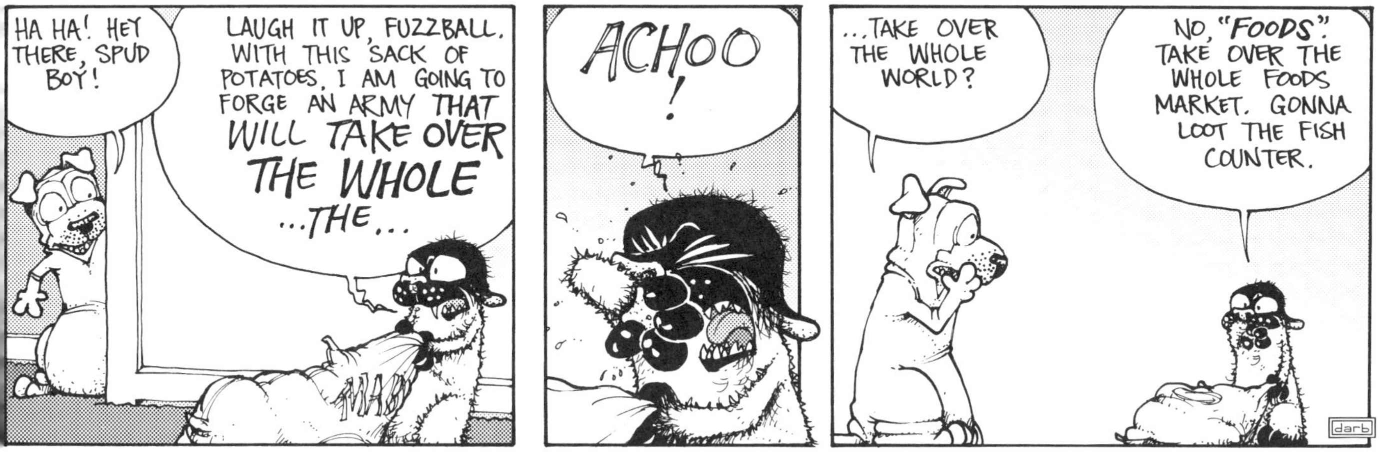
HA HA! HEY THERE, SPUD BOY!
LAUGH IT UP, FUZZBALL. WITH THIS SACK OF POTATOES, I AM GOING TO FORGE AN ARMY THAT WILL TAKE OVER THE WHOLE ...THE...
ACHOO!
...TAKE OVER THE WHOLE WORLD?
NO, "FOODS". TAKE OVER THE WHOLE FOODS MARKET. GONNA LOOT THE FISH COUNTER.
darb

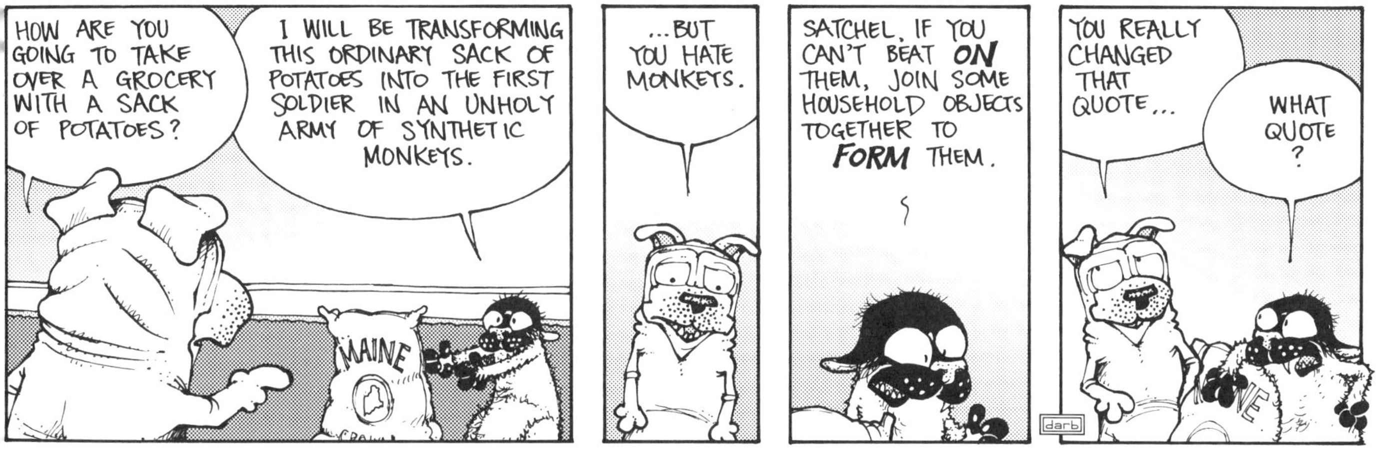
HOW ARE YOU GOING TO TAKE OVER A GROCERY WITH A SACK OF POTATOES?
I WILL BE TRANSFORMING THIS ORDINARY SACK OF POTATOES INTO THE FIRST SOLDIER IN AN UNHOLY ARMY OF SYNTHETIC MONKEYS.
MAINE
...BUT YOU HATE MONKEYS.
SATCHEL, IF YOU CAN'T BEAT ON THEM, JOIN SOME HOUSEHOLD OBJECTS TOGETHER TO FORM THEM.
darb
YOU REALLY CHANGED THAT QUOTE...
WHAT QUOTE?

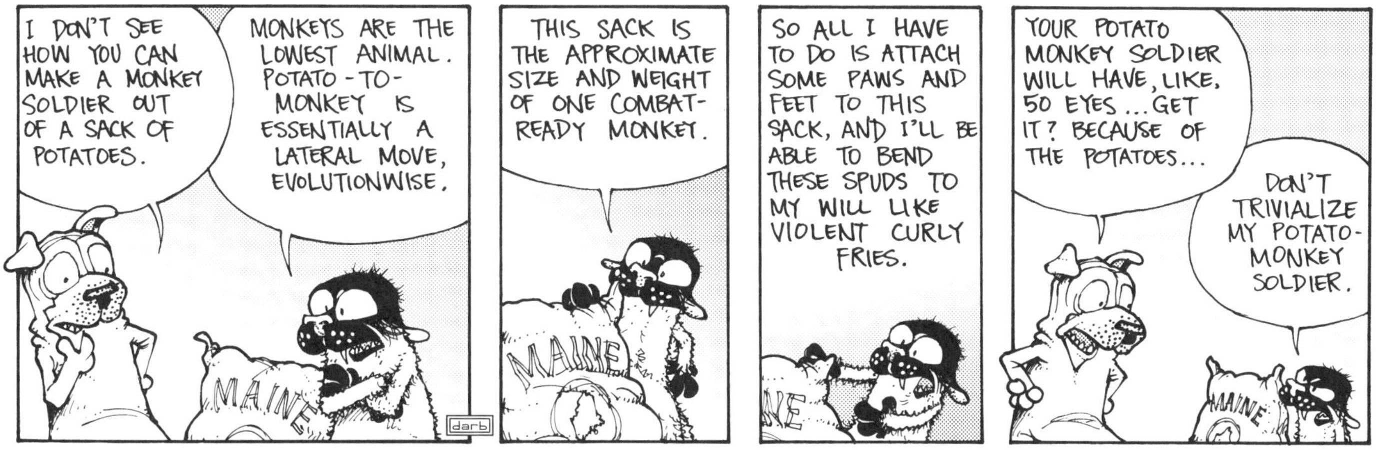
I DON'T SEE HOW YOU CAN MAKE A MONKEY SOLDIER OUT OF A SACK OF POTATOES.
MONKEYS ARE THE LOWEST ANIMAL. POTATO-TO-MONKEY IS ESSENTIALLY A LATERAL MOVE, EVOLUTIONWISE.
MAINE
darb
THIS SACK IS THE APPROXIMATE SIZE AND WEIGHT OF ONE COMBAT-READY MONKEY.
MAINE
SO ALL I HAVE TO DO IS ATTACH SOME PAWS AND FEET TO THIS SACK, AND I'LL BE ABLE TO BEND THESE SPUDS TO MY WILL LIKE VIOLENT CURLY FRIES.
YOUR POTATO MONKEY SOLDIER WILL HAVE, LIKE, 50 EYES ... GET IT? BECAUSE OF THE POTATOES...
DON'T TRIVIALIZE MY POTATO-MONKEY SOLDIER.
MAINE

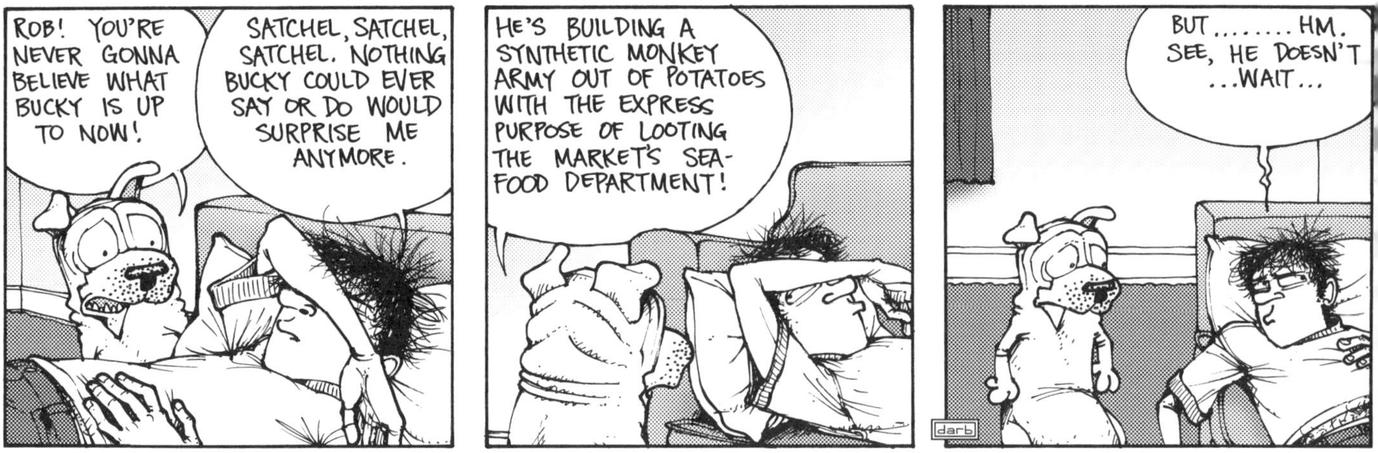
ROB! YOU'RE NEVER GONNA BELIEVE WHAT BUCKY IS UP TO NOW!
SATCHEL, SATCHEL, SATCHEL. NOTHING BUCKY COULD EVER SAY OR DO WOULD SURPRISE ME ANYMORE.
HE'S BUILDING A SYNTHETIC MONKEY ARMY OUT OF POTATOES WITH THE EXPRESS PURPOSE OF LOOTING THE MARKET'S SEA-FOOD DEPARTMENT!
BUT........HM. SEE, HE DOESN'T ...WAIT...
darb

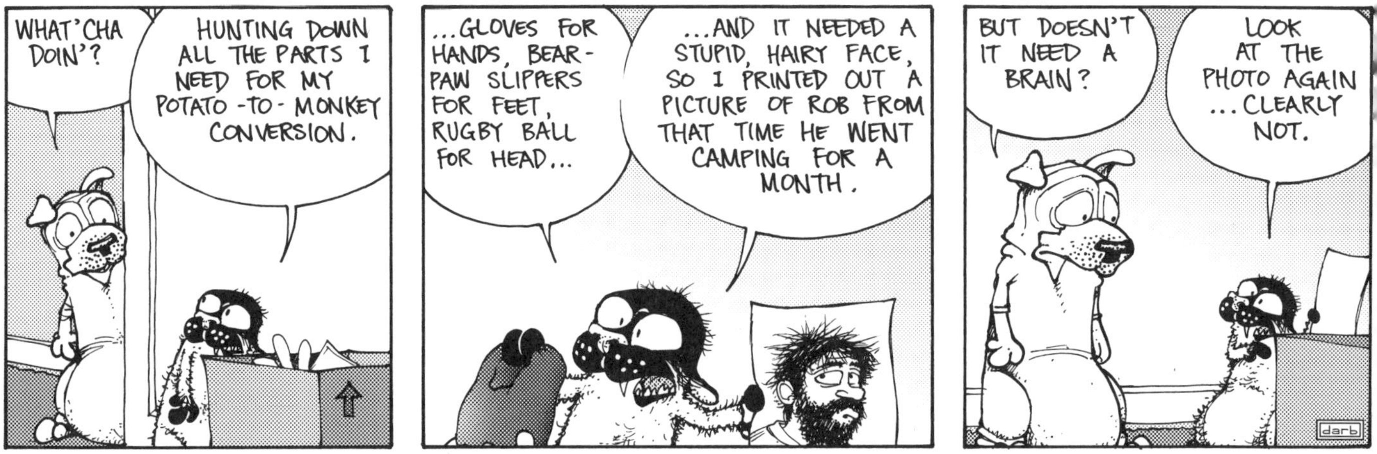
WHAT'CHA DOIN'?
HUNTING DOWN ALL THE PARTS I NEED FOR MY POTATO-TO-MONKEY CONVERSION.
...GLOVES FOR HANDS, BEAR-PAW SLIPPERS FOR FEET, RUGBY BALL FOR HEAD...
...AND IT NEEDED A STUPID, HAIRY FACE, SO I PRINTED OUT A PICTURE OF ROB FROM THAT TIME HE WENT CAMPING FOR A MONTH.
BUT DOESN'T IT NEED A BRAIN?
LOOK AT THE PHOTO AGAIN ...CLEARLY NOT.
darb

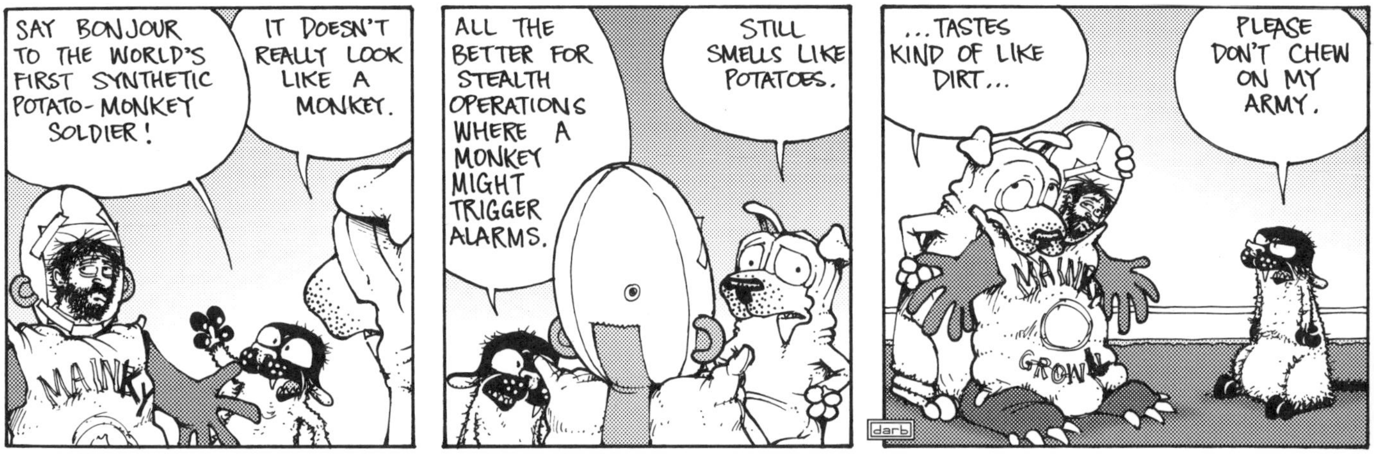
SAY BONJOUR TO THE WORLD'S FIRST SYNTHETIC POTATO-MONKEY SOLDIER!
IT DOESN'T REALLY LOOK LIKE A MONKEY.
MAINKY
ALL THE BETTER FOR STEALTH OPERATIONS WHERE A MONKEY MIGHT TRIGGER ALARMS.
STILL SMELLS LIKE POTATOES.
...TASTES KIND OF LIKE DIRT...
PLEASE DON'T CHEW ON MY ARMY.
GROWL
darb

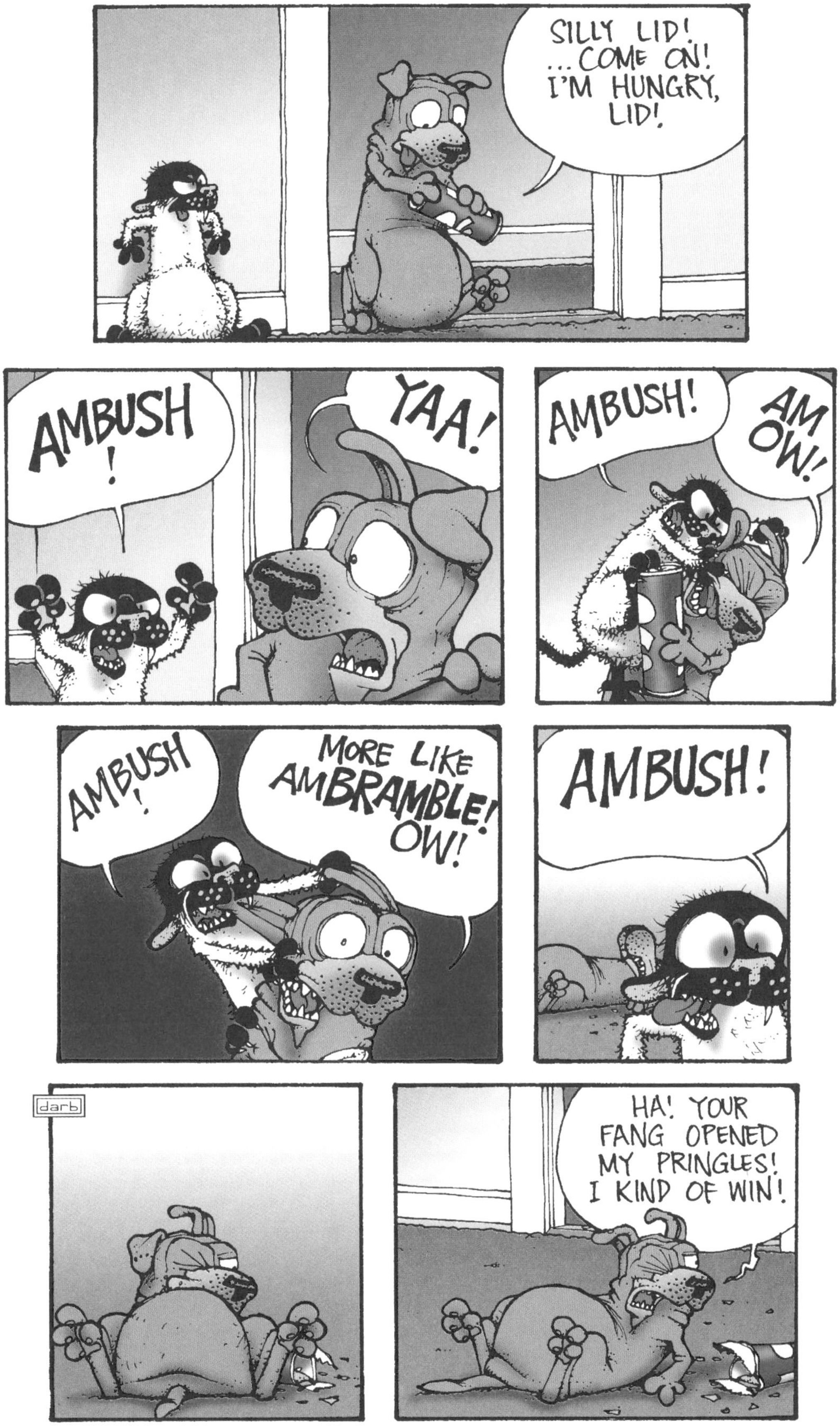
SILLY LID! ...COME ON! I'M HUNGRY, LID!
AMBUSH!
YAA!
AMBUSH!
AM OW!
AMBUSH!
MORE LIKE AMBRAMBLE! OW!
AMBUSH!
darb
HA! YOUR FANG OPENED MY PRINGLES! I KIND OF WIN!

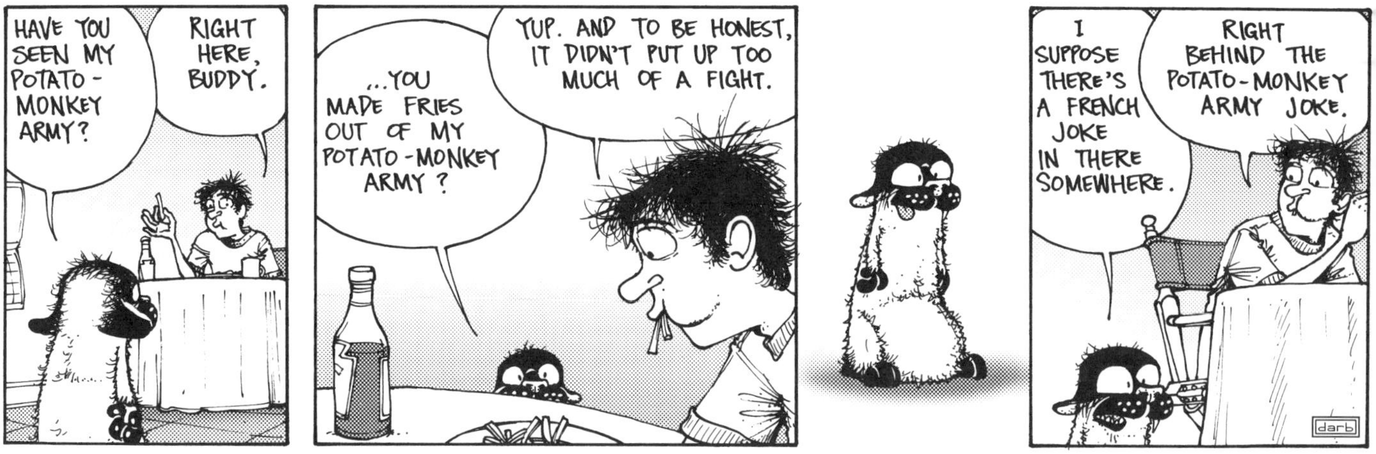
HAVE YOU SEEN MY POTATO-MONKEY ARMY?
RIGHT HERE, BUDDY.
...YOU MADE FRIES OUT OF MY POTATO-MONKEY ARMY?
YUP. AND TO BE HONEST, IT DIDN'T PUT UP TOO MUCH OF A FIGHT.
I SUPPOSE THERE'S A FRENCH JOKE IN THERE SOMEWHERE.
RIGHT BEHIND THE POTATO-MONKEY ARMY JOKE.
darb

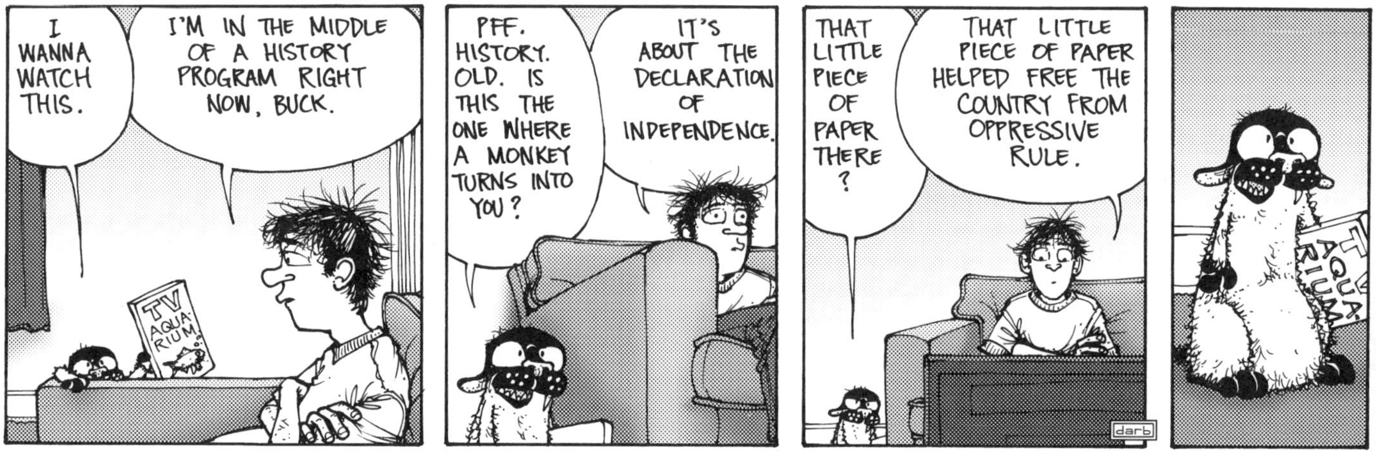
I WANNA WATCH THIS.
I'M IN THE MIDDLE OF A HISTORY PROGRAM RIGHT NOW, BUCK.
TV AQUARIUM
PFF. HISTORY. OLD. IS THIS THE ONE WHERE A MONKEY TURNS INTO YOU?
IT'S ABOUT THE DECLARATION OF INDEPENDENCE.
THAT LITTLE PIECE OF PAPER THERE?
THAT LITTLE PIECE OF PAPER HELPED FREE THE COUNTRY FROM OPPRESSIVE RULE.
darb
TV AQUARIUM

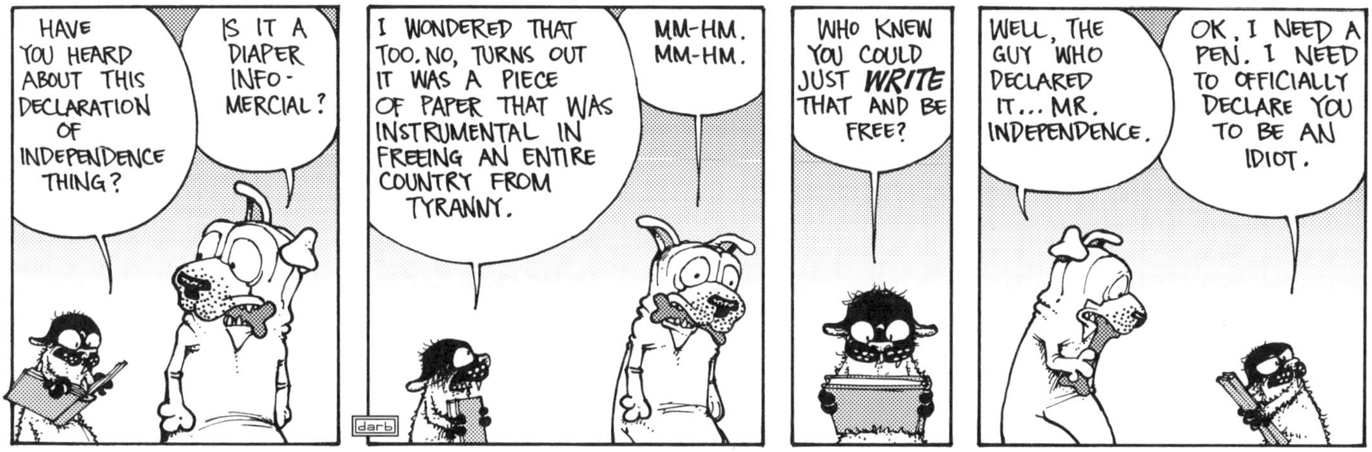
HAVE YOU HEARD ABOUT THIS DECLARATION OF INDEPENDENCE THING?
IS IT A DIAPER INFO-MERCIAL?
I WONDERED THAT TOO. NO, TURNS OUT IT WAS A PIECE OF PAPER THAT WAS INSTRUMENTAL IN FREEING AN ENTIRE COUNTRY FROM TYRANNY.
MM-HM. MM-HM.
darb
WHO KNEW YOU COULD JUST WRITE THAT AND BE FREE?
WELL, THE GUY WHO DECLARED IT... MR. INDEPENDENCE.
OK, I NEED A PEN. I NEED TO OFFICIALLY DECLARE YOU TO BE AN IDIOT.

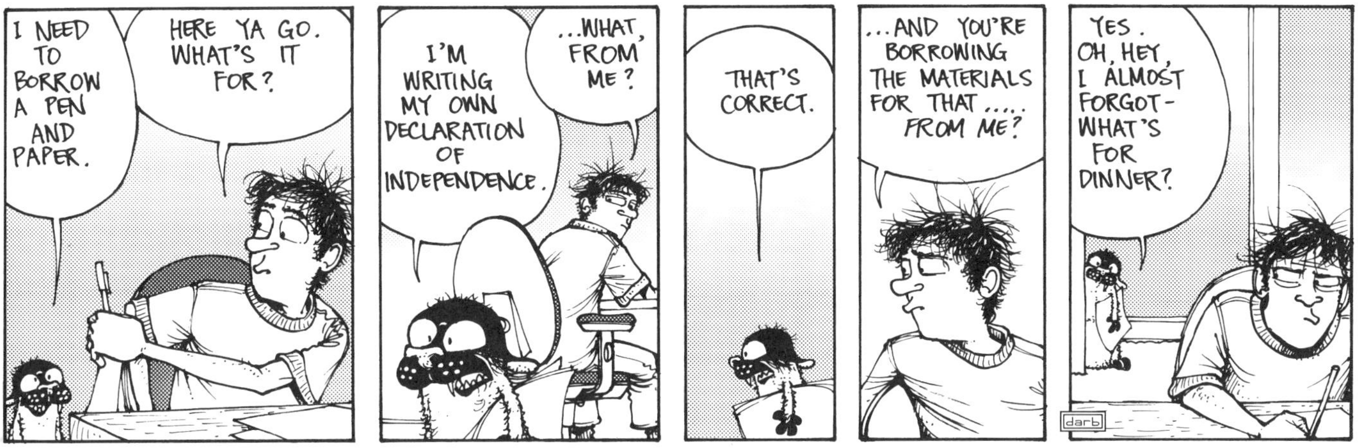
I NEED TO BORROW A PEN AND PAPER.
HERE YA GO. WHAT'S IT FOR?
I'M WRITING MY OWN DECLARATION OF INDEPENDENCE.
...WHAT, FROM ME?
THAT'S CORRECT.
...AND YOU'RE BORROWING THE MATERIALS FOR THAT..... *FROM ME?*
YES. OH, HEY, I ALMOST FORGOT- WHAT'S FOR DINNER?

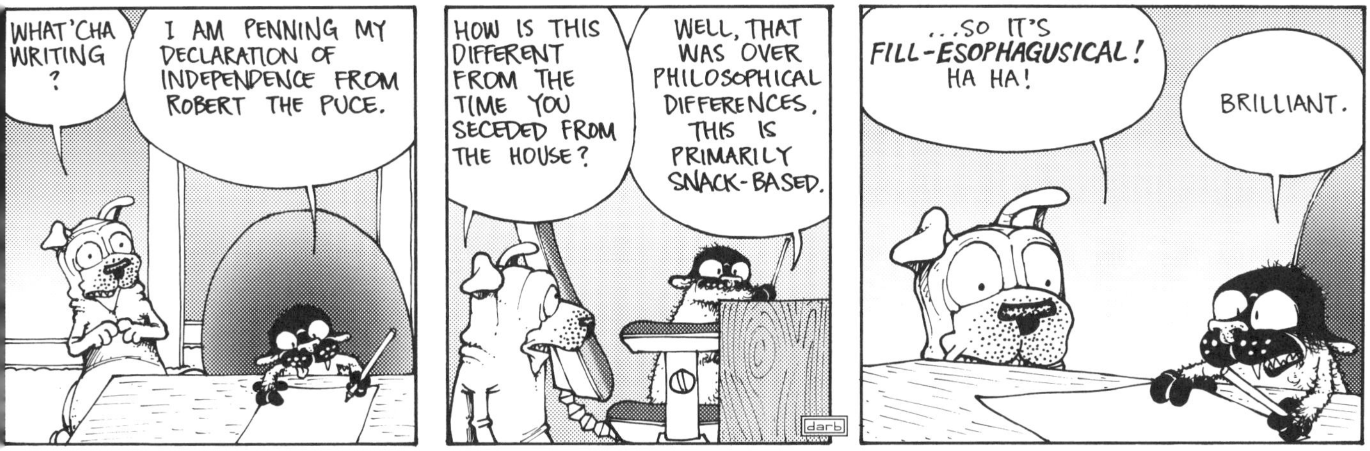
WHAT'CHA WRITING?
I AM PENNING MY DECLARATION OF INDEPENDENCE FROM ROBERT THE PUCE.
HOW IS THIS DIFFERENT FROM THE TIME YOU SECEDED FROM THE HOUSE?
WELL, THAT WAS OVER PHILOSOPHICAL DIFFERENCES. THIS IS PRIMARILY SNACK-BASED.
...SO IT'S ***FILL-ESOPHAGUSICAL!*** HA HA!
BRILLIANT.

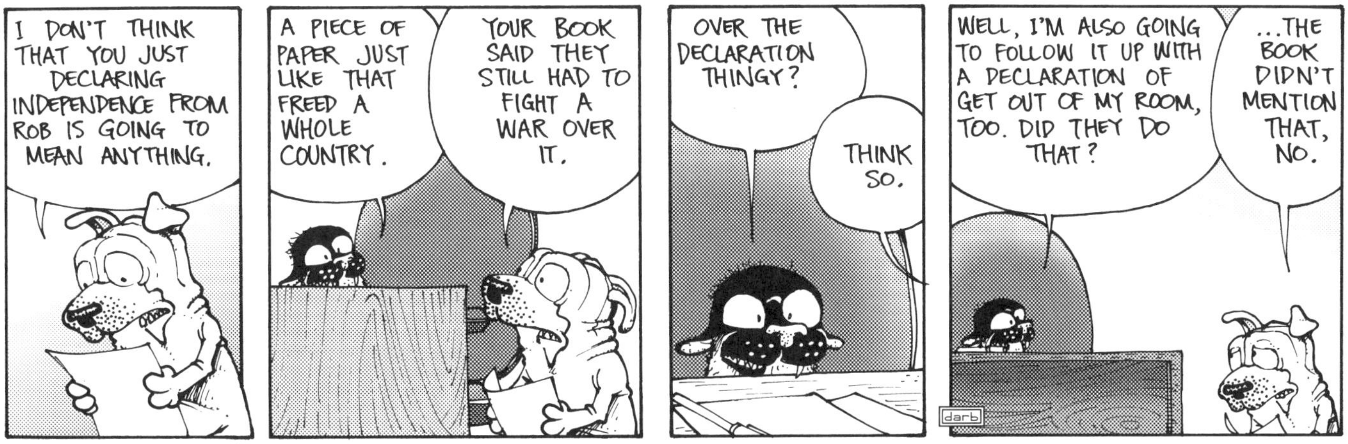
I DON'T THINK THAT YOU JUST DECLARING INDEPENDENCE FROM ROB IS GOING TO MEAN ANYTHING.
A PIECE OF PAPER JUST LIKE THAT FREED A WHOLE COUNTRY.
YOUR BOOK SAID THEY STILL HAD TO FIGHT A WAR OVER IT.
OVER THE DECLARATION THINGY?
THINK SO.
WELL, I'M ALSO GOING TO FOLLOW IT UP WITH A DECLARATION OF GET OUT OF MY ROOM, TOO. DID THEY DO THAT?
...THE BOOK DIDN'T MENTION THAT, NO.

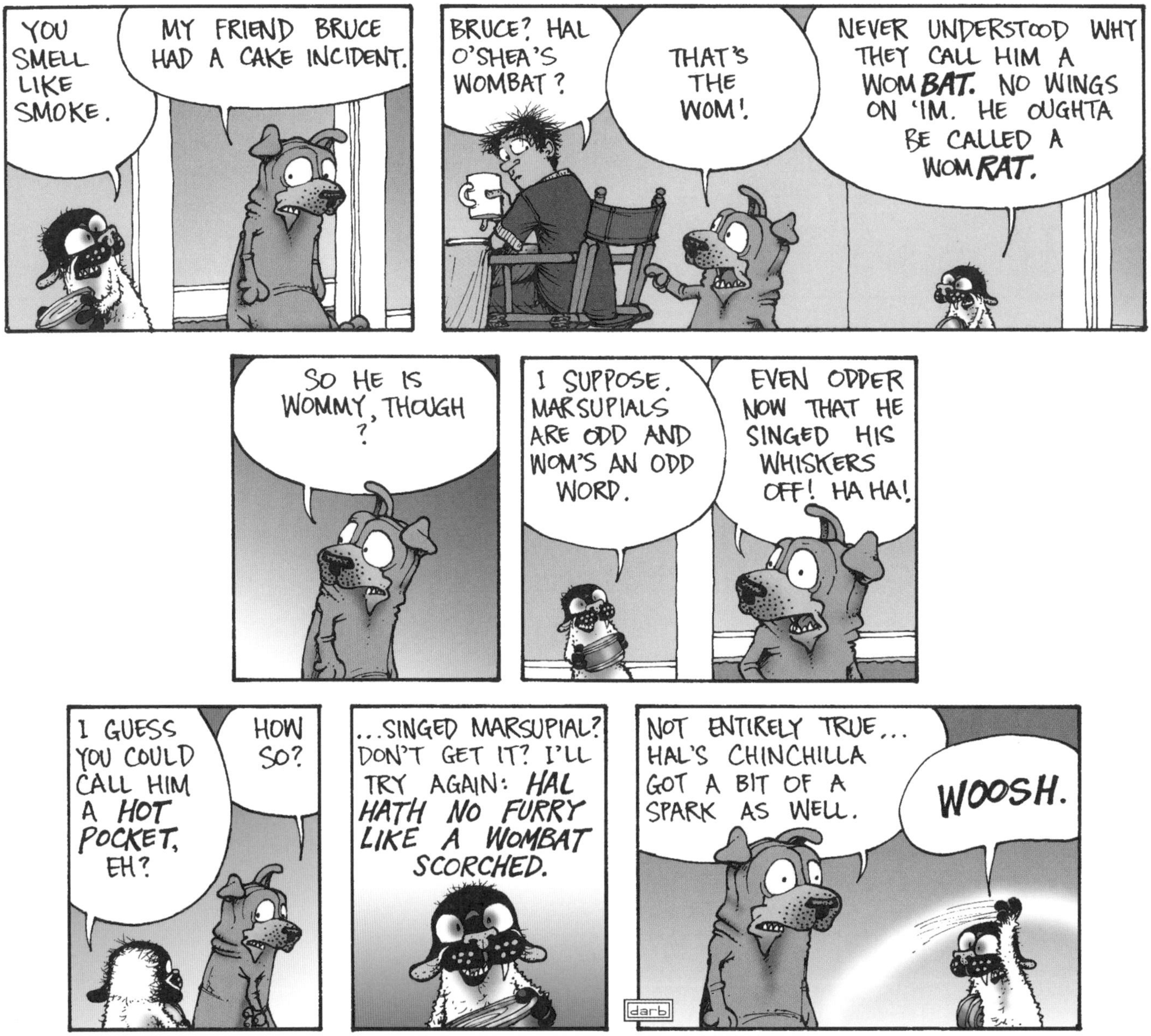
YOU SMELL LIKE SMOKE.
MY FRIEND BRUCE HAD A CAKE INCIDENT.
BRUCE? HAL O'SHEA'S WOMBAT?
THAT'S THE WOM!
NEVER UNDERSTOOD WHY THEY CALL HIM A WOM**BAT.** NO WINGS ON 'IM. HE OUGHTA BE CALLED A WOM**RAT.**
SO HE IS WOMMY, THOUGH?
I SUPPOSE. MARSUPIALS ARE ODD AND WOM'S AN ODD WORD.
EVEN ODDER NOW THAT HE SINGED HIS WHISKERS OFF! HA HA!
I GUESS YOU COULD CALL HIM A ***HOT POCKET***, EH?
HOW SO?
...SINGED MARSUPIAL? DON'T GET IT? I'LL TRY AGAIN: ***HAL HATH NO FURRY LIKE A WOMBAT SCORCHED.***
NOT ENTIRELY TRUE... HAL'S CHINCHILLA GOT A BIT OF A SPARK AS WELL.
WOOSH.
darb

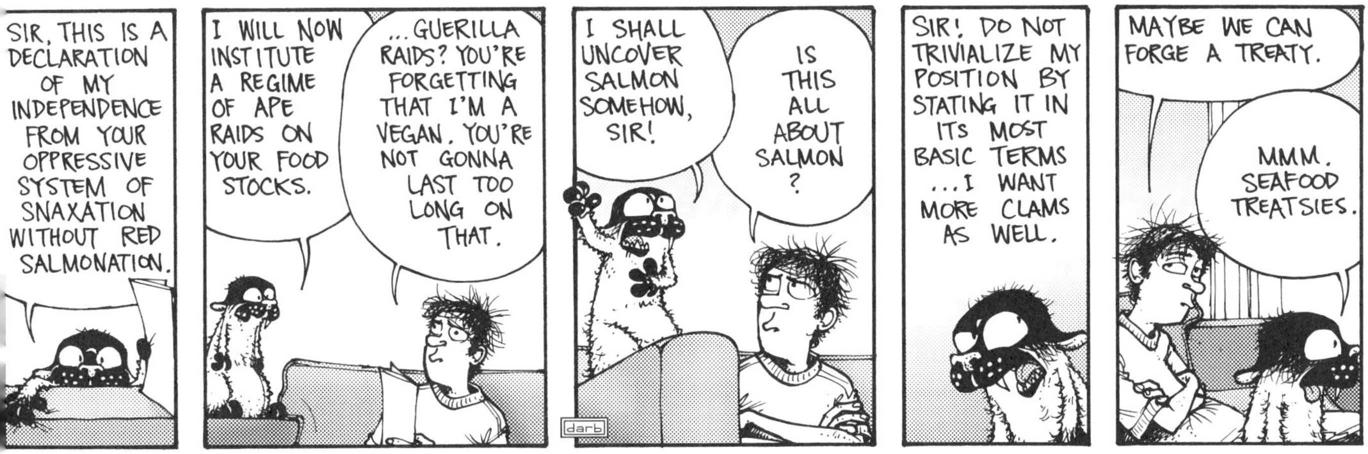
SIR, THIS IS A DECLARATION OF MY INDEPENDENCE FROM YOUR OPPRESSIVE SYSTEM OF SNAXATION WITHOUT RED SALMONATION.
I WILL NOW INSTITUTE A REGIME OF APE RAIDS ON YOUR FOOD STOCKS.
...GUERILLA RAIDS? YOU'RE FORGETTING THAT I'M A VEGAN. YOU'RE NOT GONNA LAST TOO LONG ON THAT.
I SHALL UNCOVER SALMON SOMEHOW, SIR!
IS THIS ALL ABOUT SALMON?
SIR! DO NOT TRIVIALIZE MY POSITION BY STATING IT IN ITS MOST BASIC TERMS ...I WANT MORE CLAMS AS WELL.
MAYBE WE CAN FORGE A TREATY.
MMM. SEAFOOD TREATSIES.

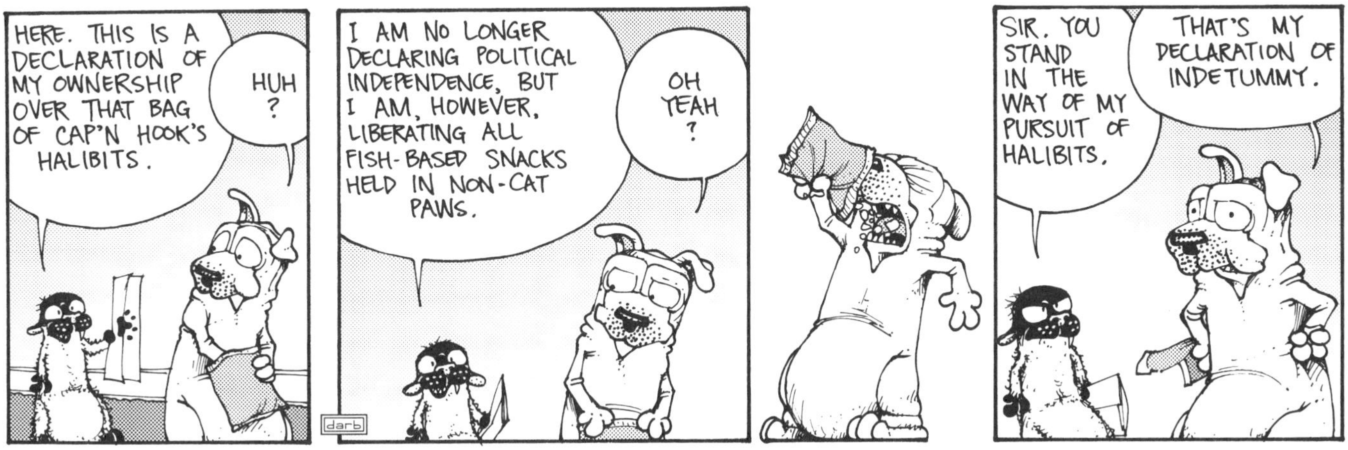
HERE. THIS IS A DECLARATION OF MY OWNERSHIP OVER THAT BAG OF CAP'N HOOK'S HALIBITS.
HUH?
I AM NO LONGER DECLARING POLITICAL INDEPENDENCE, BUT I AM, HOWEVER, LIBERATING ALL FISH-BASED SNACKS HELD IN NON-CAT PAWS.
OH YEAH?
SIR. YOU STAND IN THE WAY OF MY PURSUIT OF HALIBITS.
THAT'S MY DECLARATION OF INDETUMMY.

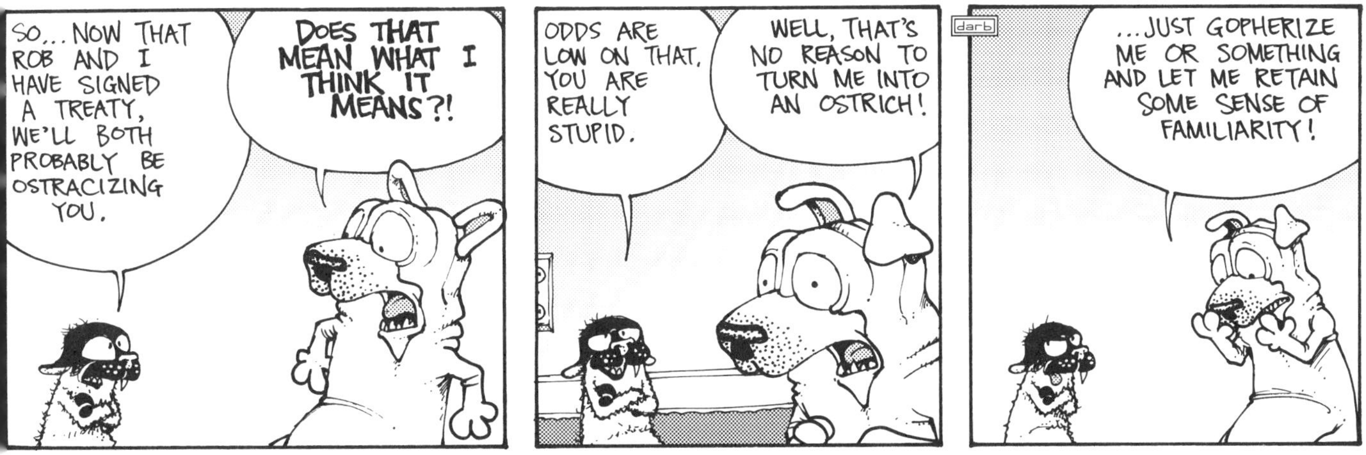
SO... NOW THAT ROB AND I HAVE SIGNED A TREATY, WE'LL BOTH PROBABLY BE OSTRACIZING YOU.
DOES THAT MEAN WHAT I THINK IT MEANS?!
ODDS ARE LOW ON THAT. YOU ARE REALLY STUPID.
WELL, THAT'S NO REASON TO TURN ME INTO AN OSTRICH!
...JUST GOPHERIZE ME OR SOMETHING AND LET ME RETAIN SOME SENSE OF FAMILIARITY!

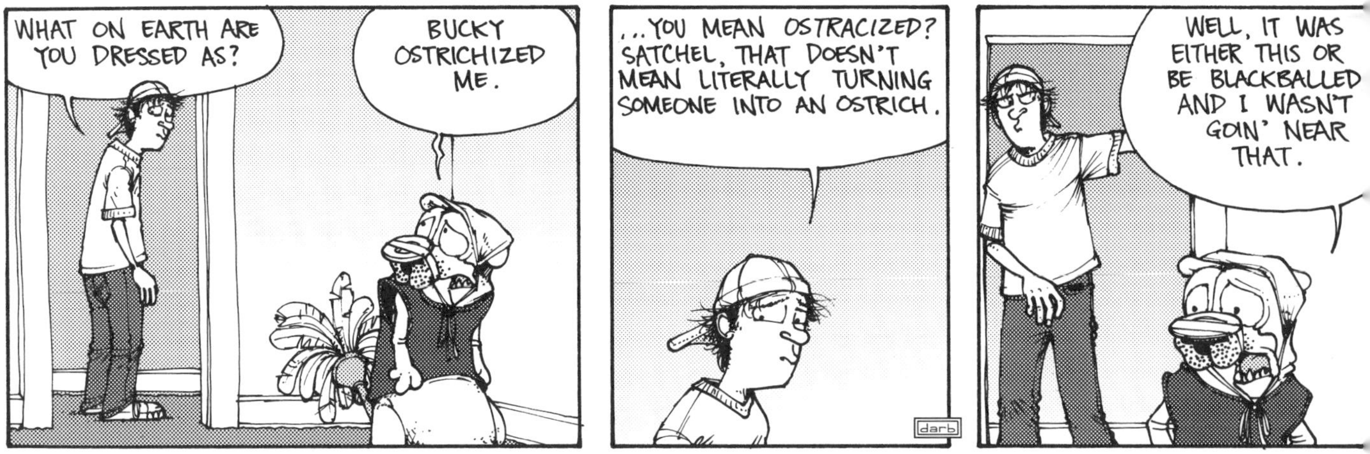
WHAT ON EARTH ARE YOU DRESSED AS?
BUCKY OSTRICHIZED ME.
...YOU MEAN OSTRACIZED? SATCHEL, THAT DOESN'T MEAN LITERALLY TURNING SOMEONE INTO AN OSTRICH.
WELL, IT WAS EITHER THIS OR BE BLACKBALLED AND I WASN'T GOIN' NEAR THAT.
darb

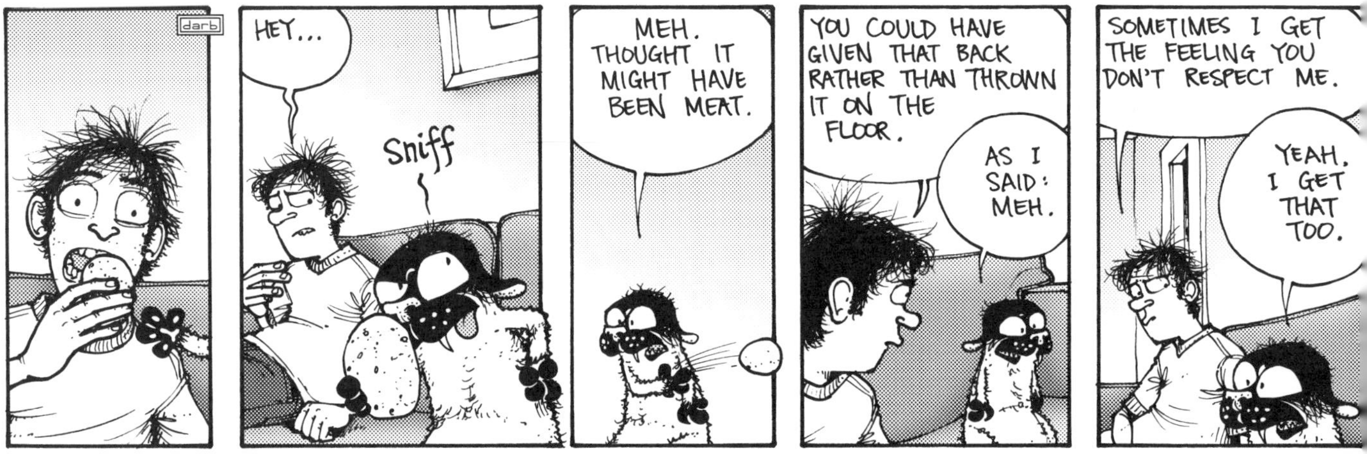
darb
HEY...
Sniff
MEH. THOUGHT IT MIGHT HAVE BEEN MEAT.
YOU COULD HAVE GIVEN THAT BACK RATHER THAN THROWN IT ON THE FLOOR.
AS I SAID: MEH.
SOMETIMES I GET THE FEELING YOU DON'T RESPECT ME.
YEAH. I GET THAT TOO.

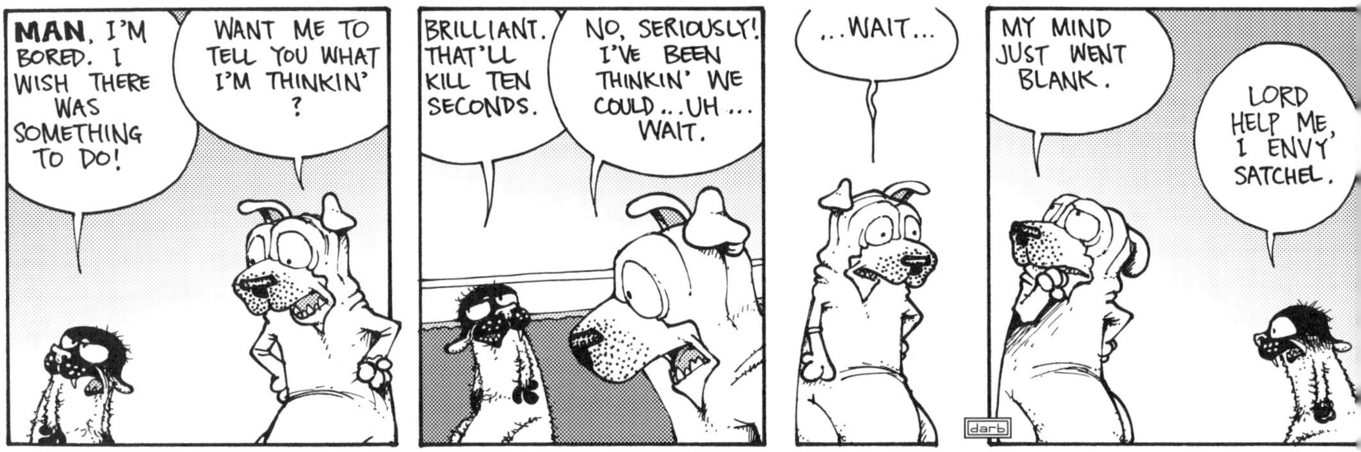
MAN, I'M BORED. I WISH THERE WAS SOMETHING TO DO!
WANT ME TO TELL YOU WHAT I'M THINKIN'?
BRILLIANT. THAT'LL KILL TEN SECONDS.
NO, SERIOUSLY! I'VE BEEN THINKIN' WE COULD...UH... WAIT.
...WAIT...
MY MIND JUST WENT BLANK.
LORD HELP ME, I ENVY SATCHEL.
darb

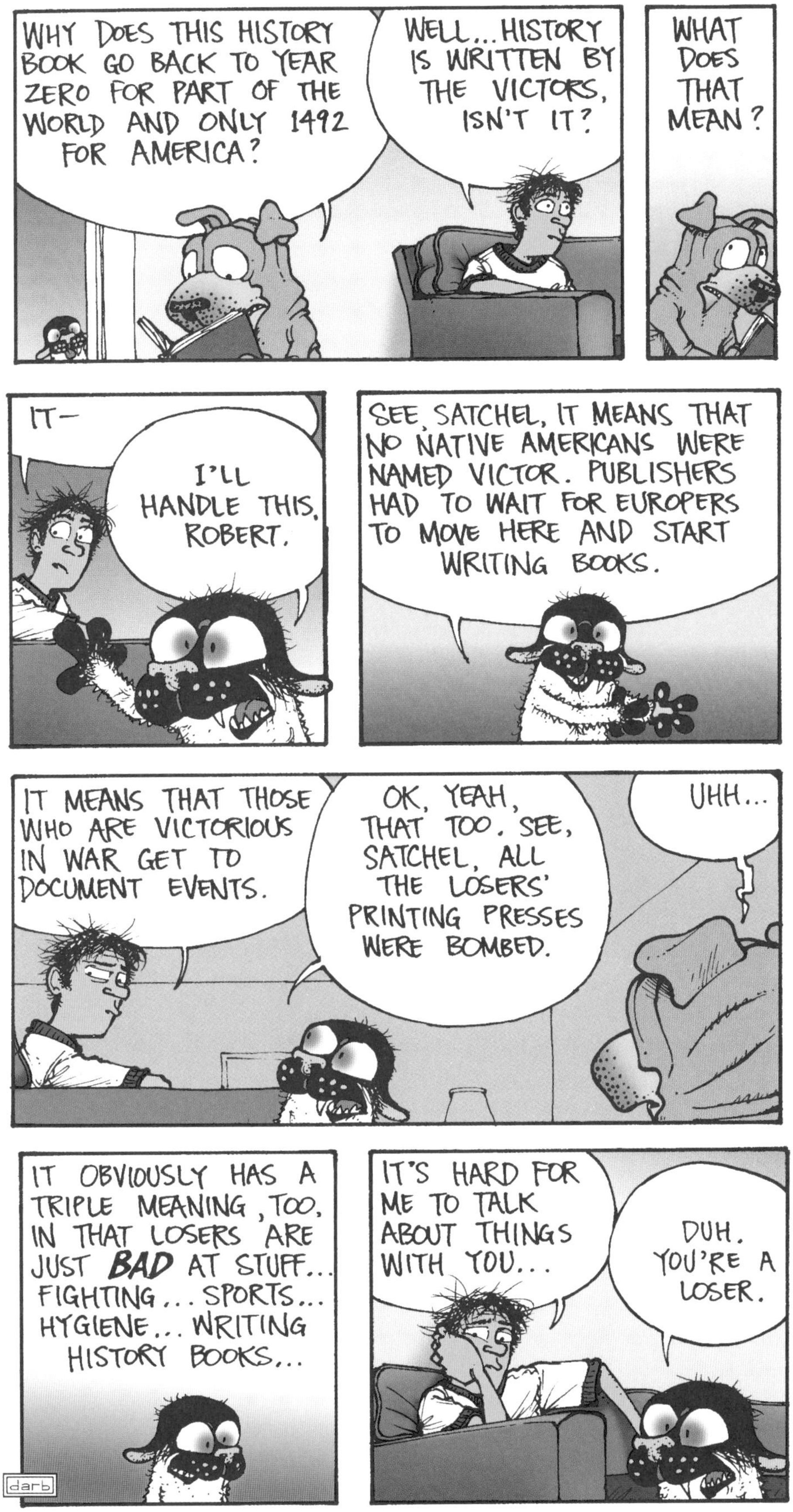
WHY DOES THIS HISTORY BOOK GO BACK TO YEAR ZERO FOR PART OF THE WORLD AND ONLY 1492 FOR AMERICA?
WELL... HISTORY IS WRITTEN BY THE VICTORS, ISN'T IT?
WHAT DOES THAT MEAN?
IT—
I'LL HANDLE THIS, ROBERT.
SEE, SATCHEL, IT MEANS THAT NO NATIVE AMERICANS WERE NAMED VICTOR. PUBLISHERS HAD TO WAIT FOR EUROPERS TO MOVE HERE AND START WRITING BOOKS.
IT MEANS THAT THOSE WHO ARE VICTORIOUS IN WAR GET TO DOCUMENT EVENTS.
OK, YEAH, THAT TOO. SEE, SATCHEL, ALL THE LOSERS' PRINTING PRESSES WERE BOMBED.
UHH...
IT OBVIOUSLY HAS A TRIPLE MEANING, TOO, IN THAT LOSERS ARE JUST BAD AT STUFF... FIGHTING... SPORTS... HYGIENE... WRITING HISTORY BOOKS...
IT'S HARD FOR ME TO TALK ABOUT THINGS WITH YOU...
DUH. YOU'RE A LOSER.
darb

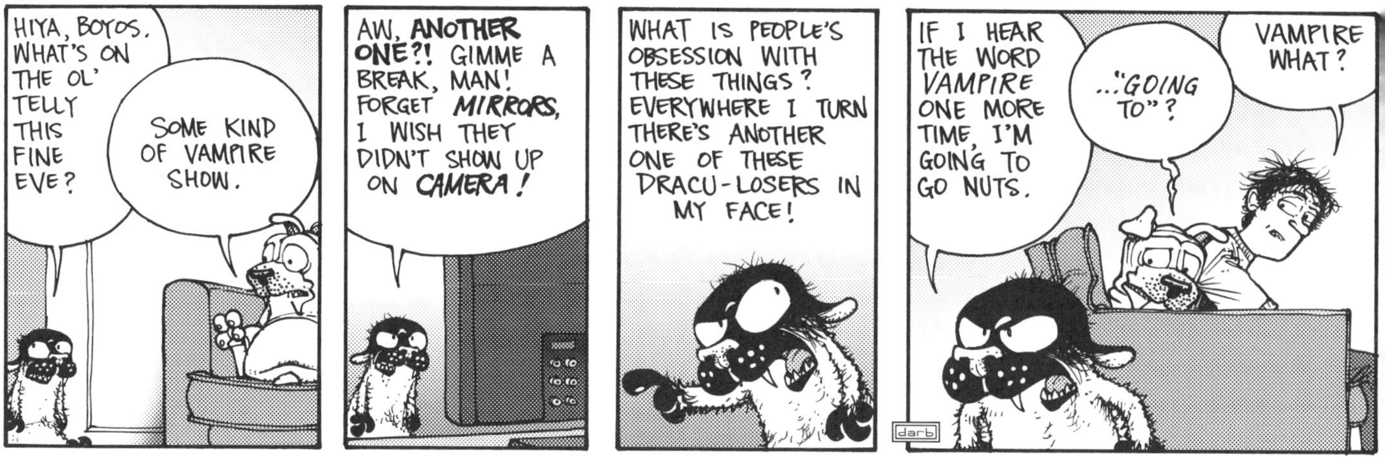
HIYA, BOYOS. WHAT'S ON THE OL' TELLY THIS FINE EVE?
SOME KIND OF VAMPIRE SHOW.
AW, ANOTHER ONE?! GIMME A BREAK, MAN! FORGET MIRRORS, I WISH THEY DIDN'T SHOW UP ON CAMERA!
WHAT IS PEOPLE'S OBSESSION WITH THESE THINGS? EVERYWHERE I TURN THERE'S ANOTHER ONE OF THESE DRACU-LOSERS IN MY FACE!
IF I HEAR THE WORD VAMPIRE ONE MORE TIME, I'M GOING TO GO NUTS.
..."GOING TO"?
VAMPIRE WHAT?
darb

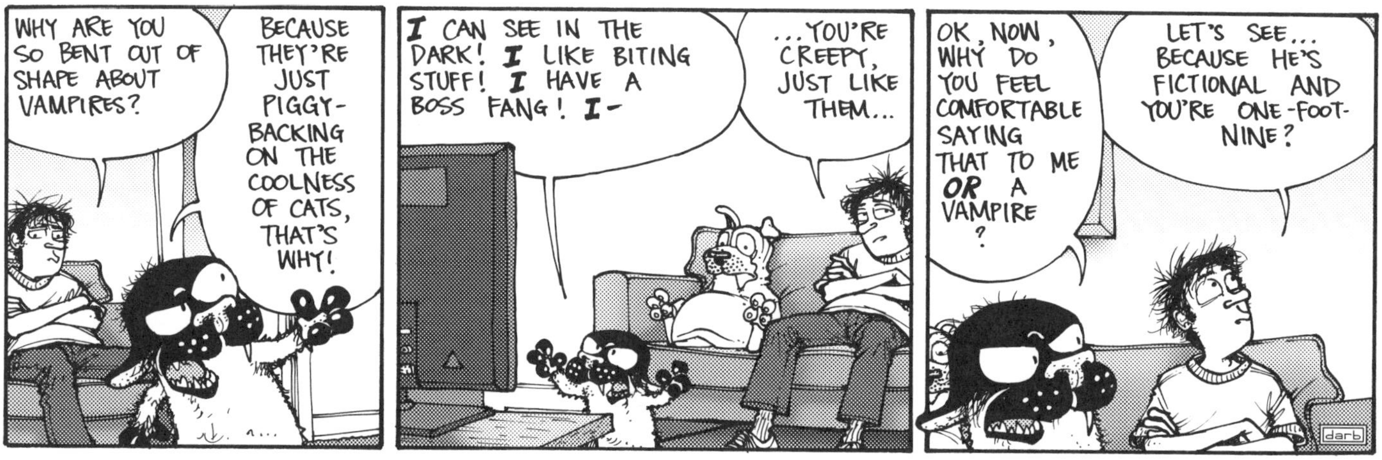
WHY ARE YOU SO BENT OUT OF SHAPE ABOUT VAMPIRES?
BECAUSE THEY'RE JUST PIGGY-BACKING ON THE COOLNESS OF CATS, THAT'S WHY!
I CAN SEE IN THE DARK! I LIKE BITING STUFF! I HAVE A BOSS FANG! I-
...YOU'RE CREEPY, JUST LIKE THEM...
OK, NOW, WHY DO YOU FEEL COMFORTABLE SAYING THAT TO ME OR A VAMPIRE?
LET'S SEE... BECAUSE HE'S FICTIONAL AND YOU'RE ONE-FOOT-NINE?
darb

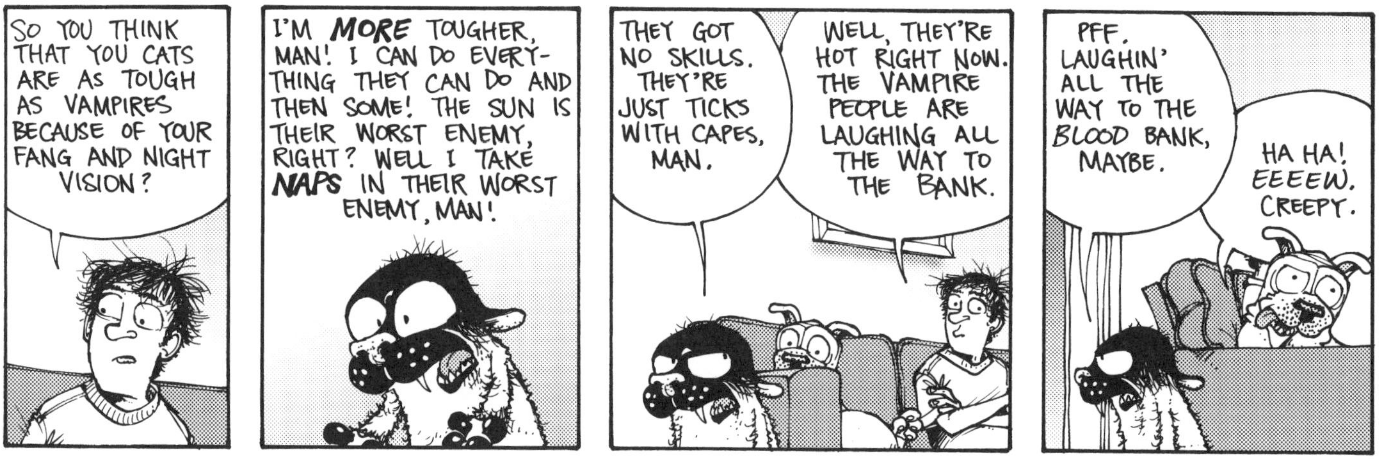
SO YOU THINK THAT YOU CATS ARE AS TOUGH AS VAMPIRES BECAUSE OF YOUR FANG AND NIGHT VISION?
I'M MORE TOUGHER, MAN! I CAN DO EVERYTHING THEY CAN DO AND THEN SOME! THE SUN IS THEIR WORST ENEMY, RIGHT? WELL I TAKE NAPS IN THEIR WORST ENEMY, MAN!
THEY GOT NO SKILLS. THEY'RE JUST TICKS WITH CAPES, MAN.
WELL, THEY'RE HOT RIGHT NOW. THE VAMPIRE PEOPLE ARE LAUGHING ALL THE WAY TO THE BANK.
PFF. LAUGHIN' ALL THE WAY TO THE BLOOD BANK, MAYBE.
HA HA! EEEEW. CREEPY.

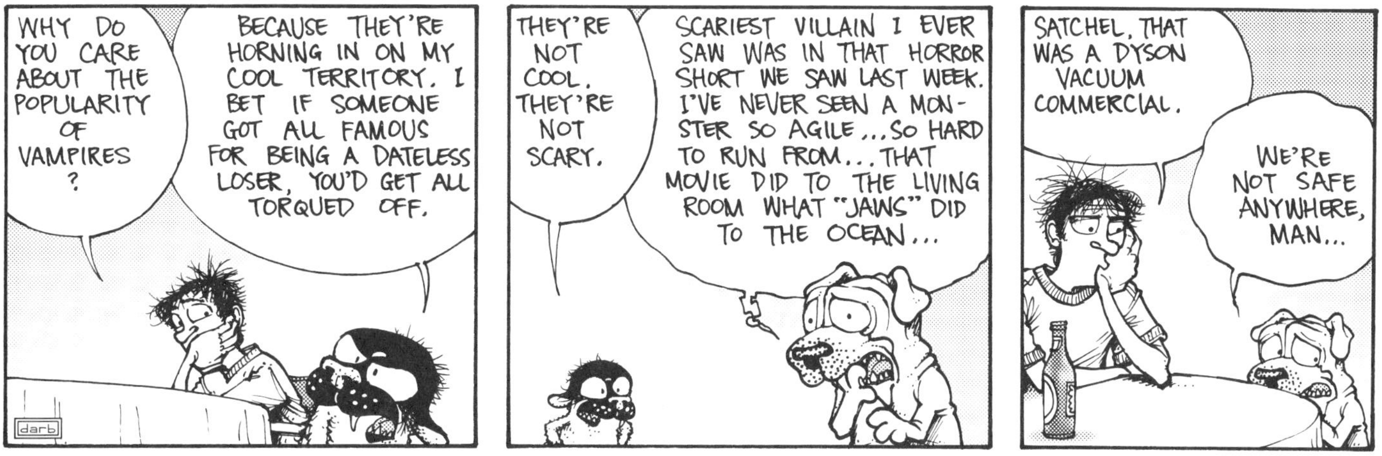
WHY DO YOU CARE ABOUT THE POPULARITY OF VAMPIRES ?
BECAUSE THEY'RE HORNING IN ON MY COOL TERRITORY. I BET IF SOMEONE GOT ALL FAMOUS FOR BEING A DATELESS LOSER, YOU'D GET ALL TORQUED OFF.
THEY'RE NOT COOL. THEY'RE NOT SCARY.
SCARIEST VILLAIN I EVER SAW WAS IN THAT HORROR SHORT WE SAW LAST WEEK. I'VE NEVER SEEN A MON-STER SO AGILE... SO HARD TO RUN FROM... THAT MOVIE DID TO THE LIVING ROOM WHAT "JAWS" DID TO THE OCEAN...
SATCHEL, THAT WAS A DYSON VACUUM COMMERCIAL.
WE'RE NOT SAFE ANYWHERE, MAN...
darb

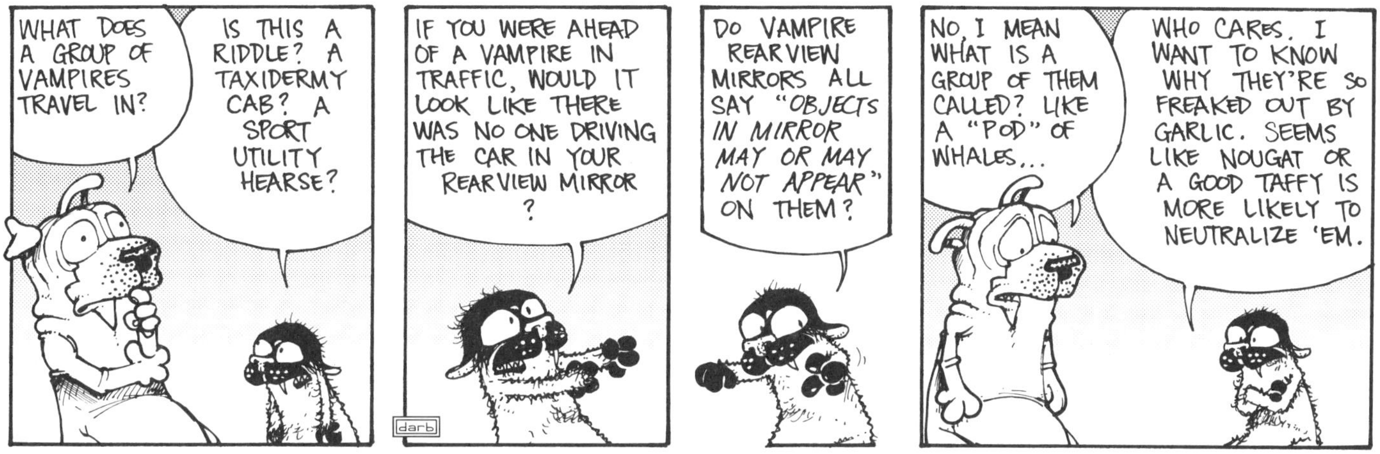
WHAT DOES A GROUP OF VAMPIRES TRAVEL IN?
IS THIS A RIDDLE? A TAXIDERMY CAB? A SPORT UTILITY HEARSE?
IF YOU WERE AHEAD OF A VAMPIRE IN TRAFFIC, WOULD IT LOOK LIKE THERE WAS NO ONE DRIVING THE CAR IN YOUR REARVIEW MIRROR ?
DO VAMPIRE REARVIEW MIRRORS ALL SAY "*OBJECTS IN MIRROR MAY OR MAY NOT APPEAR*" ON THEM?
NO, I MEAN WHAT IS A GROUP OF THEM CALLED? LIKE A "POD" OF WHALES...
WHO CARES. I WANT TO KNOW WHY THEY'RE SO FREAKED OUT BY GARLIC. SEEMS LIKE NOUGAT OR A GOOD TAFFY IS MORE LIKELY TO NEUTRALIZE 'EM.
darb

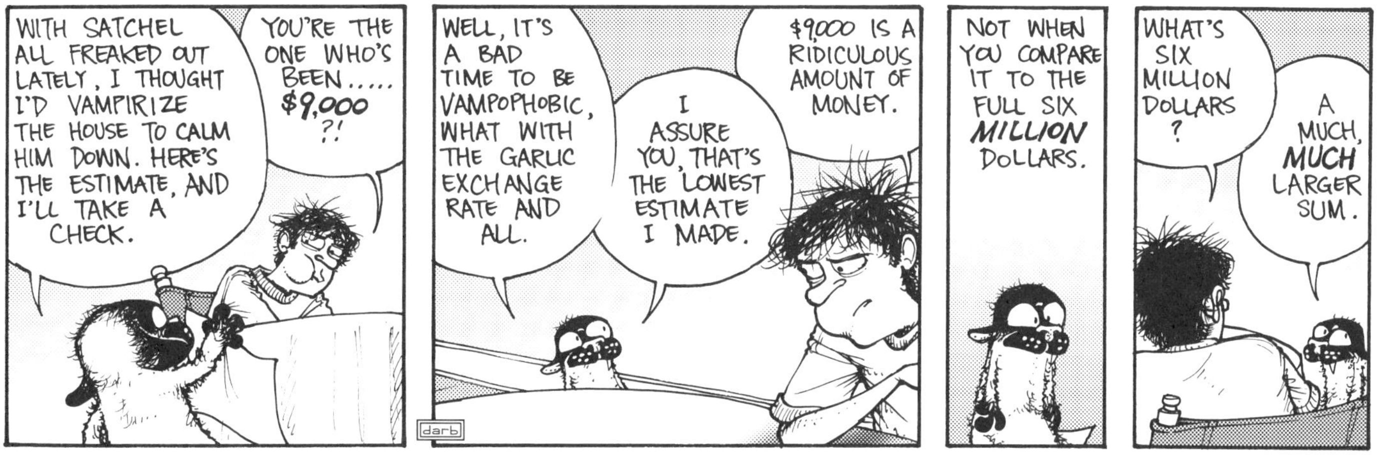
WITH SATCHEL ALL FREAKED OUT LATELY, I THOUGHT I'D VAMPIRIZE THE HOUSE TO CALM HIM DOWN. HERE'S THE ESTIMATE, AND I'LL TAKE A CHECK.
YOU'RE THE ONE WHO'S BEEN..... **$9,000** ?!
WELL, IT'S A BAD TIME TO BE VAMPOPHOBIC, WHAT WITH THE GARLIC EXCHANGE RATE AND ALL.
I ASSURE YOU, THAT'S THE LOWEST ESTIMATE I MADE.
$9,000 IS A RIDICULOUS AMOUNT OF MONEY.
NOT WHEN YOU COMPARE IT TO THE FULL SIX ***MILLION*** DOLLARS.
WHAT'S SIX MILLION DOLLARS ?
A MUCH, ***MUCH*** LARGER SUM.
darb

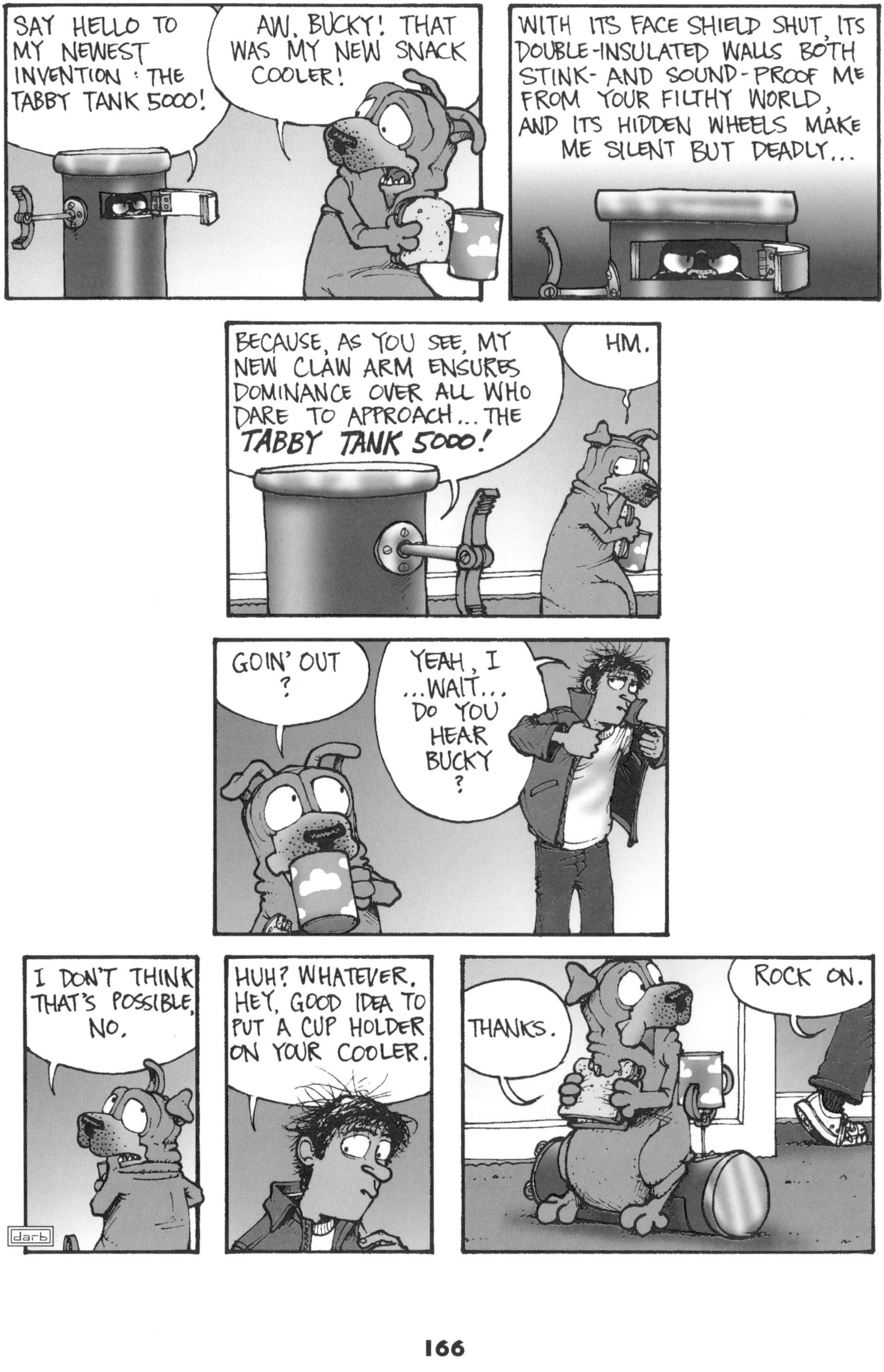
SAY HELLO TO MY NEWEST INVENTION : THE TABBY TANK 5000!
AW, BUCKY! THAT WAS MY NEW SNACK COOLER!
WITH ITS FACE SHIELD SHUT, ITS DOUBLE-INSULATED WALLS BOTH STINK- AND SOUND-PROOF ME FROM YOUR FILTHY WORLD, AND ITS HIDDEN WHEELS MAKE ME SILENT BUT DEADLY...
BECAUSE, AS YOU SEE, MY NEW CLAW ARM ENSURES DOMINANCE OVER ALL WHO DARE TO APPROACH... THE TABBY TANK 5000!
HM.
GOIN' OUT ?
YEAH, I ...WAIT... DO YOU HEAR BUCKY ?
I DON'T THINK THAT'S POSSIBLE, NO.
darb
HUH? WHATEVER. HEY, GOOD IDEA TO PUT A CUP HOLDER ON YOUR COOLER.
THANKS.
ROCK ON.

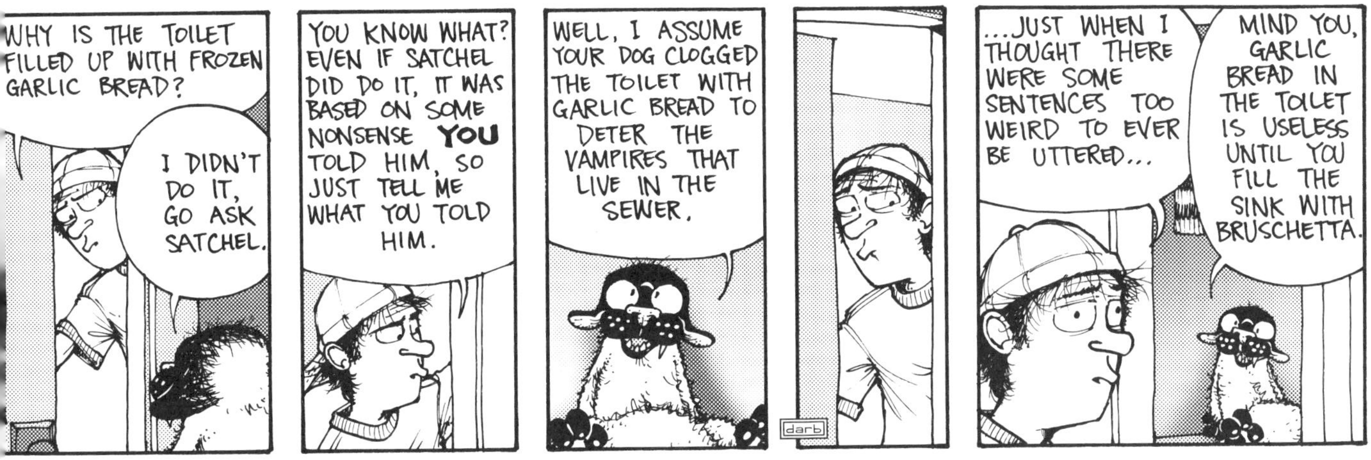
WHY IS THE TOILET FILLED UP WITH FROZEN GARLIC BREAD?
I DIDN'T DO IT, GO ASK SATCHEL.
YOU KNOW WHAT? EVEN IF SATCHEL DID DO IT, IT WAS BASED ON SOME NONSENSE **YOU** TOLD HIM, SO JUST TELL ME WHAT YOU TOLD HIM.
WELL, I ASSUME YOUR DOG CLOGGED THE TOILET WITH GARLIC BREAD TO DETER THE VAMPIRES THAT LIVE IN THE SEWER.
darb
...JUST WHEN I THOUGHT THERE WERE SOME SENTENCES TOO WEIRD TO EVER BE UTTERED...
MIND YOU, GARLIC BREAD IN THE TOILET IS USELESS UNTIL YOU FILL THE SINK WITH BRUSCHETTA.

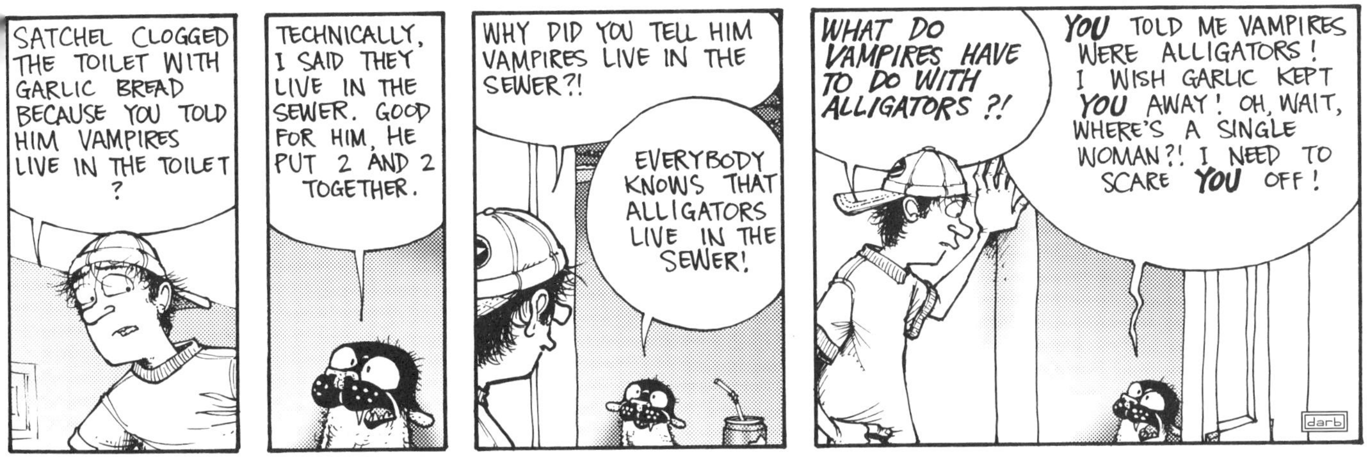
SATCHEL CLOGGED THE TOILET WITH GARLIC BREAD BECAUSE YOU TOLD HIM VAMPIRES LIVE IN THE TOILET?
TECHNICALLY, I SAID THEY LIVE IN THE SEWER. GOOD FOR HIM, HE PUT 2 AND 2 TOGETHER.
WHY DID YOU TELL HIM VAMPIRES LIVE IN THE SEWER?!
EVERYBODY KNOWS THAT ALLIGATORS LIVE IN THE SEWER!
WHAT DO VAMPIRES HAVE TO DO WITH ALLIGATORS?!
YOU TOLD ME VAMPIRES WERE ALLIGATORS! I WISH GARLIC KEPT **YOU** AWAY! OH, WAIT, WHERE'S A SINGLE WOMAN?! I NEED TO SCARE **YOU** OFF!
darb

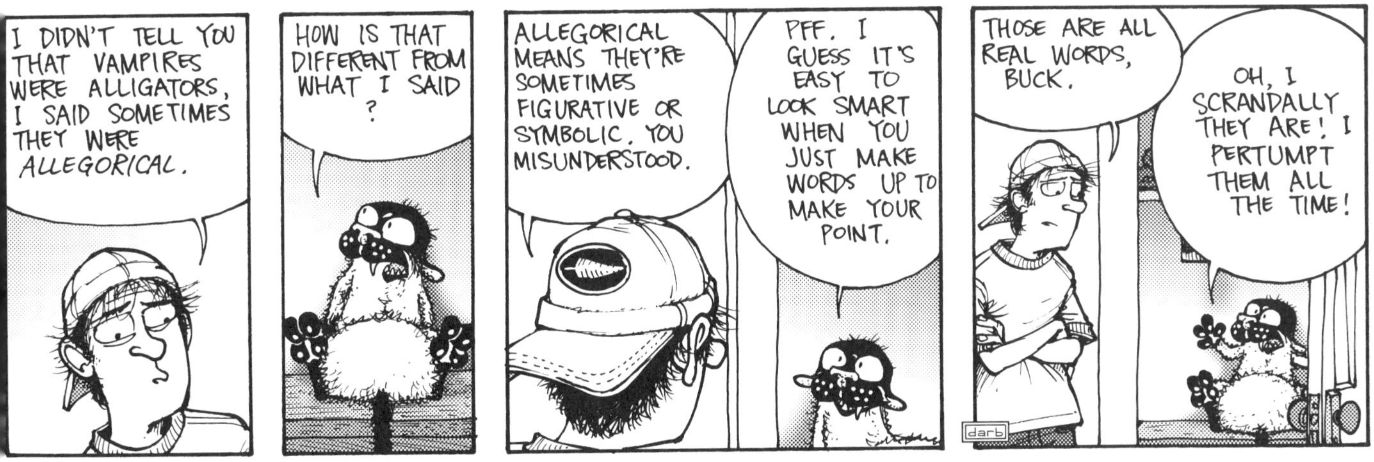
I DIDN'T TELL YOU THAT VAMPIRES WERE ALLIGATORS, I SAID SOMETIMES THEY WERE *ALLEGORICAL*.
HOW IS THAT DIFFERENT FROM WHAT I SAID?
ALLEGORICAL MEANS THEY'RE SOMETIMES FIGURATIVE OR SYMBOLIC. YOU MISUNDERSTOOD.
PFF. I GUESS IT'S EASY TO LOOK SMART WHEN YOU JUST MAKE WORDS UP TO MAKE YOUR POINT.
darb
THOSE ARE ALL REAL WORDS, BUCK.
OH, I SCRANDALLY THEY ARE! I PERTUMPT THEM ALL THE TIME!

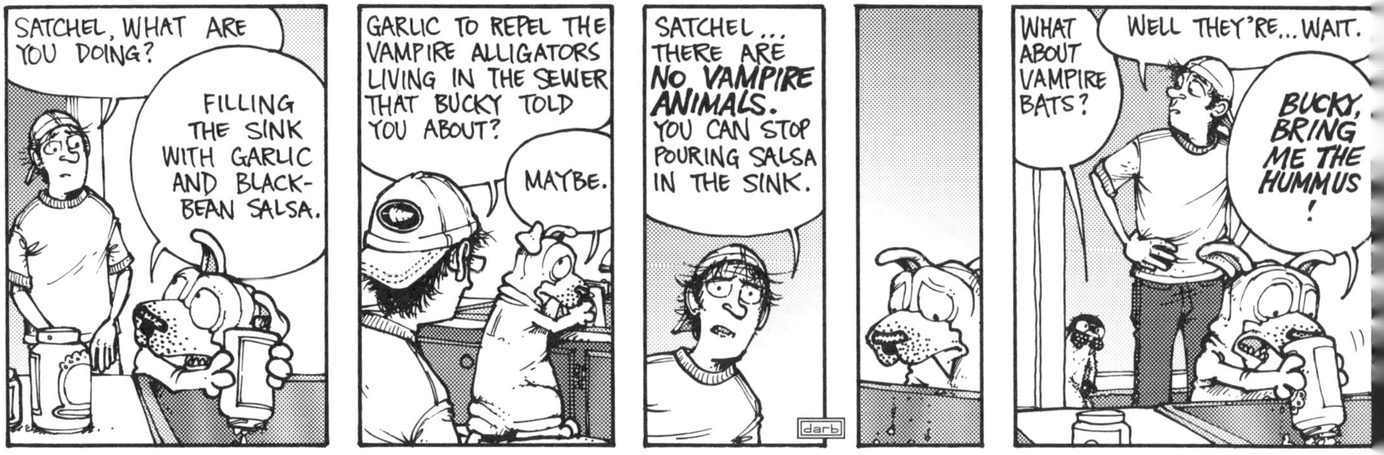
SATCHEL, WHAT ARE YOU DOING?
FILLING THE SINK WITH GARLIC AND BLACK-BEAN SALSA.
GARLIC TO REPEL THE VAMPIRE ALLIGATORS LIVING IN THE SEWER THAT BUCKY TOLD YOU ABOUT?
MAYBE.
SATCHEL... THERE ARE **NO VAMPIRE ANIMALS.** YOU CAN STOP POURING SALSA IN THE SINK.
darb
WHAT ABOUT VAMPIRE BATS?
WELL THEY'RE... WAIT.
BUCKY, BRING ME THE HUMMUS!

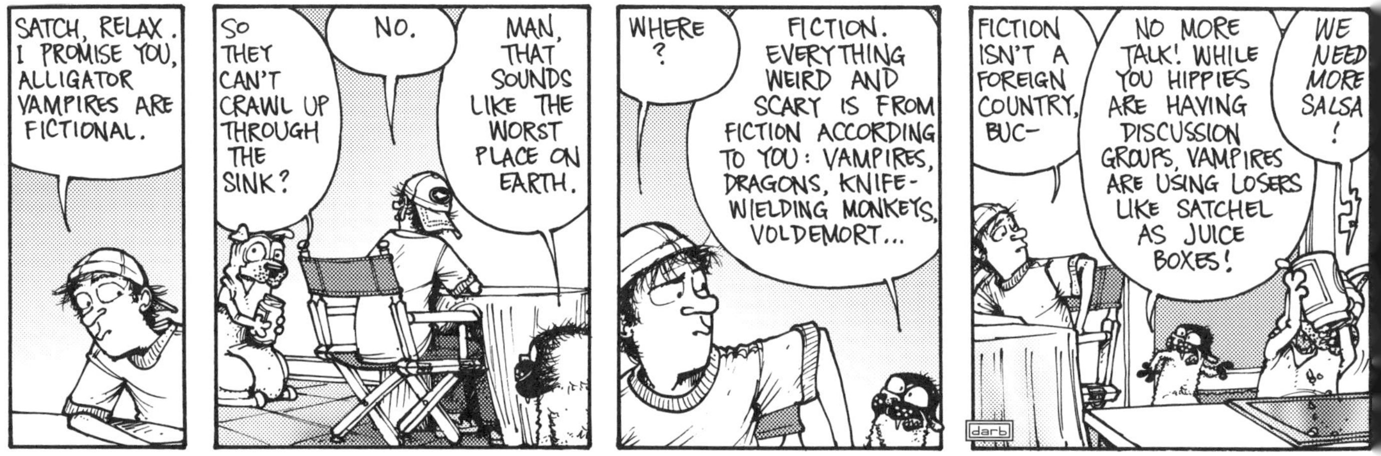
SATCH, RELAX. I PROMISE YOU, ALLIGATOR VAMPIRES ARE FICTIONAL.
SO THEY CAN'T CRAWL UP THROUGH THE SINK?
NO.
MAN, THAT SOUNDS LIKE THE WORST PLACE ON EARTH.
WHERE?
FICTION. EVERYTHING WEIRD AND SCARY IS FROM FICTION ACCORDING TO YOU: VAMPIRES, DRAGONS, KNIFE-WIELDING MONKEYS, VOLDEMORT...
darb
FICTION ISN'T A FOREIGN COUNTRY, BUC-
NO MORE TALK! WHILE YOU HIPPIES ARE HAVING DISCUSSION GROUPS, VAMPIRES ARE USING LOSERS LIKE SATCHEL AS JUICE BOXES!
WE NEED MORE SALSA!

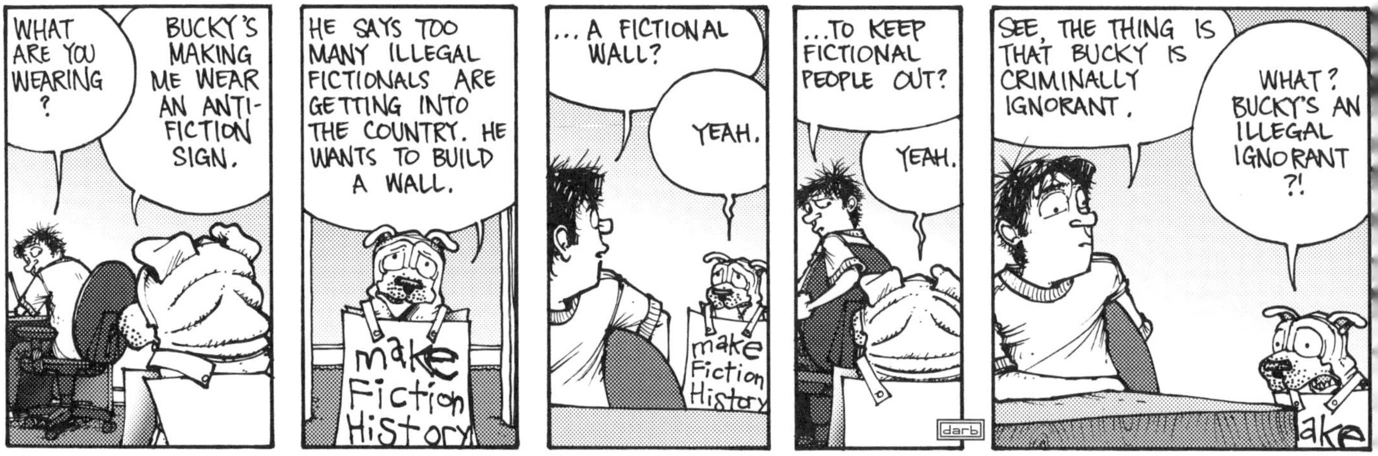
WHAT ARE YOU WEARING?
BUCKY'S MAKING ME WEAR AN ANTI-FICTION SIGN.
HE SAYS TOO MANY ILLEGAL FICTIONALS ARE GETTING INTO THE COUNTRY. HE WANTS TO BUILD A WALL.
make Fiction History
... A FICTIONAL WALL?
YEAH.
make Fiction History
... TO KEEP FICTIONAL PEOPLE OUT?
YEAH.
darb
SEE, THE THING IS THAT BUCKY IS CRIMINALLY IGNORANT.
WHAT? BUCKY'S AN ILLEGAL IGNORANT?!

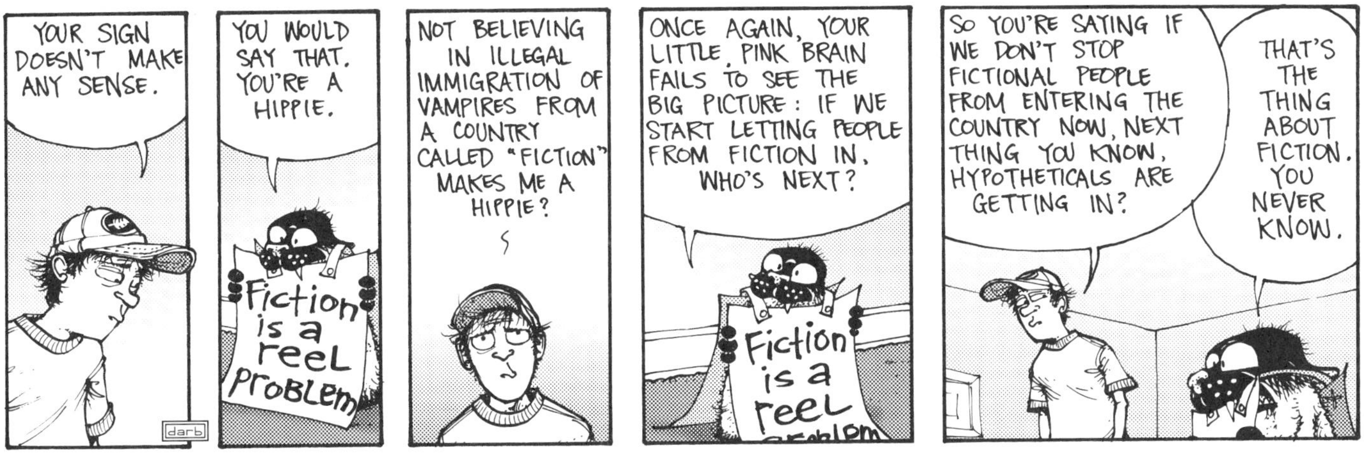
YOUR SIGN DOESN'T MAKE ANY SENSE.
YOU WOULD SAY THAT. YOU'RE A HIPPIE.
Fiction is a reel problem
NOT BELIEVING IN ILLEGAL IMMIGRATION OF VAMPIRES FROM A COUNTRY CALLED "FICTION" MAKES ME A HIPPIE?
ONCE AGAIN, YOUR LITTLE, PINK BRAIN FAILS TO SEE THE BIG PICTURE: IF WE START LETTING PEOPLE FROM FICTION IN, WHO'S NEXT?
Fiction is a reel
SO YOU'RE SAYING IF WE DON'T STOP FICTIONAL PEOPLE FROM ENTERING THE COUNTRY NOW, NEXT THING YOU KNOW, HYPOTHETICALS ARE GETTING IN?
THAT'S THE THING ABOUT FICTION. YOU NEVER KNOW.

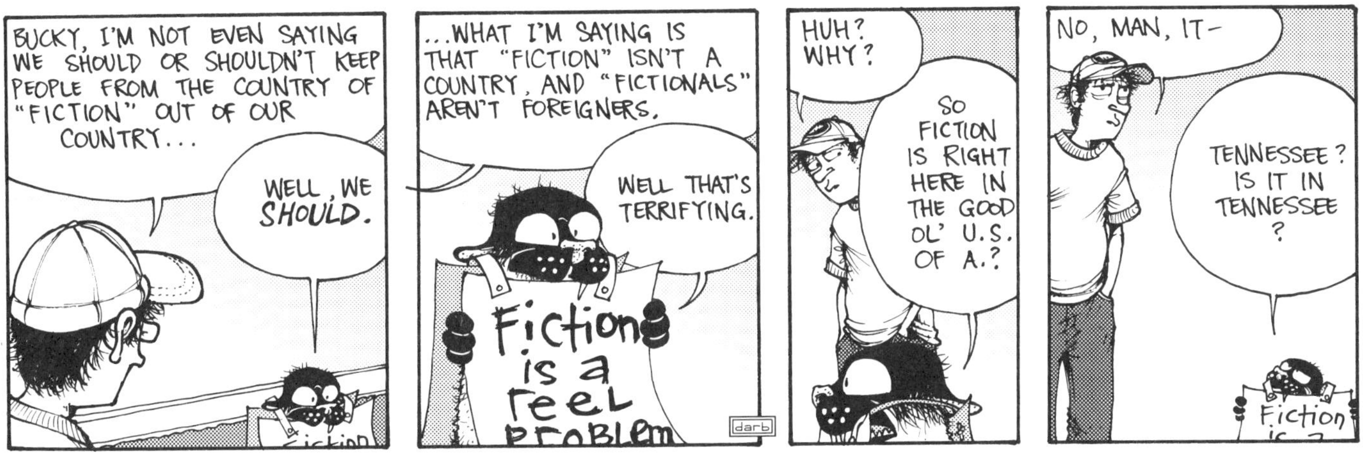
BUCKY, I'M NOT EVEN SAYING WE SHOULD OR SHOULDN'T KEEP PEOPLE FROM THE COUNTRY OF "FICTION" OUT OF OUR COUNTRY...
WELL, WE SHOULD.
...WHAT I'M SAYING IS THAT "FICTION" ISN'T A COUNTRY, AND "FICTIONALS" AREN'T FOREIGNERS.
WELL THAT'S TERRIFYING.
Fiction is a reel problem
HUH? WHY?
SO FICTION IS RIGHT HERE IN THE GOOD OL' U.S. OF A.?
NO, MAN, IT—
TENNESSEE? IS IT IN TENNESSEE?
Fiction

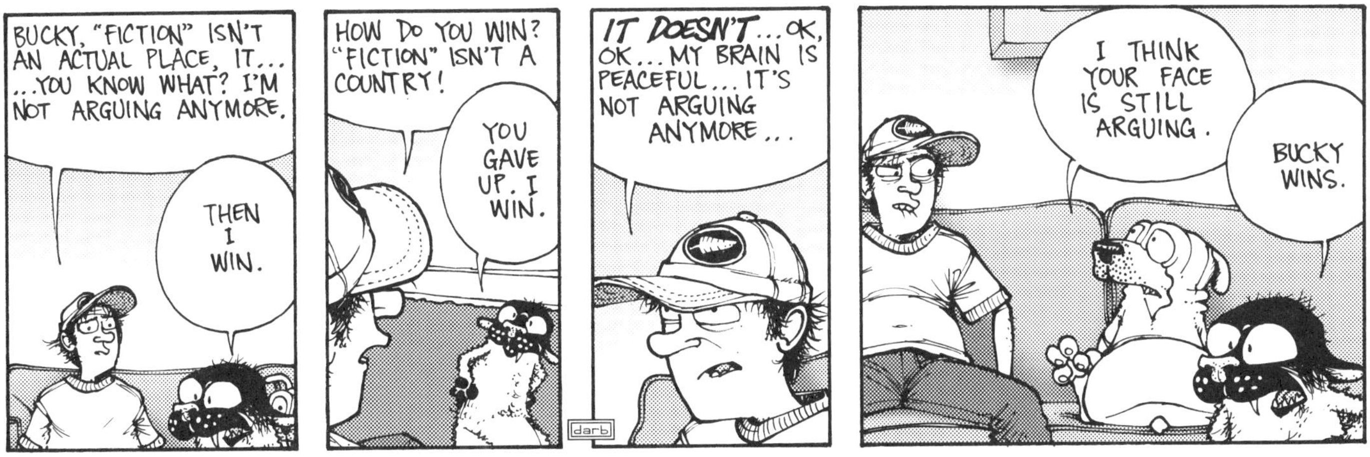
BUCKY, "FICTION" ISN'T AN ACTUAL PLACE, IT... ...YOU KNOW WHAT? I'M NOT ARGUING ANYMORE.
THEN I WIN.
HOW DO YOU WIN? "FICTION" ISN'T A COUNTRY!
YOU GAVE UP. I WIN.
IT DOESN'T... OK, OK... MY BRAIN IS PEACEFUL... IT'S NOT ARGUING ANYMORE...
I THINK YOUR FACE IS STILL ARGUING.
BUCKY WINS.

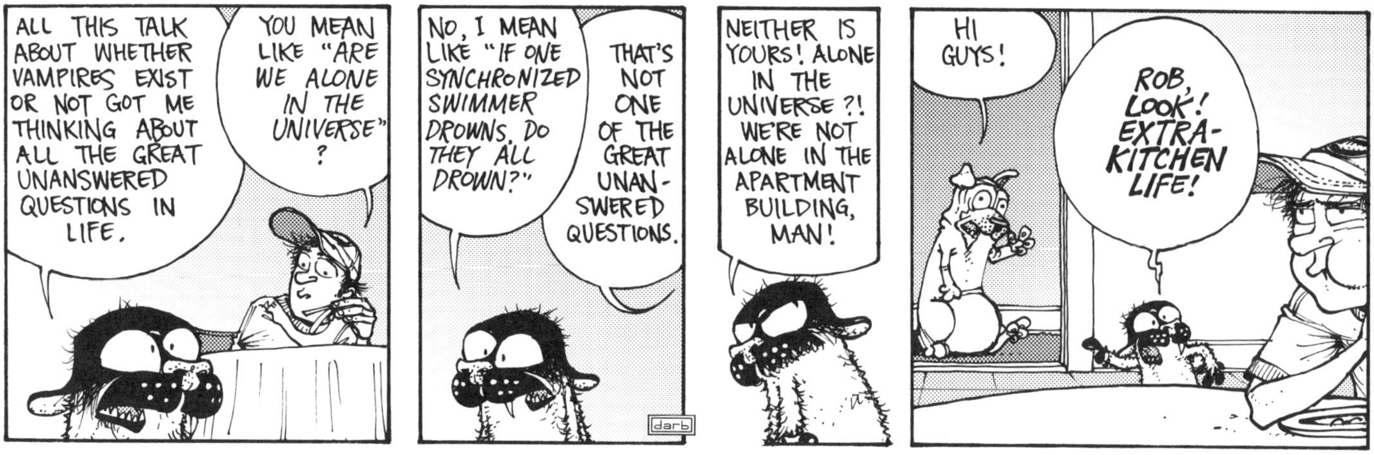
ALL THIS TALK ABOUT WHETHER VAMPIRES EXIST OR NOT GOT ME THINKING ABOUT ALL THE GREAT UNANSWERED QUESTIONS IN LIFE.
YOU MEAN LIKE "ARE WE ALONE IN THE UNIVERSE"?
NO, I MEAN LIKE "IF ONE SYNCHRONIZED SWIMMER DROWNS, DO THEY ALL DROWN?"
THAT'S NOT ONE OF THE GREAT UNANSWERED QUESTIONS.
NEITHER IS YOURS! ALONE IN THE UNIVERSE?! WE'RE NOT ALONE IN THE APARTMENT BUILDING, MAN!
HI GUYS!
ROB, LOOK! EXTRA-KITCHEN LIFE!

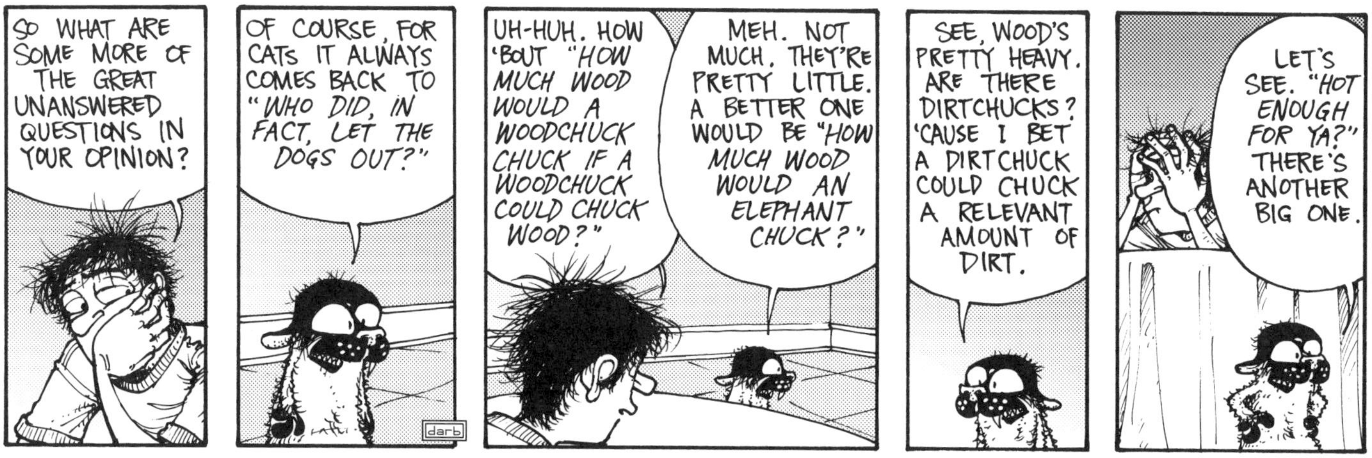
SO WHAT ARE SOME MORE OF THE GREAT UNANSWERED QUESTIONS IN YOUR OPINION?
OF COURSE, FOR CATS IT ALWAYS COMES BACK TO "WHO DID, IN FACT, LET THE DOGS OUT?"
UH-HUH. HOW 'BOUT "HOW MUCH WOOD WOULD A WOODCHUCK CHUCK IF A WOODCHUCK COULD CHUCK WOOD?"
MEH. NOT MUCH. THEY'RE PRETTY LITTLE. A BETTER ONE WOULD BE "HOW MUCH WOOD WOULD AN ELEPHANT CHUCK?"
SEE, WOOD'S PRETTY HEAVY. ARE THERE DIRTCHUCKS? 'CAUSE I BET A DIRTCHUCK COULD CHUCK A RELEVANT AMOUNT OF DIRT.
LET'S SEE. "HOT ENOUGH FOR YA?" THERE'S ANOTHER BIG ONE.

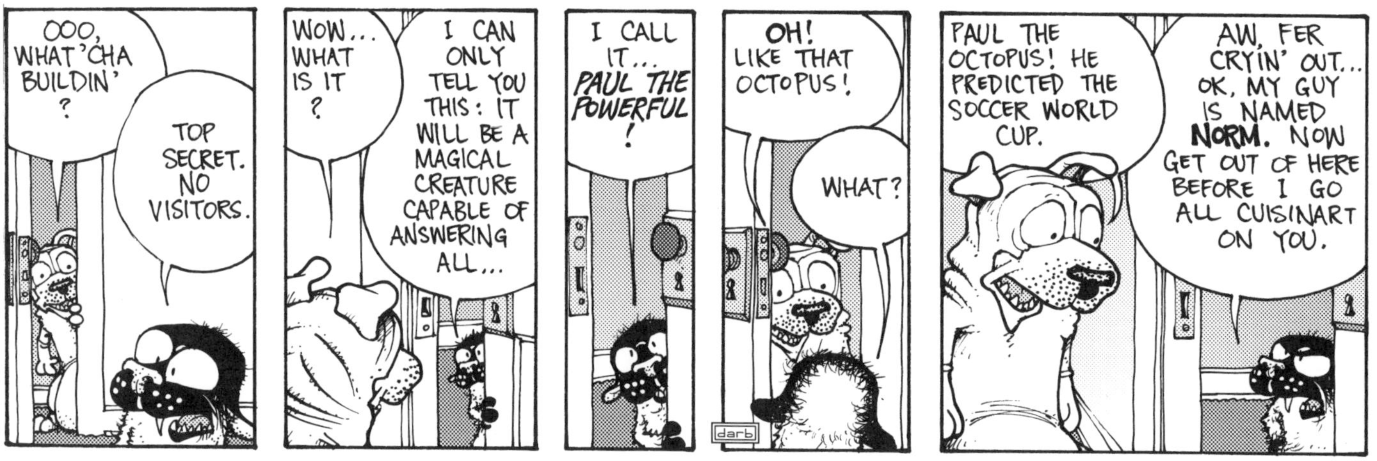
OOO, WHAT'CHA BUILDIN'?
TOP SECRET. NO VISITORS.
WOW... WHAT IS IT?
I CAN ONLY TELL YOU THIS: IT WILL BE A MAGICAL CREATURE CAPABLE OF ANSWERING ALL...
I CALL IT... PAUL THE POWERFUL!
OH! LIKE THAT OCTOPUS!
WHAT?
PAUL THE OCTOPUS! HE PREDICTED THE SOCCER WORLD CUP.
AW, FER CRYIN' OUT... OK, MY GUY IS NAMED NORM. NOW GET OUT OF HERE BEFORE I GO ALL CUISINART ON YOU.

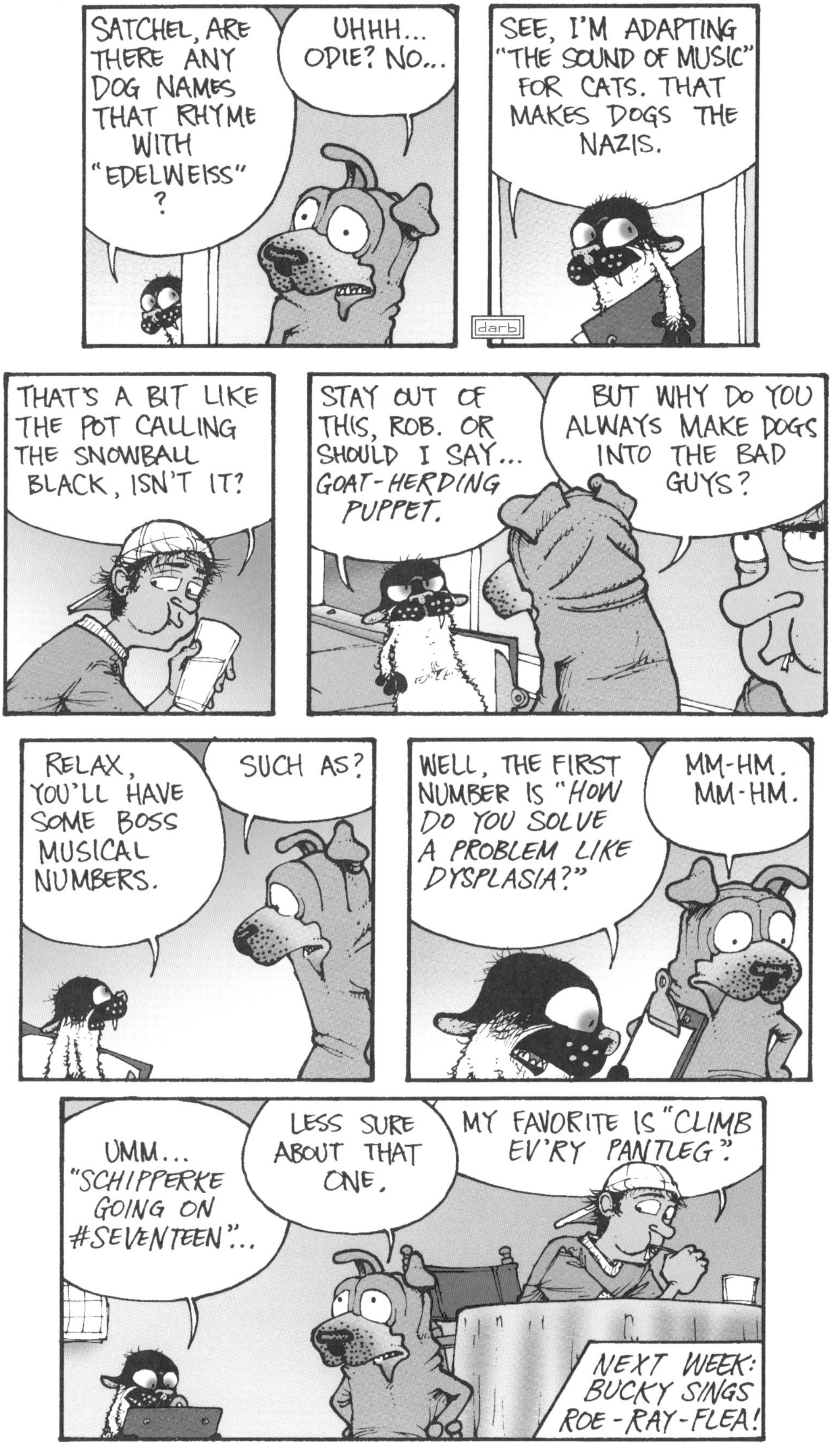
SATCHEL, ARE THERE ANY DOG NAMES THAT RHYME WITH "EDELWEISS"?
UHHH... ODIE? NO...
SEE, I'M ADAPTING "THE SOUND OF MUSIC" FOR CATS. THAT MAKES DOGS THE NAZIS.
darb
THAT'S A BIT LIKE THE POT CALLING THE SNOWBALL BLACK, ISN'T IT?
STAY OUT OF THIS, ROB. OR SHOULD I SAY... GOAT-HERDING PUPPET.
BUT WHY DO YOU ALWAYS MAKE DOGS INTO THE BAD GUYS?
RELAX, YOU'LL HAVE SOME BOSS MUSICAL NUMBERS.
SUCH AS?
WELL, THE FIRST NUMBER IS "HOW DO YOU SOLVE A PROBLEM LIKE DYSPLASIA?"
MM-HM. MM-HM.
UMM... "SCHIPPERKE GOING ON #SEVENTEEN"...
LESS SURE ABOUT THAT ONE.
MY FAVORITE IS "CLIMB EV'RY PANTLEG."
NEXT WEEK: BUCKY SINGS ROE-RAY-FLEA!

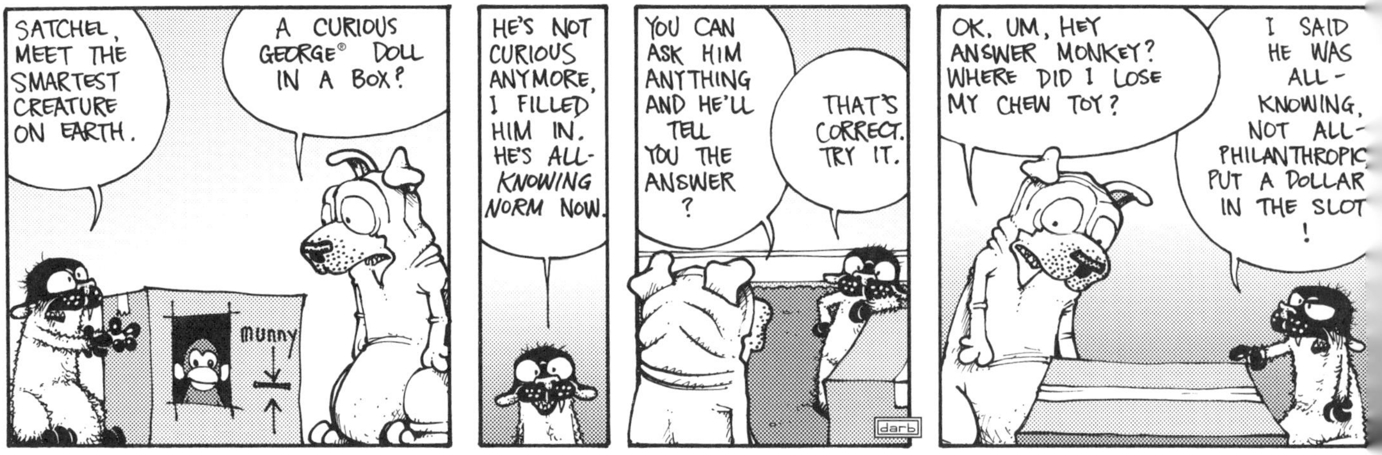
SATCHEL, MEET THE SMARTEST CREATURE ON EARTH.
A CURIOUS GEORGE® DOLL IN A BOX?
HE'S NOT CURIOUS ANYMORE, I FILLED HIM IN. HE'S ALL-KNOWING NORM NOW.
YOU CAN ASK HIM ANYTHING AND HE'LL TELL YOU THE ANSWER?
THAT'S CORRECT. TRY IT.
OK. UM, HEY ANSWER MONKEY? WHERE DID I LOSE MY CHEW TOY?
I SAID HE WAS ALL-KNOWING, NOT ALL-PHILANTHROPIC. PUT A DOLLAR IN THE SLOT!
munny
darb

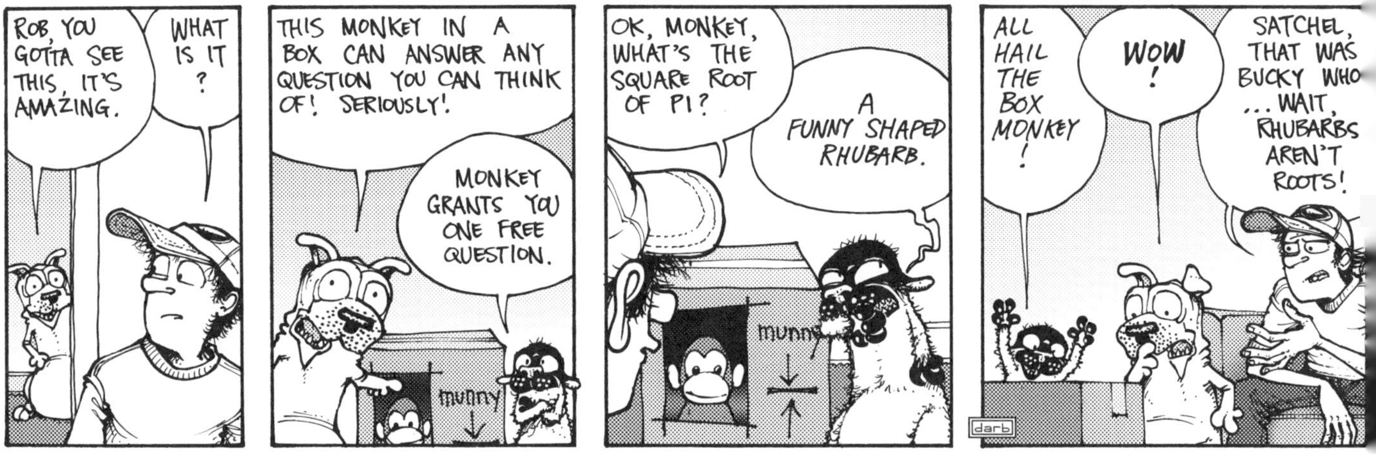
ROB, YOU GOTTA SEE THIS, IT'S AMAZING.
WHAT IS IT?
THIS MONKEY IN A BOX CAN ANSWER ANY QUESTION YOU CAN THINK OF! SERIOUSLY!
MONKEY GRANTS YOU ONE FREE QUESTION.
OK, MONKEY, WHAT'S THE SQUARE ROOT OF PI?
A FUNNY SHAPED RHUBARB.
ALL HAIL THE BOX MONKEY!
WOW!
SATCHEL, THAT WAS BUCKY WHO ... WAIT, RHUBARBS AREN'T ROOTS!
munny
darb

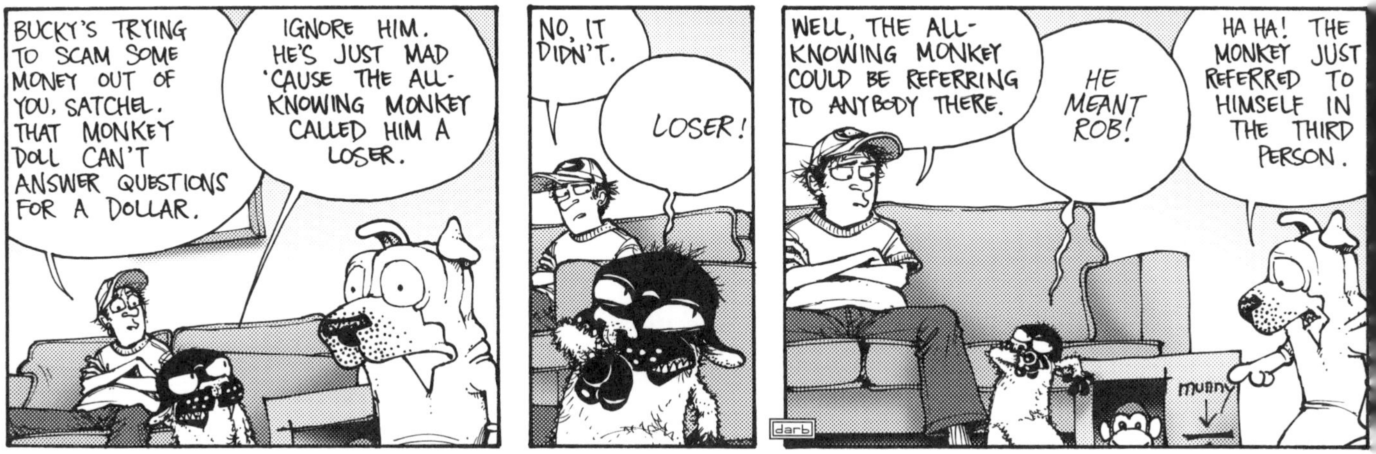
BUCKY'S TRYING TO SCAM SOME MONEY OUT OF YOU, SATCHEL. THAT MONKEY DOLL CAN'T ANSWER QUESTIONS FOR A DOLLAR.
IGNORE HIM. HE'S JUST MAD 'CAUSE THE ALL-KNOWING MONKEY CALLED HIM A LOSER.
NO, IT DIDN'T.
LOSER!
WELL, THE ALL-KNOWING MONKEY COULD BE REFERRING TO ANYBODY THERE.
HE MEANT ROB!
HA HA! THE MONKEY JUST REFERRED TO HIMSELF IN THE THIRD PERSON.
munny
darb

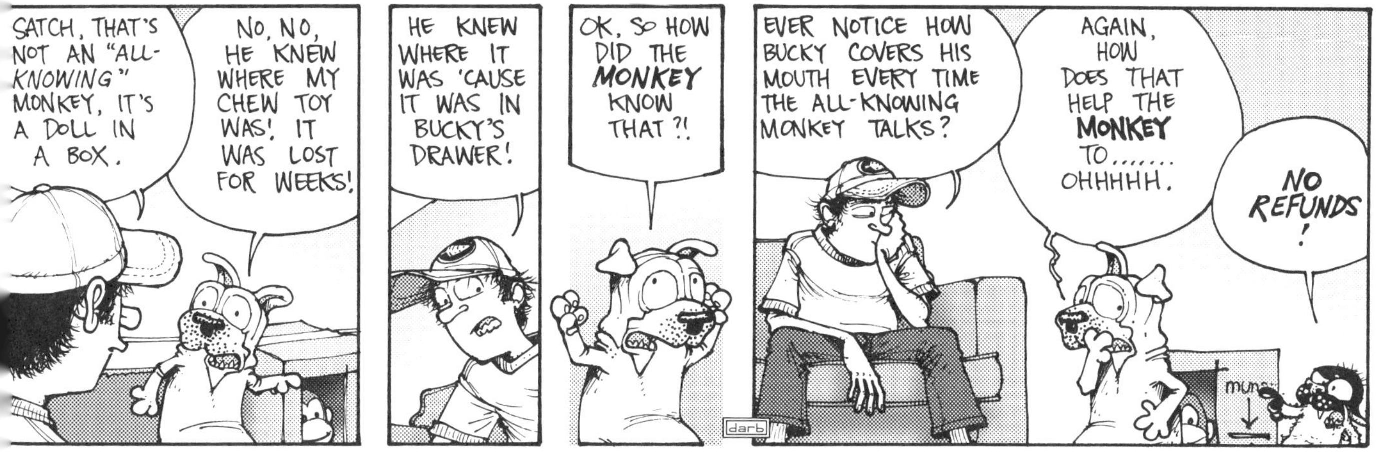
SATCH, THAT'S NOT AN "ALL-KNOWING" MONKEY, IT'S A DOLL IN A BOX.
NO, NO, HE KNEW WHERE MY CHEW TOY WAS! IT WAS LOST FOR WEEKS!
HE KNEW WHERE IT WAS 'CAUSE IT WAS IN BUCKY'S DRAWER!
OK, SO HOW DID THE MONKEY KNOW THAT ?!
EVER NOTICE HOW BUCKY COVERS HIS MOUTH EVERY TIME THE ALL-KNOWING MONKEY TALKS?
AGAIN, HOW DOES THAT HELP THE MONKEY TO....... OHHHHH.
NO REFUNDS!

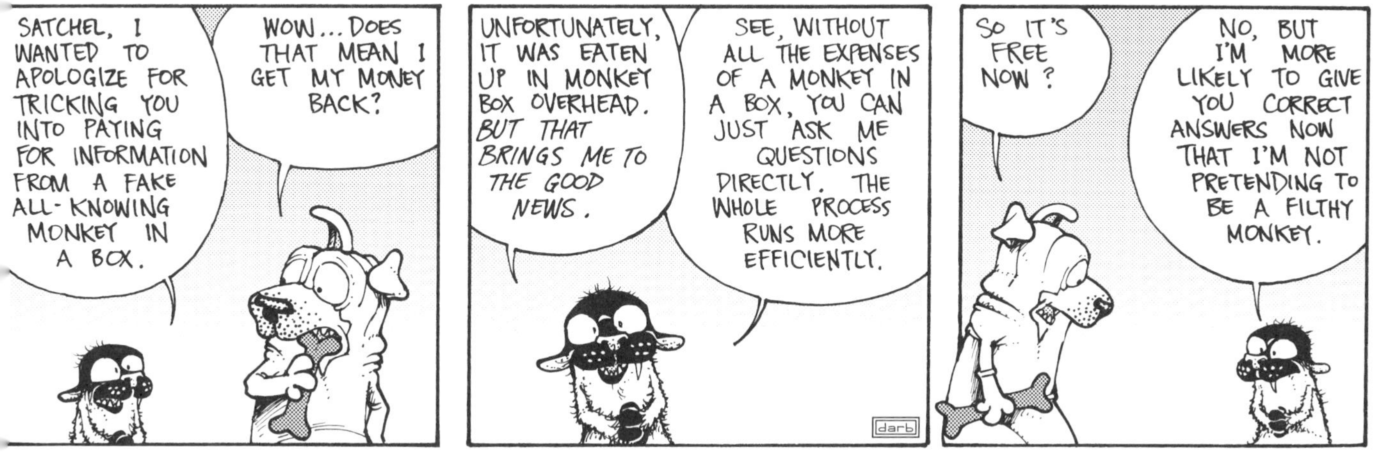
SATCHEL, I WANTED TO APOLOGIZE FOR TRICKING YOU INTO PAYING FOR INFORMATION FROM A FAKE ALL-KNOWING MONKEY IN A BOX.
WOW... DOES THAT MEAN I GET MY MONEY BACK?
UNFORTUNATELY, IT WAS EATEN UP IN MONKEY BOX OVERHEAD. BUT THAT BRINGS ME TO THE GOOD NEWS.
SEE, WITHOUT ALL THE EXPENSES OF A MONKEY IN A BOX, YOU CAN JUST ASK ME QUESTIONS DIRECTLY. THE WHOLE PROCESS RUNS MORE EFFICIENTLY.
SO IT'S FREE NOW?
NO, BUT I'M MORE LIKELY TO GIVE YOU CORRECT ANSWERS NOW THAT I'M NOT PRETENDING TO BE A FILTHY MONKEY.

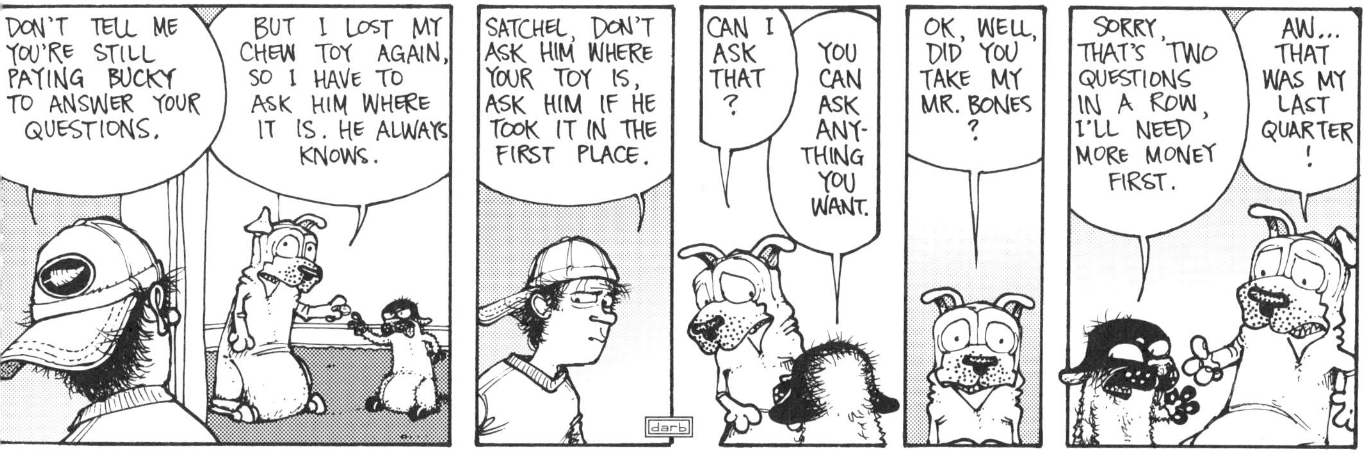
DON'T TELL ME YOU'RE STILL PAYING BUCKY TO ANSWER YOUR QUESTIONS.
BUT I LOST MY CHEW TOY AGAIN, SO I HAVE TO ASK HIM WHERE IT IS. HE ALWAYS KNOWS.
SATCHEL, DON'T ASK HIM WHERE YOUR TOY IS, ASK HIM IF HE TOOK IT IN THE FIRST PLACE.
CAN I ASK THAT?
YOU CAN ASK ANY-THING YOU WANT.
OK, WELL, DID YOU TAKE MY MR. BONES?
SORRY, THAT'S TWO QUESTIONS IN A ROW, I'LL NEED MORE MONEY FIRST.
AW... THAT WAS MY LAST QUARTER!

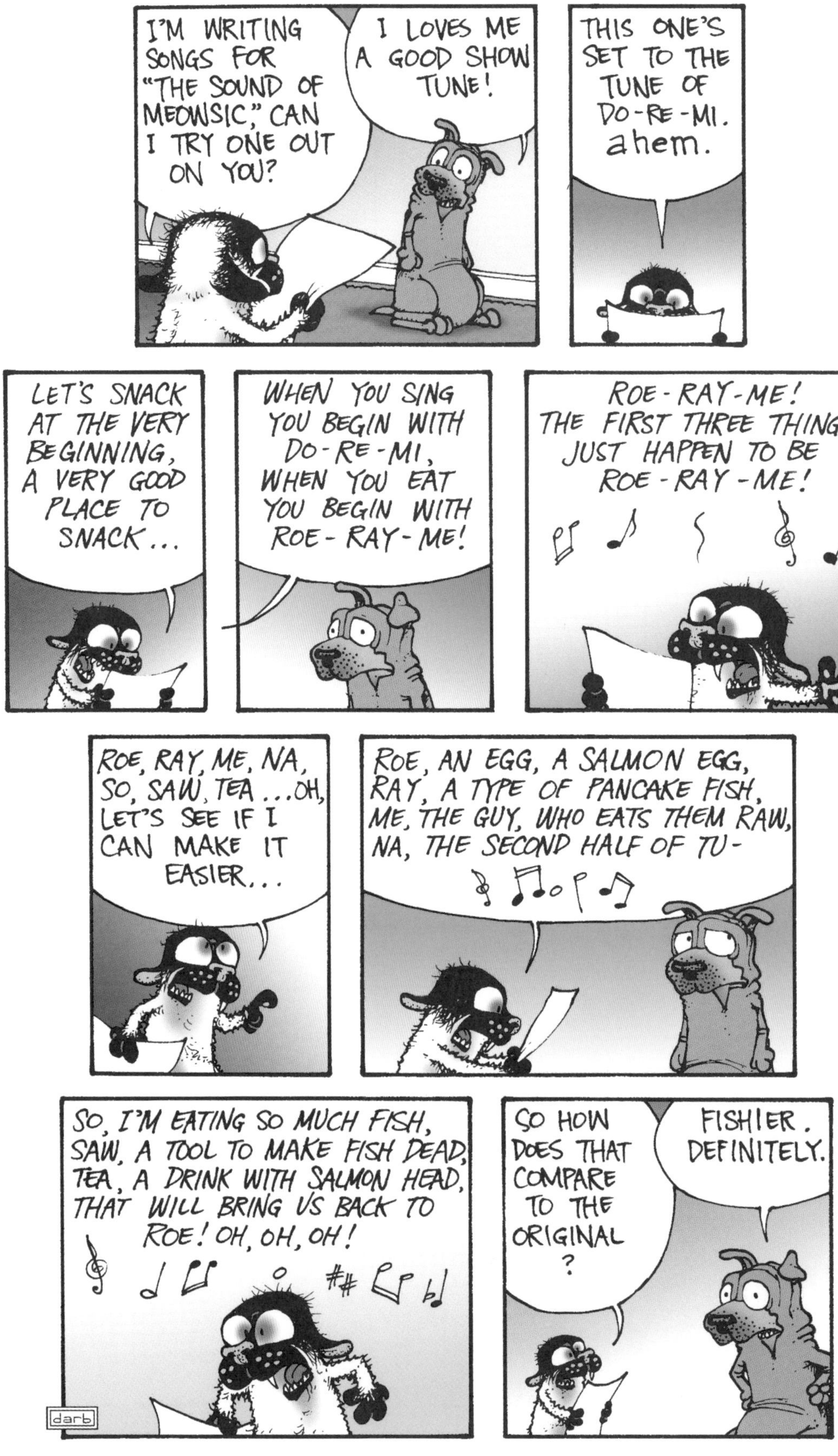

I'M WRITING SONGS FOR "THE SOUND OF MEOWSIC," CAN I TRY ONE OUT ON YOU?
I LOVES ME A GOOD SHOW TUNE!
THIS ONE'S SET TO THE TUNE OF DO-RE-MI. ahem.
LET'S SNACK AT THE VERY BEGINNING, A VERY GOOD PLACE TO SNACK...
WHEN YOU SING YOU BEGIN WITH DO-RE-MI, WHEN YOU EAT YOU BEGIN WITH ROE-RAY-ME!
ROE-RAY-ME! THE FIRST THREE THINGS JUST HAPPEN TO BE ROE-RAY-ME!
ROE, RAY, ME, NA, SO, SAW, TEA ...OH, LET'S SEE IF I CAN MAKE IT EASIER...
ROE, AN EGG, A SALMON EGG, RAY, A TYPE OF PANCAKE FISH, ME, THE GUY, WHO EATS THEM RAW, NA, THE SECOND HALF OF TU-
SO, I'M EATING SO MUCH FISH, SAW, A TOOL TO MAKE FISH DEAD, TEA, A DRINK WITH SALMON HEAD, THAT WILL BRING US BACK TO ROE! OH, OH, OH!
darb
SO HOW DOES THAT COMPARE TO THE ORIGINAL?
FISHIER. DEFINITELY.

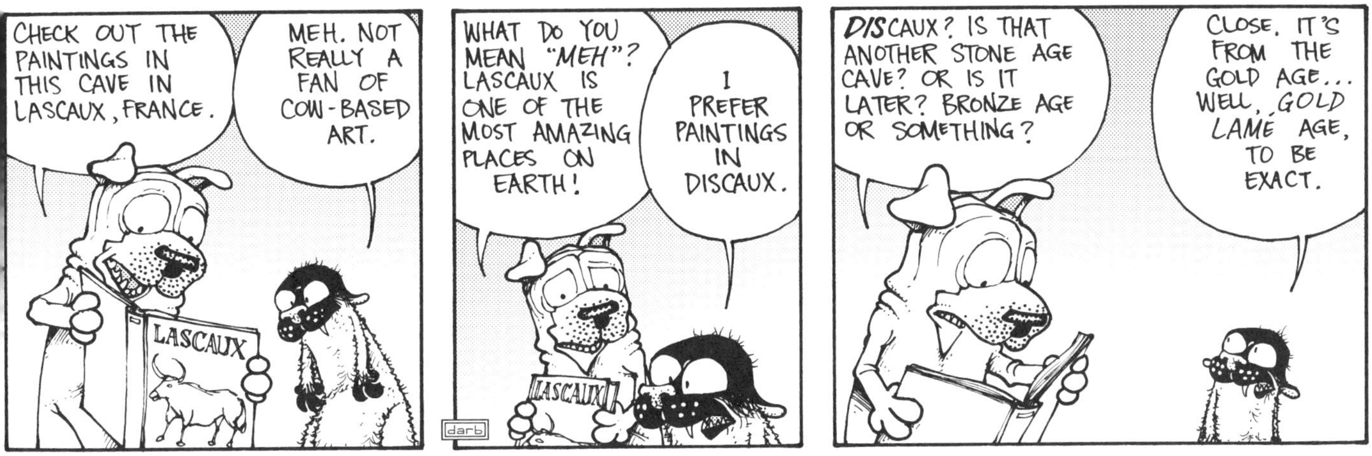
CHECK OUT THE PAINTINGS IN THIS CAVE IN LASCAUX, FRANCE.
MEH. NOT REALLY A FAN OF COW-BASED ART.
LASCAUX
darb
WHAT DO YOU MEAN "MEH"? LASCAUX IS ONE OF THE MOST AMAZING PLACES ON EARTH!
I PREFER PAINTINGS IN DISCAUX.
LASCAUX
DISCAUX? IS THAT ANOTHER STONE AGE CAVE? OR IS IT LATER? BRONZE AGE OR SOMETHING?
CLOSE. IT'S FROM THE GOLD AGE... WELL, GOLD LAMÉ AGE, TO BE EXACT.

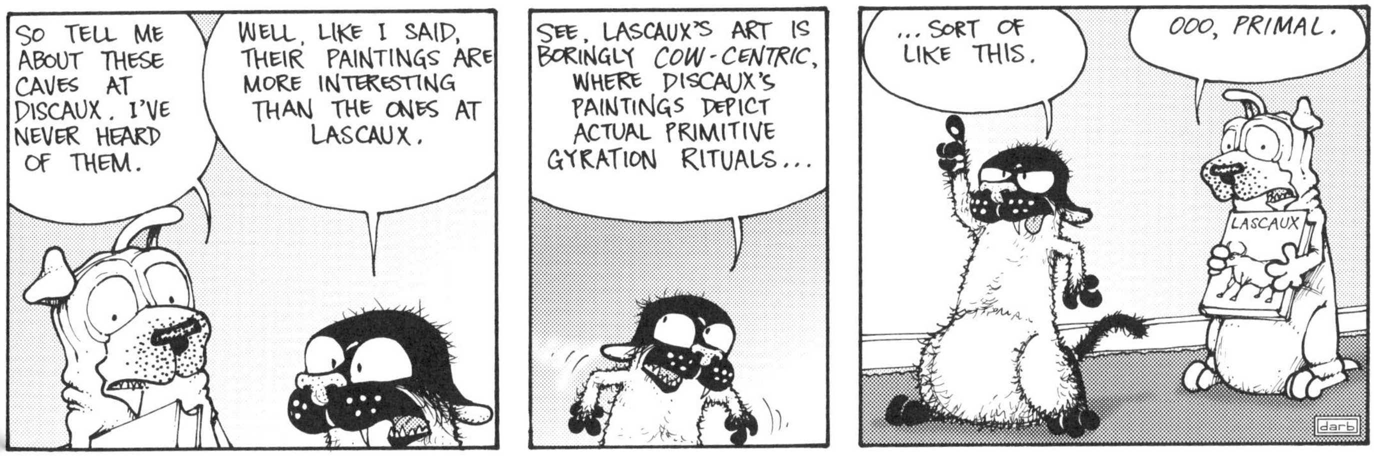
SO TELL ME ABOUT THESE CAVES AT DISCAUX. I'VE NEVER HEARD OF THEM.
WELL, LIKE I SAID, THEIR PAINTINGS ARE MORE INTERESTING THAN THE ONES AT LASCAUX.
SEE, LASCAUX'S ART IS BORINGLY COW-CENTRIC, WHERE DISCAUX'S PAINTINGS DEPICT ACTUAL PRIMITIVE GYRATION RITUALS...
...SORT OF LIKE THIS.
OOO, PRIMAL.
LASCAUX
darb

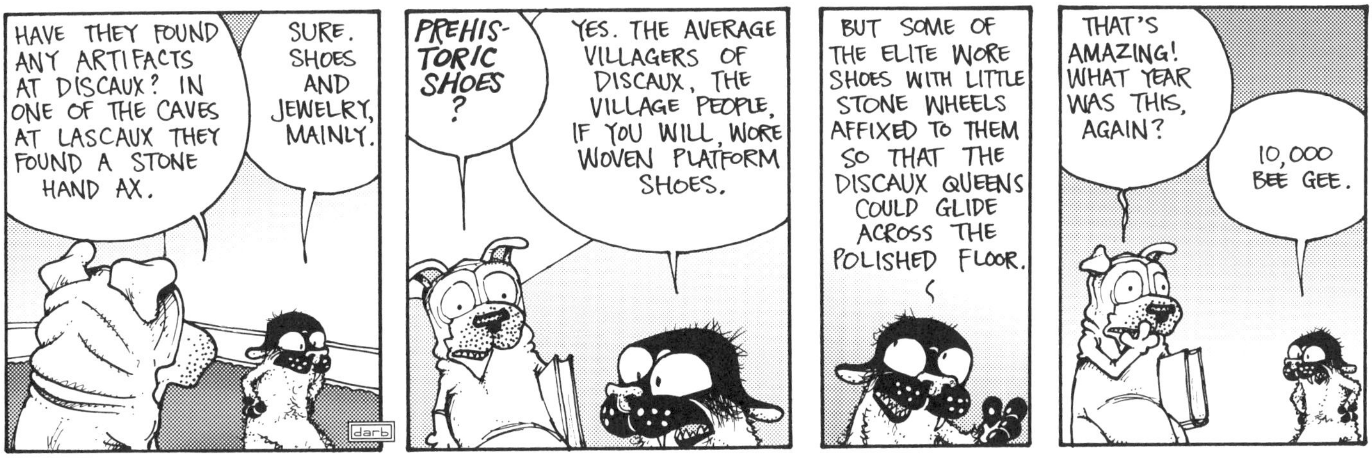
HAVE THEY FOUND ANY ARTIFACTS AT DISCAUX? IN ONE OF THE CAVES AT LASCAUX THEY FOUND A STONE HAND AX.
SURE. SHOES AND JEWELRY, MAINLY.
darb
PREHISTORIC SHOES?
YES. THE AVERAGE VILLAGERS OF DISCAUX, THE VILLAGE PEOPLE, IF YOU WILL, WORE WOVEN PLATFORM SHOES.
BUT SOME OF THE ELITE WORE SHOES WITH LITTLE STONE WHEELS AFFIXED TO THEM SO THAT THE DISCAUX QUEENS COULD GLIDE ACROSS THE POLISHED FLOOR.
THAT'S AMAZING! WHAT YEAR WAS THIS, AGAIN?
10,000 BEE GEE.

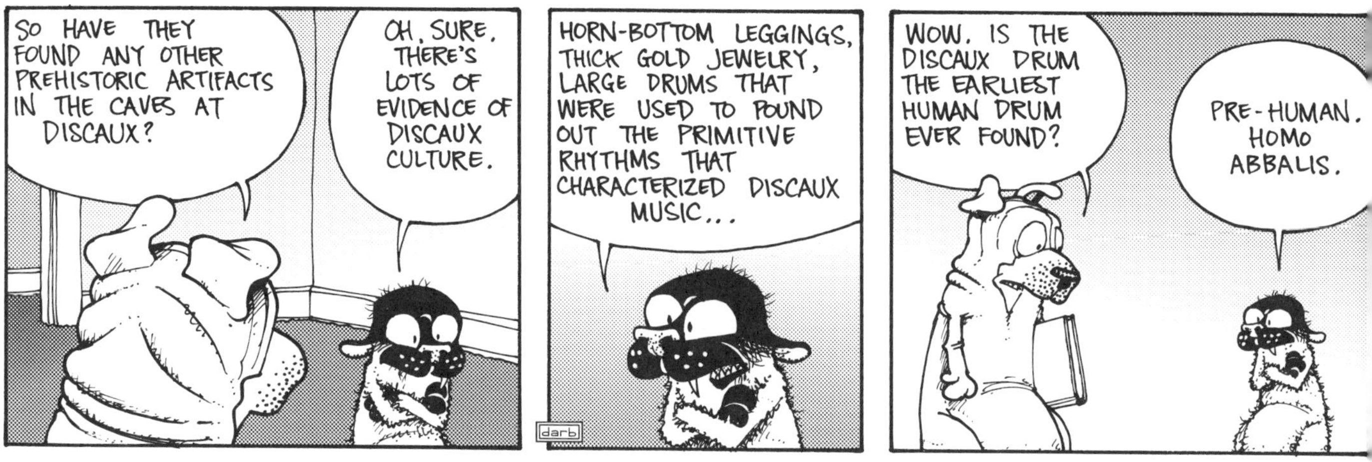
SO HAVE THEY FOUND ANY OTHER PREHISTORIC ARTIFACTS IN THE CAVES AT DISCAUX?
OH, SURE. THERE'S LOTS OF EVIDENCE OF DISCAUX CULTURE.
HORN-BOTTOM LEGGINGS, THICK GOLD JEWELRY, LARGE DRUMS THAT WERE USED TO POUND OUT THE PRIMITIVE RHYTHMS THAT CHARACTERIZED DISCAUX MUSIC...
darb
WOW. IS THE DISCAUX DRUM THE EARLIEST HUMAN DRUM EVER FOUND?
PRE-HUMAN. HOMO ABBALIS.

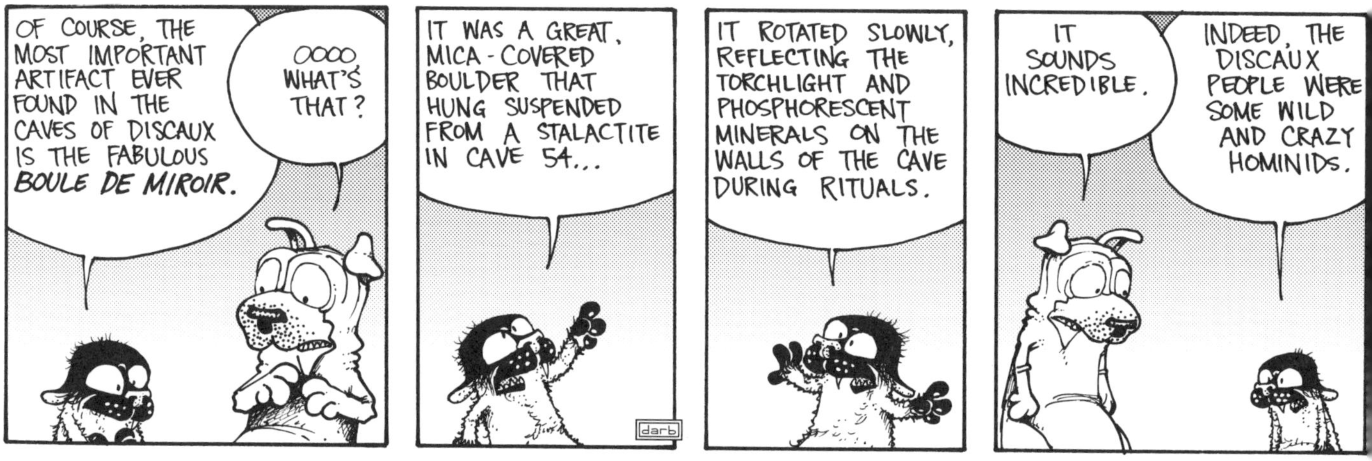
OF COURSE, THE MOST IMPORTANT ARTIFACT EVER FOUND IN THE CAVES OF DISCAUX IS THE FABULOUS *BOULE DE MIROIR*.
OOOO. WHAT'S THAT?
IT WAS A GREAT, MICA-COVERED BOULDER THAT HUNG SUSPENDED FROM A STALACTITE IN CAVE 54...
darb
IT ROTATED SLOWLY, REFLECTING THE TORCHLIGHT AND PHOSPHORESCENT MINERALS ON THE WALLS OF THE CAVE DURING RITUALS.
IT SOUNDS INCREDIBLE.
INDEED. THE DISCAUX PEOPLE WERE SOME WILD AND CRAZY HOMINIDS.

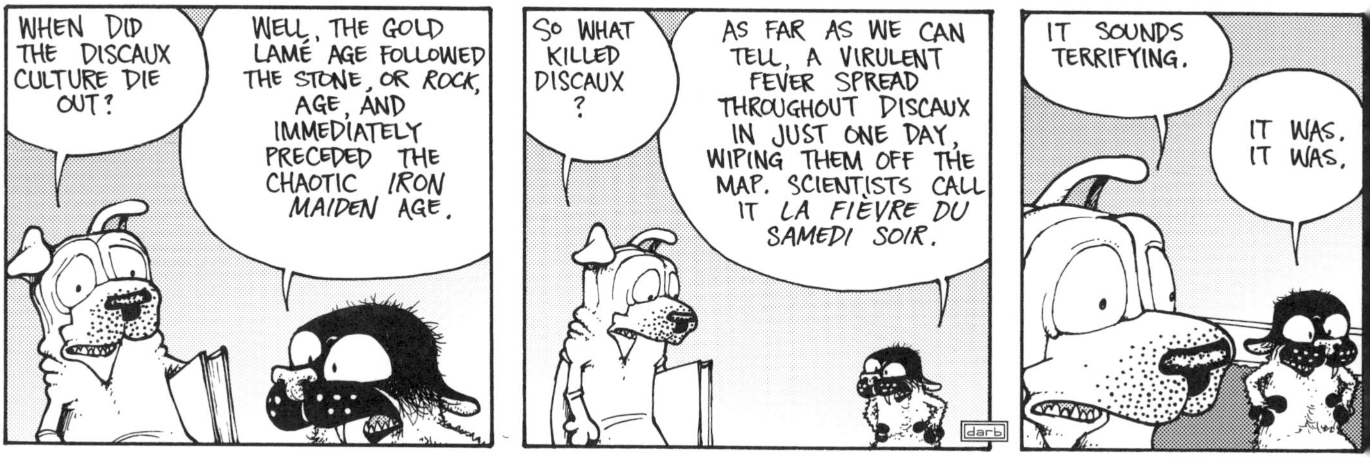
WHEN DID THE DISCAUX CULTURE DIE OUT?
WELL, THE GOLD LAMÉ AGE FOLLOWED THE STONE, OR *ROCK*, AGE, AND IMMEDIATELY PRECEDED THE CHAOTIC *IRON MAIDEN* AGE.
SO WHAT KILLED DISCAUX?
AS FAR AS WE CAN TELL, A VIRULENT FEVER SPREAD THROUGHOUT DISCAUX IN JUST ONE DAY, WIPING THEM OFF THE MAP. SCIENTISTS CALL IT *LA FIÈVRE DU SAMEDI SOIR*.
darb
IT SOUNDS TERRIFYING.
IT WAS. IT WAS.

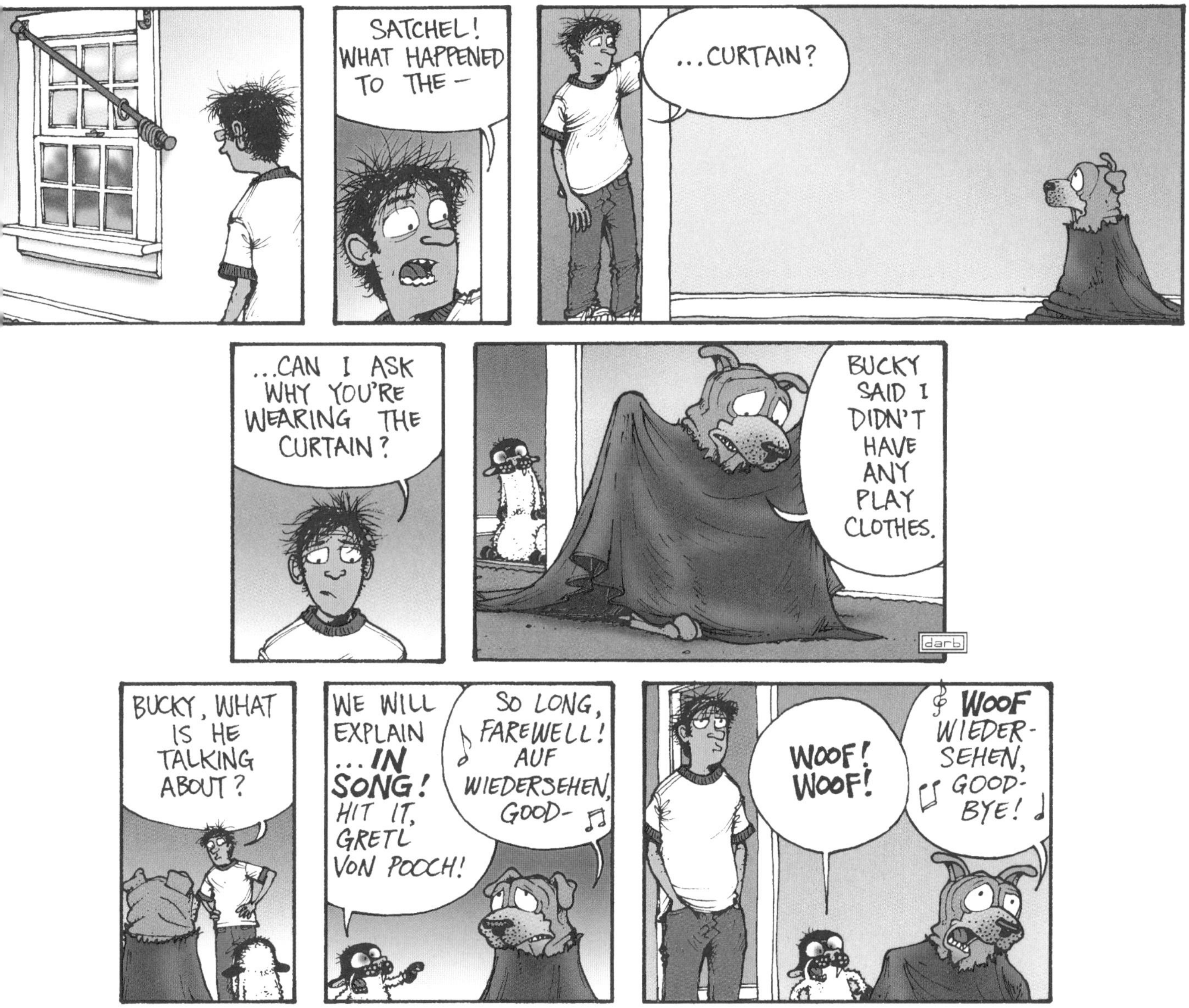
SATCHEL! WHAT HAPPENED TO THE –
...CURTAIN?
...CAN I ASK WHY YOU'RE WEARING THE CURTAIN?
BUCKY SAID I DIDN'T HAVE ANY PLAY CLOTHES.
BUCKY, WHAT IS HE TALKING ABOUT?
WE WILL EXPLAIN ...**IN SONG!** HIT IT, GRETL VON POOCH!
SO LONG, FAREWELL! AUF WIEDERSEHEN, GOOD-
WOOF! WOOF!
WOOF WIEDER-SEHEN, GOOD-BYE!

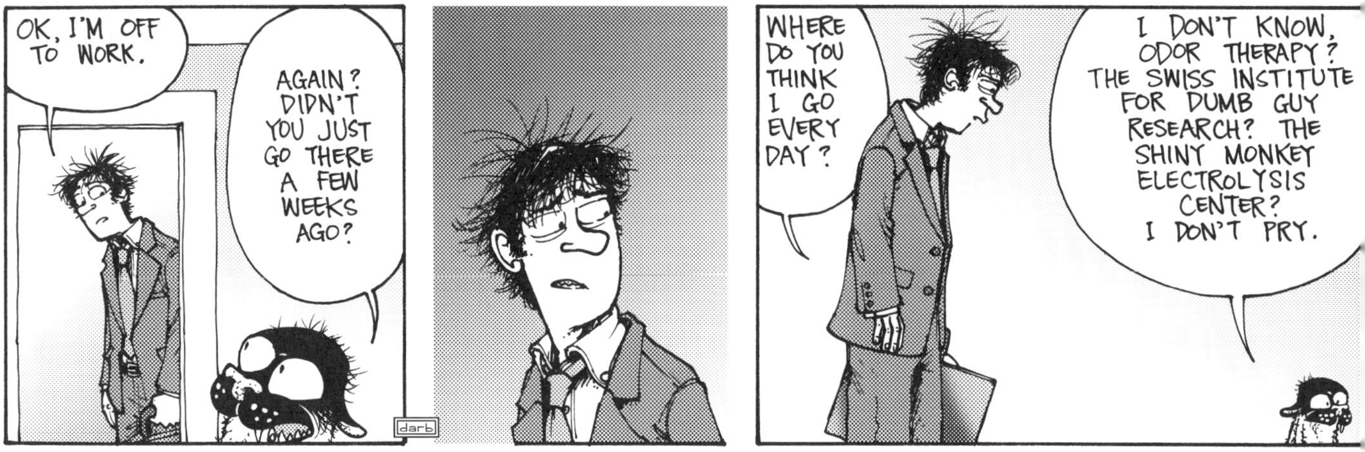
OK, I'M OFF TO WORK.
AGAIN? DIDN'T YOU JUST GO THERE A FEW WEEKS AGO?
WHERE DO YOU THINK I GO EVERY DAY?
I DON'T KNOW, ODOR THERAPY? THE SWISS INSTITUTE FOR DUMB GUY RESEARCH? THE SHINY MONKEY ELECTROLYSIS CENTER? I DON'T PRY.
darb

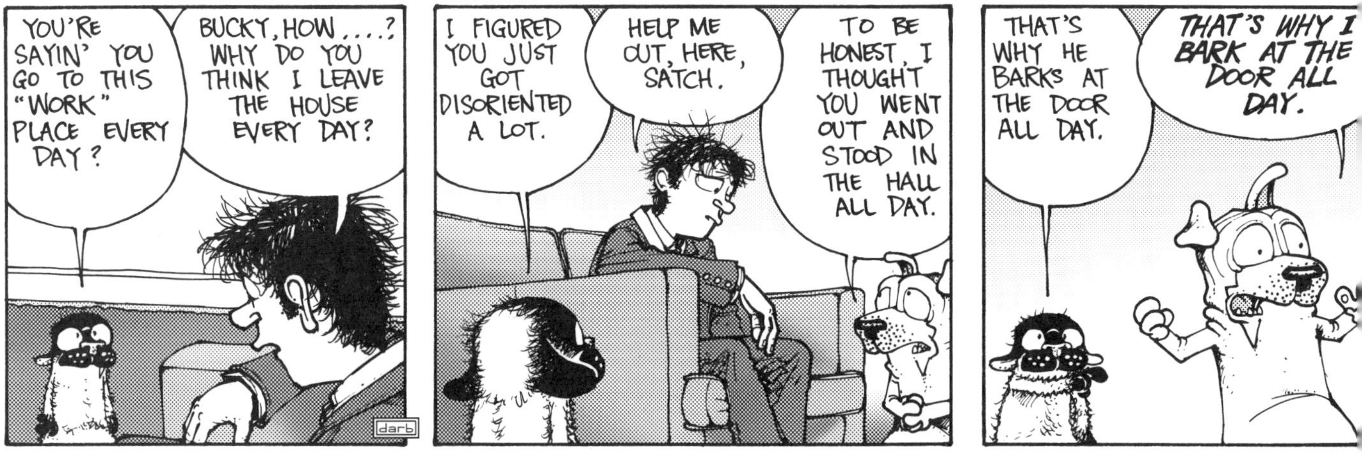
YOU'RE SAYIN' YOU GO TO THIS "WORK" PLACE EVERY DAY?
BUCKY, HOW....? WHY DO YOU THINK I LEAVE THE HOUSE EVERY DAY?
darb
I FIGURED YOU JUST GOT DISORIENTED A LOT.
HELP ME OUT, HERE, SATCH.
TO BE HONEST, I THOUGHT YOU WENT OUT AND STOOD IN THE HALL ALL DAY.
THAT'S WHY HE BARKS AT THE DOOR ALL DAY.
THAT'S WHY I BARK AT THE DOOR ALL DAY.

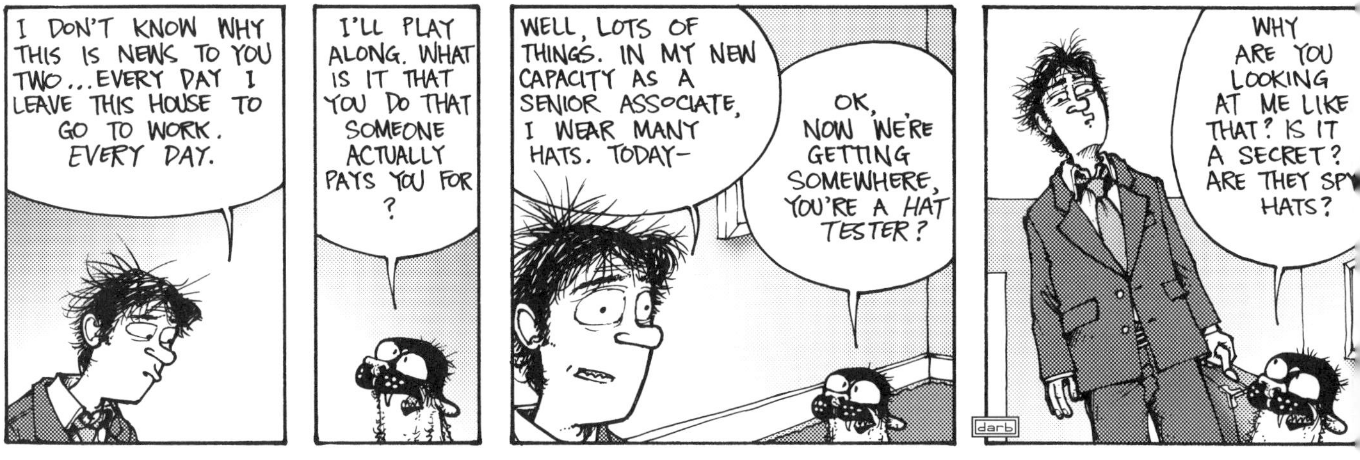
I DON'T KNOW WHY THIS IS NEWS TO YOU TWO...EVERY DAY I LEAVE THIS HOUSE TO GO TO WORK. EVERY DAY.
I'LL PLAY ALONG. WHAT IS IT THAT YOU DO THAT SOMEONE ACTUALLY PAYS YOU FOR?
WELL, LOTS OF THINGS. IN MY NEW CAPACITY AS A SENIOR ASSOCIATE, I WEAR MANY HATS. TODAY-
OK, NOW WE'RE GETTING SOMEWHERE, YOU'RE A HAT TESTER?
WHY ARE YOU LOOKING AT ME LIKE THAT? IS IT A SECRET? ARE THEY SPY HATS?
darb

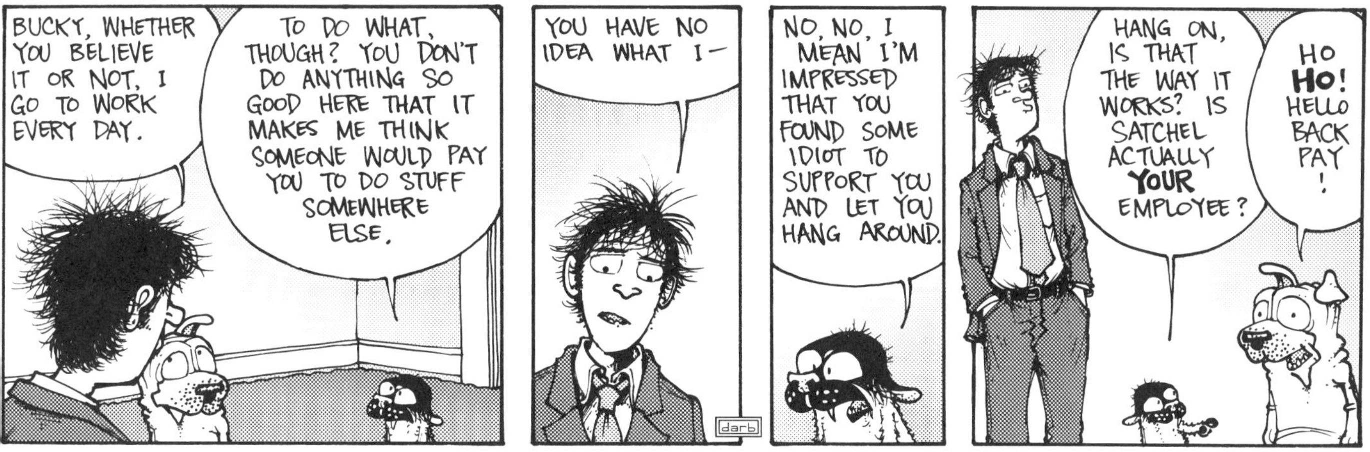
BUCKY, WHETHER YOU BELIEVE IT OR NOT, I GO TO WORK EVERY DAY.
TO DO WHAT, THOUGH? YOU DON'T DO ANYTHING SO GOOD HERE THAT IT MAKES ME THINK SOMEONE WOULD PAY YOU TO DO STUFF SOMEWHERE ELSE.
YOU HAVE NO IDEA WHAT I—
NO, NO, I MEAN I'M IMPRESSED THAT YOU FOUND SOME IDIOT TO SUPPORT YOU AND LET YOU HANG AROUND.
HANG ON, IS THAT THE WAY IT WORKS? IS SATCHEL ACTUALLY **YOUR** EMPLOYEE?
HO **HO**! HELLO BACK PAY!

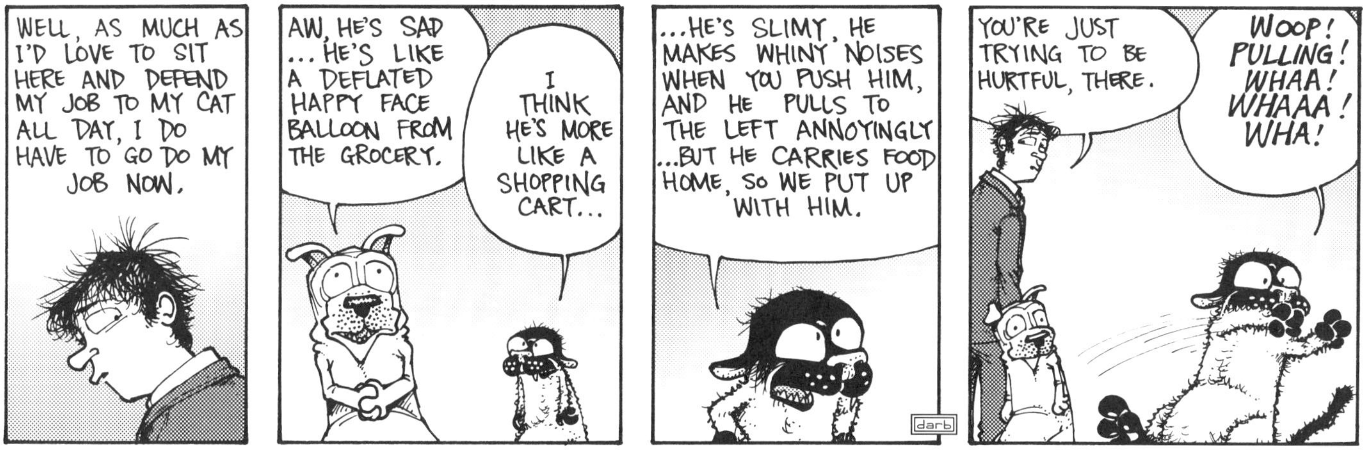
WELL, AS MUCH AS I'D LOVE TO SIT HERE AND DEFEND MY JOB TO MY CAT ALL DAY, I DO HAVE TO GO DO MY JOB NOW.
AW, HE'S SAD ... HE'S LIKE A DEFLATED HAPPY FACE BALLOON FROM THE GROCERY.
I THINK HE'S MORE LIKE A SHOPPING CART...
...HE'S SLIMY, HE MAKES WHINY NOISES WHEN YOU PUSH HIM, AND HE PULLS TO THE LEFT ANNOYINGLY ...BUT HE CARRIES FOOD HOME, SO WE PUT UP WITH HIM.
YOU'RE JUST TRYING TO BE HURTFUL, THERE.
WOOP! PULLING! WHAA! WHAAA! WHA!

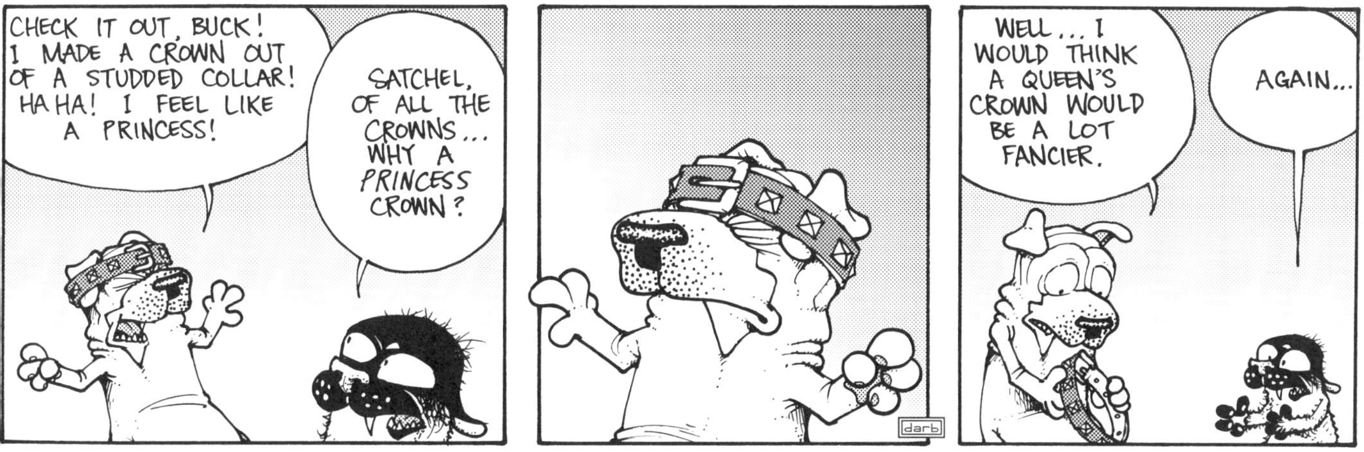
CHECK IT OUT, BUCK! I MADE A CROWN OUT OF A STUDDED COLLAR! HA HA! I FEEL LIKE A PRINCESS!
SATCHEL, OF ALL THE CROWNS... WHY A *PRINCESS* CROWN?
WELL... I WOULD THINK A QUEEN'S CROWN WOULD BE A LOT FANCIER.
AGAIN...

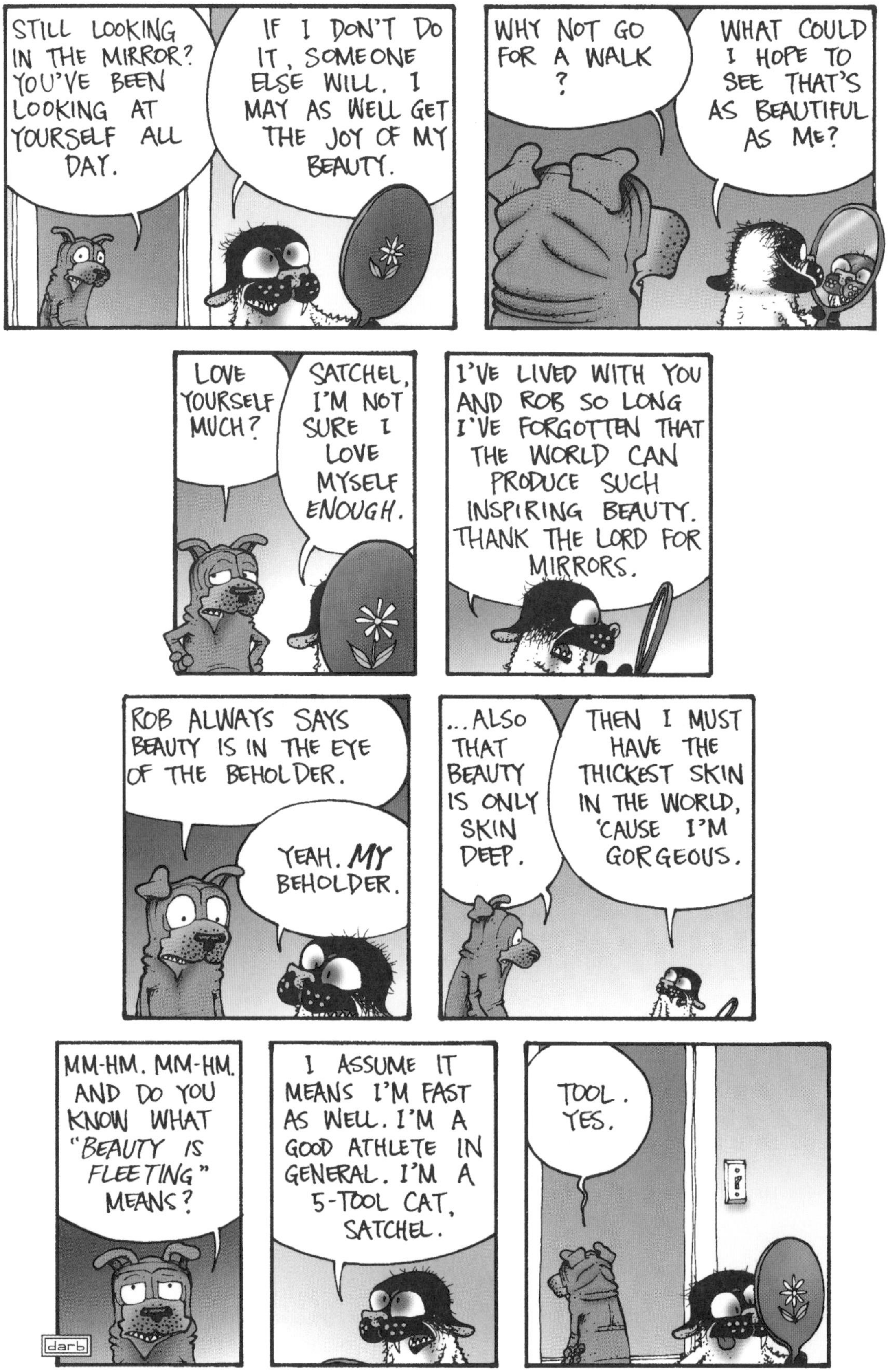
STILL LOOKING IN THE MIRROR? YOU'VE BEEN LOOKING AT YOURSELF ALL DAY.
IF I DON'T DO IT, SOMEONE ELSE WILL. I MAY AS WELL GET THE JOY OF MY BEAUTY.
WHY NOT GO FOR A WALK?
WHAT COULD I HOPE TO SEE THAT'S AS BEAUTIFUL AS ME?
LOVE YOURSELF MUCH?
SATCHEL, I'M NOT SURE I LOVE MYSELF ENOUGH.
I'VE LIVED WITH YOU AND ROB SO LONG I'VE FORGOTTEN THAT THE WORLD CAN PRODUCE SUCH INSPIRING BEAUTY. THANK THE LORD FOR MIRRORS.
ROB ALWAYS SAYS BEAUTY IS IN THE EYE OF THE BEHOLDER.
YEAH. MY BEHOLDER.
...ALSO THAT BEAUTY IS ONLY SKIN DEEP.
THEN I MUST HAVE THE THICKEST SKIN IN THE WORLD, 'CAUSE I'M GORGEOUS.
MM-HM. MM-HM. AND DO YOU KNOW WHAT "BEAUTY IS FLEETING" MEANS?
darb
I ASSUME IT MEANS I'M FAST AS WELL. I'M A GOOD ATHLETE IN GENERAL. I'M A 5-TOOL CAT, SATCHEL.
TOOL. YES.

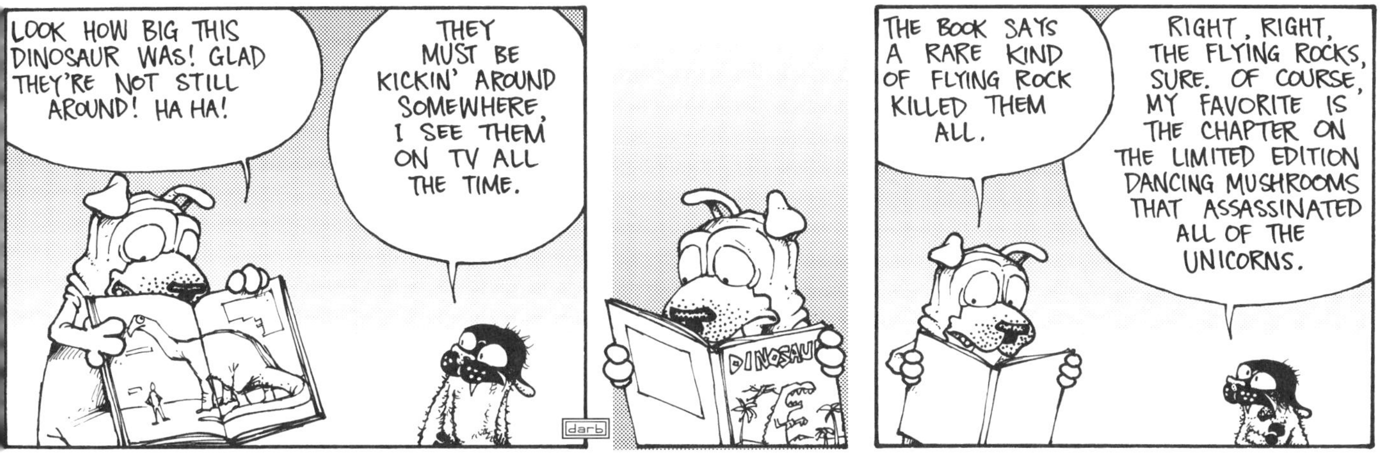
LOOK HOW BIG THIS DINOSAUR WAS! GLAD THEY'RE NOT STILL AROUND! HA HA!
THEY MUST BE KICKIN' AROUND SOMEWHERE, I SEE THEM ON TV ALL THE TIME.
DINOSAUR
THE BOOK SAYS A RARE KIND OF FLYING ROCK KILLED THEM ALL.
RIGHT, RIGHT, THE FLYING ROCKS, SURE. OF COURSE, MY FAVORITE IS THE CHAPTER ON THE LIMITED EDITION DANCING MUSHROOMS THAT ASSASSINATED ALL OF THE UNICORNS.

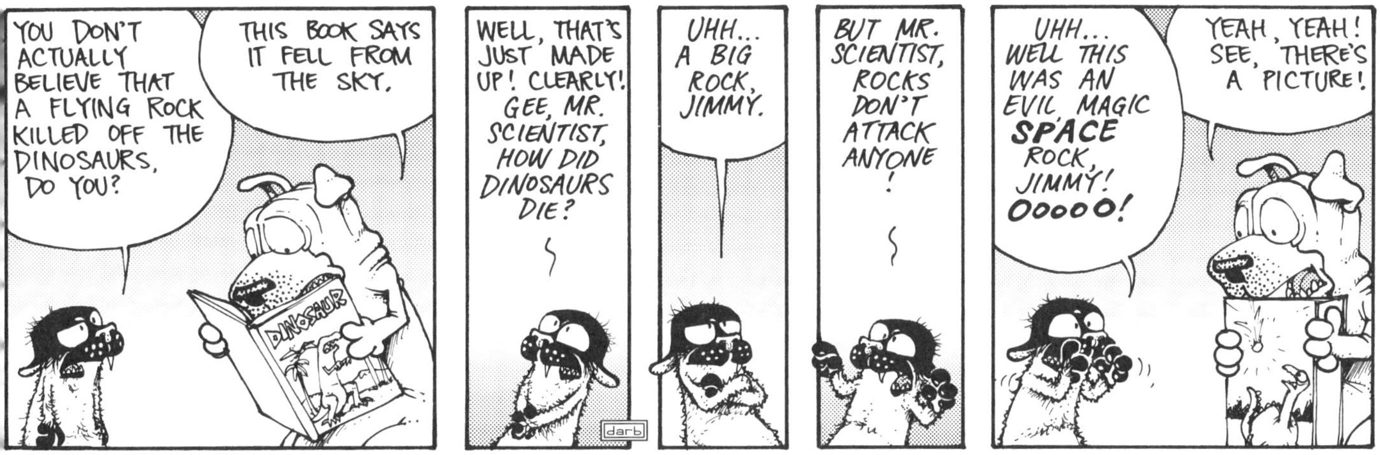
YOU DON'T ACTUALLY BELIEVE THAT A FLYING ROCK KILLED OFF THE DINOSAURS, DO YOU?
THIS BOOK SAYS IT FELL FROM THE SKY.
DINOSAUR
WELL, THAT'S JUST MADE UP! CLEARLY! GEE, MR. SCIENTIST, HOW DID DINOSAURS DIE?
UHH... A BIG ROCK, JIMMY.
BUT MR. SCIENTIST, ROCKS DON'T ATTACK ANYONE!
UHH... WELL THIS WAS AN EVIL MAGIC SPACE ROCK, JIMMY! OOOOO!
YEAH, YEAH! SEE, THERE'S A PICTURE!

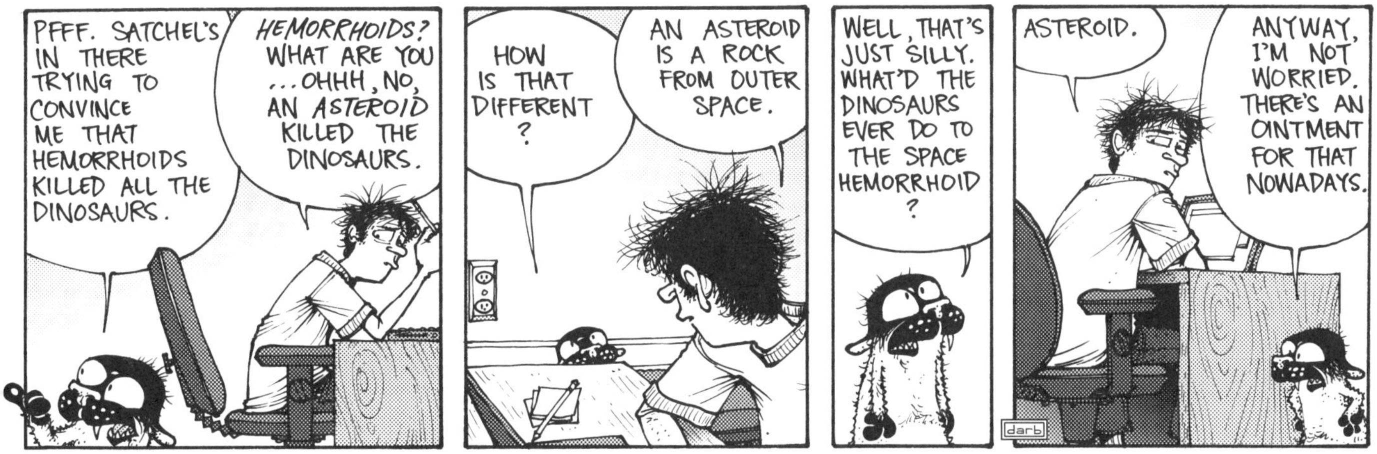
PFFF. SATCHEL'S IN THERE TRYING TO CONVINCE ME THAT HEMORRHOIDS KILLED ALL THE DINOSAURS.
HEMORRHOIDS? WHAT ARE YOU ...OHHH, NO, AN ASTEROID KILLED THE DINOSAURS.
HOW IS THAT DIFFERENT?
AN ASTEROID IS A ROCK FROM OUTER SPACE.
WELL, THAT'S JUST SILLY. WHAT'D THE DINOSAURS EVER DO TO THE SPACE HEMORRHOID?
ASTEROID.
ANYWAY, I'M NOT WORRIED. THERE'S AN OINTMENT FOR THAT NOWADAYS.

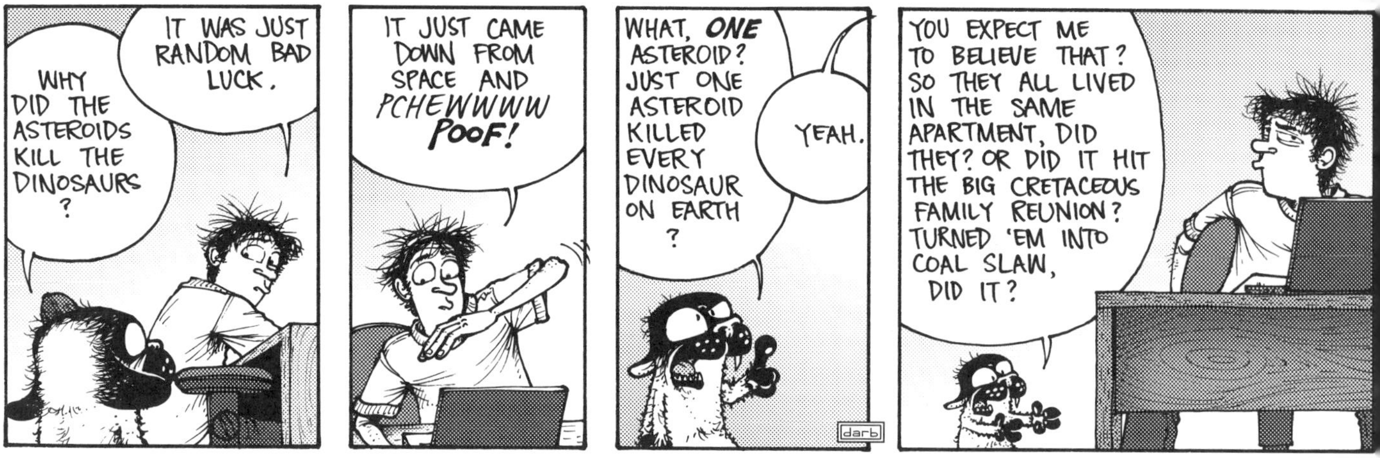
WHY DID THE ASTEROIDS KILL THE DINOSAURS?
IT WAS JUST RANDOM BAD LUCK.
IT JUST CAME DOWN FROM SPACE AND PCHEWWWW POOF!
WHAT, ONE ASTEROID? JUST ONE ASTEROID KILLED EVERY DINOSAUR ON EARTH?
YEAH.
YOU EXPECT ME TO BELIEVE THAT? SO THEY ALL LIVED IN THE SAME APARTMENT, DID THEY? OR DID IT HIT THE BIG CRETACEOUS FAMILY REUNION? TURNED 'EM INTO COAL SLAW, DID IT?
darb

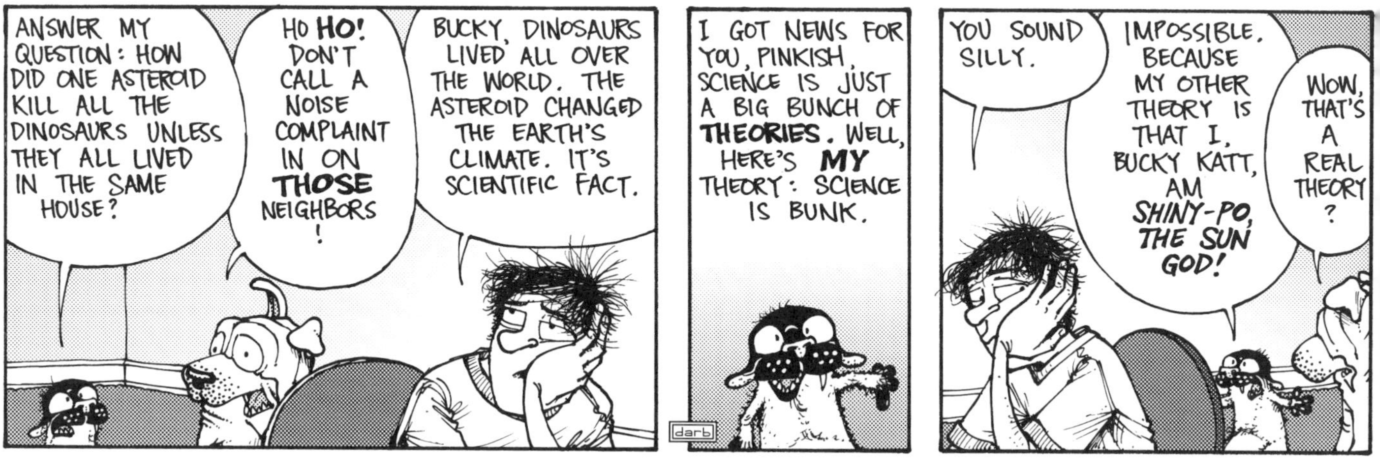
ANSWER MY QUESTION: HOW DID ONE ASTEROID KILL ALL THE DINOSAURS UNLESS THEY ALL LIVED IN THE SAME HOUSE?
HO HO! DON'T CALL A NOISE COMPLAINT IN ON THOSE NEIGHBORS!
BUCKY, DINOSAURS LIVED ALL OVER THE WORLD. THE ASTEROID CHANGED THE EARTH'S CLIMATE. IT'S SCIENTIFIC FACT.
I GOT NEWS FOR YOU, PINKISH, SCIENCE IS JUST A BIG BUNCH OF THEORIES. WELL, HERE'S MY THEORY: SCIENCE IS BUNK.
YOU SOUND SILLY.
IMPOSSIBLE. BECAUSE MY OTHER THEORY IS THAT I, BUCKY KATT, AM SHINY-PO, THE SUN GOD!
WOW, THAT'S A REAL THEORY?
darb

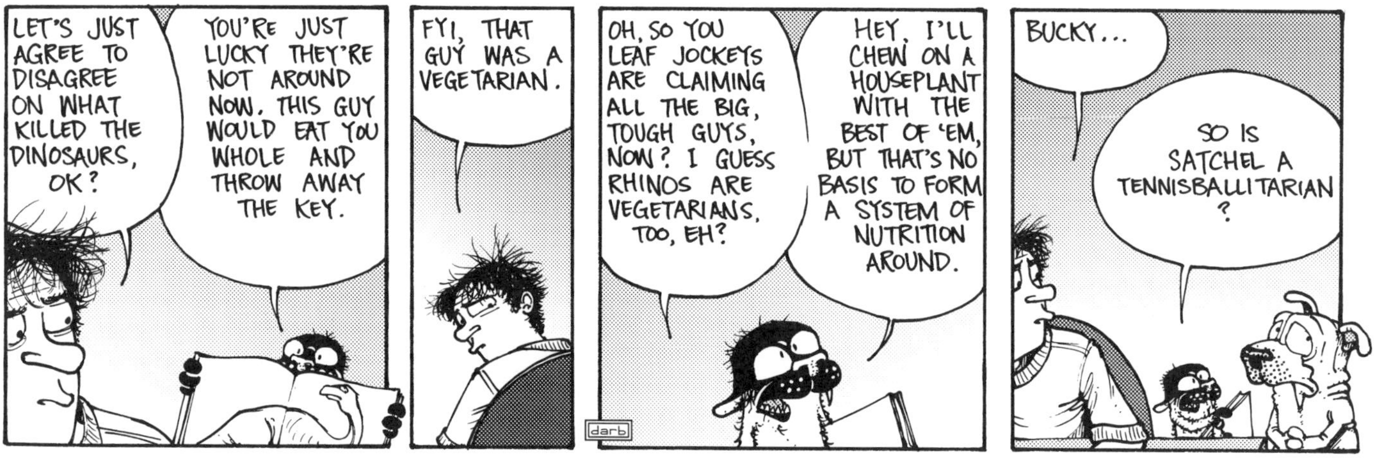
LET'S JUST AGREE TO DISAGREE ON WHAT KILLED THE DINOSAURS, OK?
YOU'RE JUST LUCKY THEY'RE NOT AROUND NOW. THIS GUY WOULD EAT YOU WHOLE AND THROW AWAY THE KEY.
FYI, THAT GUY WAS A VEGETARIAN.
OH, SO YOU LEAF JOCKEYS ARE CLAIMING ALL THE BIG, TOUGH GUYS, NOW? I GUESS RHINOS ARE VEGETARIANS, TOO, EH?
HEY, I'LL CHEW ON A HOUSEPLANT WITH THE BEST OF 'EM, BUT THAT'S NO BASIS TO FORM A SYSTEM OF NUTRITION AROUND.
BUCKY...
SO IS SATCHEL A TENNISBALLITARIAN?
darb

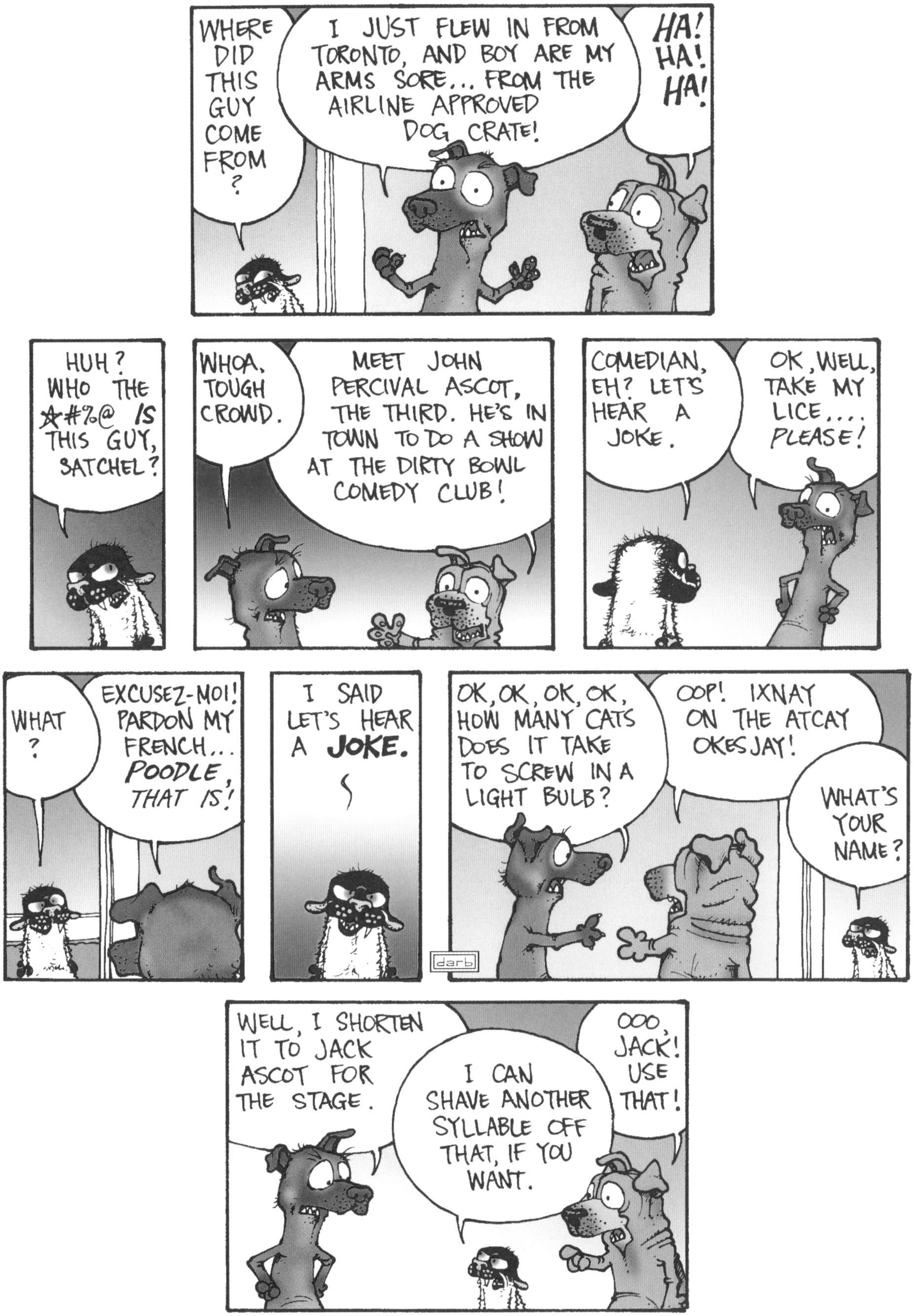
WHERE DID THIS GUY COME FROM ?
I JUST FLEW IN FROM TORONTO, AND BOY ARE MY ARMS SORE... FROM THE AIRLINE APPROVED DOG CRATE!
HA! HA! HA!
HUH? WHO THE ★#%@ IS THIS GUY, SATCHEL?
WHOA. TOUGH CROWD.
MEET JOHN PERCIVAL ASCOT, THE THIRD. HE'S IN TOWN TO DO A SHOW AT THE DIRTY BOWL COMEDY CLUB!
COMEDIAN, EH? LET'S HEAR A JOKE.
OK, WELL, TAKE MY LICE.... PLEASE!
WHAT ?
EXCUSEZ-MOI! PARDON MY FRENCH... POODLE, THAT IS!
I SAID LET'S HEAR A JOKE.
OK, OK, OK, OK, HOW MANY CATS DOES IT TAKE TO SCREW IN A LIGHT BULB?
OOP! IXNAY ON THE ATCAY OKESJAY!
WHAT'S YOUR NAME?
darb
WELL, I SHORTEN IT TO JACK ASCOT FOR THE STAGE.
I CAN SHAVE ANOTHER SYLLABLE OFF THAT, IF YOU WANT.
OOO, JACK! USE THAT!

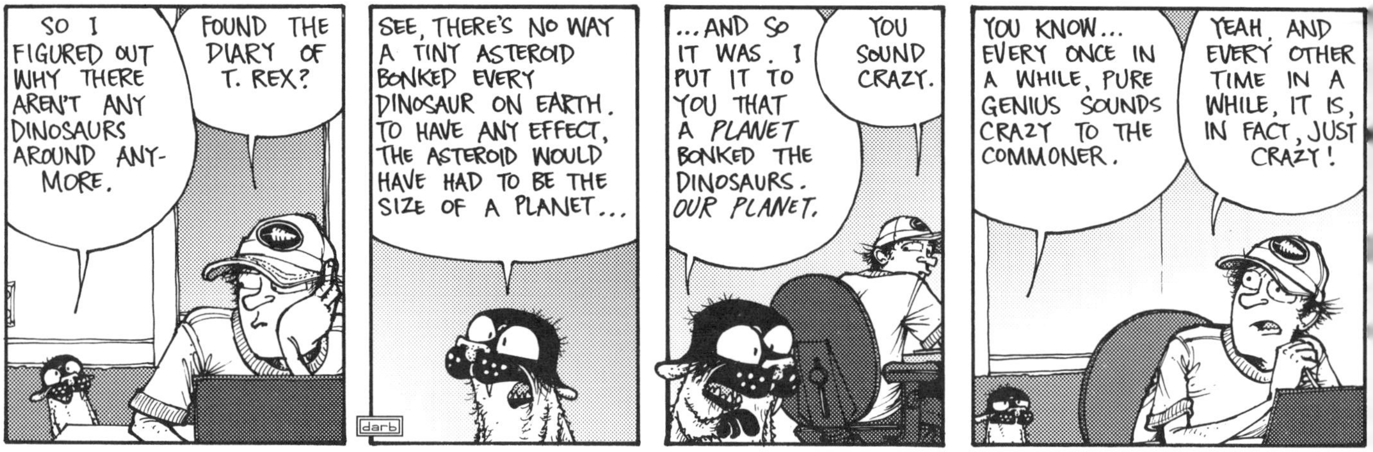
SO I FIGURED OUT WHY THERE AREN'T ANY DINOSAURS AROUND ANY-MORE.
FOUND THE DIARY OF T. REX?
SEE, THERE'S NO WAY A TINY ASTEROID BONKED EVERY DINOSAUR ON EARTH. TO HAVE ANY EFFECT, THE ASTEROID WOULD HAVE HAD TO BE THE SIZE OF A PLANET...
darb
...AND SO IT WAS. I PUT IT TO YOU THAT A *PLANET* BONKED THE DINOSAURS. *OUR PLANET.*
YOU SOUND CRAZY.
YOU KNOW... EVERY ONCE IN A WHILE, PURE GENIUS SOUNDS CRAZY TO THE COMMONER.
YEAH, AND EVERY OTHER TIME IN A WHILE, IT IS, IN FACT, JUST CRAZY!

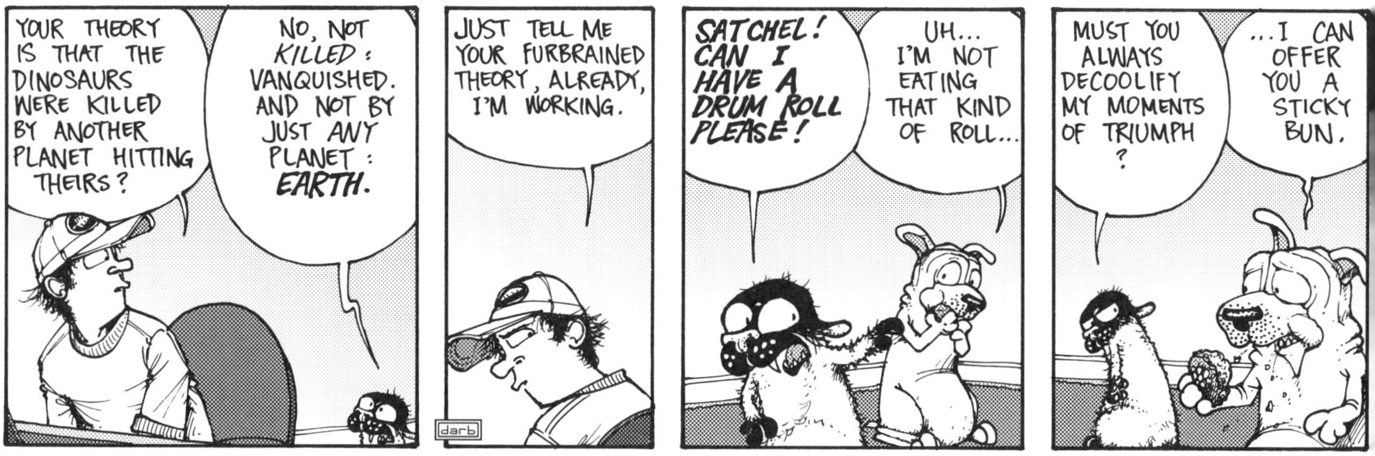
YOUR THEORY IS THAT THE DINOSAURS WERE KILLED BY ANOTHER PLANET HITTING THEIRS?
NO, NOT *KILLED*: VANQUISHED. AND NOT BY JUST *ANY* PLANET: ***EARTH.***
JUST TELL ME YOUR FURBRAINED THEORY, ALREADY, I'M WORKING.
darb
SATCHEL! CAN I HAVE A DRUM ROLL PLEASE!
UH... I'M NOT EATING THAT KIND OF ROLL...
MUST YOU ALWAYS DECOOLIFY MY MOMENTS OF TRIUMPH?
...I CAN OFFER YOU A STICKY BUN.

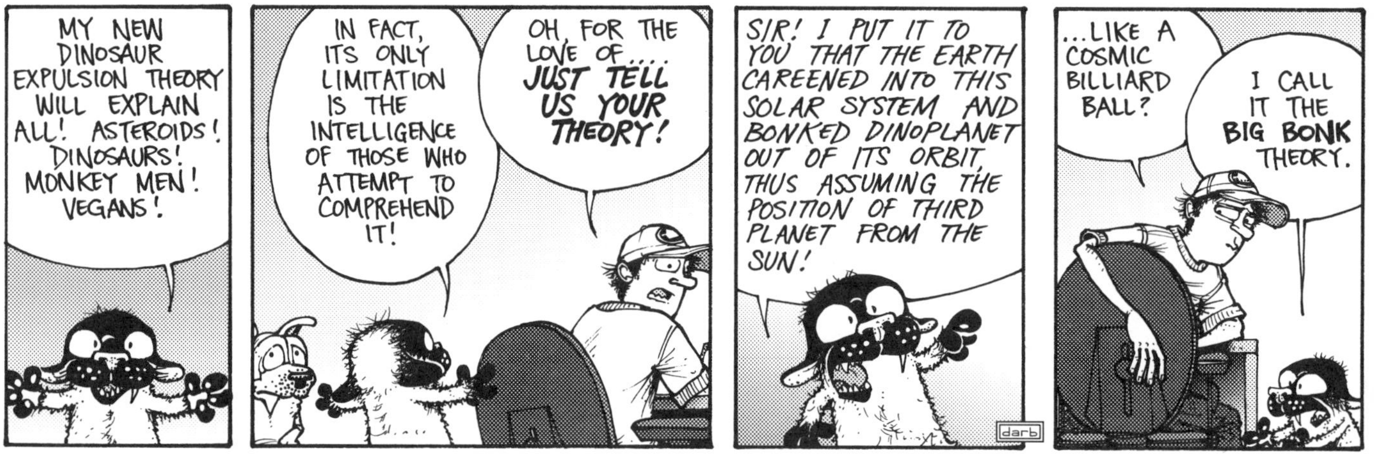
MY NEW DINOSAUR EXPULSION THEORY WILL EXPLAIN ALL! ASTEROIDS! DINOSAURS! MONKEY MEN! VEGANS!
IN FACT, ITS ONLY LIMITATION IS THE INTELLIGENCE OF THOSE WHO ATTEMPT TO COMPREHEND IT!
OH, FOR THE LOVE OF.... **JUST TELL US YOUR THEORY!**
SIR! I PUT IT TO YOU THAT THE EARTH CAREENED INTO THIS SOLAR SYSTEM AND BONKED DINOPLANET OUT OF ITS ORBIT, THUS ASSUMING THE POSITION OF THIRD PLANET FROM THE SUN!
darb
...LIKE A COSMIC BILLIARD BALL?
I CALL IT THE **BIG BONK** THEORY.

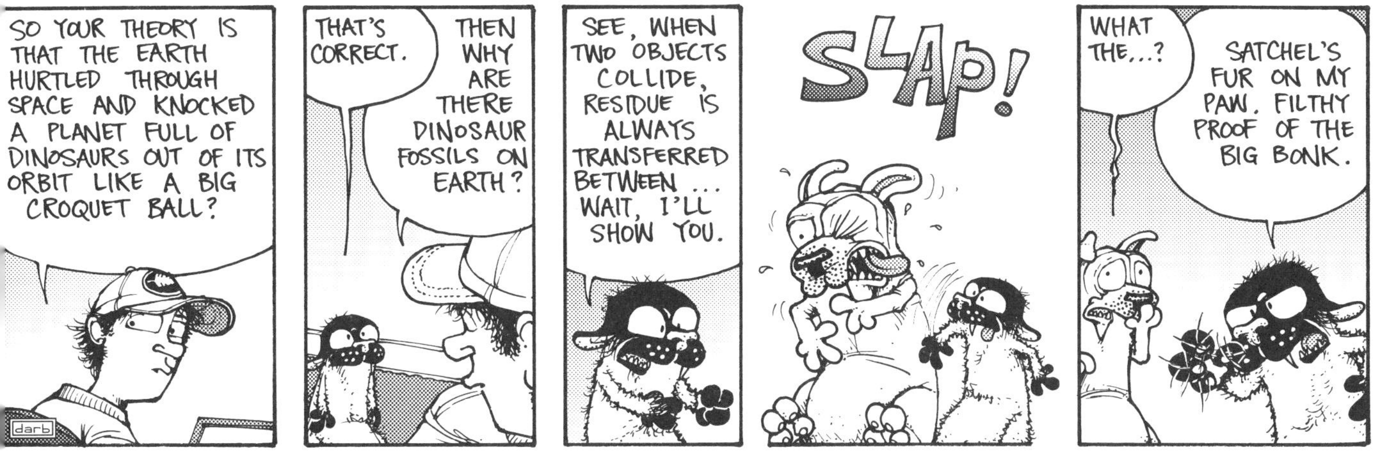
SO YOUR THEORY IS THAT THE EARTH HURTLED THROUGH SPACE AND KNOCKED A PLANET FULL OF DINOSAURS OUT OF ITS ORBIT LIKE A BIG CROQUET BALL?
THAT'S CORRECT.
THEN WHY ARE THERE DINOSAUR FOSSILS ON EARTH?
SEE, WHEN TWO OBJECTS COLLIDE, RESIDUE IS ALWAYS TRANSFERRED BETWEEN ... WAIT, I'LL SHOW YOU.
SLAP!
WHAT THE...?
SATCHEL'S FUR ON MY PAW. FILTHY PROOF OF THE BIG BONK.
darb

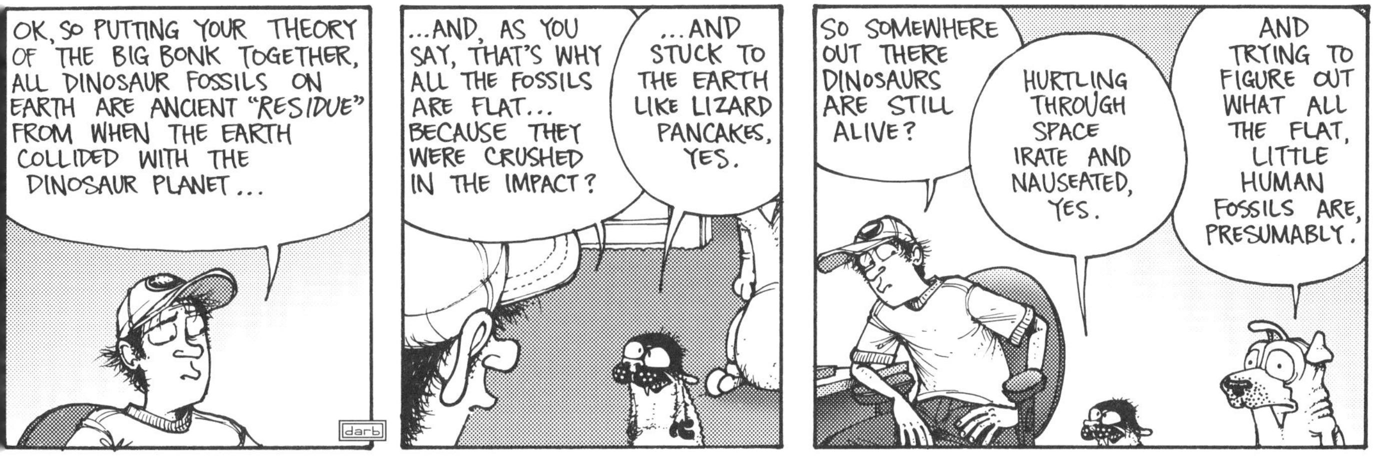
OK, SO PUTTING YOUR THEORY OF THE BIG BONK TOGETHER, ALL DINOSAUR FOSSILS ON EARTH ARE ANCIENT "RESIDUE" FROM WHEN THE EARTH COLLIDED WITH THE DINOSAUR PLANET...
...AND, AS YOU SAY, THAT'S WHY ALL THE FOSSILS ARE FLAT... BECAUSE THEY WERE CRUSHED IN THE IMPACT?
...AND STUCK TO THE EARTH LIKE LIZARD PANCAKES, YES.
SO SOMEWHERE OUT THERE DINOSAURS ARE STILL ALIVE?
HURTLING THROUGH SPACE IRATE AND NAUSEATED, YES.
AND TRYING TO FIGURE OUT WHAT ALL THE FLAT, LITTLE HUMAN FOSSILS ARE, PRESUMABLY.
darb

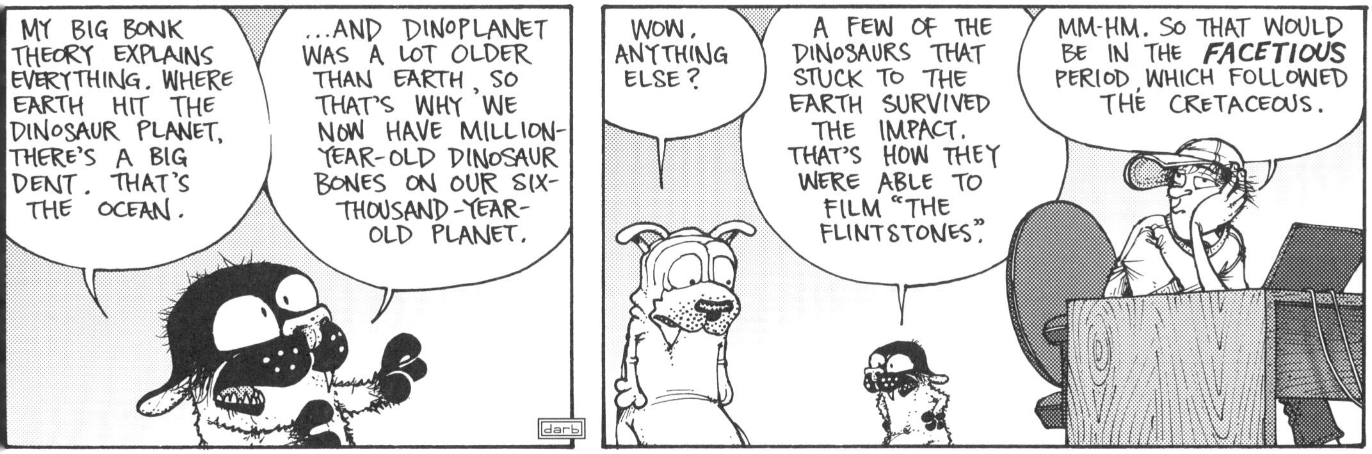
MY BIG BONK THEORY EXPLAINS EVERYTHING. WHERE EARTH HIT THE DINOSAUR PLANET, THERE'S A BIG DENT. THAT'S THE OCEAN.
...AND DINOPLANET WAS A LOT OLDER THAN EARTH, SO THAT'S WHY WE NOW HAVE MILLION-YEAR-OLD DINOSAUR BONES ON OUR SIX-THOUSAND-YEAR-OLD PLANET.
WOW. ANYTHING ELSE?
A FEW OF THE DINOSAURS THAT STUCK TO THE EARTH SURVIVED THE IMPACT. THAT'S HOW THEY WERE ABLE TO FILM "THE FLINTSTONES."
MM-HM. SO THAT WOULD BE IN THE FACETIOUS PERIOD, WHICH FOLLOWED THE CRETACEOUS.
darb

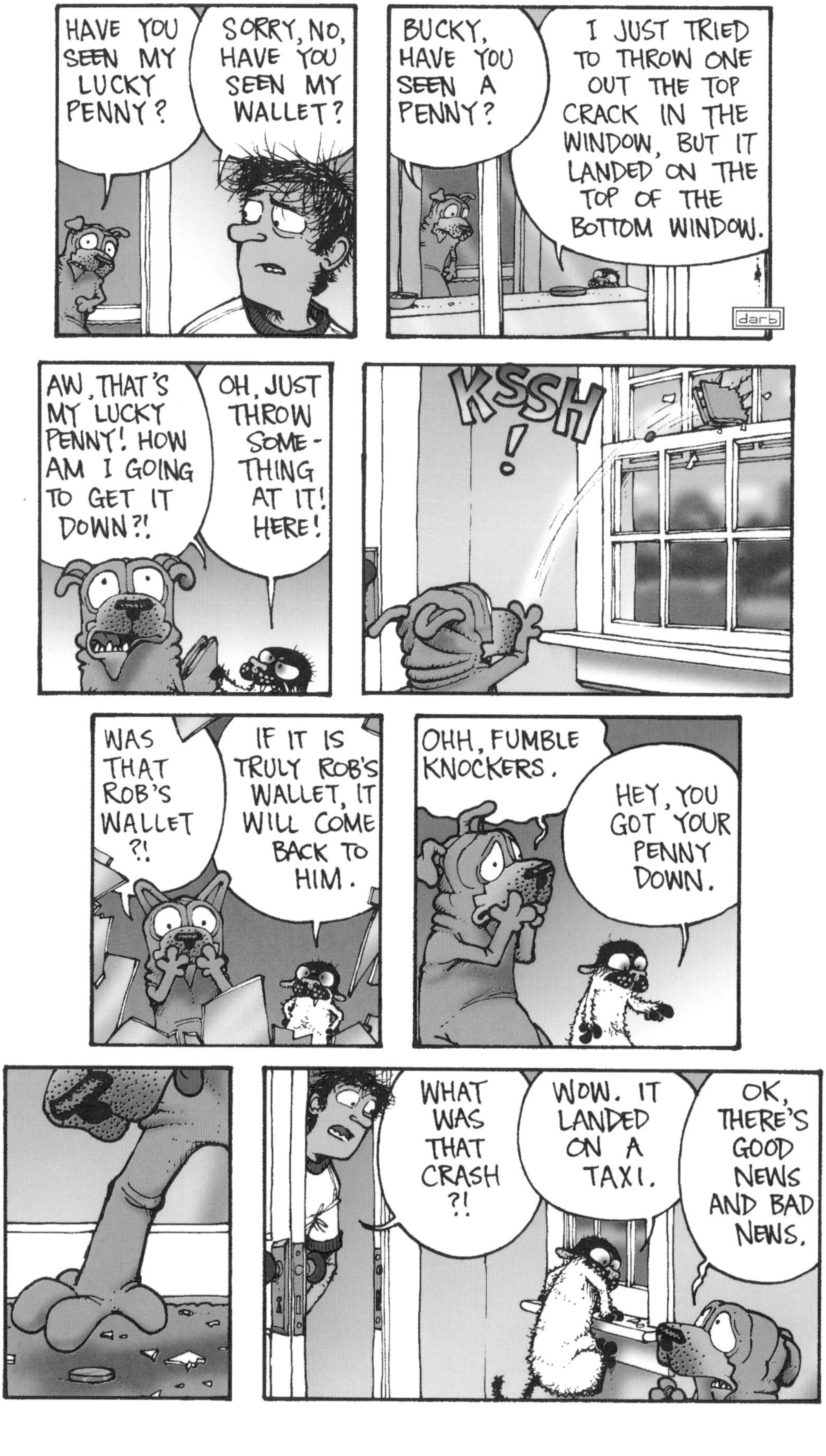
HAVE YOU SEEN MY LUCKY PENNY?
SORRY, NO, HAVE YOU SEEN MY WALLET?
BUCKY, HAVE YOU SEEN A PENNY?
I JUST TRIED TO THROW ONE OUT THE TOP CRACK IN THE WINDOW, BUT IT LANDED ON THE TOP OF THE BOTTOM WINDOW.
darb
AW, THAT'S MY LUCKY PENNY! HOW AM I GOING TO GET IT DOWN?!
OH, JUST THROW SOME-THING AT IT! HERE!
KSSH
!
WAS THAT ROB'S WALLET ?!
IF IT IS TRULY ROB'S WALLET, IT WILL COME BACK TO HIM.
OHH, FUMBLE KNOCKERS.
HEY, YOU GOT YOUR PENNY DOWN.
WHAT WAS THAT CRASH ?!
WOW. IT LANDED ON A TAXI.
OK, THERE'S GOOD NEWS AND BAD NEWS.

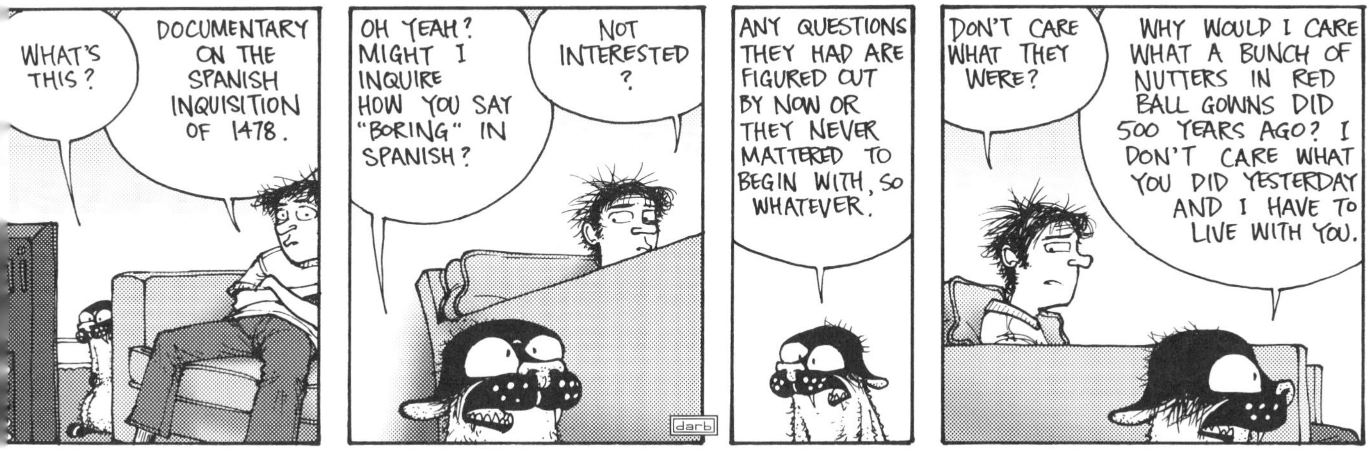
WHAT'S THIS?
DOCUMENTARY ON THE SPANISH INQUISITION OF 1478.
OH YEAH? MIGHT I INQUIRE HOW YOU SAY "BORING" IN SPANISH?
NOT INTERESTED?
ANY QUESTIONS THEY HAD ARE FIGURED OUT BY NOW OR THEY NEVER MATTERED TO BEGIN WITH, SO WHATEVER.
DON'T CARE WHAT THEY WERE?
WHY WOULD I CARE WHAT A BUNCH OF NUTTERS IN RED BALL GOWNS DID 500 YEARS AGO? I DON'T CARE WHAT YOU DID YESTERDAY AND I HAVE TO LIVE WITH YOU.
darb

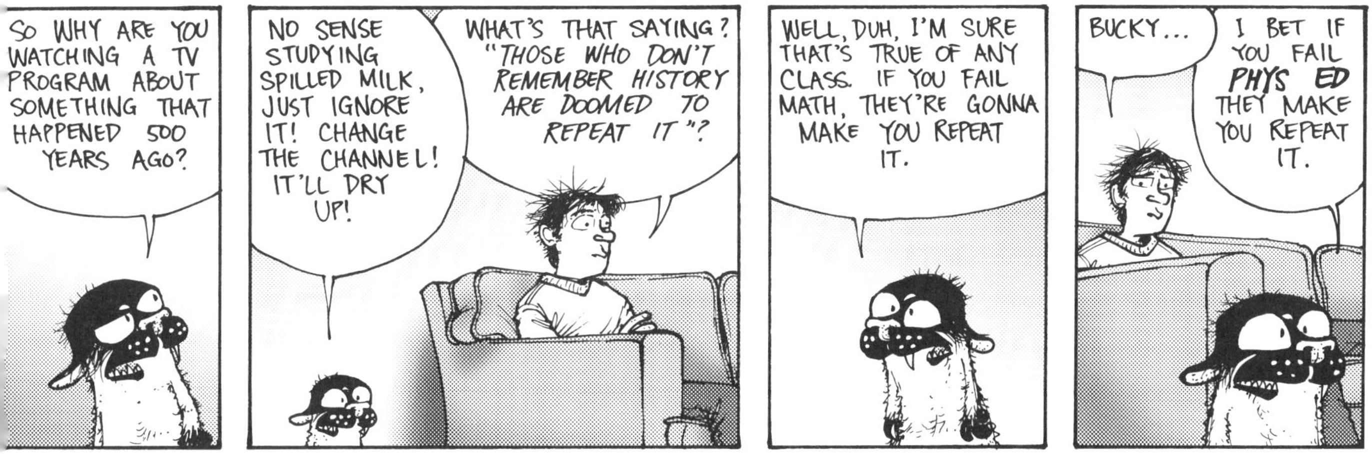
SO WHY ARE YOU WATCHING A TV PROGRAM ABOUT SOMETHING THAT HAPPENED 500 YEARS AGO?
NO SENSE STUDYING SPILLED MILK, JUST IGNORE IT! CHANGE THE CHANNEL! IT'LL DRY UP!
WHAT'S THAT SAYING? "THOSE WHO DON'T REMEMBER HISTORY ARE DOOMED TO REPEAT IT"?
WELL, DUH, I'M SURE THAT'S TRUE OF ANY CLASS. IF YOU FAIL MATH, THEY'RE GONNA MAKE YOU REPEAT IT.
BUCKY...
I BET IF YOU FAIL PHYS ED THEY MAKE YOU REPEAT IT.

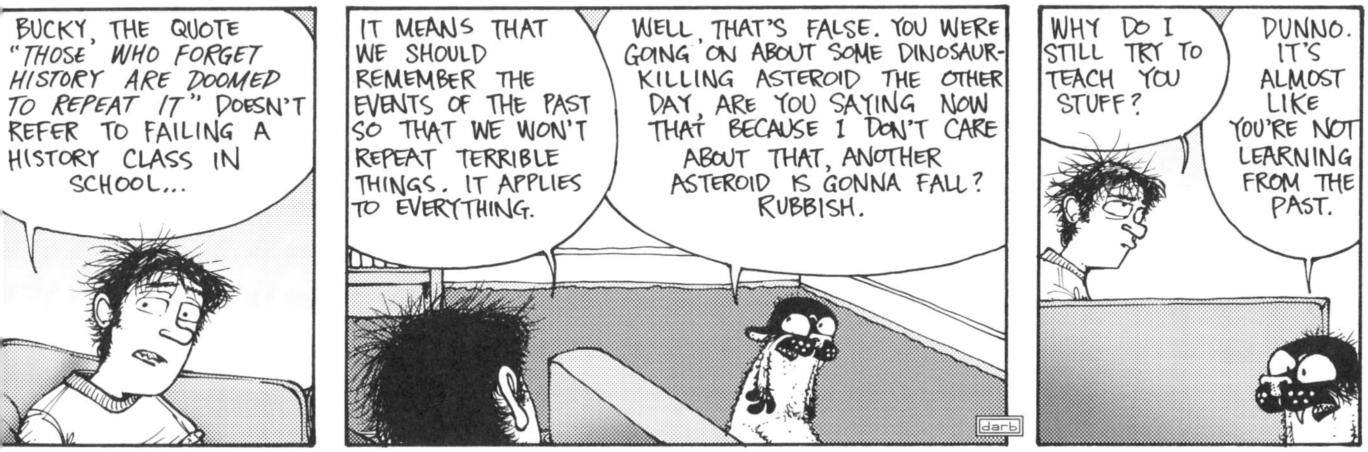
BUCKY, THE QUOTE "THOSE WHO FORGET HISTORY ARE DOOMED TO REPEAT IT" DOESN'T REFER TO FAILING A HISTORY CLASS IN SCHOOL...
IT MEANS THAT WE SHOULD REMEMBER THE EVENTS OF THE PAST SO THAT WE WON'T REPEAT TERRIBLE THINGS. IT APPLIES TO EVERYTHING.
WELL, THAT'S FALSE. YOU WERE GOING ON ABOUT SOME DINOSAUR-KILLING ASTEROID THE OTHER DAY, ARE YOU SAYING NOW THAT BECAUSE I DON'T CARE ABOUT THAT, ANOTHER ASTEROID IS GONNA FALL? RUBBISH.
darb
WHY DO I STILL TRY TO TEACH YOU STUFF?
DUNNO. IT'S ALMOST LIKE YOU'RE NOT LEARNING FROM THE PAST.

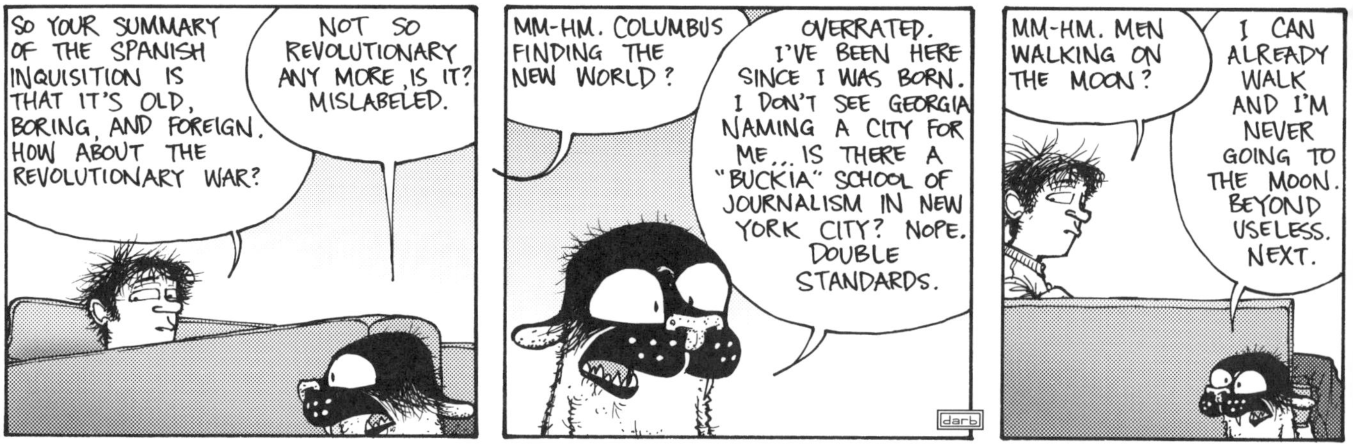
SO YOUR SUMMARY OF THE SPANISH INQUISITION IS THAT IT'S OLD, BORING, AND FOREIGN. HOW ABOUT THE REVOLUTIONARY WAR?
NOT SO REVOLUTIONARY ANY MORE, IS IT? MISLABELED.
MM-HM. COLUMBUS FINDING THE NEW WORLD?
OVERRATED. I'VE BEEN HERE SINCE I WAS BORN. I DON'T SEE GEORGIA NAMING A CITY FOR ME... IS THERE A "BUCKIA" SCHOOL OF JOURNALISM IN NEW YORK CITY? NOPE. DOUBLE STANDARDS.
darb
MM-HM. MEN WALKING ON THE MOON?
I CAN ALREADY WALK AND I'M NEVER GOING TO THE MOON. BEYOND USELESS. NEXT.

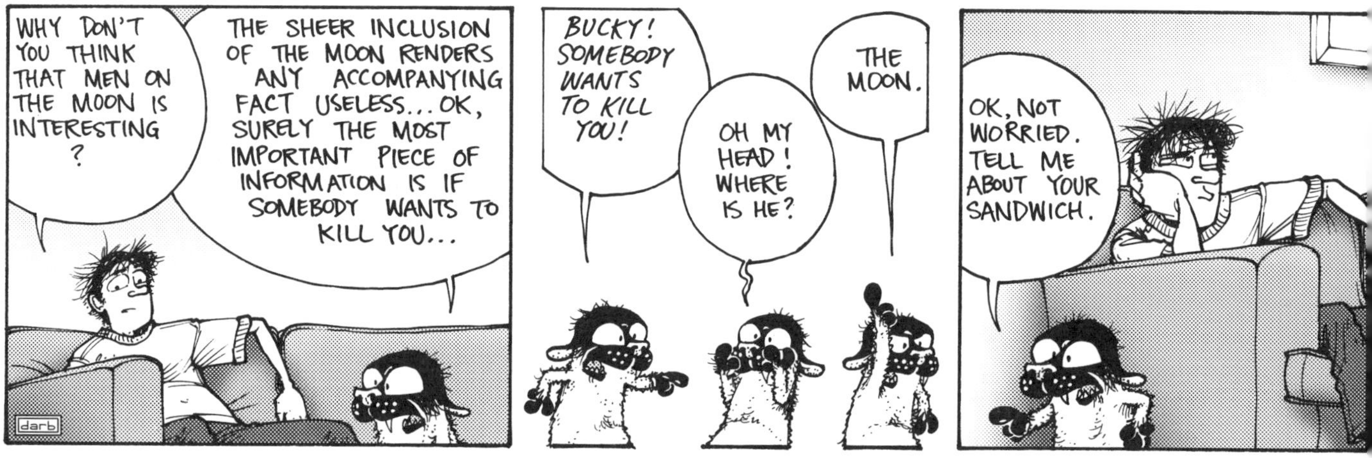
WHY DON'T YOU THINK THAT MEN ON THE MOON IS INTERESTING ?
THE SHEER INCLUSION OF THE MOON RENDERS ANY ACCOMPANYING FACT USELESS... OK, SURELY THE MOST IMPORTANT PIECE OF INFORMATION IS IF SOMEBODY WANTS TO KILL YOU...
darb
BUCKY! SOMEBODY WANTS TO KILL YOU!
OH MY HEAD! WHERE IS HE?
THE MOON.
OK, NOT WORRIED. TELL ME ABOUT YOUR SANDWICH.

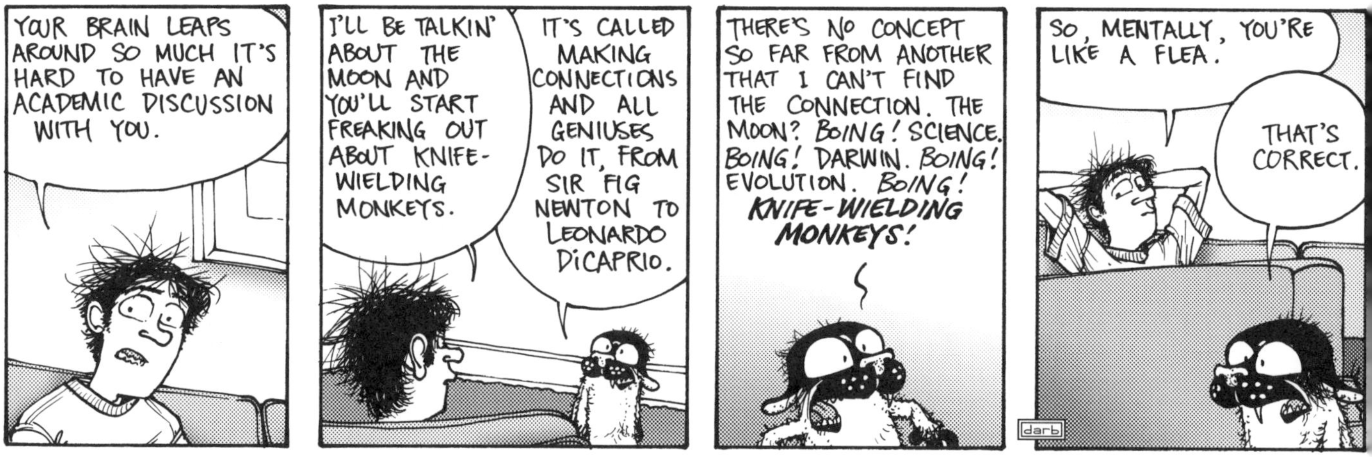
YOUR BRAIN LEAPS AROUND SO MUCH IT'S HARD TO HAVE AN ACADEMIC DISCUSSION WITH YOU.
I'LL BE TALKIN' ABOUT THE MOON AND YOU'LL START FREAKING OUT ABOUT KNIFE-WIELDING MONKEYS.
IT'S CALLED MAKING CONNECTIONS AND ALL GENIUSES DO IT, FROM SIR FIG NEWTON TO LEONARDO DiCAPRIO.
THERE'S NO CONCEPT SO FAR FROM ANOTHER THAT I CAN'T FIND THE CONNECTION. THE MOON? BOING! SCIENCE. BOING! DARWIN. BOING! EVOLUTION. BOING! KNIFE-WIELDING MONKEYS!
SO, MENTALLY, YOU'RE LIKE A FLEA.
THAT'S CORRECT.
darb

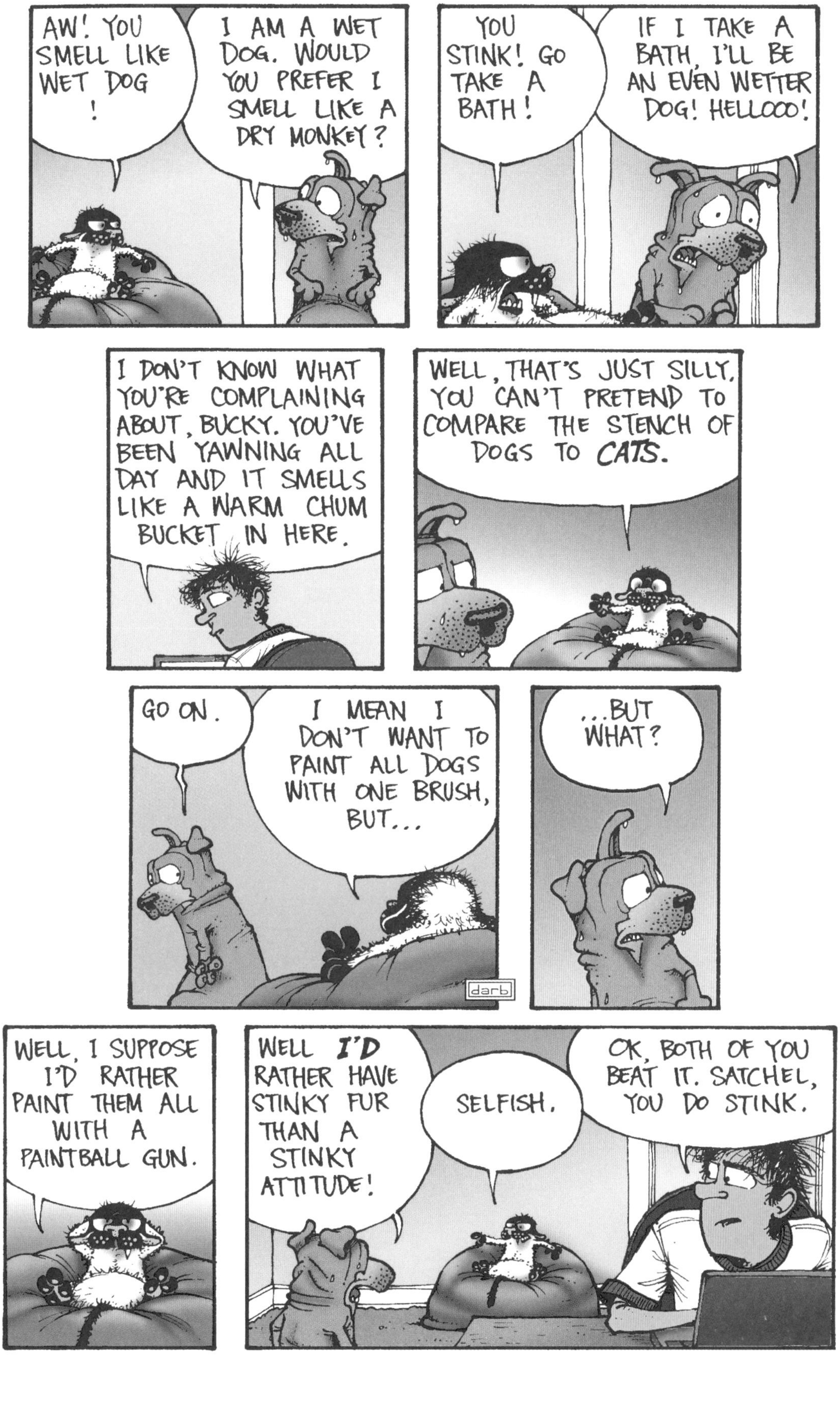
AW! YOU SMELL LIKE WET DOG!
I AM A WET DOG. WOULD YOU PREFER I SMELL LIKE A DRY MONKEY?
YOU STINK! GO TAKE A BATH!
IF I TAKE A BATH, I'LL BE AN EVEN WETTER DOG! HELLOOO!
I DON'T KNOW WHAT YOU'RE COMPLAINING ABOUT, BUCKY. YOU'VE BEEN YAWNING ALL DAY AND IT SMELLS LIKE A WARM CHUM BUCKET IN HERE.
WELL, THAT'S JUST SILLY. YOU CAN'T PRETEND TO COMPARE THE STENCH OF DOGS TO CATS.
GO ON.
I MEAN I DON'T WANT TO PAINT ALL DOGS WITH ONE BRUSH, BUT...
darb
...BUT WHAT?
WELL, I SUPPOSE I'D RATHER PAINT THEM ALL WITH A PAINTBALL GUN.
WELL I'D RATHER HAVE STINKY FUR THAN A STINKY ATTITUDE!
SELFISH.
OK, BOTH OF YOU BEAT IT. SATCHEL, YOU DO STINK.

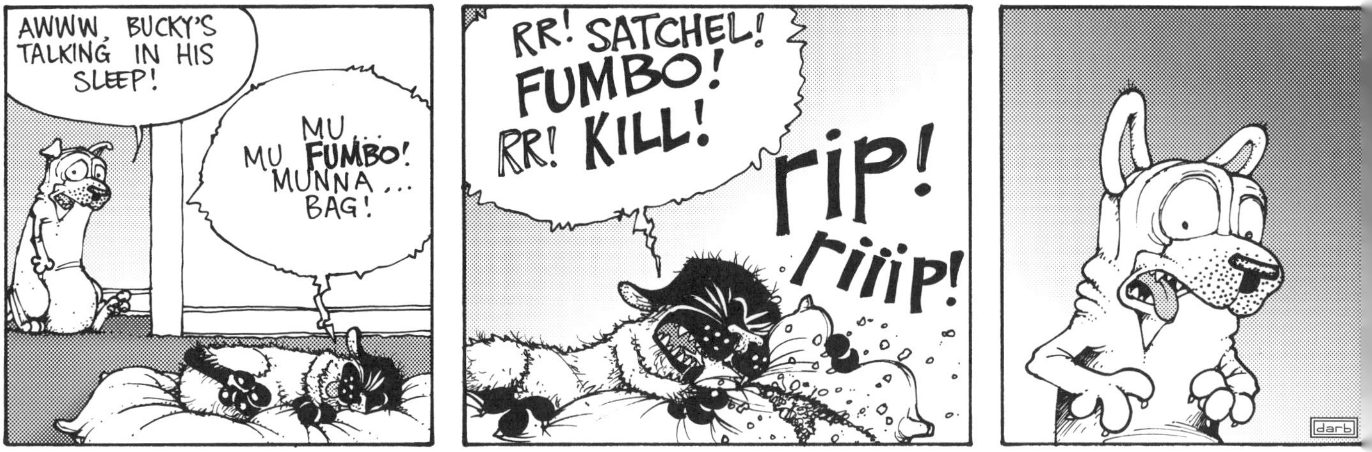
AWWW, BUCKY'S TALKING IN HIS SLEEP!
MU... MU FUMBO! MUNNA... BAG!
RR! SATCHEL! FUMBO! RR! KILL!
rip! riiip!
darb

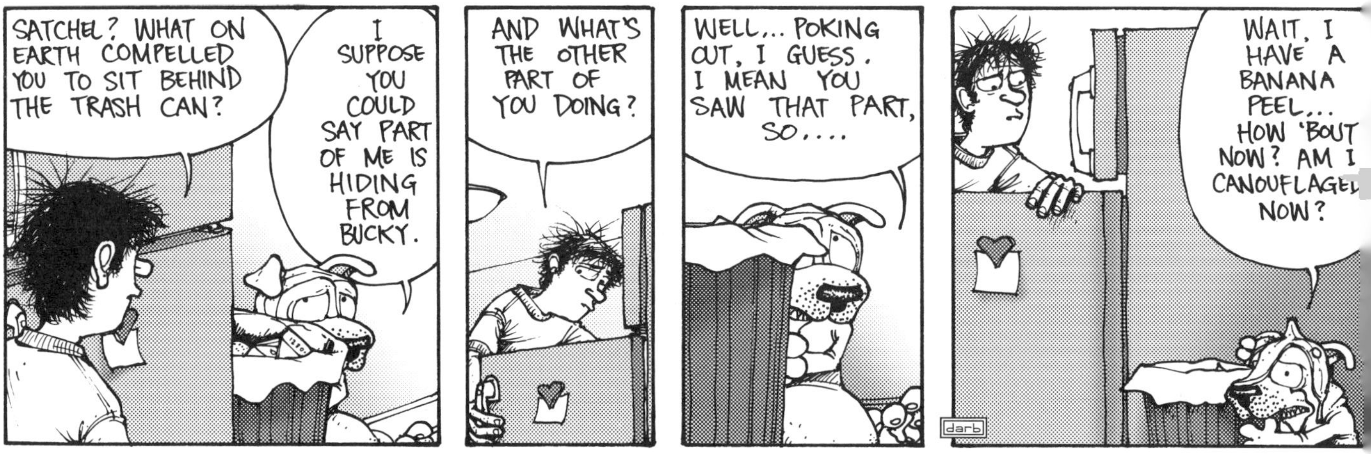
SATCHEL? WHAT ON EARTH COMPELLED YOU TO SIT BEHIND THE TRASH CAN?
I SUPPOSE YOU COULD SAY PART OF ME IS HIDING FROM BUCKY.
AND WHAT'S THE OTHER PART OF YOU DOING?
WELL,.. POKING OUT, I GUESS. I MEAN YOU SAW THAT PART, SO....
WAIT, I HAVE A BANANA PEEL... HOW 'BOUT NOW? AM I CANOUFLAGED NOW?
darb

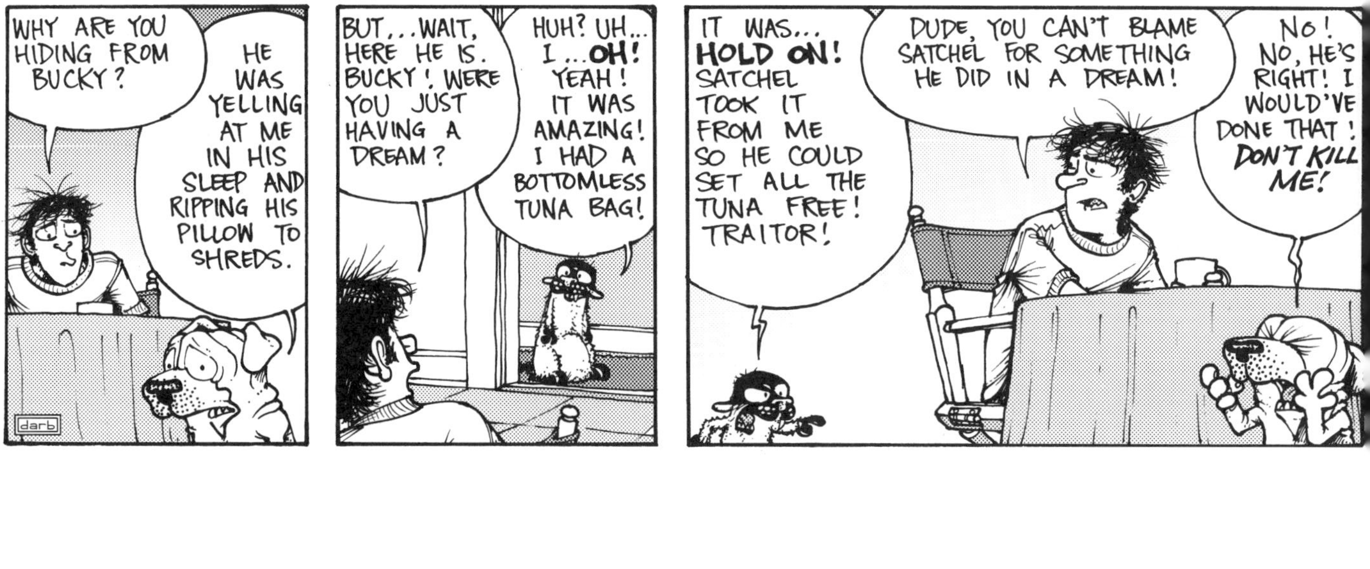
WHY ARE YOU HIDING FROM BUCKY?
HE WAS YELLING AT ME IN HIS SLEEP AND RIPPING HIS PILLOW TO SHREDS.
BUT... WAIT, HERE HE IS. BUCKY! WERE YOU JUST HAVING A DREAM?
HUH? UH... I...OH! YEAH! IT WAS AMAZING! I HAD A BOTTOMLESS TUNA BAG!
IT WAS... HOLD ON! SATCHEL TOOK IT FROM ME SO HE COULD SET ALL THE TUNA FREE! TRAITOR!
DUDE, YOU CAN'T BLAME SATCHEL FOR SOMETHING HE DID IN A DREAM!
NO! NO, HE'S RIGHT! I WOULD'VE DONE THAT! DON'T KILL ME!
darb

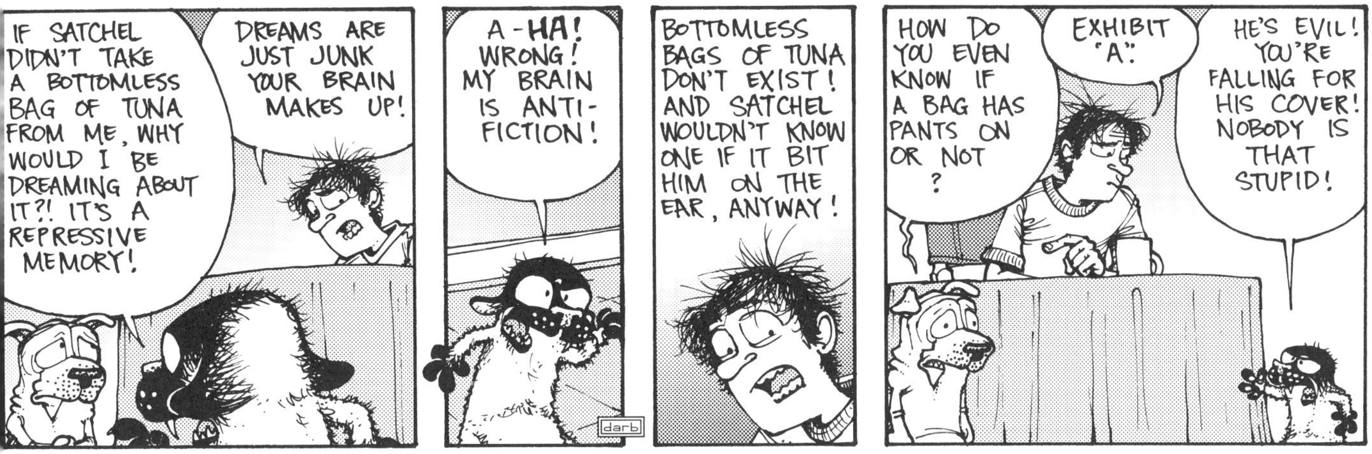
IF SATCHEL DIDN'T TAKE A BOTTOMLESS BAG OF TUNA FROM ME, WHY WOULD I BE DREAMING ABOUT IT?! IT'S A REPRESSIVE MEMORY!
DREAMS ARE JUST JUNK YOUR BRAIN MAKES UP!
A-HA! WRONG! MY BRAIN IS ANTI-FICTION!
darb
BOTTOMLESS BAGS OF TUNA DON'T EXIST! AND SATCHEL WOULDN'T KNOW ONE IF IT BIT HIM ON THE EAR, ANYWAY!
HOW DO YOU EVEN KNOW IF A BAG HAS PANTS ON OR NOT ?
EXHIBIT "A".
HE'S EVIL! YOU'RE FALLING FOR HIS COVER! NOBODY IS THAT STUPID!

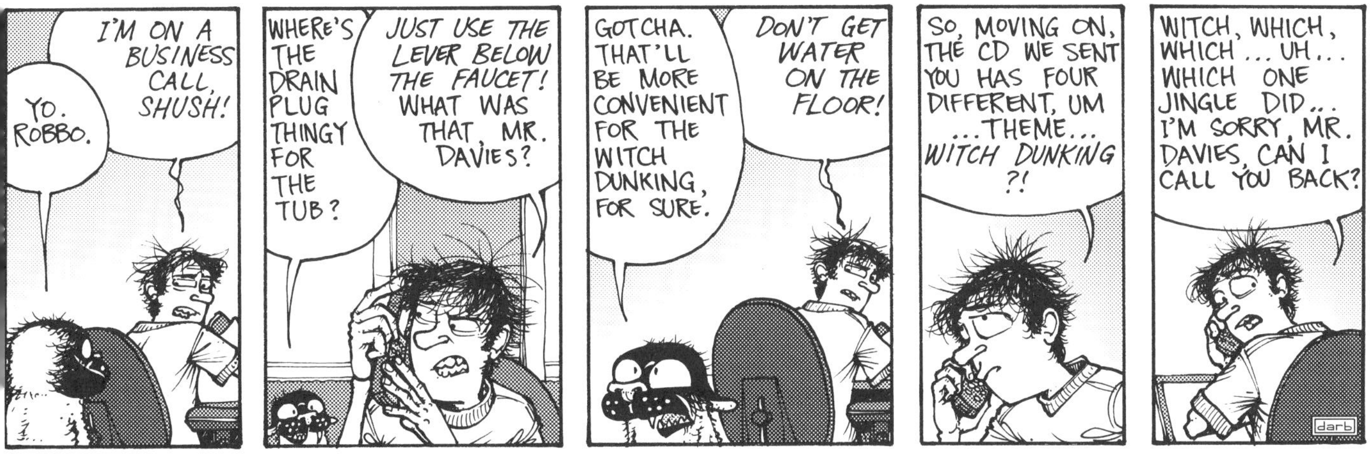
YO. ROBBO.
I'M ON A BUSINESS CALL, SHUSH!
WHERE'S THE DRAIN PLUG THINGY FOR THE TUB?
JUST USE THE LEVER BELOW THE FAUCET! WHAT WAS THAT, MR. DAVIES?
GOTCHA. THAT'LL BE MORE CONVENIENT FOR THE WITCH DUNKING, FOR SURE.
DON'T GET WATER ON THE FLOOR!
SO, MOVING ON, THE CD WE SENT YOU HAS FOUR DIFFERENT, UM ...THEME... WITCH DUNKING ?!
WITCH, WHICH, WHICH... UH... WHICH ONE JINGLE DID... I'M SORRY, MR. DAVIES, CAN I CALL YOU BACK?
darb

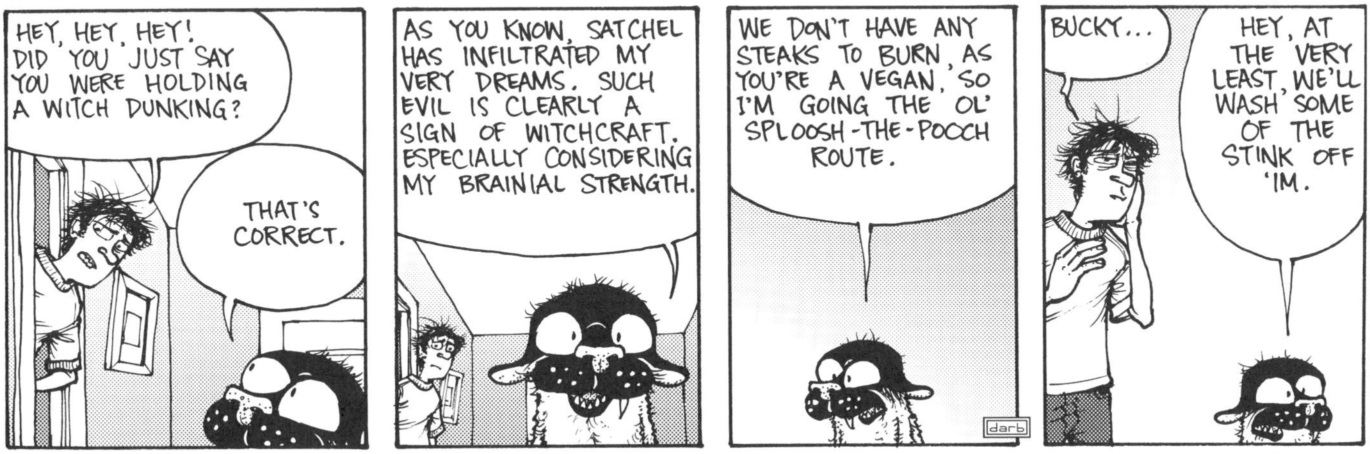
HEY, HEY, HEY! DID YOU JUST SAY YOU WERE HOLDING A WITCH DUNKING?
THAT'S CORRECT.
AS YOU KNOW, SATCHEL HAS INFILTRATED MY VERY DREAMS. SUCH EVIL IS CLEARLY A SIGN OF WITCHCRAFT. ESPECIALLY CONSIDERING MY BRAINIAL STRENGTH.
WE DON'T HAVE ANY STEAKS TO BURN, AS YOU'RE A VEGAN, SO I'M GOING THE OL' SPLOOSH-THE-POOCH ROUTE.
darb
BUCKY...
HEY, AT THE VERY LEAST, WE'LL WASH SOME OF THE STINK OFF 'IM.

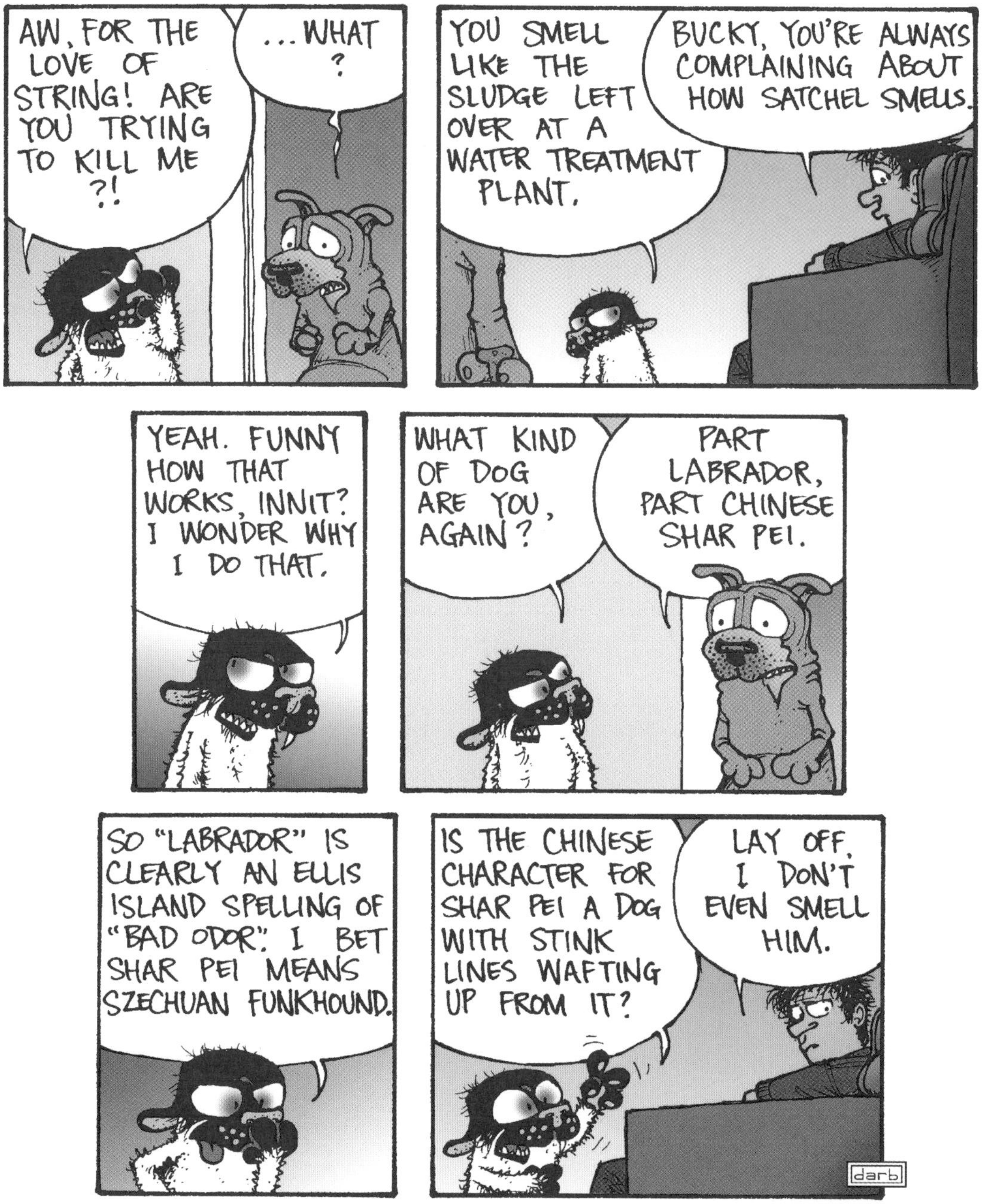
AW, FOR THE LOVE OF STRING! ARE YOU TRYING TO KILL ME ?!
...WHAT ?
YOU SMELL LIKE THE SLUDGE LEFT OVER AT A WATER TREATMENT PLANT.
BUCKY, YOU'RE ALWAYS COMPLAINING ABOUT HOW SATCHEL SMELLS.
YEAH. FUNNY HOW THAT WORKS, INNIT? I WONDER WHY I DO THAT.
WHAT KIND OF DOG ARE YOU, AGAIN?
PART LABRADOR, PART CHINESE SHAR PEI.
SO "LABRADOR" IS CLEARLY AN ELLIS ISLAND SPELLING OF "BAD ODOR". I BET SHAR PEI MEANS SZECHUAN FUNKHOUND.
IS THE CHINESE CHARACTER FOR SHAR PEI A DOG WITH STINK LINES WAFTING UP FROM IT?
LAY OFF. I DON'T EVEN SMELL HIM.
darb
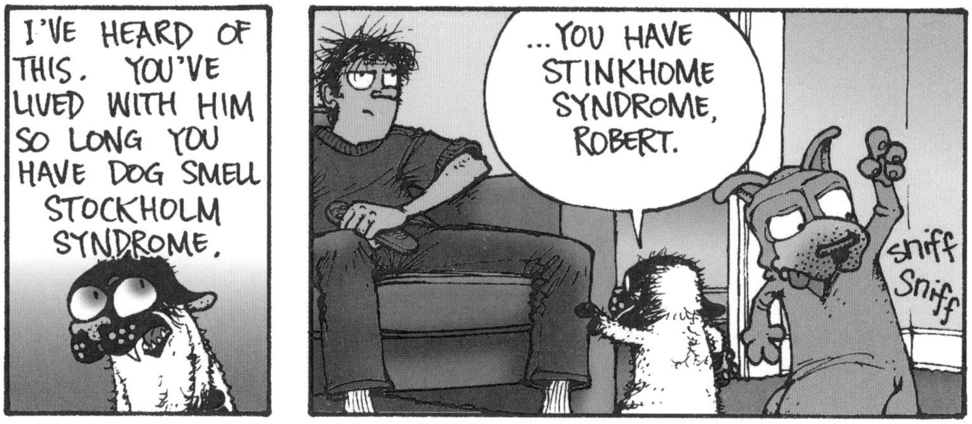
I'VE HEARD OF THIS. YOU'VE LIVED WITH HIM SO LONG YOU HAVE DOG SMELL STOCKHOLM SYNDROME.
...YOU HAVE STINKHOME SYNDROME, ROBERT.
sniff sniff

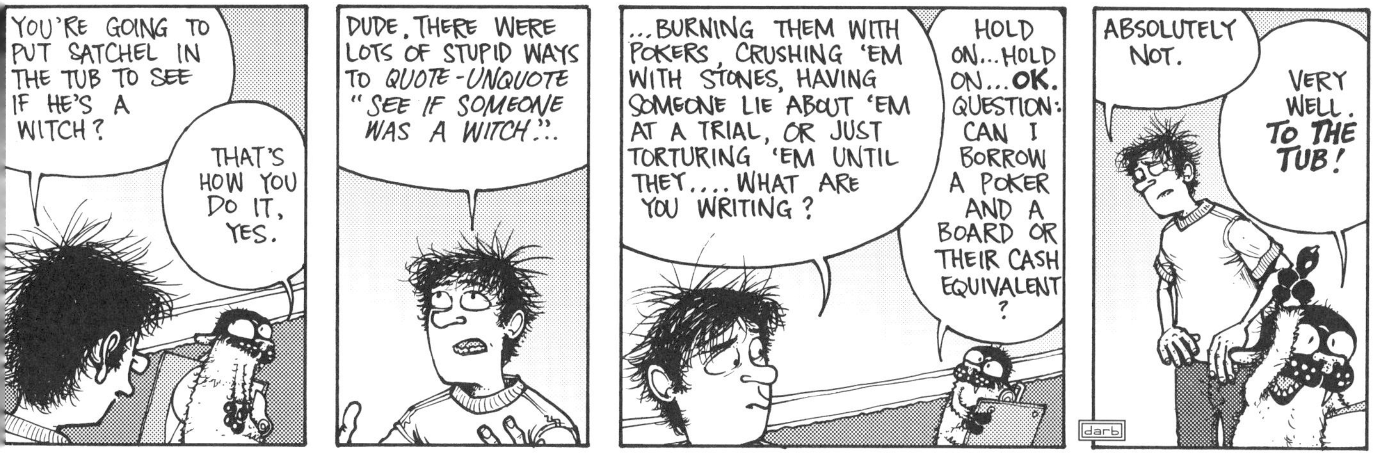

YOU'RE GOING TO PUT SATCHEL IN THE TUB TO SEE IF HE'S A WITCH?
THAT'S HOW YOU DO IT, YES.
DUDE, THERE WERE LOTS OF STUPID WAYS TO *QUOTE-UNQUOTE* *"SEE IF SOMEONE WAS A WITCH."*...
...BURNING THEM WITH POKERS, CRUSHING 'EM WITH STONES, HAVING SOMEONE LIE ABOUT 'EM AT A TRIAL, OR JUST TORTURING 'EM UNTIL THEY.... WHAT ARE YOU WRITING?
HOLD ON...HOLD ON...**OK.** QUESTION: CAN I BORROW A POKER AND A BOARD OR THEIR CASH EQUIVALENT?
ABSOLUTELY NOT.
VERY WELL. ***TO THE TUB!***
darb

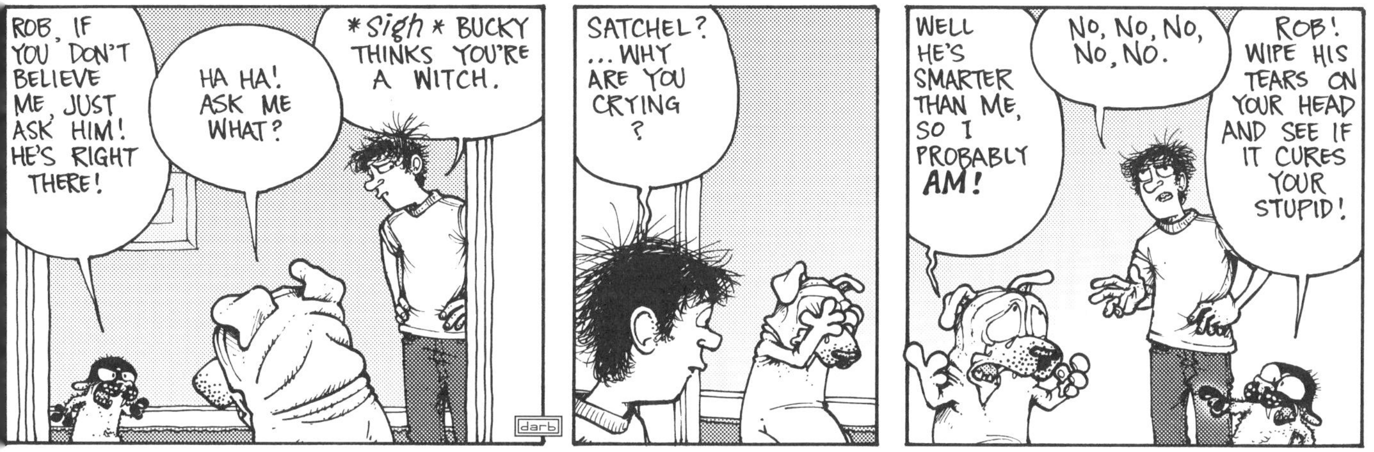

ROB, IF YOU DON'T BELIEVE ME, JUST ASK HIM! HE'S RIGHT THERE!
HA HA! ASK ME WHAT?
sigh BUCKY THINKS YOU'RE A WITCH.
darb
SATCHEL? ...WHY ARE YOU CRYING?
WELL HE'S SMARTER THAN ME, SO I PROBABLY ***AM!***
NO, NO, NO, NO, NO.
ROB! WIPE HIS TEARS ON YOUR HEAD AND SEE IF IT CURES YOUR STUPID!

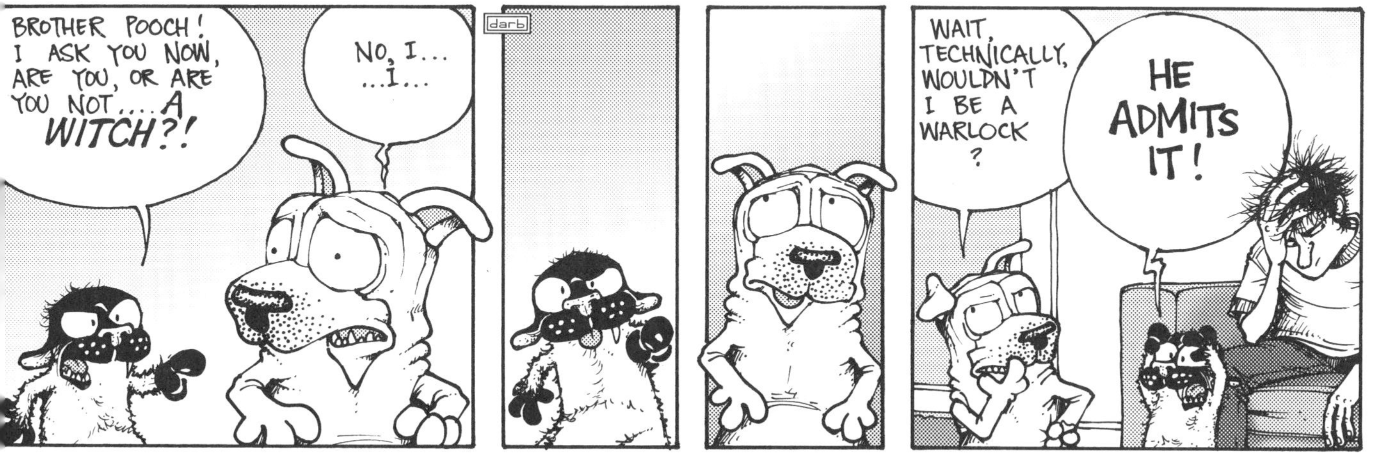

BROTHER POOCH! I ASK YOU NOW, ARE YOU, OR ARE YOU NOT.... ***A WITCH?!***
NO, I... ...I...
darb
WAIT, TECHNICALLY, WOULDN'T I BE A WARLOCK?
HE ADMITS IT!

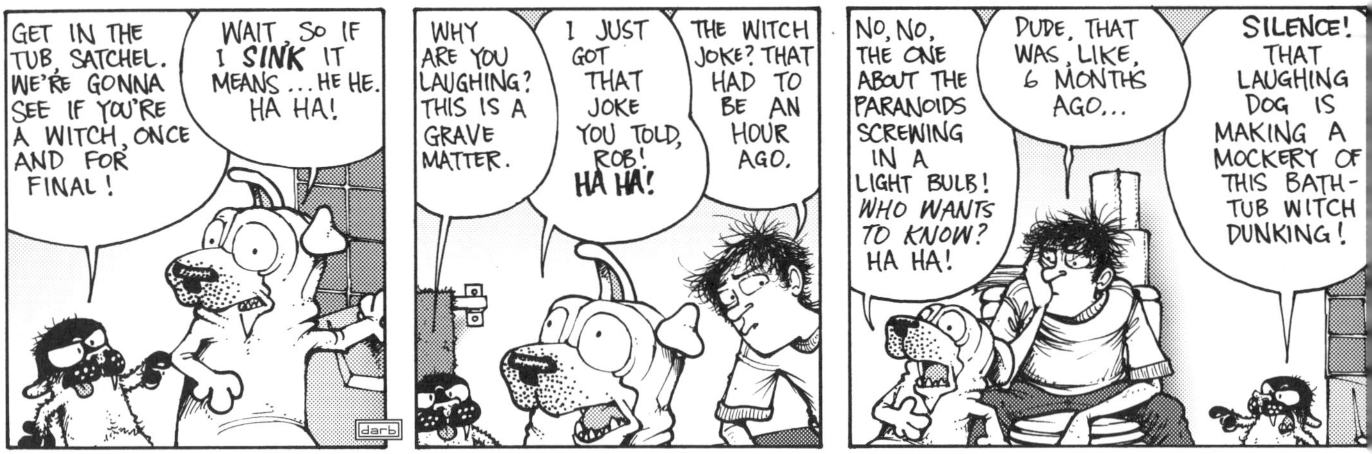
GET IN THE TUB, SATCHEL. WE'RE GONNA SEE IF YOU'RE A WITCH, ONCE AND FOR FINAL!
WAIT, SO IF I SINK IT MEANS... HE HE. HA HA!
WHY ARE YOU LAUGHING? THIS IS A GRAVE MATTER.
I JUST GOT THAT JOKE YOU TOLD, ROB! HA HA!
THE WITCH JOKE? THAT HAD TO BE AN HOUR AGO.
NO, NO, THE ONE ABOUT THE PARANOIDS SCREWING IN A LIGHT BULB! WHO WANTS TO KNOW? HA HA!
DUDE, THAT WAS, LIKE, 6 MONTHS AGO...
SILENCE! THAT LAUGHING DOG IS MAKING A MOCKERY OF THIS BATH-TUB WITCH DUNKING!
darb

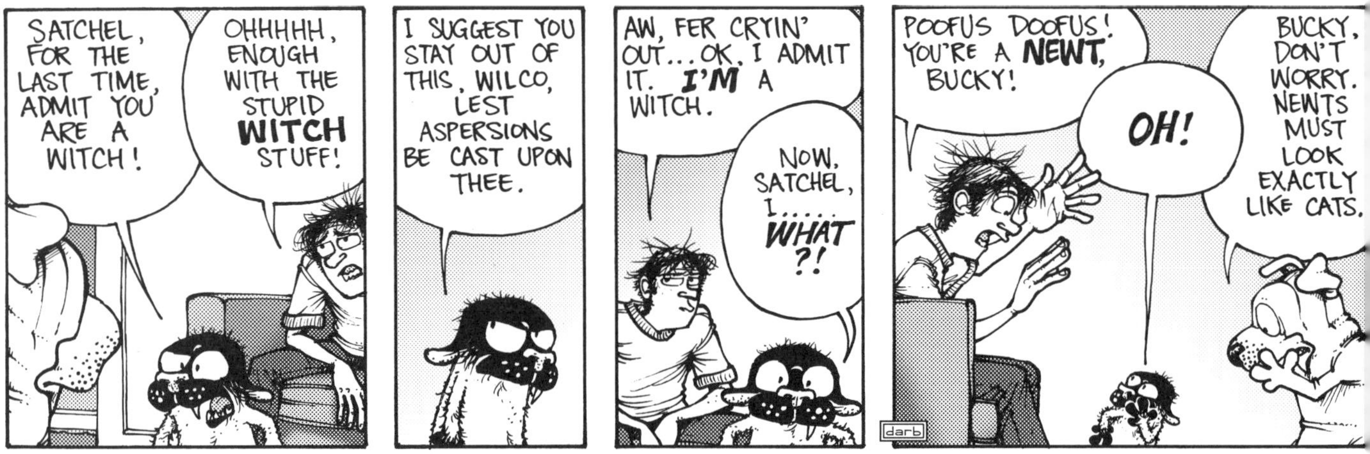
SATCHEL, FOR THE LAST TIME, ADMIT YOU ARE A WITCH!
OHHHHH, ENOUGH WITH THE STUPID WITCH STUFF!
I SUGGEST YOU STAY OUT OF THIS, WILCO, LEST ASPERSIONS BE CAST UPON THEE.
AW, FER CRYIN' OUT... OK, I ADMIT IT. I'M A WITCH.
NOW, SATCHEL, I..... WHAT?!
darb
POOFUS DOOFUS! YOU'RE A NEWT, BUCKY!
OH!
BUCKY, DON'T WORRY. NEWTS MUST LOOK EXACTLY LIKE CATS.

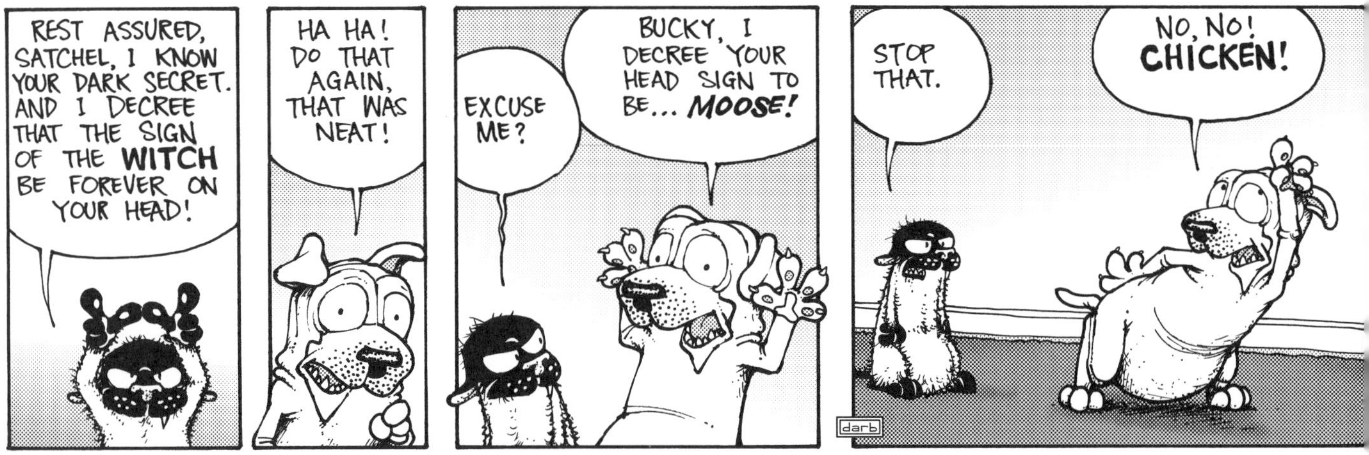
REST ASSURED, SATCHEL, I KNOW YOUR DARK SECRET. AND I DECREE THAT THE SIGN OF THE WITCH BE FOREVER ON YOUR HEAD!
HA HA! DO THAT AGAIN, THAT WAS NEAT!
EXCUSE ME?
BUCKY, I DECREE YOUR HEAD SIGN TO BE... MOOSE!
darb
STOP THAT.
NO, NO! CHICKEN!

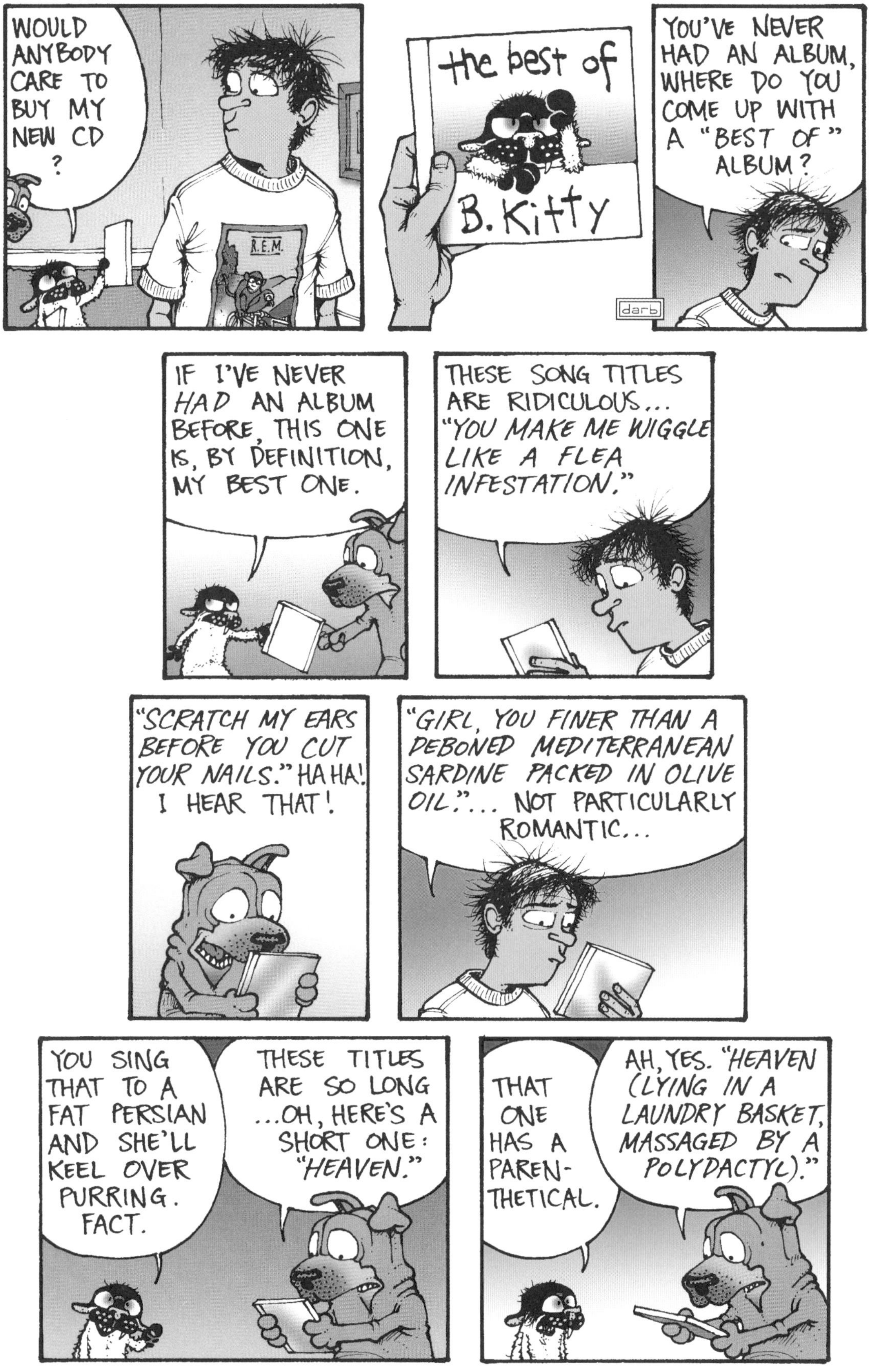

WOULD ANYBODY CARE TO BUY MY NEW CD ?
R.E.M.
the best of B. Kitty
YOU'VE NEVER HAD AN ALBUM, WHERE DO YOU COME UP WITH A "BEST OF" ALBUM?
darb
IF I'VE NEVER HAD AN ALBUM BEFORE, THIS ONE IS, BY DEFINITION, MY BEST ONE.
THESE SONG TITLES ARE RIDICULOUS... "YOU MAKE ME WIGGLE LIKE A FLEA INFESTATION."
"SCRATCH MY EARS BEFORE YOU CUT YOUR NAILS." HA HA! I HEAR THAT!
"GIRL, YOU FINER THAN A DEBONED MEDITERRANEAN SARDINE PACKED IN OLIVE OIL."... NOT PARTICULARLY ROMANTIC...
YOU SING THAT TO A FAT PERSIAN AND SHE'LL KEEL OVER PURRING. FACT.
THESE TITLES ARE SO LONG ...OH, HERE'S A SHORT ONE: "HEAVEN."
THAT ONE HAS A PAREN-THETICAL.
AH, YES. "HEAVEN (LYING IN A LAUNDRY BASKET, MASSAGED BY A POLYDACTYL)."

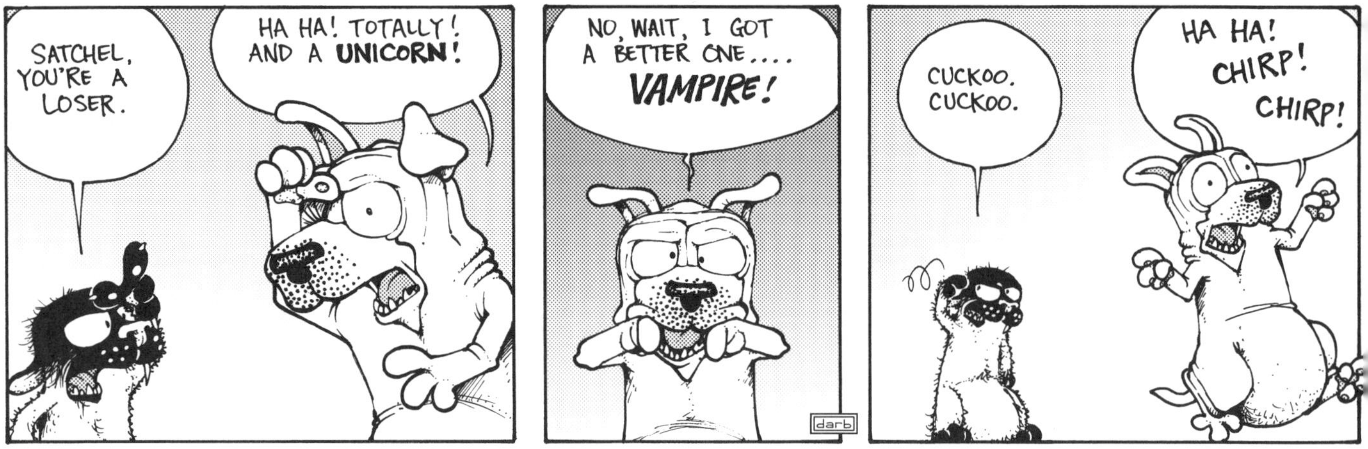
SATCHEL, YOU'RE A LOSER.
HA HA! TOTALLY! AND A **UNICORN**!
NO, WAIT, I GOT A BETTER ONE.... ***VAMPIRE!***
CUCKOO. CUCKOO.
HA HA! **CHIRP!** **CHIRP!**

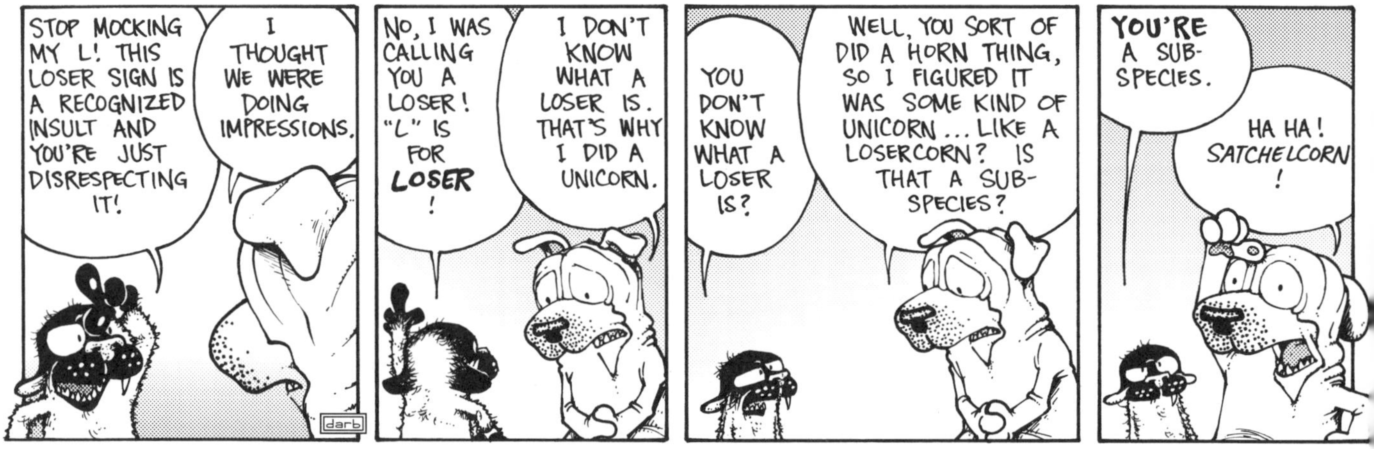
STOP MOCKING MY L! THIS LOSER SIGN IS A RECOGNIZED INSULT AND YOU'RE JUST DISRESPECTING IT!
I THOUGHT WE WERE DOING IMPRESSIONS.
NO, I WAS CALLING YOU A LOSER! "L" IS FOR ***LOSER***!
I DON'T KNOW WHAT A LOSER IS. THAT'S WHY I DID A UNICORN.
YOU DON'T KNOW WHAT A LOSER IS?
WELL, YOU SORT OF DID A HORN THING, SO I FIGURED IT WAS SOME KIND OF UNICORN... LIKE A LOSERCORN? IS THAT A SUB-SPECIES?
YOU'RE A SUB-SPECIES.
HA HA! *SATCHELCORN*!

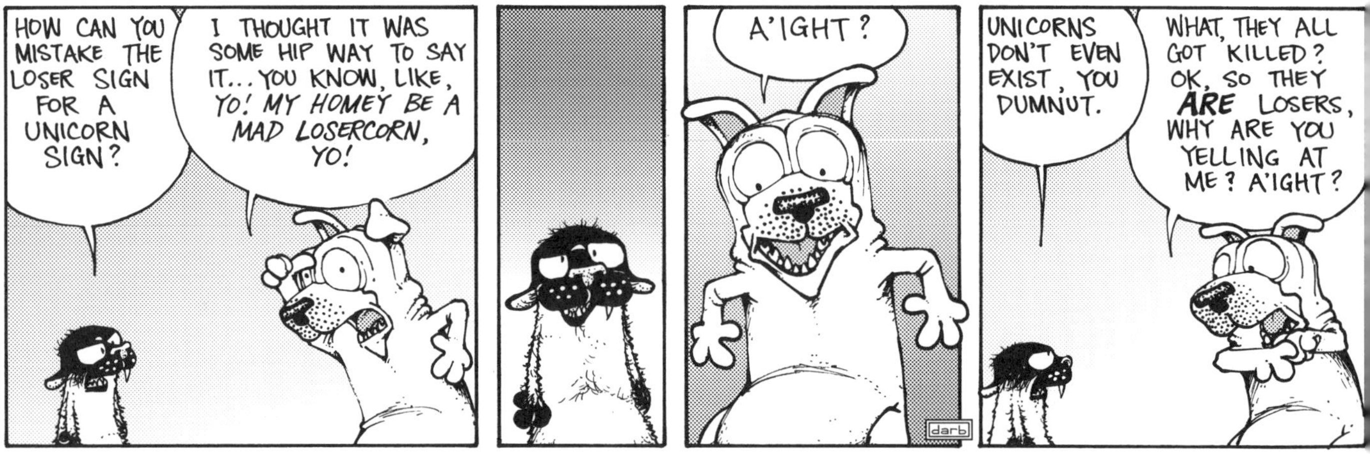
HOW CAN YOU MISTAKE THE LOSER SIGN FOR A UNICORN SIGN?
I THOUGHT IT WAS SOME HIP WAY TO SAY IT... YOU KNOW, LIKE, *YO! MY HOMEY BE A MAD LOSERCORN, YO!*
A'IGHT?
UNICORNS DON'T EVEN EXIST, YOU DUMNUT.
WHAT, THEY ALL GOT KILLED? OK, SO THEY ***ARE*** LOSERS, WHY ARE YOU YELLING AT ME? A'IGHT?

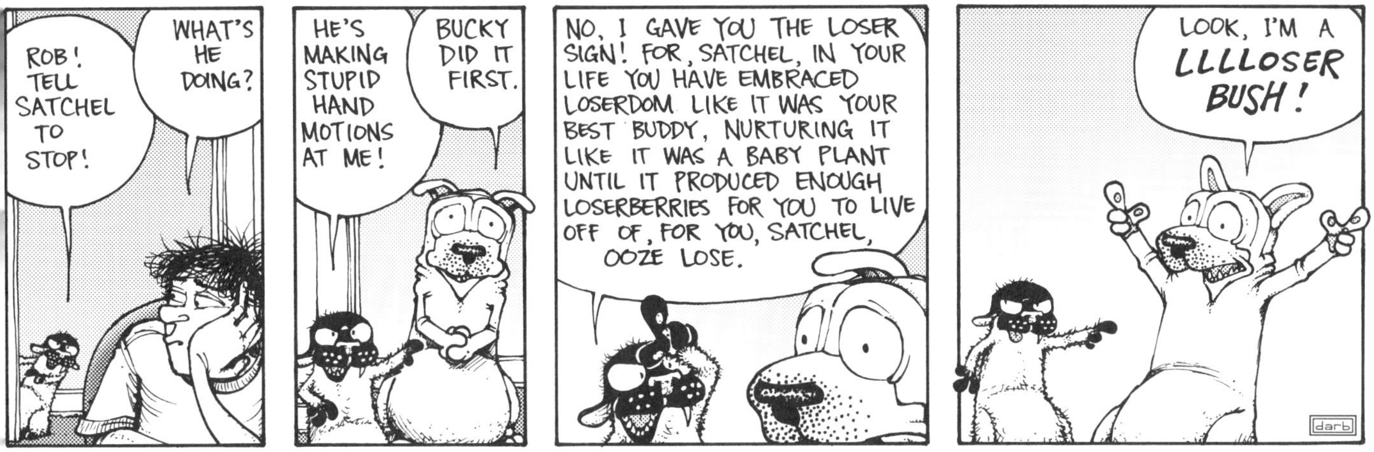
ROB! TELL SATCHEL TO STOP!
WHAT'S HE DOING?
HE'S MAKING STUPID HAND MOTIONS AT ME!
BUCKY DID IT FIRST.
NO, I GAVE YOU THE LOSER SIGN! FOR, SATCHEL, IN YOUR LIFE YOU HAVE EMBRACED LOSERDOM LIKE IT WAS YOUR BEST BUDDY, NURTURING IT LIKE IT WAS A BABY PLANT UNTIL IT PRODUCED ENOUGH LOSERBERRIES FOR YOU TO LIVE OFF OF, FOR YOU, SATCHEL, OOZE LOSE.
LOOK, I'M A LLLLOSER BUSH!
darb

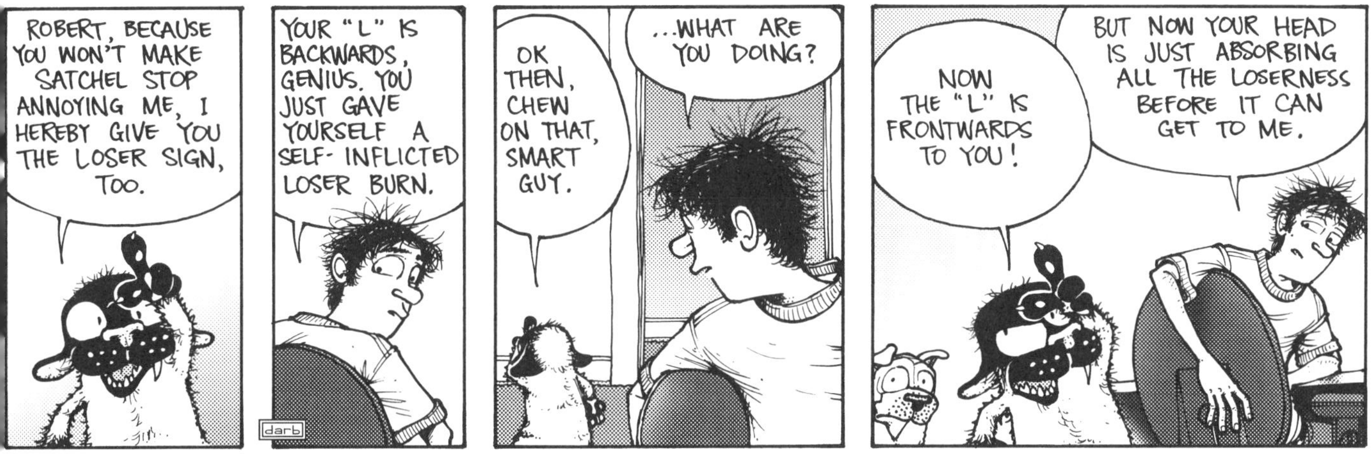
ROBERT, BECAUSE YOU WON'T MAKE SATCHEL STOP ANNOYING ME, I HEREBY GIVE YOU THE LOSER SIGN, TOO.
YOUR "L" IS BACKWARDS, GENIUS. YOU JUST GAVE YOURSELF A SELF-INFLICTED LOSER BURN.
darb
OK THEN, CHEW ON THAT, SMART GUY.
...WHAT ARE YOU DOING?
NOW THE "L" IS FRONTWARDS TO YOU!
BUT NOW YOUR HEAD IS JUST ABSORBING ALL THE LOSERNESS BEFORE IT CAN GET TO ME.

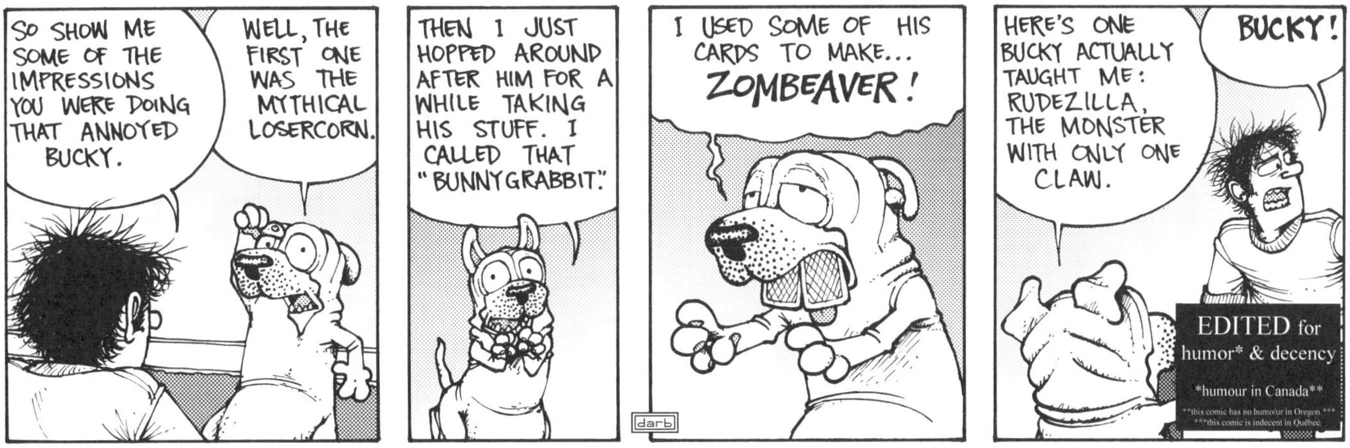
SO SHOW ME SOME OF THE IMPRESSIONS YOU WERE DOING THAT ANNOYED BUCKY.
WELL, THE FIRST ONE WAS THE MYTHICAL LOSERCORN.
THEN I JUST HOPPED AROUND AFTER HIM FOR A WHILE TAKING HIS STUFF. I CALLED THAT "BUNNYGRABBIT."
darb
I USED SOME OF HIS CARDS TO MAKE... ZOMBEAVER!
HERE'S ONE BUCKY ACTUALLY TAUGHT ME: RUDEZILLA, THE MONSTER WITH ONLY ONE CLAW.
BUCKY!
EDITED for humor* & decency
*humour in Canada**
this comic has no humo/ur in Oregon.*
***this comic is indecent in Québec.

WHOA. LAME TV SHOW.

NO, I RECORDED MY PROGRAM, SO I'M FAST-FORWARDING THE ADS.

DOESN'T THAT GO AGAINST YOUR PROFESSIONAL OATH?

MY WHAT?

WHATEVER YOU CALL THE OATH YOU TOOK WHEN YOU GOT A JOB IN ADVERTISING. LIKE THAT OATH HIPPO CRITICS TAKE.

...UHH...

OR IS THAT JUST A HIPPO THING? LIKE, IS THERE A HIPPO CABBIE OATH AND A HIPPO CASHIER OATH AND SO ON AND SO ON?

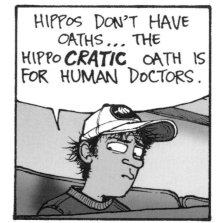

HIPPOS DON'T HAVE OATHS... THE HIPPO*CRATIC* OATH IS FOR HUMAN DOCTORS.

OH YEAH? SO DO HUMAN ACCOUNTANTS TAKE THE MONKEY PLUMBER OATH?

AND HEY, CAN YOU RECOMMEND ANY GOOD CATERERS? THEY HAVE TO HAVE TAKEN THEIR NAKED MOLE RAT CIVIL ENGINEER OATH, OF COURSE.

CLEARLY YOU DON'T UNDERSTAND WHAT HIPPOCRATIC MEANS.

OH MY. DOESN'T BEING RUDE TO A CONSUMER GO AGAINST AN ADMAN'S BEAVER DENTIST OATH?

darb

198

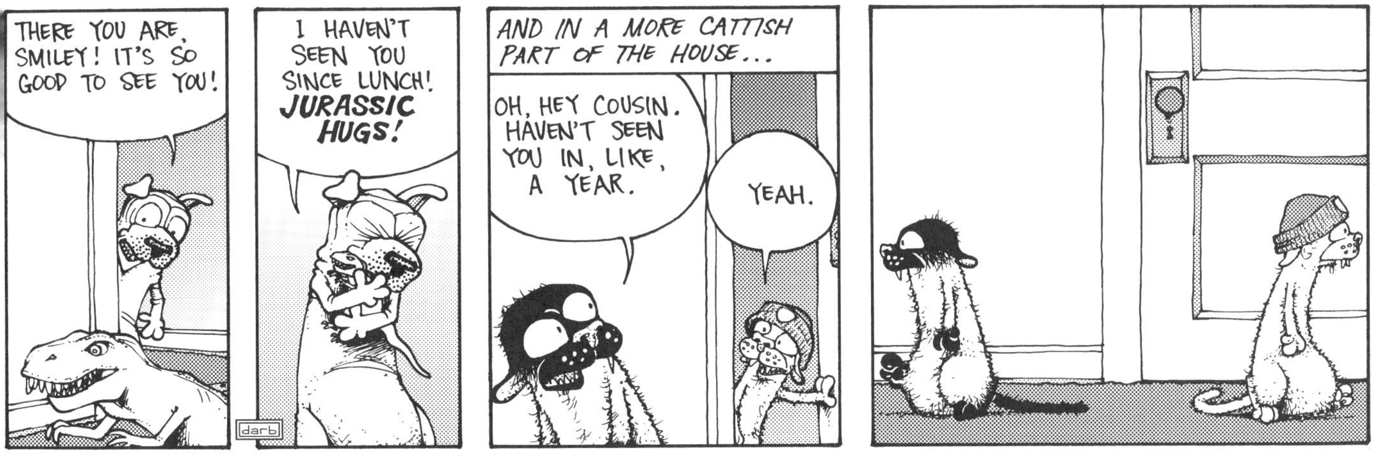
THERE YOU ARE, SMILEY! IT'S SO GOOD TO SEE YOU!
I HAVEN'T SEEN YOU SINCE LUNCH! **JURASSIC HUGS!**
AND IN A MORE CATTISH PART OF THE HOUSE...
OH, HEY COUSIN. HAVEN'T SEEN YOU IN, LIKE, A YEAR.
YEAH.

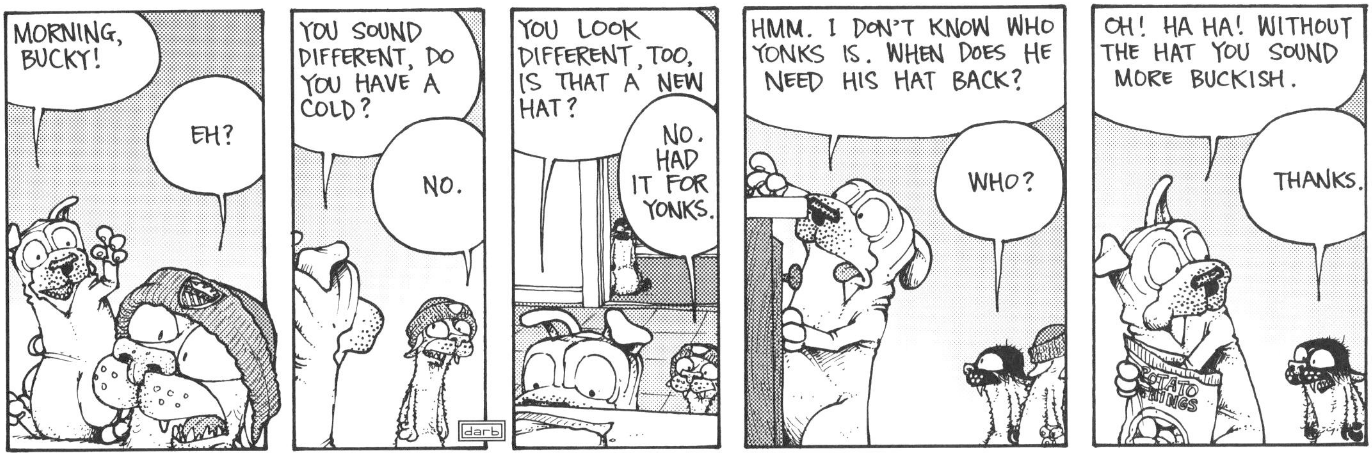
MORNING, BUCKY!
EH?
YOU SOUND DIFFERENT, DO YOU HAVE A COLD?
NO.
YOU LOOK DIFFERENT, TOO, IS THAT A NEW HAT?
NO. HAD IT FOR YONKS.
HMM. I DON'T KNOW WHO YONKS IS. WHEN DOES HE NEED HIS HAT BACK?
WHO?
OH! HA HA! WITHOUT THE HAT YOU SOUND MORE BUCKISH.
THANKS.
POTATO STRINGS

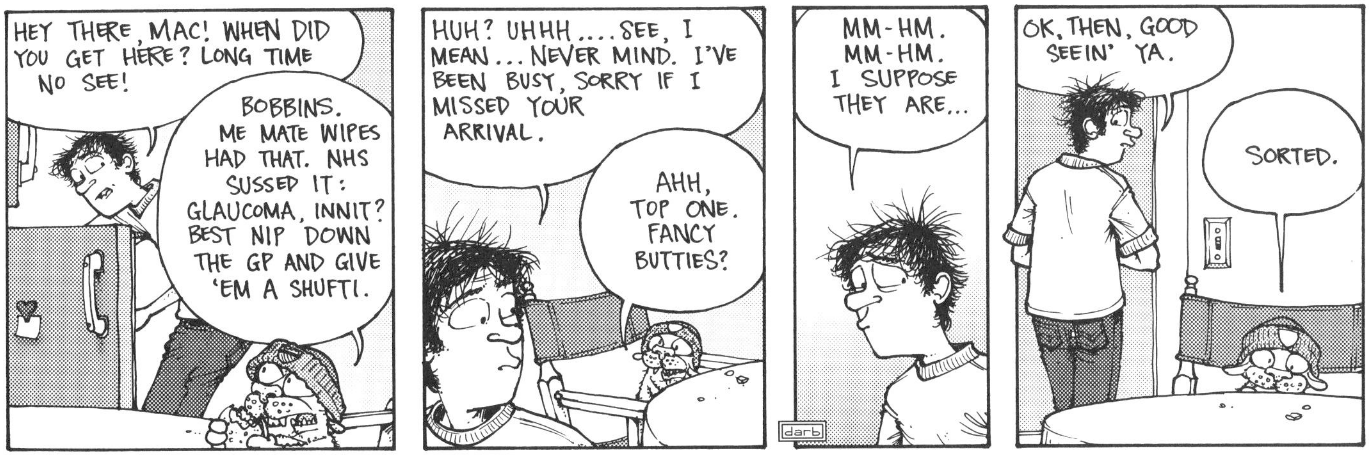
HEY THERE, MAC! WHEN DID YOU GET HERE? LONG TIME NO SEE!
BOBBINS. ME MATE WIPES HAD THAT. NHS SUSSED IT: GLAUCOMA, INNIT? BEST NIP DOWN THE GP AND GIVE 'EM A SHUFTI.
HUH? UHHH.... SEE, I MEAN... NEVER MIND. I'VE BEEN BUSY, SORRY IF I MISSED YOUR ARRIVAL.
AHH, TOP ONE. FANCY BUTTIES?
MM-HM. MM-HM. I SUPPOSE THEY ARE...
OK, THEN, GOOD SEEIN' YA.
SORTED.

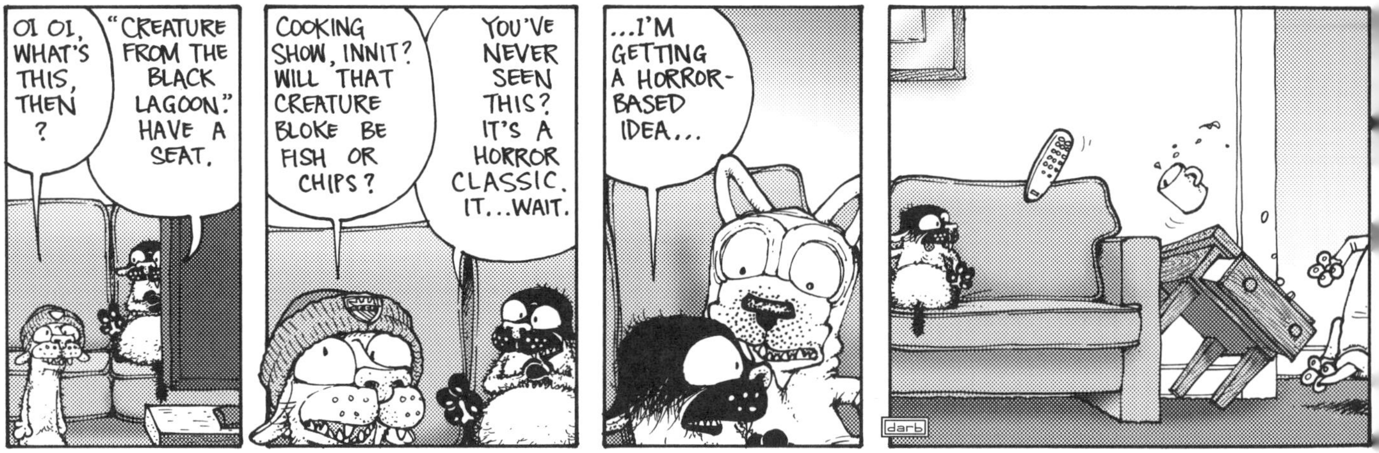
OI OI, WHAT'S THIS, THEN ?
"CREATURE FROM THE BLACK LAGOON." HAVE A SEAT.
COOKING SHOW, INNIT? WILL THAT CREATURE BLOKE BE FISH OR CHIPS?
YOU'VE NEVER SEEN THIS? IT'S A HORROR CLASSIC. IT...WAIT.
...I'M GETTING A HORROR-BASED IDEA...
darb

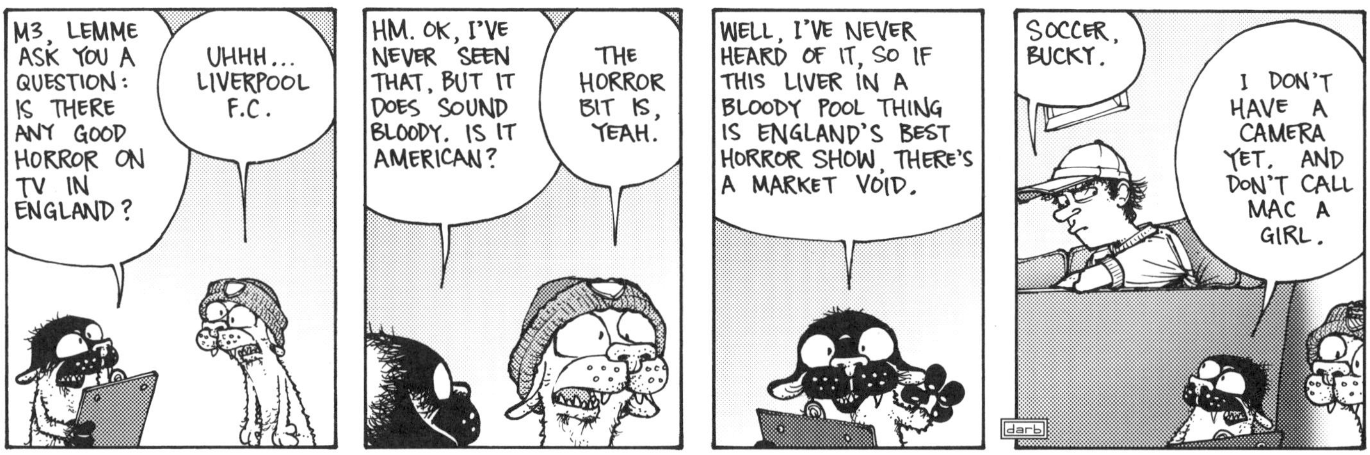
M3, LEMME ASK YOU A QUESTION: IS THERE ANY GOOD HORROR ON TV IN ENGLAND?
UHHH... LIVERPOOL F.C.
HM. OK, I'VE NEVER SEEN THAT, BUT IT DOES SOUND BLOODY. IS IT AMERICAN?
THE HORROR BIT IS, YEAH.
WELL, I'VE NEVER HEARD OF IT, SO IF THIS LIVER IN A BLOODY POOL THING IS ENGLAND'S BEST HORROR SHOW, THERE'S A MARKET VOID.
SOCCER, BUCKY.
I DON'T HAVE A CAMERA YET. AND DON'T CALL MAC A GIRL.
darb

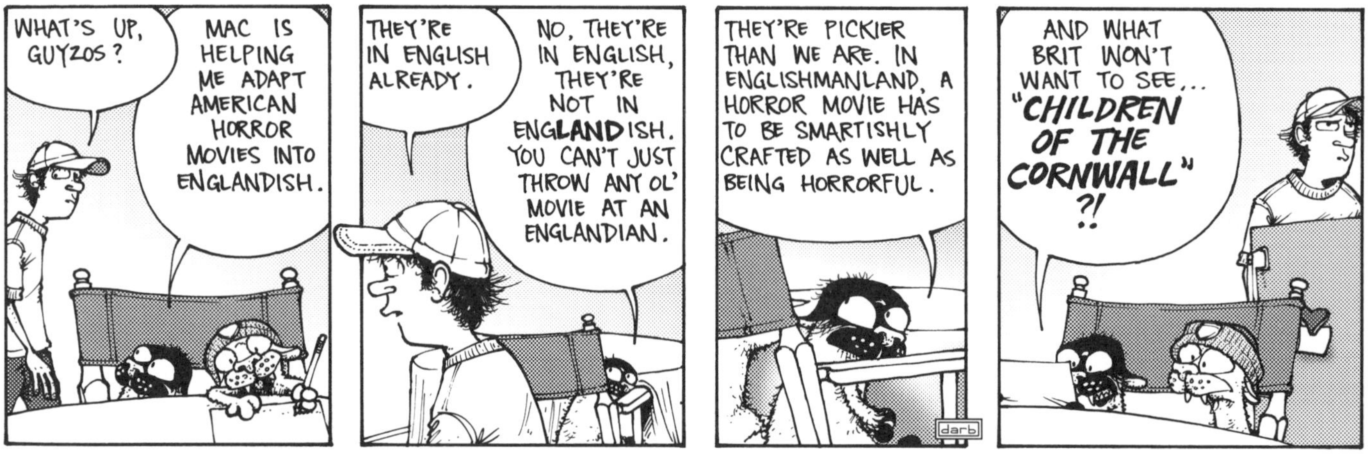
WHAT'S UP, GUYZOS?
MAC IS HELPING ME ADAPT AMERICAN HORROR MOVIES INTO ENGLANDISH.
THEY'RE IN ENGLISH ALREADY.
NO, THEY'RE IN ENGLISH, THEY'RE NOT IN ENGLANDISH. YOU CAN'T JUST THROW ANY OL' MOVIE AT AN ENGLANDIAN.
THEY'RE PICKIER THAN WE ARE. IN ENGLISHMANLAND, A HORROR MOVIE HAS TO BE SMARTISHLY CRAFTED AS WELL AS BEING HORRORFUL.
darb
AND WHAT BRIT WON'T WANT TO SEE... "CHILDREN OF THE CORNWALL" ?!

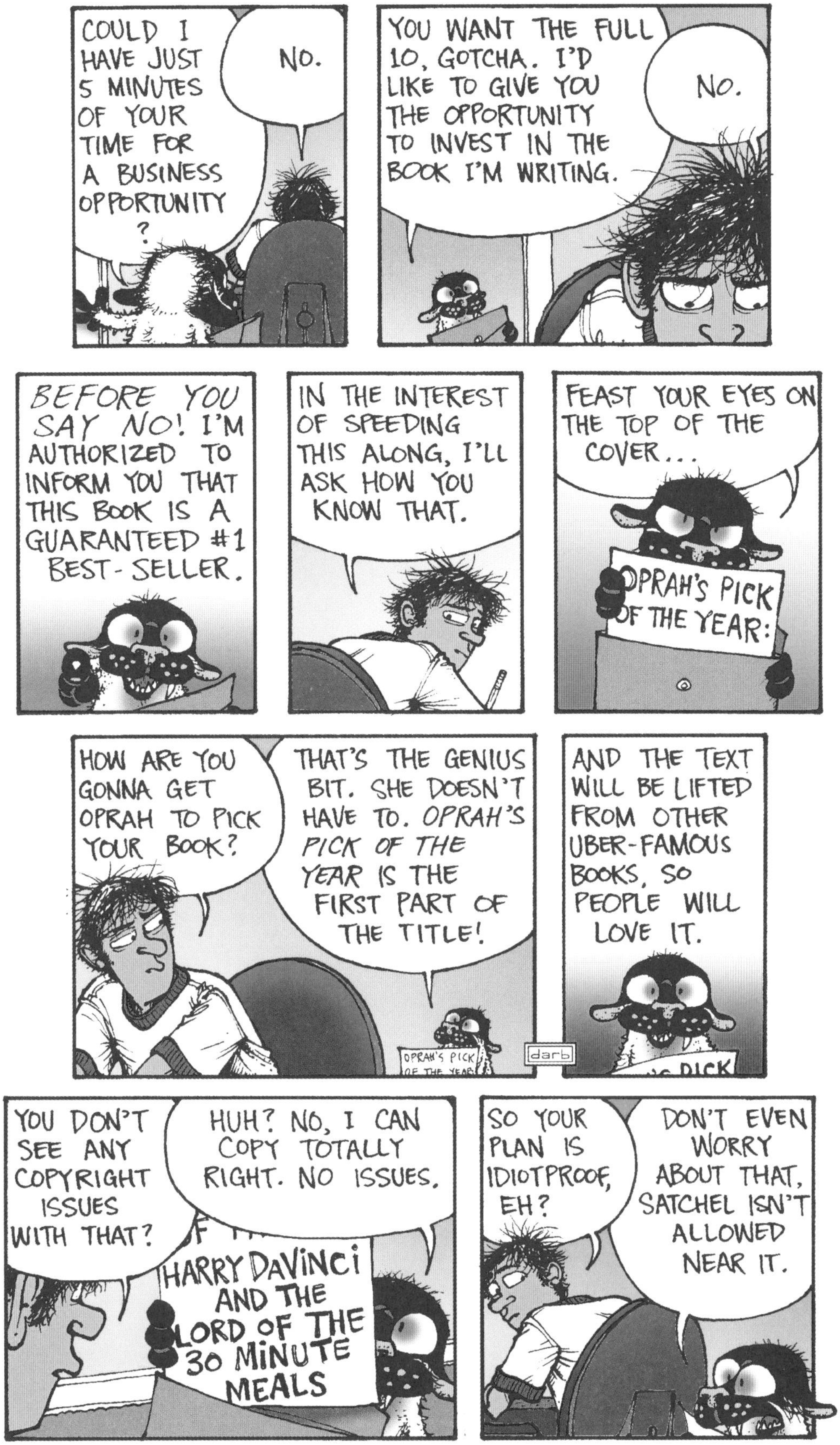
COULD I HAVE JUST 5 MINUTES OF YOUR TIME FOR A BUSINESS OPPORTUNITY ?
NO.
YOU WANT THE FULL 10, GOTCHA. I'D LIKE TO GIVE YOU THE OPPORTUNITY TO INVEST IN THE BOOK I'M WRITING.
NO.
BEFORE YOU SAY NO! I'M AUTHORIZED TO INFORM YOU THAT THIS BOOK IS A GUARANTEED #1 BEST-SELLER.
IN THE INTEREST OF SPEEDING THIS ALONG, I'LL ASK HOW YOU KNOW THAT.
FEAST YOUR EYES ON THE TOP OF THE COVER...
OPRAH'S PICK OF THE YEAR:
HOW ARE YOU GONNA GET OPRAH TO PICK YOUR BOOK?
THAT'S THE GENIUS BIT. SHE DOESN'T HAVE TO. OPRAH'S PICK OF THE YEAR IS THE FIRST PART OF THE TITLE!
OPRAH'S PICK
darb
AND THE TEXT WILL BE LIFTED FROM OTHER UBER-FAMOUS BOOKS, SO PEOPLE WILL LOVE IT.
YOU DON'T SEE ANY COPYRIGHT ISSUES WITH THAT?
HUH? NO, I CAN COPY TOTALLY RIGHT. NO ISSUES.
HARRY DAVINCI AND THE LORD OF THE 30 MINUTE MEALS
SO YOUR PLAN IS IDIOTPROOF, EH?
DON'T EVEN WORRY ABOUT THAT, SATCHEL ISN'T ALLOWED NEAR IT.

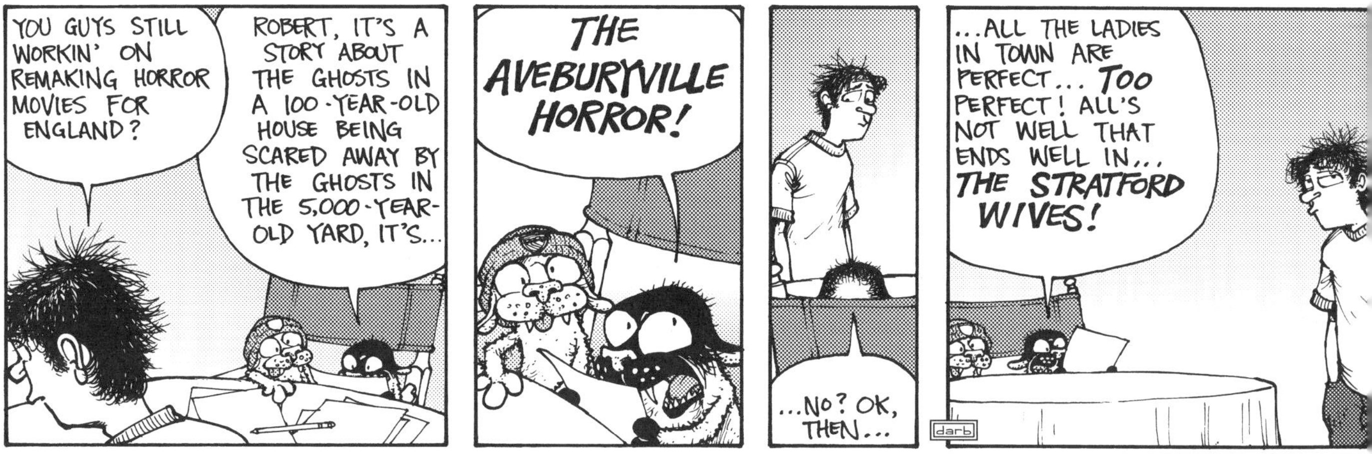
YOU GUYS STILL WORKIN' ON REMAKING HORROR MOVIES FOR ENGLAND?
ROBERT, IT'S A STORY ABOUT THE GHOSTS IN A 100-YEAR-OLD HOUSE BEING SCARED AWAY BY THE GHOSTS IN THE 5,000-YEAR-OLD YARD, IT'S...
THE AVEBURYVILLE HORROR!
...NO? OK, THEN...
...ALL THE LADIES IN TOWN ARE PERFECT... TOO PERFECT! ALL'S NOT WELL THAT ENDS WELL IN... THE STRATFORD WIVES!
darb

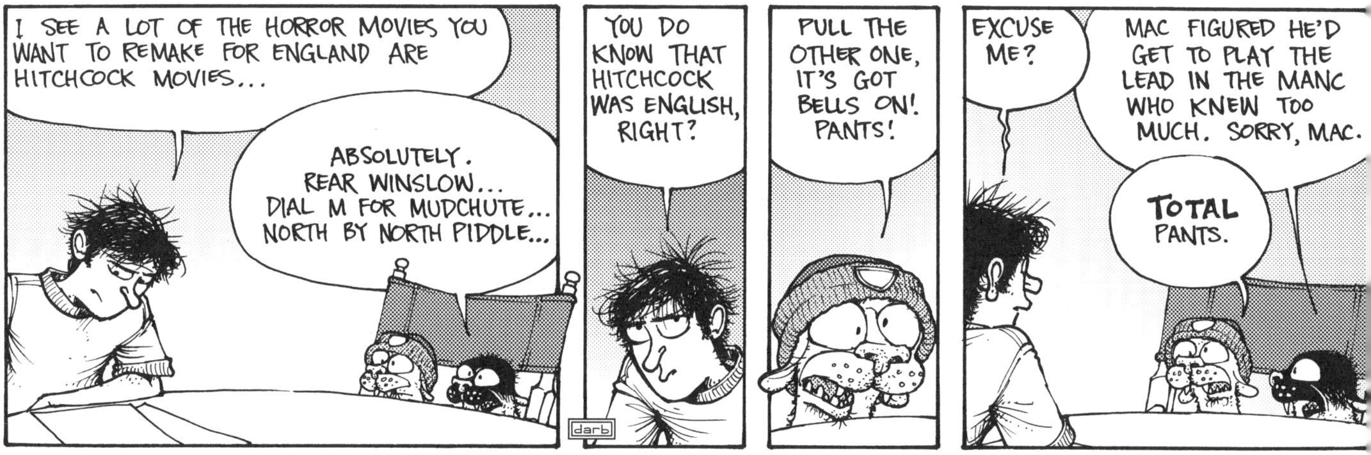
I SEE A LOT OF THE HORROR MOVIES YOU WANT TO REMAKE FOR ENGLAND ARE HITCHCOCK MOVIES...
ABSOLUTELY. REAR WINSLOW... DIAL M FOR MUDCHUTE... NORTH BY NORTH PIDDLE...
darb
YOU DO KNOW THAT HITCHCOCK WAS ENGLISH, RIGHT?
PULL THE OTHER ONE, IT'S GOT BELLS ON! PANTS!
EXCUSE ME?
MAC FIGURED HE'D GET TO PLAY THE LEAD IN THE MANC WHO KNEW TOO MUCH. SORRY, MAC.
TOTAL PANTS.

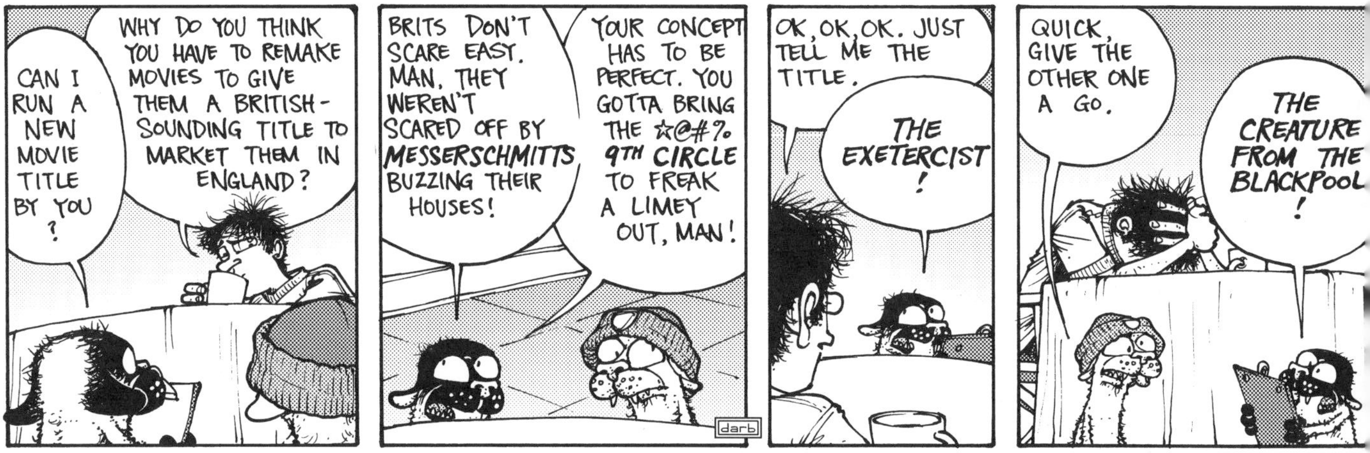
CAN I RUN A NEW MOVIE TITLE BY YOU?
WHY DO YOU THINK YOU HAVE TO REMAKE MOVIES TO GIVE THEM A BRITISH-SOUNDING TITLE TO MARKET THEM IN ENGLAND?
BRITS DON'T SCARE EASY, MAN. THEY WEREN'T SCARED OFF BY MESSERSCHMITTS BUZZING THEIR HOUSES!
YOUR CONCEPT HAS TO BE PERFECT. YOU GOTTA BRING THE ☆@#% 9TH CIRCLE TO FREAK A LIMEY OUT, MAN!
darb
OK, OK, OK. JUST TELL ME THE TITLE.
THE EXETERCIST!
QUICK, GIVE THE OTHER ONE A GO.
THE CREATURE FROM THE BLACKPOOL!

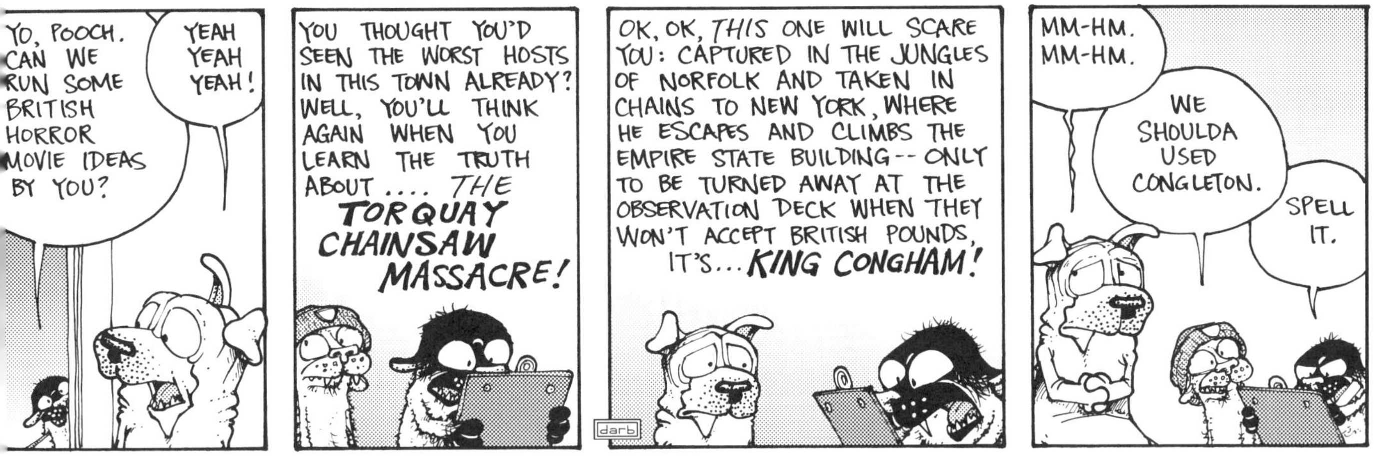
YO, POOCH. CAN WE RUN SOME BRITISH HORROR MOVIE IDEAS BY YOU?
YEAH YEAH YEAH!
YOU THOUGHT YOU'D SEEN THE WORST HOSTS IN THIS TOWN ALREADY? WELL, YOU'LL THINK AGAIN WHEN YOU LEARN THE TRUTH ABOUT.... THE TORQUAY CHAINSAW MASSACRE!
OK, OK, THIS ONE WILL SCARE YOU: CAPTURED IN THE JUNGLES OF NORFOLK AND TAKEN IN CHAINS TO NEW YORK, WHERE HE ESCAPES AND CLIMBS THE EMPIRE STATE BUILDING-- ONLY TO BE TURNED AWAY AT THE OBSERVATION DECK WHEN THEY WON'T ACCEPT BRITISH POUNDS, IT'S... KING CONGHAM!
darb
MM-HM. MM-HM.
WE SHOULDA USED CONGLETON.
SPELL IT.

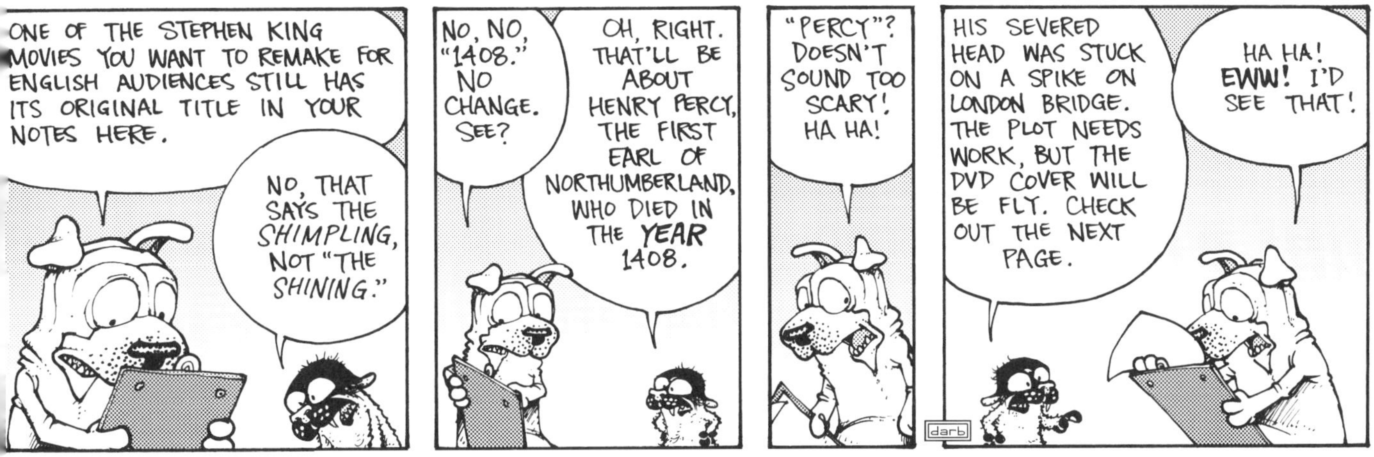
ONE OF THE STEPHEN KING MOVIES YOU WANT TO REMAKE FOR ENGLISH AUDIENCES STILL HAS ITS ORIGINAL TITLE IN YOUR NOTES HERE.
NO, THAT SAYS THE SHIMPLING, NOT "THE SHINING."
NO, NO, "1408." NO CHANGE. SEE?
OH, RIGHT. THAT'LL BE ABOUT HENRY PERCY, THE FIRST EARL OF NORTHUMBERLAND, WHO DIED IN THE YEAR 1408.
"PERCY"? DOESN'T SOUND TOO SCARY! HA HA!
darb
HIS SEVERED HEAD WAS STUCK ON A SPIKE ON LONDON BRIDGE. THE PLOT NEEDS WORK, BUT THE DVD COVER WILL BE FLY. CHECK OUT THE NEXT PAGE.
HA HA! EWW! I'D SEE THAT!

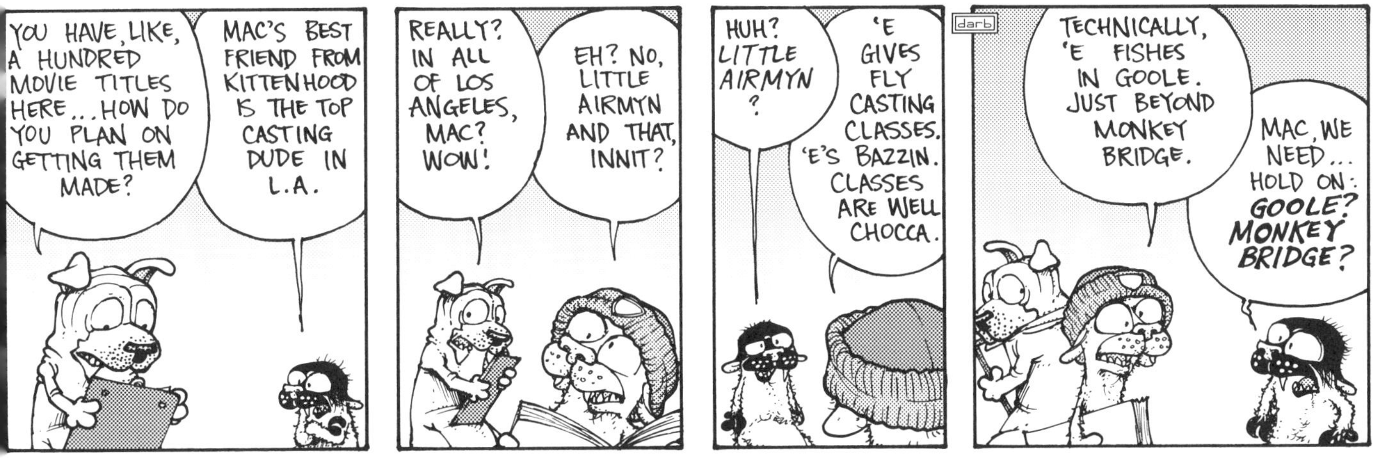
YOU HAVE, LIKE, A HUNDRED MOVIE TITLES HERE... HOW DO YOU PLAN ON GETTING THEM MADE?
MAC'S BEST FRIEND FROM KITTENHOOD IS THE TOP CASTING DUDE IN L.A.
REALLY? IN ALL OF LOS ANGELES, MAC? WOW!
EH? NO, LITTLE AIRMYN AND THAT, INNIT?
HUH? LITTLE AIRMYN?
'E GIVES FLY CASTING CLASSES. 'E'S BAZZIN. CLASSES ARE WELL CHOCCA.
darb
TECHNICALLY, 'E FISHES IN GOOLE. JUST BEYOND MONKEY BRIDGE.
MAC, WE NEED... HOLD ON: GOOLE? MONKEY BRIDGE?

HMM. I THINK MY TAN MAY HAVE WORN OFF TOO MUCH TO WEAR SHORTS.
THIS "TAN" YOU SPEAK OF... WHEN WAS THIS?
I GOT A LITTLE TAN THIS SUMMER.
ARE YOU KIDDING? YOU'RE WHITER THAN AN IRISH SUNBLOCK TESTER!
THE LOCAL KIDS' NICKNAME FOR YOU IS *FROSTY THE ADMAN*.
NASA GAUGES THE BRIGHTNESS OF A STAR BY ITS *APPARENT ROBERTUDE*.
LOOK WHO'S TALKING! MOS OF YOU IS WHITE!
BUT THAT'S A *FASHION* STATEMENT. UNDER THIS GORGEOUS FUR COAT, I'M A MANLY PUCE.
DO MOTHS FLOCK TO YOU IN THE DARKNESS?
FINISHED?
darb
IS IT TRUE THAT BENJAMIN MOORE NIXED THEIR BETA *ROB WILCO COLOR* AFTER SEVERAL FOCUS GROUP MEMBERS GOT BURNED RETINAS?
WHERE ARE MY PANTS?

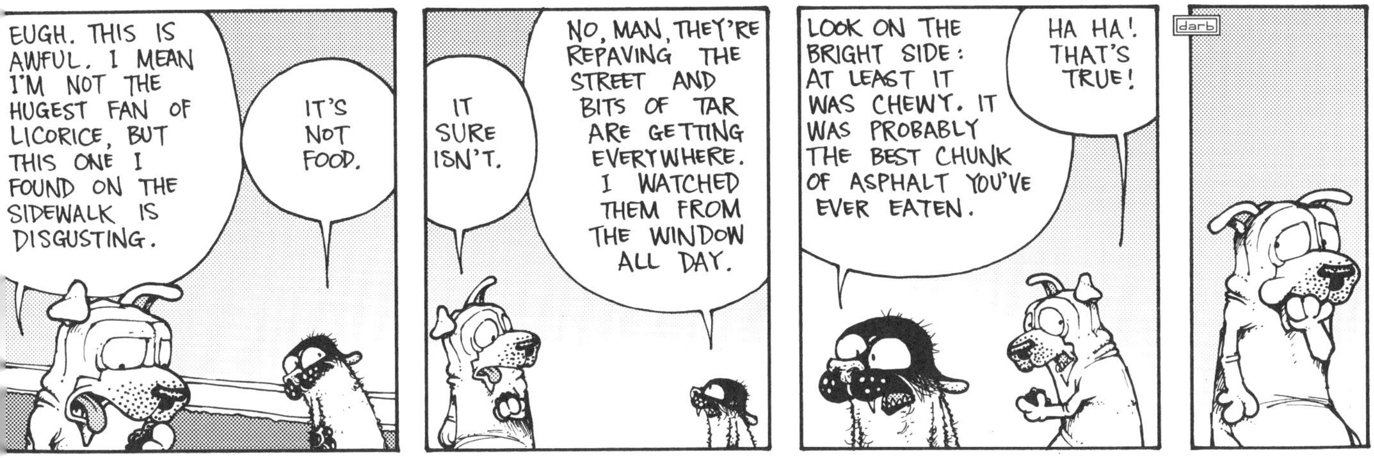
EUGH. THIS IS AWFUL. I MEAN I'M NOT THE HUGEST FAN OF LICORICE, BUT THIS ONE I FOUND ON THE SIDEWALK IS DISGUSTING.
IT'S NOT FOOD.
IT SURE ISN'T.
NO, MAN, THEY'RE REPAVING THE STREET AND BITS OF TAR ARE GETTING EVERYWHERE. I WATCHED THEM FROM THE WINDOW ALL DAY.
LOOK ON THE BRIGHT SIDE: AT LEAST IT WAS CHEWY. IT WAS PROBABLY THE BEST CHUNK OF ASPHALT YOU'VE EVER EATEN.
HA HA! THAT'S TRUE!
darb

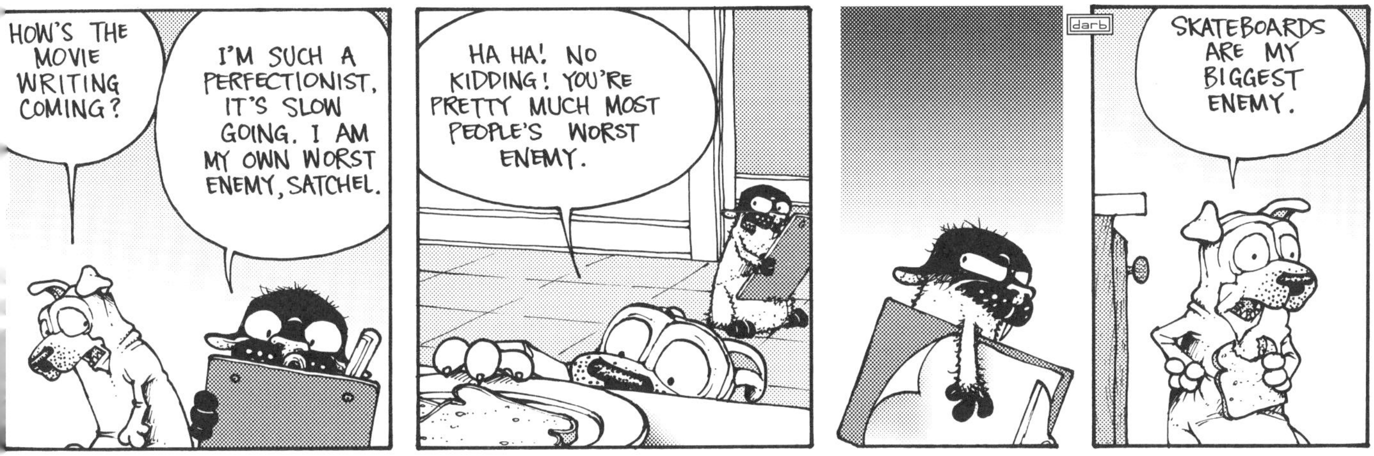
HOW'S THE MOVIE WRITING COMING?
I'M SUCH A PERFECTIONIST, IT'S SLOW GOING. I AM MY OWN WORST ENEMY, SATCHEL.
HA HA! NO KIDDING! YOU'RE PRETTY MUCH MOST PEOPLE'S WORST ENEMY.
darb
SKATEBOARDS ARE MY BIGGEST ENEMY.

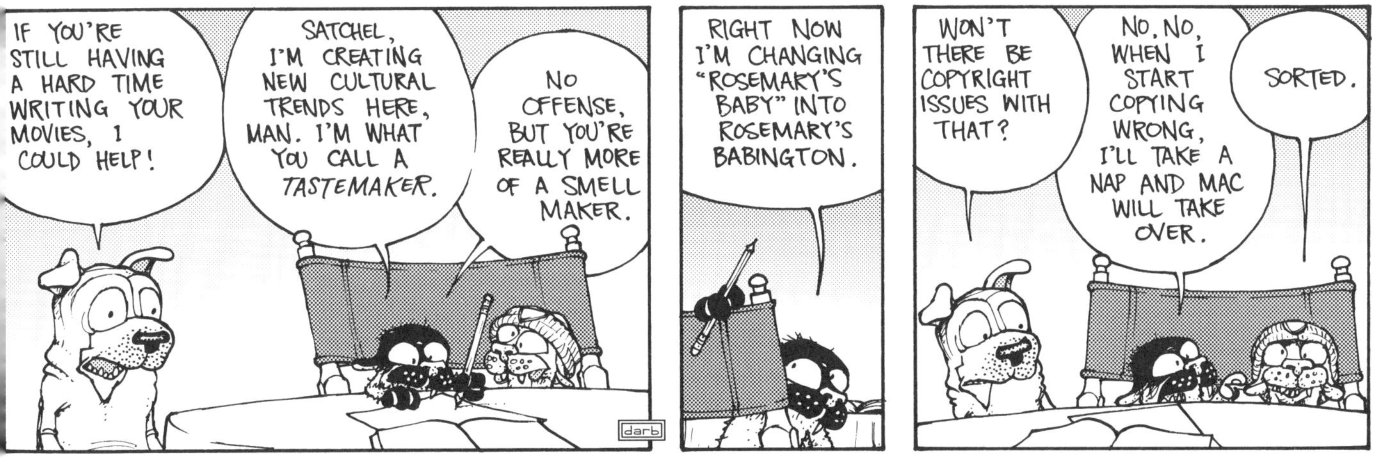
IF YOU'RE STILL HAVING A HARD TIME WRITING YOUR MOVIES, I COULD HELP!
SATCHEL, I'M CREATING NEW CULTURAL TRENDS HERE, MAN. I'M WHAT YOU CALL A *TASTEMAKER*.
NO OFFENSE, BUT YOU'RE REALLY MORE OF A SMELL MAKER.
darb
RIGHT NOW I'M CHANGING "ROSEMARY'S BABY" INTO ROSEMARY'S BABINGTON.
WON'T THERE BE COPYRIGHT ISSUES WITH THAT?
NO, NO, WHEN I START COPYING WRONG, I'LL TAKE A NAP AND MAC WILL TAKE OVER.
SORTED.

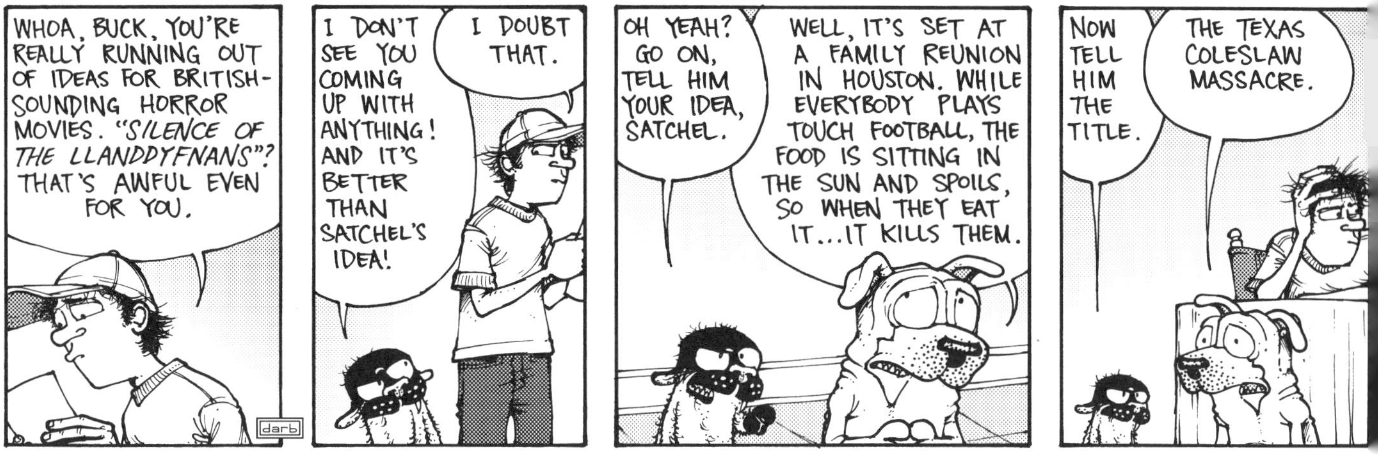
WHOA, BUCK, YOU'RE REALLY RUNNING OUT OF IDEAS FOR BRITISH-SOUNDING HORROR MOVIES. "*SILENCE OF THE LLANDDYFNANS*"? THAT'S AWFUL EVEN FOR YOU.
I DON'T SEE YOU COMING UP WITH ANYTHING! AND IT'S BETTER THAN SATCHEL'S IDEA!
I DOUBT THAT.
OH YEAH? GO ON, TELL HIM YOUR IDEA, SATCHEL.
WELL, IT'S SET AT A FAMILY REUNION IN HOUSTON. WHILE EVERYBODY PLAYS TOUCH FOOTBALL, THE FOOD IS SITTING IN THE SUN AND SPOILS, SO WHEN THEY EAT IT... IT KILLS THEM.
NOW TELL HIM THE TITLE.
THE TEXAS COLESLAW MASSACRE.
darb

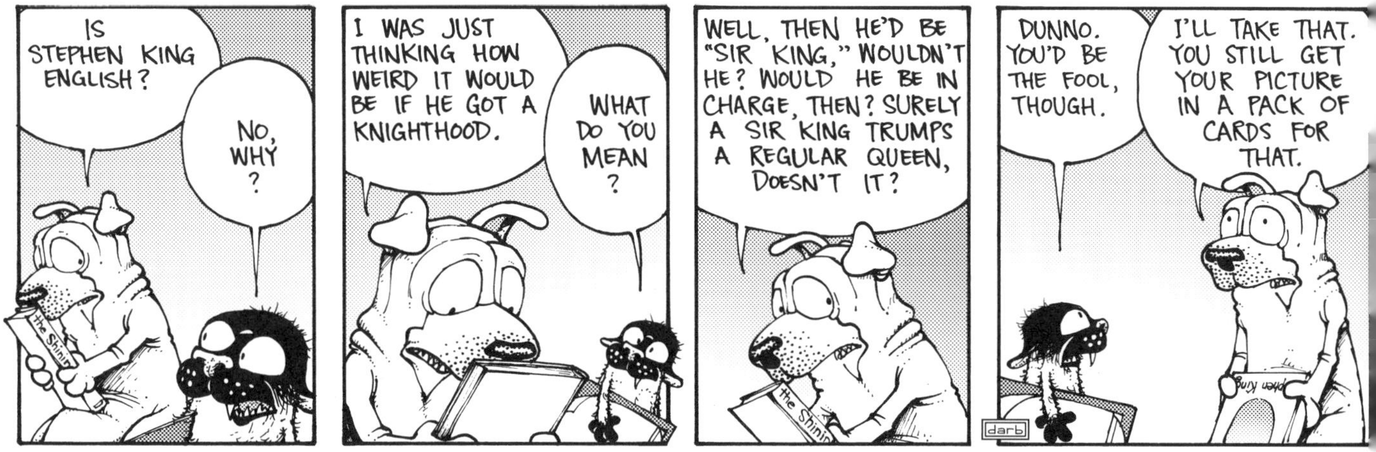
IS STEPHEN KING ENGLISH?
NO, WHY?
I WAS JUST THINKING HOW WEIRD IT WOULD BE IF HE GOT A KNIGHTHOOD.
WHAT DO YOU MEAN?
WELL, THEN HE'D BE "SIR KING," WOULDN'T HE? WOULD HE BE IN CHARGE, THEN? SURELY A SIR KING TRUMPS A REGULAR QUEEN, DOESN'T IT?
DUNNO. YOU'D BE THE FOOL, THOUGH.
I'LL TAKE THAT. YOU STILL GET YOUR PICTURE IN A PACK OF CARDS FOR THAT.
darb

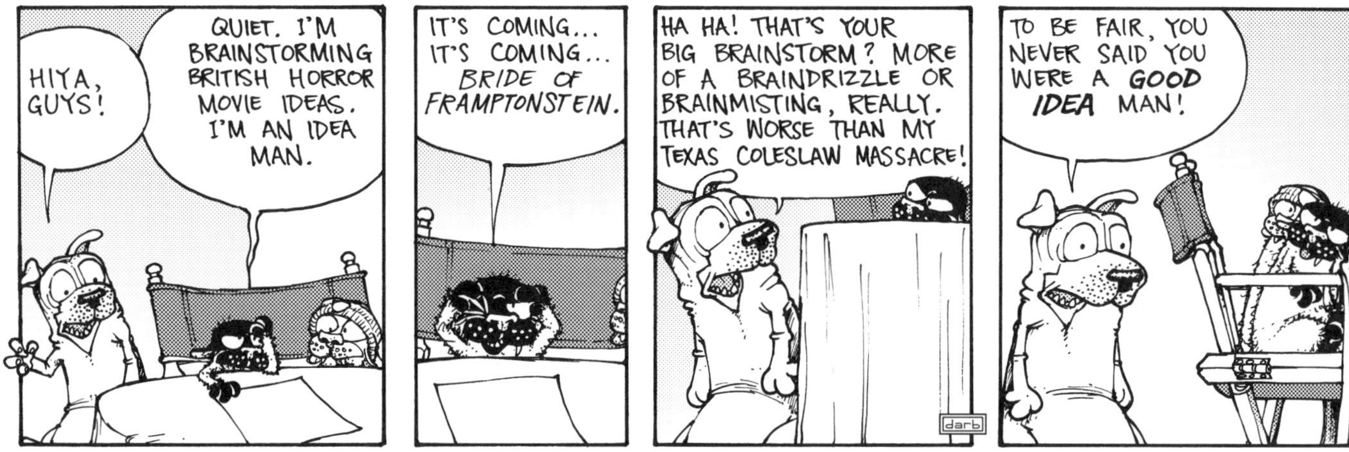
HIYA, GUYS!
QUIET. I'M BRAINSTORMING BRITISH HORROR MOVIE IDEAS. I'M AN IDEA MAN.
IT'S COMING... IT'S COMING... *BRIDE OF FRAMPTONSTEIN.*
HA HA! THAT'S YOUR BIG BRAINSTORM? MORE OF A BRAINDRIZZLE OR BRAINMISTING, REALLY. THAT'S WORSE THAN MY TEXAS COLESLAW MASSACRE!
TO BE FAIR, YOU NEVER SAID YOU WERE A ***GOOD IDEA*** MAN!
darb

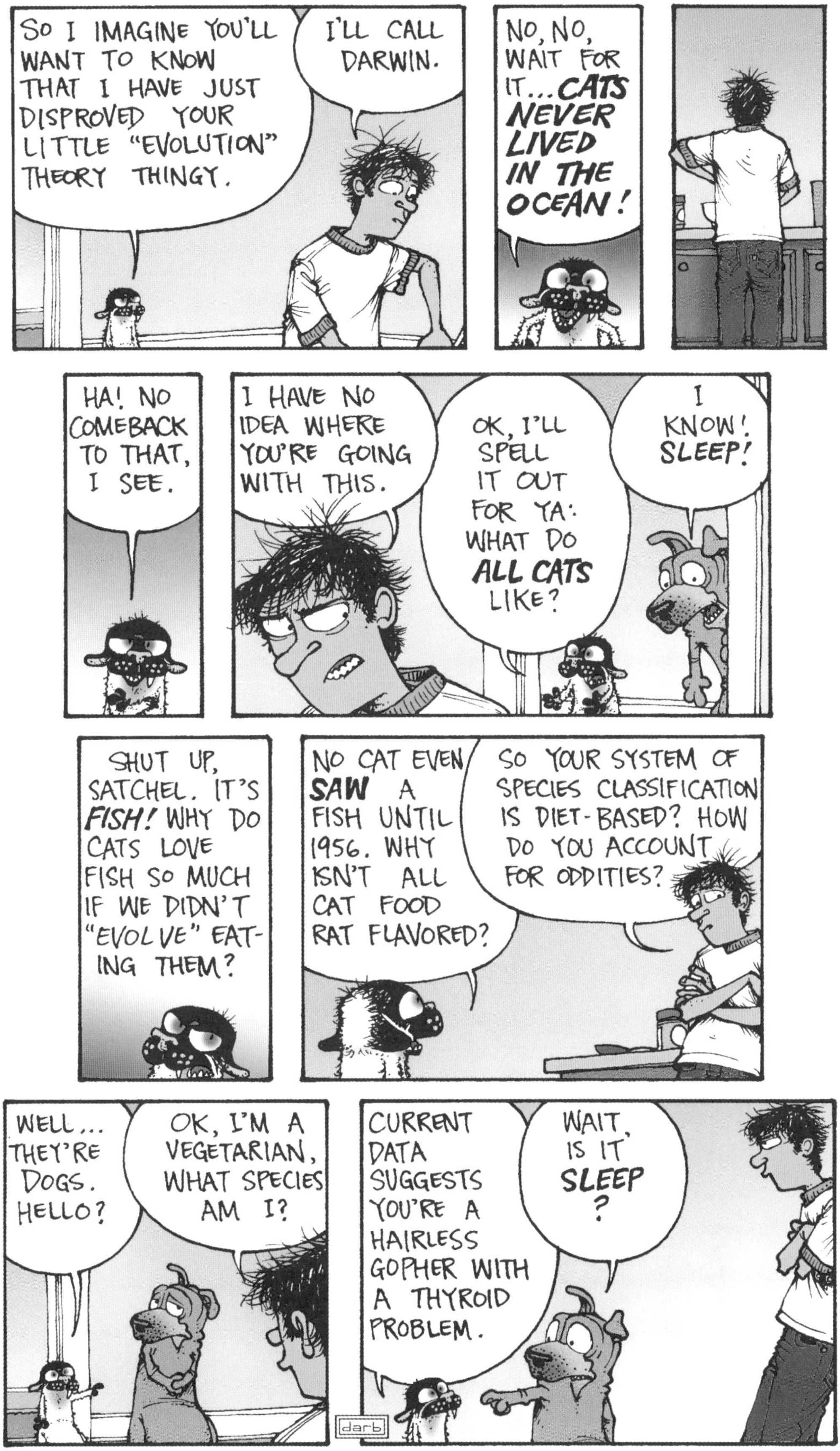
SO I IMAGINE YOU'LL WANT TO KNOW THAT I HAVE JUST DISPROVED YOUR LITTLE "EVOLUTION" THEORY THINGY.
I'LL CALL DARWIN.
NO, NO, WAIT FOR IT... CATS NEVER LIVED IN THE OCEAN!
HA! NO COMEBACK TO THAT, I SEE.
I HAVE NO IDEA WHERE YOU'RE GOING WITH THIS.
OK, I'LL SPELL IT OUT FOR YA: WHAT DO ALL CATS LIKE?
I KNOW! SLEEP!
SHUT UP, SATCHEL. IT'S FISH! WHY DO CATS LOVE FISH SO MUCH IF WE DIDN'T "EVOLVE" EATING THEM?
NO CAT EVEN SAW A FISH UNTIL 1956. WHY ISN'T ALL CAT FOOD RAT FLAVORED?
SO YOUR SYSTEM OF SPECIES CLASSIFICATION IS DIET-BASED? HOW DO YOU ACCOUNT FOR ODDITIES?
WELL... THEY'RE DOGS. HELLO?
OK, I'M A VEGETARIAN, WHAT SPECIES AM I?
CURRENT DATA SUGGESTS YOU'RE A HAIRLESS GOPHER WITH A THYROID PROBLEM.
WAIT, IS IT SLEEP?
darb

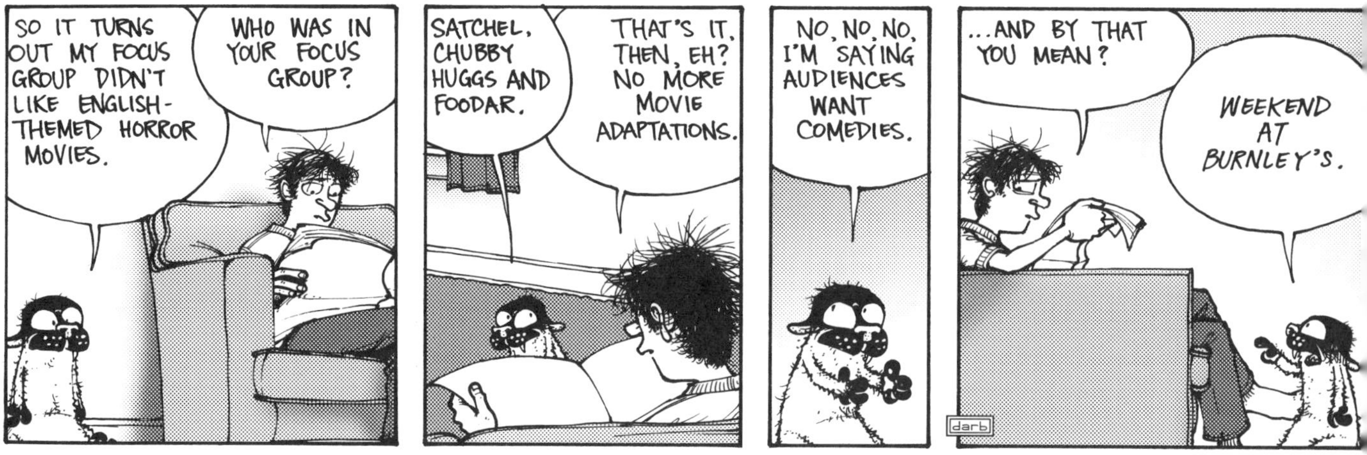
SO IT TURNS OUT MY FOCUS GROUP DIDN'T LIKE ENGLISH-THEMED HORROR MOVIES.
WHO WAS IN YOUR FOCUS GROUP?
SATCHEL, CHUBBY HUGGS AND FOODAR.
THAT'S IT, THEN, EH? NO MORE MOVIE ADAPTATIONS.
NO, NO, NO, I'M SAYING AUDIENCES WANT COMEDIES.
...AND BY THAT YOU MEAN?
WEEKEND AT BURNLEY'S.
darb

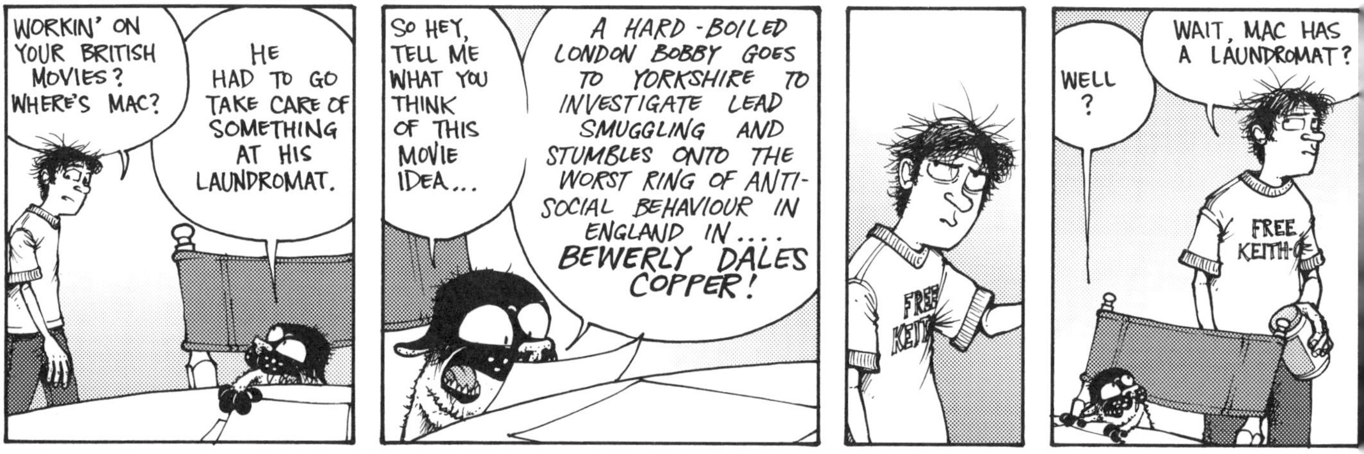
WORKIN' ON YOUR BRITISH MOVIES? WHERE'S MAC?
HE HAD TO GO TAKE CARE OF SOMETHING AT HIS LAUNDROMAT.
SO HEY, TELL ME WHAT YOU THINK OF THIS MOVIE IDEA...
A HARD-BOILED LONDON BOBBY GOES TO YORKSHIRE TO INVESTIGATE LEAD SMUGGLING AND STUMBLES ONTO THE WORST RING OF ANTI-SOCIAL BEHAVIOUR IN ENGLAND IN.... BEWERLY DALES COPPER!
FREE KEITH
WELL?
WAIT, MAC HAS A LAUNDROMAT?
FREE KEITH

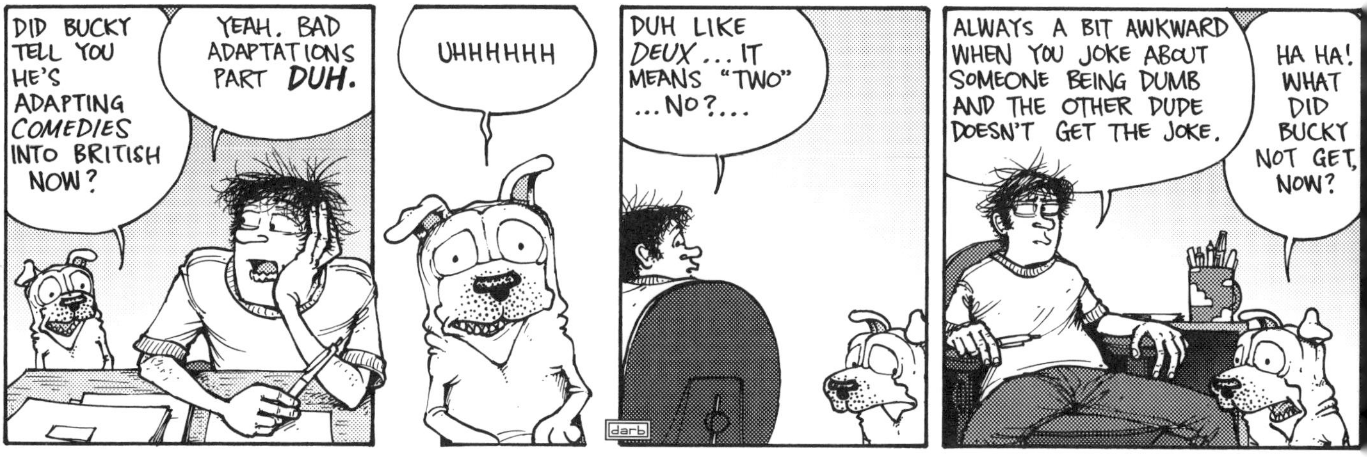
DID BUCKY TELL YOU HE'S ADAPTING COMEDIES INTO BRITISH NOW?
YEAH. BAD ADAPTATIONS PART DUH.
UHHHHHH
darb
DUH LIKE DEUX... IT MEANS "TWO" ...NO?...
ALWAYS A BIT AWKWARD WHEN YOU JOKE ABOUT SOMEONE BEING DUMB AND THE OTHER DUDE DOESN'T GET THE JOKE.
HA HA! WHAT DID BUCKY NOT GET, NOW?

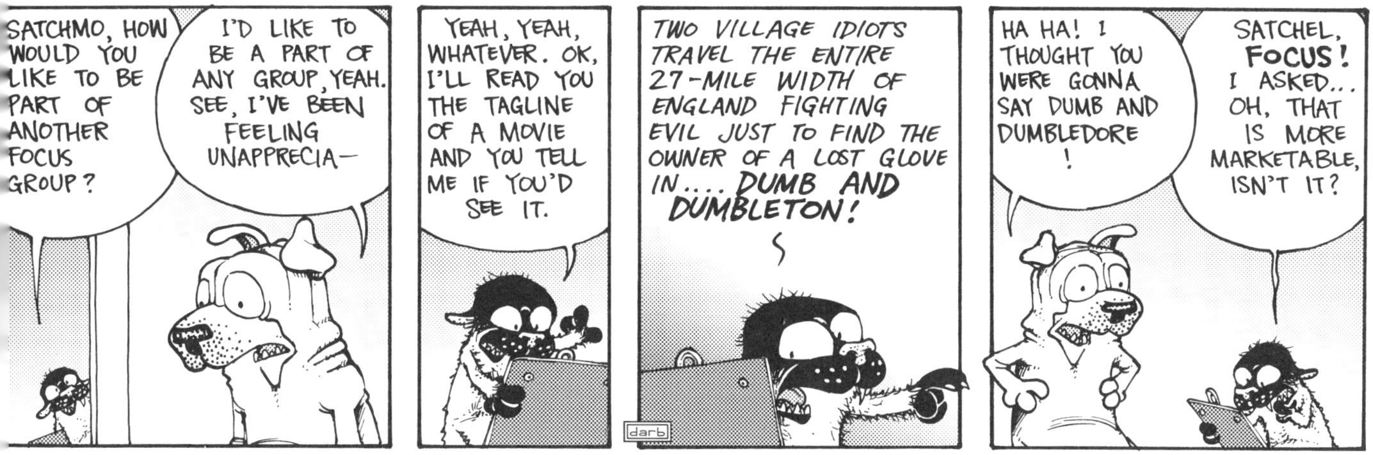
SATCHMO, HOW WOULD YOU LIKE TO BE PART OF ANOTHER FOCUS GROUP?
I'D LIKE TO BE A PART OF ANY GROUP, YEAH. SEE, I'VE BEEN FEELING UNAPPRECIA—
YEAH, YEAH, WHATEVER. OK, I'LL READ YOU THE TAGLINE OF A MOVIE AND YOU TELL ME IF YOU'D SEE IT.
TWO VILLAGE IDIOTS TRAVEL THE ENTIRE 27-MILE WIDTH OF ENGLAND FIGHTING EVIL JUST TO FIND THE OWNER OF A LOST GLOVE IN.... DUMB AND DUMBLETON!
darb
HA HA! I THOUGHT YOU WERE GONNA SAY DUMB AND DUMBLEDORE !
SATCHEL, FOCUS! I ASKED... OH, THAT IS MORE MARKETABLE, ISN'T IT?

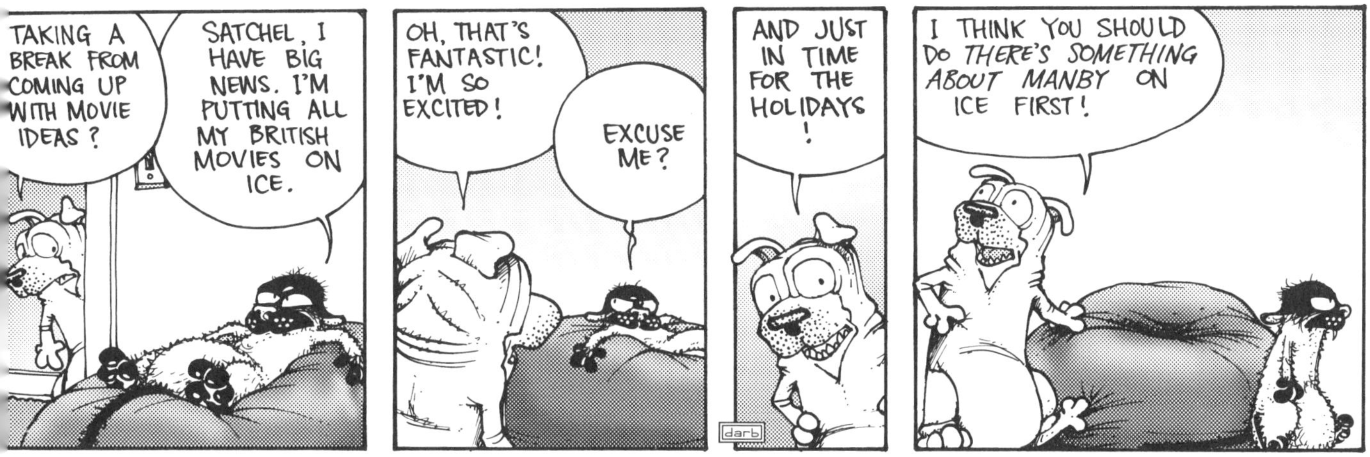
TAKING A BREAK FROM COMING UP WITH MOVIE IDEAS?
SATCHEL, I HAVE BIG NEWS. I'M PUTTING ALL MY BRITISH MOVIES ON ICE.
OH, THAT'S FANTASTIC! I'M SO EXCITED!
EXCUSE ME?
AND JUST IN TIME FOR THE HOLIDAYS !
darb
I THINK YOU SHOULD DO THERE'S SOMETHING ABOUT MANBY ON ICE FIRST!

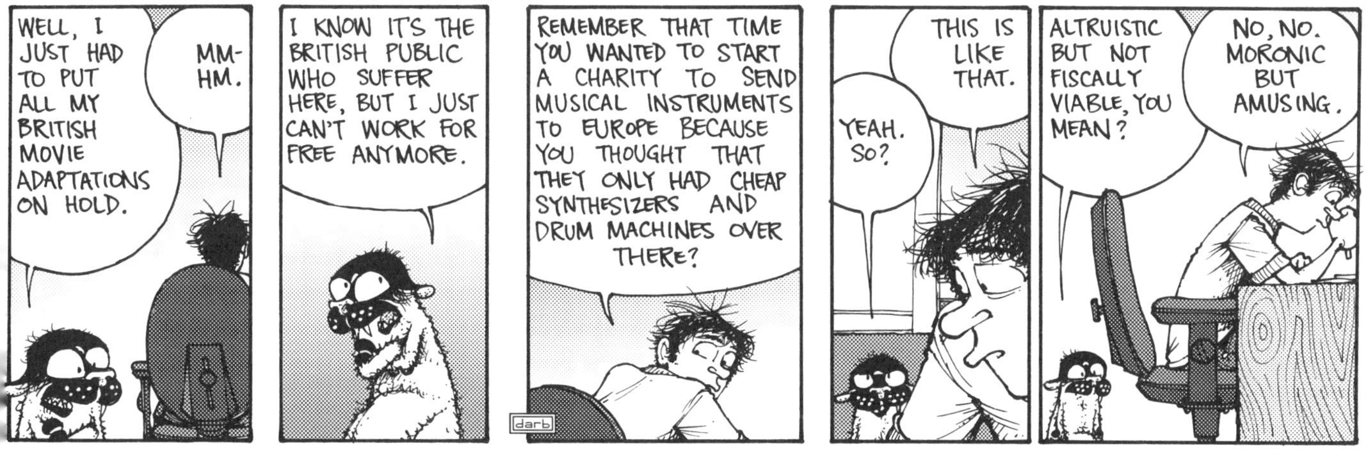
WELL, I JUST HAD TO PUT ALL MY BRITISH MOVIE ADAPTATIONS ON HOLD.
MM-HM.
I KNOW IT'S THE BRITISH PUBLIC WHO SUFFER HERE, BUT I JUST CAN'T WORK FOR FREE ANYMORE.
REMEMBER THAT TIME YOU WANTED TO START A CHARITY TO SEND MUSICAL INSTRUMENTS TO EUROPE BECAUSE YOU THOUGHT THAT THEY ONLY HAD CHEAP SYNTHESIZERS AND DRUM MACHINES OVER THERE?
darb
YEAH. SO?
THIS IS LIKE THAT.
ALTRUISTIC BUT NOT FISCALLY VIABLE, YOU MEAN?
NO, NO. MORONIC BUT AMUSING.

I WISH I COULD ENTER THIS AGILITY CONTEST. IT LOOKS SO FUN...

SO DO IT.

LOOK AT THE DOGS IN THESE PICTURES, THEY'RE ALL, LIKE, PROFESSIONAL HERDERS, I'D EMBARRASS MYSELF!

SATCHEL, LET ME TELL YOU A STORY. ONCE UPON A TIME, I WANTED TO ENTER A CAT SHOW,

BUT YOU DIDN'T AND NOW YOU REGRET IT EVERY DAY OF YOUR LIFE?

OH, NO, I DID IT. POOFED MY HAIR UP LIKE A CHIA PET AND PUT ON THE BIGGEST RIBBON I COULD FIND. I *DID IT*, SATCHEL.

SO YOU'RE SAYING IT WAS ALL ABOUT THE *EXPERI-ENCE?*

OH, NO, I WANT-ED THE $500 PRIZE.

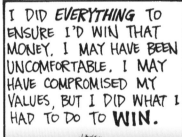

I DID *EVERYTHING* TO ENSURE I'D WIN THAT MONEY. I MAY HAVE BEEN UNCOMFORTABLE. I MAY HAVE COMPROMISED MY VALUES, BUT I DID WHAT I HAD TO DO TO **WIN.**

WOW. WHAT DID YOU DO WITH THE $500?

OH, I DIDN'T EVEN MAKE IT OUT OF THE SIAMESES. HUMILIATING.

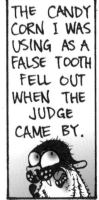

THE CANDY CORN I WAS USING AS A FALSE TOOTH FELL OUT WHEN THE JUDGE CAME BY.

BUT IT WAS A CHARACTER-BUILDING EXPERIENCE?

NOT REALLY. I HAD TO STEAL $150 TO PAY THE ENTRANCE FEE.

SO ARE YOU SAYING I SHOULD JUST TRY MY HARDEST?

GOOD LORD, NO. JUST NIP IN AND TAKE THE BLUE RIBBON WHILE ALL THE NERDLINGERS ARE RUNNING THROUGH TUBES.

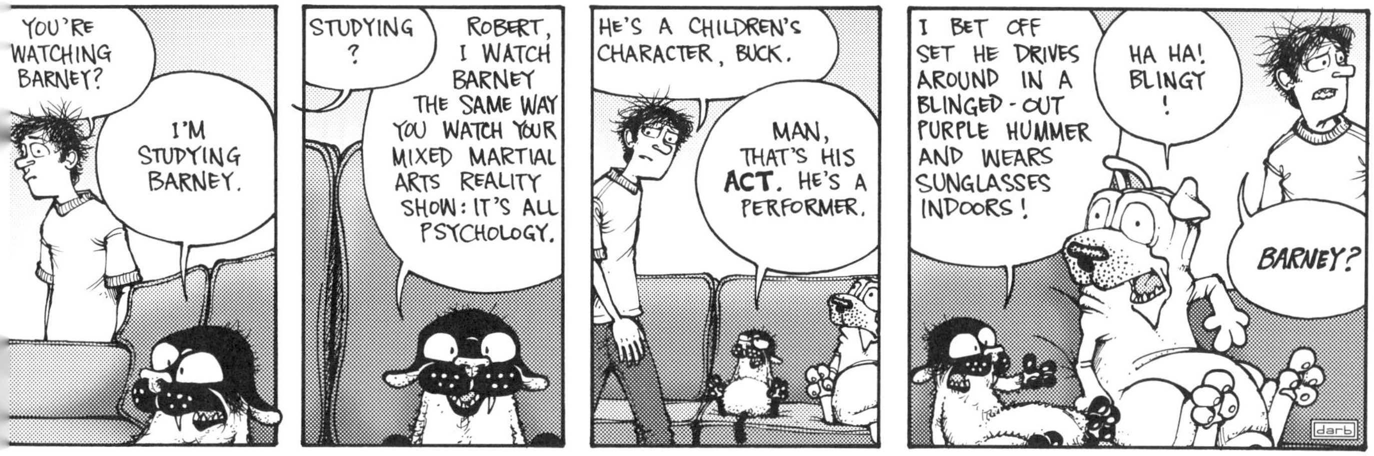
YOU'RE WATCHING BARNEY?
I'M STUDYING BARNEY.
STUDYING ?
ROBERT, I WATCH BARNEY THE SAME WAY YOU WATCH YOUR MIXED MARTIAL ARTS REALITY SHOW: IT'S ALL PSYCHOLOGY.
HE'S A CHILDREN'S CHARACTER, BUCK.
MAN, THAT'S HIS ACT. HE'S A PERFORMER.
I BET OFF SET HE DRIVES AROUND IN A BLINGED-OUT PURPLE HUMMER AND WEARS SUNGLASSES INDOORS!
HA HA! BLINGY !
BARNEY?
darb

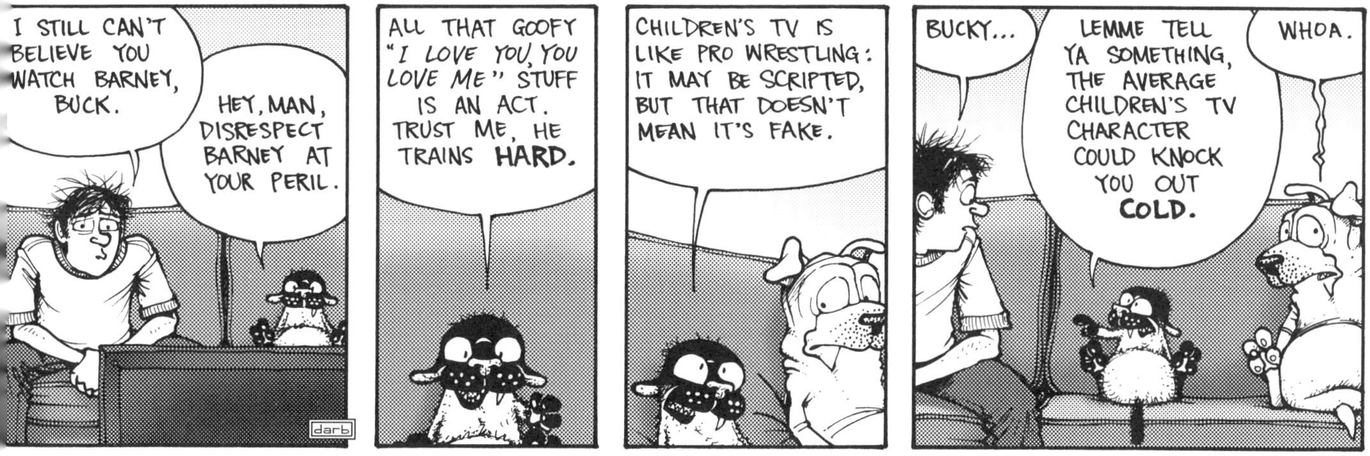
I STILL CAN'T BELIEVE YOU WATCH BARNEY, BUCK.
HEY, MAN, DISRESPECT BARNEY AT YOUR PERIL.
darb
ALL THAT GOOFY "I LOVE YOU, YOU LOVE ME" STUFF IS AN ACT. TRUST ME, HE TRAINS HARD.
CHILDREN'S TV IS LIKE PRO WRESTLING: IT MAY BE SCRIPTED, BUT THAT DOESN'T MEAN IT'S FAKE.
BUCKY...
LEMME TELL YA SOMETHING, THE AVERAGE CHILDREN'S TV CHARACTER COULD KNOCK YOU OUT COLD.
WHOA.

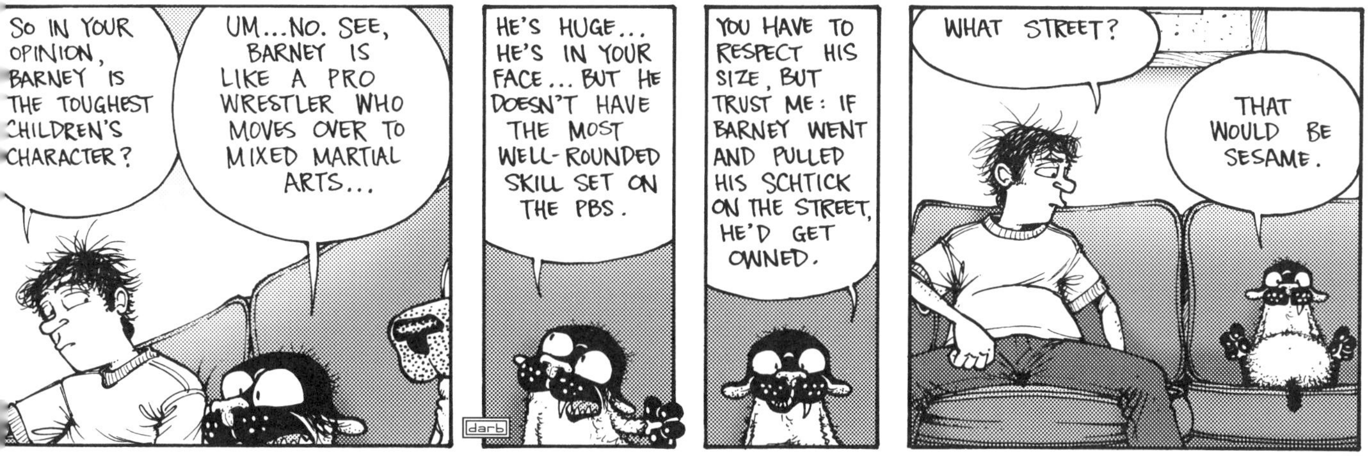
SO IN YOUR OPINION, BARNEY IS THE TOUGHEST CHILDREN'S CHARACTER?
UM...NO. SEE, BARNEY IS LIKE A PRO WRESTLER WHO MOVES OVER TO MIXED MARTIAL ARTS...
darb
HE'S HUGE... HE'S IN YOUR FACE... BUT HE DOESN'T HAVE THE MOST WELL-ROUNDED SKILL SET ON THE PBS.
YOU HAVE TO RESPECT HIS SIZE, BUT TRUST ME: IF BARNEY WENT AND PULLED HIS SCHTICK ON THE STREET, HE'D GET OWNED.
WHAT STREET?
THAT WOULD BE SESAME.

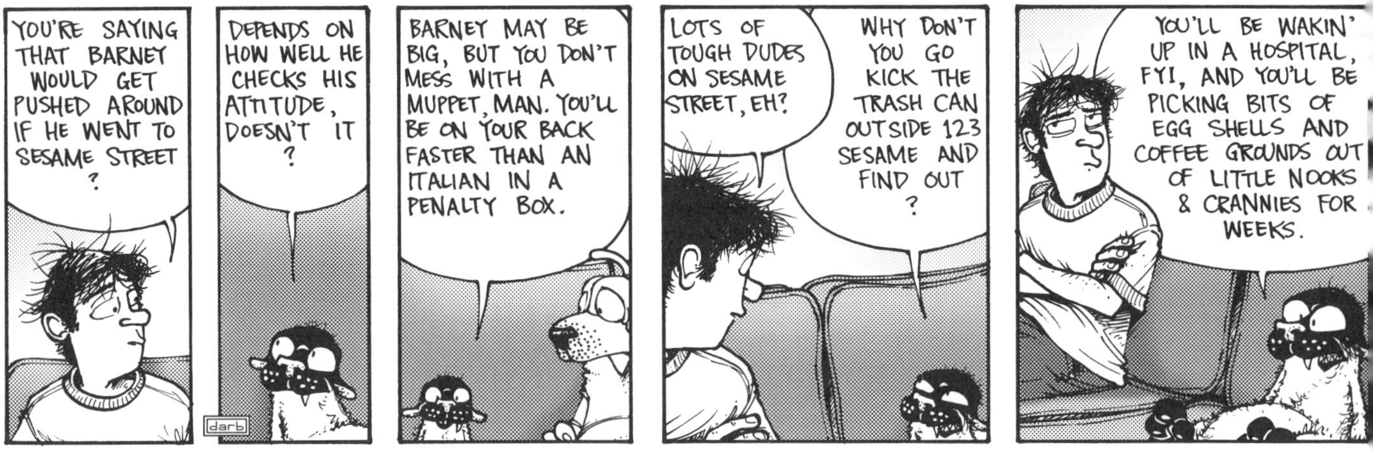
YOU'RE SAYING THAT BARNEY WOULD GET PUSHED AROUND IF HE WENT TO SESAME STREET ?
DEPENDS ON HOW WELL HE CHECKS HIS ATTITUDE, DOESN'T IT ?
darb
BARNEY MAY BE BIG, BUT YOU DON'T MESS WITH A MUPPET, MAN. YOU'LL BE ON YOUR BACK FASTER THAN AN ITALIAN IN A PENALTY BOX.
LOTS OF TOUGH DUDES ON SESAME STREET, EH?
WHY DON'T YOU GO KICK THE TRASH CAN OUTSIDE 123 SESAME AND FIND OUT ?
YOU'LL BE WAKIN' UP IN A HOSPITAL, FYI, AND YOU'LL BE PICKING BITS OF EGG SHELLS AND COFFEE GROUNDS OUT OF LITTLE NOOKS & CRANNIES FOR WEEKS.

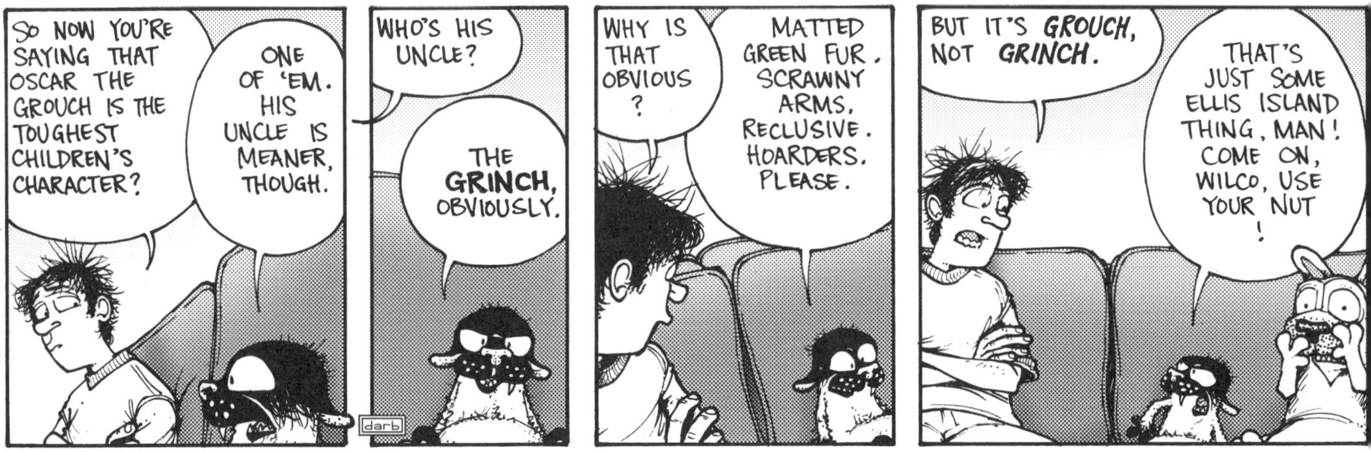
SO NOW YOU'RE SAYING THAT OSCAR THE GROUCH IS THE TOUGHEST CHILDREN'S CHARACTER?
ONE OF 'EM. HIS UNCLE IS MEANER, THOUGH.
darb
WHO'S HIS UNCLE?
THE GRINCH, OBVIOUSLY.
WHY IS THAT OBVIOUS ?
MATTED GREEN FUR. SCRAWNY ARMS. RECLUSIVE. HOARDERS. PLEASE.
BUT IT'S GROUCH, NOT GRINCH.
THAT'S JUST SOME ELLIS ISLAND THING, MAN! COME ON, WILCO, USE YOUR NUT !

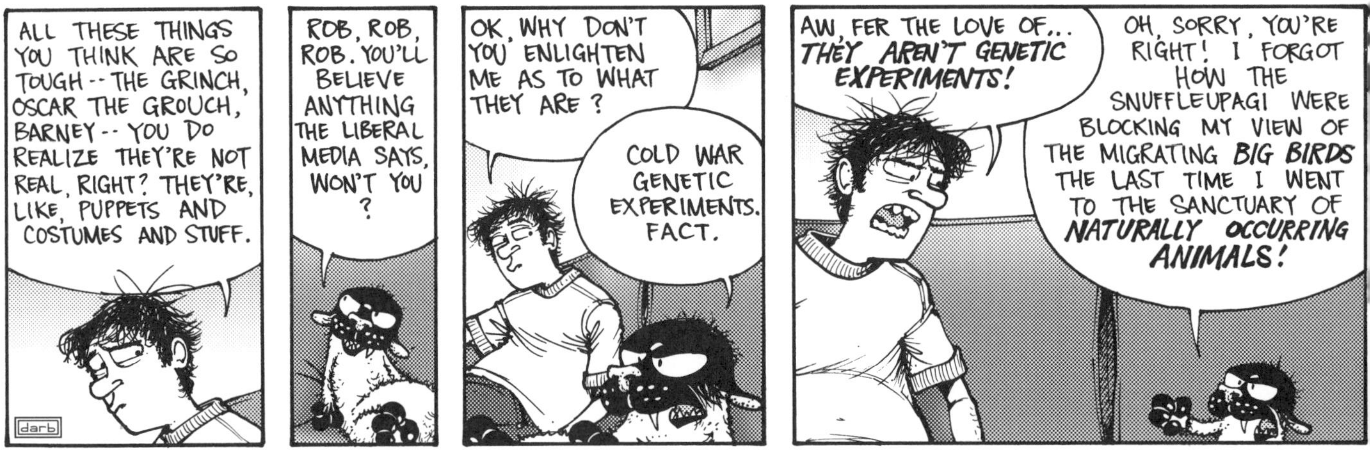
ALL THESE THINGS YOU THINK ARE SO TOUGH -- THE GRINCH, OSCAR THE GROUCH, BARNEY -- YOU DO REALIZE THEY'RE NOT REAL, RIGHT? THEY'RE, LIKE, PUPPETS AND COSTUMES AND STUFF.
darb
ROB, ROB, ROB. YOU'LL BELIEVE ANYTHING THE LIBERAL MEDIA SAYS, WON'T YOU ?
OK, WHY DON'T YOU ENLIGHTEN ME AS TO WHAT THEY ARE ?
COLD WAR GENETIC EXPERIMENTS. FACT.
AW, FER THE LOVE OF... THEY AREN'T GENETIC EXPERIMENTS!
OH, SORRY, YOU'RE RIGHT! I FORGOT HOW THE SNUFFLEUPAGI WERE BLOCKING MY VIEW OF THE MIGRATING BIG BIRDS THE LAST TIME I WENT TO THE SANCTUARY OF NATURALLY OCCURRING ANIMALS!

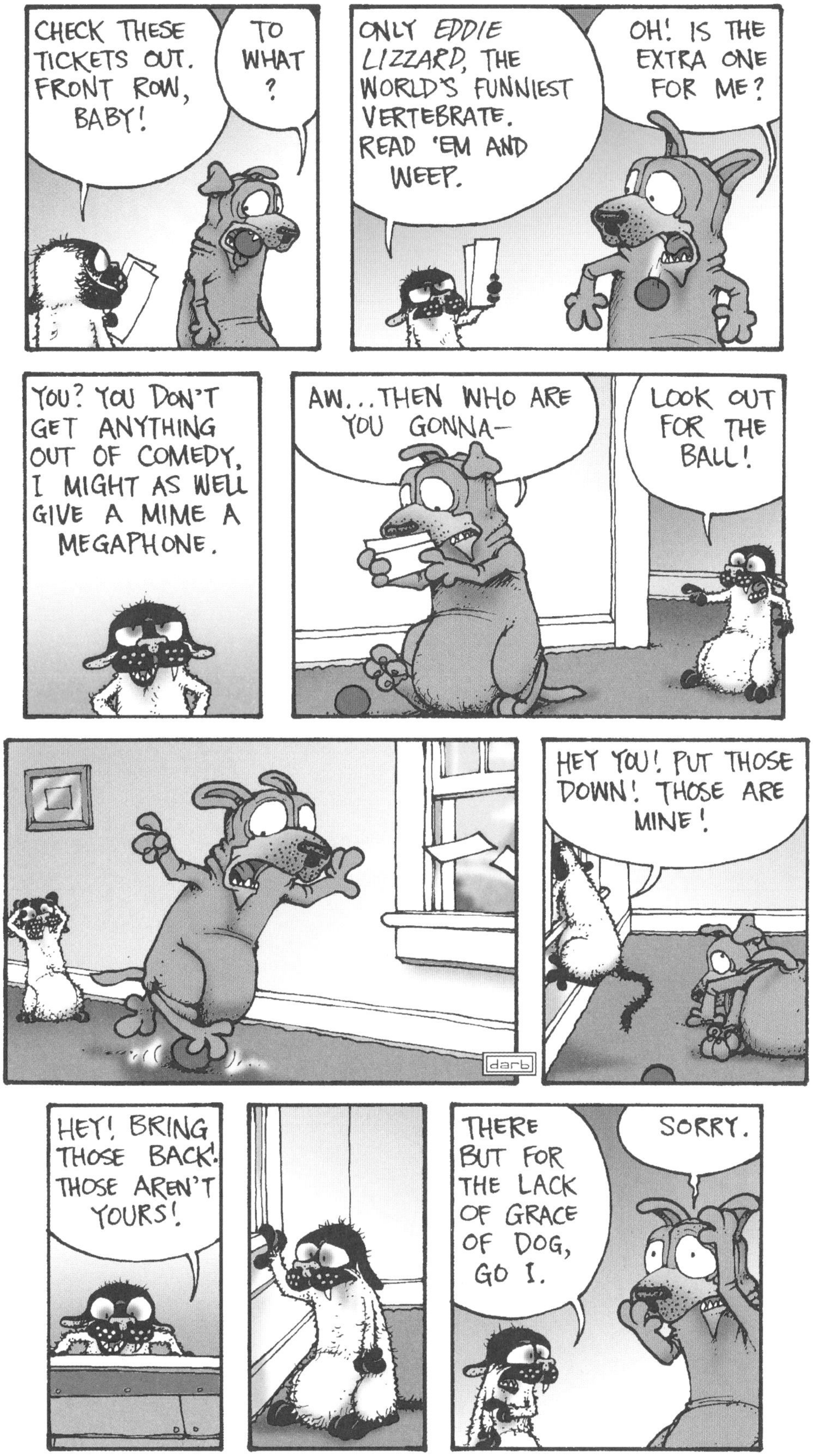
CHECK THESE TICKETS OUT. FRONT ROW, BABY!
TO WHAT ?
ONLY *EDDIE LIZZARD*, THE WORLD'S FUNNIEST VERTEBRATE. READ 'EM AND WEEP.
OH! IS THE EXTRA ONE FOR ME?
YOU? YOU DON'T GET ANYTHING OUT OF COMEDY. I MIGHT AS WELL GIVE A MIME A MEGAPHONE.
AW...THEN WHO ARE YOU GONNA—
LOOK OUT FOR THE BALL!
darb
HEY YOU! PUT THOSE DOWN! THOSE ARE MINE!
HEY! BRING THOSE BACK! THOSE AREN'T YOURS!
THERE BUT FOR THE LACK OF GRACE OF DOG, GO I.
SORRY.

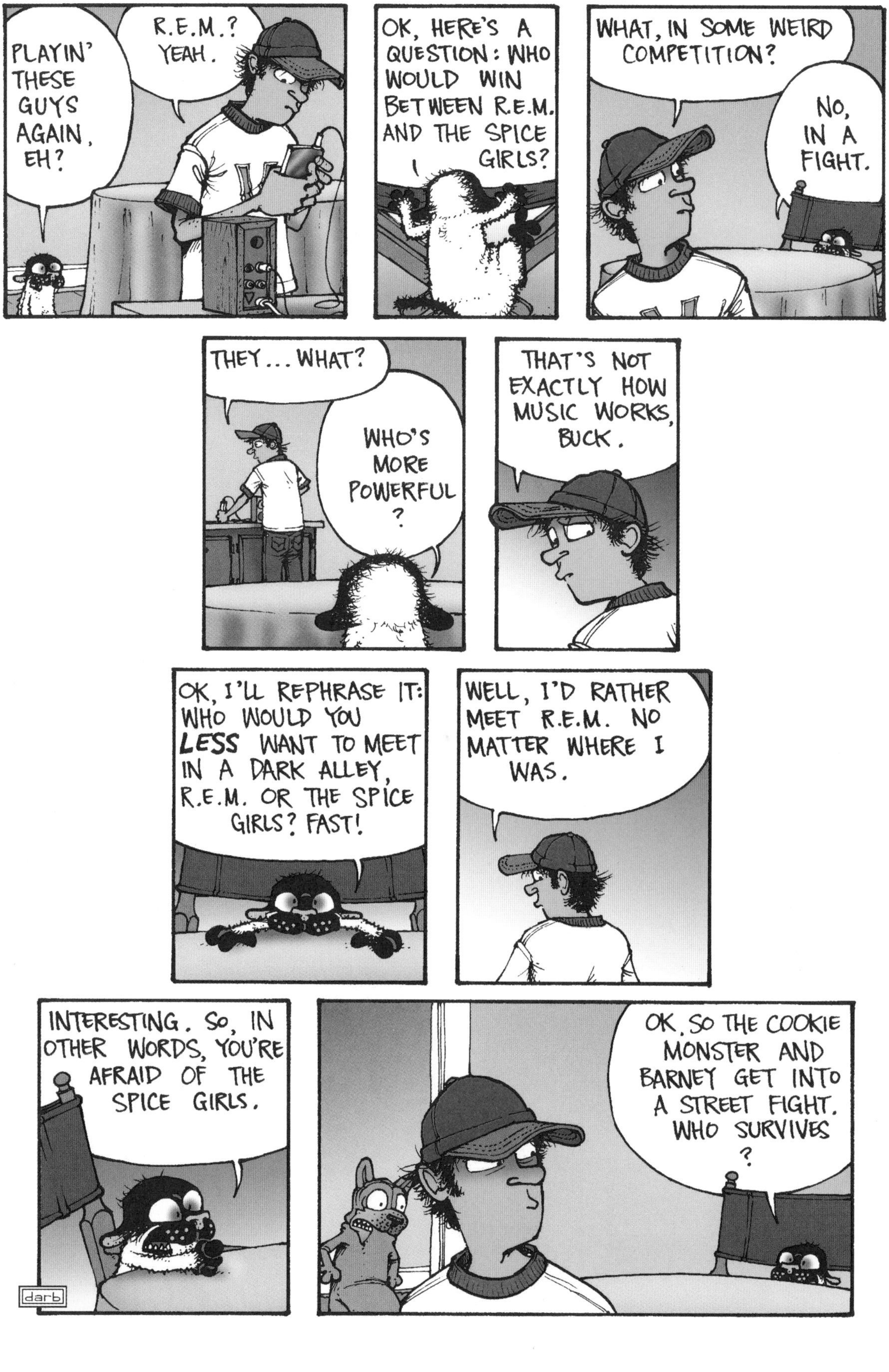
PLAYIN' THESE GUYS AGAIN, EH?
R.E.M.? YEAH.
OK, HERE'S A QUESTION: WHO WOULD WIN BETWEEN R.E.M. AND THE SPICE GIRLS?
WHAT, IN SOME WEIRD COMPETITION?
NO, IN A FIGHT.
THEY... WHAT?
WHO'S MORE POWERFUL?
THAT'S NOT EXACTLY HOW MUSIC WORKS, BUCK.
OK, I'LL REPHRASE IT: WHO WOULD YOU LESS WANT TO MEET IN A DARK ALLEY, R.E.M. OR THE SPICE GIRLS? FAST!
WELL, I'D RATHER MEET R.E.M. NO MATTER WHERE I WAS.
INTERESTING. SO, IN OTHER WORDS, YOU'RE AFRAID OF THE SPICE GIRLS.
darb
OK. SO THE COOKIE MONSTER AND BARNEY GET INTO A STREET FIGHT. WHO SURVIVES?

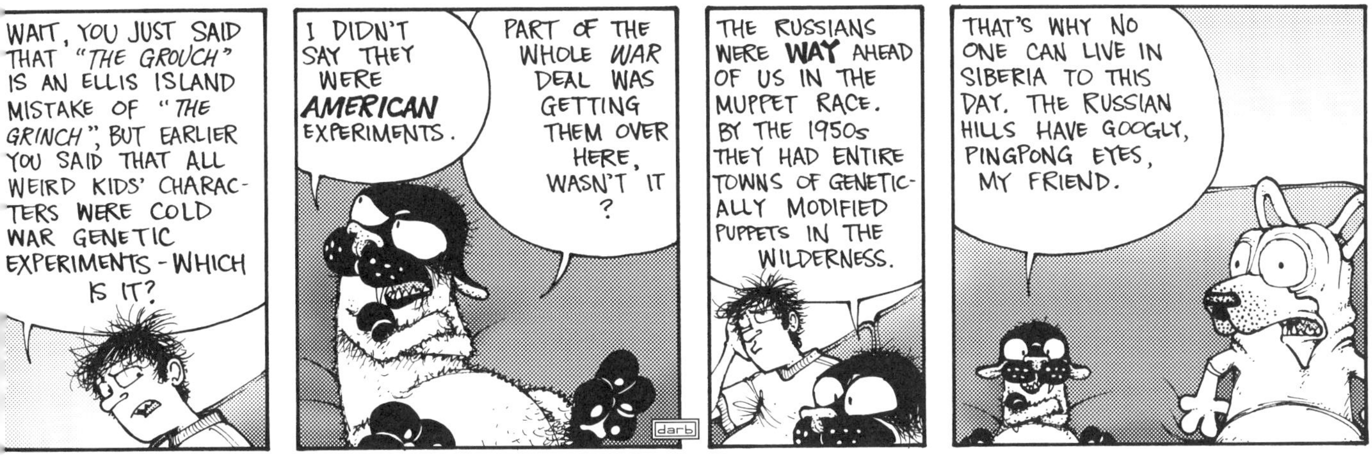
WAIT, YOU JUST SAID THAT "THE GROUCH" IS AN ELLIS ISLAND MISTAKE OF "THE GRINCH", BUT EARLIER YOU SAID THAT ALL WEIRD KIDS' CHARACTERS WERE COLD WAR GENETIC EXPERIMENTS - WHICH IS IT?
I DIDN'T SAY THEY WERE AMERICAN EXPERIMENTS.
PART OF THE WHOLE WAR DEAL WAS GETTING THEM OVER HERE, WASN'T IT?
darb
THE RUSSIANS WERE WAY AHEAD OF US IN THE MUPPET RACE. BY THE 1950s THEY HAD ENTIRE TOWNS OF GENETICALLY MODIFIED PUPPETS IN THE WILDERNESS.
THAT'S WHY NO ONE CAN LIVE IN SIBERIA TO THIS DAY. THE RUSSIAN HILLS HAVE GOOGLY, PINGPONG EYES, MY FRIEND.

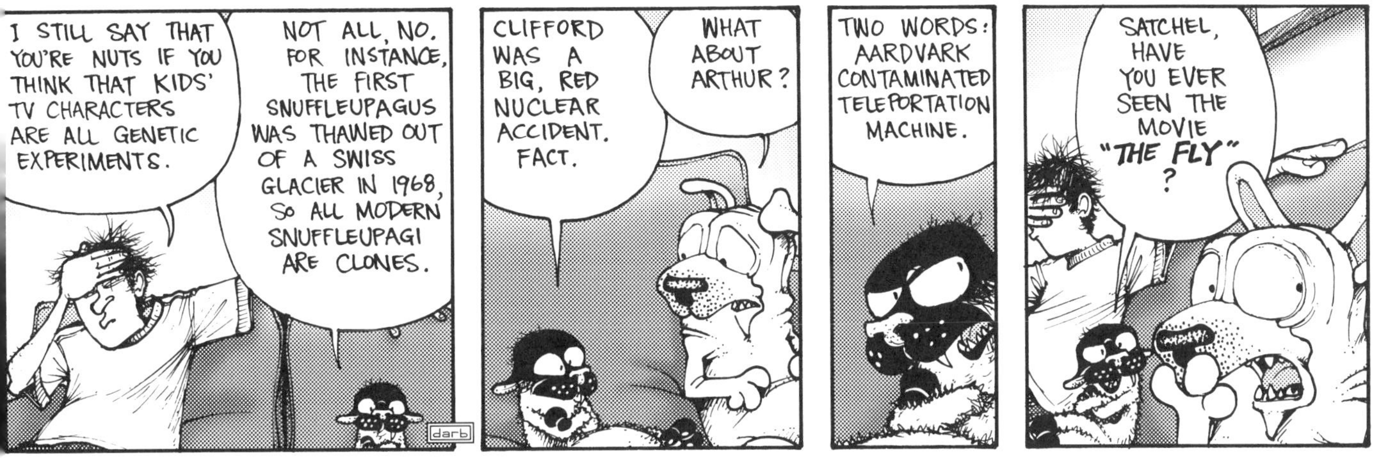
I STILL SAY THAT YOU'RE NUTS IF YOU THINK THAT KIDS' TV CHARACTERS ARE ALL GENETIC EXPERIMENTS.
NOT ALL, NO. FOR INSTANCE, THE FIRST SNUFFLEUPAGUS WAS THAWED OUT OF A SWISS GLACIER IN 1968, SO ALL MODERN SNUFFLEUPAGI ARE CLONES.
darb
CLIFFORD WAS A BIG, RED NUCLEAR ACCIDENT. FACT.
WHAT ABOUT ARTHUR?
TWO WORDS: AARDVARK CONTAMINATED TELEPORTATION MACHINE.
SATCHEL, HAVE YOU EVER SEEN THE MOVIE "THE FLY"?

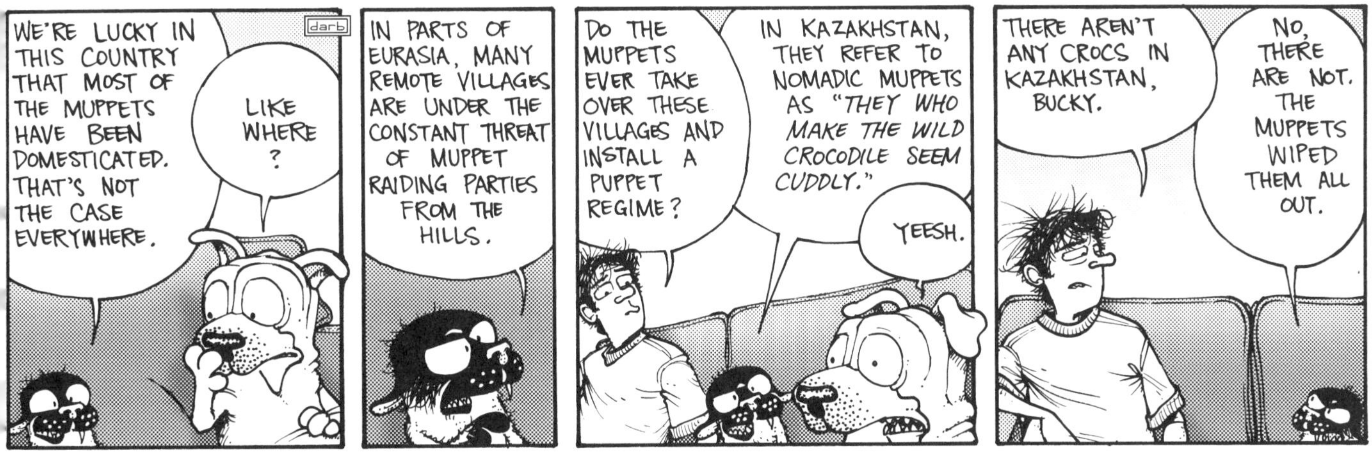
darb
WE'RE LUCKY IN THIS COUNTRY THAT MOST OF THE MUPPETS HAVE BEEN DOMESTICATED. THAT'S NOT THE CASE EVERYWHERE.
LIKE WHERE?
IN PARTS OF EURASIA, MANY REMOTE VILLAGES ARE UNDER THE CONSTANT THREAT OF MUPPET RAIDING PARTIES FROM THE HILLS.
DO THE MUPPETS EVER TAKE OVER THESE VILLAGES AND INSTALL A PUPPET REGIME?
IN KAZAKHSTAN, THEY REFER TO NOMADIC MUPPETS AS "THEY WHO MAKE THE WILD CROCODILE SEEM CUDDLY."
YEESH.
THERE AREN'T ANY CROCS IN KAZAKHSTAN, BUCKY.
NO, THERE ARE NOT. THE MUPPETS WIPED THEM ALL OUT.

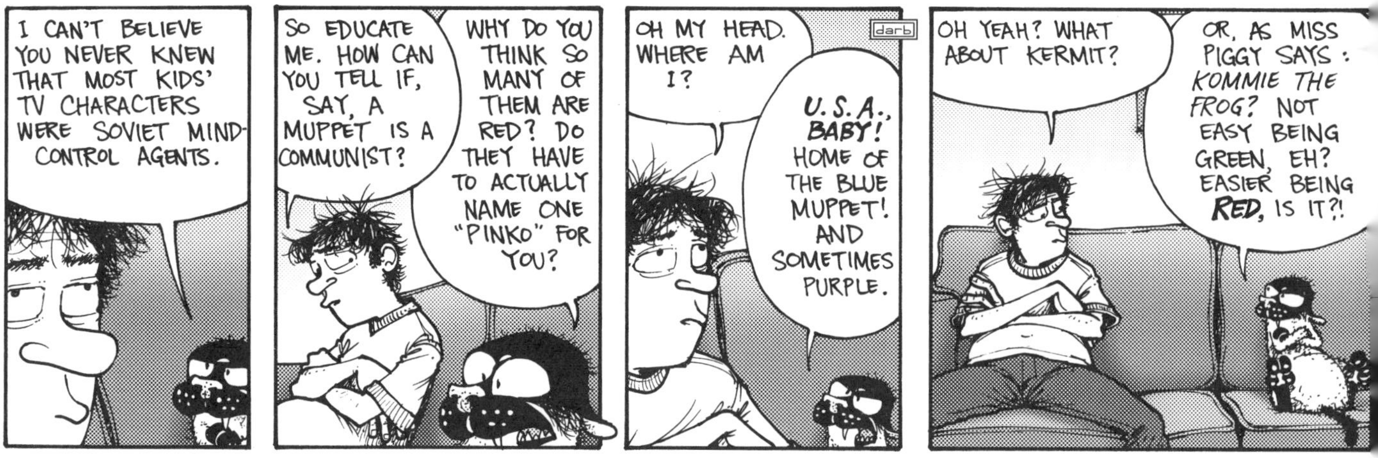
I CAN'T BELIEVE YOU NEVER KNEW THAT MOST KIDS' TV CHARACTERS WERE SOVIET MIND-CONTROL AGENTS.
SO EDUCATE ME. HOW CAN YOU TELL IF, SAY, A MUPPET IS A COMMUNIST?
WHY DO YOU THINK SO MANY OF THEM ARE RED? DO THEY HAVE TO ACTUALLY NAME ONE "PINKO" FOR YOU?
OH MY HEAD. WHERE AM I?
U. S. A., BABY! HOME OF THE BLUE MUPPET! AND SOMETIMES PURPLE.
OH YEAH? WHAT ABOUT KERMIT?
OR, AS MISS PIGGY SAYS: KOMMIE THE FROG? NOT EASY BEING GREEN, EH? EASIER BEING RED, IS IT?!

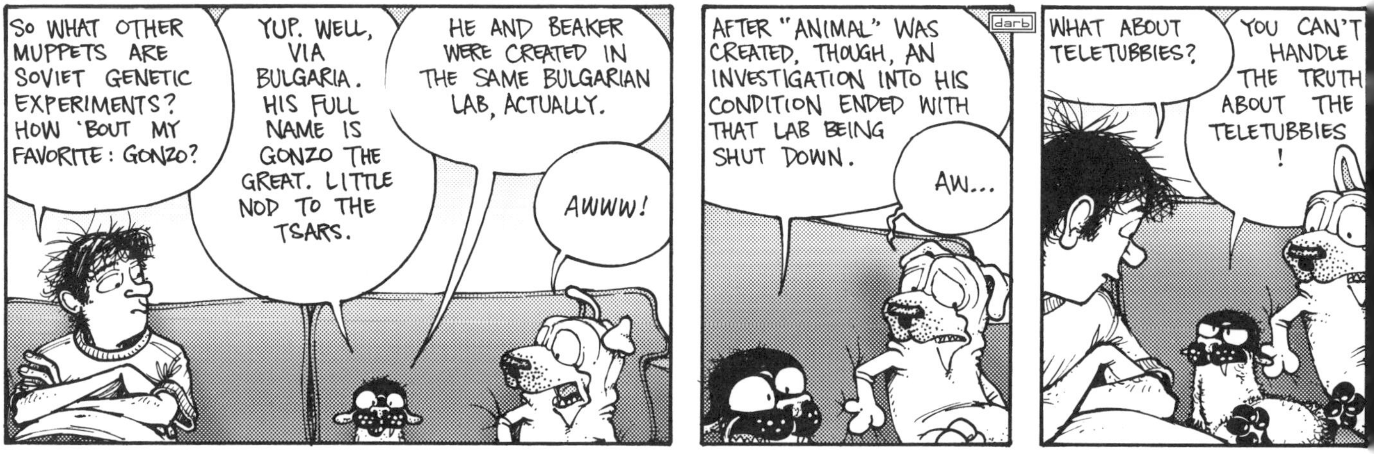
SO WHAT OTHER MUPPETS ARE SOVIET GENETIC EXPERIMENTS? HOW 'BOUT MY FAVORITE: GONZO?
YUP. WELL, VIA BULGARIA. HIS FULL NAME IS GONZO THE GREAT. LITTLE NOD TO THE TSARS.
HE AND BEAKER WERE CREATED IN THE SAME BULGARIAN LAB, ACTUALLY.
AWWW!
AFTER "ANIMAL" WAS CREATED, THOUGH, AN INVESTIGATION INTO HIS CONDITION ENDED WITH THAT LAB BEING SHUT DOWN.
AW...
WHAT ABOUT TELETUBBIES?
YOU CAN'T HANDLE THE TRUTH ABOUT THE TELETUBBIES!

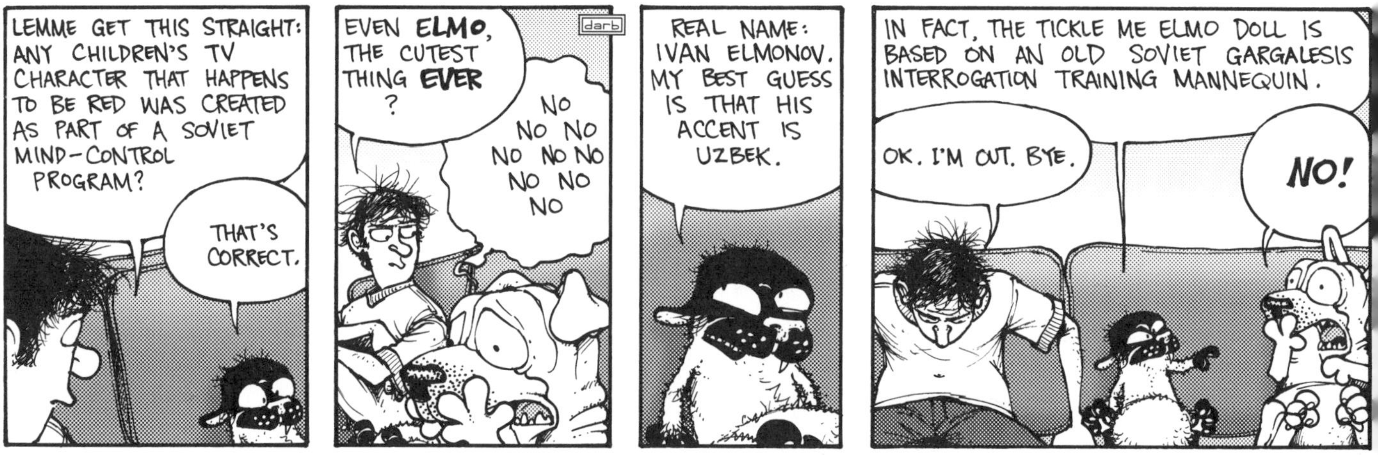
LEMME GET THIS STRAIGHT: ANY CHILDREN'S TV CHARACTER THAT HAPPENS TO BE RED WAS CREATED AS PART OF A SOVIET MIND-CONTROL PROGRAM?
THAT'S CORRECT.
EVEN ELMO, THE CUTEST THING EVER?
NO NO NO NO NO NO NO NO NO
REAL NAME: IVAN ELMONOV. MY BEST GUESS IS THAT HIS ACCENT IS UZBEK.
IN FACT, THE TICKLE ME ELMO DOLL IS BASED ON AN OLD SOVIET GARGALESIS INTERROGATION TRAINING MANNEQUIN.
OK. I'M OUT. BYE.
NO!

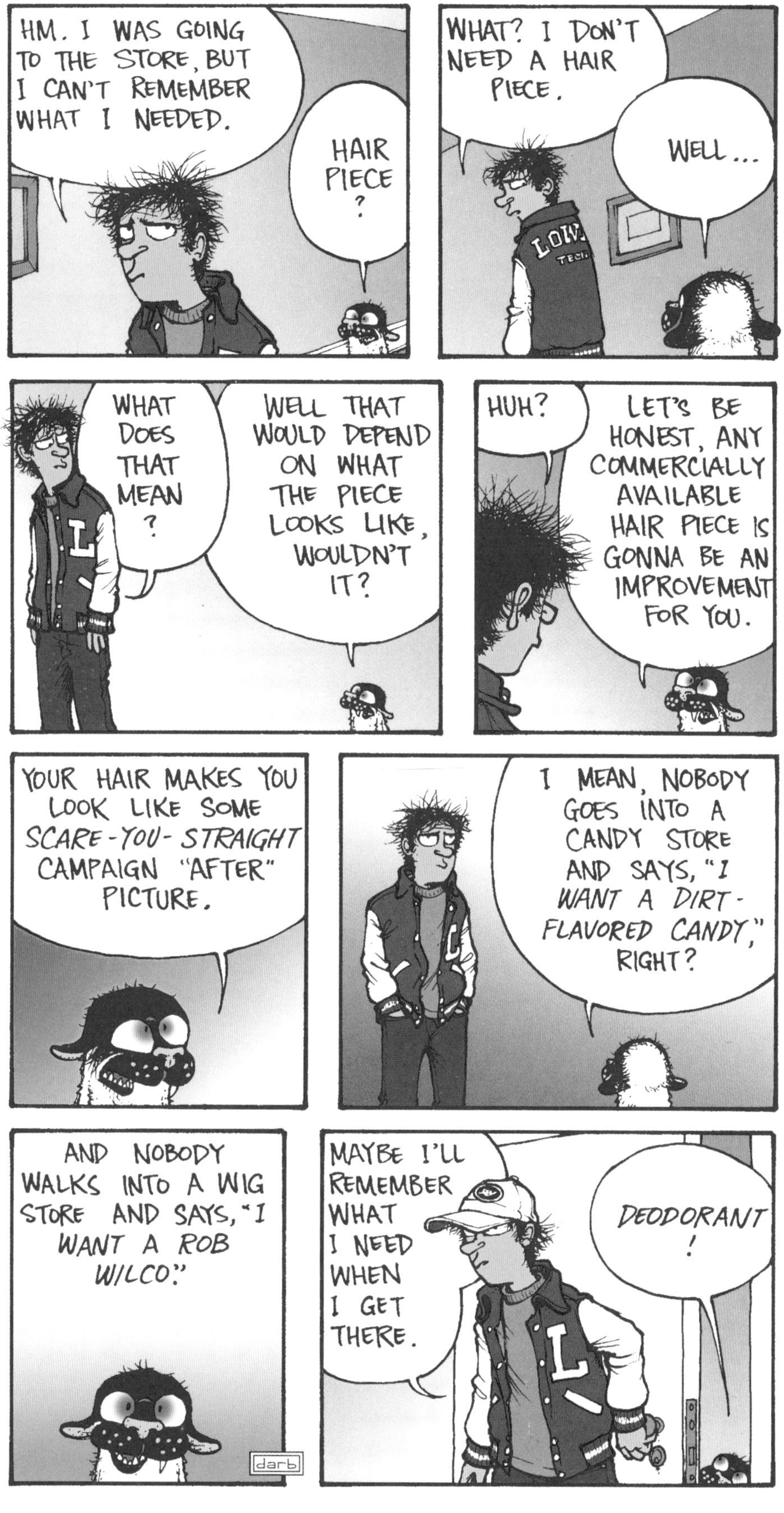
HM. I WAS GOING TO THE STORE, BUT I CAN'T REMEMBER WHAT I NEEDED.
HAIR PIECE ?
WHAT? I DON'T NEED A HAIR PIECE.
WELL...
WHAT DOES THAT MEAN ?
WELL THAT WOULD DEPEND ON WHAT THE PIECE LOOKS LIKE, WOULDN'T IT?
HUH?
LET'S BE HONEST, ANY COMMERCIALLY AVAILABLE HAIR PIECE IS GONNA BE AN IMPROVEMENT FOR YOU.
YOUR HAIR MAKES YOU LOOK LIKE SOME *SCARE-YOU-STRAIGHT* CAMPAIGN "AFTER" PICTURE.
I MEAN, NOBODY GOES INTO A CANDY STORE AND SAYS, "*I WANT A DIRT-FLAVORED CANDY,*" RIGHT?
AND NOBODY WALKS INTO A WIG STORE AND SAYS, "*I WANT A ROB WILCO.*"
darb
MAYBE I'LL REMEMBER WHAT I NEED WHEN I GET THERE.
DEODORANT !

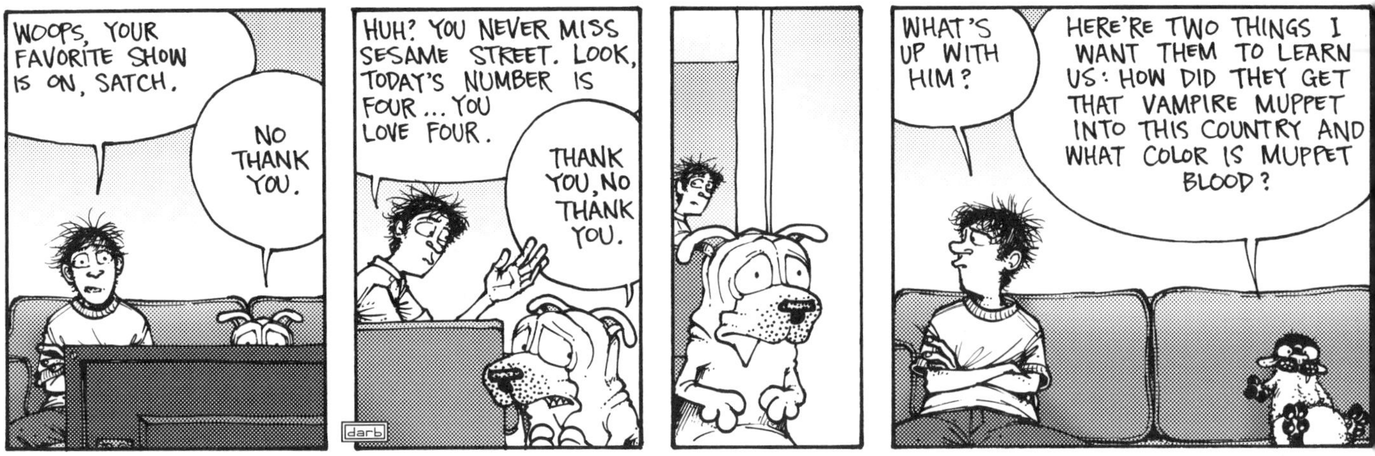
WOOPS, YOUR FAVORITE SHOW IS ON, SATCH.
NO THANK YOU.
HUH? YOU NEVER MISS SESAME STREET. LOOK, TODAY'S NUMBER IS FOUR... YOU LOVE FOUR.
THANK YOU, NO THANK YOU.
WHAT'S UP WITH HIM?
HERE'RE TWO THINGS I WANT THEM TO LEARN US: HOW DID THEY GET THAT VAMPIRE MUPPET INTO THIS COUNTRY AND WHAT COLOR IS MUPPET BLOOD?

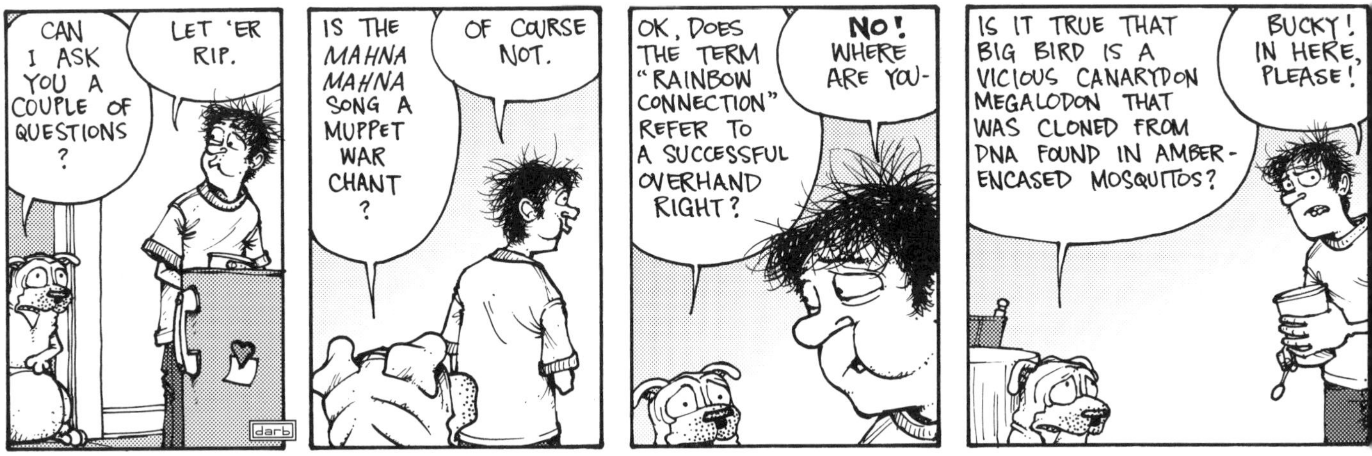
CAN I ASK YOU A COUPLE OF QUESTIONS?
LET 'ER RIP.
IS THE MAHNA MAHNA SONG A MUPPET WAR CHANT?
OF COURSE NOT.
OK, DOES THE TERM "RAINBOW CONNECTION" REFER TO A SUCCESSFUL OVERHAND RIGHT?
NO! WHERE ARE YOU-
IS IT TRUE THAT BIG BIRD IS A VICIOUS CANARYDON MEGALODON THAT WAS CLONED FROM DNA FOUND IN AMBER-ENCASED MOSQUITOS?
BUCKY! IN HERE, PLEASE!

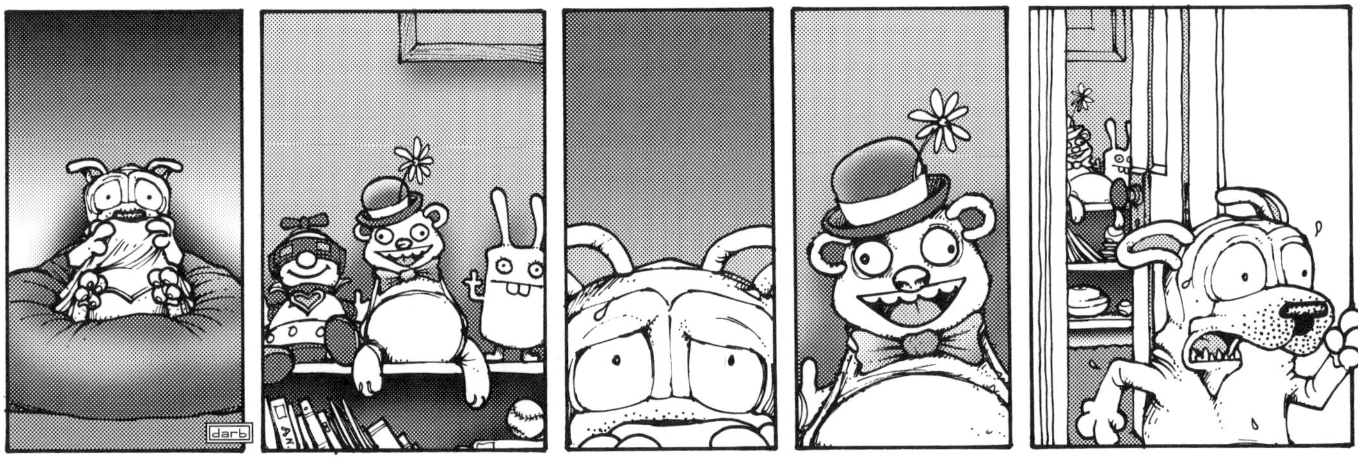

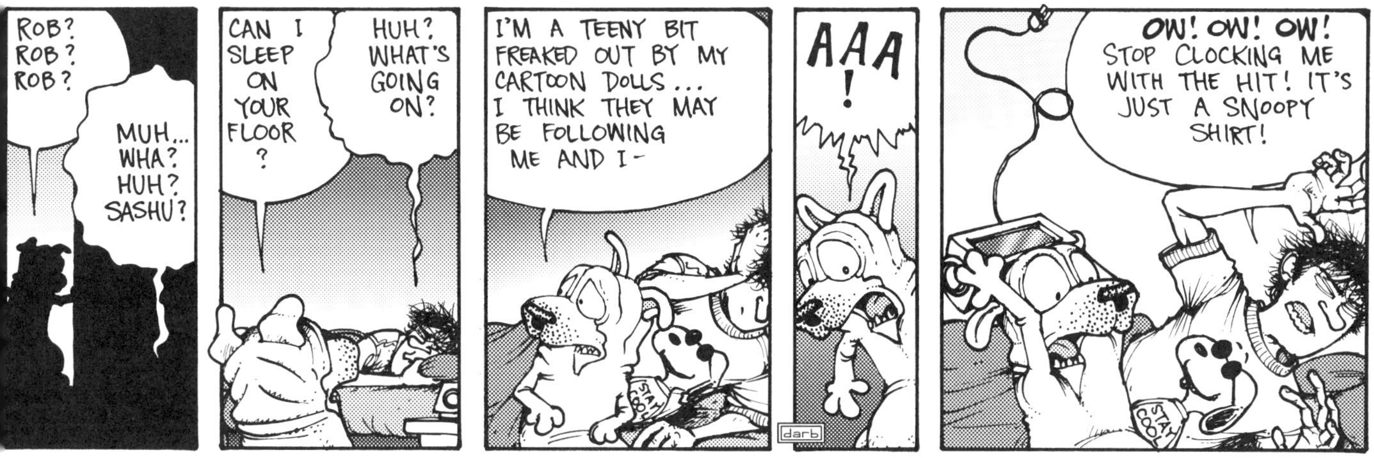
ROB? ROB? ROB?
MUH... WHA? HUH? SASHU?
CAN I SLEEP ON YOUR FLOOR?
HUH? WHAT'S GOING ON?
I'M A TEENY BIT FREAKED OUT BY MY CARTOON DOLLS... I THINK THEY MAY BE FOLLOWING ME AND I-
AAA!
OW! OW! OW! STOP CLOCKING ME WITH THE HIT! IT'S JUST A SNOOPY SHIRT!

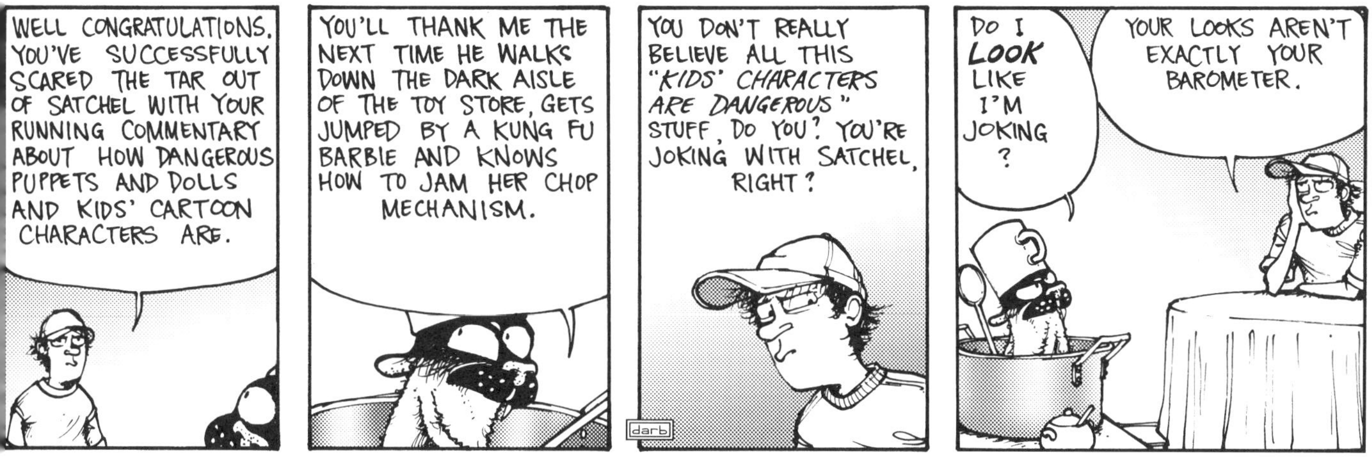
WELL CONGRATULATIONS. YOU'VE SUCCESSFULLY SCARED THE TAR OUT OF SATCHEL WITH YOUR RUNNING COMMENTARY ABOUT HOW DANGEROUS PUPPETS AND DOLLS AND KIDS' CARTOON CHARACTERS ARE.
YOU'LL THANK ME THE NEXT TIME HE WALKS DOWN THE DARK AISLE OF THE TOY STORE, GETS JUMPED BY A KUNG FU BARBIE AND KNOWS HOW TO JAM HER CHOP MECHANISM.
YOU DON'T REALLY BELIEVE ALL THIS "KIDS' CHARACTERS ARE DANGEROUS" STUFF, DO YOU? YOU'RE JOKING WITH SATCHEL, RIGHT?
DO I LOOK LIKE I'M JOKING?
YOUR LOOKS AREN'T EXACTLY YOUR BAROMETER.

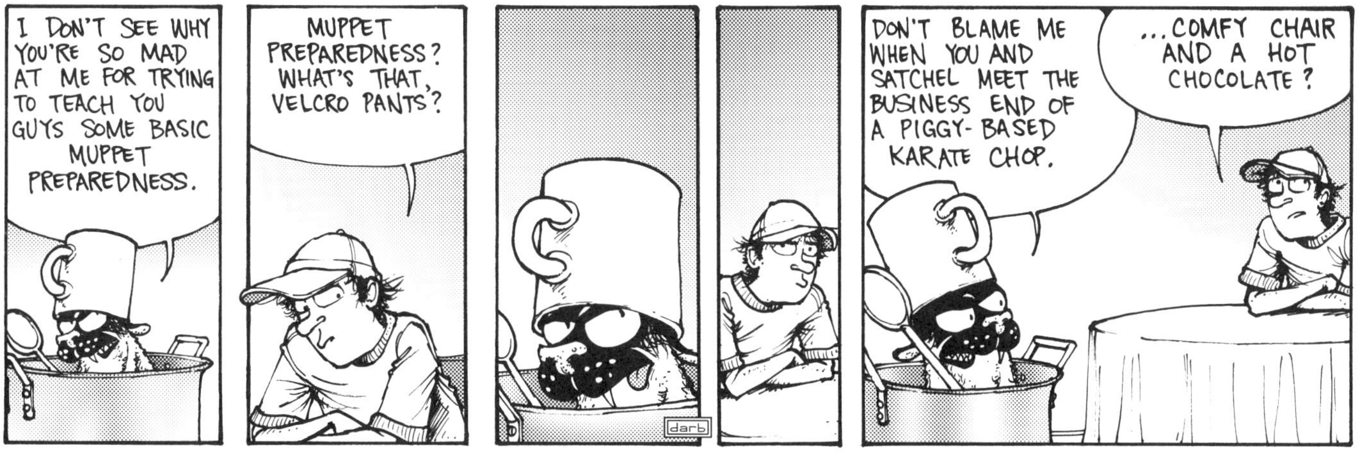
I DON'T SEE WHY YOU'RE SO MAD AT ME FOR TRYING TO TEACH YOU GUYS SOME BASIC MUPPET PREPAREDNESS.
MUPPET PREPAREDNESS? WHAT'S THAT, VELCRO PANTS?
DON'T BLAME ME WHEN YOU AND SATCHEL MEET THE BUSINESS END OF A PIGGY-BASED KARATE CHOP.
...COMFY CHAIR AND A HOT CHOCOLATE?

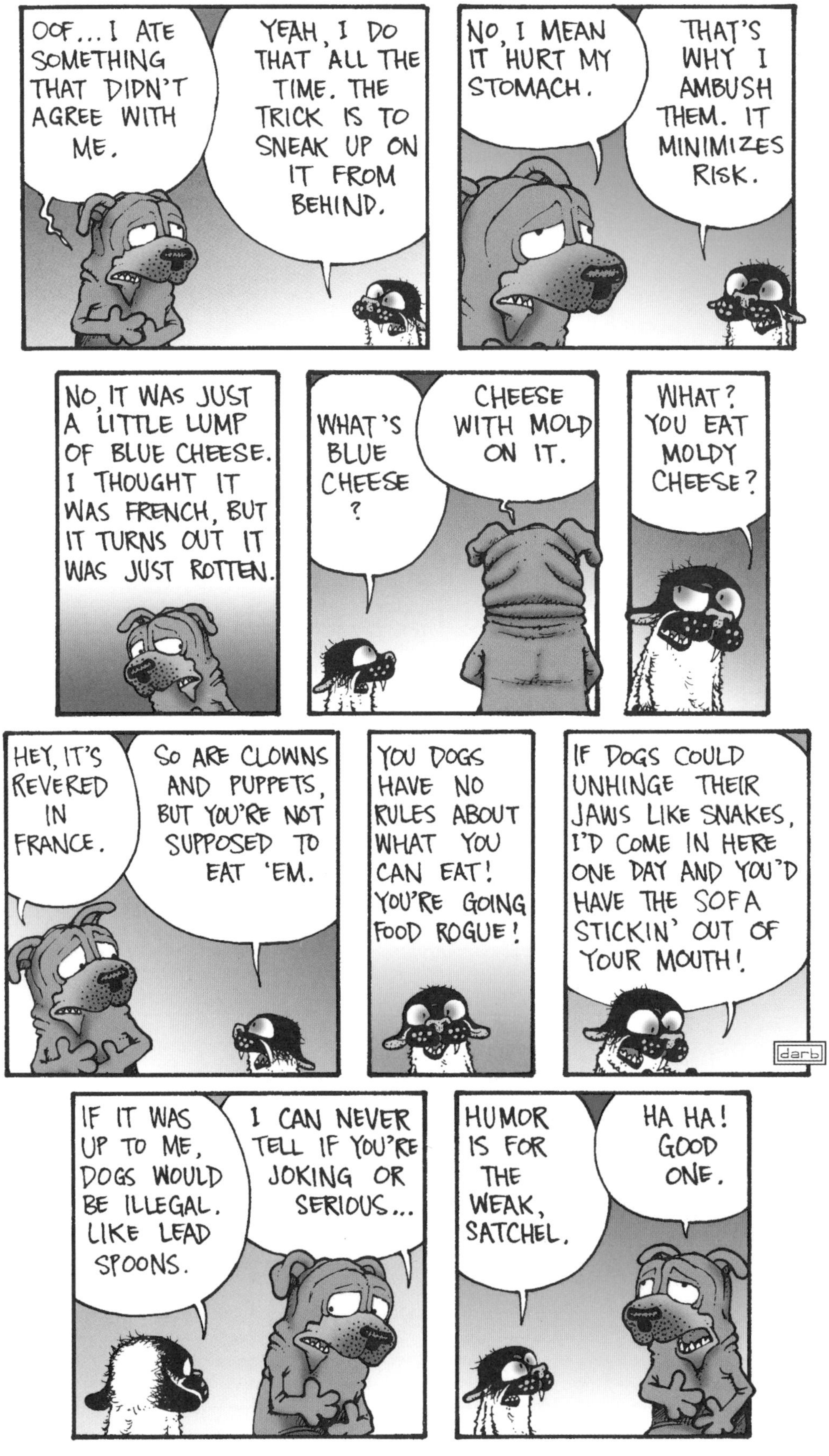

OOF... I ATE SOMETHING THAT DIDN'T AGREE WITH ME.
YEAH, I DO THAT ALL THE TIME. THE TRICK IS TO SNEAK UP ON IT FROM BEHIND.
NO, I MEAN IT HURT MY STOMACH.
THAT'S WHY I AMBUSH THEM. IT MINIMIZES RISK.
NO, IT WAS JUST A LITTLE LUMP OF BLUE CHEESE. I THOUGHT IT WAS FRENCH, BUT IT TURNS OUT IT WAS JUST ROTTEN.
WHAT'S BLUE CHEESE ?
CHEESE WITH MOLD ON IT.
WHAT? YOU EAT MOLDY CHEESE?
HEY, IT'S REVERED IN FRANCE.
SO ARE CLOWNS AND PUPPETS, BUT YOU'RE NOT SUPPOSED TO EAT 'EM.
YOU DOGS HAVE NO RULES ABOUT WHAT YOU CAN EAT! YOU'RE GOING FOOD ROGUE!
IF DOGS COULD UNHINGE THEIR JAWS LIKE SNAKES, I'D COME IN HERE ONE DAY AND YOU'D HAVE THE SOFA STICKIN' OUT OF YOUR MOUTH!
darb
IF IT WAS UP TO ME, DOGS WOULD BE ILLEGAL. LIKE LEAD SPOONS.
I CAN NEVER TELL IF YOU'RE JOKING OR SERIOUS...
HUMOR IS FOR THE WEAK, SATCHEL.
HA HA! GOOD ONE.

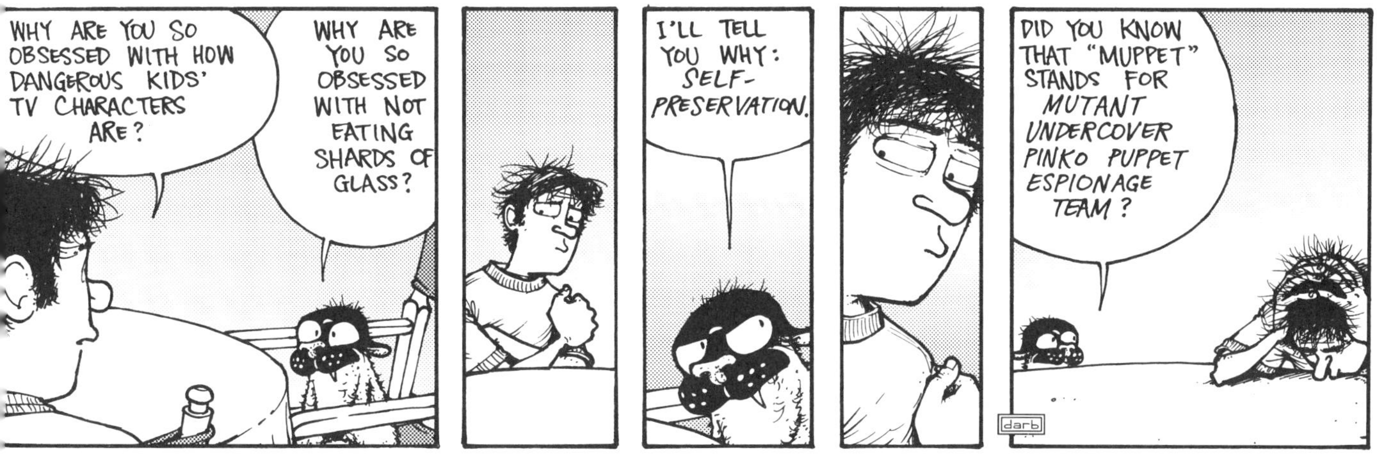
WHY ARE YOU SO OBSESSED WITH HOW DANGEROUS KIDS' TV CHARACTERS ARE?
WHY ARE YOU SO OBSESSED WITH NOT EATING SHARDS OF GLASS?
I'LL TELL YOU WHY: SELF-PRESERVATION.
DID YOU KNOW THAT "MUPPET" STANDS FOR MUTANT UNDERCOVER PINKO PUPPET ESPIONAGE TEAM?

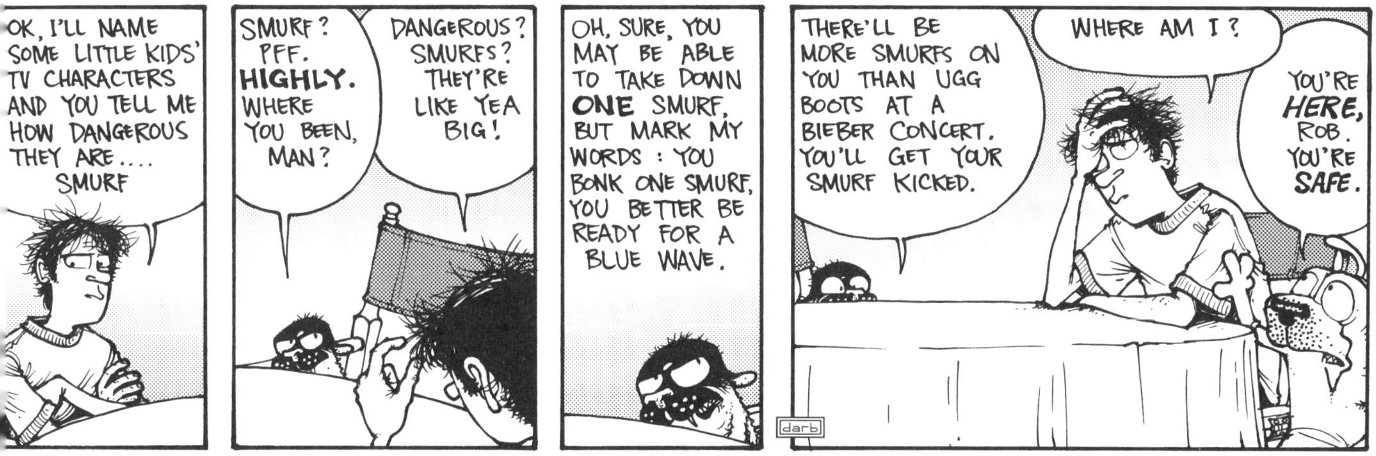
OK, I'LL NAME SOME LITTLE KIDS' TV CHARACTERS AND YOU TELL ME HOW DANGEROUS THEY ARE.... SMURF
SMURF? PFF. HIGHLY. WHERE YOU BEEN, MAN?
DANGEROUS? SMURFS? THEY'RE LIKE YEA BIG!
OH, SURE, YOU MAY BE ABLE TO TAKE DOWN ONE SMURF, BUT MARK MY WORDS: YOU BONK ONE SMURF, YOU BETTER BE READY FOR A BLUE WAVE.
THERE'LL BE MORE SMURFS ON YOU THAN UGG BOOTS AT A BIEBER CONCERT. YOU'LL GET YOUR SMURF KICKED.
WHERE AM I?
YOU'RE HERE, ROB. YOU'RE SAFE.

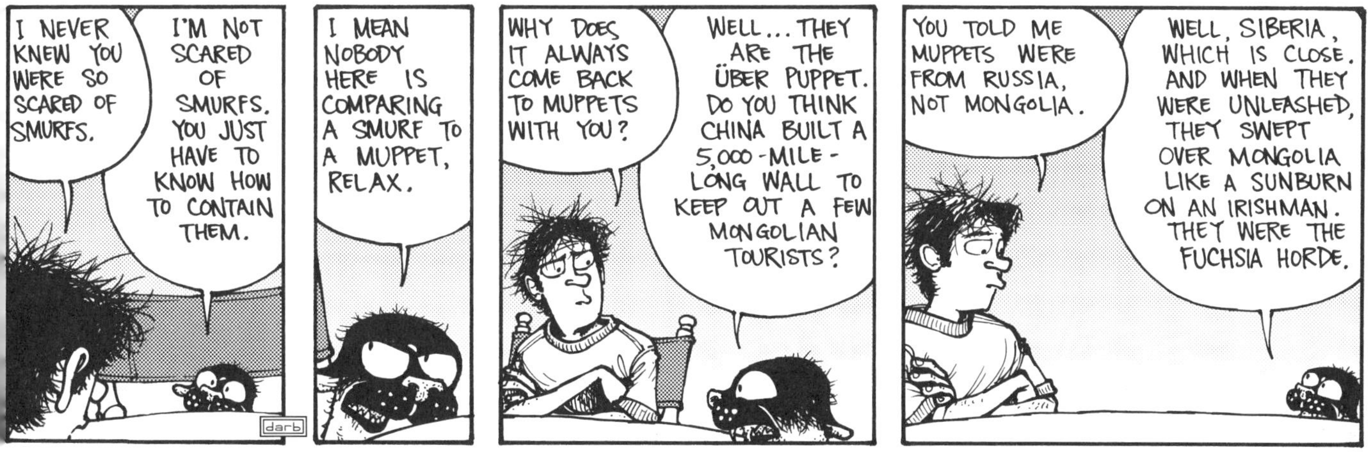
I NEVER KNEW YOU WERE SO SCARED OF SMURFS.
I'M NOT SCARED OF SMURFS. YOU JUST HAVE TO KNOW HOW TO CONTAIN THEM.
I MEAN NOBODY HERE IS COMPARING A SMURF TO A MUPPET, RELAX.
WHY DOES IT ALWAYS COME BACK TO MUPPETS WITH YOU?
WELL... THEY ARE THE ÜBER PUPPET. DO YOU THINK CHINA BUILT A 5,000-MILE-LONG WALL TO KEEP OUT A FEW MONGOLIAN TOURISTS?
YOU TOLD ME MUPPETS WERE FROM RUSSIA, NOT MONGOLIA.
WELL, SIBERIA, WHICH IS CLOSE. AND WHEN THEY WERE UNLEASHED, THEY SWEPT OVER MONGOLIA LIKE A SUNBURN ON AN IRISHMAN. THEY WERE THE FUCHSIA HORDE.

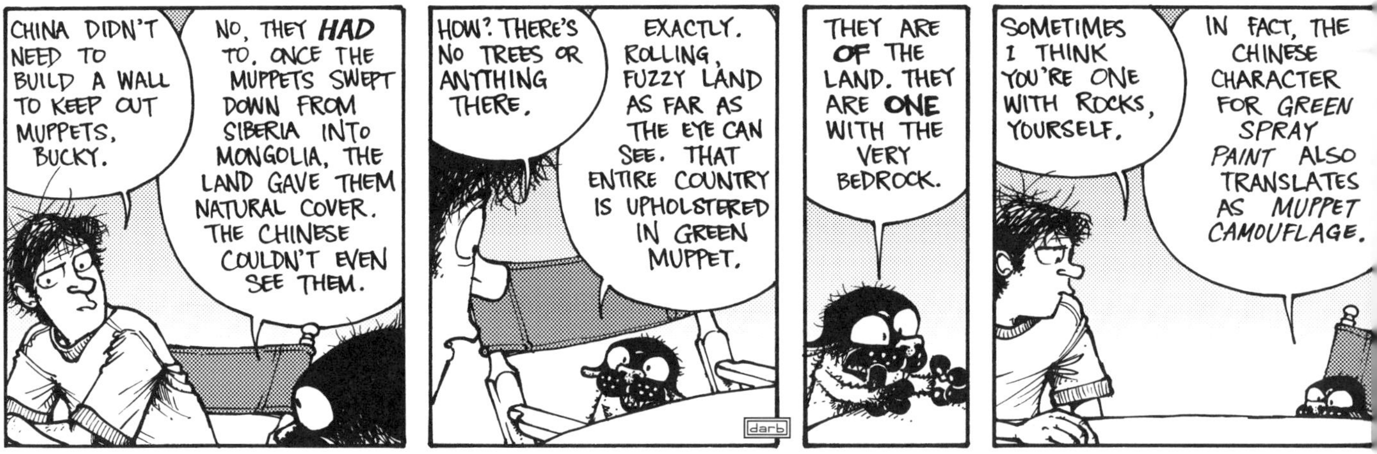
CHINA DIDN'T NEED TO BUILD A WALL TO KEEP OUT MUPPETS, BUCKY.
NO, THEY **HAD** TO. ONCE THE MUPPETS SWEPT DOWN FROM SIBERIA INTO MONGOLIA, THE LAND GAVE THEM NATURAL COVER. THE CHINESE COULDN'T EVEN SEE THEM.
HOW? THERE'S NO TREES OR ANYTHING THERE.
EXACTLY. ROLLING, FUZZY LAND AS FAR AS THE EYE CAN SEE. THAT ENTIRE COUNTRY IS UPHOLSTERED IN GREEN MUPPET.
darb
THEY ARE **OF** THE LAND. THEY ARE **ONE** WITH THE VERY BEDROCK.
SOMETIMES I THINK YOU'RE ONE WITH ROCKS, YOURSELF.
IN FACT, THE CHINESE CHARACTER FOR *GREEN SPRAY PAINT* ALSO TRANSLATES AS *MUPPET CAMOUFLAGE*.

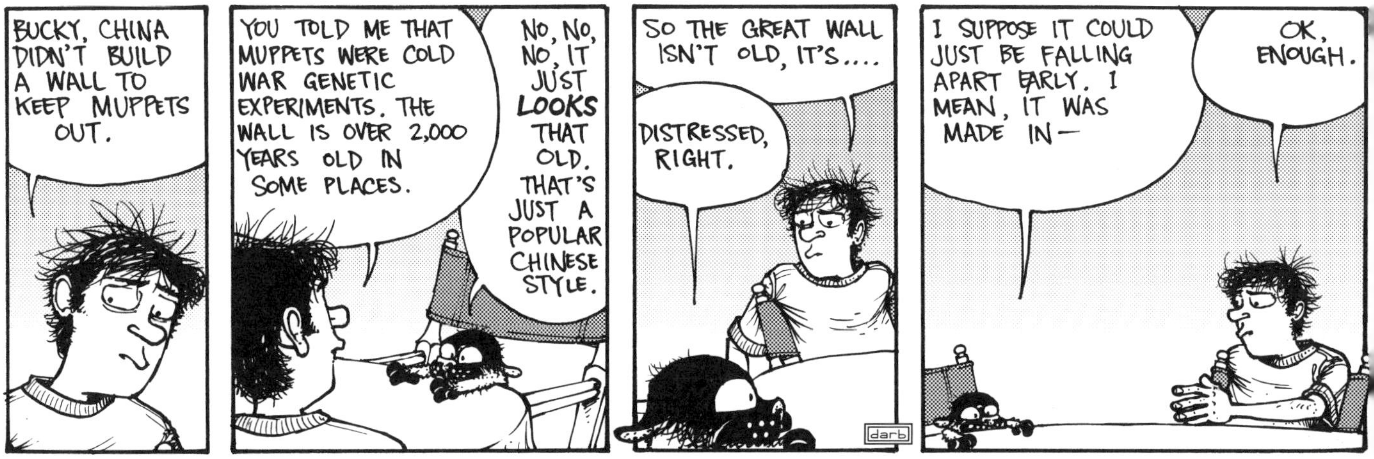
BUCKY, CHINA DIDN'T BUILD A WALL TO KEEP MUPPETS OUT.
YOU TOLD ME THAT MUPPETS WERE COLD WAR GENETIC EXPERIMENTS. THE WALL IS OVER 2,000 YEARS OLD IN SOME PLACES.
NO, NO, NO, IT JUST **LOOKS** THAT OLD. THAT'S JUST A POPULAR CHINESE STYLE.
SO THE GREAT WALL ISN'T OLD, IT'S....
DISTRESSED, RIGHT.
darb
I SUPPOSE IT COULD JUST BE FALLING APART EARLY. I MEAN, IT WAS MADE IN—
OK, ENOUGH.

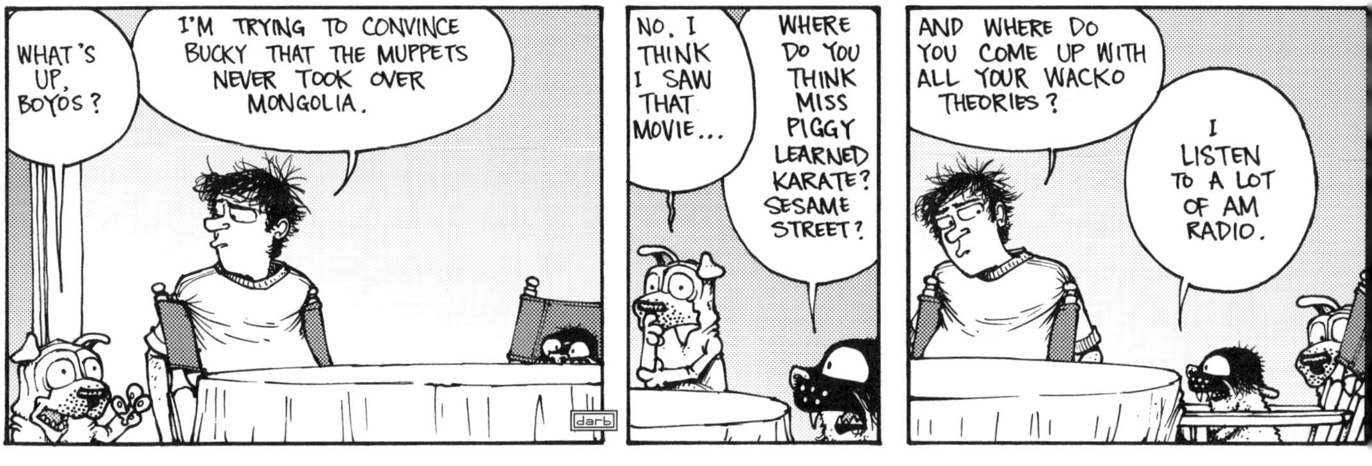
WHAT'S UP, BOYOS?
I'M TRYING TO CONVINCE BUCKY THAT THE MUPPETS NEVER TOOK OVER MONGOLIA.
darb
NO. I THINK I SAW THAT MOVIE...
WHERE DO YOU THINK MISS PIGGY LEARNED KARATE? SESAME STREET?
AND WHERE DO YOU COME UP WITH ALL YOUR WACKO THEORIES?
I LISTEN TO A LOT OF AM RADIO.

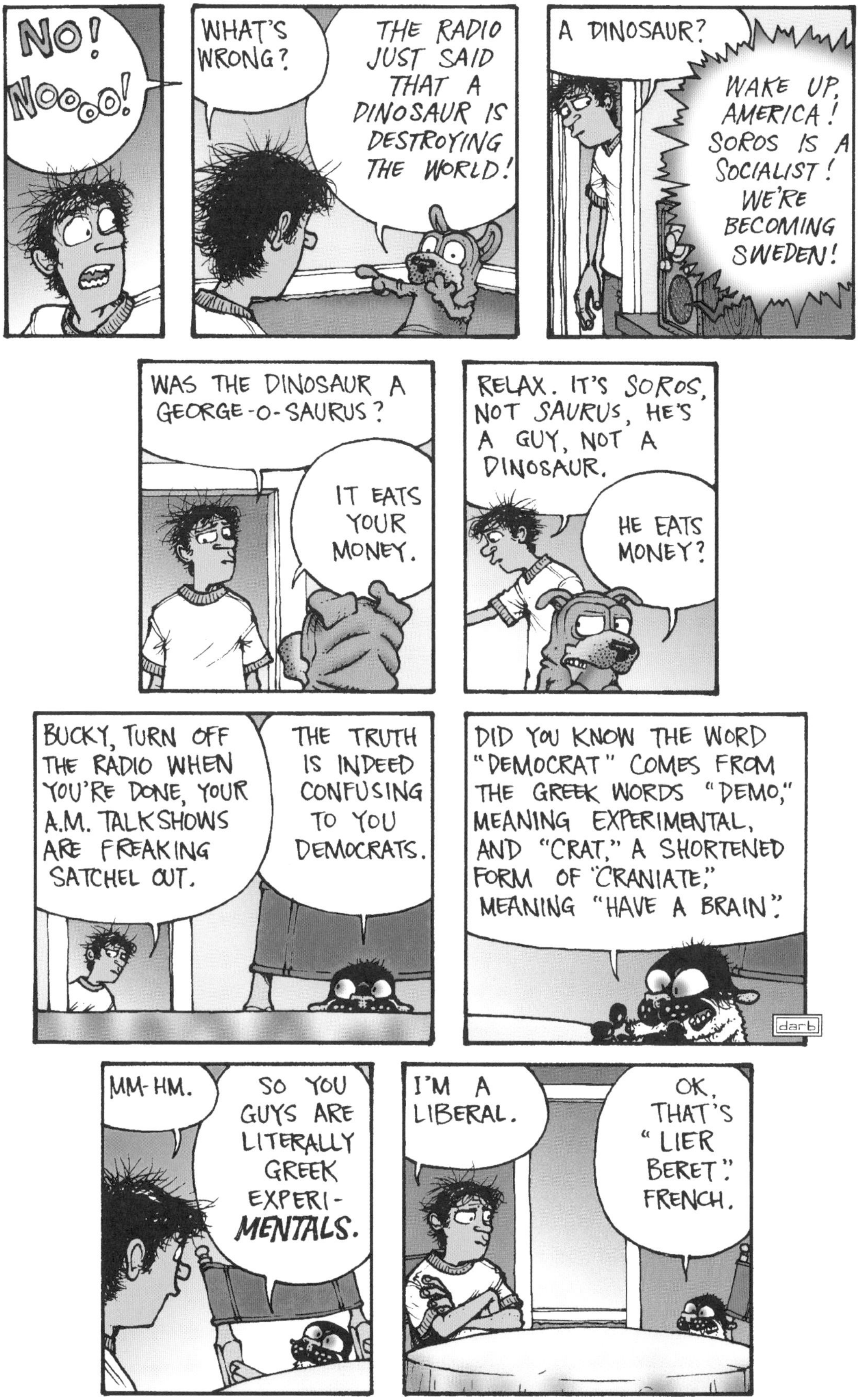
NO! NOoooo!
WHAT'S WRONG?
THE RADIO JUST SAID THAT A DINOSAUR IS DESTROYING THE WORLD!
A DINOSAUR?
WAKE UP, AMERICA! SOROS IS A SOCIALIST! WE'RE BECOMING SWEDEN!
WAS THE DINOSAUR A GEORGE-O-SAURUS?
IT EATS YOUR MONEY.
RELAX. IT'S SOROS, NOT SAURUS, HE'S A GUY, NOT A DINOSAUR.
HE EATS MONEY?
BUCKY, TURN OFF THE RADIO WHEN YOU'RE DONE, YOUR A.M. TALKSHOWS ARE FREAKING SATCHEL OUT.
THE TRUTH IS INDEED CONFUSING TO YOU DEMOCRATS.
DID YOU KNOW THE WORD "DEMOCRAT" COMES FROM THE GREEK WORDS "DEMO," MEANING EXPERIMENTAL, AND "CRAT," A SHORTENED FORM OF "CRANIATE," MEANING "HAVE A BRAIN".
darb
MM-HM.
SO YOU GUYS ARE LITERALLY GREEK EXPERI-MENTALS.
I'M A LIBERAL.
OK, THAT'S "LIER BERET". FRENCH.

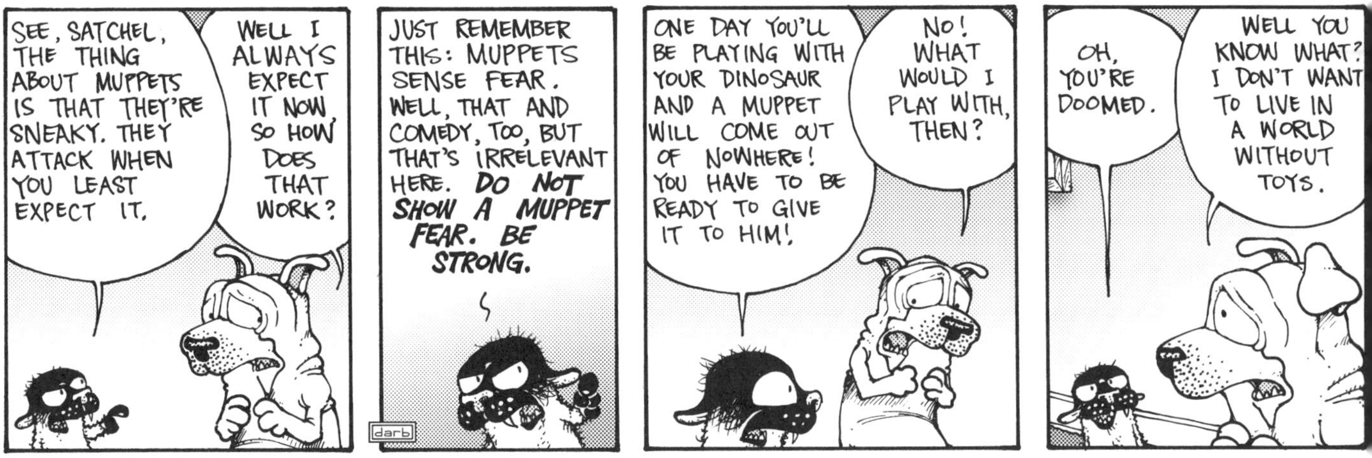
SEE, SATCHEL, THE THING ABOUT MUPPETS IS THAT THEY'RE SNEAKY. THEY ATTACK WHEN YOU LEAST EXPECT IT.
WELL I ALWAYS EXPECT IT NOW, SO HOW DOES THAT WORK?
JUST REMEMBER THIS: MUPPETS SENSE FEAR. WELL, THAT AND COMEDY, TOO, BUT THAT'S IRRELEVANT HERE. **DO NOT SHOW A MUPPET FEAR. BE STRONG.**
ONE DAY YOU'LL BE PLAYING WITH YOUR DINOSAUR AND A MUPPET WILL COME OUT OF NOWHERE! YOU HAVE TO BE READY TO GIVE IT TO HIM!
NO! WHAT WOULD I PLAY WITH, THEN?
OH, YOU'RE DOOMED.
WELL YOU KNOW WHAT? I DON'T WANT TO LIVE IN A WORLD WITHOUT TOYS.

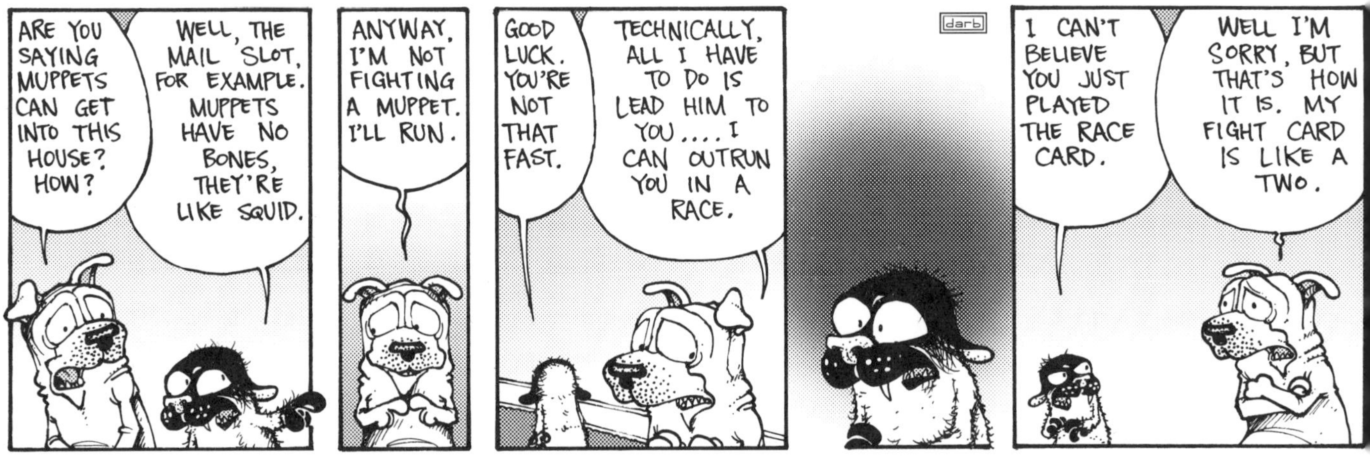
ARE YOU SAYING MUPPETS CAN GET INTO THIS HOUSE? HOW?
WELL, THE MAIL SLOT, FOR EXAMPLE. MUPPETS HAVE NO BONES, THEY'RE LIKE SQUID.
ANYWAY, I'M NOT FIGHTING A MUPPET. I'LL RUN.
GOOD LUCK. YOU'RE NOT THAT FAST.
TECHNICALLY, ALL I HAVE TO DO IS LEAD HIM TO YOU.... I CAN OUTRUN YOU IN A RACE.
I CAN'T BELIEVE YOU JUST PLAYED THE RACE CARD.
WELL I'M SORRY, BUT THAT'S HOW IT IS. MY FIGHT CARD IS LIKE A TWO.

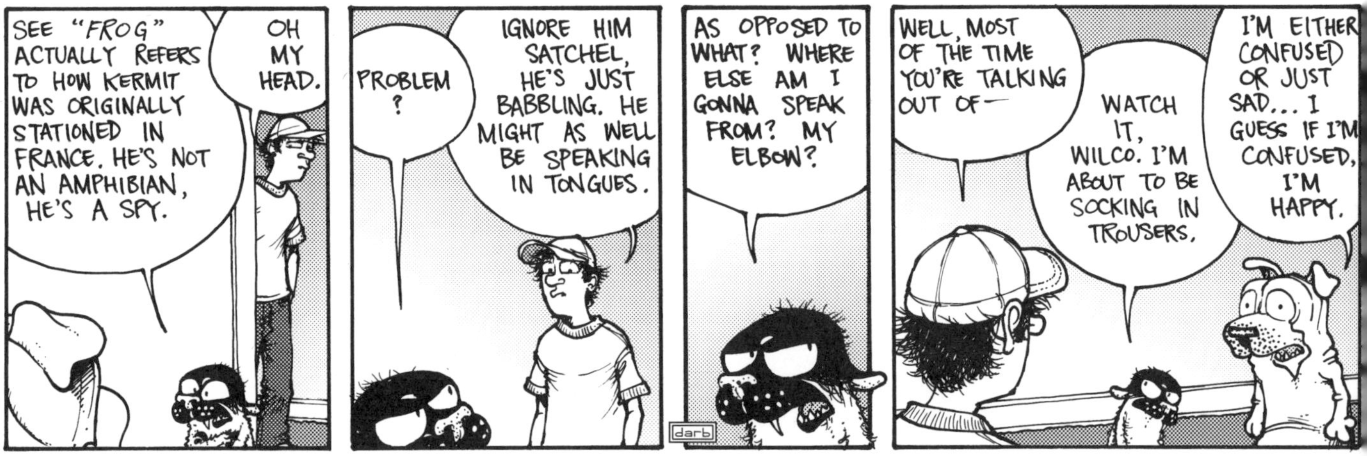
SEE "*FROG*" ACTUALLY REFERS TO HOW KERMIT WAS ORIGINALLY STATIONED IN FRANCE. HE'S NOT AN AMPHIBIAN, HE'S A SPY.
OH MY HEAD.
PROBLEM?
IGNORE HIM SATCHEL, HE'S JUST BABBLING. HE MIGHT AS WELL BE SPEAKING IN TONGUES.
AS OPPOSED TO WHAT? WHERE ELSE AM I GONNA SPEAK FROM? MY ELBOW?
WELL, MOST OF THE TIME YOU'RE TALKING OUT OF—
WATCH IT, WILCO. I'M ABOUT TO BE SOCKING IN TROUSERS.
I'M EITHER CONFUSED OR JUST SAD... I GUESS IF I'M CONFUSED, I'M HAPPY.

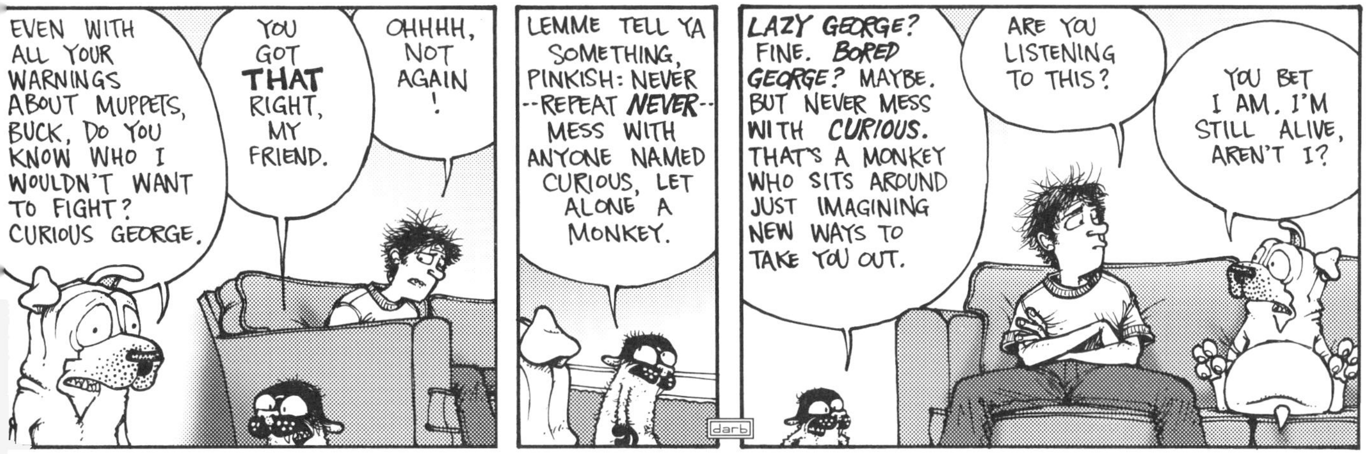
EVEN WITH ALL YOUR WARNINGS ABOUT MUPPETS, BUCK, DO YOU KNOW WHO I WOULDN'T WANT TO FIGHT? CURIOUS GEORGE.
YOU GOT **THAT** RIGHT, MY FRIEND.
OHHHH, NOT AGAIN!
LEMME TELL YA SOMETHING, PINKISH: NEVER --REPEAT ***NEVER***-- MESS WITH ANYONE NAMED CURIOUS, LET ALONE A MONKEY.
LAZY GEORGE? FINE. ***BORED GEORGE?*** MAYBE. BUT NEVER MESS WITH ***CURIOUS***. THAT'S A MONKEY WHO SITS AROUND JUST IMAGINING NEW WAYS TO TAKE YOU OUT.
ARE YOU LISTENING TO THIS?
YOU BET I AM. I'M STILL ALIVE, AREN'T I?
darb

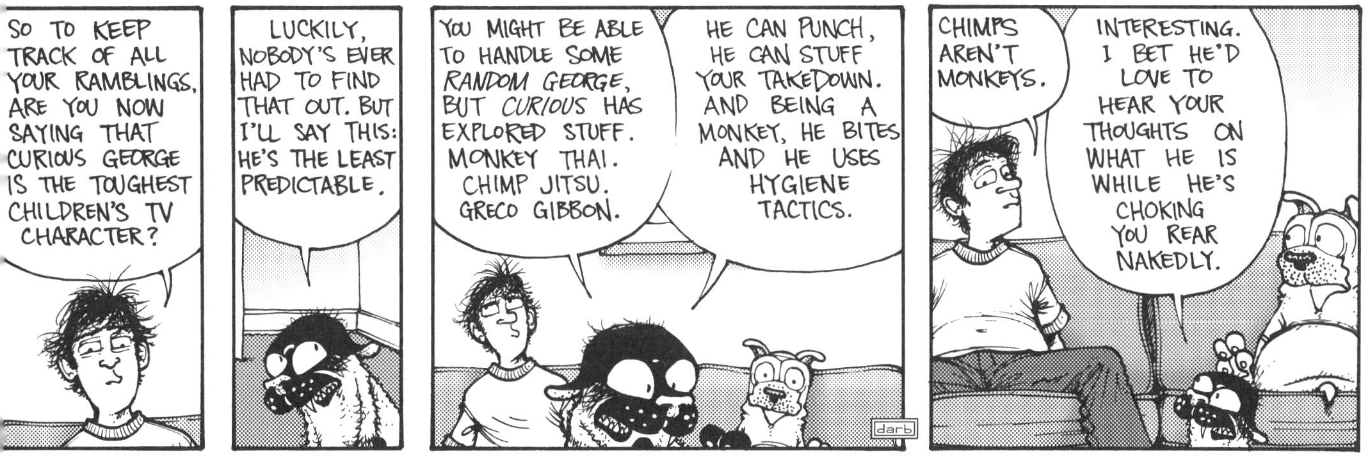
SO TO KEEP TRACK OF ALL YOUR RAMBLINGS, ARE YOU NOW SAYING THAT CURIOUS GEORGE IS THE TOUGHEST CHILDREN'S TV CHARACTER?
LUCKILY, NOBODY'S EVER HAD TO FIND THAT OUT. BUT I'LL SAY THIS: HE'S THE LEAST PREDICTABLE.
YOU MIGHT BE ABLE TO HANDLE SOME *RANDOM GEORGE*, BUT *CURIOUS* HAS EXPLORED STUFF. MONKEY THAI. CHIMP JITSU. GRECO GIBBON.
HE CAN PUNCH, HE CAN STUFF YOUR TAKEDOWN. AND BEING A MONKEY, HE BITES AND HE USES HYGIENE TACTICS.
darb
CHIMPS AREN'T MONKEYS.
INTERESTING. I BET HE'D LOVE TO HEAR YOUR THOUGHTS ON WHAT HE IS WHILE HE'S CHOKING YOU REAR NAKEDLY.

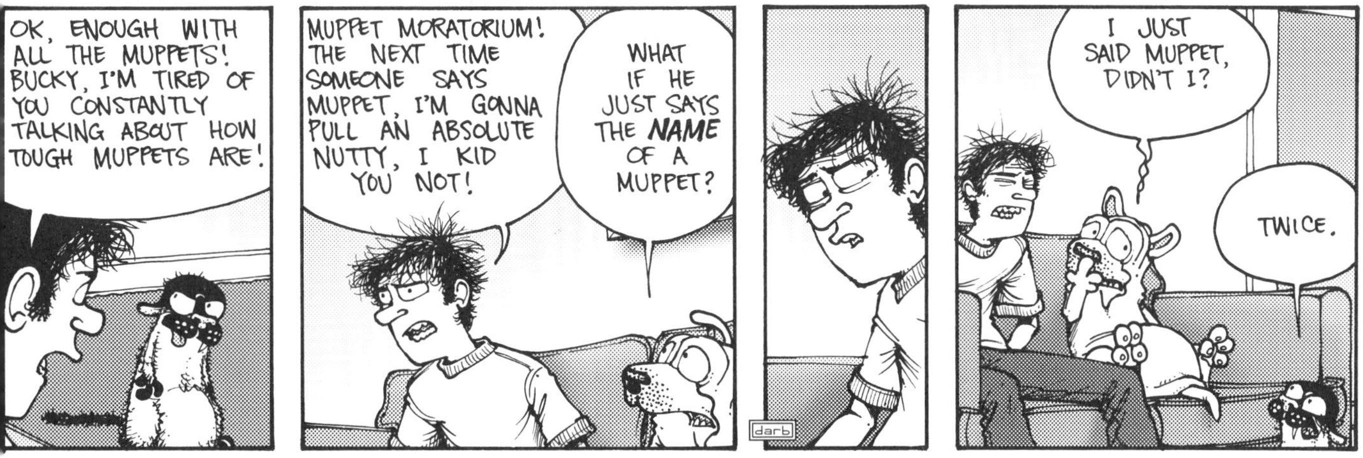
OK, ENOUGH WITH ALL THE MUPPETS! BUCKY, I'M TIRED OF YOU CONSTANTLY TALKING ABOUT HOW TOUGH MUPPETS ARE!
MUPPET MORATORIUM! THE NEXT TIME SOMEONE SAYS MUPPET, I'M GONNA PULL AN ABSOLUTE NUTTY, I KID YOU NOT!
WHAT IF HE JUST SAYS THE ***NAME*** OF A MUPPET?
darb
I JUST SAID MUPPET, DIDN'T I?
TWICE.

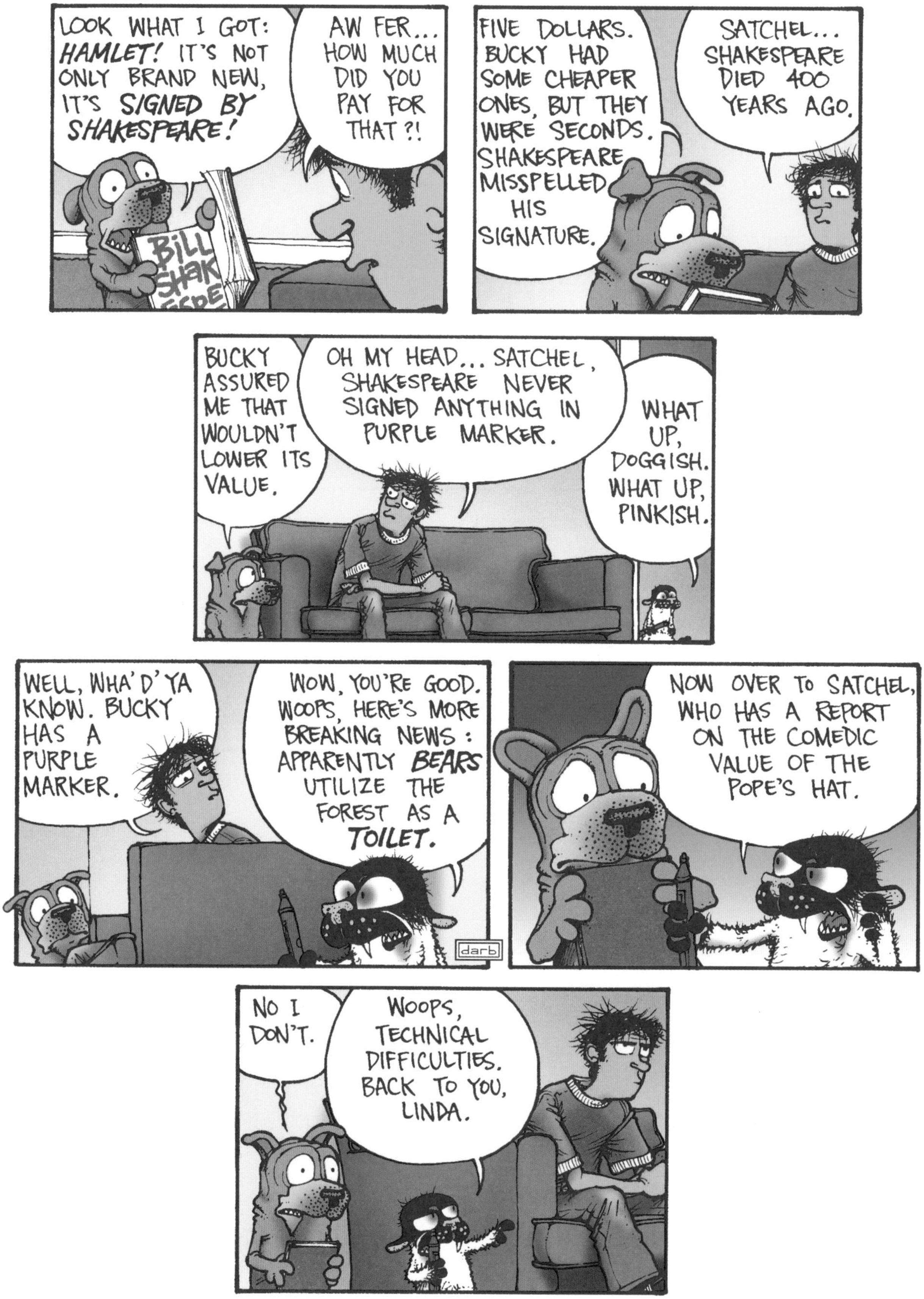
LOOK WHAT I GOT: HAMLET! IT'S NOT ONLY BRAND NEW, IT'S SIGNED BY SHAKESPEARE!
AW FER... HOW MUCH DID YOU PAY FOR THAT?!
BILL
FIVE DOLLARS. BUCKY HAD SOME CHEAPER ONES, BUT THEY WERE SECONDS. SHAKESPEARE MISSPELLED HIS SIGNATURE.
SATCHEL... SHAKESPEARE DIED 400 YEARS AGO.
BUCKY ASSURED ME THAT WOULDN'T LOWER ITS VALUE.
OH MY HEAD... SATCHEL, SHAKESPEARE NEVER SIGNED ANYTHING IN PURPLE MARKER.
WHAT UP, DOGGISH. WHAT UP, PINKISH.
WELL, WHA'D'YA KNOW. BUCKY HAS A PURPLE MARKER.
WOW, YOU'RE GOOD. WOOPS, HERE'S MORE BREAKING NEWS: APPARENTLY BEARS UTILIZE THE FOREST AS A TOILET.
darb
NOW OVER TO SATCHEL, WHO HAS A REPORT ON THE COMEDIC VALUE OF THE POPE'S HAT.
NO I DON'T.
WOOPS, TECHNICAL DIFFICULTIES. BACK TO YOU, LINDA.

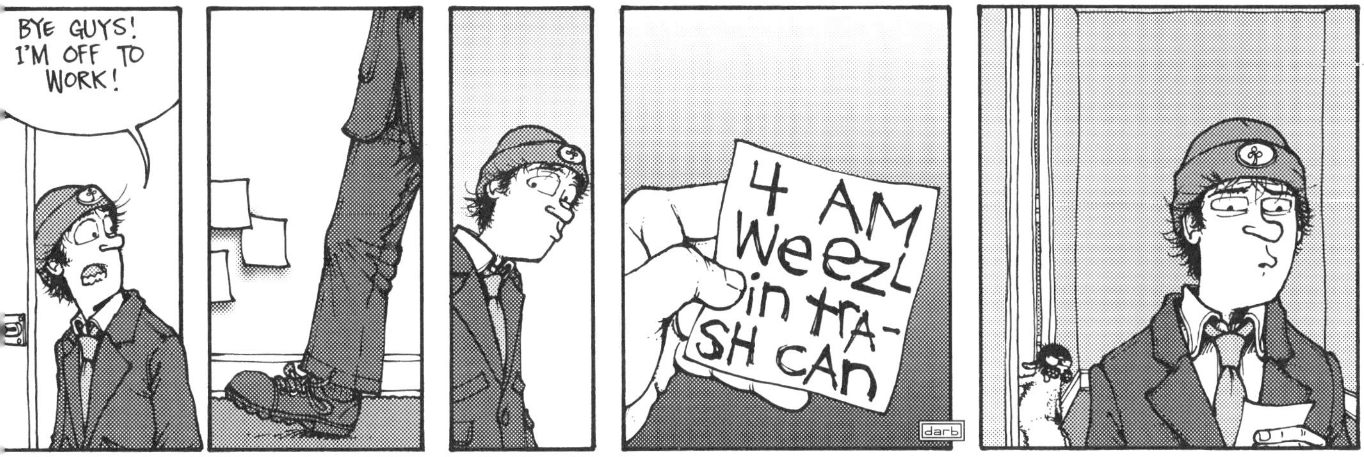

BYE GUYS! I'M OFF TO WORK!
4 AM Weezl in tra- sh can
darb

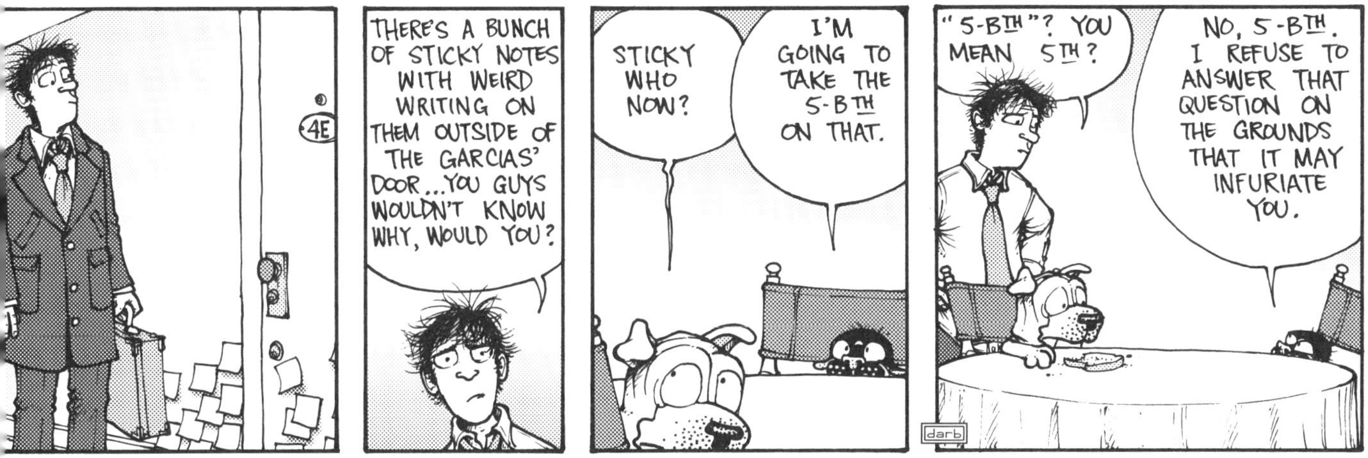

4E
THERE'S A BUNCH OF STICKY NOTES WITH WEIRD WRITING ON THEM OUTSIDE OF THE GARCIAS' DOOR...YOU GUYS WOULDN'T KNOW WHY, WOULD YOU?
STICKY WHO NOW?
I'M GOING TO TAKE THE 5-BTH ON THAT.
"5-BTH"? YOU MEAN 5TH?
NO, 5-BTH. I REFUSE TO ANSWER THAT QUESTION ON THE GROUNDS THAT IT MAY INFURIATE YOU.
darb

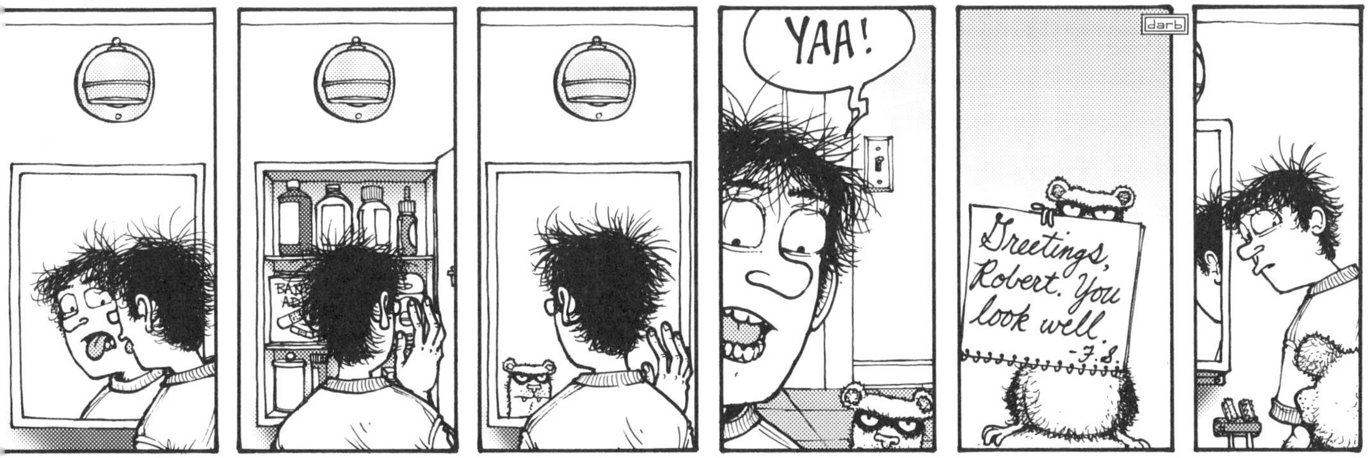

YAA!
darb
Greetings, Robert. You look well.

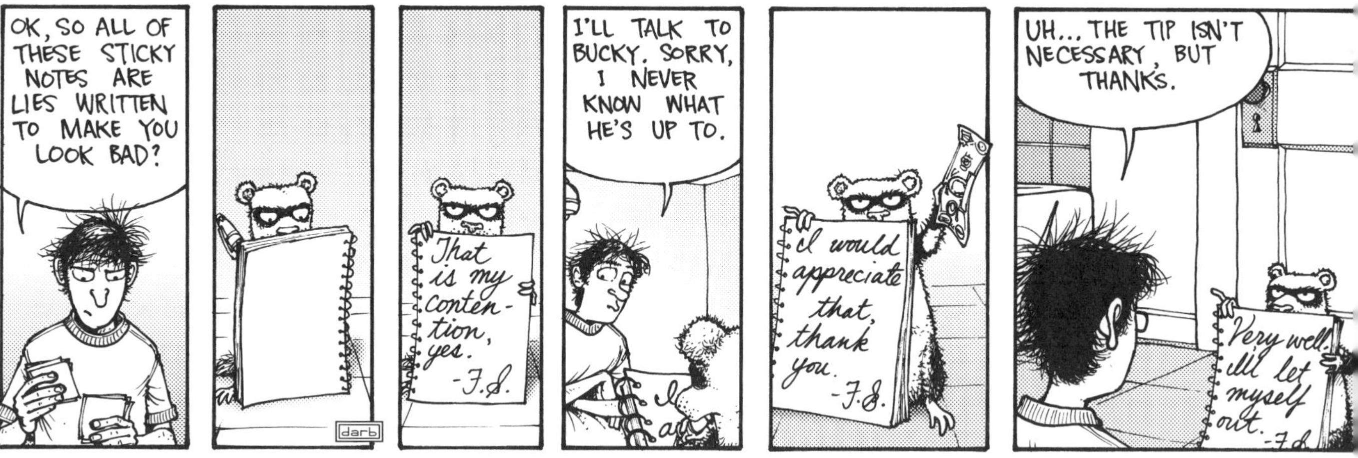
OK, SO ALL OF THESE STICKY NOTES ARE LIES WRITTEN TO MAKE YOU LOOK BAD?
That is my conten-tion, yes. -F.S.
I'LL TALK TO BUCKY. SORRY, I NEVER KNOW WHAT HE'S UP TO.
I would appreciate that, thank you. -F.S.
UH... THE TIP ISN'T NECESSARY, BUT THANKS.
Very well. I'll let myself out. -F.S.
darb

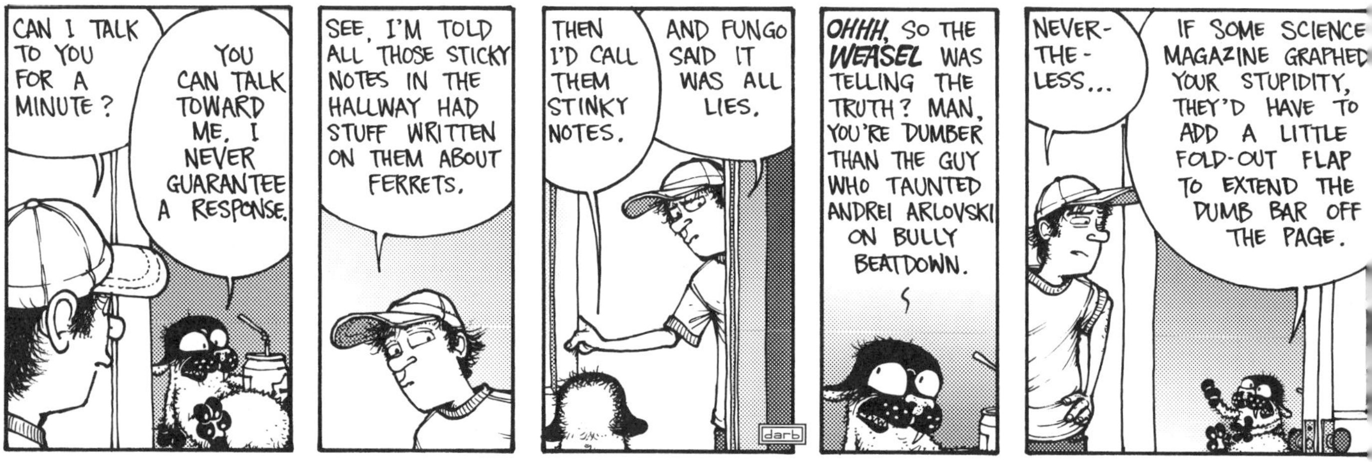
CAN I TALK TO YOU FOR A MINUTE?
YOU CAN TALK TOWARD ME. I NEVER GUARANTEE A RESPONSE.
SEE, I'M TOLD ALL THOSE STICKY NOTES IN THE HALLWAY HAD STUFF WRITTEN ON THEM ABOUT FERRETS.
THEN I'D CALL THEM STINKY NOTES.
AND FUNGO SAID IT WAS ALL LIES.
OHHH, SO THE WEASEL WAS TELLING THE TRUTH? MAN, YOU'RE DUMBER THAN THE GUY WHO TAUNTED ANDREI ARLOVSKI ON BULLY BEATDOWN.
NEVER-THE-LESS...
IF SOME SCIENCE MAGAZINE GRAPHED YOUR STUPIDITY, THEY'D HAVE TO ADD A LITTLE FOLD-OUT FLAP TO EXTEND THE DUMB BAR OFF THE PAGE.
darb

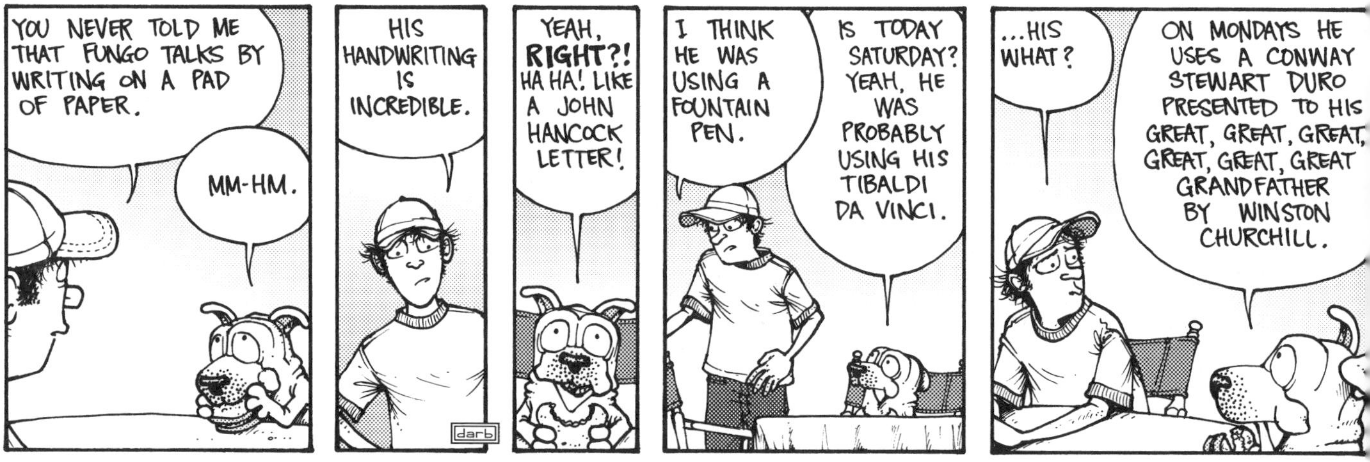
YOU NEVER TOLD ME THAT FUNGO TALKS BY WRITING ON A PAD OF PAPER.
MM-HM.
HIS HANDWRITING IS INCREDIBLE.
YEAH, RIGHT?! HA HA! LIKE A JOHN HANCOCK LETTER!
I THINK HE WAS USING A FOUNTAIN PEN.
IS TODAY SATURDAY? YEAH, HE WAS PROBABLY USING HIS TIBALDI DA VINCI.
...HIS WHAT?
ON MONDAYS HE USES A CONWAY STEWART DURO PRESENTED TO HIS GREAT, GREAT, GREAT, GREAT, GREAT, GREAT GRANDFATHER BY WINSTON CHURCHILL.
darb

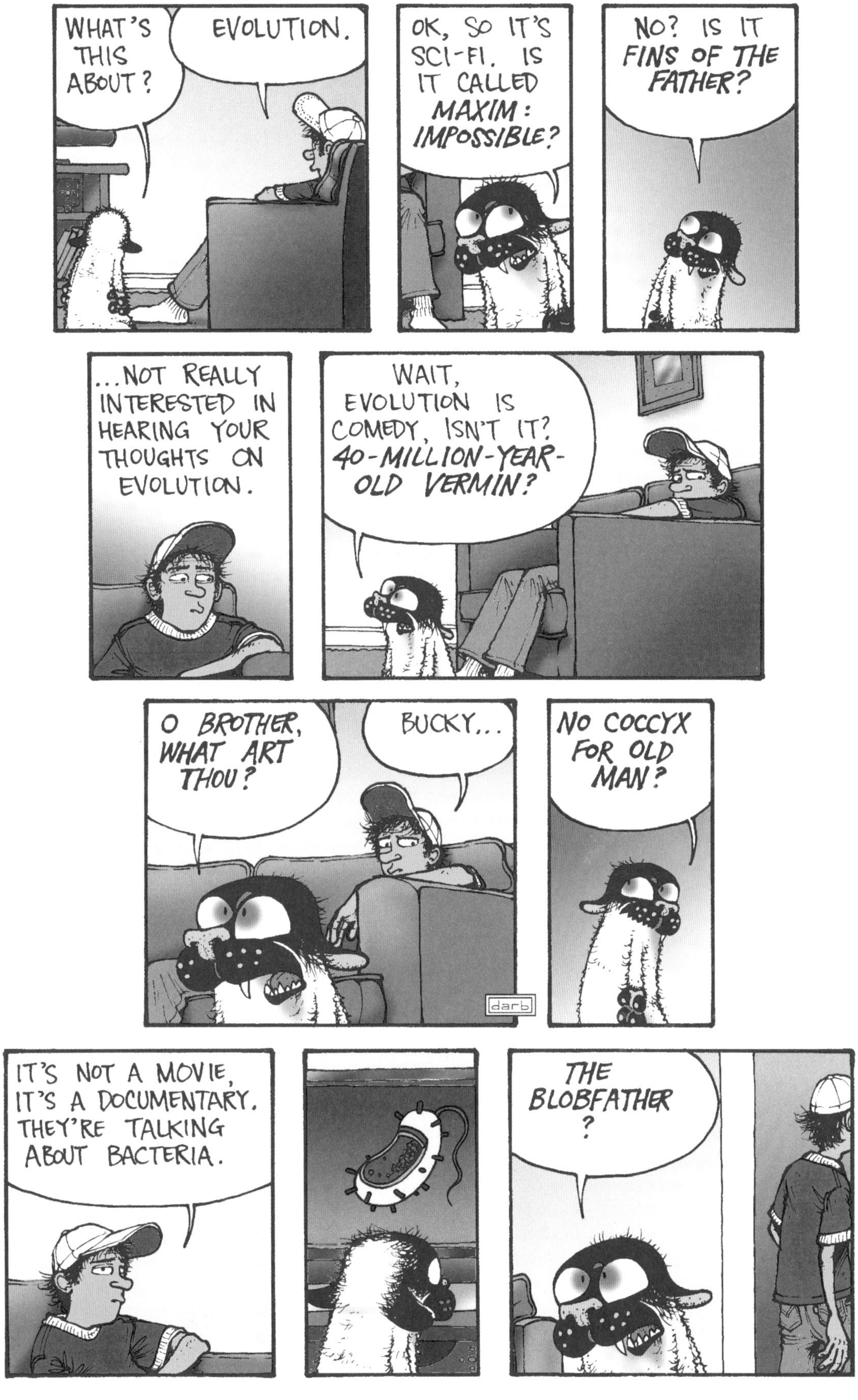
WHAT'S THIS ABOUT?
EVOLUTION.
OK, SO IT'S SCI-FI. IS IT CALLED MAXIM: IMPOSSIBLE?
NO? IS IT FINS OF THE FATHER?
...NOT REALLY INTERESTED IN HEARING YOUR THOUGHTS ON EVOLUTION.
WAIT, EVOLUTION IS COMEDY, ISN'T IT? 40-MILLION-YEAR-OLD VERMIN?
O BROTHER, WHAT ART THOU?
BUCKY...
darb
NO COCCYX FOR OLD MAN?
IT'S NOT A MOVIE, IT'S A DOCUMENTARY. THEY'RE TALKING ABOUT BACTERIA.
THE BLOBFATHER?

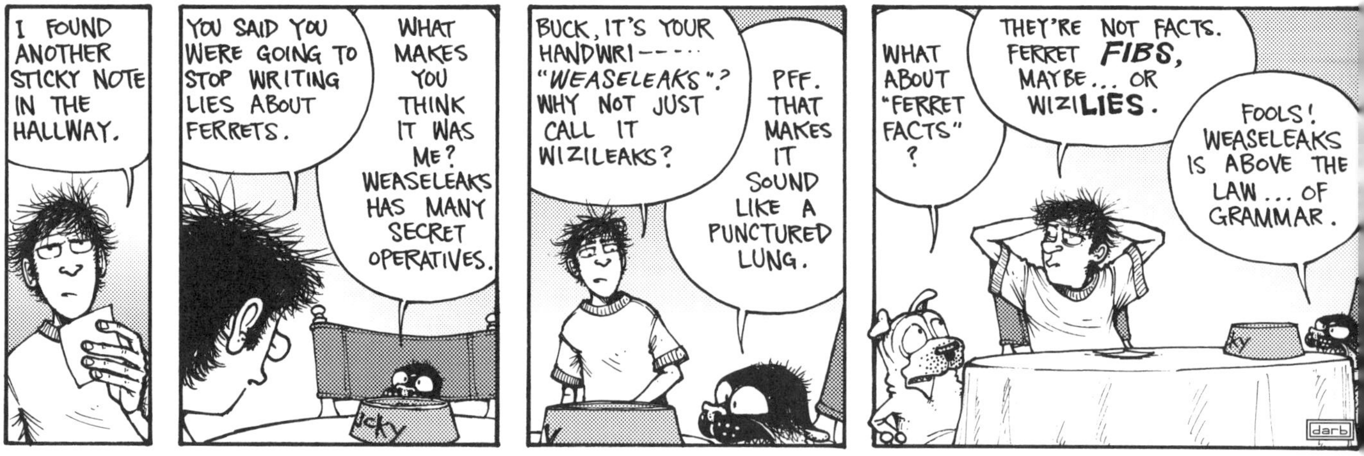
I FOUND ANOTHER STICKY NOTE IN THE HALLWAY.
YOU SAID YOU WERE GOING TO STOP WRITING LIES ABOUT FERRETS.
WHAT MAKES YOU THINK IT WAS ME? WEASELEAKS HAS MANY SECRET OPERATIVES.
BUCK, IT'S YOUR HANDWRI----- "WEASELEAKS"? WHY NOT JUST CALL IT WIZILEAKS?
PFF. THAT MAKES IT SOUND LIKE A PUNCTURED LUNG.
WHAT ABOUT "FERRET FACTS"?
THEY'RE NOT FACTS. FERRET **FIBS,** MAYBE... OR WIZI**LIES**.
FOOLS! WEASELEAKS IS ABOVE THE LAW... OF GRAMMAR.
darb

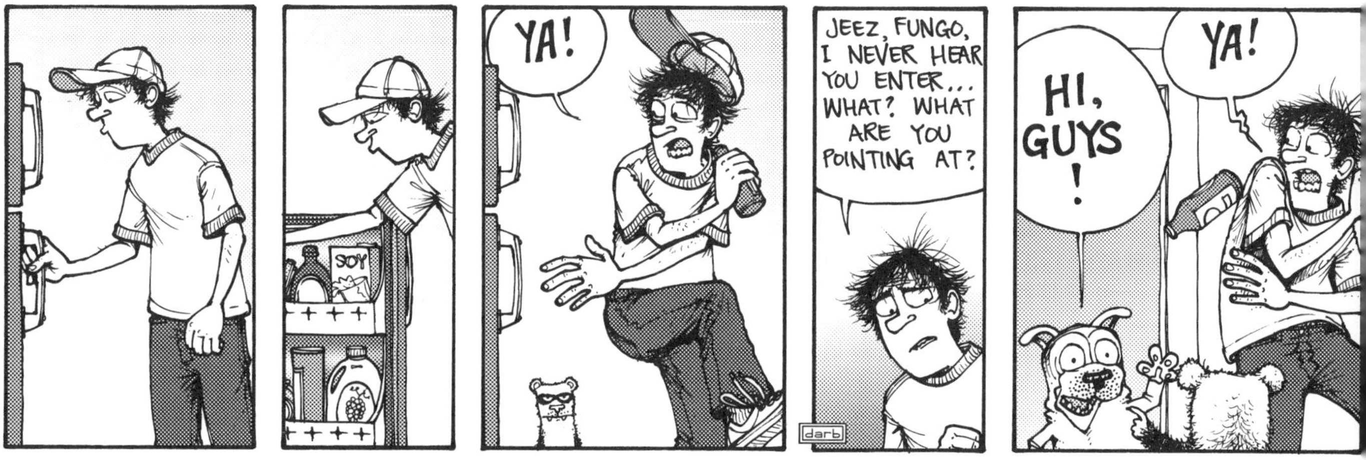
SOY
YA!
darb
JEEZ, FUNGO, I NEVER HEAR YOU ENTER... WHAT? WHAT ARE YOU POINTING AT?
HI, GUYS!
YA!

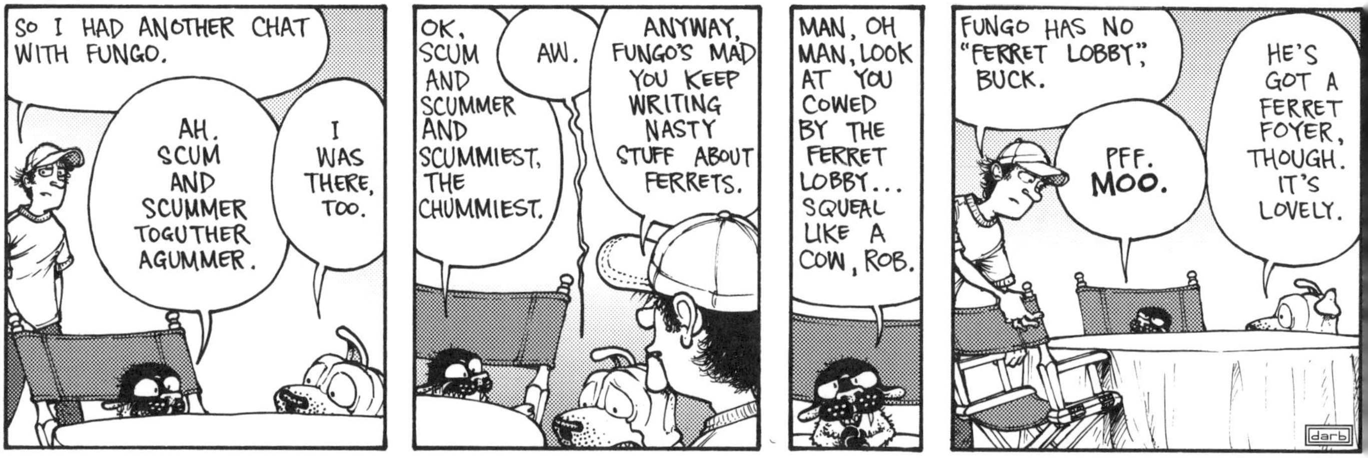
SO I HAD ANOTHER CHAT WITH FUNGO.
AH. SCUM AND SCUMMER TOGUTHER AGUMMER.
I WAS THERE, TOO.
OK, SCUM AND SCUMMER AND SCUMMIEST, THE CHUMMIEST.
AW.
ANYWAY, FUNGO'S MAD YOU KEEP WRITING NASTY STUFF ABOUT FERRETS.
MAN, OH MAN, LOOK AT YOU COWED BY THE FERRET LOBBY... SQUEAL LIKE A COW, ROB.
FUNGO HAS NO "FERRET LOBBY", BUCK.
PFF. **MOO.**
HE'S GOT A FERRET FOYER, THOUGH. IT'S LOVELY.
darb

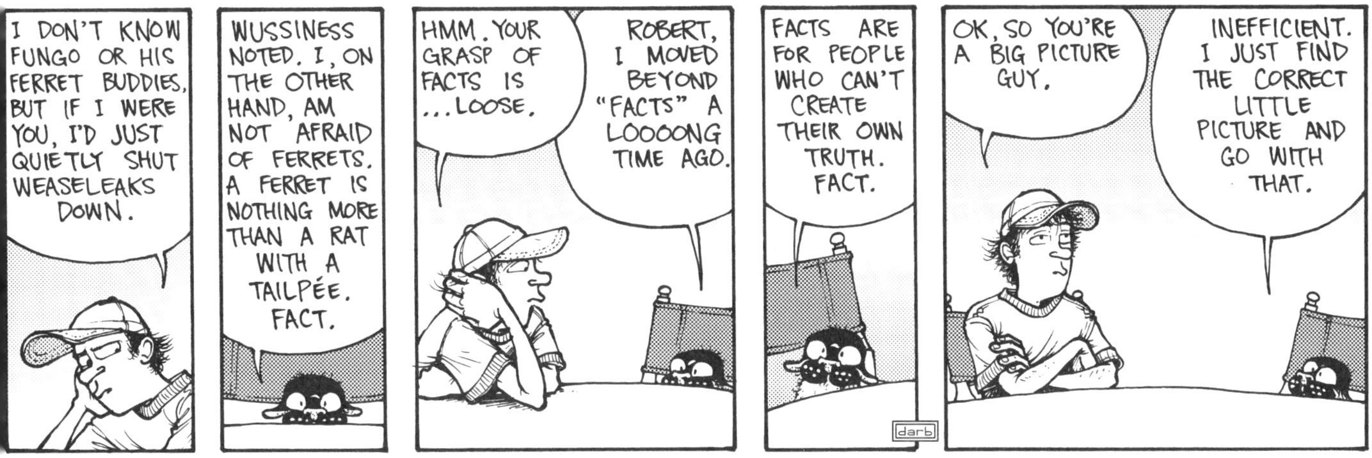
I DON'T KNOW FUNGO OR HIS FERRET BUDDIES, BUT IF I WERE YOU, I'D JUST QUIETLY SHUT WEASELEAKS DOWN.
WUSSINESS NOTED. I, ON THE OTHER HAND, AM NOT AFRAID OF FERRETS. A FERRET IS NOTHING MORE THAN A RAT WITH A TAILPÉE. FACT.
HMM. YOUR GRASP OF FACTS IS ...LOOSE.
ROBERT, I MOVED BEYOND "FACTS" A LOOOONG TIME AGO.
FACTS ARE FOR PEOPLE WHO CAN'T CREATE THEIR OWN TRUTH. FACT.
OK, SO YOU'RE A BIG PICTURE GUY.
INEFFICIENT. I JUST FIND THE CORRECT LITTLE PICTURE AND GO WITH THAT.
darb

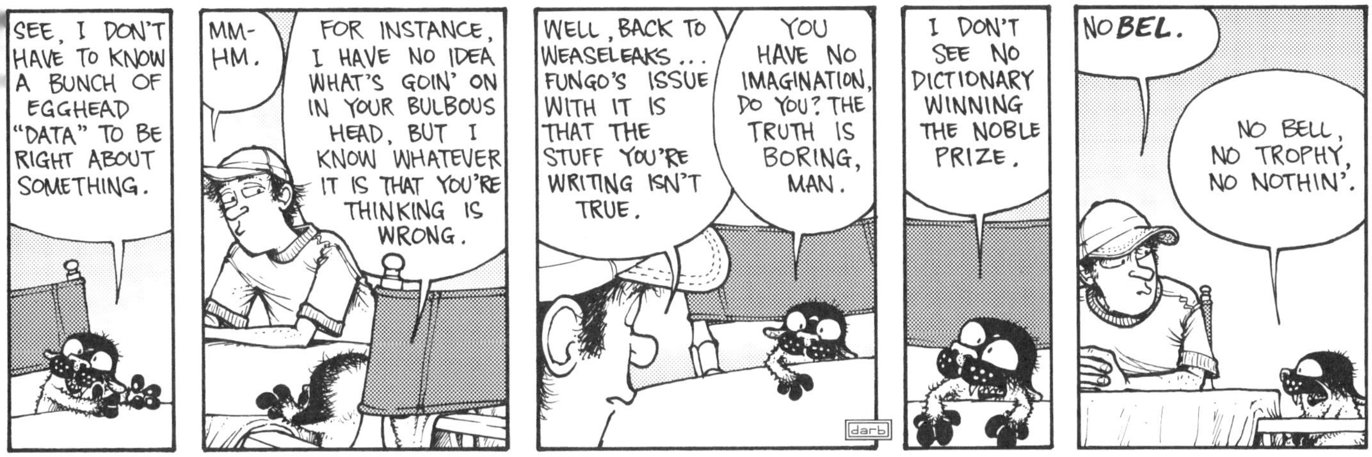
SEE, I DON'T HAVE TO KNOW A BUNCH OF EGGHEAD "DATA" TO BE RIGHT ABOUT SOMETHING.
MM-HM.
FOR INSTANCE, I HAVE NO IDEA WHAT'S GOIN' ON IN YOUR BULBOUS HEAD, BUT I KNOW WHATEVER IT IS THAT YOU'RE THINKING IS WRONG.
WELL, BACK TO WEASELEAKS... FUNGO'S ISSUE WITH IT IS THAT THE STUFF YOU'RE WRITING ISN'T TRUE.
YOU HAVE NO IMAGINATION, DO YOU? THE TRUTH IS BORING, MAN.
darb
I DON'T SEE NO DICTIONARY WINNING THE NOBLE PRIZE.
NO*BEL*.
NO BELL, NO TROPHY, NO NOTHIN'.

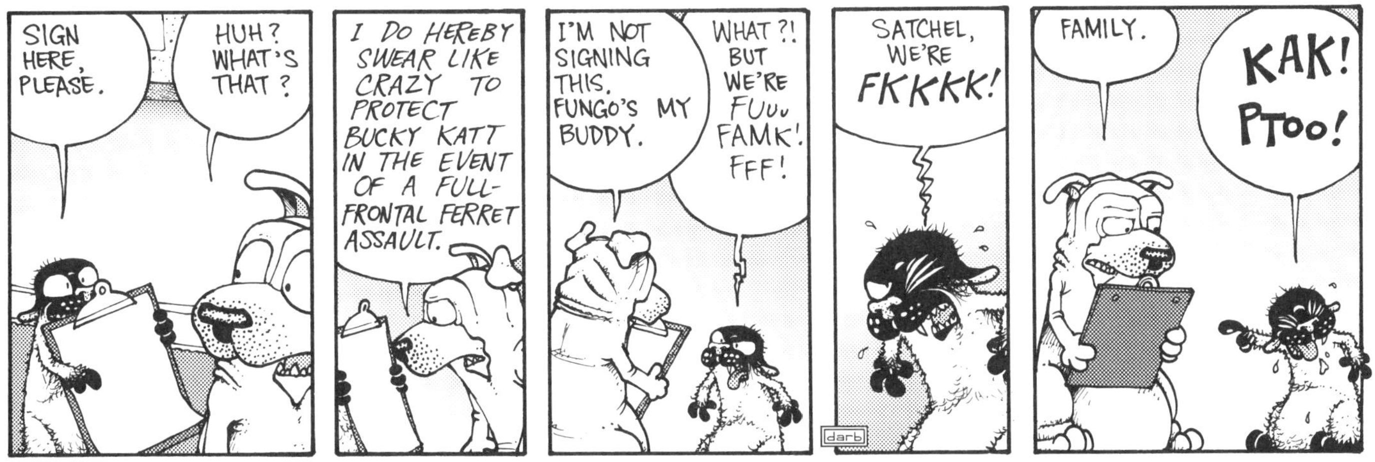
SIGN HERE, PLEASE.
HUH? WHAT'S THAT?
I DO HEREBY SWEAR LIKE CRAZY TO PROTECT BUCKY KATT IN THE EVENT OF A FULL-FRONTAL FERRET ASSAULT.
I'M NOT SIGNING THIS. FUNGO'S MY BUDDY.
WHAT?! BUT WE'RE FUU.. FAMK! FFF!
darb
SATCHEL, WE'RE FKKKK!
FAMILY.
KAK! PTOO!

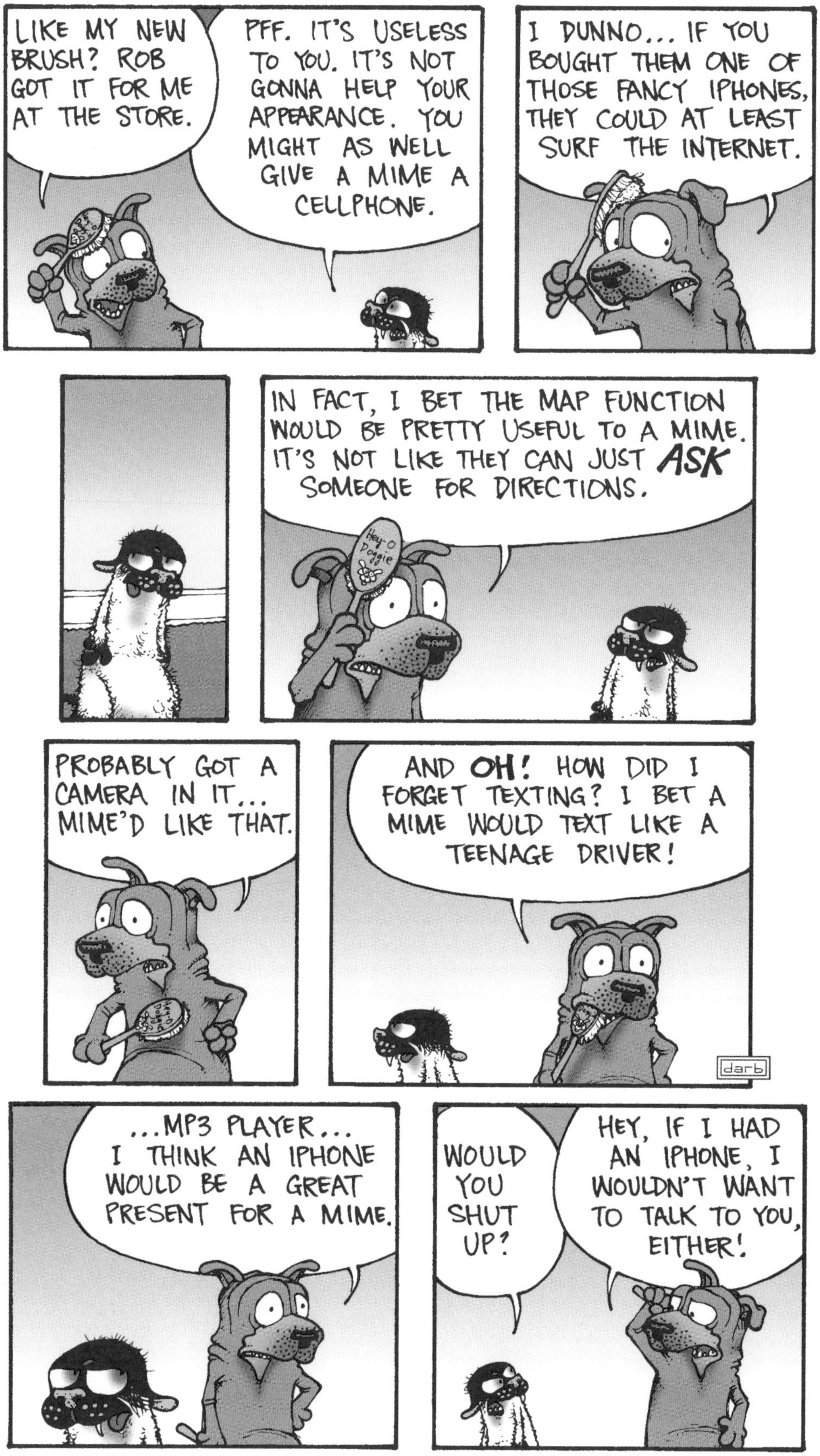

LIKE MY NEW BRUSH? ROB GOT IT FOR ME AT THE STORE.
PFF. IT'S USELESS TO YOU. IT'S NOT GONNA HELP YOUR APPEARANCE. YOU MIGHT AS WELL GIVE A MIME A CELLPHONE.
I DUNNO... IF YOU BOUGHT THEM ONE OF THOSE FANCY IPHONES, THEY COULD AT LEAST SURF THE INTERNET.
IN FACT, I BET THE MAP FUNCTION WOULD BE PRETTY USEFUL TO A MIME. IT'S NOT LIKE THEY CAN JUST ASK SOMEONE FOR DIRECTIONS.
Hey-O Doggie
PROBABLY GOT A CAMERA IN IT... MIME'D LIKE THAT.
AND OH! HOW DID I FORGET TEXTING? I BET A MIME WOULD TEXT LIKE A TEENAGE DRIVER!
darb
...MP3 PLAYER... I THINK AN IPHONE WOULD BE A GREAT PRESENT FOR A MIME.
WOULD YOU SHUT UP?
HEY, IF I HAD AN IPHONE, I WOULDN'T WANT TO TALK TO YOU, EITHER!

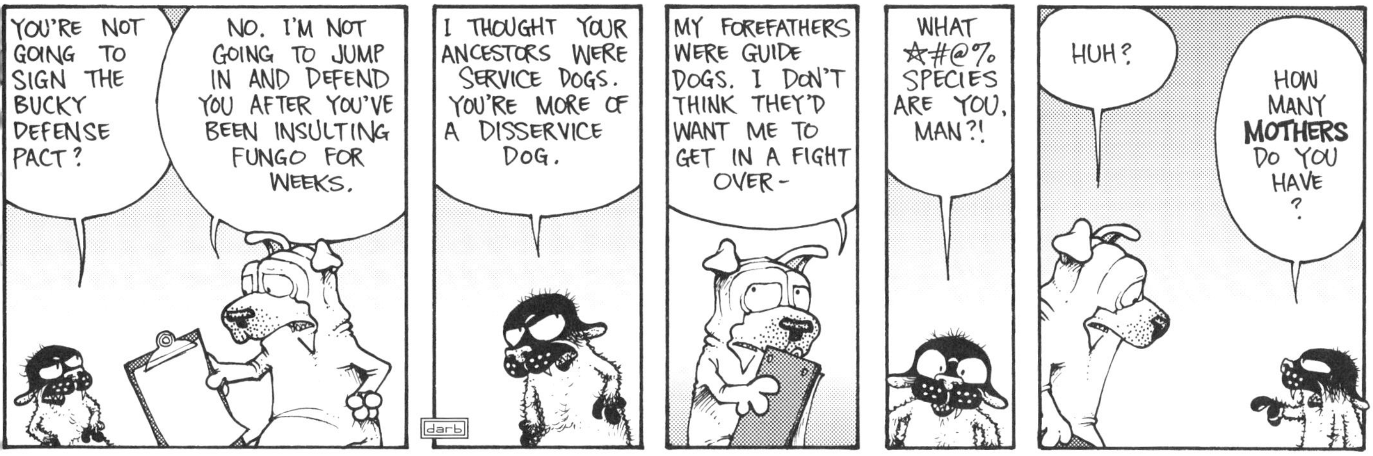
YOU'RE NOT GOING TO SIGN THE BUCKY DEFENSE PACT?
NO. I'M NOT GOING TO JUMP IN AND DEFEND YOU AFTER YOU'VE BEEN INSULTING FUNGO FOR WEEKS.
darb
I THOUGHT YOUR ANCESTORS WERE SERVICE DOGS. YOU'RE MORE OF A DISSERVICE DOG.
MY FOREFATHERS WERE GUIDE DOGS. I DON'T THINK THEY'D WANT ME TO GET IN A FIGHT OVER-
WHAT ☆#@% SPECIES ARE YOU, MAN?!
HUH?
HOW MANY **MOTHERS** DO YOU HAVE?

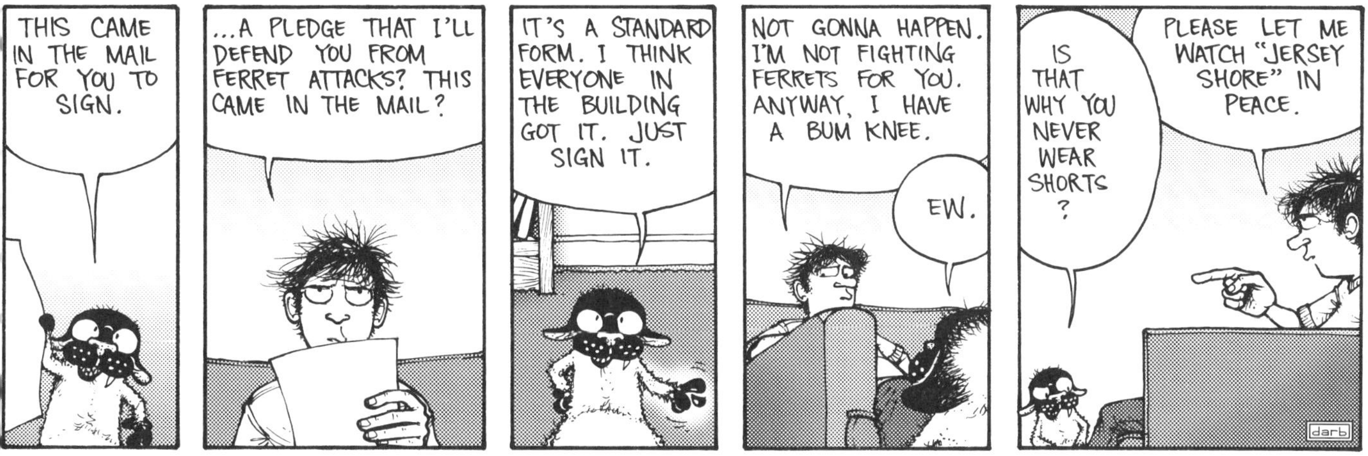
THIS CAME IN THE MAIL FOR YOU TO SIGN.
...A PLEDGE THAT I'LL DEFEND YOU FROM FERRET ATTACKS? THIS CAME IN THE MAIL?
IT'S A STANDARD FORM. I THINK EVERYONE IN THE BUILDING GOT IT. JUST SIGN IT.
NOT GONNA HAPPEN. I'M NOT FIGHTING FERRETS FOR YOU. ANYWAY, I HAVE A BUM KNEE.
EW.
IS THAT WHY YOU NEVER WEAR SHORTS?
PLEASE LET ME WATCH "JERSEY SHORE" IN PEACE.
darb

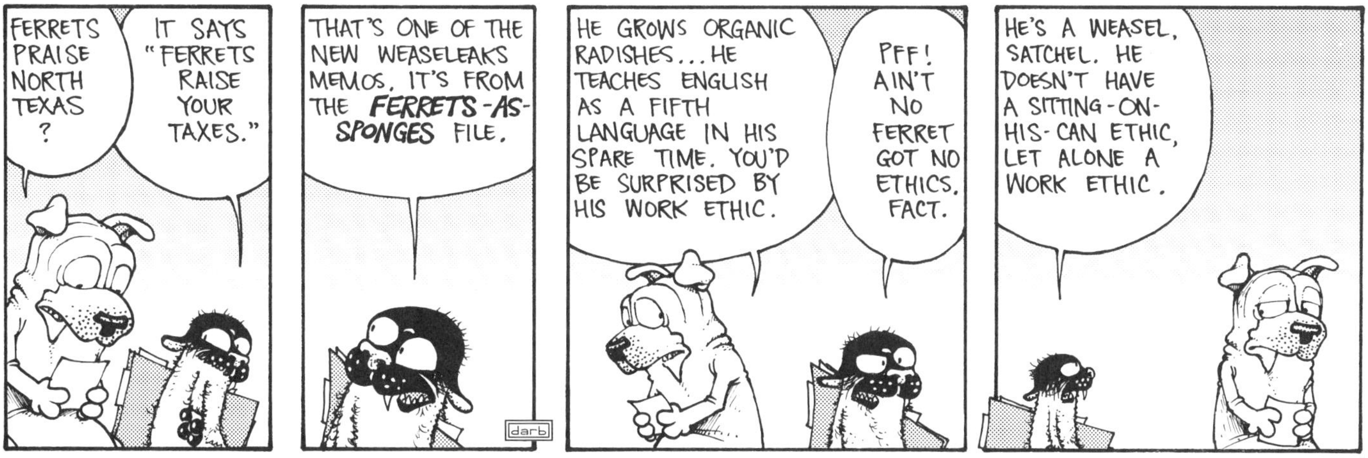
FERRETS PRAISE NORTH TEXAS?
IT SAYS "FERRETS RAISE YOUR TAXES."
THAT'S ONE OF THE NEW WEASELEAKS MEMOS, IT'S FROM THE ***FERRETS-AS-SPONGES*** FILE.
darb
HE GROWS ORGANIC RADISHES... HE TEACHES ENGLISH AS A FIFTH LANGUAGE IN HIS SPARE TIME. YOU'D BE SURPRISED BY HIS WORK ETHIC.
PFF! AIN'T NO FERRET GOT NO ETHICS, FACT.
HE'S A WEASEL, SATCHEL. HE DOESN'T HAVE A SITTING-ON-HIS-CAN ETHIC, LET ALONE A WORK ETHIC.

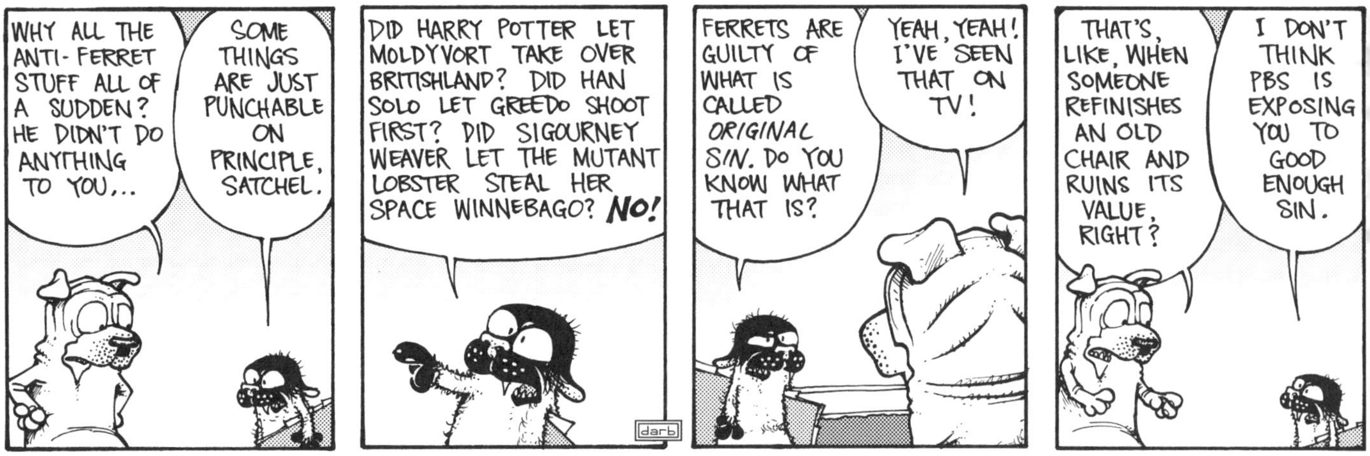
WHY ALL THE ANTI-FERRET STUFF ALL OF A SUDDEN? HE DIDN'T DO ANYTHING TO YOU...
SOME THINGS ARE JUST PUNCHABLE ON PRINCIPLE, SATCHEL.
DID HARRY POTTER LET MOLDYVORT TAKE OVER BRITISHLAND? DID HAN SOLO LET GREEDO SHOOT FIRST? DID SIGOURNEY WEAVER LET THE MUTANT LOBSTER STEAL HER SPACE WINNEBAGO? NO!
darb
FERRETS ARE GUILTY OF WHAT IS CALLED ORIGINAL SIN. DO YOU KNOW WHAT THAT IS?
YEAH, YEAH! I'VE SEEN THAT ON TV!
THAT'S, LIKE, WHEN SOMEONE REFINISHES AN OLD CHAIR AND RUINS ITS VALUE, RIGHT?
I DON'T THINK PBS IS EXPOSING YOU TO GOOD ENOUGH SIN.

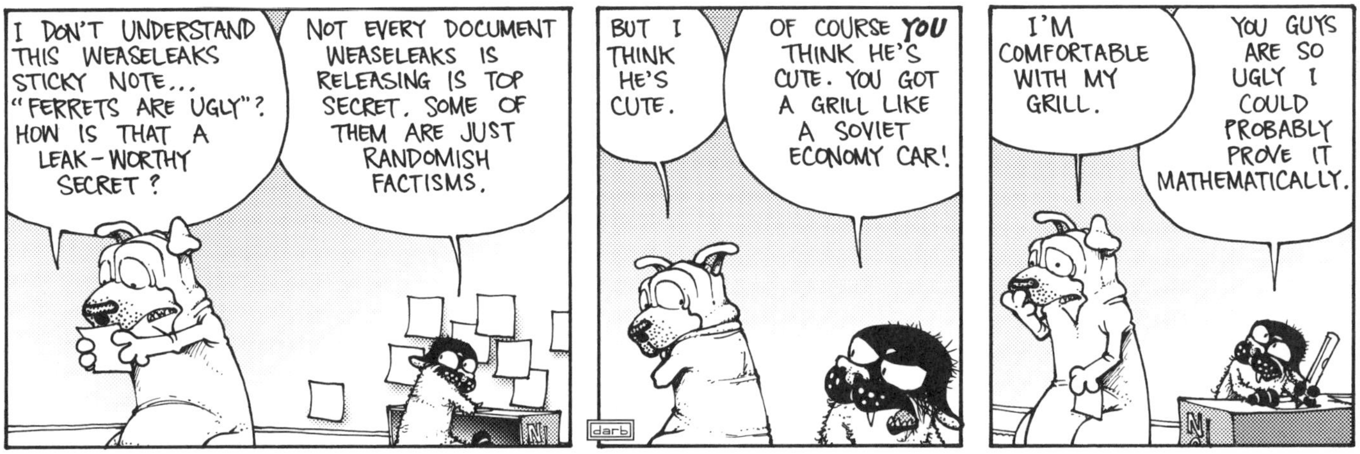
I DON'T UNDERSTAND THIS WEASELEAKS STICKY NOTE... "FERRETS ARE UGLY"? HOW IS THAT A LEAK-WORTHY SECRET?
NOT EVERY DOCUMENT WEASELEAKS IS RELEASING IS TOP SECRET. SOME OF THEM ARE JUST RANDOMISH FACTISMS.
darb
BUT I THINK HE'S CUTE.
OF COURSE YOU THINK HE'S CUTE. YOU GOT A GRILL LIKE A SOVIET ECONOMY CAR!
I'M COMFORTABLE WITH MY GRILL.
YOU GUYS ARE SO UGLY I COULD PROBABLY PROVE IT MATHEMATICALLY.

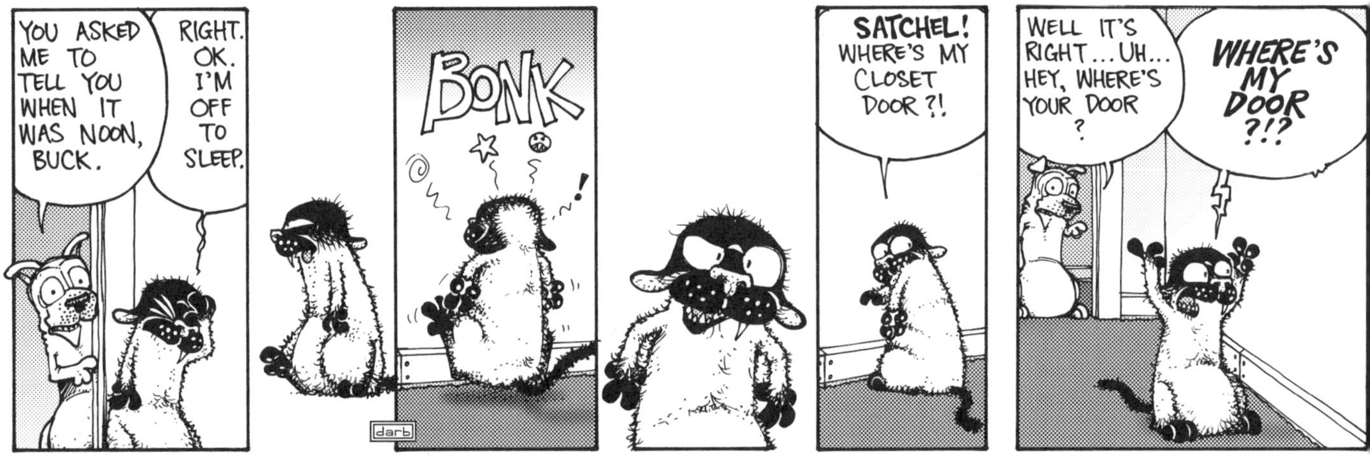
YOU ASKED ME TO TELL YOU WHEN IT WAS NOON, BUCK.
RIGHT. OK. I'M OFF TO SLEEP.
BONK
darb
SATCHEL! WHERE'S MY CLOSET DOOR?!
WELL IT'S RIGHT... UH... HEY, WHERE'S YOUR DOOR?
WHERE'S MY DOOR?!?

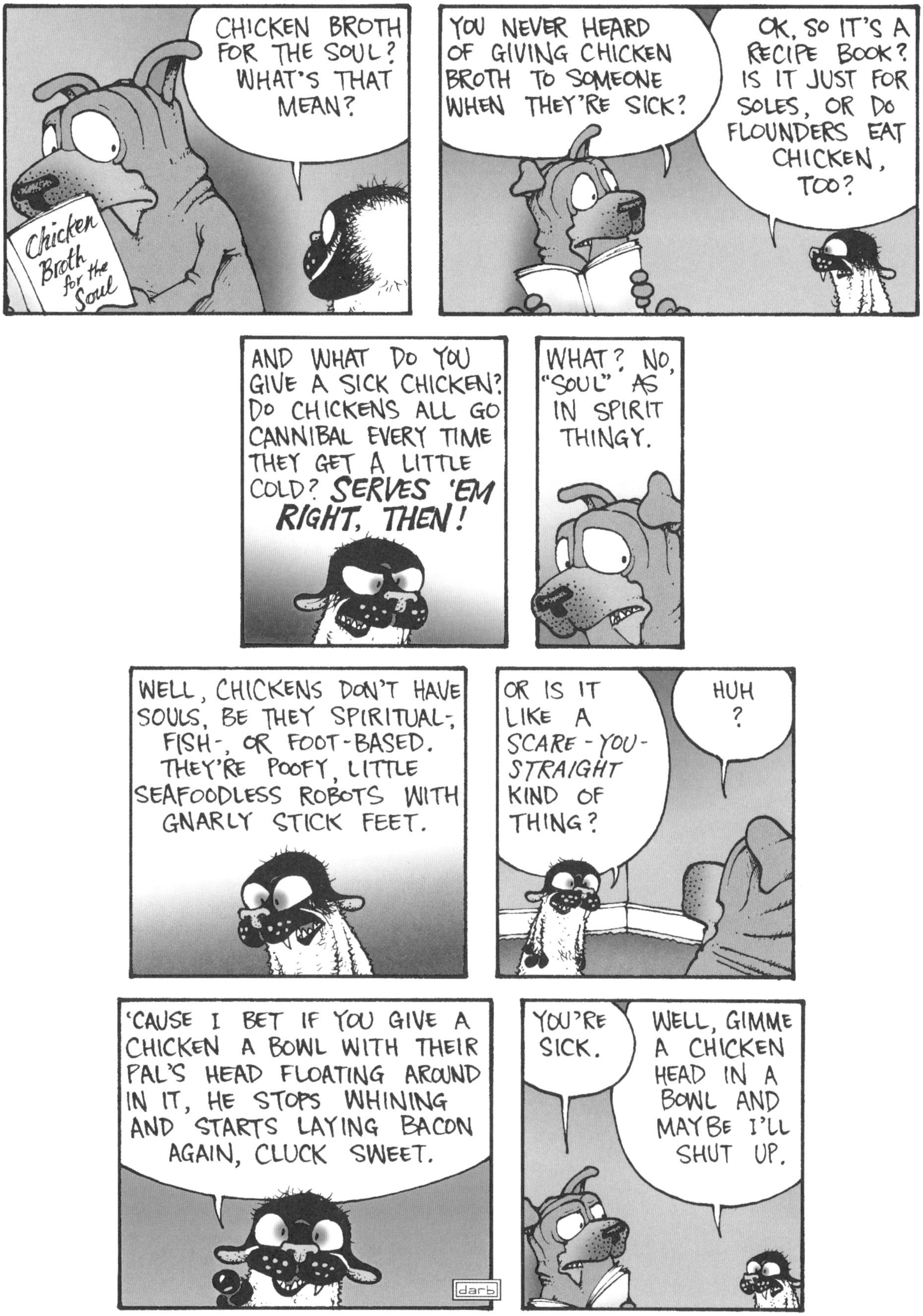
CHICKEN BROTH FOR THE SOUL? WHAT'S THAT MEAN?
Chicken Broth for the Soul
YOU NEVER HEARD OF GIVING CHICKEN BROTH TO SOMEONE WHEN THEY'RE SICK?
OK, SO IT'S A RECIPE BOOK? IS IT JUST FOR SOLES, OR DO FLOUNDERS EAT CHICKEN, TOO?
AND WHAT DO YOU GIVE A SICK CHICKEN? DO CHICKENS ALL GO CANNIBAL EVERY TIME THEY GET A LITTLE COLD? SERVES 'EM RIGHT, THEN!
WHAT? NO, "SOUL" AS IN SPIRIT THINGY.
WELL, CHICKENS DON'T HAVE SOULS, BE THEY SPIRITUAL-, FISH-, OR FOOT-BASED. THEY'RE POOFY, LITTLE SEAFOODLESS ROBOTS WITH GNARLY STICK FEET.
OR IS IT LIKE A SCARE-YOU-STRAIGHT KIND OF THING?
HUH?
'CAUSE I BET IF YOU GIVE A CHICKEN A BOWL WITH THEIR PAL'S HEAD FLOATING AROUND IN IT, HE STOPS WHINING AND STARTS LAYING BACON AGAIN, CLUCK SWEET.
darb
YOU'RE SICK.
WELL, GIMME A CHICKEN HEAD IN A BOWL AND MAYBE I'LL SHUT UP.

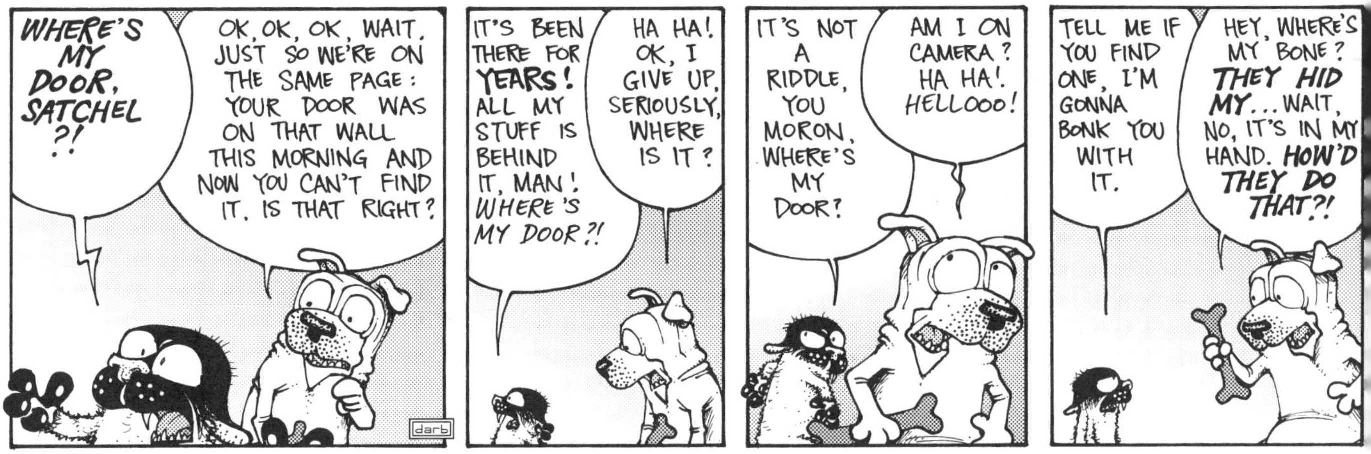
WHERE'S MY DOOR, SATCHEL ?!
OK, OK, OK, WAIT. JUST SO WE'RE ON THE SAME PAGE: YOUR DOOR WAS ON THAT WALL THIS MORNING AND NOW YOU CAN'T FIND IT. IS THAT RIGHT?
IT'S BEEN THERE FOR YEARS! ALL MY STUFF IS BEHIND IT, MAN! WHERE'S MY DOOR?!
HA HA! OK, I GIVE UP. SERIOUSLY, WHERE IS IT?
IT'S NOT A RIDDLE, YOU MORON. WHERE'S MY DOOR?
AM I ON CAMERA? HA HA! HELLOOO!
TELL ME IF YOU FIND ONE, I'M GONNA BONK YOU WITH IT.
HEY, WHERE'S MY BONE? THEY HID MY... WAIT, NO, IT'S IN MY HAND. HOW'D THEY DO THAT?!
darb

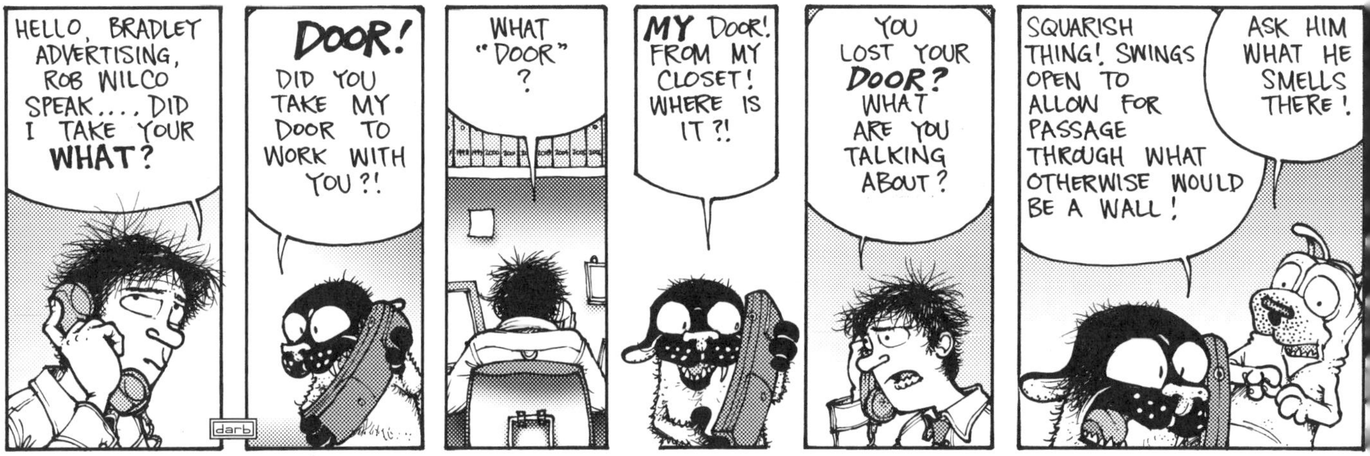
HELLO, BRADLEY ADVERTISING, ROB WILCO SPEAK.... DID I TAKE YOUR WHAT?
DOOR! DID YOU TAKE MY DOOR TO WORK WITH YOU?!
WHAT "DOOR" ?
MY DOOR! FROM MY CLOSET! WHERE IS IT?!
YOU LOST YOUR DOOR? WHAT ARE YOU TALKING ABOUT?
SQUARISH THING! SWINGS OPEN TO ALLOW FOR PASSAGE THROUGH WHAT OTHERWISE WOULD BE A WALL!
ASK HIM WHAT HE SMELLS THERE!
darb

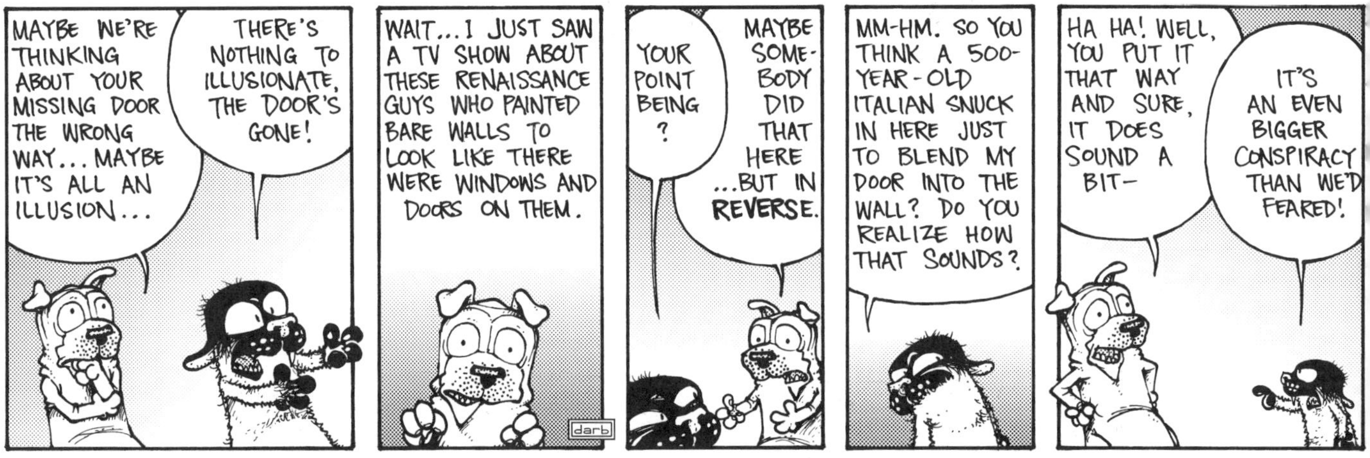
MAYBE WE'RE THINKING ABOUT YOUR MISSING DOOR THE WRONG WAY... MAYBE IT'S ALL AN ILLUSION...
THERE'S NOTHING TO ILLUSIONATE, THE DOOR'S GONE!
WAIT... I JUST SAW A TV SHOW ABOUT THESE RENAISSANCE GUYS WHO PAINTED BARE WALLS TO LOOK LIKE THERE WERE WINDOWS AND DOORS ON THEM.
YOUR POINT BEING ?
MAYBE SOME-BODY DID THAT HERE ...BUT IN REVERSE.
MM-HM. SO YOU THINK A 500-YEAR-OLD ITALIAN SNUCK IN HERE JUST TO BLEND MY DOOR INTO THE WALL? DO YOU REALIZE HOW THAT SOUNDS?
HA HA! WELL, YOU PUT IT THAT WAY AND SURE, IT DOES SOUND A BIT—
IT'S AN EVEN BIGGER CONSPIRACY THAN WE'D FEARED!
darb

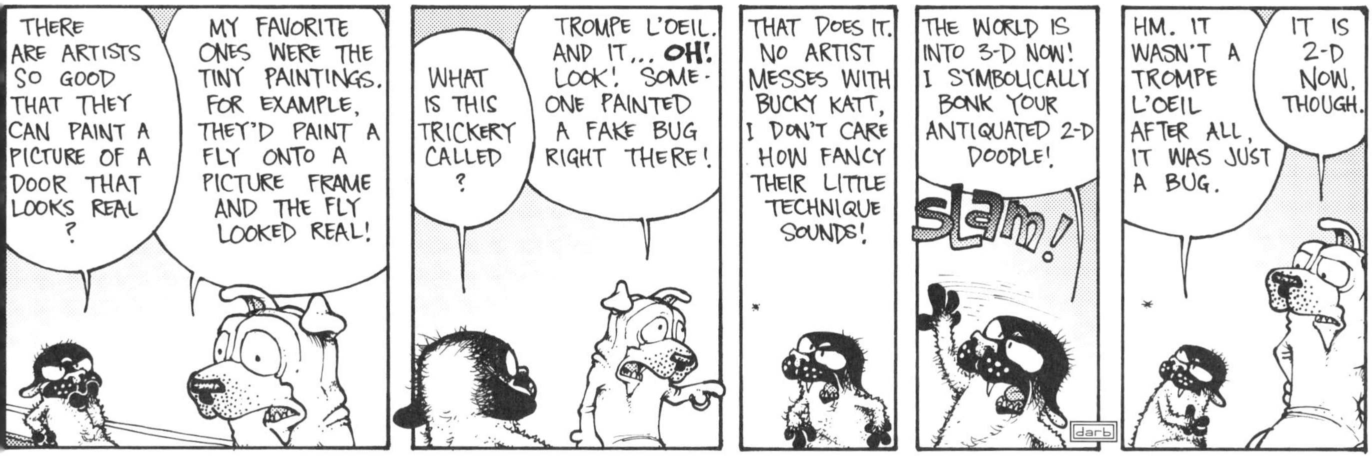
THERE ARE ARTISTS SO GOOD THAT THEY CAN PAINT A PICTURE OF A DOOR THAT LOOKS REAL?
MY FAVORITE ONES WERE THE TINY PAINTINGS. FOR EXAMPLE, THEY'D PAINT A FLY ONTO A PICTURE FRAME AND THE FLY LOOKED REAL!
WHAT IS THIS TRICKERY CALLED?
TROMPE L'OEIL. AND IT,.. OH! LOOK! SOMEONE PAINTED A FAKE BUG RIGHT THERE!
THAT DOES IT. NO ARTIST MESSES WITH BUCKY KATT, I DON'T CARE HOW FANCY THEIR LITTLE TECHNIQUE SOUNDS!
THE WORLD IS INTO 3-D NOW! I SYMBOLICALLY BONK YOUR ANTIQUATED 2-D DOODLE!
SLAM!
HM. IT WASN'T A TROMPE L'OEIL AFTER ALL, IT WAS JUST A BUG.
IT IS 2-D NOW, THOUGH.
darb

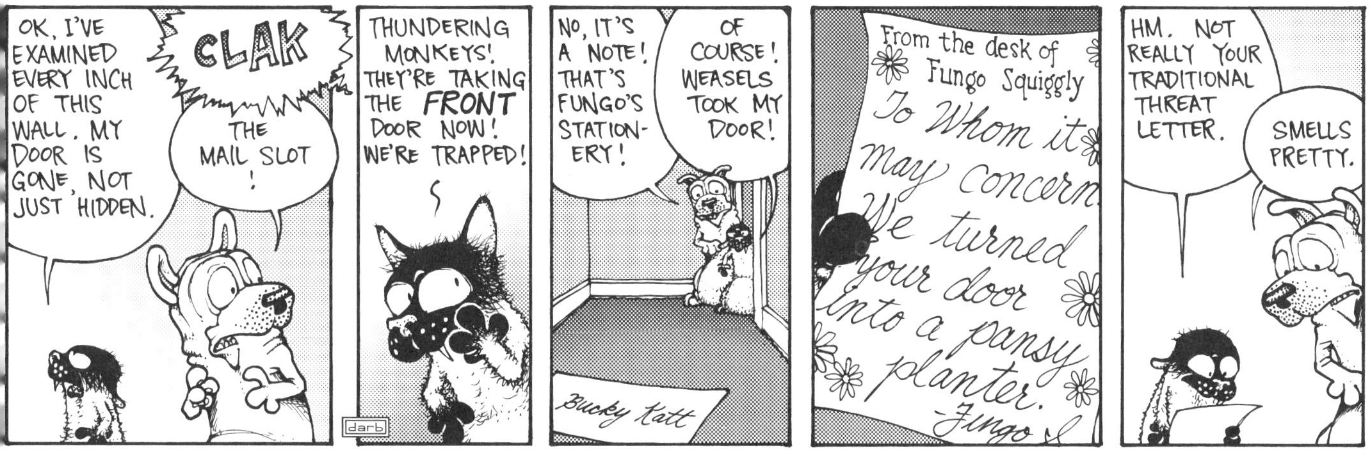
OK, I'VE EXAMINED EVERY INCH OF THIS WALL. MY DOOR IS GONE, NOT JUST HIDDEN.
CLAK
THE MAIL SLOT!
darb
THUNDERING MONKEYS! THEY'RE TAKING THE FRONT DOOR NOW! WE'RE TRAPPED!
NO, IT'S A NOTE! THAT'S FUNGO'S STATIONERY!
OF COURSE! WEASELS TOOK MY DOOR!
Bucky Katt
From the desk of Fungo Squiggly
To Whom it may concern. We turned your door into a pansy planter. -Fungo
HM. NOT REALLY YOUR TRADITIONAL THREAT LETTER.
SMELLS PRETTY.

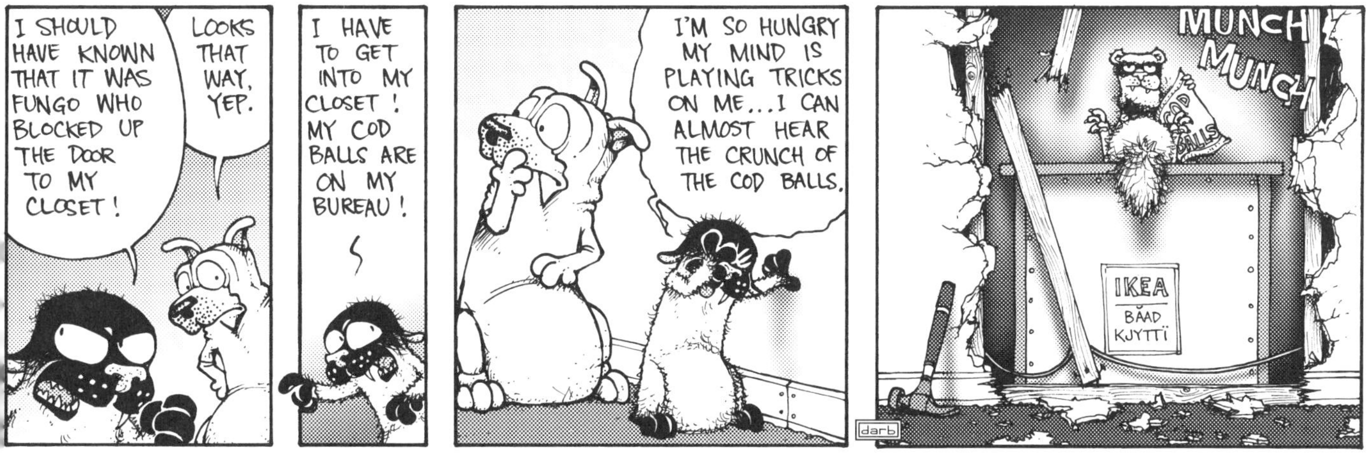
I SHOULD HAVE KNOWN THAT IT WAS FUNGO WHO BLOCKED UP THE DOOR TO MY CLOSET!
LOOKS THAT WAY, YEP.
I HAVE TO GET INTO MY CLOSET! MY COD BALLS ARE ON MY BUREAU!
I'M SO HUNGRY MY MIND IS PLAYING TRICKS ON ME...I CAN ALMOST HEAR THE CRUNCH OF THE COD BALLS.
darb
MUNCH
MUNCH
COD BALLS
IKEA
BÅAD KJYTTÏ

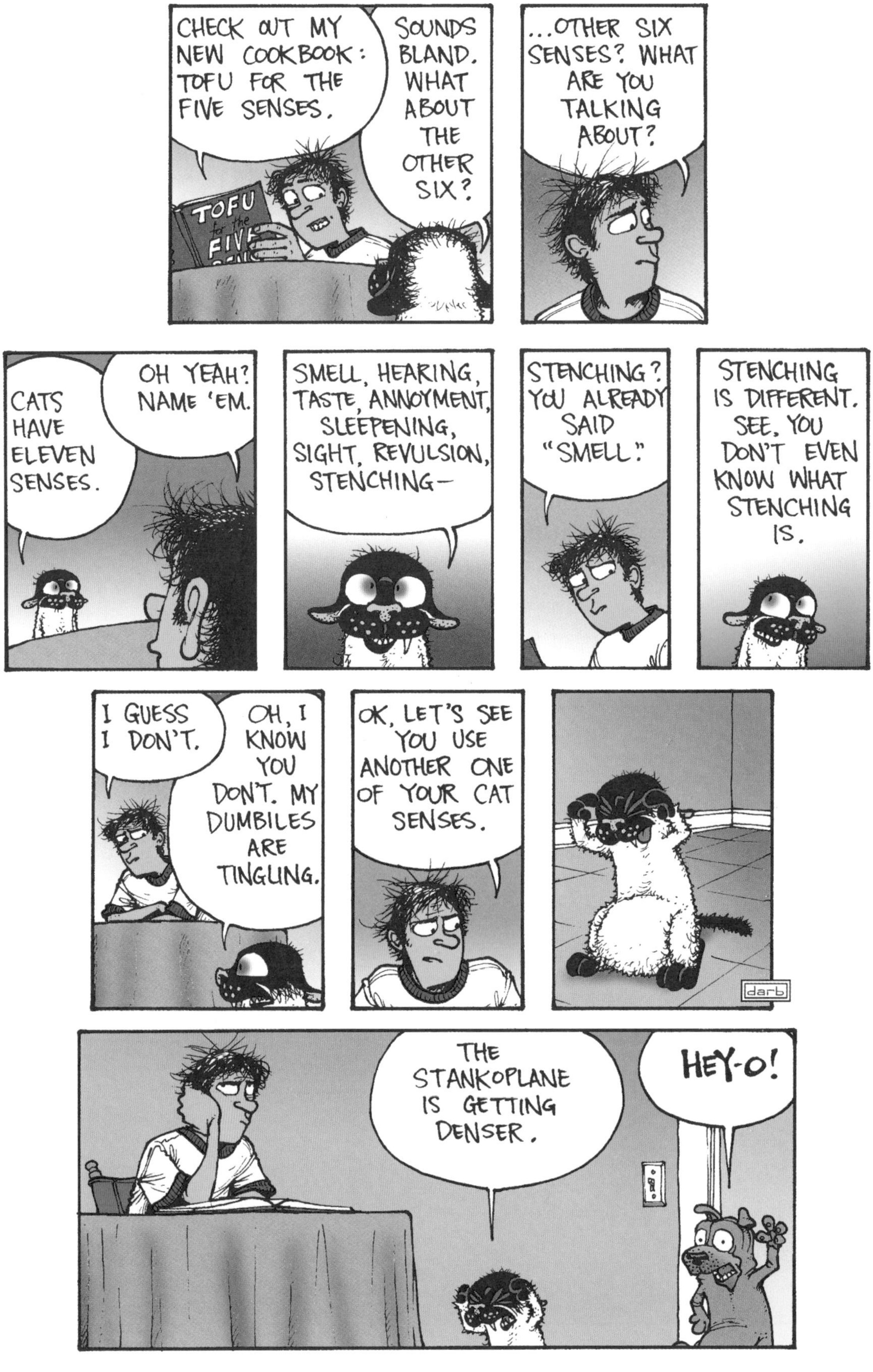
CHECK OUT MY NEW COOKBOOK: TOFU FOR THE FIVE SENSES.
TOFU for the FIVE
SOUNDS BLAND. WHAT ABOUT THE OTHER SIX?
...OTHER SIX SENSES? WHAT ARE YOU TALKING ABOUT?
CATS HAVE ELEVEN SENSES.
OH YEAH? NAME 'EM.
SMELL, HEARING, TASTE, ANNOYMENT, SLEEPENING, SIGHT, REVULSION, STENCHING–
STENCHING? YOU ALREADY SAID "SMELL."
STENCHING IS DIFFERENT. SEE, YOU DON'T EVEN KNOW WHAT STENCHING IS.
I GUESS I DON'T.
OH, I KNOW YOU DON'T. MY DUMBILES ARE TINGLING.
OK, LET'S SEE YOU USE ANOTHER ONE OF YOUR CAT SENSES.
darb
THE STANKOPLANE IS GETTING DENSER.
HEY-O!

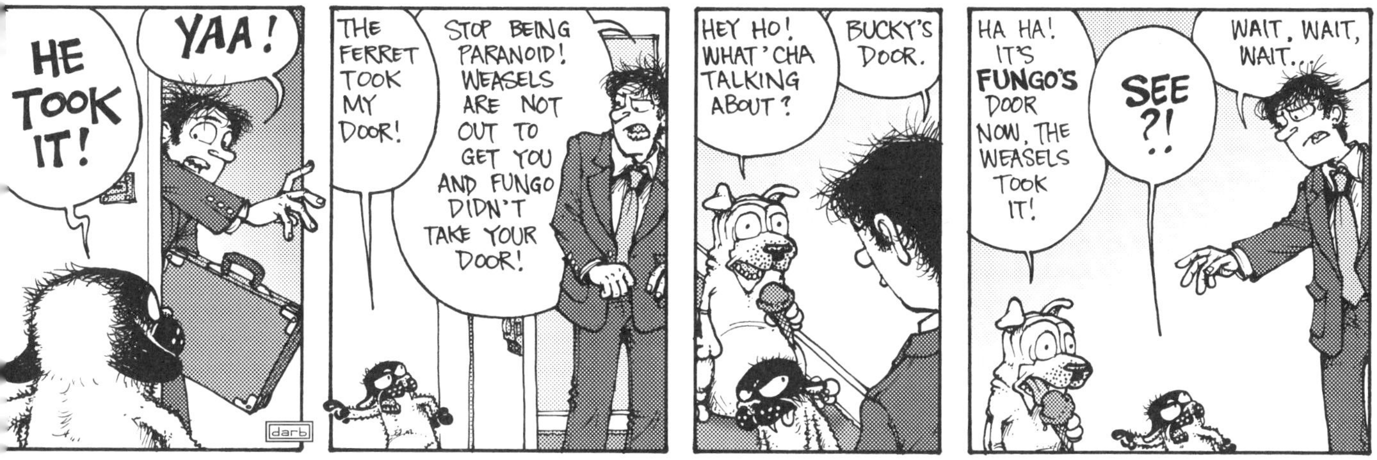
HE TOOK IT!
YAA!
darb
THE FERRET TOOK MY DOOR!
STOP BEING PARANOID! WEASELS ARE NOT OUT TO GET YOU AND FUNGO DIDN'T TAKE YOUR DOOR!
HEY HO! WHAT'CHA TALKING ABOUT?
BUCKY'S DOOR.
HA HA! IT'S FUNGO'S DOOR NOW, THE WEASELS TOOK IT!
SEE ?!
WAIT, WAIT, WAIT...

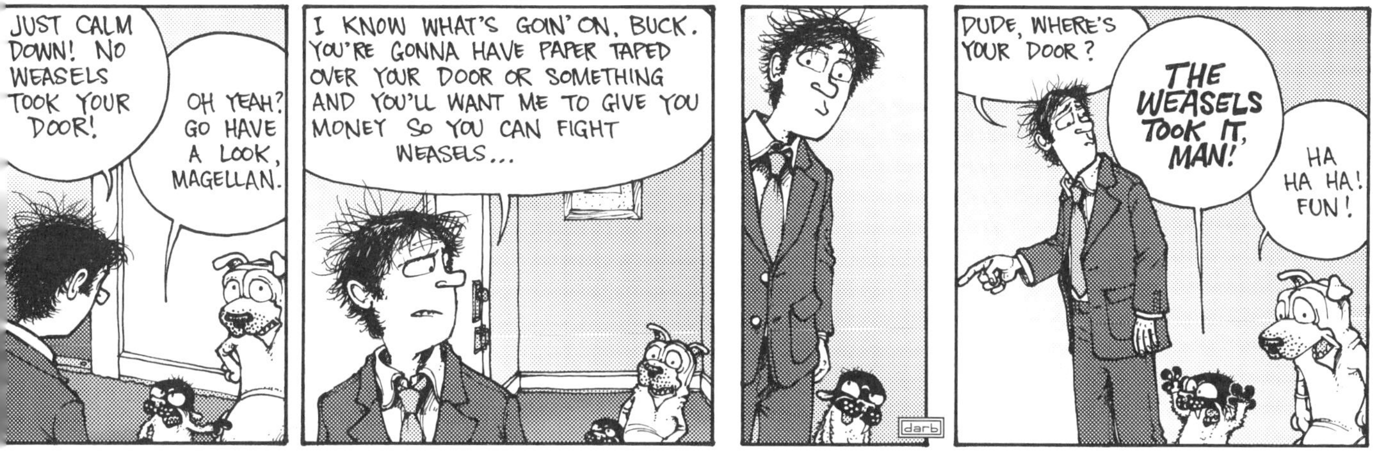
JUST CALM DOWN! NO WEASELS TOOK YOUR DOOR!
OH YEAH? GO HAVE A LOOK, MAGELLAN.
I KNOW WHAT'S GOIN' ON, BUCK. YOU'RE GONNA HAVE PAPER TAPED OVER YOUR DOOR OR SOMETHING AND YOU'LL WANT ME TO GIVE YOU MONEY SO YOU CAN FIGHT WEASELS...
darb
DUDE, WHERE'S YOUR DOOR?
THE WEASELS TOOK IT, MAN!
HA HA HA! FUN!

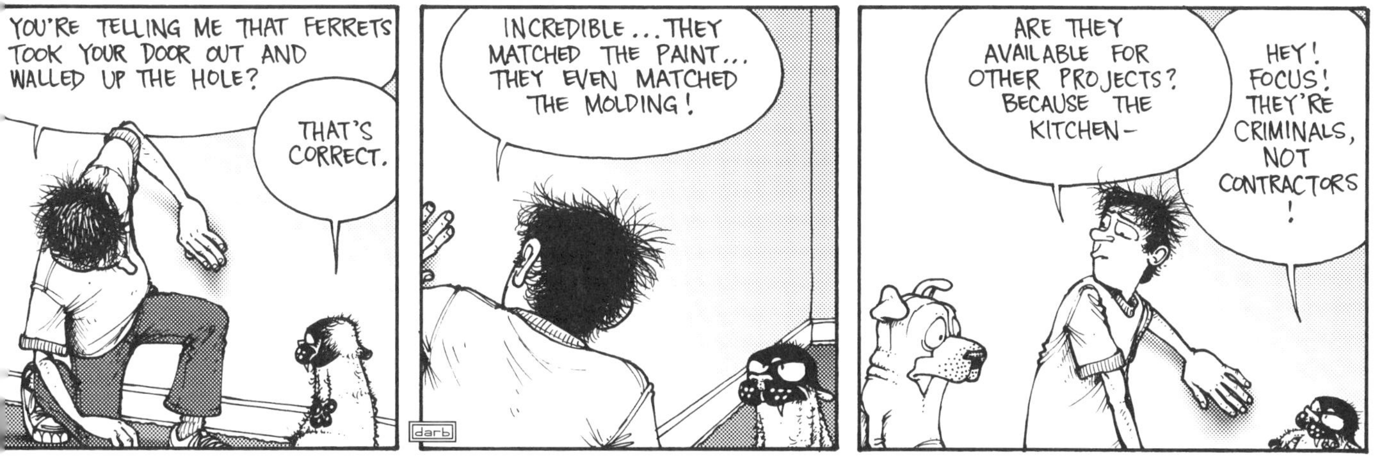
YOU'RE TELLING ME THAT FERRETS TOOK YOUR DOOR OUT AND WALLED UP THE HOLE?
THAT'S CORRECT.
darb
INCREDIBLE... THEY MATCHED THE PAINT... THEY EVEN MATCHED THE MOLDING!
ARE THEY AVAILABLE FOR OTHER PROJECTS? BECAUSE THE KITCHEN–
HEY! FOCUS! THEY'RE CRIMINALS, NOT CONTRACTORS!

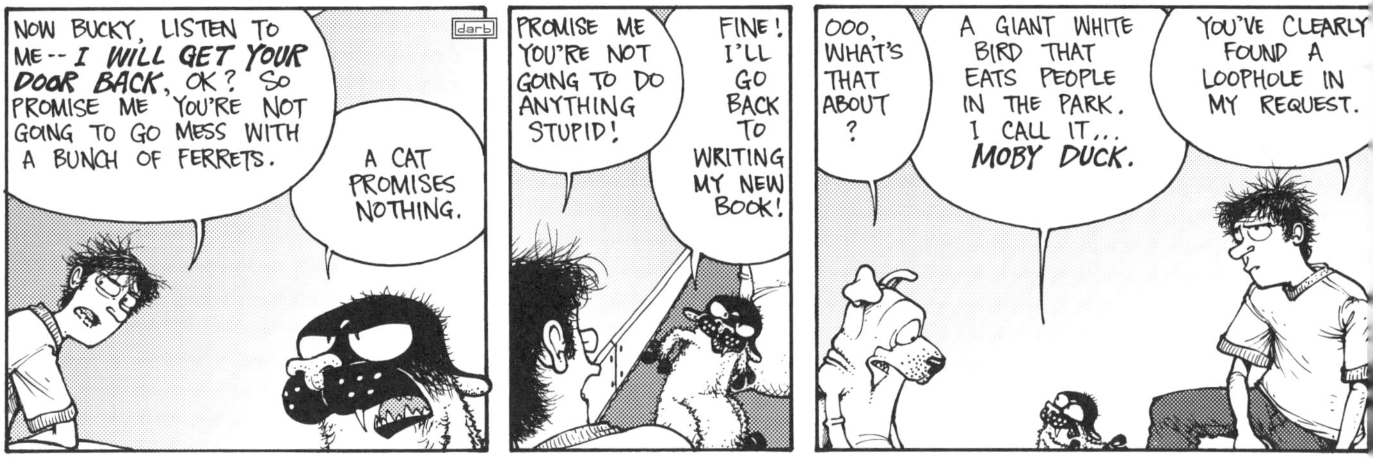
NOW BUCKY, LISTEN TO ME-- I WILL GET YOUR DOOR BACK, OK? SO PROMISE ME YOU'RE NOT GOING TO GO MESS WITH A BUNCH OF FERRETS.
A CAT PROMISES NOTHING.
PROMISE ME YOU'RE NOT GOING TO DO ANYTHING STUPID!
FINE! I'LL GO BACK TO WRITING MY NEW BOOK!
OOO, WHAT'S THAT ABOUT?
A GIANT WHITE BIRD THAT EATS PEOPLE IN THE PARK. I CALL IT... MOBY DUCK.
YOU'VE CLEARLY FOUND A LOOPHOLE IN MY REQUEST.

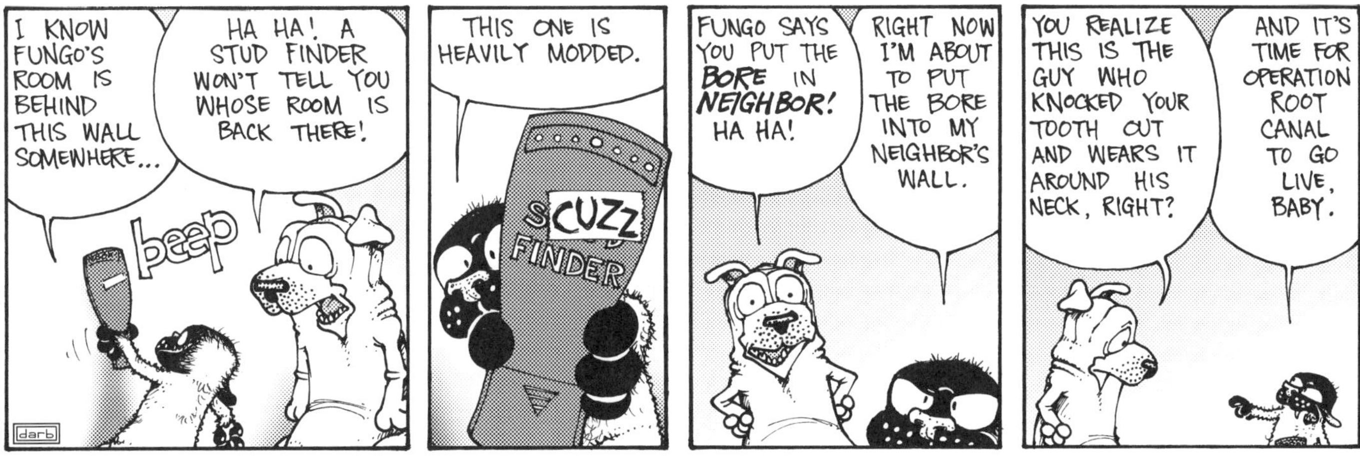
I KNOW FUNGO'S ROOM IS BEHIND THIS WALL SOMEWHERE...
beep
HA HA! A STUD FINDER WON'T TELL YOU WHOSE ROOM IS BACK THERE!
THIS ONE IS HEAVILY MODDED.
SCUZZ FINDER
FUNGO SAYS YOU PUT THE BORE IN NEIGHBOR! HA HA!
RIGHT NOW I'M ABOUT TO PUT THE BORE INTO MY NEIGHBOR'S WALL.
YOU REALIZE THIS IS THE GUY WHO KNOCKED YOUR TOOTH OUT AND WEARS IT AROUND HIS NECK, RIGHT?
AND IT'S TIME FOR OPERATION ROOT CANAL TO GO LIVE, BABY.

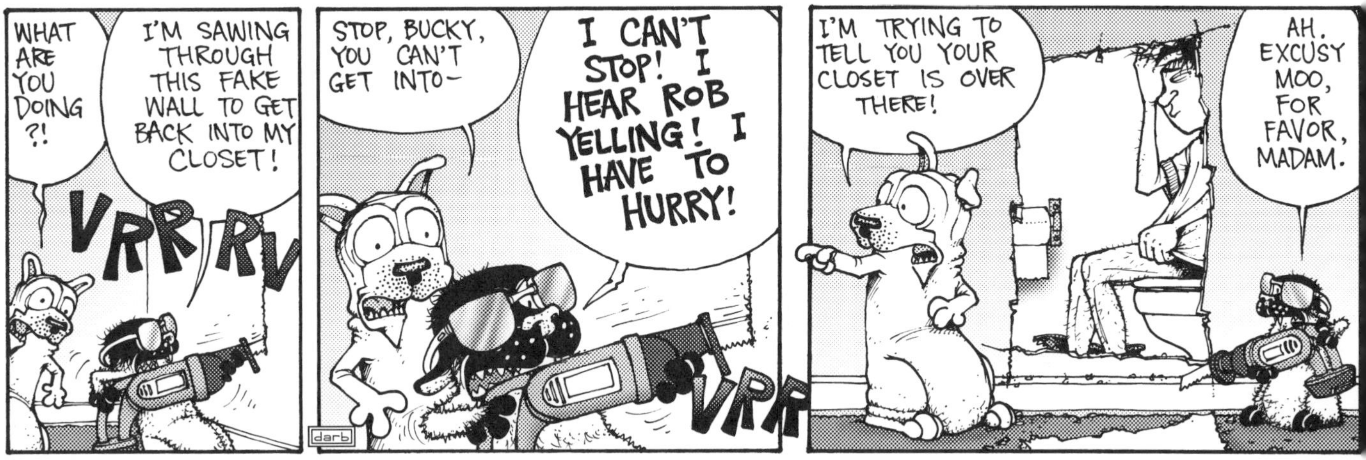
WHAT ARE YOU DOING?!
I'M SAWING THROUGH THIS FAKE WALL TO GET BACK INTO MY CLOSET!
VRRRRV
STOP, BUCKY, YOU CAN'T GET INTO-
I CAN'T STOP! I HEAR ROB YELLING! I HAVE TO HURRY!
VRR
I'M TRYING TO TELL YOU YOUR CLOSET IS OVER THERE!
AH. EXCUSY MOO, FOR FAVOR, MADAM.

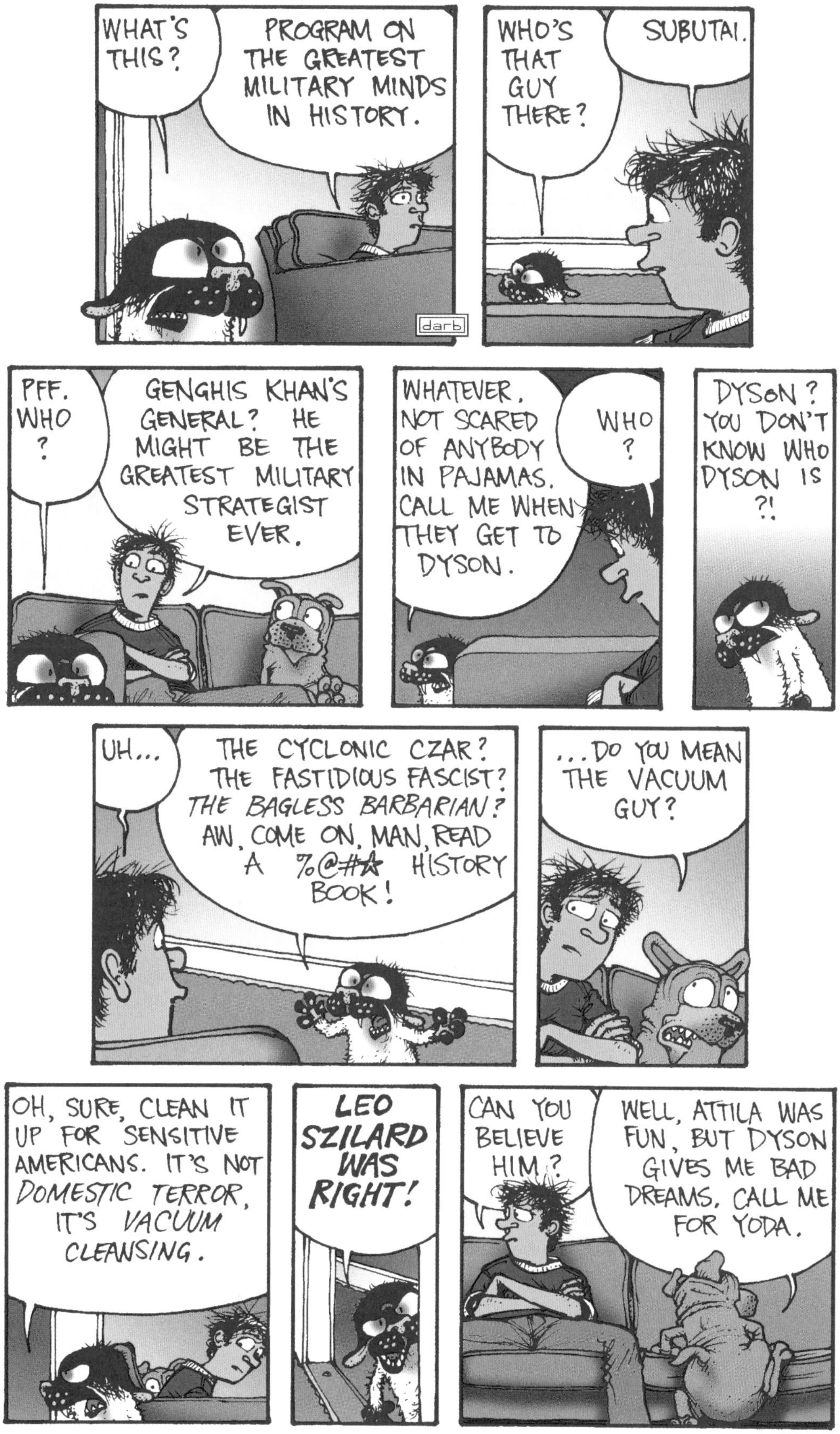
WHAT'S THIS?
PROGRAM ON THE GREATEST MILITARY MINDS IN HISTORY.
darb
WHO'S THAT GUY THERE?
SUBUTAI.
PFF. WHO?
GENGHIS KHAN'S GENERAL? HE MIGHT BE THE GREATEST MILITARY STRATEGIST EVER.
WHATEVER. NOT SCARED OF ANYBODY IN PAJAMAS. CALL ME WHEN THEY GET TO DYSON.
WHO?
DYSON? YOU DON'T KNOW WHO DYSON IS?!
UH...
THE CYCLONIC CZAR? THE FASTIDIOUS FASCIST? *THE BAGLESS BARBARIAN?* AW, COME ON, MAN, READ A %@#☆ HISTORY BOOK!
...DO YOU MEAN THE VACUUM GUY?
OH, SURE, CLEAN IT UP FOR SENSITIVE AMERICANS. IT'S NOT *DOMESTIC TERROR*, IT'S *VACUUM CLEANSING*.
LEO SZILARD WAS RIGHT!
CAN YOU BELIEVE HIM?
WELL, ATTILA WAS FUN, BUT DYSON GIVES ME BAD DREAMS. CALL ME FOR YODA.

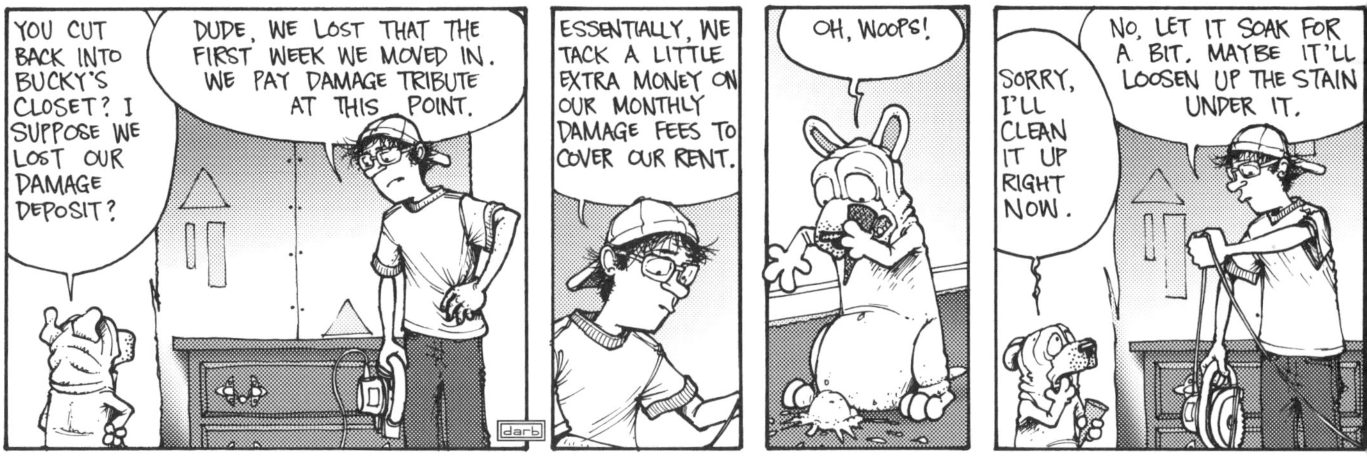
YOU CUT BACK INTO BUCKY'S CLOSET? I SUPPOSE WE LOST OUR DAMAGE DEPOSIT?
DUDE, WE LOST THAT THE FIRST WEEK WE MOVED IN. WE PAY DAMAGE TRIBUTE AT THIS POINT.
darb
ESSENTIALLY, WE TACK A LITTLE EXTRA MONEY ON OUR MONTHLY DAMAGE FEES TO COVER OUR RENT.
OH, WOOPS!
SORRY, I'LL CLEAN IT UP RIGHT NOW.
NO, LET IT SOAK FOR A BIT. MAYBE IT'LL LOOSEN UP THE STAIN UNDER IT.

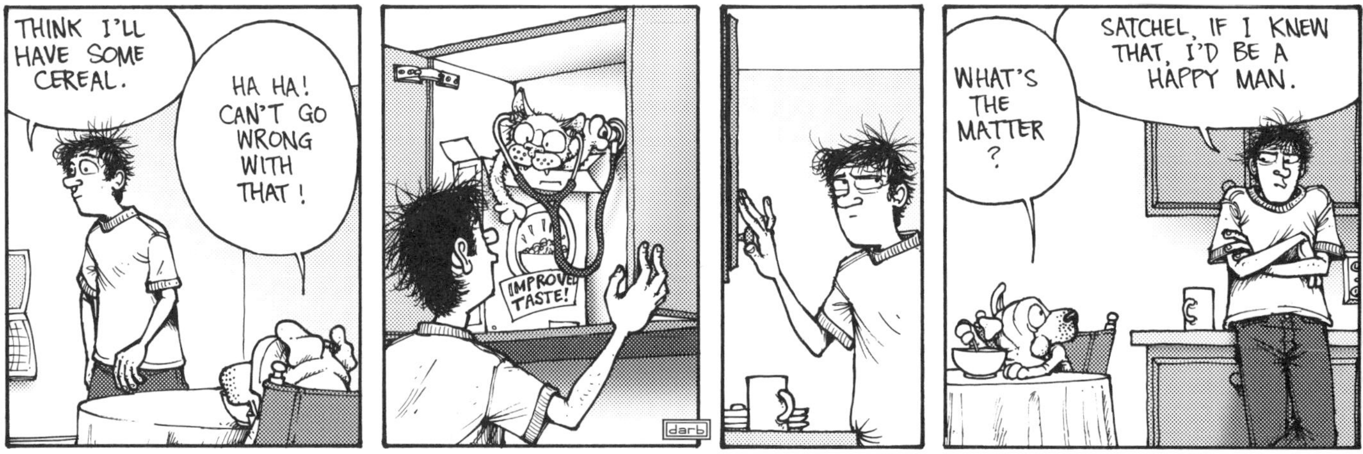
THINK I'LL HAVE SOME CEREAL.
HA HA! CAN'T GO WRONG WITH THAT!
IMPROVE TASTE!
darb
WHAT'S THE MATTER?
SATCHEL, IF I KNEW THAT, I'D BE A HAPPY MAN.

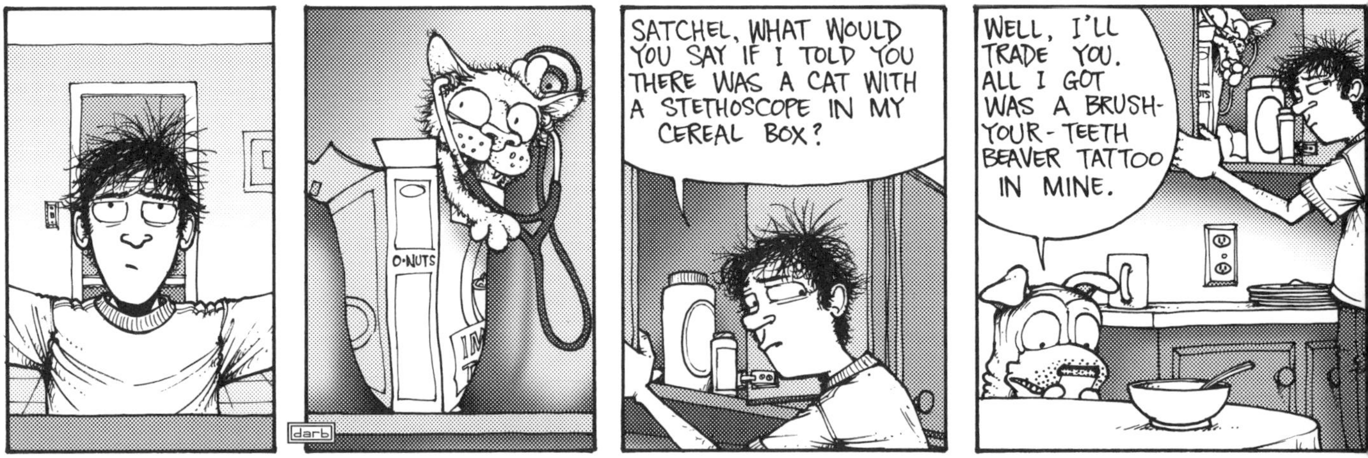
O-NUTS
darb
SATCHEL, WHAT WOULD YOU SAY IF I TOLD YOU THERE WAS A CAT WITH A STETHOSCOPE IN MY CEREAL BOX?
WELL, I'LL TRADE YOU. ALL I GOT WAS A BRUSH-YOUR-TEETH BEAVER TATTOO IN MINE.

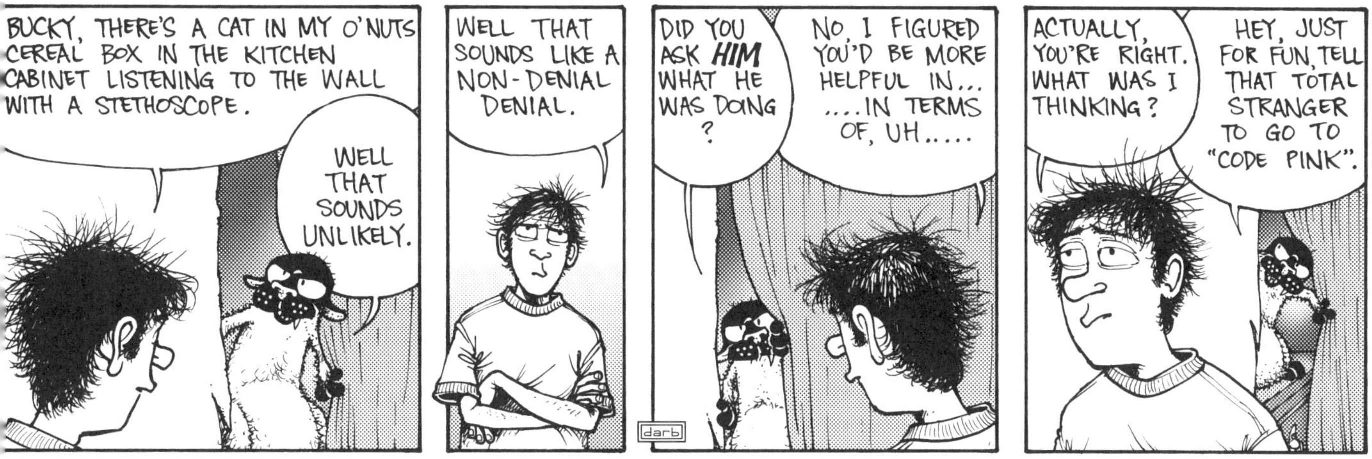
BUCKY, THERE'S A CAT IN MY O'NUTS CEREAL BOX IN THE KITCHEN CABINET LISTENING TO THE WALL WITH A STETHOSCOPE.
WELL THAT SOUNDS UNLIKELY.
WELL THAT SOUNDS LIKE A NON-DENIAL DENIAL.
DID YOU ASK **HIM** WHAT HE WAS DOING ?
NO, I FIGURED YOU'D BE MORE HELPFUL IN... ....IN TERMS OF, UH.....
ACTUALLY, YOU'RE RIGHT. WHAT WAS I THINKING ?
HEY, JUST FOR FUN, TELL THAT TOTAL STRANGER TO GO TO "CODE PINK".
darb

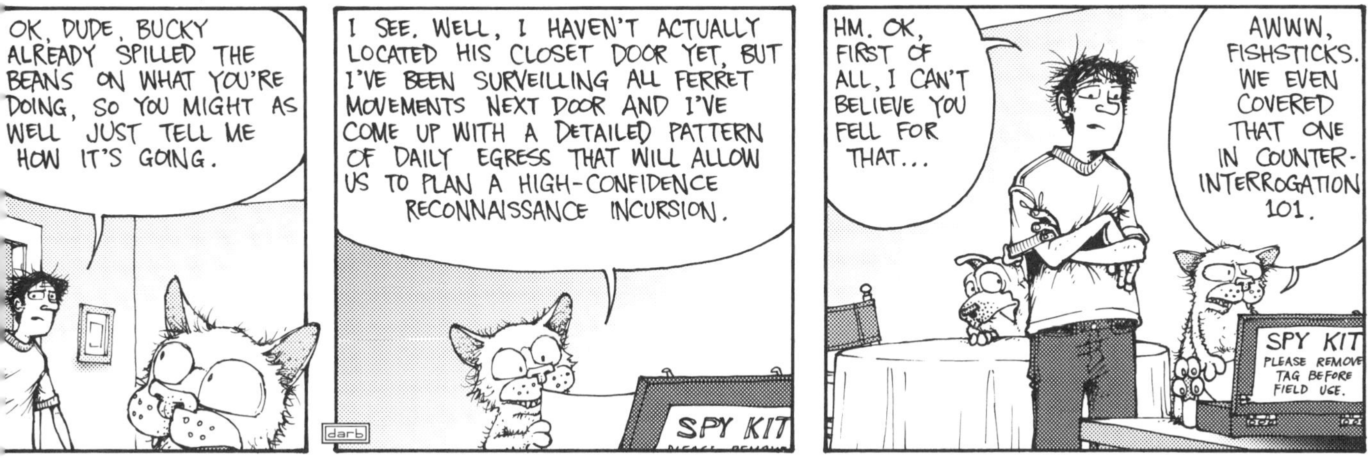
OK, DUDE, BUCKY ALREADY SPILLED THE BEANS ON WHAT YOU'RE DOING, SO YOU MIGHT AS WELL JUST TELL ME HOW IT'S GOING.
I SEE. WELL, I HAVEN'T ACTUALLY LOCATED HIS CLOSET DOOR YET, BUT I'VE BEEN SURVEILLING ALL FERRET MOVEMENTS NEXT DOOR AND I'VE COME UP WITH A DETAILED PATTERN OF DAILY EGRESS THAT WILL ALLOW US TO PLAN A HIGH-CONFIDENCE RECONNAISSANCE INCURSION.
SPY KIT
HM. OK, FIRST OF ALL, I CAN'T BELIEVE YOU FELL FOR THAT...
AWWW, FISHSTICKS. WE EVEN COVERED THAT ONE IN COUNTER-INTERROGATION 101.
SPY KIT
PLEASE REMOVE TAG BEFORE FIELD USE.
darb

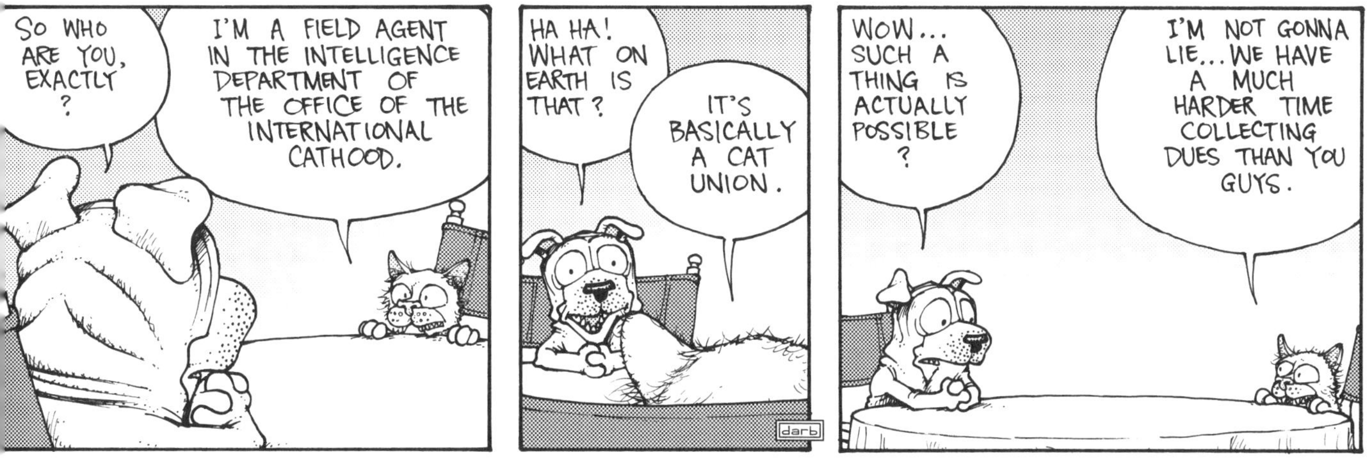
SO WHO ARE YOU, EXACTLY ?
I'M A FIELD AGENT IN THE INTELLIGENCE DEPARTMENT OF THE OFFICE OF THE INTERNATIONAL CATHOOD.
HA HA! WHAT ON EARTH IS THAT ?
IT'S BASICALLY A CAT UNION.
WOW... SUCH A THING IS ACTUALLY POSSIBLE ?
I'M NOT GONNA LIE... WE HAVE A MUCH HARDER TIME COLLECTING DUES THAN YOU GUYS.
darb

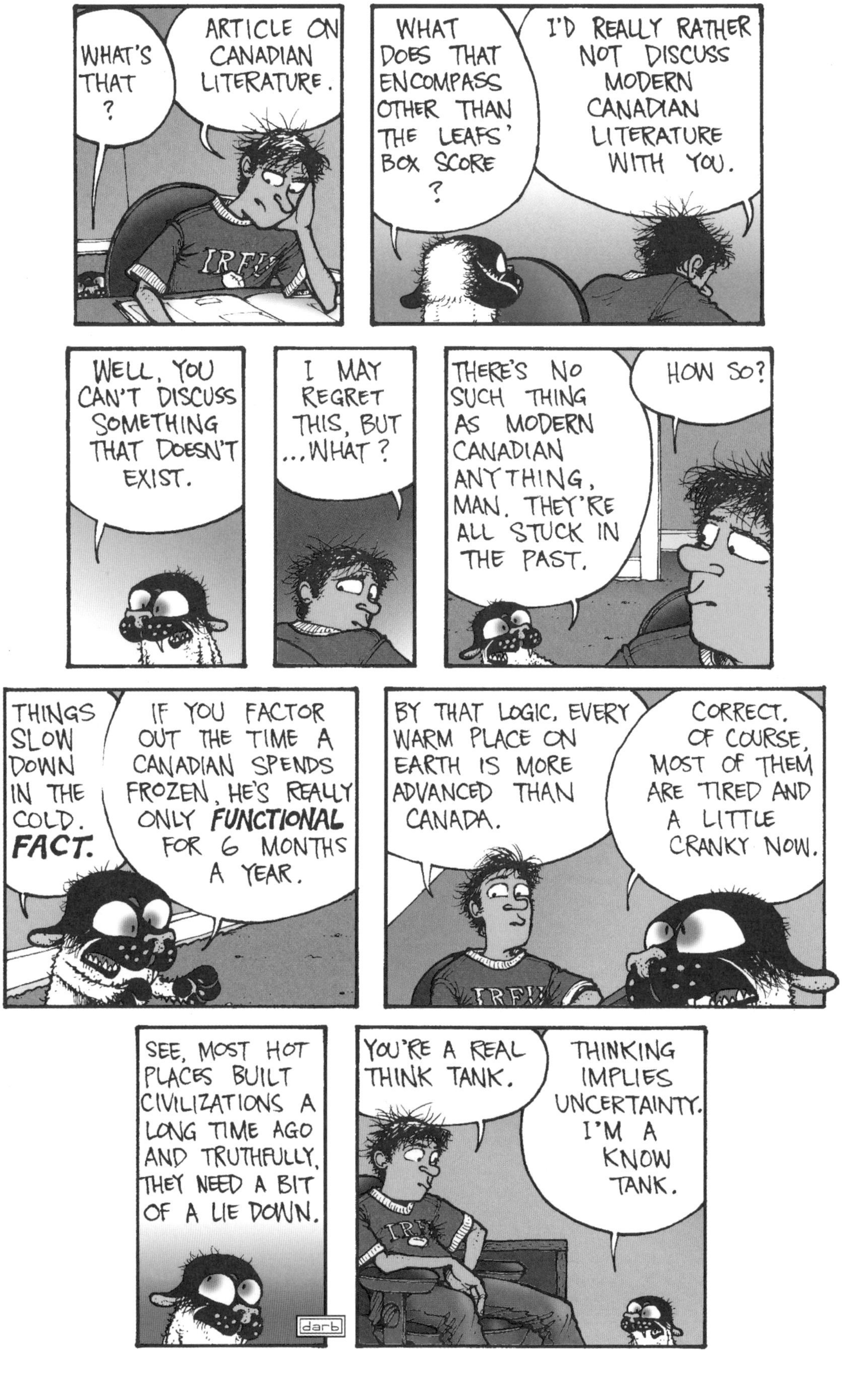
WHAT'S THAT ?
ARTICLE ON CANADIAN LITERATURE.
WHAT DOES THAT ENCOMPASS OTHER THAN THE LEAFS' BOX SCORE ?
I'D REALLY RATHER NOT DISCUSS MODERN CANADIAN LITERATURE WITH YOU.
WELL, YOU CAN'T DISCUSS SOMETHING THAT DOESN'T EXIST.
I MAY REGRET THIS, BUT ...WHAT ?
THERE'S NO SUCH THING AS MODERN CANADIAN ANYTHING, MAN. THEY'RE ALL STUCK IN THE PAST.
HOW SO?
THINGS SLOW DOWN IN THE COLD. FACT.
IF YOU FACTOR OUT THE TIME A CANADIAN SPENDS FROZEN, HE'S REALLY ONLY FUNCTIONAL FOR 6 MONTHS A YEAR.
BY THAT LOGIC, EVERY WARM PLACE ON EARTH IS MORE ADVANCED THAN CANADA.
CORRECT. OF COURSE, MOST OF THEM ARE TIRED AND A LITTLE CRANKY NOW.
SEE, MOST HOT PLACES BUILT CIVILIZATIONS A LONG TIME AGO AND TRUTHFULLY, THEY NEED A BIT OF A LIE DOWN.
darb
YOU'RE A REAL THINK TANK.
THINKING IMPLIES UNCERTAINTY. I'M A KNOW TANK.

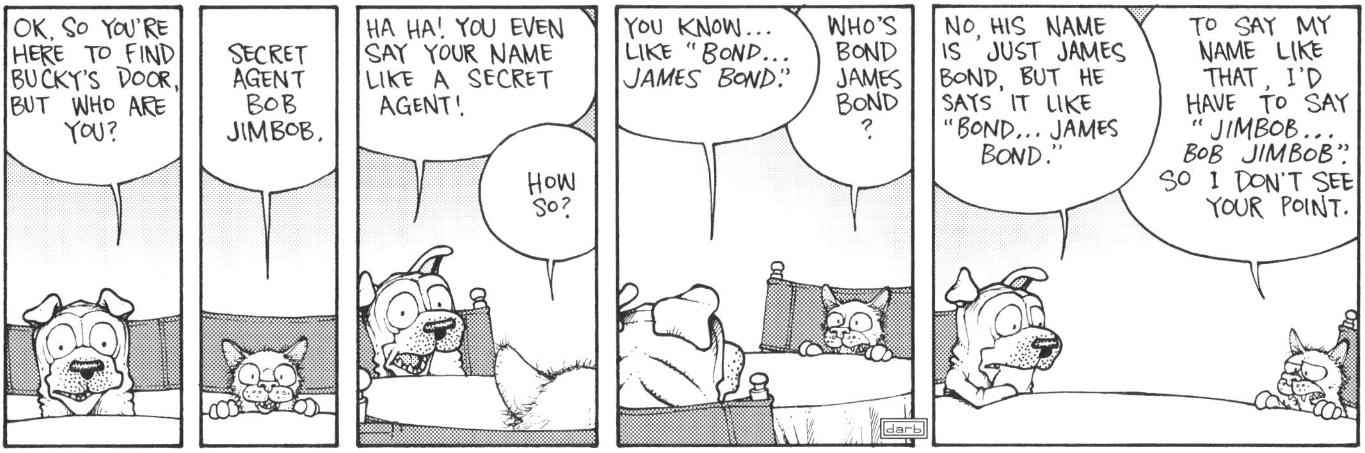
OK, SO YOU'RE HERE TO FIND BUCKY'S DOOR, BUT WHO ARE YOU?
SECRET AGENT BOB JIMBOB.
HA HA! YOU EVEN SAY YOUR NAME LIKE A SECRET AGENT!
HOW SO?
YOU KNOW... LIKE "BOND... JAMES BOND."
WHO'S BOND JAMES BOND ?
NO, HIS NAME IS JUST JAMES BOND, BUT HE SAYS IT LIKE "BOND... JAMES BOND."
TO SAY MY NAME LIKE THAT, I'D HAVE TO SAY "JIMBOB... BOB JIMBOB". SO I DON'T SEE YOUR POINT.

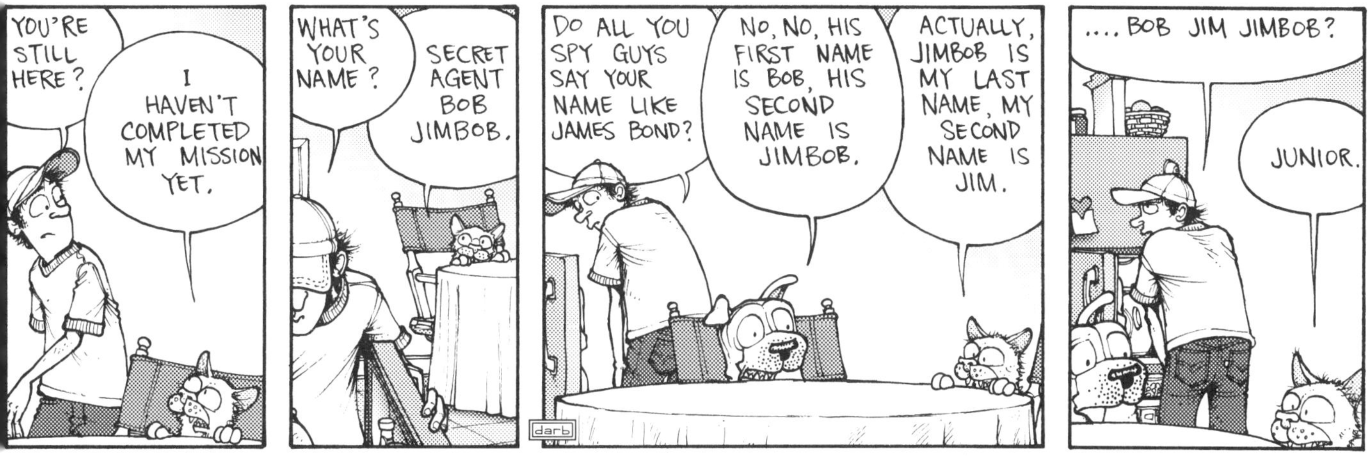
YOU'RE STILL HERE?
I HAVEN'T COMPLETED MY MISSION YET.
WHAT'S YOUR NAME?
SECRET AGENT BOB JIMBOB.
DO ALL YOU SPY GUYS SAY YOUR NAME LIKE JAMES BOND?
NO, NO, HIS FIRST NAME IS BOB, HIS SECOND NAME IS JIMBOB.
ACTUALLY, JIMBOB IS MY LAST NAME, MY SECOND NAME IS JIM.
.... BOB JIM JIMBOB?
JUNIOR.

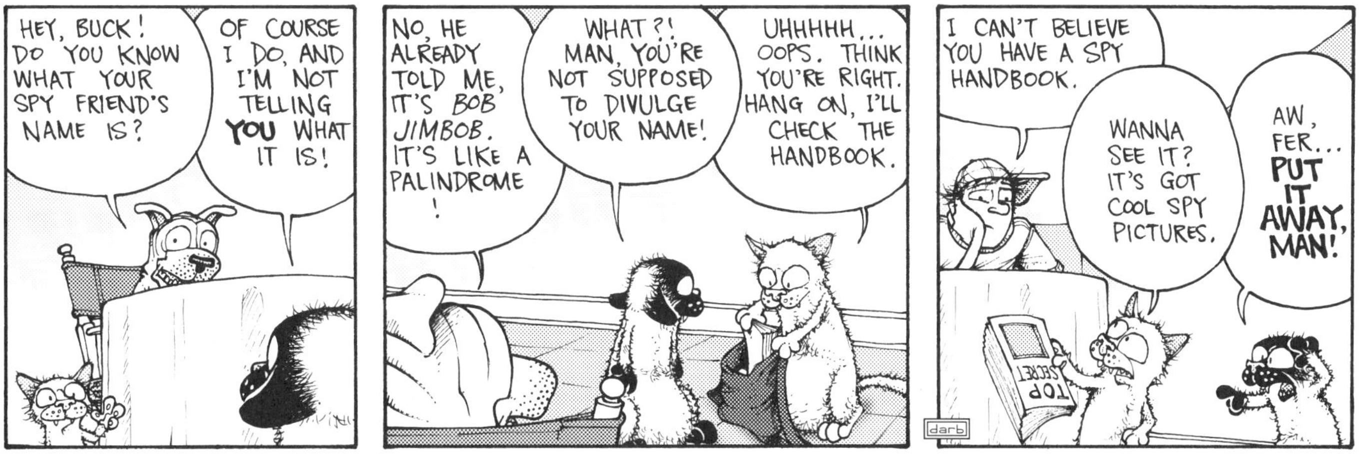
HEY, BUCK! DO YOU KNOW WHAT YOUR SPY FRIEND'S NAME IS?
OF COURSE I DO, AND I'M NOT TELLING **YOU** WHAT IT IS!
NO, HE ALREADY TOLD ME, IT'S *BOB JIMBOB*. IT'S LIKE A PALINDROME!
WHAT?! MAN, YOU'RE NOT SUPPOSED TO DIVULGE YOUR NAME!
UHHHHH... OOPS. THINK YOU'RE RIGHT. HANG ON, I'LL CHECK THE HANDBOOK.
I CAN'T BELIEVE YOU HAVE A SPY HANDBOOK.
WANNA SEE IT? IT'S GOT COOL SPY PICTURES.
AW, FER... **PUT IT AWAY, MAN!**
TOP SECRET

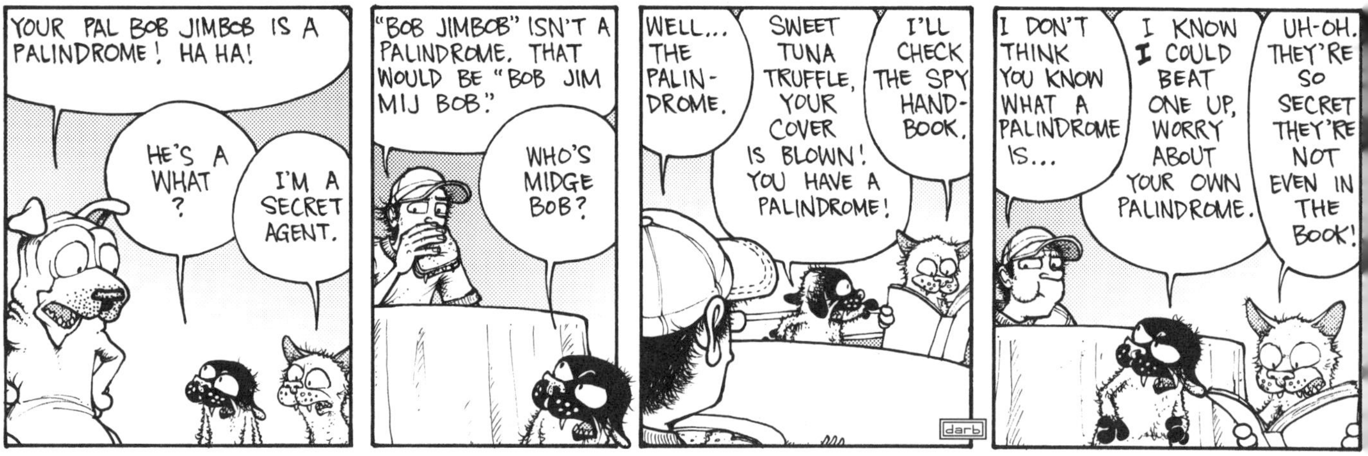
YOUR PAL BOB JIMBOB IS A PALINDROME! HA HA!
HE'S A WHAT?
I'M A SECRET AGENT.
"BOB JIMBOB" ISN'T A PALINDROME. THAT WOULD BE "BOB JIM MIJ BOB."
WHO'S MIDGE BOB?
WELL... THE PALIN-DROME.
SWEET TUNA TRUFFLE, YOUR COVER IS BLOWN! YOU HAVE A PALINDROME!
I'LL CHECK THE SPY HAND-BOOK.
darb
I DON'T THINK YOU KNOW WHAT A PALINDROME IS...
I KNOW I COULD BEAT ONE UP. WORRY ABOUT YOUR OWN PALINDROME.
UH-OH. THEY'RE SO SECRET THEY'RE NOT EVEN IN THE BOOK!

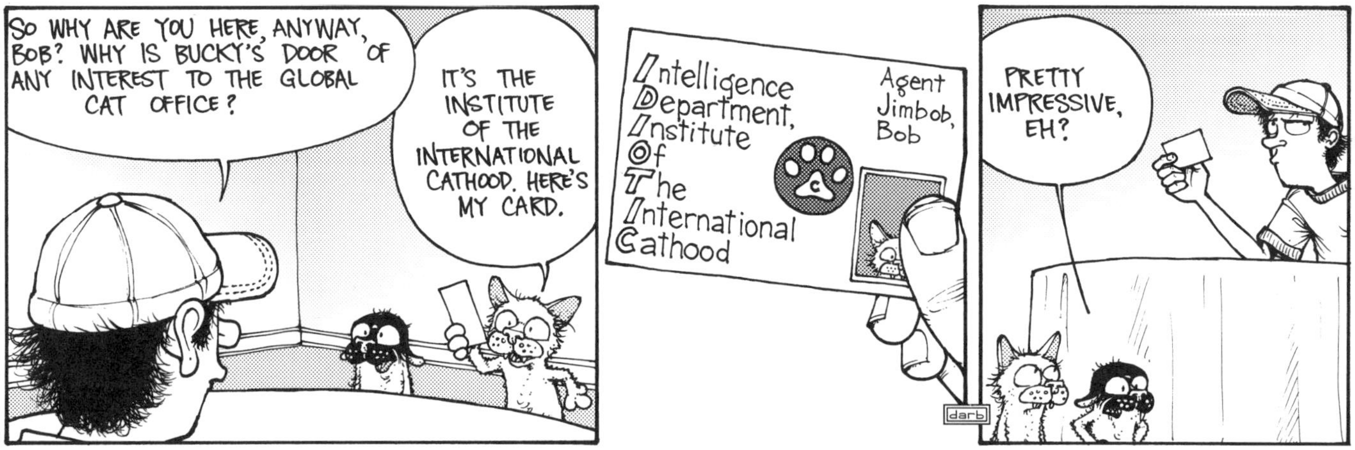
SO WHY ARE YOU HERE, ANYWAY, BOB? WHY IS BUCKY'S DOOR OF ANY INTEREST TO THE GLOBAL CAT OFFICE?
IT'S THE INSTITUTE OF THE INTERNATIONAL CATHOOD. HERE'S MY CARD.
Intelligence Department, Institute Of The International Cathood
Agent Jimbob, Bob
darb
PRETTY IMPRESSIVE, EH?

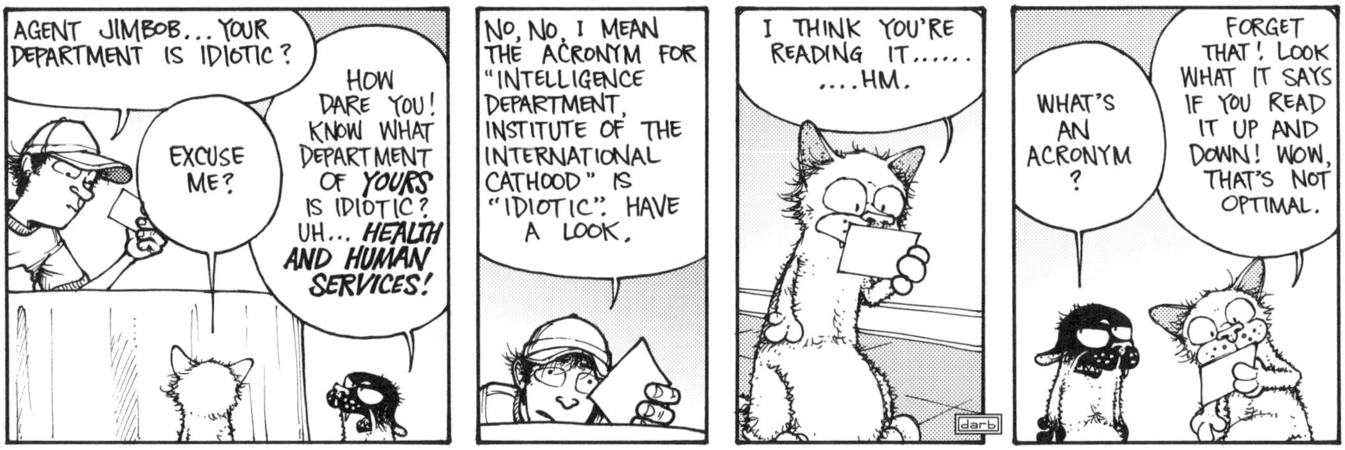
AGENT JIMBOB... YOUR DEPARTMENT IS IDIOTIC?
EXCUSE ME?
HOW DARE YOU! KNOW WHAT DEPARTMENT OF YOURS IS IDIOTIC? UH... HEALTH AND HUMAN SERVICES!
NO, NO, I MEAN THE ACRONYM FOR "INTELLIGENCE DEPARTMENT, INSTITUTE OF THE INTERNATIONAL CATHOOD" IS "IDIOTIC". HAVE A LOOK.
I THINK YOU'RE READING IT...... ....HM.
darb
WHAT'S AN ACRONYM?
FORGET THAT! LOOK WHAT IT SAYS IF YOU READ IT UP AND DOWN! WOW, THAT'S NOT OPTIMAL.

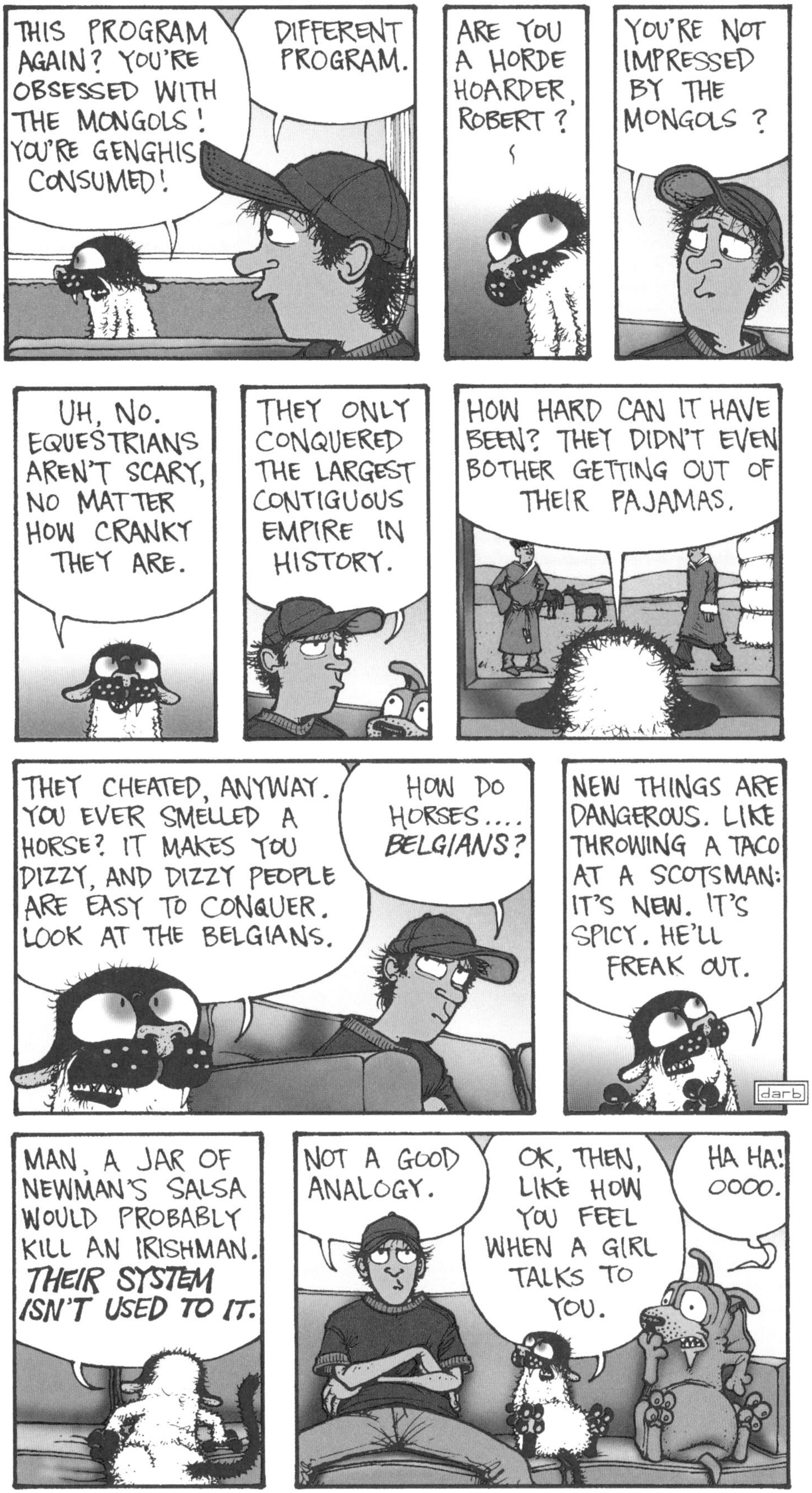
THIS PROGRAM AGAIN? YOU'RE OBSESSED WITH THE MONGOLS! YOU'RE GENGHIS CONSUMED!
DIFFERENT PROGRAM.
ARE YOU A HORDE HOARDER, ROBERT?
YOU'RE NOT IMPRESSED BY THE MONGOLS?
UH, NO. EQUESTRIANS AREN'T SCARY, NO MATTER HOW CRANKY THEY ARE.
THEY ONLY CONQUERED THE LARGEST CONTIGUOUS EMPIRE IN HISTORY.
HOW HARD CAN IT HAVE BEEN? THEY DIDN'T EVEN BOTHER GETTING OUT OF THEIR PAJAMAS.
THEY CHEATED, ANYWAY. YOU EVER SMELLED A HORSE? IT MAKES YOU DIZZY, AND DIZZY PEOPLE ARE EASY TO CONQUER. LOOK AT THE BELGIANS.
HOW DO HORSES.... *BELGIANS?*
NEW THINGS ARE DANGEROUS. LIKE THROWING A TACO AT A SCOTSMAN: IT'S NEW. IT'S SPICY. HE'LL FREAK OUT.
darb
MAN, A JAR OF NEWMAN'S SALSA WOULD PROBABLY KILL AN IRISHMAN. *THEIR SYSTEM ISN'T USED TO IT.*
NOT A GOOD ANALOGY.
OK, THEN, LIKE HOW YOU FEEL WHEN A GIRL TALKS TO YOU.
HA HA! OOOO.

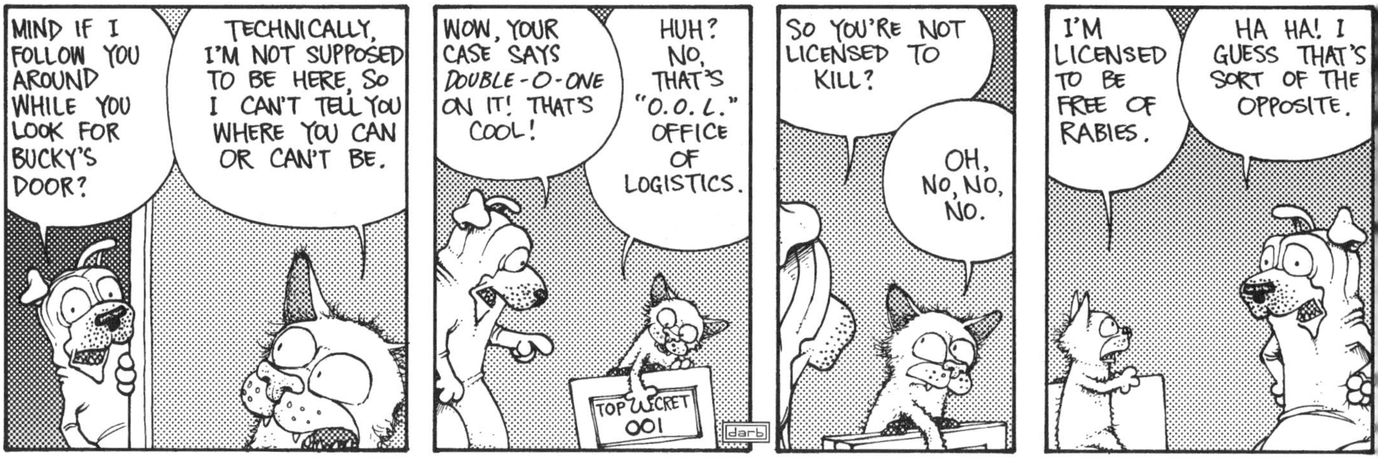
MIND IF I FOLLOW YOU AROUND WHILE YOU LOOK FOR BUCKY'S DOOR?
TECHNICALLY, I'M NOT SUPPOSED TO BE HERE, SO I CAN'T TELL YOU WHERE YOU CAN OR CAN'T BE.
WOW, YOUR CASE SAYS *DOUBLE-O-ONE* ON IT! THAT'S COOL!
HUH? NO, THAT'S "O.O.L." OFFICE OF LOGISTICS.
TOP SECRET 001
darb
SO YOU'RE NOT LICENSED TO KILL?
OH, NO, NO, NO.
I'M LICENSED TO BE FREE OF RABIES.
HA HA! I GUESS THAT'S SORT OF THE OPPOSITE.

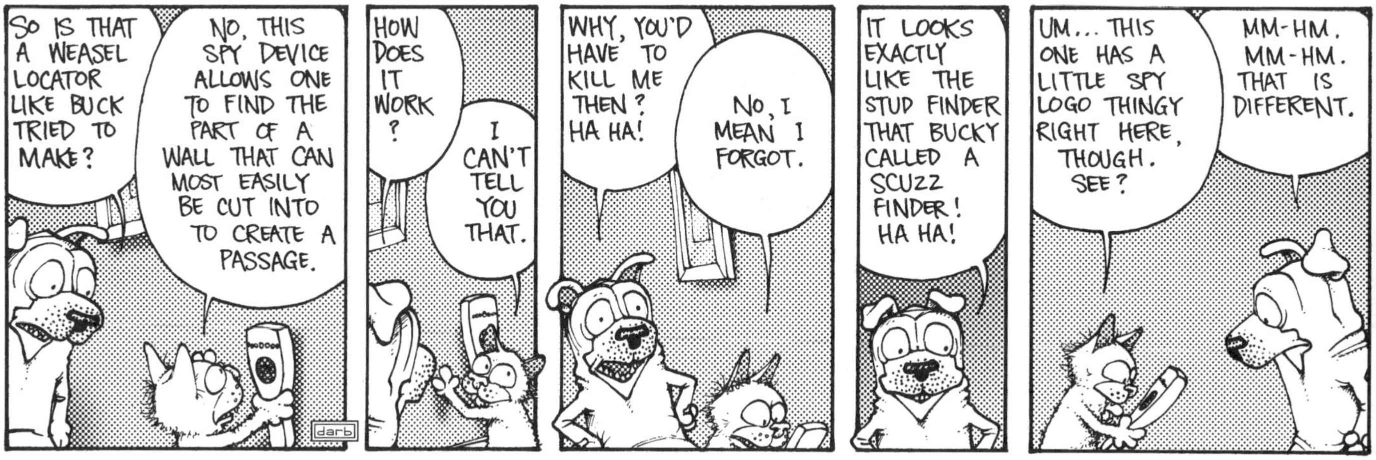
SO IS THAT A WEASEL LOCATOR LIKE BUCK TRIED TO MAKE?
NO, THIS SPY DEVICE ALLOWS ONE TO FIND THE PART OF A WALL THAT CAN MOST EASILY BE CUT INTO TO CREATE A PASSAGE.
darb
HOW DOES IT WORK?
I CAN'T TELL YOU THAT.
WHY, YOU'D HAVE TO KILL ME THEN? HA HA!
NO, I MEAN I FORGOT.
IT LOOKS EXACTLY LIKE THE STUD FINDER THAT BUCKY CALLED A SCUZZ FINDER! HA HA!
UM... THIS ONE HAS A LITTLE SPY LOGO THINGY RIGHT HERE, THOUGH. SEE?
MM-HM. MM-HM. THAT IS DIFFERENT.

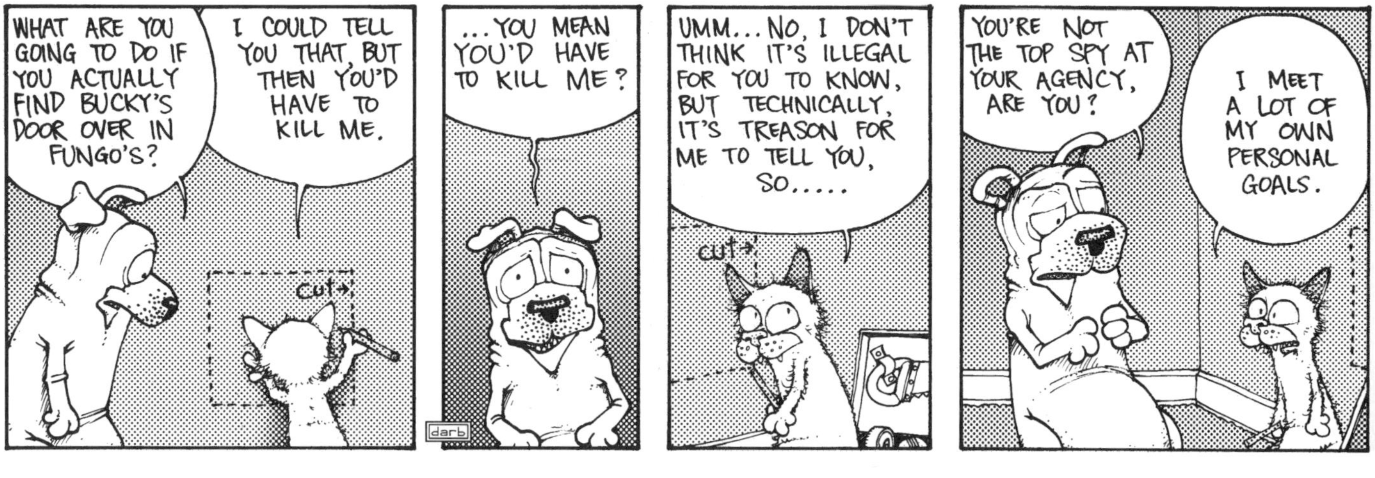
WHAT ARE YOU GOING TO DO IF YOU ACTUALLY FIND BUCKY'S DOOR OVER IN FUNGO'S?
I COULD TELL YOU THAT, BUT THEN YOU'D HAVE TO KILL ME.
CUT→
...YOU MEAN YOU'D HAVE TO KILL ME?
darb
UMM... NO, I DON'T THINK IT'S ILLEGAL FOR YOU TO KNOW, BUT TECHNICALLY, IT'S TREASON FOR ME TO TELL YOU, SO.....
CUT→
YOU'RE NOT THE TOP SPY AT YOUR AGENCY, ARE YOU?
I MEET A LOT OF MY OWN PERSONAL GOALS.

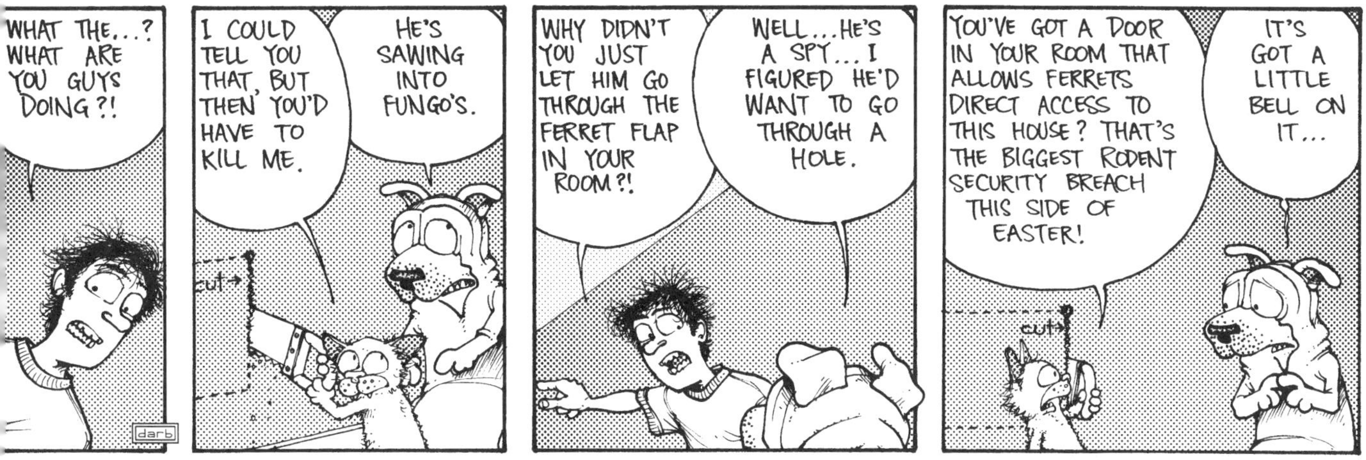
WHAT THE...? WHAT ARE YOU GUYS DOING?!
I COULD TELL YOU THAT, BUT THEN YOU'D HAVE TO KILL ME.
HE'S SAWING INTO FUNGO'S.
cut→
darb
WHY DIDN'T YOU JUST LET HIM GO THROUGH THE FERRET FLAP IN YOUR ROOM?!
WELL...HE'S A SPY... I FIGURED HE'D WANT TO GO THROUGH A HOLE.
YOU'VE GOT A DOOR IN YOUR ROOM THAT ALLOWS FERRETS DIRECT ACCESS TO THIS HOUSE? THAT'S THE BIGGEST RODENT SECURITY BREACH THIS SIDE OF EASTER!
IT'S GOT A LITTLE BELL ON IT...
cut→

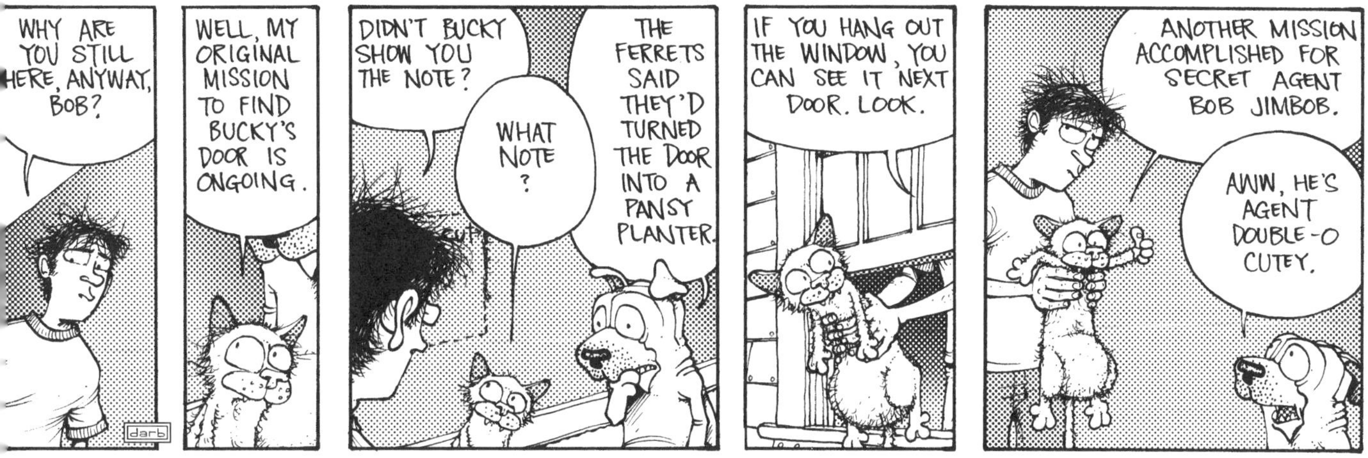
WHY ARE YOU STILL HERE, ANYWAY, BOB?
darb
WELL, MY ORIGINAL MISSION TO FIND BUCKY'S DOOR IS ONGOING.
DIDN'T BUCKY SHOW YOU THE NOTE?
WHAT NOTE?
THE FERRETS SAID THEY'D TURNED THE DOOR INTO A PANSY PLANTER.
IF YOU HANG OUT THE WINDOW, YOU CAN SEE IT NEXT DOOR. LOOK.
ANOTHER MISSION ACCOMPLISHED FOR SECRET AGENT BOB JIMBOB.
AWW, HE'S AGENT DOUBLE-O CUTEY.

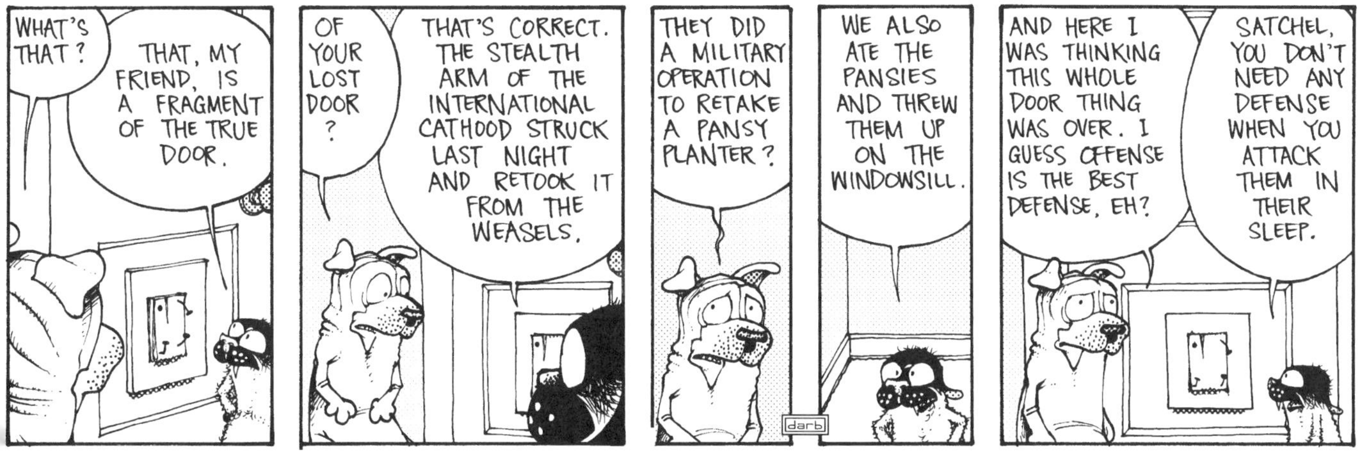
WHAT'S THAT?
THAT, MY FRIEND, IS A FRAGMENT OF THE TRUE DOOR.
OF YOUR LOST DOOR?
THAT'S CORRECT. THE STEALTH ARM OF THE INTERNATIONAL CATHOOD STRUCK LAST NIGHT AND RETOOK IT FROM THE WEASELS.
THEY DID A MILITARY OPERATION TO RETAKE A PANSY PLANTER?
WE ALSO ATE THE PANSIES AND THREW THEM UP ON THE WINDOWSILL.
darb
AND HERE I WAS THINKING THIS WHOLE DOOR THING WAS OVER. I GUESS OFFENSE IS THE BEST DEFENSE, EH?
SATCHEL, YOU DON'T NEED ANY DEFENSE WHEN YOU ATTACK THEM IN THEIR SLEEP.

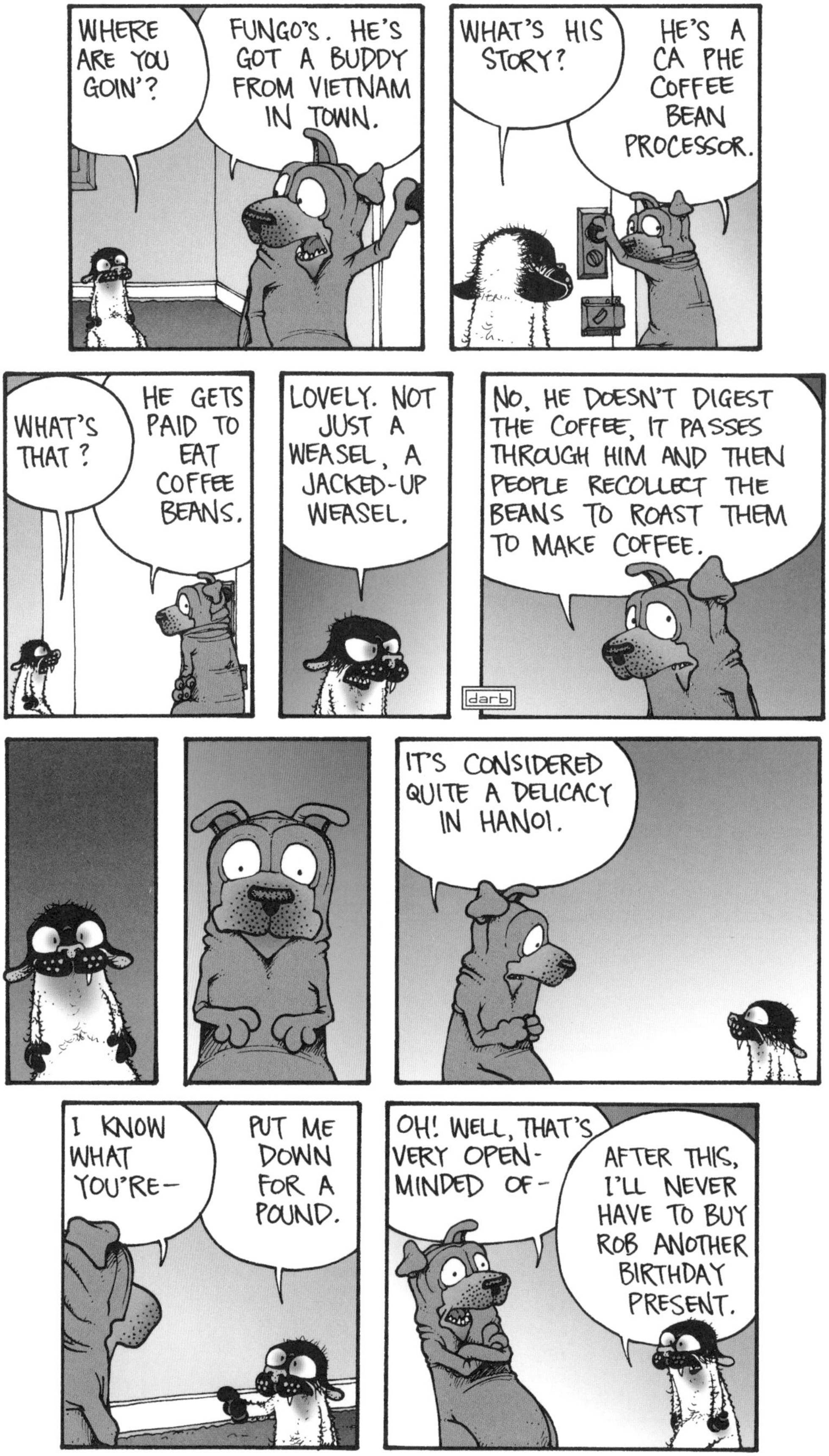
WHERE ARE YOU GOIN'?
FUNGO'S. HE'S GOT A BUDDY FROM VIETNAM IN TOWN.
WHAT'S HIS STORY?
HE'S A CA PHE COFFEE BEAN PROCESSOR.
WHAT'S THAT?
HE GETS PAID TO EAT COFFEE BEANS.
LOVELY. NOT JUST A WEASEL, A JACKED-UP WEASEL.
NO, HE DOESN'T DIGEST THE COFFEE, IT PASSES THROUGH HIM AND THEN PEOPLE RECOLLECT THE BEANS TO ROAST THEM TO MAKE COFFEE.
darb
IT'S CONSIDERED QUITE A DELICACY IN HANOI.
I KNOW WHAT YOU'RE-
PUT ME DOWN FOR A POUND.
OH! WELL, THAT'S VERY OPEN-MINDED OF-
AFTER THIS, I'LL NEVER HAVE TO BUY ROB ANOTHER BIRTHDAY PRESENT.

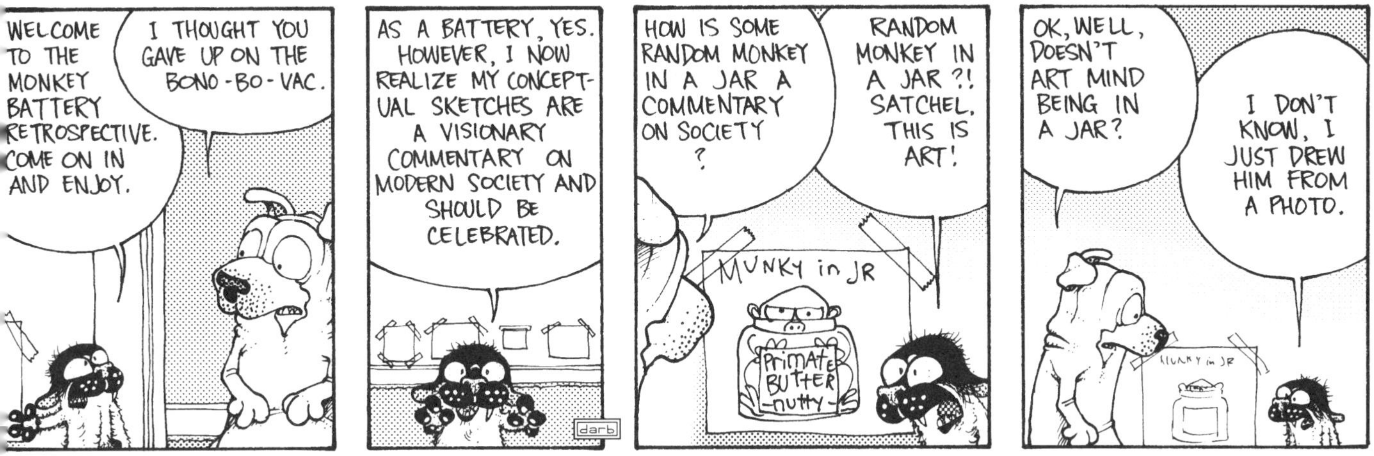
WELCOME TO THE MONKEY BATTERY RETROSPECTIVE. COME ON IN AND ENJOY.
I THOUGHT YOU GAVE UP ON THE BONO-BO-VAC.
AS A BATTERY, YES. HOWEVER, I NOW REALIZE MY CONCEPTUAL SKETCHES ARE A VISIONARY COMMENTARY ON MODERN SOCIETY AND SHOULD BE CELEBRATED.
darb
HOW IS SOME RANDOM MONKEY IN A JAR A COMMENTARY ON SOCIETY ?
RANDOM MONKEY IN A JAR ?! SATCHEL, THIS IS ART!
MUNKY in JR
Primate BUTTER nutty
OK, WELL, DOESN'T ART MIND BEING IN A JAR?
I DON'T KNOW, I JUST DREW HIM FROM A PHOTO.

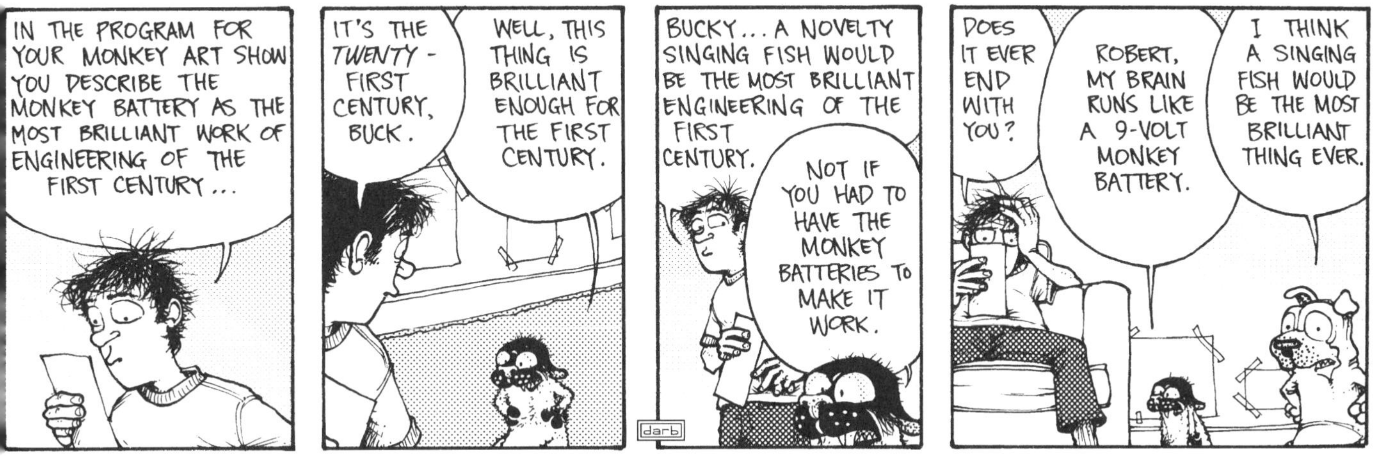
IN THE PROGRAM FOR YOUR MONKEY ART SHOW YOU DESCRIBE THE MONKEY BATTERY AS THE MOST BRILLIANT WORK OF ENGINEERING OF THE FIRST CENTURY...
IT'S THE *TWENTY*-FIRST CENTURY, BUCK.
WELL, THIS THING IS BRILLIANT ENOUGH FOR THE FIRST CENTURY.
BUCKY... A NOVELTY SINGING FISH WOULD BE THE MOST BRILLIANT ENGINEERING OF THE FIRST CENTURY.
NOT IF YOU HAD TO HAVE THE MONKEY BATTERIES TO MAKE IT WORK.
darb
DOES IT EVER END WITH YOU?
ROBERT, MY BRAIN RUNS LIKE A 9-VOLT MONKEY BATTERY.
I THINK A SINGING FISH WOULD BE THE MOST BRILLIANT THING EVER.

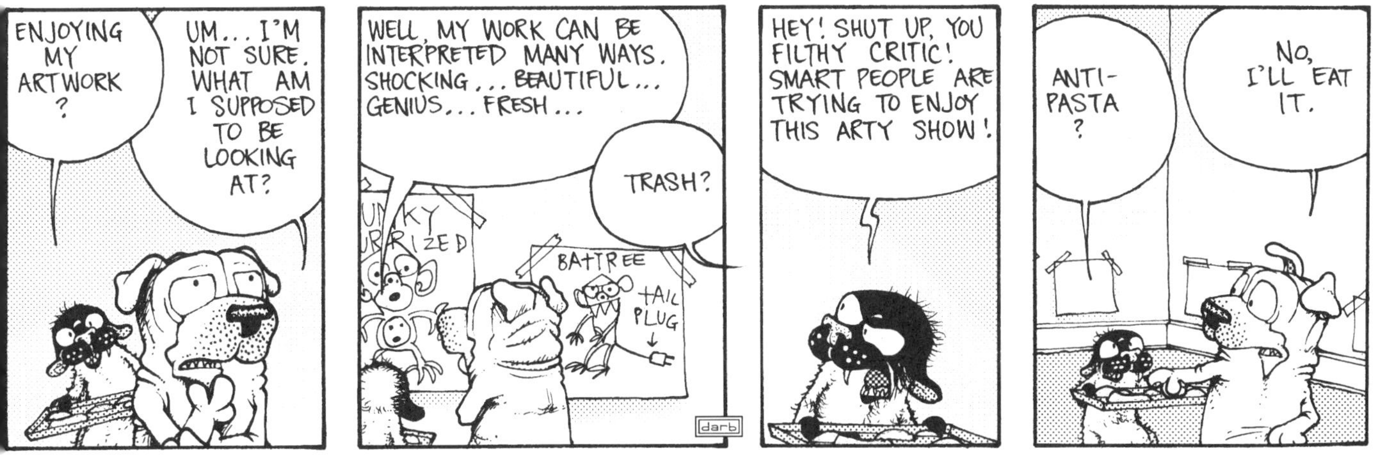
ENJOYING MY ARTWORK ?
UM... I'M NOT SURE. WHAT AM I SUPPOSED TO BE LOOKING AT?
WELL, MY WORK CAN BE INTERPRETED MANY WAYS. SHOCKING... BEAUTIFUL... GENIUS... FRESH...
TRASH?
BATTREE
TAIL PLUG
darb
HEY! SHUT UP, YOU FILTHY CRITIC! SMART PEOPLE ARE TRYING TO ENJOY THIS ARTY SHOW!
ANTI-PASTA ?
NO, I'LL EAT IT.

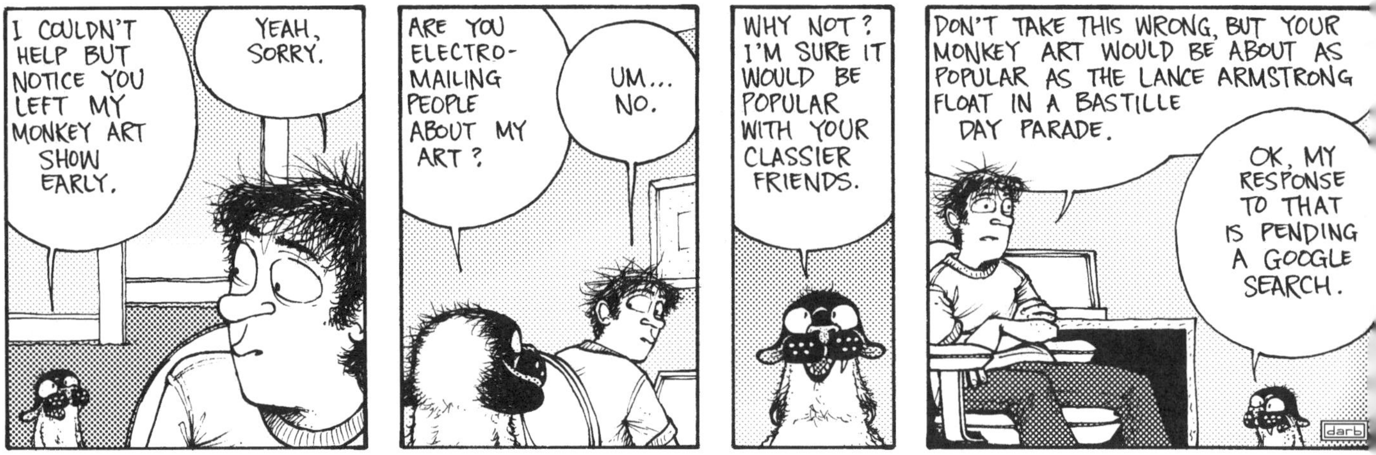
I COULDN'T HELP BUT NOTICE YOU LEFT MY MONKEY ART SHOW EARLY.
YEAH, SORRY.
ARE YOU ELECTRO-MAILING PEOPLE ABOUT MY ART?
UM... NO.
WHY NOT? I'M SURE IT WOULD BE POPULAR WITH YOUR CLASSIER FRIENDS.
DON'T TAKE THIS WRONG, BUT YOUR MONKEY ART WOULD BE ABOUT AS POPULAR AS THE LANCE ARMSTRONG FLOAT IN A BASTILLE DAY PARADE.
OK, MY RESPONSE TO THAT IS PENDING A GOOGLE SEARCH.
darb

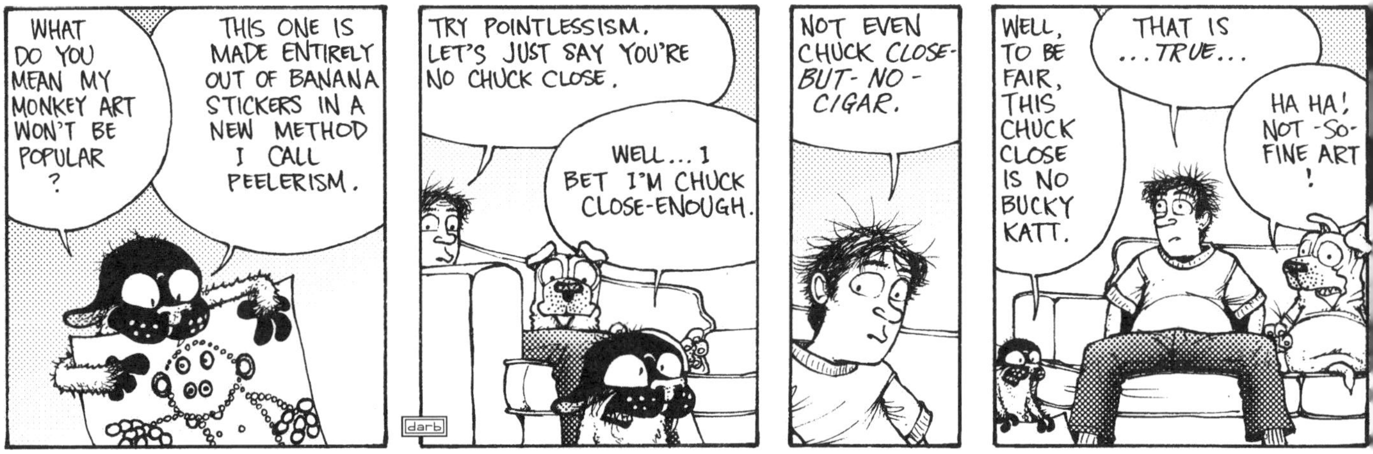
WHAT DO YOU MEAN MY MONKEY ART WON'T BE POPULAR?
THIS ONE IS MADE ENTIRELY OUT OF BANANA STICKERS IN A NEW METHOD I CALL PEELERISM.
darb
TRY POINTLESSISM. LET'S JUST SAY YOU'RE NO CHUCK CLOSE.
WELL... I BET I'M CHUCK CLOSE-ENOUGH.
NOT EVEN CHUCK *CLOSE-BUT-NO-CIGAR*.
WELL, TO BE FAIR, THIS CHUCK CLOSE IS NO BUCKY KATT.
THAT IS ...*TRUE*...
HA HA! NOT-SO-FINE ART!

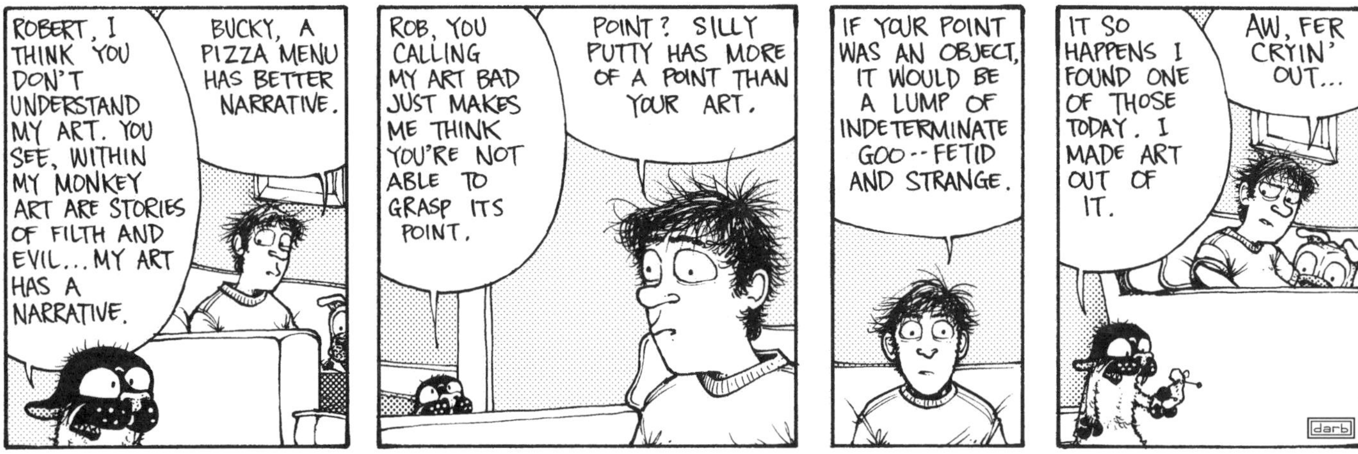
ROBERT, I THINK YOU DON'T UNDERSTAND MY ART. YOU SEE, WITHIN MY MONKEY ART ARE STORIES OF FILTH AND EVIL... MY ART HAS A NARRATIVE.
BUCKY, A PIZZA MENU HAS BETTER NARRATIVE.
ROB, YOU CALLING MY ART BAD JUST MAKES ME THINK YOU'RE NOT ABLE TO GRASP ITS POINT.
POINT? SILLY PUTTY HAS MORE OF A POINT THAN YOUR ART.
IF YOUR POINT WAS AN OBJECT, IT WOULD BE A LUMP OF INDETERMINATE GOO--FETID AND STRANGE.
IT SO HAPPENS I FOUND ONE OF THOSE TODAY. I MADE ART OUT OF IT.
AW, FER CRYIN' OUT...
darb

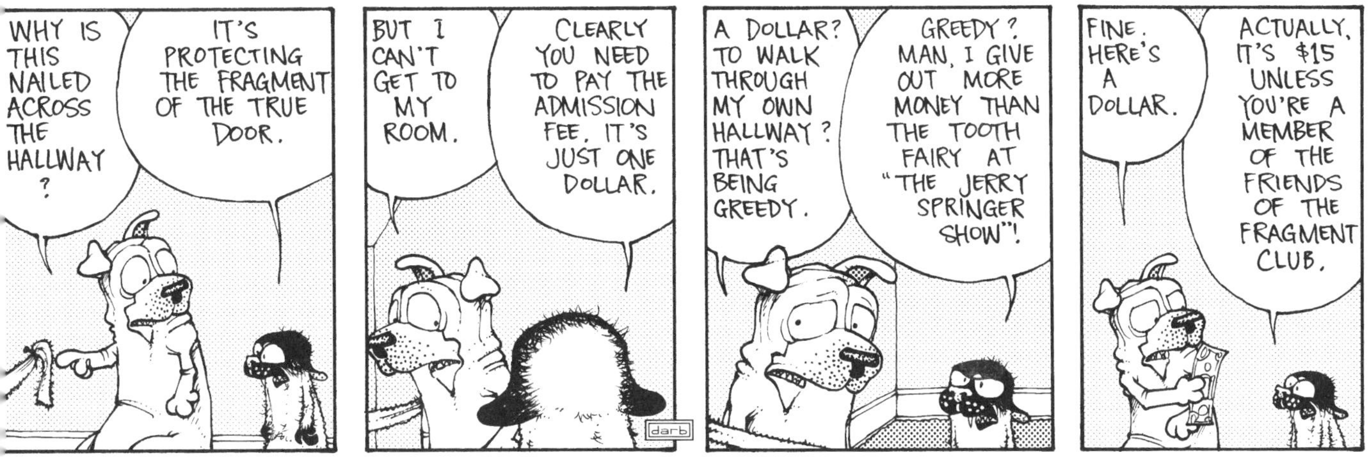
WHY IS THIS NAILED ACROSS THE HALLWAY ?
IT'S PROTECTING THE FRAGMENT OF THE TRUE DOOR.
BUT I CAN'T GET TO MY ROOM.
CLEARLY YOU NEED TO PAY THE ADMISSION FEE. IT'S JUST ONE DOLLAR.
A DOLLAR? TO WALK THROUGH MY OWN HALLWAY? THAT'S BEING GREEDY.
GREEDY? MAN, I GIVE OUT MORE MONEY THAN THE TOOTH FAIRY AT "THE JERRY SPRINGER SHOW"!
FINE. HERE'S A DOLLAR.
ACTUALLY, IT'S $15 UNLESS YOU'RE A MEMBER OF THE FRIENDS OF THE FRAGMENT CLUB.

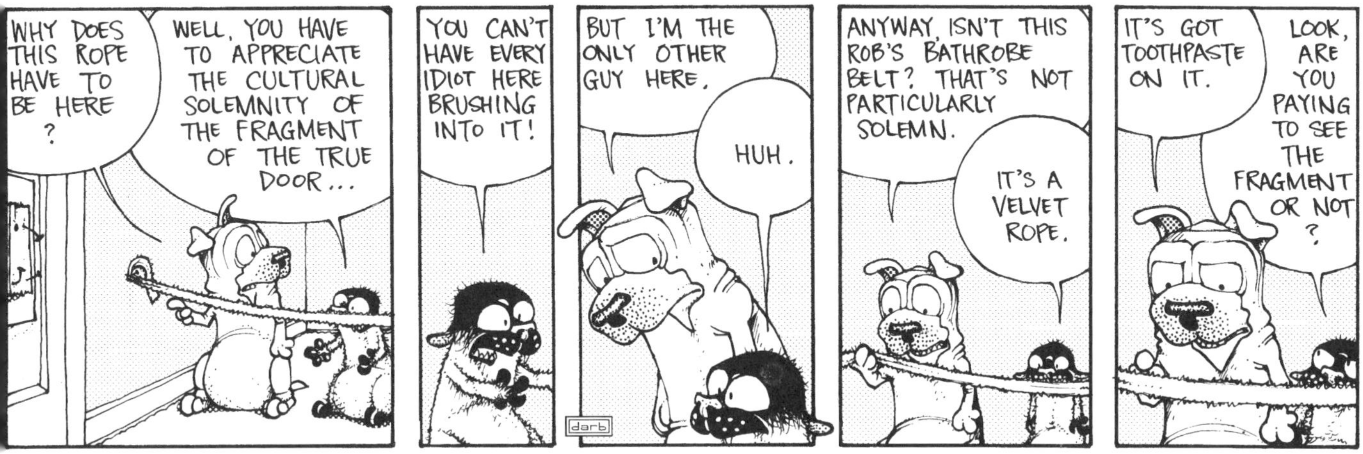
WHY DOES THIS ROPE HAVE TO BE HERE ?
WELL, YOU HAVE TO APPRECIATE THE CULTURAL SOLEMNITY OF THE FRAGMENT OF THE TRUE DOOR...
YOU CAN'T HAVE EVERY IDIOT HERE BRUSHING INTO IT!
BUT I'M THE ONLY OTHER GUY HERE.
HUH.
ANYWAY, ISN'T THIS ROB'S BATHROBE BELT? THAT'S NOT PARTICULARLY SOLEMN.
IT'S A VELVET ROPE.
IT'S GOT TOOTHPASTE ON IT.
LOOK, ARE YOU PAYING TO SEE THE FRAGMENT OR NOT ?

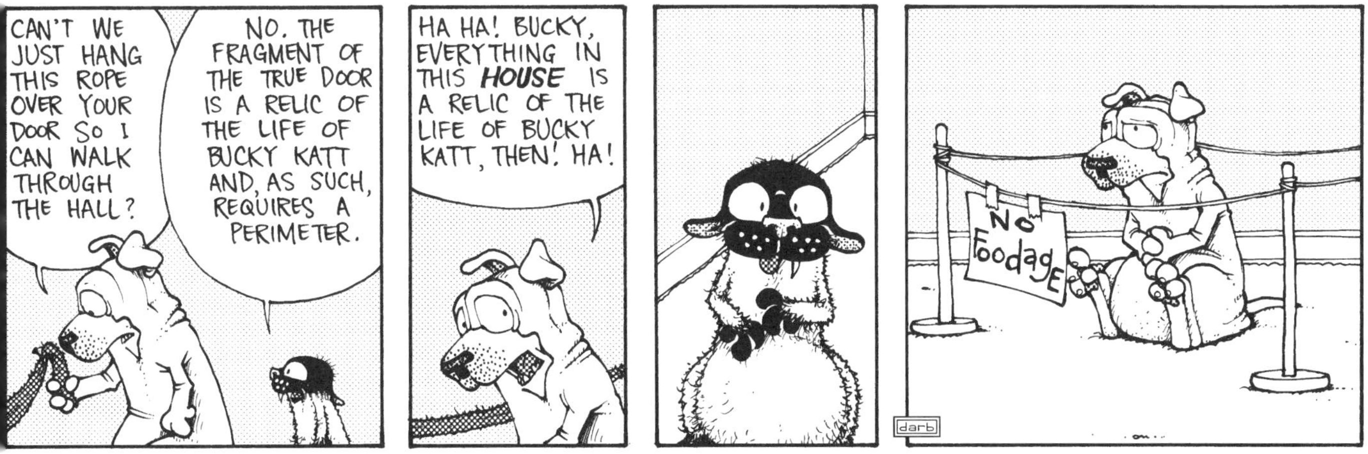
CAN'T WE JUST HANG THIS ROPE OVER YOUR DOOR SO I CAN WALK THROUGH THE HALL?
NO. THE FRAGMENT OF THE TRUE DOOR IS A RELIC OF THE LIFE OF BUCKY KATT AND, AS SUCH, REQUIRES A PERIMETER.
HA HA! BUCKY, EVERYTHING IN THIS **HOUSE** IS A RELIC OF THE LIFE OF BUCKY KATT, THEN! HA!
NO Foodage

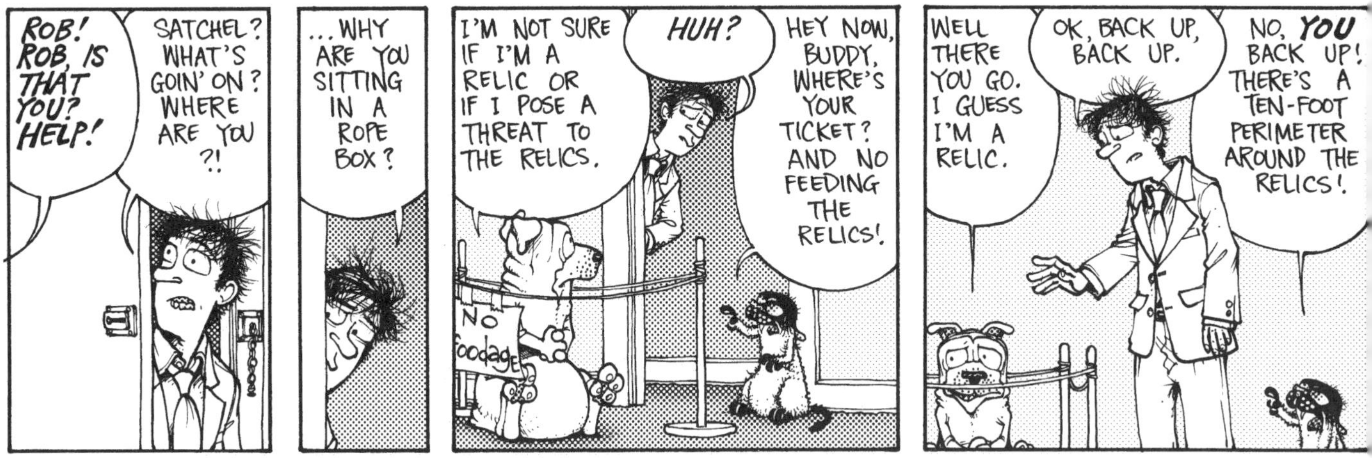
ROB! ROB, IS THAT YOU? HELP!
SATCHEL? WHAT'S GOIN' ON? WHERE ARE YOU ?!
...WHY ARE YOU SITTING IN A ROPE BOX?
I'M NOT SURE IF I'M A RELIC OR IF I POSE A THREAT TO THE RELICS.
HUH?
HEY NOW, BUDDY, WHERE'S YOUR TICKET? AND NO FEEDING THE RELICS!
NO foodage
WELL THERE YOU GO. I GUESS I'M A RELIC.
OK, BACK UP, BACK UP.
NO, YOU BACK UP! THERE'S A TEN-FOOT PERIMETER AROUND THE RELICS!

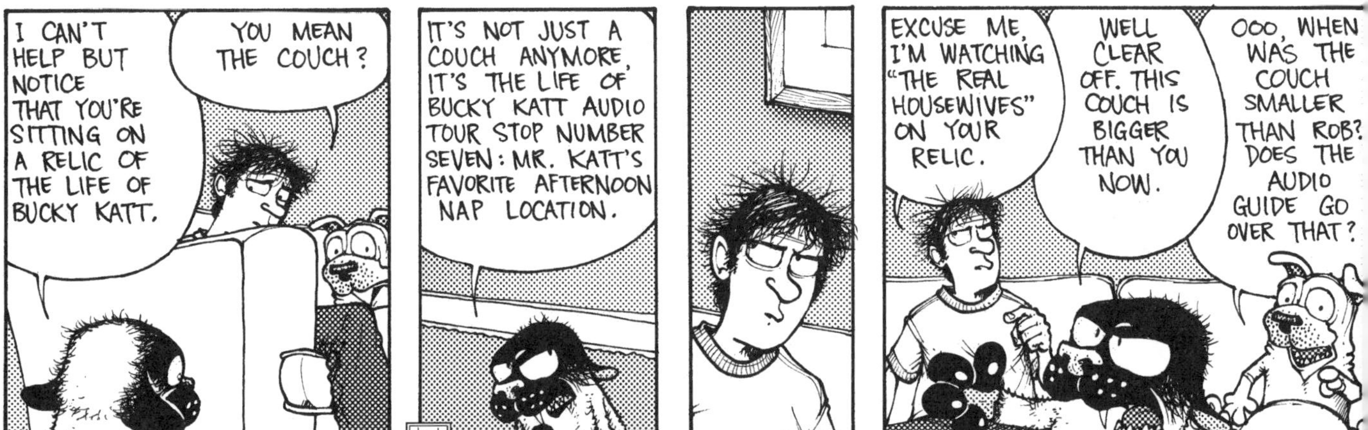
I CAN'T HELP BUT NOTICE THAT YOU'RE SITTING ON A RELIC OF THE LIFE OF BUCKY KATT.
YOU MEAN THE COUCH?
IT'S NOT JUST A COUCH ANYMORE, IT'S THE LIFE OF BUCKY KATT AUDIO TOUR STOP NUMBER SEVEN: MR. KATT'S FAVORITE AFTERNOON NAP LOCATION.
darb
EXCUSE ME, I'M WATCHING "THE REAL HOUSEWIVES" ON YOUR RELIC.
WELL CLEAR OFF. THIS COUCH IS BIGGER THAN YOU NOW.
OOO, WHEN WAS THE COUCH SMALLER THAN ROB? DOES THE AUDIO GUIDE GO OVER THAT?

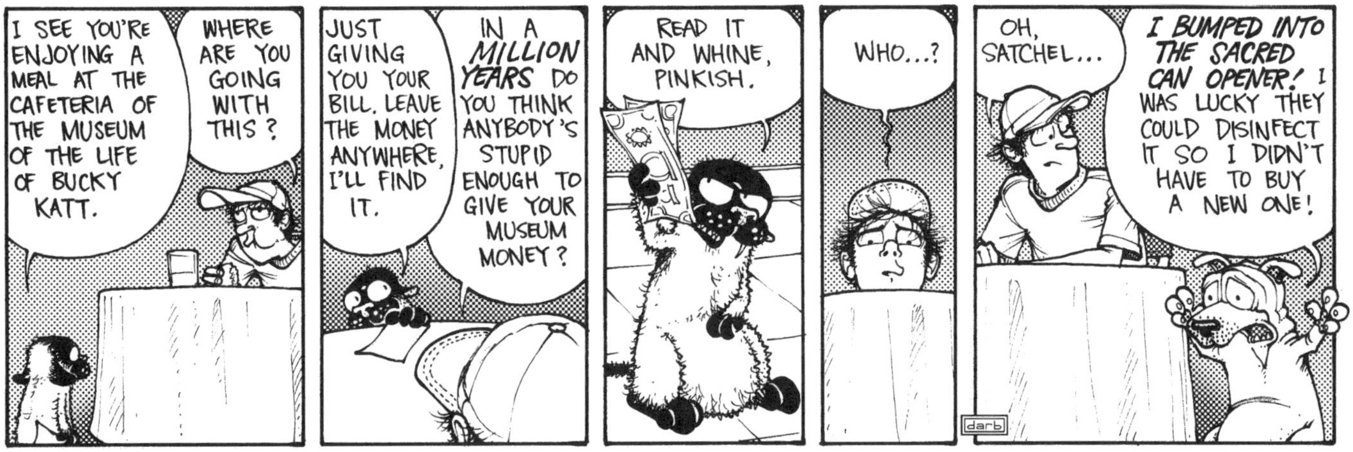
I SEE YOU'RE ENJOYING A MEAL AT THE CAFETERIA OF THE MUSEUM OF THE LIFE OF BUCKY KATT.
WHERE ARE YOU GOING WITH THIS?
JUST GIVING YOU YOUR BILL. LEAVE THE MONEY ANYWHERE, I'LL FIND IT.
IN A MILLION YEARS DO YOU THINK ANYBODY'S STUPID ENOUGH TO GIVE YOUR MUSEUM MONEY?
READ IT AND WHINE, PINKISH.
WHO...?
darb
OH, SATCHEL...
I BUMPED INTO THE SACRED CAN OPENER! I WAS LUCKY THEY COULD DISINFECT IT SO I DIDN'T HAVE TO BUY A NEW ONE!